NEW CENTURY BIBLE
COMMENTARY

General Editors

RONALD E. CLEMENTS   MATTHEW BLACK
(Old Testament)   (New Testament)

1 and 2 CHRONICLES

D1568921

THE NEW CENTURY BIBLE COMMENTARIES

EXODUS (J. P. Hyatt)
DEUTERONOMY (A. D. H. Mayes)
1 and 2 CHRONICLES (H. G. M. Williamson)
JOB (H. H. Rowley)
PSALMS Volumes 1 and 2 (A. A. Anderson)
ISAIAH 1–39 (R. E. Clements)
ISAIAH 40–66 (R. N. Whybray)
EZEKIEL (John W. Wevers)*
THE GOSPEL OF MATTHEW (David Hill)
THE GOSPEL OF MARK (Hugh Anderson)
THE GOSPEL OF LUKE (E. Earle Ellis)
THE GOSPEL OF JOHN (Barnabas Lindars)
THE ACTS OF THE APOSTLES (William Neil)
ROMANS (Matthew Black)
1 and 2 CORINTHIANS (F. F. Bruce)
GALATIANS (Donald Guthrie)
EPHESIANS (C. Leslie Mitton)
PHILIPPIANS (Ralph P. Martin)
COLOSSIANS AND PHILEMON (Ralph P. Martin)
THE PASTORAL EPISTLES (A. T. Hanson)
1 PETER (Ernest Best)*
THE BOOK OF REVELATION (G. R. Beasley-Murray)

* *Not yet available*

Other titles in preparation

NEW CENTURY BIBLE COMMENTARY

Based on the Revised Standard Version

1 and 2 CHRONICLES

H. G. M. WILLIAMSON

WM. B. EERDMANS PUBL. CO., GRAND RAPIDS

MARSHALL, MORGAN & SCOTT PUBL. LTD., LONDON

TO
MY WIFE

©Marshall Morgan & Scott 1982
First published 1982 jointly by Marshall Morgan & Scott in the UK and Common-
wealth and Wm. B. Eerdmans Publishing Company in the US

All rights reserved
Printed in the United States of America
for
Wm. B. Eerdmans Publishing Company
255 Jefferson Ave. S.E., Grand Rapids, Mich. 49503
and
Marshall Morgan & Scott
1 Bath Street, London EC1V 9LB

Library of Congress Cataloging in Publication Data

Williamson, H. G. M. (Hugh Godfrey Maturin), 1947-
1 and 2 Chronicles.

(New century Bible commentary)
Bibliography: p. xii
Includes index.
1. Bible. O.T. Chronicles — Commentaries. I. Title.
II. Title: One and two Chronicles. III. Series.
BS1345.3.W54   222′.607   82-7243
ISBN 0-8028-1925-7   AACR2

CONTENTS

PREFACE

It is not difficult to justify the appearance of a new English commentary on the books of Chronicles. The past decade has seen the publication of five substantial monographs (by Willi, Mosis, Welten, Williamson and Japhet) and numerous articles on these books, reflecting the very proper resurgence of interest in the post-exilic period of biblical history. Despite this, however, there is no substantial commentary available later than that of Rudolph in German some twenty-five years ago (1955); the work of Myers in the Anchor Bible (1965) has much useful historical comment, but is weaker in its theological and literary-critical discussion. It is to be hoped, therefore, that the present commentary (the first of any size ever to have been written by a British author) will help to mediate to a wider readership the major, positive results of recent specialised work, as well as to advance our understanding of the books in a number of fresh ways.

I should like to express my thanks to Dr. R. E. Clements for his invitation to contribute this volume to the New Century Bible series. Nine years ago, when I was a graduate student, an essay which he set first stimulated my interest in the books of Chronicles, and it led me to return to them later for my doctoral thesis. I am therefore delighted to have had this opportunity of further work on them at his request.

That essay was the first piece of academic work which I undertook after my marriage in June 1971, since when the Chronicler has dominated much of my thinking. It is therefore with a real sense of gratitude that now, at the end of this particular road, I dedicate this commentary to my wife.

H. G. M. Williamson
June 1980

ABBREVIATIONS

BIBLICAL

OLD TESTAMENT (*OT*)

Gen.	Jg.	1 Chr.	Ps.	Lam.	Ob.	Hag.
Exod.	Ru.	2 Chr.	Prov.	Ezek.	Jon.	Zech.
Lev.	1 Sam.	Ezr.	Ec.	Dan.	Mic.	Mal.
Num.	2 Sam.	Neh.	Ca.	Hos.	Nah.	
Dt.	1 Kg.	Est.	Isa.	Jl	Hab.	
Jos.	2 Kg.	Job	Jer.	Am.	Zeph.	

APOCRYPHA (*Apoc.*)

1 Esd.	Tob.	Ad.Est.	Sir.	S.3Ch.	Bel	1 Mac.
2 Esd.	Jdt.	Wis.	Bar.	Sus.	Man.	2 Mac.
			E. Jer.			

NEW TESTAMENT (*NT*)

Mt.	Ac.	Gal.	1 Th.	Tit.	1 Pet.	3 Jn
Mk	Rom.	Eph.	2 Th.	Phm.	2 Pet.	Jude
Lk.	1 C.	Phil.	1 Tim.	Heb.	1 Jn	Rev.
Jn	2 C.	Col.	2 Tim.	Jas.	2 Jn	

GENERAL

A	The Alexandrian Codex of the Septuagint
ABR	*Australian Biblical Review*
AI	R. de Vaux, *Ancient Israel: its Life and Institutions*, ET, London, 2nd edn., 1965
AJSL	*American Journal of Semitic Languages and Literatures*
ANEP	*The Ancient Near East in Pictures Relating to the Old Testament*, edited by J. B. Pritchard, Princeton, 1954
ANET	*Ancient Near Eastern Texts Relating to the Old Testament*, edited by J. B. Pritchard, 3rd edn, Princeton, 1969
Ass.Mos.	*The Assumption of Moses*

AV	*Authorised Version* (1611)
B	The Vatican Codex of the Septuagint
BA	*Biblical Archaeologist*
BASOR	*Bulletin of the American Schools of Oriental Research*
BDB	*Hebrew and English Lexicon of the Old Testament*, edited by F. Brown, S. R. Driver and C. A. Briggs, Oxford, 1907
BHS	*Biblia Hebraica Stuttgartensia*, edited by K. Elliger and W. Rudolph, Stuttgart, 1977
BibOr	*Bibliotheca Orientalis*
BJPES	*Bulletin of the Jewish Palestine Exploration Society*
BT	*The Bible Translator*
B.Yoma	A Tractate of the Babylonian Talmud called 'Yoma'
BZ	*Biblische Zeitschrift*
CBQ	*Catholic Biblical Quarterly*
CM	*The Books of Chronicles*, by E. L. Curtis and A. A. Madsen, Edinburgh, 1910
CTM	*Concordia Theological Monthly*
DBS	*Supplément au Dictionnaire de la Bible*, edited by L. Pirot, A. Robert, H. Cazelles and A. Feuillet, Paris, 1928—
DOTT	*Documents from Old Testament Times*, edited by D. Winton Thomas, Edinburgh and London, 1958
EAEHL	*Encyclopedia of Archaeological Excavations in the Holy Land*, edited by M. Avi-Yonah and E. Stern, Jerusalem, 1975–8
EI	*Eretz-Israel*
ET	English Translation
ExpT	*Expository Times*
ETL	*Ephemerides Theologicae Lovanienses*
Exod.R.	Exodus Rabbah
GCW	G. von Rad, *Des Geschichtsbild des chronistischen Werkes*, Stuttgart, 1930
GK	*Gesenius' Hebrew Grammar as edited and enlarged by the late E. Kautzsch*, edited by A. E. Cowley, 2nd edn, Oxford, 1910
GTTOT	J. Simons, *The Geographical and Topographical Texts of the Old Testament*, Leiden, 1959
HDB	*Dictionary of the Bible*, edited by J. Hastings, Edinburgh, 1898
HTR	*Harvard Theological Review*
HUCA	*Hebrew Union College Annual*

IBC	*Israel in the Books of Chronicles*, by H. G. M. Williamson, Cambridge, 1977
IDB	*The Interpreter's Dictionary of the Bible*, edited by G. A. Buttrick, Nashville, 1962
IDBS	*IDB, Supplementary Volume*, edited by K. Crim, Nashville, 1976
IEJ	*Israel Exploration Journal*
IJH	*Israelite and Judaean History*, edited by J. H. Hayes and J. M. Miller, London, 1977
JANES	*Journal of the Ancient Near Eastern Society of Columbia University*
JAOS	*Journal of the American Oriental Society*
JB	*Jerusalem Bible*
JBL	*Journal of Biblical Literature*
JJS	*Journal of Jewish Studies*
JNES	*Journal of Near Eastern Studies*
JPOS	*Journal of the Palestine Oriental Society*
JQR	*Jewish Quarterly Review*
JSJ	*Journal for the Study of Judaism*
JSOT	*Journal for the Study of the Old Testament*
JSS	*Journal of Semitic Studies*
JTS	*Journal of Theological Studies*
KS	*Kleine Schriften*
Kt.	*Kethibh*
L	The Lucianic Recension of the Septuagint
LXX	The Septuagint
mg	margin
MGWJ	*Monatsschrift für Geschichte und Wissenschaft des Judentums*
MIO	*Mitteilungen des Instituts für Orientforschung*
MS(s)	manuscript(s)
MT	The Massoretic Text
NEB	*New English Bible*
NM	Nehemiah Memoir
ns	new series
NT	New Testament
Num.R.	Numbers Rabbah
OrBibLov	*Orientalia et Biblica Lovaniensia*
OT	Old Testament
OTS	*Oudtestamentische Studiën*
P	Peshitta
Par.	Paralipomena (the translation of Chronicles in LXX)

PEQ	*Palestine Exploration Quarterly*
PJB	*Palästinajahrbuch*
1QapGn	The Genesis Apocryphon from Qumran Cave 1
1QIsaᵃ	The First Isaiah Scroll from Qumran Cave 1
4QSamᵃ	The First Samuel Scroll (very fragmentary) from Qumran Cave 4
Qr.	*Qere*
RB	*Revue Biblique*
RH	*Das erste Buch der Chronik*, by J. W. Rothstein and J. Hänel, Leipzig, 1927
RHPhR	*Revue d'histoire et de philosophie religieuses*
RSR	*Recherches de science religieuse*
RSV	*Revised Standard Version*
RTK	*Realencyklopädie für Theologie und Kirche*
RTP	*Revue de Théologie et de Philosophie*
RV	*Revised Version*
SEA	*Svensk Exegetisk Årsbok*
SJT	*Scottish Journal of Theology*
SVT	Supplements to *Vetus Testamentum*
T	Targum
TDOT	*Theological Dictionary of the Old Testament*, edited by G. J. Botterweck and H. Ringgren, ET, Grand Rapids, 1977—
TGUOS	*Transactions of the Glasgow University Oriental Society*
ThLZ	*Theologische Literaturzeitung*
ThQ	*Theologische Quartalschrift*
ThZ	*Theologische Zeitschrift*
TI	*Tradition and Interpretation*, edited by G. W. Anderson, Oxford, 1979
TynB	*Tyndale Bulletin*
UF	*Ugarit-Forschungen*
US	M. Noth, *Überlieferungsgeschichtliche Studien* 1, Halle, 1943
V	Vulgate
vrs	(ancient) versions
VT	*Vetus Testamentum*
ZAW	*Zeitschrift für die alttestamentliche Wissenschaft*
ZDMG	*Zeitschrift des Deutschen Morgenländischen Gesellschaft*
ZDPV	*Zeitschrift des Deutschen Palästina-Vereins*
ZThK	*Zeitschrift für Theologie und Kirche*

SELECT BIBLIOGRAPHY

Note In the text, commentaries and some monographs are
cited by author's name alone and other works listed
here by an abbreviated title. Works not included in
this select bibliography are cited in full in the text.

COMMENTARIES

P. R. Ackroyd, *I & II Chronicles, Ezra, Nehemiah* (*Torch
Bible Commentaries*), London, 1973.

W. E. Barnes, *The Books of Chronicles* (*The Cambridge Bible
for Schools and Colleges*), Cambridge, 1899

I. Benzinger, *Die Bücher der Chronik* (*Kurzer Hand-
Commentar zum Alten Testament*), Tübingen and Leipzig,
1901.

E. Bertheau, *Die Bücher der Chronik*, Leipzig, 1854.

H. Cazelles, *Les Livres des Chroniques* (*La Sainte Bible*),
Paris, 1954.

R. J. Coggins, *The First and Second Books of the Chronicles*
(*The Cambridge Bible Commentary*), Cambridge, 1976.

E. L. Curtis and A. A. Madsen, *A Critical and Exegetical
Commentary on the Books of Chronicles* (*International
Critical Commentary*), Edinburgh, 1910.

H. L. Ellison, 'I and 2 Chronicles', in D. Guthrie, *et al.*
(eds), *The New Bible Commentary Revised*, London, 1970,
pp. 369–94.

W. A. L. Elmslie, *The Books of Chronicles* (*The Cambridge
Bible for Schools and Colleges*), Cambridge, 1916.

— 'The First and Second Books of Chronicles', in G. A.
Buttrick, *et al.* (eds), *The Interpreter's Bible*, Vol. 3,
Nashville, 1954, pp. 341–548.

K. Galling, *Die Bücher der Chronik, Esra, Nehemia* (*Das
Alte Testament Deutsch*), Göttingen, 1954.

J. Goettsberger, *Die Bücher der Chronik oder Paralipomenon*
(*Die heilige Schrift des Alten Testaments*), Bonn, 1939.

W. R. Harvey-Jellie, *Chronicles* (*The Century Bible*),
London, 1906.

A. S. Herbert, 'I and II Chronicles', in M. Black and H. H.
Rowley (eds), *Peake's Commentary on the Bible*, London
and Edinburgh, 1962, pp. 357–69.

C. F. Keil, *The Books of the Chronicles (Biblical Commentary on the Old Testament)*, ET, Edinburgh, 1872.

R. Kittel, *Die Bücher der Chronik (Handkommentar zum Alten Testament)*, Göttingen, 1902.

F. Michaeli, *Les livres des Chroniques, d'Esdras et de Néhémie (Commentaire de l'Ancien Testament)*, Neuchâtel, 1967.

J. M. Myers, *I Chronicles* and *II Chronicles (The Anchor Bible)*, Garden City, 1965.

R. North, 'The Chronicler: 1–2 Chronicles, Ezra, Nehemiah', in R. E. Brown *et al* (eds), *The Jerome Biblical Commentary*, London, Dublin and Melbourne, 1968, pp. 402–38.

J. W. Rothstein and J. Hänel, *Das erste Buch der Chronik (Kommentar zum Alten Testament)*, Leipzig, 1927.

K. Roubos, *I & II Kronieken (De Prediking van het Oude Testament)*, 2 vols., Nijkerk, 1969 and 1972.

W. Rudolph, *Chronikbücher (Handbuch zum Alten Testament)*, Tübingen, 1955.

I. W. Slotki, *Chronicles (Soncino Books of the Bible)*, London, Jerusalem and New York, 1952.

SPECIAL STUDIES

F.-M. Abel, *Géographie de la Palestine*, Paris, 1933.

P. R. Ackroyd, *The Age of the Chronicler*, Auckland, 1970.

— 'The Chronicler as Exegete', *JSOT* 2 (1977), pp. 2–32.

— 'History and Theology in the Writings of the Chronicler', *CTM* 38 (1967), pp. 501–15.

— 'The Theology of the Chronicler', *Lexington Theological Quarterly* 8 (1973), pp. 101–16.

Y. Aharoni, *The Land of the Bible*, ET, London, 1967.

W. F. Albright, *Archaeology and the Religion of Israel*, Baltimore, 1946.

— 'The Date and Personality of the Chronicler', *JBL* 40 (1921), pp. 104–24.

— "The Judicial Reform of Jehoshaphat', in *Alexander Marx Jubilee Volume*, New York, 1950, pp. 61–82.

L. C. Allen, *The Greek Chronicles. The Relation of the Septuagint of I and II Chronicles to the Massoretic Text. Part 1: The Translator's Craft (SVT 25); Part 2: Textual Criticism (SVT 27)*, Leiden, 1974.

A. Alt, *Kleine Schriften zur Geschichte des Volkes Israel*, Vols. 1 and 2, Munich, 1953; Vol. 3, Munich, 1959.

G. W. Anderson (ed.), *Tradition and Interpretation*, Oxford, 1979.

D. Baly, *Geography of the Bible*, rev. edn, Guildford, 1974.

D. Barag, 'The Effects of the Tennes Rebellion on Palestine', *BASOR* 183 (1966), pp. 6–12.

W. Baumgartner, *Hebräisches und Aramäisches Lexikon zum Alten Testament*, Leiden, 1967—.

A. Bendavid, *Parallels in the Bible*, Jerusalem, 1972.

G. Beyer, 'Beiträge zur Territorialgeschichte von Südwestpalästina im Altertum. 1. Das Festungssystem Rehabeams', *ZDPV* 54 (1931), pp. 113–34.

G. J. Botterweck, 'Zur Eigenart der chronistischen Davidgeschichte', *ThQ* 136 (1956), pp. 402–35.

R. L. Braun, 'Chronicles, Ezra, and Nehemiah: Theology and Literary History', *SVT* 30 (1979), pp. 52–64.

— 'The Message of Chronicles: Rally 'Round the Temple', *CTM* 42 (1971), pp. 502–14.

— 'A Reconsideration of the Chronicler's Attitude toward the North', *JBL* 96 (1977), pp. 59–62.

— 'Solomon, the Chosen Temple Builder: the Significance of 1 Chronicles 22, 28, and 29 for the Theology of Chronicles', *JBL* 95 (1976), pp. 581–90.

— 'Solomonic Apologetic in Chronicles', *JBL* 92 (1973), pp. 502–14.

A.-M. Brunet, 'Le Chroniste et ses Sources', *RB* 60 (1953), pp. 481–508; 61 (1954), pp. 349–86.

— 'Paralipomènes (Livres des) ou des Chroniques', *DBS* 6 (1960), cols. 1220–61.

— 'La Théologie du Chroniste. Théocratie et Messianisme', *Sacra Pagina. Miscellenea Biblica Congressus Internationalis Catholici de Re Biblica* (= *Bib. Eph. Th. Lov.* 12–13), ed. J. Coppens, A. Descamps, É. Massaux, Vol. 1, Paris, 1959, pp. 384–97.

H. van den Bussche, 'Le Texte de la prophétie de Nathan sur la dynastie davidique', *ETL* 24 (1948), pp. 354–94.

T. C. Butler, 'A Forgotten Passage from a Forgotten Era (1 Chr. xvi 8–36)', *VT* 28 (1978), pp. 142–50.

A. Caquot, 'Peut-on parler de messianisme dans l'oeuvre du Chroniste?', *RTP*, 3me série, 16 (1966), pp. 110–20.

F. M. Cross, 'A Reconstruction of the Judean Restoration',

JBL 94 (1975), pp. 4–18.

R. Le Déaut and J. Robert, *Targum des Chroniques*, Rome, 1971.

S. R. Driver, *An Introduction to the Literature of the Old Testament*, Edinburgh, 1913⁹.

A. B. Ehrlich, *Randglossen zur Hebräischen Bibel*. Vol. 7, Leipzig, 1914.

D. N. Freedman, 'The Chronicler's Purpose', *CBQ* 23 (1961), pp. 436–42.

G. Gerleman, *Studies in the Septuagint II. Chronicles*, Lund, 1946.

H. Gese, 'Zur Geschichte der Kultsänger am zweiten Tempel', in *Vom Sinai zum Zion. Alttestamentliche Beiträge zur biblischen Theologie*, Munich, 1974, pp. 147–58.

J. C. L. Gibson, *Syrian Semitic Inscriptions, Volume 1: Hebrew and Moabite Inscriptions*, Oxford, 1971: *Volume 2: Aramaic Inscriptions*, Oxford, 1975.

M. Gil, 'Israel in the Books of Chronicles' (Hebrew), *Beth Mikra* 13 (1968), pp. 105–15.

J. Goldingay, 'The Chronicler as a Theologian', *Biblical Theology Bulletin* 5 (1975), pp. 99–126.

D. W. Gooding, *Relics of Ancient Exegesis*, Cambridge, 1976.

H. Haag, 'Das Mazzenfest des Hiskia', in H. Gese and H. P. Rüger (eds), *Wort und Geschichte. Festschrift für Karl Elliger zum 70. Geburtstag*, Neukirchen-Vluyn, 1973, pp. 87–94.

M. Haran, *Temples and Temple Service in Ancient Israel*, Oxford, 1978.

J. H. Hayes and J. M. Miller (eds), *Israelite and Judaean History*, London, 1977.

S. Japhet, 'Conquest and Settlement in Chronicles', *JBL* 98 (1979), pp. 205–18.

— 'Chronicles, Book of', *Encyclopaedia Judaica*, Vol. 5, Jerusalem, 1971, cols. 517–34.

— *The Ideology of the Book of Chronicles and its Place in Biblical Thought* (Hebrew), Jerusalem, 1977.

— 'The Supposed Common Authorship of Chronicles and Ezra-Nehemiah Investigated Anew', *VT* 18 (1968), pp. 330–71.

M. D. Johnson, *The Purpose of the Biblical Genealogies*,

Cambridge, 1969.

E. Junge, *Der Wiederaufbau des Heerwesens des Reiches Juda unter Josia*, Stuttgart, 1937.

H. G. Kippenberg, *Garizim und Synagoge. Traditionsgeschichtliche Untersuchungen zur samaritanischen Religion der aramäischen Periode*, Berlin, 1971.

H.-J. Kraus, *Worship in Israel*, ET, Oxford, 1966.

A. Kropat, *Die Syntax des Autors der Chronik verglichen mit der seiner Quellen*, Giessen, 1909.

W. E. Lemke, 'The Synoptic Problem in the Chronicler's History', *HTR* 58 (1965), pp. 349–63.

J. Liver, *Chapters in the History of the Priests and Levites: Studies in the Lists of Chronicles and Ezra and Nehemiah* (Hebrew), Jerusalem, 1968.

— *Studies in Bible and Judean Desert Scrolls* (Hebrew), Jerusalem, 1971.

A. Malamat, 'Josiah's Bid for Armageddon: the Background of the Judean-Egyptian Encounter in 609 B.C.', *JANES* 5 (1973), pp. 267–78.

J. W. McKay, *Religion in Judah under the Assyrians*, London, 1973.

G. E. Mendenhall, 'The Census Lists of Numbers 1 and 26', *JBL* 77 (1958), pp. 52–66.

T. N. D. Mettinger, *Solomonic State Officials. A Study of the Civil Government Officials of the Israelite Monarchy*, Lund, 1971.

K. Möhlenbrink, 'Die levitischen Überlieferungen des Alten Testaments', *ZAW* 52 (1934), pp. 184–231.

F. L. Moriarty, 'The Chronicler's Account of Hezekiah's Reform', *CBQ* 27 (1965), pp. 399–406.

R. Mosis, *Untersuchungen zur Theologie des chronistischen Geschichtswerkes*, Freiburg, 1973.

J. M. Myers, 'The Kerygma of the Chronicler', *Interpretation* 20 (1966), pp. 259–73.

J. D. Newsome, 'Toward a New Understanding of the Chronicler and his Purposes', *JBL* 94 (1975), pp. 201–17.

A. Noordtzij, 'Les Intentions du Chroniste', *RB* 49 (1940), pp. 161–8.

R. North, 'Does Archeology Prove Chronicles Sources?', in H. N. Bream, R. D. Heim and C. A. Moore (eds), *A Light Unto My Path: Old Testament Studies in Honor of Jacob M. Myers*, Philadelphia, 1974, pp. 375–401.

—'Theology of the Chronicler', *JBL* 82 (1963), pp. 369–81.

M. Noth, *Aufsätze zur biblischen Landes– und Altertumskunde*, 2 vols., Neukirchen, 1971.

— 'Eine palästinische Lokalüberlieferung in 2. Chr. 20', *ZDPV* 67 (1944–5), pp. 45–71.

— 'Eine siedlungsgeographische Liste in 1. Chr. 2 und 4', *ZDPV* 55 (1932), pp. 97–124.

— *Überlieferungsgeschichtliche Studien I*, Halle, 1943 (cited in the text as *US*).

J. B. Payne, 'Validity of Numbers in Chronicles', *Near East Archaeological Society Bulletin* ns 11 (1978), pp. 5–58.

D. L. Petersen, *Late Israelite Prophecy: Studies in Deutero-Prophetic Literature and in Chronicles*, Missoula, 1977.

O. Plöger, 'Reden und Gebete im deuteronomistischen und chronistischen Geschichtswerk', in *Aus der Spätzeit des Alten Testaments*, Göttingen, 1971, pp. 50–66.

— *Theocracy and Eschatology*, ET, Oxford, 1968.

E. Podechard, 'Le Premier Chapitre des Paralipomènes', *RB* 13 (1916), pp. 363–86.

K.-F. Pohlmann, *Studien zum dritten Esra. Ein Beitrag zur Frage nach dem ursprünglichen Schluss des chronistischen Geschichtswerkes*, Göttingen, 1970.

R. Polzin, *Late Biblical Hebrew: Toward an Historical Typology of Biblical Hebrew Prose*, Missoula, 1976.

G. von Rad, *Das Geschichtsbild des chronistischen Werkes*, Stuttgart, 1930 (cited in the text as *GCW*).

— *Der heilige Krieg im alten Israel*, Zürich, 1951.

— 'The Levitical Sermon in I and II Chronicles', ET, in *The Problem of the Hexateuch and Other Essays*, Edinburgh and London, 1966, pp. 267–80.

M. Rehm, *Textkritische Untersuchungen zu den Parallelstellen der Samuel-Königsbücher und der Chronik*, Münster, 1937.

G. Rinaldi, 'Quelques remarques sur la politique d'Azarias (Ozias) de Juda en Philistie (2 Chron. 26, 6ss.)', *SVT* 9 (1963), pp. 225–35.

I. L. Seeligmann, 'Der Auffassung von der Prophetie in der deuteronomistischen und chronistischen Geschichtsschreibung', *SVT* 29 (1978), pp. 254–84.

J. Simons, *The Geographical and Topographical Texts of the Old Testament*, Leiden, 1959 (cited in the text as *GTTOT*).

W. F. Stinespring, 'Eschatology in Chronicles', *JBL* 80 (1961), pp. 209–19.

C. C. Torrey, 'The Chronicler as Editor and as Independent Narrator', *AJSL* 25 (1908–9), pp. 157–73 and 188–217.

E. C. Ulrich, *The Qumran Text of Samuel and Josephus*, Missoula, 1978.

P. Vannutelli, *Libri Synoptici Veteris Testamenti seu Librorum Regum et Chronicorum Loci Paralleli*, 2 vols., Rome, 1931 and 1934.

R. de Vaux, *Ancient Israel: its Life and Institutions*, ET, London, 2nd edn, 1965 (cited in the text as *AI*).

W. G. E. Watson, 'Archaic Elements in the Language of Chronicles', *Biblica* 53 (1972), pp. 191–207.

A. C. Welch, *Post-Exilic Judaism*, Edinburgh and London, 1935.

—*The Work of the Chronicler. Its Purpose and its Date*, London, 1939.

J. Wellhausen, *Prolegomena to the History of Israel*, ET, Edinburgh, 1885.

P. Welten, *Geschichte und Geschichtsdarstellung in den Chronikbüchern*, Neukirchen, 1973.

—'Lade—Tempel—Jerusalem: zur Theologie der Chronikbücher', in A. H. J. Gunneweg and O. Kaiser (eds), *Textgemäss: Aufsätze und Beiträge zur Hermeneutik des alten Testaments*, Göttingen, 1979, pp. 169–83.

J. W. Wenham, 'Large Numbers in the Old Testament', *TynB* 18 (1967), pp. 19–53.

T. Willi, *Die Chronik als Auslegung. Untersuchungen zur literarischen Gestaltung der historischen Überlieferung Israels*, Göttingen, 1972.

H. G. M. Williamson, 'The Accession of Solomon in the Books of Chronicles', *VT* 26 (1976), pp. 351–61.

— 'The Dynastic Oracle in the Books of Chronicles', in A. Rofé (ed.), *Seeligmann Anniversary Volume*, Jerusalem (forthcoming).

—'Eschatology in Chronicles', *TynB* 28 (1977), pp. 115–54.

—*Israel in the Books of Chronicles*, Cambridge, 1977 (cited in the text as *IBC*).

—'The Origins of the Twenty-Four Priestly Courses: a Study of 1 Chronicles xxiii–xxvii', *SVT* 30 (1979), pp. 251–68.

—'Sources and Redaction in the Chronicler's Genealogy of

Judah', *JBL* 98 (1979), pp. 351–9.

—' "We are yours, O David": the Setting and Purpose of 1
Chronicles xii 1–23', *OTS* 21 (1981), pp. 164–76.

Y. Yadin, *The Art of Warfare in Biblical Lands*, ET,
London, 1963.

A. Zeron, 'Die Anmassung des Königs Usia im Lichte von
Jesajas Berufung', *ThZ* 33 (1977), pp. 65–8.

—'Tag für Tag kam man zu David, um ihm zu helfen,
1. Chr. 12, 1–22', *ThZ* 30 (1974), pp. 257–61.

INTRODUCTION

to

1 and 2 Chronicles

THE GENEALOGIES

1 Chr. 1–9

Few biblical passages are more daunting to the modern reader than the opening chapters of 1 Chronicles. Nevertheless, their very extent suggests that they were a matter of great concern to the author and that concentrated effort to recover his methods and purposes may be rewarding. Even though the comments below aim to deal mainly with the Chronicler's own interests in this material, rather than the light they may shed on the periods of history from which they purport to come, a few overall guidelines may be helpful by way of introduction.

Looking first at the 'vertical' dimension of the lists, it is to be noted that they cover three main periods. Chapter 1 moves along the line of God's election from Adam to Israel (Jacob). Chapters 2–8 then deal in much greater detail with the sons of Israel; nearly all the material refers to the pre-exilic period, and the impression is conveyed that much relates specifically to the time of David, to whose reign over a united Israel the first major narrative section is devoted. Finally, ch. 9 narrows the spectrum again to list the chief representatives of the post-exilic community, with whom the Chronicler and his readers would most readily identify themselves. This simple scheme, it will be argued, is not arbitrary. On the contrary, just as ch. 1 clearly points to the special election of Israel within the family of the nations, so ch. 9 balances this by indicating that the community it portrays stands in unbroken succession to the nation whose history is about to be related. In this dimension, therefore, the themes of election, continuity and restoration are prominent (cf. Ackroyd, *Age*, p. 48).

With the apparently exclusive attitude of this outlook must be compared the much broader concerns of the 'horizontal' dimension of the lists. This comes to expression chiefly in the central section, where, quite in contrast with what is generally regarded as the narrow-mindedness of the Chronicler's community, we are presented with an effort to include within the family of Israel all who could mount any legitimate claim to participation. A great variety of sources has here been combined in an effort to attend to all the tribes, even those who were either long since lost to history, or whose descendants would have been regarded as quite unacceptable by the Jerusalem community. Moreover, there is no attempt to cover up the inclusion of foreigners through mixed marriages. The obvious reason of space it has not been possible to include full discussion of such issues in every case, though clearly the decision made about them will often exercise a considerable influence on the commentator's appreciation of the Chronicler's presentation.

Finally, for passages where the Chronicler's source has not survived, or where he may have been engaging in free composition, the commentary aims to deal as far as possible with the whole range of problems raised by the text. Here, however, it should be remembered that there are two steps involved in the exercise. The less important one is the determination of the nature and extent of the material which the Chronicler inherited. Precisely because of its inevitably hypothetical nature, this step needs often to be treated at greater length. This should not allow the reader's attention to be deflected, however, from the ultimately more significant step of seeking to appreciate the purpose for which the Chronicler has himself included this material and also the way he has handled it. In a few cases, this twofold exercise has demanded more extensive discussion than could reasonably be accommodated in a commentary. These studies have had to be published separately (see Bibliography) and only their results are summarised here.

B. NAME AND PLACE IN THE CANON

In the Hebrew Canon, 1 and 2 Chronicles were counted as a single book and called *dibrê hayyāmîm*, 'the events of the days', hence 'annals'. This expression occurs quite frequently in the *OT*, particularly in the books of Kings, where it is usually qualified in order to give it a more precise definition, e.g. 'the Book of the Chronicles of the Kings of Judah', 1 Kg. 14:29. However, in three cases (Neh. 12:23; Est. 2:23; 6:1) it is used, as in our title, without further qualification. For a book whose historical scope stretches from Adam (1 Chr.1:1) to the establishment of the Persian empire (2 Chr. 36:20) any more precise definition would be inappropriate.

That this appreciation remained alive in Jewish tradition may be seen from the fuller title provided by the Targum, which starts 'This is the book of genealogies, the Chronicles from days of antiquity'. It is quite probable that Jerome would have been familiar with this tradition, for while he retained the Greek title (see below) for his translation, he suggested in his so-called *Prologus galeatus* (i.e. the prologue to his translation of the books of Samuel and Kings) that 'we might more significantly call it the *chronikon* of the whole of sacred history'. Jerome's use of a Greek word here indicates that he intended it as a title that should serve as an equivalent to that in Hebrew. By way of his influence on Luther, Jerome's suggestion has finally come to be the most widely used name for our books.

An alternative tradition, however, has also survived. In the MSS of LXX, the work is divided into two and called *paraleipomenōn a* and *b* (and cf. V's *Paralipomenon*), that is, '(The Books) of things left out'. This is a reference to the fact that in a number of passages Chronicles supplements the account of the history in Samuel and Kings. Such a name is clearly misleading, however, for it obscures the fact that Chronicles also repeats much material from Samuel and Kings and, more importantly, it fails to do justice to the Chronicler's own positive purpose which he had in writing and which has determined his selection and arrangement of material. Indeed, it may be said that the influence of this misnomer in LXX and V on the Christian church has contributed significantly to the undervaluing and consequent neglect of these books until comparatively recent times.

As already mentioned, the books of Chronicles were treated as a single work in the Massoretic tradition until the Middle Ages. Apart from the Syriac tradition, we have no evidence to suggest that their canonical status was ever seriously questioned. Hints from Josephus (*Contra Apionem* 1.40) and the *NT* (see on 2 Chr. 24:21) suggest that their position was assured by the first century in the main traditions of both Judaism and Christianity.

In the Hebrew Canon, Chronicles usually comes at the very end of the third division, 'the Writings'; cf. The Babylonian Talmud, Baba Bathra 14b. In a few lists, however, it stands at the head of that division; for a convenient presentation of the evidence, cf. L. B. Paton, *Esther* (1908), pp. 1–3. In LXX, however, which has exercised the dominant influence on the Christian Bible in this regard, it is grouped with the other historical books, between 2 Kings and Ezra, as is to be expected on the basis of its content.

The position of Chronicles at the end of the Hebrew Canon has been frequently explained on the supposition that it was originally joined to Ezra-Nehemiah. It is argued that Ezra and Nehemiah were detached from the original work and canonised because they were regarded as of greater value, continuing, as they do, the history already recorded in Samuel and Kings. Being supplementary, Chronicles came to be accepted only later. H. Cazelles, *VT* 29 (1979), pp. 379–80, has sought to refine this view further by arguing that the very positive role which Chronicles ascribes to the Levites would have been unacceptable to the Sadducees in the period of the second temple, whereas the portrayal of Ezra and Nehemiah would have caused less difficulty. He thus thinks that only later, presumably after the Pharisaic tradition became normative following the destruction of the temple, was Chronicles accepted into the Canon.

Such speculations, however, are highly questionable. Not only do they postulate a quite unparalleled process in the canonisation of this work for which, *pace* Cazelles, no compelling explanation has been offered, but they totally misrepresent the process of canonisation itself. As rightly stressed by Willi, pp. 180f., canonisation was never a selective act, but rather a declaration of a work's inherent authority, already recognised by the religious community over a considerable period of time. In addition to this, we have absolutely no tangible evidence for the canonisation of Chronicles later than Ezra-Nehemiah, while their separate acceptance in LXX, which cannot be later than the middle of the second century BC (cf. *IBC*, pp. 14f., and Allen, 1, pp. 11f.), provides strong evidence for both their separate treatment and canonisation from comparatively early times. Their joining in the apocryphal 1 Esdras, intelligible enough on the basis of content, is nevertheless to be regarded as a secondary activity. It has sometimes been argued (most fully and recently by Pohlmann) that this latter work (which comprises, roughly speaking, 2 Chr. 35–36, Ezr. 1–10 and Neh. 8, together with some supplementary additions and involving some changes in order) should be regarded as a fragment of the 'original Septuagint' translation of the Chronicler's work before its separation into two parts. To this it may be replied that 1 Esdras is indeed probably to be regarded as a fragment. However, a number of considerations, not least the fact that 1 Esd. 9:37 shows that the author was following a *Vorlage* in which Neh. 8 followed Neh. 7, not Ezr. 10, demonstrate conclusively that the work is a compilation, and hence secondary as far as the conjoining of Chr. with Ezr.-Neh. is concerned (cf. *IBC*, pp. 12–36).

The precise reason for the position of Chronicles at the end of the Hebrew Canon thus remains unexplained, but within the context of the miscellaneous collection of which the third division, the Writings, is made up this need occasion no surprise.

C.   THE EXTENT OF THE CHRONICLER'S WORK

There are two main areas of disagreement in discussions concerning the extent of the Chronicler's work. First, it is disputed whether he was also responsible for the whole or part of the books of Ezra and Nehemiah, and, second, there is little agreement concerning the question of possible secondary material within the books of Chronicles themselves. We shall deal in this section with only the first of these two points, reserving the second for the next section. Needless to say, the commentator's attitude to both issues will profoundly affect his interpretation of the Chronicler's presentation.

For at least the last 150 years the overwhelming majority of scholars has accepted the view that the books of Chronicles are directly continued in the books of Ezra and Nehemiah, that the division between them in the Canon is secondary, and that their theology must be expounded as a whole. I have already examined this consensus in some detail in *IBC*, pp. 5–70. It will be possible here to rehearse only the main points at issue, while at the same time I shall try to take some account of criticisms of my earlier work as well as of other recent publications.

This consensus is based on four main arguments. First, there is an almost exact overlap between the end of Chronicles (2 Chr. 36:22f.) and the beginning of Ezra (Ezr. 1:1–3). It is suggested that this was a conscious device to stress the unity of the two parts of the work when Ezra-Nehemiah was separated off and canonised in advance of Chronicles. This argument, however, depends on an understanding of the process of canonisation already criticised above in section B. Moreover, there are other more plausible suggestions to account for the phenomenon, so that 2 Chr. 36:22f. need be no more than a secondary addition to the original conclusion at 36:21; see the commentary *ad loc*.

Second, the evidence of 1 Esdras has been adduced to suggest continuity of authorship. Certainly the work is of interest in demonstrating that the chronological relationship between the books was recognised already in antiquity. However, 1 Esdras is itself a compilation (see section B above), not the direct translation of an original work. Its 'author' presumably selected his material for a particular purpose. Since it may readily be agreed that there are various important points which Chronicles and Ezra-Nehemiah hold in common because of their origin within the same somewhat restricted community, it is not surprising that the compiler of 1 Esdras should have drawn on them both. In no way, however, does this prove that they were originally joined, while the separate translation of Chronicles and Ezra-Nehemiah in LXX at a time and place of origin very close to 1 Esdras points rather to their separate existence as far back as purely formal, textual evidence will allow us to reach.

If these first two arguments in favour of unity of authorship are quite inconclusive, the third might appear to offer hope of more tangible results. It is the argument from the alleged similarity of vocabulary and style. The position over this until comparatively recently may be simply summarised. A number of older works, such as Driver, *Introduction*, pp. 535–40, and CM, pp. 27–36, listed various lexical and syntactical features in order to illustrate the characteristics of the Chronicler's style. These lists were not drawn up primarily with a view to determining the precise extent of the Chronicler's work, for which purpose they are quite unsuitable, but rather started with the unity of Chronicles, Ezra and Nehemiah as a presupposition. However, these lists were generally considered by other scholars to have demonstrated the unity of Chronicles, Ezra and Nehemiah as well.

This consensus remained unexamined until 1968, when it was forcefully challenged by Japhet, *VT* 18 (1968), pp. 330–71. She selected a number of items, primarily of vocabulary, which pointed in the opposite direction. Nevertheless, this left unanswered the evidence of the older lists, and it was to this specific topic that I addressed my earlier study of the matter (*IBC*, pp. 37–59). It should be emphasised that this was not an attempt at a full analysis of the language and style of these books, but only a more restricted inquiry into the question whether the published evidence for unity of authorship on this basis retained validity. It was found that in fact most of the evidence published was not relevant; for instance, much was simply characteristic of post-exilic Hebrew as a whole, some of the items listed did not appear in both Chronicles and Ezra-Nehemiah, and so on. Nevertheless, it was suggested that in a number of cases the evidence of the lists could in fact point in the opposite direction since it betrayed significant differences of usage between the two bodies of writing.

This exercise has been criticised along two lines. First, it is said that, with the exception of the Nehemiah Memoir, it did not take sufficiently into account the various sources, particularly in Ezra-Nehemiah, which the writer will have used. This, in fact, was a conscious decision, for such an analysis would have been out of place in the context of the examination of the earlier published lists. It is, however, quite obvious that a full study of the characteristic language of these books would demand such attention to sources. It is less clear, however, that this would undermine my main conclusions. Japhet, for instance, isolated some characteristic features of the language of the books of Chronicles which are totally absent from Ezra-Nehemiah, and it will be seen later that some of these are, moreover, features by which the Chronicler expressed his most fundamental theological convictions. Naturally a source-analysis of Ezra-Nehemiah would be a quite irrelevant exercise. In addition, it should be remembered that such an analysis would also cut through a good deal of the alleged evidence in favour of unity of authorship.

A second criticism concerns my concentration on items of vocabulary rather than on grammar and syntax. (This too, of course, was determined by the restricted nature of the undertaking.) Fortunately, it is possible now to use the study of Polzin (1976), which does indeed concentrate on just such matters. A superficial reading of Polzin's book might suggest a completely contrasting position with that outlined above, for he speaks of 'an extremely strong case for similarity in authorship of Chr. and Ezr.' (p. 71). This statement too, however, must be understood in the context of Polzin's own objectives. His aim is to establish what he calls a 'typology of late biblical Hebrew prose', and to see where the Priestly strand in the Pentateuch fits into this. In moving towards this objective, he analyses the language of most of the certainly post-exilic biblical books, and finds that in this respect Chronicles, Ezra and the non-Nehemiah Memoir portions of Nehemiah share certain features which set them apart from Esther and the NM. (It is a weakness that Polzin does not undertake a similar comparison with the Hebrew portions of Daniel, for in many cases they too stand close to the former group.) He further argues that Esther and the NM are consciously archaising compositions, whereas the other books best represent 'the actual state of the language at the time of its composition'.

Two points may therefore be made in applying Polzin's results to our specific purpose. First, in so far as Chronicles, Ezra and parts of Nehemiah reflect a living language at a particular stage in its development, similarities between them are to be expected, and I take this to be Polzin's point when he speaks of 'similarity' rather than 'identity' of authorship. After working carefully through Polzin's evidence, I have found this conclusion to be repeatedly confirmed, for he himself very fairly shows how the features discussed are often found in other late biblical Hebrew texts, as would be expected.

Secondly, it is not germane to Polzin's purpose to draw attention to the differences already alluded to between Chronicles and Ezra-Nehemiah, differences which, it may be claimed, are significant in suggesting the existence of separate authors, albeit authors writing within a single stage in the development of the language. On the one occasion where he does take such evidence into account (pp. 54f.), he has artificially to ascribe the difference to later scribal tradition, while this element is significantly omitted from his summarising chart (p. 75). I thus conclude that Polzin's work, which, it must be stressed, is not directed primarily at our present concern, suggests that an approach to our problem along such lines would not materially affect the conclusions already reached on the basis of vocabulary.

The fourth and final area of discussion concerning the extent of

the Chronicler's work is the decisive one. This concerns the Chronicler's outlook, interests and theology. In addition to such shared
interests as genealogies, the temple, details of temple worship and
the prominence of the cultic officials, there is also the larger question
to be considered whether the books of Chronicles may be regarded
as a self-contained work in their own right or whether they demand
for a full understanding at least the account of the restoration after
the exile in the opening chapters of Ezra, if not more.

As regards the points of shared interest, it should be readily
agreed that not much can be built on them. The post-exilic community in Jerusalem undoubtedly centred on the temple as its focal
point, so that any writer dealing with history, whether recent or
remote, would have been likely to give particular attention to it and
its service. This probability is borne out by the fact that several of
these common interests are also shared by the Priestly portions of
the Pentateuch.

More striking, therefore, will be any differences of outlook which
can be detected between the two books. If it can be established that
these affect fundamental concerns of the respective works, then they
should be decisive in establishing that Ezra and Nehemiah were not
an original part of the Chronicler's work.

I argued in *IBC*, pp. 60–9, that there were such differences, and
dealt with some of them in varying degrees of detail. The point has
subsequently been urged that no account was taken of the influence
of sources in Ezra-Nehemiah. This criticism is justified. Fortunately, however, some of the main points at issue have been treated
along precisely these lines by Braun, *SVT* 30 (1979), pp. 52–64.
His study shows that although greater attention to the influence of
sources should lead to a reappraisal of which points are the most
significant, the overall picture of a real diversity between the two
works in areas which are crucial to their ideology is in no way
affected. (Contrast S. J. L. Croft, *JSOT* 14 [1979], pp. 68–72, some
of whose criticisms are answered in the following paragraphs.)

Some of the major distinctive themes of the books of Chronicles
will be outlined in section G below. Here, therefore, it may be
simply observed that most of these themes are handled in all the
major levels of Ezra-Nehemiah in ways which contrast with Chronicles. The doctrine of retribution, for instance, which the Chronicler
expounds with distinctive, stereotyped vocabulary and with an emphasis often on the prophetic word, is 'almost entirely lacking in
Ezra-Nehemiah' (Braun, p. 55). It is broached only in the prayers
of Ezr. 9 and Neh. 9, but even then with significantly contrasting
concepts and without the Chronicler's distinctive vocabulary. Again,
the importance of the covenant with David and his dynasty, includ-

ing the hope for its future restoration, is nowhere raised in Ezra-Nehemiah. It is not sufficient merely to say that it would have been inappropriate in a work describing the post-exilic restoration. Rather, in Chronicles it concerns a fundamental development in the covenantal basis of God's relationship with Israel, which results in a shift away from the emphasis of the Deuteronomic historian on the Exodus and Sinai (see on 2 Chr. 6). In Ezra-Nehemiah, however, we find throughout, and especially in those areas where the redactor's hand is most probably to be seen, a position that takes no account of this development, but retains instead the importance of the Sinai covenant and the promises to the patriarchs.

A third major area of divergence relates to the understanding of 'Israel' in the two works. Several writers (e.g. H. Cazelles, *VT* 29 [1979], pp. 377f.) have contested this point, but without, in my judgment, appreciating the totally different attitudes which pervade the two works in this respect. This is particularly striking with regard to the status of the inhabitants of the old northern kingdom (though it is to be seen elsewhere as well). The Chronicler clearly believes that many Israelites continued to live in the north after the fall of Samaria and that strenuous, and sometimes moderately successful, attempts were made to regain their adherence to the Jerusalem temple (cf. 2 Chr. 29–36, *passim*). In Ezra-Nehemiah, however, this situation is nowhere recognised. Even in Ezr. 3:1–4:5, the passage which perhaps stands nearest of all to the thought of the Chronicler, the contrast is most marked. Here, the only recognised inhabitants of the north are foreigners resettled by the Assyrians, and they are refused any share in the Jerusalem community. Yet the Chronicler has said nothing of this resettlement in his work, despite the opportunity provided by his *Vorlage* (2 Kg. 17). If, as many scholars hold, the Chronicler included parts of Ezra-Nehemiah within his work with the intention of offering guidelines for the thought and policy of the community in his own day, this unexplained and total change of outlook would surely have been confusing to the point of bewilderment.

Fourthly, it is remarkable that while Ezra and Nehemiah do not, on the whole, refer back to the distinctive traditions of the Chronicler when they deal with the past history of the nation (the only exception is a certain paralleling of the account of Ezr. 3 with the building of the first temple as recorded by the Chronicler), there are several points at which they are certainly dependent on other presentations. In Chronicles, for instance, Jacob is consistently called 'Israel' (see on 1 Chr. 1:34) and was regarded by the Chronicler as of some importance for the nation's history. This distinctive nomenclature and appraisal is completely lacking in Ezra-Nehemiah. Furthermore, the presentation of the resettlement of the old northern kingdom (Ezr. 4) has already been stated to diverge from that in Chronicles, as has the prominence of the Exodus traditions. Finally, although Neh. 13:26 is probably to be attributed to the NM, yet it still contrasts strikingly with the Chronicler's own portrayal of Solomon's reign (2 Chr. 1–9).

Although much more could be said, one further example of such divergence must suffice. It concerns the approach to history-writing itself. It will be frequently noted that the Chronicler supplies theological commentary on the events he is recording in the form of what, following von Rad, have come to be called 'Levitical sermons'. They combine his confessional standpoint with citations from the canonical prophets, clearly regarded by now as authoritative. Moreover, these sermons frequently accompany and explain those dramatic reversals in the people's fortunes which are so characteristic of his narrative. None of this, however, is found in Ezra-Nehemiah (cf. Newsome), even though there would have been ample opportunity for its compiler either to combine such forms with his earlier sources (e.g. at Ezr. 5) or to include them in passages where it has often been thought he may have been composing more freely (e.g. at Ezr. 3 and 9). This distinction, too, gives the strong impression that another writer is here at work, employing his own rather different methods for communicating his beliefs to his readers.

It may thus be concluded that the books of Chronicles and Ezra-Nehemiah are separate works. While Ezra and Nehemiah are not our present concern, it would appear to be possible to make sense without difficulty of their starting point in Ezr. 1:1. Their complicated literary history leads on any view to problems in outlining a fully satisfactory exposition of their thought, but the solution of these problems is at no point dependent on the need for reference back specifically to the books of Chronicles.

Chronicles too, it may be claimed, can be well understood and appreciated as a work in its own right. The retelling of sacred history was no innovation in Israel or Judah, and certainly did not demand that the story must be brought right down to the writer's own day. Enough hints (e.g. 1 Chr. 3; 9; 2 Chr. 36:20f.) were included to point forward to the eventual restoration, the broad outline of which would, of course, have been familiar to the Chronicler's readers. Nevertheless the lessons of the past are satisfactorily communicated in the work as it stands, and again there are no references forward which demand the presence of any part of Ezra-Nehemiah within it.

D. UNITY

The second area of disagreement with regard to the extent of the Chronicler's work concerns its internal unity. Since the question was first raised, three main periods of scholarly discussion may be distinguished, although of course they cannot be rigidly separated.

During the first phase, which reached its peak in the 1920s and 1930s, the results of the dominant documentary hypothesis of Pentateuchal origins exercised a profound influence on the study of Chronicles. Thus RH, for instance, argued in detail in their commentary on 1 Chronicles for a basic narrative which continued the tradition of the P source in the Pentateuch, and they proposed an elaborate series of subsequent redactions, which gradually accommodated Chronicles more closely to the Pentateuch as a whole, including, as of particular importance, Deuteronomy. Welch, on the other hand, argued in exactly the opposite direction. For him, the Chronicler's work is to be dated before the post-exilic restoration, and was written by a member of the community who had never been in exile. It 'must be set alongside the proposals in Ezekiel as one of the programmes which were put forward, before the final settlement was reached ' (WC, p. 156). This, of course, involves regarding not only 1 Chr. 1–9 as secondary, but also all passages which betray the influence of P. Thus the bulk of Welch's monograph is given over to isolating the work of a reviser who shared the outlook of P. The original Chronicler, he argued, compiled his book within a community which still accepted D as its authoritative law-code. Finally, mention should be made of a work from the middle of this period, a work which includes the most thorough examination ever published of the relationship of Chronicles to the various strands of the Pentateuch, G. von Rad's *Das Geschichtsbild des chronistischen Werkes* (1930). This was in many respects a reaction to the rather extreme views of RH, and so was concerned to emphasise the importance of Deuteronomy for the Chronicler. Nevertheless, it avoided going to the other extreme later espoused by Welch. This result was perhaps to be expected in a writer who based himself on the Deuteronomistic history, and yet knew the Pentateuch in substantially its present shape rather than as separate documents. Nevertheless, von Rad still argued that Chronicles had been subjected to a measure of secondary editing, particularly with regard to the position of the Levites. His moderate stance over the relationship between the Chronicler and the Pentateuch has continued to exert considerable influence down to the present day.

The second phase of discussion about the unity of Chronicles took on a very different appearance from the first and its results are still widely held. Pioneered by Noth (*US*, pp. 110–23) and Rudolph, this approach sees in Chronicles essentially the work of a single author. Nevertheless, evidence is adduced to suggest that it has been subjected to all manner of later additions. These, however, appear to be isolated, and not the result of a single or consistent redaction. (A notable exception here is the commentary by Galling [1954], who argues that the work of two authors, whose individual characteristics can be clearly identified, is to be traced throughout Chronicles. His position is not, however, dependent on the results of Pentateuchal analysis, as in the first phase of research. Galling's suggestions, which were soon to be overshadowed by the appearance of Rudolph's magisterial commentary [1955], have attracted little support, and none of any lasting importance. For a response to Galling, cf. Welten, pp. 191–3.) Thus both Noth and Rudolph find a great deal of secondary material in the first nine chapters, though they retain a basic core of this for the Chronicler, a good deal in the account of David's reign, especially 1 Chr. 23–27 and parts of 15–16, and then rather less in the remainder of the work (i.e. 2 Chronicles). No commentary has attempted so detailed an analysis since Rudolph (though cf. Willi, pp. 194–204); nevertheless, several follow him in referring in unspecific terms to the probability of later additions in these sections.

Thirdly, mention should be made of a recent trend amongst a number of American scholars, in particular, namely, that of linking the question of the unity of Chronicles with the larger topic of the development of Chronicles–Ezra–Nehemiah. Though briefly adumbrated by Freedman, *CBQ* 23 (1961), pp. 436–42, this trend has been most fully developed by Cross, *JBL* 94 (1975), pp. 4–18, though see also Newsome, *JBL* 94 (1975), pp. 201–17, and Petersen, pp. 57–60. Cross argues for three separate editions of the Chronicler's work. The latest, labelled Chr$_3$ and dated to about 400 BC, is made up of the whole of Chronicles, Ezra and Nehemiah. Cross then uses the evidence of 1 Esdras and Josephus, *Jewish Antiquities*, to argue for a Chr$_2$ dated about 450 BC. Not surprisingly, he suggests that this included at its end the whole of the *Vorlage* of 1 Esdras (including the story of the three guardsmen, subsequently dropped by Chr$_3$). It is impossible, however, because of the dates involved, for him to retain the genealogies of 1 Chr. 1–9, and in consequence he does not regard them as part of the earlier editions of Chronicles. No evidence from the genealogies themselves, however, is adduced for this suggestion. Finally, in rather closer dependence on Freedman, Cross suggests that the original work of the Chronicler, Chr$_1$, was made up of 1 Chr. 10 – 2 Chr. 34 plus the

Vorlage of 1 Esd. 1:1–5:65 (= 2 Chr. 34:1 – Ezr. 3:13). It comes from the period of the building of the second temple, whose restoration, together with the proposed restoration of the kingdom under Zerubbabel, it was designed to support.

The approach to our problem outlined by Cross is open to a number of serious objections (see also *Tyn B* 28 [1977], pp. 120–30). Only a few of the more salient points need be mentioned here. First, he has not taken account of at least two solid pieces of evidence from the irreducible core of Chronicles which demand a date considerably later than 520–515 BC; see on 1 Chr. 29:7; 2 Chr. 16:9, and section E below. Second, his analysis depends on evidence from 1 Esdras already seen to be inadmissable. Third, his denial of 1 Chr. 1–9 to the original work of the Chronicler is dependent entirely on the demands of his theory as based on the conclusion of his work in 1 Esdras or Ezra—Nehemiah. He has not brought forward any arguments based on the evidence of Chronicles itself. It may therefore be concluded that, although there are signs of the increasing popularity of this approach to the question of composition, it is nevertheless to be rejected as unsatisfactory.

In the present commentary the question of the literary status of the disputed passages is treated fully. Study of this subject has remained virtually static since Rudolph's commentary, but it is to be hoped that some further progress has now been made. Since each passage has to be discussed on its own merits, it is possible only to summarise the chief results which emerge.

It is argued throughout that Chronicles constitutes a substantial unity, including the genealogies of 1 Chr. 1–9 (see the introduction to that section). In many cases where secondary additions have formerly been detected, it is found either that the arguments do not stand up to critical examination or that they overlook the demands of the literary structure and theological cohesion of the sections in question. It will often be found that the problem has arisen because the Chronicler has not always cared to harmonise every detail of the sources on which he has drawn.

Secondly, however, evidence will be presented in a few cases, notably in 1 Chr. 15–16 and 23–27, but also in one or two other less extensive passages, which points to secondary expansion of the Chronicler's original work. These are not nearly so numerous as the passages isolated by Rudolph, but unlike his seemingly miscellaneous collection they all share certain clear characteristics which enable us to attribute them to the hand of a priestly reviser. (Their predominance in 1 Chr. 15–16 and 23–27 is thus in no way surprising.) The Chronicler himself advanced a very favourable portrayal of the Levites, but about a generation after his work the priesthood

in Jerusalem was reformed on the basis of the twenty-four courses
more familiar from later times; cf. *SVT* 30 (1979), pp. 251–68. The
reviser, it may be surmised, was anxious both to correct what he
may have seen as the Chronicler's undue neglect of the importance
of the priests in their relationship to the Levites, and to present
Davidic legitimation for the recently emerged priestly and Levitical
orders.

The isolation of this single, relatively slight, redaction of the
Chronicler's work depends primarily on internal literary-critical
arguments. It does not represent a return to the first phase of study
in this field outlined above. Rather, it seeks to advance in a modest
way the approach of Noth and Rudolph. Its chief virtues are its
simplicity and coherence.

E. DATE, SETTING AND AUTHORSHIP

The Chronicler has left very few clues by which we may date his
work with any certainty. Absolute limits are set on the one hand by
a reference to 'the establishment of the kingdom of Persia' in
2 Chr. 36:20, which precludes a date earlier than 539 BC, and on
the other hand by textual attestation of the existence of Chronicles
before the middle of the second century BC, namely the citation of
LXX of Chronicles by Eupolemos. In fact, since time must be allowed
for Chronicles to have become established in Alexandria, and then
for the translation to be known and used by Eupolemos, and since
it is probable that for his description of David Ben Sira was dependent on Chronicles (cf. Sir. 47:8–10), it is clear that this lower limit
should be raised somewhat, thereby excluding the Maccabean date
which has occasionally been proposed.

Dates throughout this long period of over 300 years have at
various times been suggested. Nevertheless, it is possible to eliminate some of the most extreme proposals. A date very early in the
Persian period was favoured by Welch, and, as already noted, has
recently been revived by Cross, Newsome and others. The reference
to Darics at 1 Chr. 29:7, discussed in full in *Tyn B* 28 (1977),
pp. 123–6, tells strongly against this, however, for this coin was not
minted before 515 BC at the earliest, and sufficient time must be
allowed for the anachronism to have been tolerated. Second, at
2 Chr. 16:9, there is a citation of Zech. 4:10. Since this comes in a
'Levitical sermon', the citation is put on a level footing with citations
from pre-exilic, canonical prophets; form-critically, it cannot simply
be explained away as a reference to the saying of a contemporary.
Time must therefore be allowed for the prophecies of Zechariah to

have acquired authoritative status. Third, it is accepted in this commentary that the bulk of 1 Chr. 1–9 comes from the Chronicler himself. Although there are difficulties surrounding the text of 1 Chr. 3:17–24, it certainly requires a date at least two generations later than Zerubbabel, and possibly more. The combination of these points suggests that we should not look for a date too early in the Persian period.

Switching now to the lower limit, we note that nearly all the arguments which have been advanced in favour of a late date for Chronicles have been based on Ezra—Nehemiah. If the two works are separate, however, this carries no weight. Moreover, there is no indication, linguistic or ideological, of any Hellenistic influence on Chronicles (cf. Ackroyd, *Age*, pp. 7f.). In view of the considerable impact (both positively and by reaction; cf. M. Hengel, *Judaism and Hellenism* [1974]) of Hellenism on later Jewish religion and literature, a dating within the Persian period is much more likely. I am aware of only one piece of internal evidence which has been thought to point to a later date, but this rests on a misunderstanding of the text in question; see on 2 Chr. 26:15.

It may thus be concluded that a date for Chronicles within the fourth century BC is most probable, but that in the circumstances dogmatism is out of the question. With this clearly understood, perhaps a speculation may be allowed. It is probable, to judge from 1 Chr. 23–27, that the priestly reviser worked no more than a generation after the Chronicler, and that he did so under the impact of the institution of the twenty-four priestly courses. It has been suggested (cf. *SVT* 30 [1979], pp. 251–68) that two incidents from very late in the Persian period may have caused this development. If so, Chronicles itself would come from about the middle of the fourth century BC.

Regrettably little is known about the situation in Judah at that time. However, D. Barag, *BASOR* 183 (1966), pp. 6–12, has argued strongly that the effects of the Persian suppression of the abortive revolt led by the Sidonian Tennes were felt in Judah, so that it would be attractive to seek a setting for Chronicles at this time. The crushing of rising hopes of independence would certainly have necessitated the kind of encouragement to faith which the Chronicler holds out. It must be emphasised, however, that our understanding and appreciation of the work are in no way dependent on this conjecture.

There can be no doubt, in view of the character of Chronicles as a whole, that its author lived in or near Jerusalem, and that he was an ardent supporter of the temple and its services. However, this does not imply that he was an exclusive ritual purist; rather the reverse, as our sketch of some of his characteristic themes (section G below) will indicate.

He has often been identified in Jewish tradition with Ezra. This view was revived by Albright, *JBL* 40 (1921), pp. 104–24, and it is regarded with cautious favour by Myers. The most scientific evidence that could be advanced in its favour would be the demonstration of a similarity of language between the (hypothetical) Ezra Memoir in Ezr. 7–10 and the Chronicler. Despite the efforts of A. S. Kapelrud, *The Question of Authorship in the Ezra Narrative* (1944), it has not been possible to prove this. Furthermore, as seen above, the picture which can be gained of Ezra does not accord well with that of the Chronicler. Finally, though in itself this is not conclusive, authorship by Ezra would demand a rather earlier date for Chronicles than that favoured here.

Because of the prominence afforded to the Levites in his work, it used to be thought that our author was to be found amongst their number. This view has gone out of fashion since Noth and Rudolph relegated much of this material to the status of later additions. Their position is not fully shared in this commentary, however, and indeed the fact that someone with strong pro-priestly leanings felt the need to make some revisions does rather point back to a Levitical origin for the work. Also in favour of this conclusion is the fact that the Chronicler's own thought comes most clearly to expression in a form of preaching that was probably used by teaching Levites. Finally, this hypothesis adequately explains his access to the various types of source material at his disposal.

F. SOURCES

(a) Source citation formulae

In the past commentators have expended much effort in their attempts to uncover information about the nature and extent of the sources used by the Chronicler from his apparent references to them (see the survey of opinions in Willi, pp. 231–3). These source citation formulae have been repeatedly analysed and grouped. Excepting for the moment the various references in the genealogies, it is generally agreed that these formulae fall into two main groups. First, there are what appear to be references to official records: 'The Book of the Kings of Judah and Israel' (2 Chr. 16:11) and the like. Second, there are references to prophetic records: 'The Chronicles of Samuel the seer' (1 Chr. 29:29) and the like. Since the latter are clearly thought by the Chronicler to have been included within the former (cf. 2 Chr. 20:34; 32:32), many scholars have gone on to argue that in fact all these titles refer to a single work, often termed 'The Midrash of the Book of Kings', following 2 Chr. 24:27 (and cf. 13:22). This work is conceived of as a source parallel with Samuel and Kings, but including additional material which the Chronicler has in turn woven into his own composition.

This approach to the Chronicler's citation of sources is fundamentally in error, however, in not taking into account the relationship of these formulae to those of his *Vorlage* in Samuel and Kings. In fact, with the apparent exception of 2 Chr. 35:26–27 (see the commentary), and, of course, 1 Chr. 29:29 (where the Chronicler is composing freely by analogy with the formulae found at the close of the reigns of other kings), he always refers to his 'sources' at precisely the same point in the text as did the Deuteronomic historian before him. This fact is particularly noteworthy at 2 Chr. 16:11; 20:34 and 25:26, where the formulae do not come at the end of the king's reign. Conversely, with the exception of 1 Chr. 29:29 already noted, the Chronicler does not supply such references in passages where they are absent in the earlier history. It is thus evident that in all such cases the Chronicler was dependent on his *Vorlage*. A further pointer in this direction comes from the reign of such a king as Solomon, for whom, it will be argued in the commentary, the Chronicler drew on no source other than Kings. This fact is surprising, if indeed, as 2 Chr. 9:29 implies, the Chronicler had access to other, prophetic sources for this reign.

While we must, therefore, conclude that these formulae cannot assist us in a search for the Chronicler's extra-biblical sources, they are nevertheless of considerable interest in their own right. We may take first the group which links prophets with the written sources, namely, 1 Chr. 29:29; 2 Chr. 9:29; 12:15; 13:22; 20:34; 26:22; 32:32; 33:19. Two observations must be made about this group. First, it is clear from 2 Chr. 26:22 ('Now the rest of the acts of Uzziah, from first to last, Isaiah the prophet the son of Iddo wrote') that the references to prophets in these citations are intended as a statement about authorship. Second, it will be noted in the commentary that for at least 1 Chr. 29:29 and 2 Chr. 9:29 the Chronicler intends us to understand his remarks as referring to the Deuteronomic history itself. This receives confirmation from the statements of 2 Chr. 20:34 and 32:32 that the prophetical writings were included in 'the Book of the Kings of (Judah and) Israel'. It is thus evident that he already stands within the tradition of interpretation, maintained also in the normative divisions of the Hebrew canon, which regarded these historical books as 'Former Prophets', and suggests that they had an authority for him superior

to that of other available sources (see further, below). It is, furthermore, of interest to observe that he only ever uses this particular
formula of kings whom, either in part or in whole, he judges favourably; they are never used in the case of wholly bad kings. This
may reflect a stage in the process of the interpretation of the prophets
which has attracted increasing attention in recent study. It is observed that, from a historical perspective, most of the pre-exilic
prophets uttered mainly oracles of judgment. In later times, however, the books of the canonical prophets were regarded as
forward-looking promises of salvation; cf. R. E. Clements, 'Patterns
in the Prophetic Canon', in G. W. Coats and B. O. Long (eds),
Canon and Authority (1977), pp. 42–55. It may be that the Chronicler
is a witness to this shift in the interpretation of the primary thrust
of the prophetic message.

The second group of citation formulae is closer to those found
already in the books of Kings, and must be intended to refer to the
same type of annals as do they themselves; cf. 2 Chr. 16:11; 20:34;
24:27; 25:26; 27:7; 28:26; 32:32; 33:18; 35:27; 36:8 (and cf.
1 Chr. 9:1). Here it is of interest to note, however, that although
the Chronicler allows himself some freedom in the titles he uses, he
nevertheless goes out of his way to insist, unlike his *Vorlage*, that
'Israel' is always mentioned in this connection. Not once do we find
a title like 'The Book of the Kings of Judah' (or equivalents) alone.
He thus demonstrates his appreciation of the fact that his *Vorlage*
is no mere political history, but should, rather, be interpreted as
the religious history of the one people of God. This, too, reflects an
approach which is close to that re-emphasised by much redaction-
critical study of both the histories and the prophets.

(b) Sources available to the Chronicler

In the light of the previous section it is clear that we can approach
the question of what sources were available to the Chronicler only
indirectly. It is universally agreed nowadays that his major source
was the books of Samuel and Kings (albeit in a sometimes slightly
different form from MT; cf. section A, above), and that he has also
drawn in varying degrees on a number of other biblical books.
Beyond that, however, we must be content with informed
conjecture.

The question of the availability of additional sources cannot be
dealt with at the level of generalities. Sound method demands that
each passage be examined in its own right first of all, and that all
the tools available to the modern critical historian must be em-

ployed. Within the limitations imposed by reasons of space and, in several areas, restricted expertise, this has been attempted in the commentary below. No useful service would be rendered by dealing with the issues here as well. A few summarising conclusions must therefore suffice.

First, it may be stated, with as strong a degree of certainty as is ever possible in such circumstances, that the Chronicler did have access to sources since lost to us. There has always been a minority of scholars who have denied this, usually arguing that no such material could have survived the fall of Jerusalem and the exile of much of its population. This is a presupposition, however, for which there is no evidence whatsoever other than surmise. The very existence of a large part of the Old Testament is sufficient to prove that written materials did survive, and it seems quite arbitrary to limit these to works which were eventually to be included within the canon. At the same time, the portrayal of the Chronicler which emerges from such a presupposition lacks credibility. Certainly, many passages dealt with in the commentary will be attributed to his own personal composition. But the suggestion that the long tracts of material such as those found in the genealogies of 1 Chr. 1–9, with their clear testimony to earlier literary and oral layers, and within a society that set considerable store by genealogical purity (cf. Ezr. 2:59–63) are complete fabrication is in my opinion far more difficult to believe than the view which all the evidence supports, namely, that here as elsewhere the Chronicler was reworking inherited material.

Second, some of the passages where there is reason to suspect such a source can be grouped together on the basis of content in such a way as to suggest that this material did not all reach the Chronicler in short, detached units, but may on occasion have been already taken up into more extensive compositions. From time to time, for instance, it will be suggested that authentic material relating to the conscript army has been preserved; cf. some of the 'genealogies' of 1 Chr. 1–9, which are probably based on a military census for conscript purposes, and the passages treated together at 2 Chr. 14:8. All this material, together, perhaps, with other which reflects interest in military affairs, could have been joined in a single source on which the Chronicler drew. Other such similarities between one passage and another, again suggestive of more extensive sources, are alluded to here and there in the commentary.

Thirdly, however, we should avoid the danger of jumping to the conclusion that attribution of the basis of a passage to an earlier source will automatically guarantee its historicity as judged by modern standards. On the one hand there are some passages (e.g.

2 Chr. 14:9ff.; 20) where the Chronicler's handling of his source is such as to create an impression quite other than that which would be acceptable to a modern historian; see further, below. On the other hand, the sources themselves, could they be reconstructed, would equally need to be critically examined. The result is that undoubtedly on some occasions Chronicles can be used with caution to fill out our knowledge of the history of Israel. At other times, however, such as in the case of passages pertaining to the cult, it will be argued that although the Chronicler is drawing on a source, that source itself may nevertheless be of only post-exilic origin, and so reflect more nearly the conditions of the Chronicler's own day than, say, those of David's time. Finally, there are other occasions (e.g. 1 Chr. 2–4; cf. *JBL* 98 [1979], pp. 351–9) where it can be seen that the sources themselves have already passed through more than one stage of redaction; in such cases too they should be used only with the greatest caution for the purposes of historical reconstruction.

(c) Use of sources and nature of composition

Discussion of the nature of the Chronicler's composition cannot be separated from the question of the way in which he has used his sources. The easiest starting point remains, of course, his use of earlier biblical material, since here it is possible to analyse his method in some detail. His approach has been characterised in several different ways: Targum (W. E. Barnes, *ExpT* 8 [1896–7], pp. 316–19), Midrash (W. E. Barnes, *The Expositor*, 5th series 4 [1896], pp. 426–39; R. Bloch, *DBS* 5 (1957), cols. 1263–81, *et al.*), and, most recently and fully, 'exegesis' (Willi).

These designations all relate to the work of secondary authors on an authoritative text. Their aim is to explain their text for later readers by a variety of devices such as translation, the addition of illustrative stories, the substitution of modern equivalents for outdated terms, the harmonisation of difficulties in the text, often on the basis of other biblical passages, and so on. Much useful work has been done in recent years which has led to a fuller appreciation of these methods not only in later Jewish writings whence such terms as Targum and Midrash originally derive, but also in much earlier periods, as attested both in works such as LXX (e.g. Gooding, *Relics of Ancient Exegesis*) and within the text of the *OT* itself; cf. I. L. Seeligmann, *SVT* 1 (1953), pp. 150–81.

The importance for the Chronicler of his biblical *Vorlage* can scarcely be overestimated. Willi is right to dismiss any attempt to appreciate his purpose based only on the non-synoptic passages. He frequently presupposes knowledge of passages in his *Vorlage* which he himself has not included, and indeed as a general rule the overall shape and order of his work is dependent on the earlier composition. Thus by his detailed analysis of the various techniques which the Chronicler has used as an exegete of his biblical *Vorlage*, Willi has contributed significantly to our understanding of his work. In the comments on the parallel passages below, examples will be found of many such exegetical techniques on the part of the Chronicler as harmonisation, typology, explanation of obscurities by appeal to other passages, and so on.

Nevertheless, just as it is mistaken to undervalue the importance of the parallel passages, so it must be insisted that any attempt to categorise Chronicles as a whole on the basis of these sections alone is also to be avoided, and this for several reasons. First, by his heavily selective use of Samuel and Kings the Chronicler has shown that he is not attempting simply to expound it as a text in its own right. This very fact of selection shows that he is using the earlier work as a source, and that some purpose other than mere exposition must have governed his decisions concerning what to include and what to omit.

Second, although some of the additional material is attributable to a concern to explain and amplify the presentation of the earlier biblical text, it is doubtful whether this purpose alone is sufficient to account for it all. Thus, just as Willi is right to protest against those who ignore the parallel passages, so it must be said that his own proposals do not do justice to the great bulk of extra material which the Chronicler has used. (Here, in fairness, it should be added that the present commentary is more positive than Willi towards the availability of written sources and that less is attributed to later additions than in Willi's work.)

Finally, there is strong evidence for the Chronicler's use of techniques other than the purely exegetical. Only the most striking can be summarised here. Mention must first be made of the recognition by Mosis (and to a lesser extent by Ackroyd) of an overall, paradigmatic patterning of his narrative by the Chronicler. While by no means all of Mosis' suggestions are acceptable, his exposition of the various phases of the history on the pattern of 'exile' and 'restoration' is generally convincing; see especially on 1 Chr. 10. Yet in order to create these patterns, the Chronicler has to use equally his biblical sources, other material, and his own personal composition. All are enlisted without distinction in the interests of the wider purpose.

Next, it must be observed that, in connection with some of the issues with which he is most deeply concerned, the Chronicler does not always expound his position in a single passage, but develops it often through the course of an extended narrative sequence. His attitudes towards the Davidic dynasty and towards the composition of Israel as the people of God are both impressive examples of this (see section G below). However, they do not arise directly and exclusively out of the biblical *Vorlage*. Rather, it would seem that the aim of the composition has determined which material shall be selected, regardless of its source.

As a final example of the Chronicler's highly developed skill in composition, we may note his ability to shape material within a shorter narrative unit in order that it should serve his purpose most effectively. Here again, it must be noted, there is often evidence that points towards a variety of origins for the materials which he has employed. Amongst other examples to be developed more fully in the commentary, mention may be made of the genealogy of Judah (1 Chr. 2–4; cf. *JBL* 98 [1979], pp. 351–9), the support for David before and at his coronation at Hebron (1 Chr. 11–12; cf. *OTS* 21 [1981] pp. 164–76) and his patterning of the transition of rule from David to Solomon on that from Moses to Joshua (1 Chr. 22; 28–29; cf. *VT* 26 [1976], pp. 351–61).

In conclusion, therefore, it emerges that we should beware of attempts simplistically to reduce to a single category the nature of the Chronicler's composition or his use of sources which was determined by it. It may be accepted that the various exegetical techniques referred to above are used by him. Furthermore, it is true that on the whole he has handled his biblical sources more conservatively than others—perhaps because he accorded them a greater authority, or perhaps because the Deuteronomic redaction had already supplied these accounts with the 'pan-Israelite' orientation which the Chronicler himself seems to have brought to local traditions which he inherited directly. Again, it is clear, as Welten has well shown, that he uses certain motifs, such as building, in stereotyped ways as a means of passing a theological verdict on the reign being described. But overall the Chronicler shows himself as the master, not the servant, of his sources. His is the last example of Israel's genius for retelling her sacred history in a way which applies its lessons creatively to the demands of a developing community. Those who followed him in this enterprise, by contrast, found themselves explicitly tied to the shape of the history which had emerged as settled and authoritative by their own day.

G.   SOME CHARACTERISTIC THEMES

Writing in the later part of the *OT* period, the Chronicler is heir to most of the traditions which flow through the main stream of *OT* thought. Since it is not his purpose to make a systematic present-ation of all that has gone before, there is much which he can therefore take for granted, in both the realms of antecedent history (cf. von Rad, *GCW*, pp. 64–80) and of thought. It is thus more appropriate here to highlight a few of his most characteristic themes than to attempt an overall appraisal of his 'theology'. These themes are, of course, more fully developed in the commentary itself. The two most helpful recent works in this area are undoubtedly Japhet, *Ideology* (though on occasions she underestimates the importance of what the Chronicler simply assumed, and therefore drives a thicker wedge than is always necessary between him and the rest of the *OT*), and Mosis.

(a) The People

Since the early days of critical study of the books of Chronicles it has been recognised that they contain a distinctive approach to the question of Israel as the people of God. This is not surprising in view of the fact that the Chronicler was writing at a time when one of the major issues for the Jewish people was the precise definition of the extent of its own community. There is evidence of consider-able disagreement at that time concerning how 'open' or 'exclusive' a stance should be taken to those outside the confines of the group centred on Jerusalem.

During the central decades of this century, the Chronicler's con-tribution to this debate was misunderstood. He was portrayed as adopting an anti-Samaritan stance and as justifying this from the course of the nation's past history. This misunderstanding has been dramatically reversed during the past decade, however. All the scholarly monographs published on Chronicles in recent years in-veigh against it, as do several other works, including some whose primary interest is in the history of the Samaritans themselves (cf. Kippenberg; R. J. Coggins, *Samaritans and Jews* [1975]; Braun, *JBL* 96 [1977], pp. 59–62, and *SVT* 30 [1979], pp. 56–9, etc.). What, then, is the true position?

The Chronicler opens his account with a genealogical portrayal of Israel in its ideal extent of twelve tribes. It is noteworthy that Jacob, the father of the tribal ancestors, is always called 'Israel' in Chron-icles, and is accorded a prominence virtually unique in the *OT*. The line of God's election is traced directly from Adam to him in ch. 1, while in ch. 9, following the tribal lists, it focuses on the post-exilic Jerusalem community. In the central section (chs. 2–8), however, the primary tribes of that community (Judah, Benjamin and Levi) are used to provide a framework for the other tribes, rather than being grouped separately.

If it may be assumed that this introduction presents the reader with the Chronicler's inclusive ideal, then his subsequent narrative has as one of its purposes the aim of showing that there is no historical barrier to its practical realisation in his own day. He thus presents a fresh interpretation of past history which can be appreciated only as a narrative whole, and not on the basis of isolated texts.

The reigns of David and Solomon, it has long been agreed, are portrayed as a 'united monarchy' indeed. Virtually all commentators are unanimous in observing that the Chronicler passes over adumbrations of the later division, that he emphasises, often against his *Vorlage*, the participation of 'all Israel' in the major events of the time, and that he portrays David and Solomon as active in their concern for all their people without distinction.

It might have been felt by some of his readers, however, that this unity was irretrievably lost with the division of the monarchy after Solomon's death. The Chronicler is therefore anxious to show first that the division itself did not irretrievably put either group outside the boundary of Israel (understood as a religious, rather than a purely political, title), and, secondly, that in fact from a historical perspective the two groups had theoretically, if not in every case in practice, been subsequently brought together again.

As regards the first point, he shows carefully that the northern tribes did not forfeit their position as children of Israel. They were to be regarded, rather, as those who had 'forsaken' the Lord, a position into which the southern tribes also fell sometimes, and from which return by way of repentance was always considered possible (see further on 2 Chr. 13:4–12).

The Chronicler establishes the second point by the combination of a number of factors at about the time of the fall of the northern kingdom: the end of separate political rule in the north, confession of sin by the northern tribes, apostasy by Judah, its defeat at the hand of the northerners, and the carrying into captivity of many from both parts (on all this, see 2 Chr. 28). This reverses in every particular the situation which developed after the division as described in 2 Chr. 13. At this point, the Chronicler portrays Hezekiah as a second Solomon, thus restoring fully the position that was lost at the time of the division. In principle, therefore, the whole population is reunited in worship under a Davidic king at the

Jerusalem temple. Nothing in the subsequent narrative reverses this position.

By thus bringing forward into the historical arena the fulfilment of the prophetic hopes for the reunification of the one people of Israel, the Chronicler was no doubt attempting to mediate between the extreme 'exclusivists' and the extreme 'assimilationists' of his own day. He achieved this by demonstrating from the history of the divided monarchy that a faithful nucleus does not exclude others; it is, rather, a representative centre, to which all the children of Israel should be welcomed if they will return (cf. *IBC*, pp. 87–140).

(b) Kingship

The first of the distinctive aspects of the Chronicler's conception of kingship is his direct equation of kingship in Israel with the kingdom of God. This comes to expression both in passages where there is reason to suppose that the Chronicler is composing freely in order to make a significant theological statement and in places where he has departed slightly from his *Vorlage*. In the former category come 1 Chr. 28:5, 'he has chosen Solomon my son to sit upon the throne of the kingdom of the Lord over Israel'; 1 Chr. 29:23, 'then Solomon sat on the throne of the Lord as king instead of David his father'; and 2 Chr. 13:8, 'the kingdom of the Lord in the hand of the sons of David'. In the latter category we should note 1 Chr. 17:14, where God speaks of 'my house' and 'my kingdom', as opposed to 2 Sam. 7:16, 'your house' and 'your kingdom'; and 2 Chr. 9:8, where the Queen of Sheba says to Solomon that God has 'set you on his throne as king for the Lord your God', as opposed to 1 Kg. 10:9, 'set you on the throne of Israel'.

In a time when the days of Israel as an independent monarchy must have seemed remote in the extreme, it was almost inevitable that some of the ideology surrounding the monarchy should be transferred to the heavenly court. The Chronicler thus testifies to the beginnings of a movement which was to reach its extreme expression in the later apocalyptic literature. Indeed, there are occasions when he severs the link with the human sphere altogether, and ascribes kingship to God without further qualification; cf. 1 Chr. 29:11; 2 Chr. 20:6. Normally, however, he portrays God's kingship as being exercised in Israel through the human representative of his choice. We need not doubt that for his original readers this approach to kingship would have been a source of assurance and hope: Israel's kingdom was secure and everlasting because it was in God's hands. Just as he had specifically 'turned the kingdom over to David' (1 Chr. 10:14) in order to rescue Israel after the 'exilic' disaster of Saul's death, so he was well able to intervene again to re-establish his kingdom when he so chose.

For the Chronicler, therefore, there was no question about the continuity of kingship, since it was grounded in God. The only live issue in his time was through whom God would manifest that rule when eventually it was asserted publicly again (cf. Dan. 4:17 for an independent expression that reflects the Chronicler's thought quite closely). The theoretical possibility of change in this regard is clear from his particular description of the transition from Saul to David in 1 Chr. 10:14 noted above. This leads us directly to the second charateristic aspect of the Chronicler's conception of kingship, for in fact, despite 1 Chr. 10:14, he makes clear in other ways that by the time of Solomon's death the kingship had been entrusted inalienably into the hands of the Davidic dynasty. Indeed, already in 1 Chr. 17:13 it is promised that a transfer such as that from Saul to David would not happen again.

The details of his presentation in this regard (which, it may be noted, are again expressed through a developing narrative rather than a single, specific text) are outlined in the introductory comments to 1 Chr. 17; see further my 'Dynastic Oracle', and *TynB* 28 (1977), pp. 115–54. It is therefore unnecessary to repeat that summary here. Suffice it to say that, as might be expected from the emphasis of the passages listed at the start of this discussion, the Chronicler ascribes to Solomon a far greater role in the establishment of the dynasty than does the Deuteronomic historian, and that this is in line with his portrayal, expressed in various ways, of the reigns of David and Solomon as a single episode in the history of Israel. Once this position has been reached, the Chronicler does not refer to it very frequently thereafter. Sufficient passages remain, however, to make it clear that he is simply assuming it to continue, rather than seeking in any way to play it down; cf. 2 Chr. 13:5; 21:7; 23:3.

Third, it has already been pointed out as a distinctive characteristic of the Chronicler that once the Davidic dynasty is regarded as established it tends to displace in importance the earlier stress on the Exodus and Sinai traditions. One must beware here of the danger either of playing down this element to the point at which the Chronicler is simply assimilated to the more normal *OT* presentation, or of so stressing this feature that it leads to a denial of his recognition of the earlier traditions at all. Rather, we should see that he is attempting his own distinctive resolution of the often-observed tension between the Mosaic and Davidic covenants. Up until the establishment of the dynasty, Exodus and conquest are fundamental for the people's self-understanding; cf. 1 Chr. 17:21f., etc. Thereafter, however, that covenantal basis of the people's existence has to lose ground to the stress on the new, Davidic covenant; cf. 2 Chr. 6, etc.

Beyond these three points, the Chronicler seems not to have been concerned to present the nature and role of kingship in Israel in any particularly distinctive light. There is, it is true, a tendency towards 'democratisation', in that we frequently find the king consulting with his people and involving them closely in the major events of the history. Furthermore, as will be seen later, the Chronicler regards the role of the king as being of particular importance in terms of leadership of and provision for the temple cult, while at the same time he carefully limits the part the king may personally play in the ritual. These concerns, however, are not at all unprecedented, and probably reflect the interpretation of older texts current in the Chronicler's day rather than forming a positive part of the message which he wished to convey.

(c) The Temple and Worship

It is clear from even a casual reading of the books of Chronicles that one of their central concerns is the temple of Jerusalem and the worship associated with it. There can be little doubt that many of the positions adopted reflect the customs and practices current in the post-exilic period. The Chronicler will have shared with his readers a recognition that the second temple and its cult provided one of the most powerful elements of continuity with pre-exilic Israel and that their sense of identity was in no small measure bound up with their faithfulness towards them.

It follows that not all the material in Chronicles which is relevant to this theme is necessarily peculiar to the Chronicler. At the same time, however, justice must be done to his loyal adherence to the temple cult, a loyalty which comes to fullest expression in Abijah's speech in 2 Chr. 13:10–12. In this and many other passages he makes it abundantly clear that there can be no question of participation in the Jerusalem community except on the basis of full acceptance of the exclusive claims of its temple's authority. It is noteworthy in this connection that his assessment of the Davidic kings is frequently based directly on their behaviour with regard to the temple.

At first sight this rather exclusive position might seem to conflict with his more 'ecumenical' stance outlined in section (a) above. It must be emphasised, however, that it is balanced by his particular presentation of the steps which led up to the building and dedication of the temple. The account of this preparation, which dominates the reigns of David and Solomon, manages to include at various points references and allusions to most of the major cult symbols from the earlier period of Israel's history (e.g. the ark, the tabernacle, the holy vessels, etc.). In addition, such important sites as Mount Moriah and Gibeon are also introduced. The Chronicler, however, portrays the completed temple as the fulfilment of all these various traditions, as the centre to which they have all contributed. It may thus be claimed that he intends his portrayal to smooth the way for return by those groups of his own time which may have set particular store by one or other of these traditions and so distanced themselves from the Jerusalem community.

More controversial will probably have been the relationship of the king to the temple which the Chronicler describes. There are two aspects of this issue which he may have had some difficulty in holding together. On the one hand there was the point of view that he wished to convey to the members of his own community. It is well known that during the post-exilic period there was an increasing tendency for the High Priest to take on more and more of the functions which had formerly been reserved for the Davidic king. In line with this, several commentators have argued that the Chronicler portrayed the king as having importance only in so far as he established and provided for the temple cult. In this way, it is suggested, he could present the second temple as embodying a fulfilment of the old Davidic promises.

This interpretation (which is in part dependent upon Ezra and Nehemiah) does not appear to do justice to the dominant role which the king in Chronicles continues to exercise in regard to the temple. It is certainly true that his selection of material for the reigns of David and Solomon is largely governed by its relevance to the theme of temple building (cf. especially Braun, *JBL* 95 [1976], pp. 581–90), but that does not therefore make their role dispensable thereafter. Indeed, it is striking how little attention the Chronicler gives to the role of the High Priest except in the execution of certain specific rituals (cf. 2 Chr. 26:16–21), and the most distinguished of them all, Jehoiada, is singled out because he worked for the restoration of the Davidic monarchy at a time when it was under considerable threat (2 Chr. 23–24). Generally speaking, as the reigns of Hezekiah and Josiah demonstrate most clearly, the Chronicler believed that a Davidic king was necessary for the successful maintenance of the temple cult even after the period of the united monarchy. We may thus conclude that he wished to retain this ideal in contradistinction to those who were attempting to see in the post-exilic high priests the legitimate successors of the kings.

On the other hand, it might be considered that this concentration on the role of the Davidic king in connection with the temple poses a difficulty for the Chronicler's portrayal of 'all Israel' united in worship at a single sanctuary. This he overcomes, however, by stressing the concern of David and Solomon (and to a lesser extent of some of their more illustrious successors) to involve all the people in the preparations for the building of the temple, and in their care for the ark which preceded it. By this distinctive portrayal of the united monarchy in which he reaches back before the time of the later division, he presents his readers with an ideal upon which they can all agree and which might enable them to unite around the post-exilic temple as being the direct successor of the Solomonic building.

The next aspect of this topic which deserves mention is the role of David in the establishment of the temple worship. Here it should be noted that, despite appearances, there is no superseding of the Mosaic regulations. The Chronicler repeatedly affirms, either by explicit reference or by allusion, that as far as was practicable the worship of the temple was ordered in conformity with the stipulations of the Pentateuch; sacrifices and festivals provide the clearest examples of this. Alongside this, however, and in conformity with his literary methods already discussed, he has a rather definite appreciation of historical development. The result is that, particularly with regard to the Levites, he saw the need for a redefining of their tasks once the significance of the ark and tabernacle had been taken over by the temple (cf. 1 Chr. 6:31–32 and the references listed there). It may well be that the presentation of the role of these junior officials as singers, gatekeepers, teachers, and so on, was determined by tensions within the ranks of the clergy—tensions created by the continuing development of their orders in the post-exilic period. If so, he will have been claiming Davidic authorisation for the scheme which he outlines (cf. North, *JBL* 82 [1963], pp. 369–81). To this extent, the priestly reviser stands in the same tradition, though the emphasis which he lays on the Aaronic priests is certainly out of proportion with the Chronicler's own favoured position.

Finally in this section, a strong corrective needs to be entered against the portrayal of the Chronicler as a strict and unyielding ritualist. It is probable that commentators have come to think of him in this way because they expect him so to be on the basis of their approach to the religion of the post-exilic period as a whole. In fact, however, against such a background it is strange that the contrary tendencies in the Chronicler's work have been so consist-

ently undervalued, for it is they which make up one of the distinctive
characteristics of his work. Three points may be summarised here.

First, the Chronicler stresses the note of great joy at the conclusion of nearly all the major religious celebrations which he describes;
cf. on 1 Chr. 12:38–40 with selected references listed there. He
introduces this theme so frequently and consistently that it is difficult not to suppose that it emerges directly from his own experience. Secondly, in the Levitical sermons especially, he puts a
considerable emphasis on faith in God as the path to blessing, but
rarely on ritual perfection. To do this, as is well known, he cites
freely from the major canonical prophets. It is true that he frequently expresses the faithfulness of the kings by their attention to
the temple and its rituals, but in the light of his presentation as a
whole this is to be seen as expressive of their underlying devotion
rather than as its sum total. Finally, it is noteworthy that ultimately
the Chronicler does not regard the temple and its rituals as indis-
pensable for piety. Frequently he records effective prayer in quite
other settings; in line with his *Vorlage* he envisages the possibility
of non-cultic religion (e.g. 2 Chr. 6:34ff.; 7:14, etc.);   and on one
occasion he even portrays sincerity of heart as overruling ritual
impurity (2 Chr. 30:18–20). In these ways he successfully demonstrates that his religion was not grounded in a cold formality. Naturally, obedience to the ritual law was part of his ideal, but that fact
should not blind us to his awareness of the vital reality of a living
God who was not tied down to working through such channels
alone. This aspect of his theology is apparent too in the next topic
to be considered.

(d) Retribution and Repentance

One of the best-known features of the Chronicler's work is what has
been called (not quite accurately) his doctrine of immediate retribution; cf. Wellhausen, *Prolegomena*, pp. 203–10, for a survey of
the main examples. Briefly stated, the Chronicler goes even further
than the Deuteronomic historian in attempting to correlate blessing
with faithfulness and judgment with disobedience within each separate generation. Generally speaking it is the kings who demonstrate
faithfulness who are rewarded with success in building and military
operations, with a large family, wealth, the respect of foreign nations, etc., while those who 'forsake' God suffer defeat in war,
disease, conspiracy, and so on.

The basic premise of this doctrine is expressed in its negative
aspect at 1 Chr.10:13–14 and in its positive aspect at 1 Chr. 28:9,

both of which passages introduce some of the Chronicler's key vocabulary ('unfaithfulness', 'seek', 'forsake', etc.; cf. Braun, *SVT* 30 [1979], pp. 53–6). However, even more important for the Chronicler's message is the fact that this doctrine is not worked out purely mechanically. Two points should be emphasised here. First, the possibility of repentance is always held out as a way of averting, or at the very least of moderating the threatened judgment. The basis for this aspect of the Chronicler's message is laid in the addition which he makes to God's answer to Solomon's prayer at the dedication of the temple, 2 Chr. 7:14. The significance of this verse for the understanding of the Chronicler can hardly be exaggerated. In it, he gives four possible responses of the people to imminent or actual disaster, each response sufficient to cause God to intervene with forgiveness and restoration. These four words are then used in the subsequent narrative as markers at one point or another to introduce one of the miraculous interventions that are such a characteristic feature of the work. Although these narratives do sometimes give rise to historical difficulties, they nevertheless stand out as an impressive testimony to the Chronicler's overriding conviction that God is more willing to bless than to condemn, and that he looks only for a change of heart by king or people to enable him to restrain his judgment.

Secondly, there is an aspect of this doctrine to which only Japhet, *Ideology*, pp. 154–66, has really done justice, namely that of prophetic warning before judgment finally falls. Expressed quite often in the form of 'Levitical sermons', these warnings have a beneficial effect in a number of cases (e.g. 2 Chr. 12:5). Where they are rejected, however (e.g. 2 Chr. 16:7–10; 24:19–22; 25:15f.; 26:16–21, etc.), then punishment is forthcoming. Nonetheless, this generally overlooked feature of the Chronicler's thought further illustrates God's compassion for his people (cf. 2 Chr. 36:15f.) and again removes his understanding of retribution from the purely mechanical sphere.

Even with this more nuanced approach, there may still be many who remain critical of this aspect of the Chronicler's theology. Certainly, from the perspective of the Old Testament as a whole, it needs to be balanced by other writers who make clear that it must not be interpreted as a rigid rule which admits of no exceptions; indeed, the Chronicler himself will be seen here and there to have acknowledged this fact. Nevertheless, his underlying motive here should be appreciated, for it formed a vital part of his attempt to encourage his readers to faith. Living probably at a time when Persian power seemed invincible, they needed to be reminded that their God was one who acts, often against all the odds, and that the present generation need not be heir to the judgments on their predecessors. As von Rad, *Old Testament Theology*, Vol. I (1962), p. 349, has put it,

'the Chronicler is at pains to show that Jahweh's judgment or salvation still affected each generation individually. . . We must not fail to catch what it is that the writer wants to hammer home to his readers in this critique, namely, that each generation stands immediately before Jahweh, and stands or falls with its anointed. To understand this presentation, which is certainly a very forced one, we must recognise that here the Chronicler is making his contribution to one of the hardest problems which cropped up in late Jahwism, namely, the question of the share of the individual in Jahweh.'

The Chronicler's doctrine of retribution and repentance thus becomes another of his ways of demonstrating the openness of the future. The ideals of the past which his work traces were not simply the products of wishful thinking. They could be paradigms for future blessing. Indeed, there are even occasional passages (e.g. 2 Chr. 20) where he seems to encourage the belief that an attitude of faith can usher in an apocalyptic-type intervention; but these are exceptional. His general policy is to demonstrate from a retelling of the people's history that there is no barrier from that quarter to the hopes for a restoration of one people united under one king around one temple. His work as a whole thus itself takes on the parenetic purpose of a 'Levitical sermon', warning and encouraging his contemporaries to a responsive faith which may again call down the mercy of their God:

Hear me, Judah and inhabitants of Jerusalem!
Believe in the Lord your God, and you will be
established; believe his prophets, and you will
succeed (2 Chr. 20:20).

H. OUTLINE OF CONTENTS

1 Chronicles

A. SCOPE OF THE COMMENTARY

Substantial sections of the books of 1 and 2 Chronicles reproduce with varying degrees of exactitude passages already found in earlier books of the *OT*, particularly Samuel and Kings. The commentator has therefore to decide what approach is to govern his work in handling these passages.

The primary aim throughout the present commentary has been to elucidate the message which the Chronicler himself sought to convey. For this reason, questions of history, geography and the like in the parallel passages have not generally been treated. For these topics the reader must be referred to the commentaries on the earlier books of the *OT*, together with such other more recent literature as will be cited from time to time. In these parts of the commentary, therefore, discussion will focus on the purpose behind the Chronicler's inclusion of such passages and on the ways in which he has handled them.

This last point also raises difficulties over the selection of material, for between parallel texts there are often small points of difference whose precise significance it is not always easy to judge. Many, for instance, are due simply to differences in spelling and stylistic conventions, or to the accidents of textual transmission, and it would be inappropriate to dwell at length on these in the present commentary. The interested reader will find the fullest and most easily available collection of such material in the commentary of Curtis and Madsen, while a synoptic presentation of the data itself is available in the works of Vannutelli and of Bendavid.

Recent study, however, has tended to confirm that in addition to these problems there is the further consideration that the text of Samuel/Kings which the Chronicler used (his *Vorlage*) was not always of the same type as the MT found in our printed Hebrew Bibles. Evidence of this comes not only from the earliest known Greek translations of Samuel and Kings, which are sometimes closer to the form of text found in Chronicles (though this evidence must be handled with care; cf. Rehm and Allen), but also from some fragments of a scroll of the Hebrew text of Samuel from Qumran (4QSam[a]). Unfortunately, this text has still not been published in its entirety, but such of it as is known (cf. Lemke and Ulrich) shows clearly that sometimes differences between our texts of Samuel/Kings and Chronicles should be ascribed not to the Chronicler's own bias or interests, but to the Hebrew text he was using. For the

commentary will endeavour to show rather that the chief tribes of
the faithful southern kingdom, Judah, Benjamin and Levi, were
regarded as a framework to enclose, not a fence to exclude, the
others, and in a lesser way this comes to expression too in the
reference to members of Ephraim and Manasseh amongst the restored community (9:3; contrast Neh. 11:4).

It follows from these first two concerns of the genealogies that
their purpose is not simply to legitimise a narrowly defined circle of
people to the exclusion of others. After all, most of the material
stops well short of the writer's own day, and so would be useless
for such a purpose. In this they are quite unlike the lists in Ezra
and Nehemiah (cf. Ezr. 2:59–63; Neh. 7:61–65). Rather, their aim
is to paint a portrait of the people of God in its ideal extent as a
symbol of both the particularity of his election and the breadth of
his grace.

A third concern is geographical. Details of the settlement of the
tribes are noted with surprising frequency. Coupled with indications
from the later narrative, it would seem that, despite the tiny area of
the Persian province of Judah in which he lived, the Chronicler
retained a concern for the full extent of the land promised to the
patriarchs and realised in the Davidic empire (cf. 1 Chr. 28:8; 2
Chr. 20:7 and 11, with Johnson, *Purpose*, pp. 37–60, and Japhet,
Ideology, pp. 327–33). In all these elements he stands as a witness
to some fundamental concerns of much *OT* thought in a period
when the effects of geographical dispersion and increased awareness
of the implications of individualism were coaxing his contemporaries
in quite contrary directions (cf. W. D. Davies, *The Gospel and the
Land* [1974], Part 1).

These remarks clearly presuppose the essential unity of 1 Chr. 1–
9, and their part within the work of the Chronicler as a whole. An
attempt to justify the first presupposition will be made at the relevant points of the commentary, though it will be argued there too
that a few brief passages are most probably to be regarded as secondary additions. Concerning the second, it may be observed that
only a few scholars have ever denied this section as a whole to the
Chronicler. There is a considerable number of points of contact
between the genealogies and the narrative (most of which have been
summarised by Johnson, *Purpose*, pp. 47–55) such as a concern for
'all Israel', an emphasis on David and his dynasty, the centrality of
Judah and Jerusalem, immediate retribution, lack of attention to
Moses and the Exodus, and so on. Even more telling, however, are
common stylistic features, not paralleled elsewhere, such as the
attention to Jacob in the history of the nation and the fact that he
is regularly called Israel (see the comments on 1:34*b* and 2:1–2),

and the description of the battle in 5:20 which coincides very closely indeed with accounts in the later narrative (see the commentary, *ad loc.*).

One of the few to argue against this consensus was A. C. Welch, *Post-exilic Judaism* (1935), pp. 185f.; but his reasons, based on the apparent confusions in the lists, fail to take into account the careful structure of much of the material as analysed in this commentary. More recently, Freedman, *CBQ* 23 (1961), pp. 436–42, Cross, *JBL* 94 (1975), pp. 4–18, and Newsome, *JBL* 94 (1975), pp. 201–17, have all taken a similar line as a result of their very early date for the original work of the Chronicler. However, since they adduce no argument at all from the genealogies themselves but simply dismiss them as secondary because certain passages (especially ch. 3) contradict their dating, their position in this regard must be rejected as being based entirely on circular reasoning. Moreover, neither their early dating, nor the literary history of the text from which they set out, is accepted in this commentary (see the Introduction, sections D and E, and *TynB* 28[1977], pp. 120–30).

FROM ADAM TO ISRAEL

I:I–2:2

Within the genealogies, this introductory section shows Israel's place among the nations by tracing the line of descent from Adam to Jacob (Israel). Although the chapter almost exactly follows the book of Genesis, which will have been the Chronicler's only source for this period, there are nevertheless two elements which suggest that he consciously followed this pattern in order to emphasise the element of divine election and grace inherent in the material.

First, by abstracting a bare list of names from his more variegated source, he shows that he appreciated its intricate pattern, and indeed wished to emphasise it. Details of secondary lines within a family are consistently treated first (vv. 5–16, 20–23, 29–33, 35–54), each section thus finishing with the stress on the line that was to lead eventually to Israel (cf. *IBC*, pp. 62–3). Secondly, assuming that 2:1–2 is based on Gen. 35:23–26*a*, he has on this occasion altered the order of material in Genesis (since 1:35–54 comes from Gen. 36) so as to make it conform with the overall scheme.

It is noteworthy that within this presentation no particular attention is drawn to Abraham. Rather, the break comes only with Israel (2:1), after whom the genealogies are arranged on a quite different principle. This is the first of a number of hints which suggest that the Chronicler traced the immediate origins of Israel to Jacob (see further on 1:34, 2:1–2, 16:13 and 2 Chr. 1:8–10), probably betraying thereby one of the reasons for his well-known stress on the full complement of twelve tribes as 'all Israel'. At the same time, however, it is clear from this chapter that if Israel's election was realised in Jacob, it was implicit already in Adam (see W. Eichrodt, *Theology of the Old Testament*, Vol. 1 [1961], p. 64). This constitutes a marked development in *OT* thought which is paralleled in some Samaritan literature (see J. Macdonald, *The Theology of the Samaritans* [1964], p. 277), but taken much further in later Jewish writings (e.g. *Ass. Mos.* 1:12–13; 4 Ezr. 6:54, 59; 7:11, etc.; cf. Japhet, *Ideology*, pp. 104–9) and the *NT* (Eph. 1:4, on which see M. Barth, *Ephesians 1– 3* [1974], pp. 105–12).

Substantial sections of this chapter (namely vv. 4b–23, 32f., 43– 54) are regarded as secondary additions by a number of commentators (e.g. Benzinger, Rudolph), but their reasons are generally unconvincing (see E. Podechard, *RB* 13 [1916], pp. 363–86; Noth, *US*, pp. 159f.; Johnson, *Purpose*, pp. 73f.):

(a) In the B text of LXX, vv. 11–16 and 17b–24a are omitted, whilst 47b–49a are misplaced and now follow 51a. The second two cases, however, are clearly the result of homoioteleuton (Allen, 2, pp. 134 and 136), and whereas no such mechanical reason is apparent for the first passage, it is unlikely to represent the Chronicler's original text, since it unnaturally truncates the otherwise complete genealogy of the sons of Ham (v. 8). Moreover, LXX does not coincide with the reconstructed text.

(b) Verses 24f. repeat in summary form the substance of vv. 17–19; furthermore, here and elsewhere there are differences of style in the way the genealogies are presented. These features do not, however, necessarily argue in favour of secondary expansion. Apart from vv. 32f. (on which, see below), the text follows Genesis exactly, so that all its apparently uneven features can be explained on the basis of faithful adherence to this *Vorlage*.

(c) Some of the material serves no real purpose in the chapter. This argument is double-edged, for it then becomes equally difficult to explain why a later editor should have wished to include it. In fact, however, we have already noted that all the material in the chapter has been carefully arranged to serve its total purpose, while at the same time virtually all genealogical matter from Genesis has been included. These two factors argue strongly for the essential unity of the whole.

1–4. The Chronicler moves directly from **Adam** to **Noah** by a bare list of names compiled from Gen. 5. Since for him the flood meant a completely fresh start in the spread of mankind, it is not surprising that he omits the genealogy of Cain from Gen. 4:17–26. This is the only time he omits such material from Genesis.

4. It is not apparent from this list that **Shem, Ham, and Japheth** were all sons of **Noah**. LXX, however, includes the words 'sons of Noah'. If the Chronicler drew on Gen. 5:32, he may have relied on his readers' knowledge of the true position. More probably, however, he began at this point to follow Gen. 10:1ff., as in the following verses, in which case the words $b^e n\hat{e}$ $n\bar{o}ah$, presupposed by LXX, will have been lost by parablepsis.

5–23. The genealogies of the three sons of Noah (vv. 5–7, 8–16, 17–23) closely follow Gen. 10. However, in line with the Chronicler's purpose in this chapter, historical and geographical material is omitted from Gen. 10:5, 9–12, 18b–21, 30–32.

6. Diphath: read 'Riphath' with a number of Hebrew MSS, LXX, V and Gen. 10:3. *r* and *d* are very similar in Hebrew script. This is the first of a large number of such differences, usually due to scribal error, between the various parallel lists. In this case, there is little doubt that MT of Chr. is at fault; elsewhere, the situation is reversed, while sometimes (see v. 7) there can be no certainty either way. Unless the variants are of more than textual significance, they will not be noted in the remainder of this commentary.

7. Rodanim: Gen. 10:4: 'Dodanim'. The versional evidence is indecisive and either are possible. Chr., at any rate, refers to the inhabitants of Rhodes.

10. Gen. 10:8ff. gives two reasons why **Nimrod** was a **mighty one** (*gibbôr*). Originally, Gen. 10:8 seems to have been followed immediately by vv. 10–12 (see C. Westermann, *Genesis*, I [1974], p. 689), indicating that Nimrod was a powerful ruler (or tyrant; cf. Isa. 49:24). Verse 9, which calls him 'a mighty hunter', was added later. By omitting vv. 9–12, the Chronicler leaves *gibbôr* ambiguous, probably expecting his readers to be able to supply their own interpretation from Gen. LXX indicates its preference by adding *kynēgos*, 'hunter', but most modern commentators favour the alternative. **began to be:** i.e. 'was the first to be'.

17. After **Aram**, probably restore 'the sons of Aram:', with Gen. 10:23 and LXX^A; compare v. 4 for a similar situation.

24–27. The line from **Shem** to **Abraham** is compiled on the basis of Gen. 11:10–26, using the same method as in vv. 1–4. That this involves slight repetition of material already found in vv. 17ff. is thus due to the position in the Chronicler's sources, and does not necessarily support theories of secondary expansion.

27. If, as was argued above, this chapter is substantially the Chronicler's own composition, then there is nothing here to support

Myers' view that **Abraham** 'was the center of interest for the writer'.
Nor is he at all prominent in the later narrative.
Abram: this older form of the name is faithfully reproduced from
Gen. 11:26. However, as the source from which the Chronicler goes
on to draw in the following verses refers to him as Abraham, he
connects the two (cf. Gen. 17:5) as briefly as possible: **that is,
Abraham** (Goettsberger). Thus even this comment is imposed on
the Chronicler by his close adherence in this chapter to his sources,
and need not indicate particular interest in Abraham himself.

28–34a. The sons of Abraham: as usual, the secondary lines
(Ishmael and Keturah) are dealt with first before the line of election
through Isaac.

29–31 is drawn from Gen. 25:13–16a.

32–33. A number of factors combine to suggest that this section
on **the sons of Keturah** was added later to the Chronicler's composition: (a) The list is quite out of place in its present context.
Verse 28 has led us to expect treatment of the descendants of
Ishmael and Isaac, whereas **Zimran**, etc., were themselves the sons
of Abraham. We would therefore have expected to find them in v.
28, not amongst the descendants of Ishmael. (b) This is confirmed
by v. 29, where the context shows that **their genealogies** (*tōlᵉḏōt-
ām*) refers only to Ishmael and Isaac. We would thus expect Isaac's
genealogy immediately to follow Ishmael's. (c) Although the section
is based on Gen. 25:1–4, a number of small changes have been
introduced. This is quite out of character with what has already
been noted of the Chronicler's procedure in this chapter. (d) By
following the genealogy of Ishmael, these verses reverse the order
in Genesis, but not for the theological reasons that motivated the
Chronicler at 2:1–2. If, for these reasons, we regard vv. 32–33 as
secondary, v. 34a will also be an addition to explain the now confused position of the sons of Isaac. Otherwise, it would have been
unnecessary after 28–29a.

It must be noted, on the other hand, that we should certainly
have expected the Chronicler to include this material in view of his
completeness elsewhere in the chapter. Perhaps this very observation motivated the interpolator; or did the material originally
stand at v. 28, and get accidentally moved to its present position in
the course of transmission? Though satisfying most of the problems,
this suggestion nevertheless leaves the variant form of text
unexplained.

34b–2:2. The sons of Isaac: Esau's descendants are listed first,
so as to end this whole section on **Israel** and his children, the
progenitors of the twelve tribes. The Chronicler uses this name
consistently for Jacob, twelve times in all (but cf. 1 Chr. 16:13 and

17), so that we should not emend v. 34*b* to 'Jacob' on the basis of LXX. By this device the Chronicler probably wished to stress that the Israel of his day, if it was to be true to its history, could consist only of the full complement of twelve tribes.

35-37. The Chronicler has condensed and slightly rearranged material from Gen. 36:4-5 and 10-14 in order to compile this list of **Esau**'s family.

36. Timna, and Amalek appear here as sons of **Eliphaz**, whereas in Gen. 36:12 Timna was his concubine, and Amalek her son. It has been suggested (Kittel) that this was a deliberate alteration by the Chronicler who, regarding these as the names of tribes, wished to emphasise the greater prominence of Timna in his own day. It seems more likely, however, that, whatever the position in Gen., the Chronicler thought of these names as individuals. Moreover, in v. 39 he has retained Timna's female identity (which the form of name would in any case suggest). Perhaps, therefore, clarity has fallen victim to compression: the names alone were loosely attached to the preceding list (note that there is an 'and' before Timna in the MT), with the Chronicler once again relying on his readers' knowledge of Genesis for the full position.

38-42. The sons of Seir: see Gen. 36:20-28. Whatever may have originally been the case (cf. J. R. Bartlett, *JTS* ns 20 [1969], pp. 1-20), the Chronicler believed that their connection with Esau's family was that both inhabited the territory of Edom (cf. 2 Chr. 25:11, 14). This explanation (Gen. 36:8, 20, 21, etc.) is again omitted by the Chronicler, however, making for confusion without prior knowledge of Genesis.

43-54. This list of **kings** (43-51*a*) and **chiefs** (51*b*-54) **of Edom** closely follows Gen. 36:31-43, with a few omissions and very slight changes; cf. J. R. Bartlett, *JTS* ns 16 (1965), pp. 301-14. No clear motive for its inclusion is apparent, a problem which is even more acute for those who regard it as secondary. Ackroyd suggests that the Chronicler was here reminding his readers that 'physical descent is not everything, and also that their neighbours are not unrelated to them', but this is unlikely in view of the total lack of evidence for any such viewpoint in the rest of the work. Probably, therefore, we have a further indication of the Chronicler's desire for completeness in this chapter (Johnson, *Purpose*, p. 74), though his omission of 'the chiefs of the sons of Esau' from Gen. 36:15-19 shows that he was not fully consistent in this purpose.

2:1-2. the sons of Israel: the elaborate pattern of genealogical arrangement reaches its climax in these verses. That this is intentional is suggested both by the fact that the arrangement hereafter is explicitly based on the contrary principle of placing the most important tribe (Judah) first (see 1 Chr. 5:1–2), and by the Chronicler's alteration of the order in Genesis on this one occasion in order to achieve his effect (see below). He thus succeeds in demonstrating that God's purposes of election through the primeval and patriarchal history reach their fulfilment in the full complement of twelve sons of Israel. This list appears to be drawn from Gen. 35:23–26. An alternative possibility is Exod. 1:2–5, but **Joseph** is not integrated into that list, as the context there demands, and it is, moreover, further removed from Gen. 36, which the Chronicler has just been using.

2. Dan is in an unexpected position on any showing, appearing here two places higher up the list. Most commentators attribute this to scribal error; alternatively, Keil and Brunet (*RB* 60 [1953], pp. 490f.) have detected the influence of Gen. 30:1–6, which suggests the adoption of Dan by Rachel. On this view, the Chronicler then reckoned Dan as the oldest of Rachel's children, and listed him accordingly. Should this be correct, it would be a further pointer to the use of Gen. 35:23–26 as the basis for this list as a whole. The suggestion of J. M. Sasson, *ZAW* 90 (1978), pp. 171–85, that the seventh place in a genealogy is often a mark of special favour, does not seem to help explain this particular case.

THE TRIBES OF ISRAEL

2:3–9:1

The purpose of these chapters and their place in the Chronicler's work as a whole was explained in the general introduction to chs. 1–9. Two further matters remain for discussion, namely, the sources used here and the order in which the tribes are listed.

Several types of source material can be clearly detected. First, other passages from the *OT*, notably the comparable lists of Gen. 46 and Num. 26, have again been exploited, though not on the same principles as those noted for ch. 1. Secondly, a number of the genealogies are characterised by brief notes of a very localised nature such as concern for pasture, inter-tribal skirmishes, and so on (e.g. 1 Chr. 4:39–43; 5:9–10, 19–21; 7:21). A close parallel for this type of material within a genealogical context has been found in the Safaitic inscriptions (see Johnson, *Purpose*, pp. 61f.; *IBC*, pp. 77–9), discovered mainly in the basaltic area to the south east of Damascus, and dating from the last century BC and first century AD. Though these lists, which sometimes cover many generations, are principally intended to identify the writers, unlike the immediate situation in Chronicles, they nevertheless indicate both the type of

material which the Chronicler (or the compiler of a source before
him) could have used to assemble these sections, and that what
appears to us as a rather haphazard conglomeration of interests need
not necessarily result from separate levels of composition. Thirdly,
a number of phrases (e.g. 1 Chr. 5:24; 7:2, 4f., 7, 9, 11, 40, etc.)
appear to refer to a military census list (see Johnson, *Purpose*, pp.
62–8; J. Liver, *Studies in Bible and Judean Desert Scrolls* [1971], pp.
234–48), which could itself have been organised to a certain extent
in genealogical form (see G. E. Mendenhall, *JBL* 78 [1958], pp. 52–
66). Finally, though we cannot go here beyond conjecture, it seems
reasonable to postulate the use of miscellaneous smaller sources,
perhaps preserved particularly amongst the leading families of the
post-exilic community, who mainly traced their ancestry to Judah,
Benjamin and Levi. It is at any rate noteworthy that the Chronicler
has far more material on these tribes in his genealogies.

The question of the order in which the tribes are listed here has
occasioned much debate, but as yet no satisfactory solution has been
found. There are three main suggestions. Noth (*US*, pp. 118–22)
argues that the Chronicler followed Num. 26 almost exclusively,
while Rudolph holds that 2:1–2 set the pattern for him. Neither
suggestion stands up to examination, however, for the order in 1
Chr. 2–8 is quite different from both suggested patterns, and the
arguments adduced to explain the variation are unconvincing. (For
a detailed examination, see *IBC*, pp. 72–82.) The third suggestion
thus seems more promising, namely, that the arrangement is geographical (CM; RH; Brunet, *RB* 60 [1953], pp. 485f.; Keil argued
for a combination of the historical importance of the tribes with
geographical considerations). On this view, the movement starts
with Judah (cf. 1 Chr. 5:1–2) and its southern neighbour Simeon,
goes through the transjordanian tribes to Levi at the centre, then to
the north, and back through Ephraim and Manasseh to Benjamin
on Judah's border again. Though superficially attractive, this
scheme also breaks down at a number of points. In particular, Asher
(7:30–40) is quite out of place between Ephraim and Benjamin, and
the first list of Benjamin (7:6–12) is here located amongst the northern tribes. CM's attempt to reconstruct a genealogy of Zebulun
from these verses has convinced no one who does not already sub-
scribe to their theory. There is thus justification for a fresh explanation of the Chronicler's ordering of material in these chapters.

Our survey of possible sources indicated that the Chronicler devotes fullest attention to Judah (2:3–4:23), Levi (6:1–81) and Benjamin (8:1–40). It is noteworthy that these three lists, dealing with
the main components of the post-exilic community, seem to provide
a framework for the whole section (so too Michaeli, p. 71). Judah,

it is explicitly stated, comes first because he 'became strong among his brothers and a prince was from him' (5:2). Levi, appropriately, is central, and Benjamin rounds off the section. In view of the quasi-symbolic nature of presentation noted in ch. 1 (and compare Ezek. 48 for a similar effect), we need not be surprised if the Chronicler is here suggesting that the three tribes which, in his view, remained faithful to the Davidic kingship and the temple in the pre-exilic period, are thus presented as the framework of the true Israel of his own day. Consistent with his view elsewhere, however, the other tribes are not excluded, but rather enclosed, by this framework. Here, the detailed ordering was not of great significance, and seems to have been dictated partly by the demands of his sources, and partly by editorial tidiness. All that mattered was that several tribes should appear each side of Levi. Thus, Simeon's close connection with Judah (4:27) led the Chronicler to juxtapose their two genealogies.

Now, the Simeonite genealogy concludes with features that suggest it was drawn from the second block of source material referred to above; so too do the Reuben (5:1–10) and Gad (5:11–17) genealogies which immediately follow. Consequently, it was logical for the Chronicler here to deal in full with the two and a half transjordanian tribes, even though part of the material in 5:18–26 may have had to be taken from one of his other sources (see the commentary for details). Chapter 7, by contrast, which comes between Levi and Benjamin, is mainly characterised by material of the military census list type, and the internal order here will then have been influenced by this source. The only exception is Ephraim (7:20–9; for Manasseh, see the commentary), which looks as though it should come in the first main section. However, since at the end of ch. 5 the Chronicler departed from his source in order to deal fully with the two and a half transjordanian tribes, a reference there to Ephraim would have been out of place. Consequently, he held this material over and placed it after its near neighbour Manasseh. We may thus conclude that, as in ch. 1, the Chronicler's main contribution to this long section is its overall structure, by which he again conveyed his picture of the ideal Israel. The individual details of the genealogies usually concerned him less.

It is noteworthy that Zebulun and Dan are omitted. It is often suggested that there may have been a serious textual corruption early in ch. 7, to which the genealogy of Zebulun fell victim, and that Dan was originally mentioned at 7:12. This position is rejected in the commentary (and cf. *IBC*, p. 75). It is possible, however, that the brevity of the Naphtali genealogy (7:13) and the confusion at the start of the Manasseh paragraph immediately following are a better indication of textual loss, and this may perhaps account for the absence of these two tribes.

Judah

2:3–4:23

At first sight, these chapters present a totally confused mass of diverse material, presented in a disorderly manner. The fragmentary nature of many of the parts, together with the apparent tensions between them (e.g. compare 2:31 with 2:34, or 4:1 with 2:3–8), indicate that the Chronicler's purpose did not lie in the simple tracing of a family tree. Nor is it likely that his interests here coincided with those of the sources on which he drew, for research has shown that often these have been overlaid by the new context in which they are now placed. (For attempts to salvage parts of this earlier stage of the text, together with the history they may reflect, see particularly, in addition to the larger commentaries, J. Wellhausen, *De Gentibus et Familiis Judaeis* [1870]; M. Noth, *ZDPV* 55 [1932], pp. 97–124; R. de Vaux, 'The Settlement of the Israelites in Southern Palestine and the Origins of the Tribe of Judah', in H. T. Frank and W. L. Reed [eds.], *Translating and Understanding the Old Testament* [1970], pp. 108–34; W. Beltz, *Die Kaleb-Traditionen im Alten Testament* [1974].) Our attention here, therefore, must be restricted only to the contribution which the Chronicler himself made to the ordering of the material, but that in turn depends on isolating the sources at his disposal. For a more detailed defence of the position outlined below, cf. *JBL* 98 (1979), pp. 351–9.

Clearly there was, first, a good deal that could be derived from earlier biblical texts, or at least their near equivalents (2:3–8, 10–17, 20; 3:1–16). Secondly, 2:25–33 and 42–50a stand out as a related unit by their exactly parallel opening and closing formulae. Since nowhere else in the *OT* are Jerahmeel and Caleb called brothers, nor made the sons of Hezron, this pattern was probably already found in the Chronicler's source. A third possible source, though now broken up in several places, can be reconstructed from 2:18–19, 24, 50b–52 and 4:2–8. The evidence for this view is summarised below in the comments on the various passages. This source seems to have comprised an independent genealogy of the family of Caleb and Ephrath through their two sons Hur and Ashhur. Finally, it is reasonable to suppose that through those families which survived the exile, other fragments would have been available to him in either written or oral form.

It is important to notice next that 2:53–55 was also probably in

its present position before the time of the Chronicler. These are the
verses that will have initially disrupted the connection between 2:52
and 4:2 in the third of the sources noted above. 4:1 is a clear
editorial link to remind the reader where he was, so to speak, before
the interruption. The names mentioned quickly trace the line again
(father to son) from Judah to Shobal, the father of Reaiah, the point
at which the interruption had occurred. It is clear, however, that
4:1 was not composed by the Chronicler, because it does not trace
quite the same line as he himself did from Judah (contrast 2:3ff.,
noting particularly the position of Carmi), and also because when
the Chronicler uses the expression 'the sons of X', he never introduces a bare list of names as father to son, but as brothers. It follows
that, once ch. 3 is removed, the surrounding material was already
in substantially its present shape before the time of the Chronicler.
The apparent break with 4:1, however, provided a convenient point
before which he could include his material in ch. 3.

In the earlier part of ch. 2, v. 9 is evidently of importance, for it
introduces the following substantial section. It will be argued in the
commentary that it is the Chronicler's own editorial composition,
whereby he combined for the first time the genealogies of Jerahmeel
and Caleb from the second source with that of Ram (vv. 10–17).

It follows from these considerations that an important part of the
Chronicler's contribution to these chapters was the introduction and
positioning of 2:10–17 and ch. 3. Both deal with David, the one
tracing his ancestors, the other his descendants. The significance of
this observation may be emphasised by the structure of the section
as a whole (cf. CM, Michaeli):

Descendants of Ram (as far as David)   – 2:10–17
   Descendants of Caleb   – 2:18–24
      Descendants of Jerahmeel   – 2:25–33
      Supplementary material on Jerahmeel   – 2:34–41
   Supplementary material on Caleb   – 2:42–55
Supplementary material on Ram (David's descendants) – ch. 3

This chiastic pattern, which both cuts across the main outlines of
the Chronicler's main source and uses the Davidic material as an
inclusio, can thus be seen as the Chronicler's own work. The emphasis placed on David within the tribe of Judah is apparent, and
fully in line with his interests later on in the work. We see again
how the Chronicler uses a genealogical pattern to express his theological convictions.

It only remains to deal with 4:1–23. Verses 21–23 treat the sons
of Shelah. The whole genealogy thus ends with the oldest surviving
son of Judah from 2:3—a further *inclusio*. 4:1–20 gives supplementary material on the sons of Perez, and thus may be said to balance

2:4–8. Thus the whole genealogy is arranged in a chiastic manner, with the sons of Hezron (2:9–3:24) as the middle element. This too draws attention to the centrality of David's family in the tribe.

This positive appreciation of the Chronicler's contribution to the ordering of these chapters is in marked contrast to the position of Rudolph, who plays on the tensions in the material to argue that most of it was added after the Chronicler's own time. Whilst his position cannot be examined in detail here, it should be said that on our understanding many of these tensions were present already in the material adopted by the Chronicler, but that since his interest was in the overall presentation they need not have worried him. Rudolph seems to confuse the earliest stage in the development of the sources with the Chronicler's own work, an unwarranted assumption. It has the further defect of deflecting attention from an attempt to do justice to the present shape of the book.

2:3–4. The distressing story of the birth of the five **sons of Judah** is found in Gen. 38, from which the Chronicler will have abstracted this summary. Of the first three sons, by **Bathshua** (= 'the daughter of Shua'; her own name is not recorded in Gen. 38), only **Shelah** survived, a fragment of his genealogy being preserved at the end of this section, 4:21–23. Surprisingly, no reference is made to the death of **Onan**. Knowledge of Gen. 38:10 may be presupposed, but Rudolph conjectures that a line may have been lost by homoioteleuton ('And Onan too, his second son, was wicked in the sight of the Lord, and he slew him').

4. For Judah to have had children by **his daughter-in-law Tamar** was against the law of Lev. 18:15, 20:12. The electing grace which tolerated this situation in the family which led to David (and cf. Mt. 1:3) is emphasised by the contrast with the Lord's action in slaying Er (v. 3). Rudolph and Myers find it significant that this is the first reference to 'the Lord' in the book.

5. Cf. Gen. 46:12; Num. 26:21. No more is heard of **Hamul**, and, despite v. 6, little can be said in support of equating him with the Mahol of 1 Kg. 4:31.

6–8. **The sons of Zerah** are quickly dealt with before the Chronicler returns to his main interest, the line of Perez through Hezron.

6. **Zimri:** on the basis of Jos. 7:1, we might have expected 'Zabdi'. In view of the names following, there may have been some early confusion with the similar root *zmr*, 'to make music'. **Ethan** is called an 'Ezrahite' in 1 Kg. 4:31 (where he occurs in conjunction with the others listed here), and this apparently justifies his inclusion with the sons of Zerah. There, they are traditional wise men; elsewhere (e.g. the headings to Pss. 88 and 89) they are associated with the musical guilds (cf. Albright, *Archaeology*, pp. 126–8). They were

thus 'adopted' into the tribe of Judah, their position being determined by an early midrashic form of word-play.

7. Either knowledge of Jos. 7:1 is presupposed, or words to the effect of 'And the sons of Zimri: Carmi and . . . ' have dropped out from the start of the verse. **Achar** (*ᶜāk̠ār*) = Achan. The Chronicler thus introduces a word play on **the troubler** (*ᶜôk̠ēr*) **of Israel**.

8. Not known from elsewhere. Throughout 2:3-17 there are enough small divergences of this nature from other comparable parts of the Hebrew Bible to suggest that the Chronicler's *Vorlage* may have been an expanded or parallel version of the MT.

9. With **the sons of Hezron**, the Chronicler reaches the heart of his interest in Judah. Since this verse combines the two originally independent sources of vv. 10-17 and 25-33, 42-50*a*, it is probable that he composed it himself so as then to be able to order this whole section in the manner described above. Support for this view comes from the fact that Caleb is here called **Chelubai**, unlike v. 42, and from the fact that the expression **that were born to him** (*ᵃšer nôlad̠ -lô*) is found again only where the Chronicler is himself constructing a genealogical introduction on the basis of his sources (3:1; and cf. 2:3; 3:4, 5, etc.).

Two small problems remain unexplained. First, the position of **Ram**: if it is correct, the Chronicler has put him in the middle. This would be intelligible on the basis of the structure of the genealogy as a whole, discussed above. CM, however, consider it possible that it originally followed Chelubai (cf. LXX; the *y* of *kᵉlûb̠āy* might then be the corruption of an original *w* in *wᵉᵓet̠ rām*), in which case the following lists would deal with the three sons in reverse order, rather like in parts of ch. 1. Secondly, the name **Chelubai**: this spelling, though attested, is not found elsewhere in the *OT*. It appears to be a familiar form, which, unless it is the result of corruption (as in CM's suggestion above), may have simply been the form most familiar to the Chronicler himself.

10-17: cf. Ru. 4:19-22; Num. 2:3 and 1 Sam. 16:6ff. The precise relation of the Chronicler to these texts is uncertain: some, for instance, argue that Ruth borrowed from Chr.; again, part of the family of David (vv. 14-17) is not paralleled at all elsewhere. The authenticity of this material is widely acknowledged, however, for it is plausible that a record of David's family should have been preserved (Noth, *US*, pp. 119f.; A. Malamat, *JAOS* 88 [1968], pp. 170f.), and since 1 Sam. makes David the eighth son of Jesse, the slight difference here militates against its being pure fabrication (Rudolph). Myers thus suggests that both this list and Ruth go back to 'an original temple source'.

15. David the seventh: contrast 1 Sam. 16:10f., 17:12; but should we compare 1 Chr. 3:24? On the basis of 1 Chr. 27:18, P has tried to harmonise by reading here 'Elihu the seventh and David the eighth', but this is clearly secondary (see the commentary *ad loc.*). Although we have seen the centrality of David in the Chronicler's structure of this genealogy, his sober estimate of him as an individual is made clear by the inclusion without any break of his sisters and their families.

16-17. Zeruiah and Abigail (2 Sam. 17:25, etc.) are called **sisters** of David only here, though 2 Sam. 19:13 indicates that **Amasa** was related to him. **the Ishmaelite:** we note again that the Chronicler does not seem to have been troubled by the inclusion of non-Israelites; contrast Ezr.–Neh. This is highlighted by the fact that, whether through accident or deliberate revision, **Jether** has erroneously become an 'Israelite' in 2 Sam. 17:25.

18-24. A rather disjointed section, centring on the family of **Caleb.** It is evident that fragments have been extracted from their original contexts: vv. 18f. have their direct continuation in 50*b*ff.; the formula in v. 23*b* suggests that the preceding verses probably once had a more extensive setting, whilst v. 20 is related to Exod. 31:2; 35:30. Rudolph makes the consequent unevenness of this section the springboard for an extensive rearranging of the genealogy of Judah, as a result of which it is suggested that a good deal of the present text was added only secondarily. His difficulties, however, start from a probable misunderstanding of v. 24 (see below) and from his failure to attempt an appreciation of the Chronicler's motives in making this compilation. The most important member of Caleb's family will have been **Bezalel**, because of his association with the tabernacle; hence the joining of v. 20 to 18-19. This introduced Caleb's marriage to **Ephrathah**, however, and since this passage was intended as the main (though not the longest) statement of the family of Caleb, it was natural that v. 24 should also have been included. The mention there of **the death of Hezron**, however, could best be given a context by the inclusion of the otherwise admittedly rather out-of-place reference to Hezron's second marriage (21-23). Despite most commentators, this would have been inappropriate after v. 9, because of the Chronicler's desire there to move straight to the descendants of Ram. No more suitable context than the present setting was thus available to him for this fragment.

18. The Chronicler did not equate **Caleb** with the spy of Num. 13:6, etc., since the latter was a contemporary of Bezalel, Caleb's great-grandson (v. 20), or more, if some generations have been passed over. Furthermore, the spy is referred to explicitly in a different context (4:15). **by his wife Azubah, and by Jerioth:** MT ('[begat] Azubah, a woman, and Jerioth') is clearly corrupt, because,

apart from other difficulties, v. 19 shows that **Azubah** was Caleb's
wife, not daughter. *RSV* rightly follows the slightly emended text
presupposed by V and P (read *'ištô* for *'iššāh wᵉ*), but misleadingly
retains the word 'and' as well, making **Jerioth** a second wife or
concubine. It is better either to take the first *'eṯ* as a preposition or
preferably to construe *hôlîḏ* with a double accusative (not attested
elsewhere, but cf. Isa. 55:10; 66:9, and GK §117cc), thus making
Jerioth the daughter of **Caleb** and **Azubah** (Keil); cf. *NEB*: 'Caleb
. . . had Jerioth by Azubah his wife'.

19. cf. v. 50*b*.

20. By including **Bezalel**, the builder of the tabernacle (cf. Exod.
31ff.; 2 Chr. 1:5), the Chronicler has characteristically juxtaposed
the themes of king and temple in the genealogies of Ram and Caleb.

21. Afterward need be taken as no more than a stereotyped
literary formula of transition (U. Cassuto, *Biblical and Oriental
Studies* 2 [1975], p. 23), so that it is not necessary to link this verse
directly with v. 9. **Machir** was a son of Manasseh who settled in
Transjordan (Num. 32:39-41), the area in which the names found
in the following verses are located (Noth, *Aufsätze* 1, pp. 347ff.).
The history which underlies this surprising association between
Judah and Manasseh is uncertain, but appears to be early if v. 23*a*
is to be believed.

23. The association of **Aram** with **Geshur** suggests that it may
refer, not to the later state of Aram Damascus, but rather to Maa-
cath, one of the smaller kingdoms, which, together with its neighbour Geshur, was later absorbed by Aram Damascus (cf. B. Mazar,
JBL 80 [1961], pp. 16-28). The two are associated several times
(Dt. 3:14; Jos. 12:5; 13:13), while in 1 Chr. 19:6 we have the
compound 'Aram-maacah' (Rudolph). Their capture of the **sixty
towns** (which we would rather call villages) could thus be dated any
time before the expansion of Aram Damascus (*contra* J. M. Miller,
JNES 28 [1969], pp. 60f.).

24. The direct continuation of vv. 18-19. Together, these verses
will have been the heading for the third of the Chronicler's sources.
MT appears to be corrupt here: 'And after the death of Hezron in
Caleb-ephrathah, and the wife of Hezron was Abijah, and she bore
. . . '. *RSV* accepts the widely adopted emendation (Wellhausen)
of reading *bâ kālēb* for *bᵉkālēb*(**Caleb went in to**), deleting the
wᵉ before *'ēšeṯ* and reading *'ābîhû* (**his father**) for *ᵃbiyyāh* (Abijah). The first alteration makes excellent sense and is supported by
LXX and V; the second two, however, are conjectural, and have the
disadvantage of suggesting that **Ephrathah** was married twice, which
is mentioned nowhere else, and of leading to a confusion with v.
19. It may therefore be suggested rather that the words 'and the

wife of Hezron was Abijah' are a misplaced gloss on v. 21, where the daughter of Machir is not named, perhaps mistakenly incorporated here to make some sort of sense after the initial corruption earlier in the verse. P omits the phrase. Though normally a man's name, Abijah is used for a woman at 2 Chr. 29:1. The verse should thus be translated, 'After the death of Hezron, Caleb went in to Ephrath, and she bore him Ashhur, the father of Tekoa'.

25-33. The sons of Jerahmeel are listed in a straightforward genealogy, whose general reliability there is no reason to doubt. The lack of any *OT* parallels makes further detailed evaluation impossible. **Jerahmeel** seems originally to have been a clan on Judah's southern frontier (1 Sam. 27:10; 30:29), sharing a common faith (note the Yahwistic names **Ahijah** [25] and **Jonathan** [33]) and eventually 'adopted' by Judah.

34-41. It is clear that these verses have been added to the foregoing, probably by the Chronicler himself, because (a) they follow the concluding formula of v. 33*b*, (b) they comprise a vertical, as opposed to horizontal, genealogy, leading straight to **Elishama**, and (c) v. 34 is in tension with v. 31. Originally, the paragraph will have been compiled as a certification of **Elishama**'s pedigree (41), necessary, perhaps, because of an Egyptian amongst his ancestors (34). In the light of present knowledge, there are no means of identifying him further. The scribe of Jehoiakin (Jer. 36:12, 20f.) has been suggested, but this is no more than a guess. For **Jekamiah** (41; cf. 3:18), cf. C. Graesser, *BASOR* 220 (1975), pp. 63-6.

42-55. In the Chronicler's scheme, this passage is to be understood in its entirety as additions to the genealogy of Caleb (vv. 18-24). As explained above, however, it is made up of parts of at least two originally separate sources.

42. The designation of **Caleb** as **the brother of Jerahmeel** shows that the following list (42-50*a*) originally dealt with another clan that was adopted by Judah (1 Sam. 25:3, 30:14, and see on vv. 25-33). The formula 'x, the father of y' (e.g. **Mareshah . . . the father of Ziph**), in which 'y' is a place name, begins here to occur regularly. In an important study, M. Noth, *ZDPV* 55 (1932), pp. 97-124, sought to isolate one of the Chronicler's sources on this basis. However, since his reconstruction cuts across the Chronicler's immediate sources as analysed above, his detailed conclusions cannot be accepted. Nevertheless, the feature from which he set out remains striking in its frequency here and absence from the rest of the *OT*. It is probable, therefore, that an earlier tradition dealing with the area of Calebite settlement was broken up even before the composition of the sources available to the Chronicler. Since it centres mainly on **Hebron** (cf. Jos. 14:13, 15:13; Jg. 1:20), with several of the settlements lying beyond the borders of the post-exilic province of Judah but coinciding with the earlier situation, a date for this original tradition from the united monarchy (Rudolph) or shortly after (Noth) seems plausible.

Mareshah: MT has Mesha; *RSV* follows the harmonisation of LXX. At the end of the verse, MT has 'the father of Hebron' (*RSV*: **Hebron**). It is impossible now to be sure of the original reading. *RV* follows MT exactly, while *NEB* offers a reasonable alternative conjecture: 'Mesha the eldest, founder of Ziph, and Mareshah founder of Hebron'.

49. and the daughter of Caleb was Achsah: cf. Jos. 15:16f. and Jg. 1:12f., passages which clearly deal with Caleb the son of Jephunneh, the spy. It was noted at v. 18, however, that the Chronicler did not make this identification. Theoretical harmonisation, e.g. that there were two Calebs each with a daughter called Achsah, or that **daughter** here means a much later female descendant, is possible, but not very convincing. More probably, the different adoptive positions of Caleb reflect its increasing significance within Judah; this phrase must then be regarded as a later addition by one who did not appreciate the Chronicler's position.

50. These were the sons of Caleb: the conclusion of the section begun in v. 42. The abrupt opening of the next section with the words **the sons of Hur** (so rightly with LXX and V; MT: 'son') is accounted for by the Chronicler's removal of the start of the list to vv. 18–19, 24. The original conclusion of this section of the Chronicler's source is still clearly visible in the resumptive 4:4*b*.

52. Haroeh (= 'the seer') is not a personal name; Noth correctly established that we should read 'Reaiah' (*rᵉʾāyāh*), as in 4:2, which was at an earlier stage the direct continuation of this verse.

53–55. An obscure fragment, attached before the Chronicler's time because of the link through **Kiriath-jearim**.

55 remains a mystery. **scribes** (*sōp̄ᵉrîm*) has no article in MT, and, unlike other professional guilds, they were probably not restricted to a particular locality. We therefore expect a proper name, perhaps 'Siphrites', i.e. inhabitants of (Kiriath-)sefer (cf. *BHS*). The associated names are otherwise unknown, but that is no reason to 'translate' them as some versions and commentators do (e.g. as religious functionaries). **from Hammath**: *NEB* apparently follows S. Talmon, *IEJ* 10 (1960), pp. 410–16, in deriving this word from a noun *ḥmt* = 'family-in-law': 'These were Kenites who were connected by marriage with the ancestor of the Rechabites'. **the house of Rechab**: it would not be surprising if the Rechabites (2 Kg. 10:15f.; Jer. 35) were related to the **Kenites**, but in the context of this list we expect a place name after **the father of**; MT has

'Beth-rekeb', with which S. Klein, *MGWJ* 70 (1926), pp. 410–16, compares Beth-markaboth (4:31). Certainty in this verse is, however, unattainable.

Chapter 3 deals with the descendants of David. For the positioning of this chapter by the Chronicler in the genealogy and its significance as a whole, see the introduction to 2:3–4:23.

1–9. The sources for this list of **the sons of David** are: 2 Sam. 3:2–5 for those who **were born to him in Hebron** (vv. 1–4*a*); 2 Sam. 5:5 for the length of his reign **in Hebron** and **in Jerusalem** (v. 4*b*), though the explicit reference to the division between Israel and Judah is here passed over; 2 Sam. 5:14–16 for the sons **born to him in Jerusalem** (vv. 5–8, and cf. 1 Chr. 14:4–7). The note about **Tamar, their sister,** is based on 2 Sam. 13:1. Some of the slight variants (of which the most significant is **Daniel,** v. 1, for 'Chileab', 2 Sam. 3:3) may be due either to scribal error or to an alternative text of the *Vorlage*. **Eliphelet** (6) and **Nogah** (7) are lacking in 2 Sam., and are secondary, the former because the name appears again in v. 8, and the latter as a dittograph of the following name. That they recur in 1 Chr. 14 indicates that the error had already arisen in the Chronicler's source.

10–16. The pre-exilic kings are listed according to their appearance in the books of Kings. This accounts, for instance, for the fact that Uzziah (2 Chr. 26) appears here as **Azariah** (12), and does not, in consequence, mean that this chapter could not have been included by the Chronicler himself. As **Josiah** (14) was not succeeded by his eldest son, the form of presentation changes with him. At the same time, material from some other source starts here to be introduced.

15. Johanan is otherwise unknown. The continuation of the verse precludes our following LXX and those commentators who identify him as Jehoahaz. He may have died before his father, and so not have ascended the throne. **Shallum** took the throne name Jehoahaz (cf. Jer. 22:11). The four sons of Josiah are here listed by their age, not their order of accession, which was Jehoahaz, **Jehoiakim** (then Jehoiachin, his son), **Zedekiah.** This agrees with the situation in 2 Kg. 23–24 except for the case of **Zedekiah,** whom 2 Kg. 24:18 makes younger than **Shallum** (Jehoahaz: 2 Kg. 23:31). Since Chr. here goes against both the age and order found in 2 Kg., error by confusion is improbable; the simplest solution is to suppose that the age of Zedekiah in 2 Kg. 24:18 has been corrupted in the course of transmission, perhaps precisely because it was found odd that an elder brother should succeed a younger.

16. Jeconiah: so Jer. 24:1; 29:2; = Jehoiachin in 2 Kg. 24:8ff., Coniah in Jer. 22:24, 28; 37:1. **Zedekiah his son:** probably not a son of Jeconiah, because his sons are listed in the next two verses,

nor a confusion with the last king of Judah, since the spelling is
slightly different from v. 15; rather an otherwise unknown son of
Jehoiakim (Rudolph; Myers. Note the plural **the descendants** =
'sons'). However, cf. 2 Chr. 36:10, whose confusion may be related
to the problem of this verse.

17–24. The exilic and post-exilic line. Parts of this list, which is
not found elsewhere, and most of whose names are otherwise unknown to us, are difficult to unravel in detail. Moreover, on the
vital question of relationships between the various names, MT and
the versions often differ in ways that are textually slight, but genealogically of considerable moment. Since the list appears to trace
the Davidic family down to the time of the Chronicler, or shortly
before, it has attracted considerable attention and much conjecture
in order to accommodate it to wider theories of date and authorship.
For reasons of space, a full treatment of all these issues cannot be
undertaken here (in addition to the commentaries, see especially the
speculations of J. W. Rothstein, *Die Genealogie des Königs Jojachin
und seiner Nachkommen* [1902]).

17–18. the sons of Jeconiah: *RSV*'s **the captive** represents a
slight, and correct, emendation of MT, which has a name here,
'Assir' (so *AV*; read *hā'assîr* for *'assîr*, haplography). **his son**
(*bᵉnô*) is senseless in this context. Either delete with V and 2 MSS
of LXX (so *NEB*) or emend to *bᵉkōrô*, 'his firstborn'. **Shenazzar:**
contrary to a very widely held conjecture, it now appears that this
name is quite unconnected with the Sheshbazzar of Ezr. 1:8, 11;
5:14, 16 (cf. P.-R. Berger, *ZAW* 83 [1971], pp. 98–100).

19. Zerubbabel: in Ezr. 3:2, 8; 5:2; Neh. 12:1; the book of Hag.
passim and the *NT* (Mt. 1:12; Lk. 3:27), Zerubbabel is called the
son of Shealtiel, Jehoiachin's oldest son (see v. 17), but here of the
younger **Pedaiah**. Since our list, which is to be dated later, puts
him in an apparently less exalted position, it is likely to rest on
sound tradition. (Contrast LXX, which here substitutes Shealtiel for
Pedaiah.) An explanation which has found very wide acceptance is
that, Shealtiel having died childless, Zerubbabel was born to Pedaiah as the result of levirate marriage (cf. Dt. 25:5–10) with Shealtiel's widow (Keil).

20. and Hashubah . . . , five: Zerubbabel's sons in this verse are
grouped separately from his three other children in v. 19. Since the
text already makes this distinction clear, there is no need to spell it
out with further emendation, or to make this group 'the children of
Meshullam'. It may well be that they were born after the return
from exile. 'The names of Zerubbabel's children have been thought
to express the hopes of Israel at that time' (CM); e.g. **Hasadiah**,
'the Lord is kind' and **Jushab-hesed**, 'may kindness be returned'.

21. The second half of this verse (from **his son Rephaiah** on) is the most difficult of the passage, with no sure way of deciding between the three main possibilities: (a) the MT (cf. *AV*, *RV*) reads 'the sons of Rephaiah, the sons of Arnan', etc. On this view, there is no connection between these various groups, or between them and the grandsons of Zerubbabel in the first half of the verse. Consequently, it cannot be dated (Keil). In its favour are the absence of the copula at the start of the list, and the principle of *lectio difficilior potior*; (b) these names somehow represent further **sons of Hananiah**. RH and Rudolph conjecture the simple reading of 'and' instead of **his son** before each name (*w* for *bnw*), while Myers apparently retains MT, but introduces the words 'also there were' at the start of the list to make the connection. In favour of this suggestion is that it makes good sense in the context, but it is purely conjectural, lacking any textual support; (c) *RSV* and *NEB* follow LXX (and cf. V and P) in emending MT *bᵉnê* to *bᵉnô*, **his son**, four times, with the effect that the genealogy as a whole stretches many generations from Zerubbabel. In favour of this reading is its partial versional support and the fact that it makes good sense. On the other hand, the versions may well represent the secondary easing of a difficulty under the influence of vv. 10–13, and LXX's mistaken addition of a further 'his son' at the very end of the verse tells against its textual purity. In view of this, for lack of better evidence and for all its difficulties, MT should, perhaps, be retained, as in (a) above.

22. The **six** at the end of the verse, preceded by only five names, points to some corruption. It is simplest to delete **the sons of Shemaiah** as a confused dittograph. This makes possible the identification of **Hattush** with Ezr. 8:2, but it cannot be certain because of the textual difficulties of the latter verse, the problems of the dating of Ezra, the uncertainty of the date of this genealogy in view of v. 21 and the fact that Hattush was a common name (cf. Neh. 3:10; 10:4[5]; 12:2).

23–24. Nothing is known of the remaining names in this genealogy, though some of them are attested in extra-biblical sources of the same period (see Myers). Perhaps a hint of the Chronicler's hopes is hidden in his concluding **seven** when compared with 2:15 after the climactic **five** and **six** of vv. 20 and 22. But it is veiled at best, and the **three** of v. 23 interrupts the ascending sequence.

4:1–20. Supplementary material on the sons of **Perez**. Many unrelated fragments have been brought together here in the interests of completeness. Apart from the opening verses, there seems to be no way of telling how much had already been collected before the Chronicler, or indeed how much was added to his work later.

1. A pre-chronistic editorial connection (see above); consequently, despite the contrast with 2:5–9, we should not emend **Carmi** to Caleb. At an earlier stage, there may have been confusion with Gen. 46:9 (cf. 1 Chr. 5:3).

2–4. The continuation of 2:52, though 2:54 must also have been included at some stage. The position of **the Zorathites** is different from 2:53. It is this variant that will have originally led to the disruption of 4:2 from 2:52.

3. These were the sons of: so LXX (and V?). MT: 'and these were the father of'. The slight problem with *RSV* is that it leaves this verse unconnected with its context, contrary to what we would expect from v. 4*b*. A few commentators therefore make the attractive, though admittedly conjectural, suggestion that this verse treats the family of Hareph, the third son of Hur (2:51) and the only one not dealt with so far, restoring something like: 'And these are the sons of Hareph, the father of Beth-gader, Elah . . . '. **and the name of their sister was Hazzelelponi:** normally in these lists, sisters are put at the end, but not so here; also, the name is very curious. P omits the phrase. Rudolph conjectures that it is a confused marginal gloss on v. 5*b*, to indicate that the names there are in the wrong order: (*š^emāh*) *huṣṣaḇ lip̄nê šēm* ^a*ḥôṯāh*: '(her name) is put before the name of her sister'.

5–8. The descendants of **Ashhur** by his **two wives:** cf. 2:24. On our understanding of that verse, he is not to be equated with Hur, but is his younger brother. This short list, therefore, stands exactly where we would expect it in the genealogical source which the Chronicler used.

6. Ha-ahashtari: perhaps intended as a clan, 'the Ahashtarites'. Being apparently a Persian loan-word (cf. *hā^aḥašt^erānîm*, Est. 8:10, 14), it must be secondary to the original compilation of the genealogy.

7. *w^eḳôṣ* ('and Koz') has been lost from the end of the verse by haplography. It should be restored, with some T MSS, to supply the link with what follows.

9–10. With this attractive fragment about **Jabez**, the end has been reached of the Chronicler's main sources traced thus far through the genealogies of Judah, unless Jabez and Zobebah (v. 8) are corrupt forms of the same name (Kittel). In theory, this or any other of the following fragments could have been added later. Nor is there any substantial contact with the place-name in 2:55. The episode turns on a double word-play: **Jabez** (*ya ʿbēṣ*), so named because his mother **bore him in pain** (b^eʿōṣeḇ), prays that the ill omen of his own name **might not hurt me** (ʿoṣbî; on this unusual form, cf. GK §§61*a*, 115*c*). The passage accords well with the Chronicler's belief in the efficacy of prayer, much emphasised later in his narrative. **and keep me** is not a translation of MT ($w^e{}^{\varsigma}\bar{a}\acute{s}\hat{\imath}t\bar{a}$): perhaps 'and turn'; cf. D. Winton Thomas, *BT* 17 (1966), p. 193.

11-12. Chelub: otherwise unknown. Despite several of the versions, nothing about his family as listed here favours identification with, or emendation to, Caleb. For **Recah**, LXX has 'Rechab', whereby Rudolph finds a link between this fragment and 2:55, but this is far from certain. **Irnahash:** literally, 'city of the craftsman', which may account for the position of the following verses.

13-15. The sons of Kenaz: The Kenizzites seem to have been another southern tribe that attached itself to Judah. **Othniel** and **Caleb the son of Jephunneh** are linked as brothers in Jos. 15:17; Jg. 1:13, though that is not mentioned here. **Caleb** is further described several times as a Kenizzite: Num. 32:12; Jos. 14:6, 14.

13. and Meonothai is correctly restored in *RSV* with LXX and V, having been lost from MT by haplography.

14. Ge-harashim: 'the Valley of craftsmen'; cf. Neh. 11:35 and M. Har-El, *PEQ* 109 (1977), pp. 75-86.

15. Kenaz: MT: 'and Kenaz'. From this it might appear as though some names have been lost. (Note also the plural, **the sons of Elah**.) However, in view of the context as a whole, it is attractive to transpose two words in MT, so as to read '*ēlleh b^enê k̲^enaz*, 'these are the sons of Kenaz' (CM; RH). The error was due to the fact that **Elah** and the pronoun 'these' are identical in an unpointed text. The restored text makes a satisfactory conclusion to the section.

16-20. Very little can be made of this passage, since it is quite unconnected with its context and the names are not otherwise certainly attested. Moreover, vv. 19-20 are themselves a collection of isolated fragments. The probable southern location of the geographical names suggests that it may have been part of a pre-exilic Calebite genealogy.

17-18. The transposition of 18*b* to follow 17*a* (Bertheau, as in *RSV*) provides a neat solution to the problems of MT (cf. *RV*), namely, the lack of a subject for **she conceived** (*wattahar*) and the confusion in v. 18, where one list of sons is attributed to two different women. In such a context, however, any suggestion can only be tentative (cf. the main alternative approach to the passage, postulating a substantial lacuna between vv. 17 and 18; G. Richter, *ZAW* 49 [1931], p. 266; Galling; Rudolph).

20. Ben-zoheth: 'the son of Zoheth'. Evidently the list has been mistakenly broken off.

21-23. The sons of Shelah: the genealogy of Judah concludes with attention to his oldest surviving son; cf. 2:3. It sheds welcome light on the existence of guilds (**families**) of craftsmen in ancient

Israel, for which the evidence is otherwise only indirect or circumstantial; cf. I. Mendelsohn, *BASOR* 80 (1940), pp. 17–21; de Vaux, *AI*, pp. 76–8; A. Demsky, *IEJ* 16 (1966), pp. 212–15. The comment at the end of v. 22 that **the records are ancient** and the reference to **the king** in v. 23 both point to a pre-exilic date.

22. who ruled in Moab: only here is *b'l* followed by the preposition *l*, and the sense is not altogether appropriate to the context, especially the verse following. Many prefer to translate 'who married Moabites' with T, and cf. Ru. 1, while to others LXX ('who settled in') has suggested an emendation to *'ābᵉrû*, 'crossed over to'; but nowhere else does LXX translate *'br* thus. Perhaps, however, we should understand *bāᵃlû* as *pāᵃlû*, 'who worked for', either as a scribal error (for confusion of *b* and *p*, cf. 1 Chr. 17:6) or even as a dialectal variant (cf. M. Dijkstra, *VT* 25 [1975], pp. 671–4, with other examples). **and returned to Lehem:** so V, T (and cf. LXX) and most commentators, emending to *wayyāšubû bêt lāḥem*; MT: 'and Jashubi-lehem' (*AV*, *RV*), apparently intends a place-name. On the alternative suggestion offered above, however, repoint to *wᵉyōšᵉbê lāḥem*, 'and (were) inhabitants of (Beth)lehem'.

23. there may refer to Lehem, indicating that these potters moved for a period of royal service. The frequently suggested connection between this verse and the jars stamped *lmlk* from the late pre-exilic period is problematic; cf. P. Welten, *Die Königs-Stempel* (1969), pp. 127–30.

Simeon

4:24–43

The tribe of Simeon was always closely associated with Judah (Jos. 19:1, 9; Jg. 1:3f.), and this doubtless governed its position here (cf. v. 27). The genealogy is in three parts: (a) genealogy proper (24–27); (b) geographical material (28–33); (c) fragments of tribal history, preceded by a list of Simeonite princes (34–43). The purpose of this material and the probable sources used have already been discussed (pp. 38f. and 45ff.). There is thus no reason to deny any part of the passage to the Chronicler. (For a fuller defence of this position, cf. *IBC*, pp. 76–81.)

24–27. The sons of Simeon: v. 24 follows Num. 26:12–14 closely (except for **Jarib**), though Gen. 46:10 and Ex. 6:15 show greater divergence. Thereafter, the Chronicler draws on an otherwise unknown source. From v. 27 it looks as though the source was once much fuller, but that it has been abbreviated.

25. Mibsam and **Mishma**: cf. 1:29f. This may again reflect the absorption of Ishmaelite clans by an Israelite tribe.

28-33. This list of Simeonite settlements is drawn with only slight changes from Jos. 19:2-8. A comparable list is found in Jos. 15:26–32, where it is but part of a larger description of Judah's southern territory. Y. Aharoni (*IEJ* 8 [1958], pp. 26–38; and cf. independently Z. Kallai-Kleinmann, *VT* 8 [1958], pp. 158–60) explains that our passage represents the town list of Simeon before its absorption into the larger, and later, administrative district of 'the Negeb of Judah'. In consequence, the note that **these were their cities until David reigned** (31*b*) will reflect the date of the final administrative change, since several of the cities listed were no longer Simeonite before David's reign; cf. 1 Sam. 27:6; 30:26–30.

33. and they kept a genealogical record: literally 'and their genealogical enrolment to them' (*wᵉhityaḥᵉśām lāhem*), indicating an unusual emphasis on the personal pronoun. The Chronicler may have wished to stress the separate tribal identity of Simeon in view of its being later overshadowed by Judah.

34-38. This list of Simeonite **princes** serves as an introduction to the following historical notes with which it was probably already combined in the Chronicler's source (see vv. 38 and 41). Thus, although none of the names is directly related to the Simeonite genealogy, v. 42 shows that it has been correctly placed.

39-43. Under pressure of an increasing population (38), the Simeonites expanded in two different directions.

39. Gedor: LXX, 'Gerar', very probably correct (cf. Y. Aharoni, *IEJ* 6 [1956], pp. 26–32).

40. Cf. Jg. 18:7. Both Philistines and Canaanites, whom we would expect to inhabit this district, were reckoned as sons of **Ham** (Gen. 10:6 and 14).

41. A westward expansion into Philistine territory **in the days of Hezekiah** is plausible in view of his successful campaign as far as Gaza (2 Kg. 18:8), which lies further west of Gerar (cf. B. Oded in *IJH*, pp. 444f.). **the Meunim:** unexpected here, both because of geographical location (cf. on 2 Chr. 26:7) and because of the close syntactical association with **their tents**. There is considerable textual uncertainty, reflected in the Qr. and the variety of versional renderings. Only LXX translates with a proper name; P has 'springs' (*hammaʿyānîm*), V and T 'dwellings'. This latter is most appropriate; with transposition of one consonant, read *mᵉʿônêhem*, 'their dwellings'.

42-43. A separate expansion, usually thought to be south-eastwards. Bartlett, however, *JTS* ns 20 (1969), p. 6, argues rather that

Seir should be located in the southern part of the Negeb. On the syntax of 42a, cf. J. R. Porter, *JTS* ns 14 (1963), p. 372.

Reuben

5:1–10

The genealogy of Reuben shows a similar structure to that of Simeon, although the geographical section (vv. 8–9) is very limited, and is fused with the historical notes. These (9–10) reflect the same outlook as those for Simeon, and so probably came from the same source, whose order the Chronicler may have taken over.

1–2 is primarily concerned to explain why **Judah**, not **Reuben**, was placed first in the Chronicler's genealogies. The repetition of the introductory phrase, **the sons of Reuben the first-born of Israel**, in v. 3 suggests that this is the Chronicler's own statement, not the insertion of a later editor. Two themes are juxtaposed in these verses, however. What really mattered for the Chronicler's immediate purpose was that **he** (Reuben) **is not enrolled in the genealogy according to the birthright, for Judah became strong among his brothers** (as stressed by the Chronicler's very detailed listing analysed above) **and a prince was from him** (i.e. David, who we have seen was made the focus of attention in the genealogy, as in the later narrative). To this reasoning, a separate, and in the context strictly unnecessary, tradition has been appended, namely, that Reuben's **birthright**, forfeited **because he polluted his father's couch** (cf. Gen. 35:22; 49:4), **was given to the sons of Joseph**, an idea emphasised by repetition at the end of v. 2. This tradition is not directly attested anywhere else in the *OT* (not even in Gen. 48, which is dealing with a separate issue), so that its more common occurrence in post-biblical texts must derive from these verses. Despite the attempts of von Rad (*GCW*, pp. 72–4) and Rudolph (whose conjectures for these verses are partly followed by *NEB*), more difficulties are created than solved by following LXX, which substitutes 'blessing' (*brkh*) for **birthright** (*bkrh*) on its first and third occurrences. (A full discussion of the textual problems may be found in *IBC*, pp. 89–95.) We should rather retain MT (with *RSV*) and conclude that the Chronicler has gone out of his way here to safeguard the highly honoured place of **the sons of Joseph**, the core of the old northern kingdom, within the whole family of Israel.

3. the sons of Reuben are listed in conformity with Num. 26:5f. (cf. Gen. 46:9).

4–6. The sons of Joel: there are no means available for connecting this fragment with the main genealogy of Reuben. It is certainly not

long enough in its present form to stretch from the sons of Reuben
(v. 3) to the exile (v. 6). The inclusion of the name **Baal** suggests
authentic tradition, pointing as it does to an early and/or northern
provenance (cf. G. B. Gray, *Studies in Hebrew Proper Names* [1896],
pp. 120–36).

6. Tilgath-pilneser: regularly in Chronicles (cf. 5:26 and 2 Chr.
28:20) for 'Tiglath-pileser' in 2 Kg. (on which see A. R. Millard,
JSS 21 [1976], pp. 1–14), and so clearly not accidental (*contra
NEB*). The shift is perhaps due to euphonic reasons; cf. the similar
metathesis of *'almuggîm* (1 Kg. 10:11) to *'algûmmîm* in 2 Chr. 9:10,
and Willi, p. 87. For the exile of the transjordanian tribes, cf. 2
Kg. 15:29.

7–8a. his kinsmen: namely, of Beerah. *'eḥâw*, 'his brothers', need
not denote so close a relative as in English usage. There is thus no
difficulty in keeping both vv. 5f. and 8 together. **their families:**
MT, 'his families', perhaps an error of assimilation to the ending of
the previous word. Several of the versions support the very slight
change presupposed by *RSV* (*lᵉmišpᵉḥōtām*).

8b. Aroer . . . Nebo and Baalmeon occur in earlier lists of
Reubenite settlements (Num. 32:38; Jos. 13:15ff.), but by the time
of the Moabite Stone (*c.* 830 BC) they were clearly under Moabite
control (lines 9, 14, 26; cf. *DOTT*, pp. 196f.; *ANET*, p. 320). Since
the immediately preceding context deals with a period later than
this, and what follows is from an earlier period, it would seem that
who dwelt (lit. 'he dwelt', perhaps marking the start of a new
sentence) should be referred to the tribe of Reuben as a whole, not
just Bela (Rudolph).

9–10 may reflect in part the unsettled existence of Reuben, who
was eventually absorbed by Gad. **Hagrites:** cf. vv. 19f. Ps. 83:6[7]
classes them with the Ishmaelites and Moabites as enemies of Israel,
but more detailed identification is inevitably uncertain; cf. E.
Meyer, *Die Israeliten und ihre Nachbarstämme* (1906), pp. 326–8;
Simons, *GTTOT*, §102; J. Van Seters, *Abraham in History and
Tradition* (1975), pp. 62–4.

Gad

5:11–17

This paragraph is distinctive in not including any material from
other *OT* lists (notably Num. 26). It is the only 'genealogy' to open
with a geographical note (v. 11) and this is distinctly connected with
the end of the previous section (**over against them**). Moreover,
there are several features in common with vv. 4–10: (a) both passages

have a similar structure—main list (4–6, 12), attention to their **kinsmen** (7–8a; 13–15) and notes about areas of tribal pasture (9–10; 16); (b) it follows from this that they reflect identical interests; (c) terms in common, notably *hārō'š*, **the chief** (7; 12), and compare **his kinsmen by their families** (7) with **their kinsmen according to their fathers' houses** (13). It thus looks as though the Chronicler here continued straight on with the source he had already been using, without on this occasion expanding it with other biblical material.

11. Bashan: as elsewhere in the *OT* (e.g. Dt. 3:10), considered adjacent to Gilead (v. 10). Both terms are used with a certain elasticity, so that no problem need be found with this juxtaposition (cf. Abel, *Géographie* I, pp. 275f.; Baly, *Geography*, pp. 219ff.).

12. and Shaphat: in view of the titles given to **Joel** and **Shapham**, T and LXX are perhaps right in seeing **Janai**'s title in these words; read *haššōpēṭ*, 'the judge'.

16. and in its towns: lit. 'and in its daughters', which usually presupposes the name of a town before it. **Bashan**, however, is a region. Unless this is a usage of the phrase for which we otherwise have no evidence, we must suppose that a name has dropped out. **Sharon:** clearly not the coastal plain south of Carmel, but an area in Transjordan, mentioned on the Moabite Stone (line 13), but whose exact location is unknown (cf. Simons, *GTTOT*, §301).

17. in the days of Jotham king of Judah, and in the days of Jeroboam king of Israel: since Jotham ruled as co-regent after his father Uzziah contracted leprosy (2 Kg. 15:5), it is possible that this refers to a single enrolment. In that case, it would have been undertaken by **Jeroboam** II, since Gad was part of the northern kingdom. **Jotham** may have already been mentioned in the Chronicler's source, if the theory of 'a synchronistic chronicle written in two columns' is correct (cf. Mettinger, *Solomonic State Officials*, p. 39, with references); otherwise the Chronicler will himself have added it in accordance with 'his scheme of making the Davidic dynasty the chronologico-religious backbone of his work' (Myers).

The Transjordanian Tribes

5:18–22

The editorial hand of the Chronicler is apparent in this paragraph. Verse 20 is so typical of his very characteristic battle reports (cf. 2 Chr. 13:13–19; 14:9–15; 18:31; 20:1–27; 26:7; 32:7–8, 20–22) that he must have rewritten his source at this point in his own words. Moreover, v. 18 is the only occasion on which figures for the two and a half transjordanian tribes are added together. Since originally they would have been given separately, as in Num. I and 26, it looks as though the Chronicler has himself supplied the total on the basis of the separate figures in his source.

These observations help to explain the fact that, judging by v. 18, the paragraph is not based on the source which the Chronicler has been using previously, but on the military census list referred to above (p. 46). As he had just dealt with Reuben and Gad, the influence of the tradition of the two and a half tribes and concern for editorial tidiness caused him here to abandon strict adherence to the earlier source and to compile a summarising paragraph on the basis of whatever material was available to him. In consequence, it is possible that vv. 19–22 are an alternative account of the war mentioned in v. 10, the differing emphasis being due to the different interests and concerns of the two sources, though the likelihood of prolonged skirmishing between rival settlers in the region makes certainty about this impossible.

18. forty-four thousand seven hundred and sixty: the number is no doubt computed from the Chronicler's source. Though large, it is considerably less than the totals in Num. I and 26.

19. the Hagrites: cf. v. 10. **Jetur, Naphish, and Nodab:** Arabian tribes; cf. Gen. 25:15; I Chr. 1:31; Lk. 3:1 ('Iturea' = **Jetur**) and W. F. Albright, *Studi Orientalistici in onore di Giorgio Levi della Vida*, I (1956), pp. 13f.

21. The numbers certainly seem to be exaggerated in this case.

22. for many fell slain: apparently an explanation why even more captives were not taken. **the exile:** vv. 6 and 26 suggest that the Chronicler is referring to the deportation of the transjordanian tribes in 734 BC (cf. 2 Kg. 15:29), more than ten years before the fall of Samaria.

The Half-Tribe of Manasseh

5:23–26

It seems unlikely that this paragraph formed part of the Chronicler's original composition: (a) a reference to the half-tribe of Manasseh *after* the more general editorial treatment of the two and a half tribes in the previous paragraph is awkward; (b) vv. 25–26 are a mere expansion of v. 22, based on 2 Kings, 26b indicating that they refer not just to Manasseh, but to the whole group; (c) such detailed attention to the fate of the northern tribes is quite foreign to the Chronicler's method elsewhere; (d) the material in vv. 23–24, clearly drawn from the military census list, would be more at home in

7:14-19, where such material, expected on the basis of the other lists in that chapter, is missing. On this view, it could be argued that a later editor was disturbed by the lack of attention to half-Manasseh in this context, and so compiled a suitable entry on the basis of 1 Chr. 7 and 2 Kg. 15-18.

23. they were very numerous should stand (as in MT) at the end of the verse, as a separate sentence (cf. 4:27). **from Bashan**, etc. will then define that part of **the land** which they inhabited. **Senir:** according to Dt. 3:9, to be identified with **Hermon**. Here, it may refer to the whole range, as opposed to just the southern part known specifically as **Mount Hermon**, or the **and** may be epexegetic, in which case translate as 'even Mount Hermon'.

24. the heads of their fathers' houses: this expression is used in several different ways in the *OT*; cf. J. P. Weinberg, *VT* 23 (1973), pp. 400-14. In the genealogies, however (especially ch. 7), its context shows clearly that it is being used for 'military commanders'; cf. Johnson, *Purpose*, pp. 62ff. **Epher:** MT has 'and Epher', which suggests that a name has dropped out from the start of the list. The evidence of the versions for deleting 'and' in such a case is of little value.

mighty warriors: a phrase whose precise significance is difficult to determine owing to its flexible usage, but in the context of a military census, *RSV* is not unreasonable; cf. W. McKane, *TGUOS* 17 (1957-8), pp. 28-37; de Vaux, *AI*, p. 70.

25. they: the two and a half tribes; cf. 26*b*.

25-26 is composed on the basis of 2 Kg. 15:19, 29; 17:6; 18:11, together with a brief summary of 17:7-23. Its effect is to transfer to the earlier deportation of the two and a half tribes the description and explanation of the later exile of the main part of the northern kingdom; for the Chronicler's handling of this latter, see on 2 Chr. 28. **Pul . . . Tilgath-pilneser** (cf. v. 6): both names refer to the same person. It is possible that MT intends this, and so *RSV* translates with an appositional phrase (more literally, $w^e\,^\prime et\text{-}r\hat{u}a\d{h}$ could be rendered 'even the spirit of . . . '). However, it is also possible that the author was here misled by the separate references to Pul and Tiglath-pileser in 2 Kg. 15:19 and 29 into thinking of them as different people (in which case translate 'and the spirit of . . . '). **Hara and:** absent from 2 Kg. 17:6; 18:11, some LXX MSS and P, and mentioned nowhere else. It also interrupts the close geographical connection between **Habor** and **the river Gozan**. In consequence, many delete, finding here a corruption either of $n^e har$ ('river of'), which follows, or of $h\bar{a}r\hat{e}\ m\bar{a}day$ ('the mountains of Media') which probably stood in the writer's *Vorlage* in 2 Kg. (cf. LXX); cf. Simons, *GTTOT*, §§99, 938-41.

Levi

6:1–81
NB. In the Hebrew Bible, **6:1–15** is numbered as 5:27–41, and in consequence **6:16–81** as 6:1–66.

With Levi, the Chronicler reaches the central point of his genealogical lists, doubtless reflecting his estimation of the significance of
this priestly tribe for the community of his own day. As in the case
of Judah and Benjamin, much more detail is provided than for the
other tribes which these three enclose.

Internal analysis of the chapter is again hampered by the fact that
most commentators find a considerable amount of secondary
addition here, without agreement as to its extent. In an attempt to
resolve this problem, however, it may be suggested that the most
convenient starting point is the list of their dwelling places in vv.
54–81.

The verses are clearly parallel with Jos. 21:5–39, though it is
disputed which passage is the earlier; the usual view that Chronicles
drew on Joshua has recently been forcefully challenged by A. G.
Auld, *JSOT* 10 (1978), pp. 26–40, and *ZAW* 91 (1979), pp. 194–
206. Whatever be the truth in this issue, a comparison of the two
texts reveals that the most significant difference between them lies
in the order of the material. The Chronicler's order is governed by
the following scheme:

sons of Aaron of the families of the Kohathites (54–60)
the rest of the Kohathites (61)
Gershomites (62)
Merarites (63)
Kohathites—supplement (66–70)
Gershomites—supplement (71–76)
Merarites—supplement (77–81).

This order, it may now be observed, is identical with that of the
main body of the lists in vv. 1–49, the sons of Aaron heading the
section in vv. 1–15, with two parallel lists linked to the three sons
of Levi in 16–30 and 31–48. The only exception to this correspondence is the repetition of part of the list of the sons of Aaron in 50–
53, but this is already to be regarded as a later expansion on quite
other grounds (see the commentary). Assuming that the ordering of
54–81 is the work of the Chronicler, this parallel pattern in the first
half of the chapter strongly suggests that he was responsible for its
arrangement too.

The main argument usually levelled against such a unity is the
repetition of the opening of the Levitical genealogy in vv. 1ff. and
16ff. Closer examination shows, however, that the differences be-

tween these two passages (vertical contrasted with horizontal genealogy) so serve the interests of their respective contexts that no
difficulty need be felt in attributing the inclusion of both to a single
hand (see the commentary).

What significance did the Chronicler see in this structure? First,
the pre-eminence of the high priests, the sons of Aaron, is evident.
Second, however, it has long been observed that there is a close
connection between vv. 16–30 and 31–48. The former apparently
deals with 'ordinary' Levites, the latter with Levitical singers. Each
of the six lists involved leads back to one of the three sons of Levi:
Gershom, Kohath and Merari. Further, however, those in the first
group are traced through the elder son of these three, those in the
second list through the younger son. (On apparent exceptions to
this otherwise clear pattern, see the commentary.) Finally, we learn
from vv. 39 and 44 that the Kohathites were stationed centrally,
with the Gershomites and Merarites to right and left respectively.
Since the sons of Aaron were also Kohathites, it may thus be seen
that the whole sevenfold structure of the Levitical lists in this
chapter is based on a regular pattern which could be expressed
diagrammatically thus:

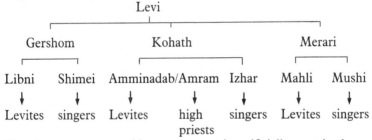

That in some respects this arrangement is artificially contrived may
be seen first from the fact that the Chronicler has omitted some
material that we know he had available in order to achieve it (e.g.
Exod. 6:21ff.), secondly from the fact that he omitted any listing of
Levitical priests who were not also high priests, even though later
parts of his work show that he considered them important, and
thirdly from the frequent dependence of vv. 33–47 on 20–30, even
though they purport to be tracing independent lines within the
genealogy. The whole is thus to be interpreted as what, on the basis
of a far more restricted investigation, has been called a work of art,
rather than a legal or even biological description (A. Lefèvre, *RSR*
37 [1950], pp. 287–92). In the Chronicler's symbolism, at the heart
of the theocracy this perfectly arranged tribe is seen to revolve
around the person of the high priest. Though his methods are
strange to us, he must be allowed to paint his portrait in his own

way, and we must beware of asking of his material the kind of questions which it was never arranged to answer.

Some additional studies dealing with the general question of Levites in Chronicles may appropriately be listed here: J. Köberle, *Die Tempelsänger im Alten Testament* (1899); von Rad, *GCW*, pp. 80–119; K. Möhlenbrink, *ZAW* 52 (1934), pp. 184–231; de Vaux, *AI*, pp. 345–405; A. H. J. Gunneweg, *Leviten und Priester* (1965), pp. 204–16; A. Cody, *A History of Old Testament Priesthood* (1969), pp. 156ff.

1–15. Although the introduction (1–4) to the list of high priests is based on Exod. 6:16ff., the Chronicler has abstracted only what he needed to construct a vertical genealogy; as has been noted on previous such occasions, he moves straight along the line leading to the figure at the centre of attention (in this case, **Phinehas**), without dealing at all with the other lines; contrast vv. 16–19. The form is entirely appropriate to the purpose in hand. **Gershom** (1): more accurately, 'Gershon', the normal biblical spelling. The Chronicler himself usually uses the form Gershom (though even so, cf. 2 Chr. 29:12). The present spelling may be due to the influence of his source.

4b–15. Though appearing to give a full list of pre-exilic high priests, ordered on a hereditary basis, this passage is in some respects clearly an artificial construction: several high priests mentioned elsewhere are omitted here (Jehoiada, 2 Chr. 22:11–24:17; Azariah, 2 Chr. 26:20; Urijah, 2 Kg. 16:11ff.); **Azariah** (9) is the son, not grandson, of **Zadok** (8), according to 1 Kg. 4:2; study of the process of the composition of the list in the light of its parallels elsewhere (1 Chr. 9:10f.; Ezr. 7:1–5; Neh. 11:10f., etc.) and of material from the historical books strongly suggests that the Chronicler (or his source) here combined several traditional groups of names of high priests and that not all those mentioned were the son of their predecessor (cf. J. R. Bartlett, *JTS* ns 19 [1968], pp. 1–18). Furthermore, once the note of v. 10 about **Azariah . . . who** (first) **served as priest in the house that Solomon built in Jerusalem** is restored to its right place in connection with the **Azariah** of v. 9 (rather than **Zadok**, as proposed by E. Robertson, *The Old Testament Problem* [1950], pp. 175f., together with the intriguing suggestion that this list is of Samaritan origin), it emerges that there are twelve generations between Aaron and the building of the temple, which looks very much like a construction based on the principle of 12 × 40 = the 480 years of 1 Kg. 6:1. Similarly, eleven generations then take us down to the **exile** of **Jehozadak** (15), whose son Joshua (Hag. 1:1) was high priest at the time of the building of the second temple. Thus two sets of twelve generations link these three significant events (cf. K. Koch, *VT* 18 [1978], pp. 438f.), comparable to the three sets of fourteen generations in Mt. 1:1–17. It follows from these considerations that **was the father of** (4, and in fact repeated before each name) is to be understood as the metaphorical expression for succession in office, and the list as a whole as portraying the divine orderliness that we have noted as a characteristic of the Chronicler's presentation of Levi.

16–30. The first two generations of **the sons of Levi** are listed (16–19) in accordance with Num. 3:17–20 (cf. Exod. 6:16–19). The horizontal construction of the genealogy (contrast 6:1–4) here suits the parallel development of the three branches of Levites in the following verses. From **Gershom** (20) and **Merari** (29), seven generations are then listed through the line of the elder son (**Libni, Mahli**). It is probable that this is meant to span the period to the reign of David, who reorganised the duties of the Levites, since **Asaiah** (30) of the sons of Marari is also mentioned at 1 Chr. 15:6. Nothing is known of the Chronicler's source for this material, though its presentation is again evidently schematic.

22–28. **The sons of Kohath** do not appear at first to fit into this pattern, both because their line is traced through the otherwise unknown **Amminadab** (22), and because the list is so much longer. The first problem cannot be easily resolved. Amminadab is not listed among the sons of Kohath in v. 18 or anywhere else. On the basis of Exod. 6:21, we might have expected Izhar. This is found in the LXX^A, and is adopted by a number of commentators. On the other hand, the listing of Izhar in v. 38 would lead us, by analogy with the other lists, to expect Amram here. This is adopted by RH and Möhlenbrink (p. 201). The following list might then have originally referred to Levitical priests. It is just possible that a copyist found 'Amram' difficult in view of vv. 3ff., and so substituted Amminadab (the first two letters of each name are the same) under the influence of 15:10 or Exod. 6:23. LXX^A would then represent a secondary harmonisation, witnessing to a failure to appreciate the parallel pattern of vv. 16–30 with 31–48.

The difficulty of the length of the genealogy seems to have been solved by A. Lefèvre, *RSR* 37 (1950), pp. 287–92 (followed by Johnson, *Purpose*, pp. 71–3). He notes that the expression **the sons of** in vv. 25 and 28 is inappropriate in a vertical genealogy, that **Elkanah** occurs five times (twice at the start of v. 25, obscured by *RSV*) and that the conjunction 'and' occurs on several occasions as a disturbing influence. *RSV* and *NEB* have omitted some of these, but cf. *AV*, *RV*. Lefèvre shows that if these points are given due weight, and the indication of Exod. 6:24 followed up, vv. 22–25 present the following genealogy:

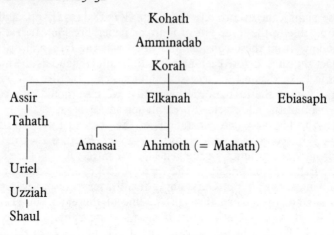

It will be observed that seven generations thus follow **Kohath**, bringing the list into line with the other two in this section.

25. and Ahimoth: read $w^e\,{}^{\flat}\bar{a}h\hat{\imath}w\ mah\underline{a}t,$ 'and his brother, Mahath' (*BHS*); cf. v. 35. The very slight variant may have arisen once it was forgotten that this genealogy included horizontal, not just vertical, elements.

26–28. Part of the genealogy of **Samuel** is here appended, without any direct contact with the foregoing. (In MT, 26*a* reads, in the *Qere*, 'Elkanah. The sons of Elkanah, Zophai his son', etc.) Despite a number of orthographic variants, the list is clearly the same as that in I Sam. 1:1 and 8:2, perhaps in a different textual recension. It was presumably added at this point because of the link with the name Elkanah. It is not impossible that Samuel was of Levitical descent, 'an Ephraimite' of I Sam. 1:1 meaning 'a resident of Ephraim'; cf. Jg. 17:7. Alternatively, we may be witnessing here the first step in the 'adoption' of one whose priestly function indicated Levitical affinities. In this passage, his family is simply juxtaposed, without genealogical link, but by vv. 33–38 he has been completely absorbed into the tribe.

28. Joel his first-born, the second Abijah: an unquestionably correct emendation, on the basis of I Sam. 8:2 and with some versional support, of MT: 'the firstborn Vashni, and Abiah' (*AV*). **Joel** will have been lost after **Samuel** by homoioteleuton, and then **and the second** ($w^e hass\bar{e}n\hat{\imath}$) necessarily read as a name 'Vashni' ($wa\check{s}n\hat{\imath}$), probably formed by analogy with the Persian name Vashti (Est. 1:9).

31–32. The list of Levitical singers is prefaced by a note of David's rearrangement of their duties **after the ark rested**; cf. I Chr. 15:16ff.; 23–26; 2 Chr. 35:3, etc., and von Rad, *GCW*, pp. 98–115.

That David should have had a particular interest in the music of
the cult, and made arrangements for it, is in itself highly probable.
His association with music is known from ancient traditions (e.g. 2
Sam. 6:5; 23:1; Am. 6:5, if MT there is sound; and the early stories
about David's playing to Saul in 1 Sam.), and the existence of guilds
of singers in Israel from earliest times is rendered likely by analogy
with the evidence from surrounding cultures (cf. S. Mowinckel, *The
Psalms in Israel's Worship* 2 [1962], pp. 79–81). David's transfer of
the ark to Jerusalem (2 Sam. 6) and the inclusion of Zadok the
priest in the lists of his officials (2 Sam. 8:16–18; 20:23–26) further
show that, as we would expect, the cult was not exempt from the
very far-reaching reforms that David initiated during his reign.

It is difficult to believe, however, that the lists which follow
prèsent the precise form of Davidic arrangement: as genealogies,
they are constructed artificially from vv. 20–30, while in terms of
cultic history they seem to show a more developed stage over against
the distinction of Levites and singers in Ezr. 2, Neh. 7, etc. Moreover, 'the headings of the psalms represent a somewhat earlier
conception than that of the Chronicler. They know but two families
of singers, Asaph and the sons of Korah' (Mowinckel, *Psalms* 2, p.
97); see further on Chs 15–16. We should therefore conclude that
the Chronicler's presentation both here and in comparable passages
implies the claim that the guilds of singers of his own day, whose
idealised origins he here describes, stand in legitimate and unbroken
continuity with the innovations of David. The particular stress on
the ark will be to reinforce the singers' rightful place within the
service of **the house of the Lord in Jerusalem**.

33–38. the sons of the Kohathites: this is clearly the same list as
in vv. 22–27, but read now as a vertical genealogy with the family
of **Samuel** fully integrated. In consequence, the list is considerably
longer (22 generations) than the two which follow. As in these,
however, and as befits the Chronicler's scheme, the first name,
Heman the singer, is additional, while at the end the line is traced
through the younger son of Levi's three children, in this case, Izhar.
Apart from these intentional points, the differences between the
lists are easily accounted for as transcriptional variations, except for
Zephaniah, which does not correspond to **Uriel** (24). **Azariah** and
Uzziah (24) are interchangeable; compare 2 Kg. 15:1–7 with 2 Chr.
26. Assir and Elkanah (22*b*, 23*a*) are omitted.

39–43. For the family of **Asaph**, the first few names are 'late
. . . and favourites with the Chronicler' (CM). Beyond this, their
source is unknown. With **Ethni**, however, a close parallel with vv.
20–21 begins, with similar variations to those noted above. **Jahath**
should not be deleted (*contra* Möhlenbrink, pp. 202f.), but reversed

with **Shimei** just before it. It then corresponds to the Jahath of v.
20, while Shimei takes the place of Libni in that verse as being the
younger son of Gershom (cf. v. 17).

44–47. Although the genealogy of **Ethan** is again traced through
Merari's younger son, **Mushi**, it does not this time correspond to
vv. 19f. This strongly suggests that these lists were not pure inventions by the Chronicler, but were rather reflections of the guilds of
his own day, whose legitimacy his elaborate scheme was intended
to uphold.

48–49. The Levitical lists are rounded off with a brief indication
of the chief duties of the Levites and priests, that of the singers
having already been mentioned (vv. 31f.).

48. As in the final form of the Pentateuch, **the Levites** served as
assistants to the priests (Num. 18:1–7), initially in **the tabernacle**
(cf. Num. 3:5ff.), and later in the Jerusalem temple (e.g. 2 Chr.
30:16; 35:11).

49. The family of **Aaron** as a whole was set aside for the priesthood, only the descendants of his grandson Phinehas filling the role
of high priest (cf. vv. 3–4). Their chief duties as summarised here
conform to the Pentateuchal regulations, e.g. Lev. 1:3–9; 4f.; Num.
4:5ff.; 18:5, etc.

50–53. The list of high priests is here followed again down to the
time of David. It is clearly a secondary addition to the Chronicler's
composition, however, because (a) the context has been dealing with
all the priests, the sons of Aaron, not just the high priestly duties,
and (b) it is secondary to vv. 3–7. There, a genealogical narrowing
to Phinehas was noted, whereas here a bare list of successive names
has simply been abstracted (Möhlenbrink, p. 205). To argue that
this list must be earlier than 3ff. because it is shorter (e.g. Willi, p.
214) overlooks the fact that it intends only to come down to the
period of David, whose reorganisation of the cult has already been
noted (v. 31).

54–81. This list of Levitical **dwelling places** is parallel with Jos.
21:5–39; see the introduction to this chapter above. The only major
point of difference which can with reasonable certainty be attributed
to the Chronicler himself concerns the order of material at the start,
for which see above, p. 68. The general interest of the Chronicler
in geographical matters in these lists has already been mentioned
(p. 39), but we may presume that he found this passage particularly
significant, since it indicates the residence of Levites throughout the
tribal territory of Israel, a further indication of their centrality to
the life and well-being of the nation; see also Japhet, *JBL* 98 (1979),
pp. 211f. Attempts to argue that this passage was added to his work

in at least two separate stages (Benzinger, RH) are thus unconvincing (see further, CM).

Minor variations between the parallel texts can again often be attributed to errors in transcription. In several cases (e.g. vv. 59, **Ashan**, and 78*a*, lacking in MT of Jos. 21:36) the Chronicler appears to preserve a better text. A few of the differences do not appear to be mechanical, however (e.g. **Tabor**, v. 62), and suggest the possibility of the Chronicler drawing on a slightly different recension of the text of Joshua from that preserved to us (or *vice versa*). The Chronicler's version is usually a little shorter, summarising numbers of cities (e.g. Jos. 21:24, 25, 31, 32, etc.), for instance, being frequently omitted. Again, references to Dan in Jos. 21:5 and 23 are omitted at vv. 61 and 69. Although it is equally striking that Dan is not given a genealogy in these lists at all (see on 7:12), it is doubtful whether we should detect bias on the part of the Chronicler here (cf. *VT* 23 [1973], p. 379). If the omission is not due to scribal accident, it can be more easily explained on the supposition that the Chronicler's *Vorlage* came to him from southern circles which, unlike the Chronicler himself, were totally opposed to all northern traditions.

A detailed explanation of the earlier history of the text and its geographical allusions lies beyond the scope of this commentary. In addition to the commentaries on Jos. 21, cf. W. F. Albright, *Louis Ginzberg Jubilee Volume*, 1 (1945), pp. 49–73; Alt, *KS* 2, pp. 294ff. and 306–15; B. Mazar, *SVT* 7 (1960), pp. 193–205; Haran, *Temples and Temple Service*, pp. 112–31; Aharoni, *Land*, pp. 269–73; A. Cody, in *Homenaje a Juan Prado* (1975), pp. 179–89; and the articles of Auld noted above.

54. the lot: either understand, or supply from Jos. 21:10, *rî'š-ōnāh*: 'first'.

57. cities: Jos. 21:13 has 'city', since of the following only **Hebron** was a city **of refuge.**

60. throughout their families: Jos. 21:19 has *ûmigrᵉšêhen*, 'and their pasture lands'. Since either text is possible in the context, textual emendation should be resisted. **thirteen:** only eleven cities have been listed by the Chronicler; Juttah and Gibeon may be restored to vv. 59 and 60 respectively on the basis of Jos. 21:16f.

61. The second half of the verse is muddled, even in the English. We should probably restore ' . . . the tribe of Ephraim, from the tribe of Dan and the half-tribe of Manasseh . . . ' with Jos. 21:5.

62. Manasseh in Bashan: Jos. 21:6 is correct in its qualification: 'The half tribe of Manasseh'.

67. cities: cf. v. 57.

69. Before **Aijalon**, Jos. 21:23 has 'and out of the tribe of Dan,

Elteke with its pasture lands, Gibbethon with its pasture lands'. Since we know from Jos. 19:42 and 45 that **Aijalon** and **Gath-rimmon** both belonged to Dan, not Ephraim, the longer text is here to be preferred.

70. Aner (*'et̲–'ānēr*): an error for the orthographically very similar 'Taanach' (*'et̲–ta'nak*), Jos. 21:25.

72. Kadesh belongs in v. 76; Jos. 21:28 here reads Kishion.

75. Hukok was a city of Naphtali (Jos. 19:34), not Asher: read 'Helkath' (Jos. 21:31).

77. This verse diverges considerably from Jos. 21:34–35. Two names have dropped out, and the two which remain are different. While **Rimmon(o)** may be correct (Jos. 21:35 has Dimnah), no possible connection is apparent between **Tabor** (probably an abbreviation of Chisloth-tabor, Jos. 19:12) and Nahalal of Jos. 21:35. This is a further indication of varying recensions of the text.

Issachar

7:1–5

Chapter 7 consists of the second block of smaller genealogies enclosed by the Judah-Levi-Benjamin framework. Most of the material comprises a combination of a short introduction based on Num. 26 (cf. Gen. 46) and details drawn from a military census list arranged in genealogical form (see above, p. 46). No particular significance appears to attach to the internal order of the chapter, which may have been dictated by the order of the Chronicler's extra-biblical source.

1. Cf. Num. 26:23f. and Gen. 46:13. **The sons of** (*wᵉlib̲nê*): cf. GK §143e for the *l* of introduction. This usage, characteristic of late biblical Hebrew, is a favourite of the Chronicler (cf. Driver, *Introduction*, p. 539, and *IBC*, pp. 50f.), so that there is no need to emend (*contra RSV* and most commentators).

2. For the military terminology, see on 5:24. **David:** we know of a census from David's time: 2 Sam. 24; 1 Chr. 21. Since his reign marks the start of the Chronicler's narrative proper, his administrative reforms are noted elsewhere in the genealogies as the point of reference; cf. 4:31; 6:31.

3. five: either **Izrahiah** and his sons are all included together, or **And the sons of Izrahiah** should be deleted as a dittograph (Rudolph), so making for five **sons of Uzzi**.

4. for they had many wives and sons: an explanation of the larger number than in v. 2.

5. Their kinsmen: there is a slight illogicality in MT here, since

this verse gives a total for **all the families of Issachar**, not excluding
the sons of Uzzi. If the context is judged insufficiently clear to allow
MT to stand regardless (*sc.* 'they and their brethren'), the simplest
solution is to postulate the loss of a comparative *m* from the start of
the verse (*mēᵃḥêhem*) by haplography, and to join the word to the
preceding verse: 'for they had more wives and sons than their
kinsmen. All the families of Issachar totalled . . . ' (CM; Rudolph).

Benjamin

7:6–12

This paragraph is marked by three curious features: (a) it starts
with the single word **Benjamin**. *RSV*'s **The sons of** is restored
conjecturally on the basis of a few MSS and the Versions, but despite
most commentators these may reflect only a secondary easing of the
difficulty; (b) the opening does not follow either Gen. 46:21 or
Num. 26:38–41 as closely as is usual in these lists. In fact, only **Bela**
and **Becher** are found in common, and this is not enough to establish
dependence at all, since both were clearly present in the source
which the Chronicler uses for the rest of the paragraph (cf. vv. 7
and 8); (c) Benjamin is dealt with in greater detail in ch. 8. These
verses are thus unexpectedly placed.

A few scholars (notably CM, followed by Brunet, *RB* 60 [1953],
pp. 485f.) have sought to explain these anomalies by suggesting that
the passage in fact presents a very corrupt form of the genealogy of
Zebulun, otherwise lacking in the genealogies. However, the textual
emendations proposed are too violent to inspire confidence. On the
omission of Zebulun (and Dan), see above, p. 47. Rudolph, by
contrast, finds evidence here of a very heavy textual corruption,
which enables him to conjecture that the original order of tribes in
this chapter was Issachar, Zebulun, Benjamin, Dan, Naphtali, Gad,
Asher, Manasseh, Ephraim, but his reasoning is both circular and
e silentio (see *IBC*, pp. 75f.).

We may therefore suggest rather that the Chronicler has here
continued straight on with the source he was using in the preceding
verses in just the same manner as was seen above for Gad, 5:11–17.
Benjamin at the start may then be regarded as the form of heading
used there, adopted without alteration; lack of reference to the
Pentateuch is automatically explained, and the problem of two separate genealogies of Benjamin is at least eased.

In further support of this suggestion, the list in vv. 6–11 is
completely regular, with a section in order on each of the three sons
mentioned in v. 6, namely **Bela** in v. 7, **Becher** in vv. 8–9 and

Jediael in vv. 10–11. This order no doubt accurately reflects the situation in the source here used.

Several features suggest that the list is late, perhaps even post-exilic, in its final form (e.g. the use of papponomy in v. 10; the name **Elioenai** in v. 8, etc.; cf. Myers). This is in no way surprising, for lists such as these for a tribe which continued to maintain a measure of self-identity would doubtless have been kept up-to-date. Although often the material is linked to David (see v. 2), this is by no means always the case (e.g. 5:17), and 9:1 indicates a period at least as late as the exile.

12. **Shuppim and Huppim:** cf. 'Muppim', 'Huppim', Gen. 46:21, and 'Shephupham . . . Hupham', Num. 26:39, both in the Benjaminite genealogies. This suggests that the verse is a rather disjointed addition to the preceding. For the remainder of the verse, nearly all commentators now follow Klostermann (*RTK* 4, p. 94) in emending to *bᵉnê ḏān ḥušîm bᵉnô 'eḥāḏ*, 'The sons of Dan: Hushim, his son, one'. Hushim is understood as the same as Shuham in the Dan genealogy of Num. 26:42. A number of difficulties attend this reconstruction, however (cf. *VT* 23 [1973], pp. 375–9), so that it is easier to construe the names as a continuation of the Benjaminite fragmentary addition: for **Ir**, cf. 'Iri', v. 7; for **Hushim**, cf. the same name amongst Benjaminites at 8:8 and 11. **Aher** ('another') may be a slip for 'Addar' (= Ard), whom we expect here on the basis of 8:3 and Num. 26:40.

Naphtali

7:13

This genealogy corresponds with Gen. 46:24f.; Num. 26:48f. On any showing its brevity is noteworthy, and this may conceivably be due to an extensive scribal loss (see further on vv. 14–19). This is the only evidence we have for such mutilation, which might account also for the absence of Dan and Zebulun. Though it has at least this much in its favour, against those who without any such evidence whatever postulate large lacunae earlier in the chapter, it should be stressed that the suggestion remains otherwise entirely conjectural (cf. above, p. 47).

Manasseh

7:14–19

It was suggested above at 5:23–26 that material found there had
been removed from its original position following this paragraph.
What remains here is the introductory section which, as in the other
lists in this chapter, is closest to Pentateuchal passages. This
accounts for the fact that it does not appear to fit so well in a context
based on a military census list.

MT, which is faithfully followed by *RSV* throughout, reveals a
number of internal difficulties. Chief amongst these are (a) the
position of **Maacah**, who in v. 15 is the **sister**, but in v. 16 the
wife, of **Machir**. (b) The absence of a satisfactory 'first' to match
the **second** of v. 15. (c) The presence in v. 15 of **Huppim** and
Shuppim. Is this a misplaced marginal correction of v. 12, where
they also appear? Others have suggested that the words should be
translated as something like 'defaced and worn away,' a desperate
copyist's comment. Rudolph, however (see below), thinks they are
corrupt forms of Hepher and Shechem, two of the sons of Gilead.
(d) Verse 17*b* starts **These were the sons of Gilead**, but he is
omitted from the preceding list (16–17*a*). (e) Verse 19 is not attached
to its context in any way. Moreover, comparison with Num. 26:29–
34 and Jos. 17:2 leads to even further problems of linking all the
evidence together.

Unless our understanding is gravely at fault, it would thus appear
that there has been some serious textual disruption here. The nature
of the damage suggests physical causes at an early stage of transmission rather than simple scribal error. This has given the commentators on the Hebrew text ample scope for the exercise of
ingenuity whose results we cannot even begin to summarise here.
As a general guide, however, parallels between the opening of the
other genealogies of this chapter suggest that Rudolph (pp. 68–71,
and cf. *BHS*) may be nearest the mark in following Num. 26:29–34
quite closely. We set out his reconstruction here accordingly,
although with full recognition of its highly speculative character:

14. The sons of Manasseh whom his Aramean concubine bore:
she bore Machir, the father of Gilead. **15**. And the sons of Gilead:
Abiezer the first-born, then Helek, Asriel, Hepher, Shechem and
Shemida; and the name of their sister was Maacah. And the sons
of Hepher: . . . the first-born, and the name of the second was
Zelophehad, and Z. had only daughters. **19**. And the sons of
Shemida were Ahian, etc. **16**. And Maacah, the wife of . . ., bore
a son, etc.

Ephraim

7:20–29

The interests of this paragraph in tribal history and geography place
its origins squarely within the material on which the Chronicler
drew at 4:24–5:22. It was suggested above that having gone on there
for reasons of editorial tidiness to deal in full with the two and a
half transjordanian tribes, he held over this section on Ephraim in
order to introduce it alongside its close neighbour, Manasseh. In
the present text, three originally separate elements have been
combined.

20–21a, 25–27. Though headed **The sons of Ephraim**, these
verses, which seem certainly to have belonged together at one time,
in fact give a vertical genealogy of **Joshua**, the son of **Nun** (v. 27).
It appears artificial, however, first because the three names at the
start (**Shuthelah, Bered, Tahath**) are to be compared with the three
brothers, sons of Ephraim, at Num. 26:35–6 (Shuthelah, Becher,
Tahan), and second because of the considerable repetition of names
within the list, which has been obscured to some extent in the
present text by variations in spelling; cf. H. W. Hogg, *JQR* 13
(1900–1), pp. 147–54. This was an unusual practice in early times,
though common in the Chronicler's own day. The list therefore
seems to have been compiled in a manner similar to that found
already at 6:33ff. The Chronicler probably received it in this form
from his source, for it contradicts his usual habit of starting the
genealogies with a close representation of the material in Num. 26,
and because the list focuses attention on Joshua, for whom elsewhere
he shows little particular interest.

21b–24. This fascinating fragment interrupts the genealogy of
Joshua, and so may have been inserted here by the Chronicler
himself, although his reasons are not fully clear. It seems necessary
to distinguish between its original setting and the Chronicler's own
interpretation of it. By inserting it halfway through the Joshua
genealogy he himself dates it well after the time of the patriarch
Ephraim, thus making the **Ephraim** of v. 22 a later descendant (so
Keil). This positioning will have encouraged the interpretation of
the event found in the Targum and much other midrashic literature
which, combining these verses with Exod. 13:17 and Ps. 78:9ff.,
found here a reference to a premature and unsuccessful Exodus of
the tribe of Ephraim from Egypt (cf. J. Heinemann, *HTR* 68 [1975],
pp. 1–15; M. J. Mulder, *JSJ* 6 [1975], pp. 141–66). **They came
down** (*yārᵉdû*, v. 21) would perhaps not have been felt as a difficulty by the Chronicler, since it might have become by his time a

standard verb to use with the northern Ephraim, comparable to the sometimes inexact English expression 'to go up to town'.

This is unlikely to reflect the original sense of the fragment, however, in which **Ephraim** can hardly be understood as other than the Patriarch, despite the historical problems this raises. The suggestion, with reference to Jer. 31:15, that **Ephraim** (22) refers to the whole of the later tribe (e.g. Rudolph) founders on the clearly individual continuation that he **went in to his wife**, etc. The fragment seems originally to have suggested the residence of Ephraim in Israel (*contra* Gen. 48:5, etc.) and the setback to the westward expansion of his family. In this setting, **they came down** will retain its natural sense. If it is true that the Chronicler has given the story a new historical setting, then it cannot be used to support the view that he himself reckoned with continuous habitation of the land without reference to the Exodus and Conquest (Japhet, *JBL* 98 [1979], pp. 205-18). Nor is it wise to draw far-reaching consequences about which tribes were or were not in Egypt from a fragment whose interpretation is so much disputed. Myers, for instance, suggests that the conditions of the patriarchal period are here reflected, but that the association with Ephraim is an anachronism, based on the location of the incident.

21. Gath: Gittaim, rather than the more remote Gath of the Philistines; B. Mazar, *IEJ* 4 (1954), pp. 227-35; A. F. Rainey, *EI* 12 (1975), pp. 63-76. **who were born in the land:** as opposed to either the patriarch or the Israelites of the Judges period, who were not considered part of the autochthonous population. To later midrashic writers, however, a contrast may have been suggested rather with Ephraimites who were born in Egypt, thus furthering the development of the tradition about a premature Exodus. **their cattle:** i.e. of the men of Gath. The contrary view (e.g. that the men of Gath went down to Goshen to raid the Ephraimites' cattle) stretches credulity to breaking point.

23. because evil (*rāʿāh*) **had befallen his house.** A name etiology which depends for its force on the whole preceding narrative; cf. B. O. Long, *The Problem of Etiological Narrative in the Old Testament* (1968), p. 38. Mulder, *JSJ* 6 (1975), pp. 141-66, suggests that the whole incident is a midrashic expansion on the name **Beriah** in the light of anti-Samaritan polemic in the Chronicler's day. This runs counter to the positive outlook of the Chronicler to the north, however (cf. section G of the Introduction), as well as overlooking the affinity of this material with that discussed above in chs 4 and 5.

24. After Ephraim's westward expansion was checked, they were able to settle instead in **Lower and Upper Beth-horon**, which lie close together further to the east. **Uzzen-sheerah** has not been identified with any certainty.

28–29. The two preceding paragraphs are here drawn together in a brief description of the dwelling places of **the sons of Joseph**. Though comparison with Jos. 16–18 leads to some questions about the details, for the Chronicler the presentation of the people in the land will have been the chief concern, rather than the problems of historical geography.

Asher

7:30–40

Asher is the last tribe to be drawn from the military census list (cf. v. 40) on which the Chronicler based most of this chapter. The introduction is closer to Gen. 46:17 than Num. 26:44–47, but otherwise the material in the paragraph has no known parallel.

40. twenty-six thousand: a noteworthy reduction from the 41,500 of Num. 1:40f. and 2:27f. and the 53,400 of Num. 26:47, no doubt reflecting accurately the situation in a later period.

Benjamin

8:1–40

The Chronicler rounds off his survey of the Israelite tribes with a more extended treatment of Benjamin, thereby concluding the Judah-Levi-Benjamin framework which encloses the whole (cf. above, p. 46f.).

The chapter raises several problems which have not yet found a fully satisfactory solution. Unlike the genealogies of Judah and Levi, no clearly discernible structure is apparent in the present form of the text, whilst attempts to impose a more coherent pattern upon it demand such radical and conjectural textual emendation that they cannot inspire confidence; cf. H. W. Hogg, *JQR* 11 (1898–9), pp. 102–14; J. Marquart, *JQR* 14 (1901–2), pp. 343–51. More promising is Rudolph's approach. Finding complete breaks in the genealogy following vv. 7, 12 and 28, and that each of the resulting four sections has a geographical reference, he postulates that we have here parallel lists of Benjaminite families and their dwelling places at a particular time, either during the reign of Josiah or the post-exilic period. Since, in addition, A. Demsky, *BASOR* 202 (1971), pp. 16–23, has suggested that the genealogy of Saul (vv. 29–40; cf. 9:35–44) may reflect the social and ethnic background of

Gibeon at the end of the monarchy, this approach would seem best to suit the material. If this is correct, it should be observed that the expression **sons of** in this chapter will often refer to clan affiliation rather than direct family relationships.

The divergent types of material (e.g. vv. 6, 13, 40) suggest that earlier sources may have already been used to make the compilation which was available to the Chronicler. For the apparent duplication of a genealogy of Benjamin, see the comments at 7:6–12. In fact, there are hardly any points of contact between the two passages. This is to be explained on the basis of their different dates. For the duplication of 8:28–38 and 9:34–44, see the comments *ad loc.*

1–7. The list's interest in these verses will be in **the sons of Ehud**, dwelling at **Geba** (v. 6), rather than in the family tree of **Benjamin** (v. 1). That the opening verses cannot be harmonised with Num. 26:38–41 or 1 Chr. 7:6 is thus not surprising, for the differences will reflect alterations in which clans were prominent at a given period.

1. first-born: although it is true that in Hebrew this word has the same consonants as 'Becher' (7:6), it should be evident from the comments above that a harmonistic emendation is not demanded. The continuation, **the second, . . . the third**, etc., further supports the present form of the text.

3. Since it is unlikely that there were two sons of **Bela** called **Gera**, it is probable that we should follow the proposal to read 'and' **Abihud** as *waᵃbî ᵉhûd*, 'even the father of Ehud' (cf. D. W. Baker, *VT* 30 [1980], p. 133), followed then by v. 6a 'These are the sons of Ehud'. It may be reasonably conjectured that this latter phrase was omitted by homoioteleuton, subsequently written in the margin, only then to be reinserted in the wrong place, being understood as a postscript rather than a heading. Ehud may then be identified with the Benjaminite judge of Jg. 3:15.

6. and they were carried into exile to Manahath: more literally, 'and they carried them captive to . . . ' (*RV*). There can be no certainty in understanding this allusion. Rudolph thinks it may refer to the exile of part of Benjamin to **Manahath** in Edom (cf. 1:40), perhaps even in the post-exilic period. But it is clear from v. 1 (and cf. v. 33, etc.) that not all the material in the list must refer to the later period, even if the conclusion towards which each section moves (in this case, v. 7b) probably does. Thus a quite alternative suggestion, such as that of A. Bartel, *Beth Mikra* 39 (1969), pp. 24–27, cannot be ruled out, which, seeing the narrative here as very compressed, finds a reference to the expulsion by Benjamin of the indigenous inhabitants of **Geba** to **Manahath** in Judah (cf. 2:52, 54). Verse 13 provides a comparable situation. More speculatively,

he links this with the narrative of 2 Sam. 21:1–6; but against such
an identification of **Geba** with Gibeon, cf. J. Maxwell Miller, *VT*
25 (1975), pp. 145–66.

7. Naaman, Ahijah: delete as repetitions of v. 4*b* ('Ahoah' and
'Ahijah' are almost identical in Hebrew script), inserted to give
some sense to the verse after the displacement of 'These are the sons
of Ehud' (v. 6).

and Gera, that is, Heglam, who: read 'and Gera (he is the one that
carried them into exile) was the father . . . '; cf. mg. The words in
brackets represent an explanatory gloss, giving fuller details of the
incident of v. 6*b*, and thus supporting Bartel's general line of approach there. **Uzza and Ahihud** will thus be the clans that are
contemporaneous with the original compilation of the list.

8–12. Reference to Israelites resident in **Moab** (v. 8) shows that
this section too starts back in earlier times, for such conditions,
paralleled for instance by 1 Sam. 22:3f. and Ru. 1, would have been
unlikely after Moab regained its independence from Israel except in
cases of dire emergency (Jer. 40:11). The allusions to the family
difficulties of **Shaharaim** are insufficient for more detailed
reconstruction.

12. **The sons of Elpaal:** these will be the ones towards whom
this section has been moving (cf. v. 7).

built: since both towns are attested as early as the middle of the
second millennium BC in the list of Thutmose III (cf. J. Simons,
*Handbook for the Study of Egyptian Topographical Lists relating to
Western Asia* [1937], p. 117; *ANET*, p. 243), we must understand
either as 'rebuilt' or 'fortified'. **Ono and Lod:** according to Ezr. 2:33
with 1, these towns were resettled in the post-exilic period by the
families who had previously lived there, but just when in the period
of the monarchy they were first settled by Benjaminites is uncertain:
Myers thinks it may have been as early as the time of Rehoboam,
but Rudolph favours the brief period of expansion under Josiah.

13–28. At first sight, this section seems directly to continue the
preceding without a break. Rudolph is correct in noting, however,
that the heads of families which follow (cf. vv. 16*b*, 21*b*, 25*b* and
27*b*) deal only with those mentioned in 13–14. **Elpaal** in 18*b*, which
might be thought to refer back to 11f., is apparently an exception.
However, this is unlikely both because 18*b* would be quite out of
place in what is otherwise a regular ordering, and because there is
no link whatever between those listed as his 'sons'. The same name
may refer to two quite different people, or may reflect a strong clan
whose branches developed independently in different areas.

13. On the basis of the above considerations, Rudolph further
conjecturally restores 'and Elpaal' after **Beriah.** **who put to flight**

the inhabitants of Gath: cf. v. 6. If this refers to the early expansion and settlement of the tribe, then, as in the previous two sections, so here, the list starts well back in time in order to identify the clans which had developed by the time of composition. **Gath:** cf. 7:21. Despite the reference to **Beriah** in this verse and 7:23, no direct association between the incidents alluded to is apparent.

14. and Ahio: read *wa*ᵃ*ḥêhem*, 'and their brothers', as suggested by LXX.

20. Shimei will be the same as 'Shema' in v. 13.

27. Jeroham and 'Jeremoth' (v. 14) are similarly to be identified, though it is not certain which form is correct.

28. This verse starts the passage which is paralleled at 9:34ff. Questions of priority will be dealt with there. **These dwelt in Jerusalem:** it is not at all surprising that during the period of the divided monarchy many Benjaminites should have taken up residence in the capital city, which lay on the border between Judah and Benjamin. The list thus closes with the locality in which the clans surviving at that time resided. Rudolph, Myers and others who link Aijalon and Gath (v. 13) with this thus fail to distinguish between the history of the clans and the time of their being recorded in the list.

29-40. The chapter concludes with the Benjaminites centred on Gibeon, whose most illustrious family was that of Saul, here traced down through many generations.

Most scholars argue against the unity of this section, finding in vv. 29-32 a treatment of those living at Gibeon and Jerusalem, the family of Saul then being attached because of a false identification of Kish. The arguments for this division are not compelling, however. We have noted that each previous section starts with the earlier history of part of the tribe, then passing rapidly to the descended clans or families of the writer's day. If vv. 29-40 are read as a single unit, the same will apply, whereas if vv. 29-32 are treated separately, the pattern there is broken. Moreover, A. Demsky, *BASOR* 202 (1971), pp. 16-23, has suggested that the list combines both vertical and horizontal elements, which helps to explain the tension concerning the position of Kish, while A. Malamat's study (*JAOS* 88 [1968], pp. 163-73), comparing biblical and Babylonian royal genealogies, also favours the unity of the list as a whole.

30. Baal: this name points to the very early origin of this section of the list, for it seems most unlikely that it could have been used in a Benjaminite family of the later period; contrast its use in a northern context at 5:5. This point supports our interpretation of this part of the list as reflecting the early history of the tribe.

Nadab: *RSV* curiously fails to restore 'Ner' before Nadab (haplography) with 9:36 and LXX, although it did correctly restore 'Jeiel' on the same grounds at v. 29. That **Kish** appears here as his brother, but in v. 33 as his son, is to be explained on the basis of the increasing prominence of Kish within the tribe in later times (Demsky).

32. Now these also dwelt opposite their kinsmen in Jerusalem: it seems that part of the family moved from Gibeon to Jerusalem, but the context does not make clear quite how many were involved. The context as a whole, however, implies that the majority stayed in Gibeon. **with their kinsmen** is explanatory of 'opposite their kinsmen'. Without it, it would be possible to take the verse as suggesting that none of the families listed, but only their kinsmen, in fact dwelt in Jerusalem.

33. Although it is possible to harmonise Saul's father and grandfather with I Sam. 9:1 and 14:50f. by postulating the loss of 'the son of Ner' from I Sam. 9:1 (Goettsberger, followed now by most commentators), his earlier ancestors cannot be so reconciled. This again is to be explained on the basis of the totally different natures of the two lists.

Eshbaal: 'a man of Baal'. This will be the original form of the name; texts that were more frequently read in public had to be altered to satisfy religious sensibilities. Thus we find the same man being called Ishvi, 'man of the Lord', at I Sam. 14:49, and Ishbosheth, 'man of shame', at 2 Sam. 2:8, etc.

34. Merib-baal: 'Baal contends'; the parallel 9:40 has both this form and 'Meri-baal', 'man, hero of Baal' (obscured by *RSV*). This too may reflect accommodation to religious sensibility (cf. Jg. 6:31f.), as the form 'Mephibosheth' (2 Sam. 4:4, etc.) certainly does. (For a contrary view, see M. Tsevat, *HUCA* 46 [1975], pp. 71–87.)

35–38. The remainder of Saul's line is not known from earlier sources. It seems to come down to late pre-exilic times, which would fit with the other sections of the chapter. Compare also the comments at 10:6.

39–40. These two verses, which are attached rather loosely, are omitted from the end of ch. 9.

Conclusion

9:1

It is now generally agreed that this verse stands as a summarising conclusion to chs 2–8; if it be agreed that the following list is intended to refer to the post-exilic community, this verse would be unsuitable as an introduction to it.

the Book of the Kings of Israel: cf. 2 Chr. 20:34. It is probable that, although this might appear to refer to all the preceding material, it covers most immediately those sections which we have argued come from a genealogically styled census list; cf. J. Liver, *Studies in Bible and Judean Desert Scrolls* (1971), pp. 234–48. See further, section F of the Introduction.

And Judah: *RSV* here follows the Masoretic pointing, while others prefer to link the words with the previous sentence. The present text makes adequate sense, however, and balances 5:25 well. 'Transgressed' there translates a word from the same root as **unfaithfulness** here. It occurs a number of times as a key theological word in the Chronicler's narrative (cf. 10:13), including at 2 Chr. 36:14, where it is again used to explain the exile of the Southern Kingdom.

THE POST–EXILIC COMMUNITY

9:2–44

The closing section of the Chronicler's introductory genealogies gives a summary of the members of the restored community after the exile. It may be seen as a balance to the first chapter, for just as there the line of God's election was seen to narrow down to Israel and his sons, so here the post-exilic community is portrayed as being in direct continuity with them in terms of descent, cult and geographical inheritance (see vv. 2–3). It is thus the vital link whereby the Chronicler associates the community of his own day with the people whom he has introduced and whose history he is about to relate. The chapter ends (vv. 35–44) with a repetition of the family of Saul, which serves as an appropriate introduction to the narrative of ch. 10.

Most of vv. 2–17 are paralleled in Neh. 11:3–19. On the view taken in this commentary that both are parts of separate works, this causes no difficulty. The differences between the lists (which cannot all be dealt with in the following comments) are rather greater than usual for the Chronicler's parallel passages. Some may be explained as consistent with his general outlook (cf. S. Japhet, *VT* 18 [1968], pp. 352f., 355, and U. Kellermann, *ZDPV* 82 [1966], pp. 212f.), but the remainder should perhaps rather be explained either as due to the list having reached each writer through a different channel or because of the need to accommodate them to their new literary and historical contexts.

Many scholars (e.g. Rudolph; S. Mowinckel, *Studien zu dem Buch*

Ezra-Nehemia 1 [1964], pp. 145–51; Kellermann; but contrast Myers) argue that our chapter must be directly dependent on Neh. 11, because v. 2 is parallel to Neh. 11:3 which is itself not part of the list, but of the editorial framework supplied for it in Neh. This would eliminate the first explanation above of the differences between the two lists, and is in many ways a strong argument. Nevertheless, it is difficult now to be sure that the original list did not itself have a heading which could have given rise independently to both 1 Chr. 9:2 and Neh. 11:3, while on a theory of direct literary dependence, some explanations of the differences between them (e.g. at vv. 7–9) are strained. Evidence for a firm decision on the matter is thus lacking.

In either case, it seems clear that the Chronicler used only so much of his *Vorlage* as he needed to give a representative picture, and that thereafter he abandoned it in order to include greater detail of a rather different nature on the minor cultic officials and their duties (vv. 18ff.). There is an indication at v. 33 that this too was once part of a more extensive source.

2. the first: or 'the principal'; either would fit the context well. The view that the list refers rather to the pre-exilic inhabitants of Jerusalem is not strengthened by the alternative translation, it being ruled out by the concluding reference to the exile of the southern kingdom in the previous verse. **in their cities:** the following list deals only with inhabitants of Jerusalem; but contrast Neh. 11:25–36. This point alone, though suggesting, does not prove direct dependence on Neh. 11, since the source for the material might well have included settlement in towns other than Jerusalem.

Israel: i.e. laity. **the temple servants:** 'Nethinim'; a group, possibly of foreign origin, who were dedicated to service in the temple (cf. B. A. Levine, *JBL* 82 [1963], pp. 207–12). Though they occur regularly in Ezr.–Neh., the Chronicler mentions them nowhere else. As the remainder of the chapter follows the order of 2*b* regularly, it would appear that he identified them with the gatekeepers and other functionaries of vv. 17ff., though for some reason which we cannot now establish he preferred to avoid use of the collective term.

3. Ephraim and Manasseh: since members of these tribes are not listed separately in the remainder of the chapter, it seems far more probable that the Chronicler has added these words here than that they were omitted from Neh. 11 for polemical reasons (*contra* Rudolph). Following the Chronicler's portrayal of the restoration of Israel's unity under Hezekiah, he is anxious to emphasise that the later community was representative of all Israel, not just the former southern kingdom alone, so that it could act as a nucleus for the return of any who had a legitimate claim to participation.

4–6. Those **of Judah** are listed under the three sons of the patriarch, **Perez**, Shelah and **Zerah** (cf. 2:3–4).

5. the Shilonites: vocalise rather as 'Shelanites' (cf. Num. 26:20), i.e. sons of Shelah.

6. six hundred and ninety: Neh. 11:6 records that there were 468 sons of Perez, but omits any reference to **Zerah**. Consequently, the two sets of numbers should not be contrasted with each other. Since in v. 9 (not paralleled in Neh. 11) the summarising number refers to the whole of Benjamin, that here may be intended to refer to all three clans of Judah.

7–9. the Benjaminites: four clans are listed, which is more plausible than the one of Neh. 11:7–9. The differences between the two texts in this paragraph seem greater than can be explained on the basis of scribal error alone.

10–13. the priests: this passage is closer to Neh. 11:10–14 than the foregoing, though not without abbreviation and some differences of spelling. The main difficulty centres on the first few names in the list, for whereas in the remainder three priestly families are traced over several generations, these are apparently unconnected. The names are quite common in priestly lists, **Jedaiah** and **Jehoiarib** occurring together three times elsewhere (1 Chr. 24:7; Neh. 12:6, 19); radical emendation, such as that of Rudolph who wants to read 'Jedaiah, the son of Jehoiakim, son of Azariah . . . ', should thus be avoided. Neh. 11:10 may be right in suggesting that they too were related, but this is not certain.

10. Though preceded by 'and' in MT here, in Neh. 11:10 **Jachin** is introduced without any connection. J. R. Bartlett, *JTS* ns 19 (1968), p. 4, n. 1, suggests that, since the Jachin of Gen. 46:10 is replaced by a Jarib at 1 Chr. 4:24, his name appears here as an added note on **Jehoiarib**. While this is possible, it should be remembered that a Jachin does appear among the priestly courses at 1 Chr. 24:17.

11. the chief officer of the house of God: it is in fact the line of high priests which has just been traced (cf. 6:12–15).

13. one thousand seven hundred and sixty: Neh. 11:12–14 gives a total of 1,192 (822+242+128), but whether the difference is due to scribal error, the situation at the time of the writers or other causes we cannot now tell. The Chronicler's figure does not give the appearance of deliberate exaggeration in this case.

14–16. the Levites: the text here adds a few names to that of Neh. 11, which may represent an updating either by the Chronicler himself or a later editor.

16. who dwelt in the villages of the Netophathites: Neh. 12:28 mentions these villages as the home of the Levitical singers. This addition to Neh. 11 may reflect the increasing importance of this class in later times.

17–26a. The gatekeepers: after a brief introductory list, the duties of the gatekeepers are set out in a disproportionate amount of detail. Since at this point the parallel with Neh. 11 ceases, and since a good deal of the paragraph is not strictly relevant to a listing of the members of the restored community, it would appear that the Chronicler here switches to a different source which vigorously maintained their Levitical status and the significance of their service.

17. Only two of these names are mentioned at Neh. 11:19, whereas three occur in the list of families of gatekeepers at Ezr. 2:42. There is thus no need to postulate that the Chronicler depended on Neh. 11 or a common source here; the verse could well have stood at the head of a separate source which he here began to follow.

18. the king's gate on the east side: cf. Ezek. 46:1ff. The name may also have lived on from pre-exilic times.

19. Son of Korah: one of the main emphases of this passage is the maintainance of Levitical descent of the gatekeepers; cf. vv. 18*b*, 26. The other is to stress that their duty was in strict continuity with that of the Levites who previously had been responsible for the maintainance of the tabernacle (Num. 4:1ff.); compare the expression here **as their fathers had been in charge of the camp of the Lord** with the evidently conscious ambivalence throughout between tent and temple terminology, culminating in the curious explanation given in v. 23: **the house of the Lord, that is, the house of the tent.** The need for such functionaries is obvious, and is assumed rather than asserted in earlier periods, as, for instance, in the case of Samuel (1 Sam. 3:15). Nevertheless, a source such as that followed here by the Chronicler suggests that during the post-exilic reconstruction there was in addition a certain amount of 'jockeying for position' on the part of the minor cultic officials (cf. von Rad, *GCW*, pp. 115–19).

20. Association with **Phinehas** the high priest (Num. 25:11ff.; cf. 3:32 for the similar role of his father **Eleazar**) would further have enhanced their position. **the Lord was with him:** better (with *NEB*), 'the Lord be with him!'

21. Zechariah the son of Meshelemiah: cf. 26:2, 14. This verse thus brings us down from the Mosaic period to that of David (in the Chronicler's presentation).

22. For the Chronicler's understanding of **David**'s reorganisation of the cult in view of the projected temple building, see on 6:31–2.

This verse provides the only statement of **Samuel**'s involvement, however. Since he died before David's reign (1 Sam. 25:1; 28:3), the statement can only be understood in terms of his general influence on David arising from his struggle for the purity of the cult at Shiloh after its degeneration in the hands of Eli's sons.

26b–32. The shift from the specific duties of the gatekeepers to those of a more general Levitical nature is slightly obscured, but might be clarified by translating **who were Levites** as 'They were the Levites who . . . '. There then seems to follow a general outline of Levitical duties, including that of the gatekeepers (v. 27), but covering also their charge of the temple **chambers** and **treasures** (26b), furnishings (28–29a) and materials for the offerings and shewbread (29b, 31–32).

30. A note (whether interpolated by the priestly reviser or not, we cannot say) reminds the reader that in accordance with the regulations of Exod. 30:22ff. (see especially v. 33) the actual preparation of **the spices** was the duty of the priests exclusively.

33 looks as though it should introduce a list of the Levitical **singers**. It cannot refer to the foregoing in view of the explicit statement that they were **free from other service** (literally, 'in the chambers free'). This strongly indicates that the Chronicler was not composing freely here, but following a source that has been broken off rather abruptly.

34. This concluding verse has been adapted from 8:28. An attempt was made there to show that 8:28–38 comes from two separate sections of the four part list of which ch. 8 is made up, and that it fits into the structure and purpose of that chapter in a natural way. Here, however, the situation is different. The verse is not fully appropriate to its context which has dealt more with Levitical functions than lists, and furthermore the statement that they **lived in Jerusalem**, which is the point towards which in ch. 8 the previous verses have been moving, is not of importance in this chapter, and is strictly speaking in contradiction to vv. 16, 22 and 25. It is thus hard to escape the conclusion that this and the following verses are dependent on 8:28–38. Demsky's arguments to the contrary (*BASOR* 202 [1971], p. 16) are unconvincing. 8:39–40 are not necessarily later additions, and even if they were, that would not prove the priority of 9:34–44. In addition, the better state of the text in ch. 9 is no guarantee of its priority either, since errors could arise in either form of a parallel text independently, and tell us nothing about which was the borrower.

35–44. The genealogy of Saul and his family is repeated from 8:29–38. It is very appropriate in this position as an introduction to ch. 10, and so could well have been included here as well by the

Chronicler. We have to understand that when he took this paragraph over, he felt that the previous verse could also be retained as a conclusion to the previous section. For details, cf. 8:28–38.

THE UNITED MONARCHY

1 Chr. 10:1–2 Chr. 9:31

The reigns of Saul, David and Solomon over a united Israel are central to the concerns of the Chronicler, about half his narrative material being devoted to these three kings alone. Nearly all the major themes of his work are developed here, and it is in their light that the subsequent history of the people is assessed.

Saul

10:1–14

The Chronicler's narrative opens abruptly with a brief account of the death of Saul. It is clearly based on 1 Sam. 31; but there are some significant changes, as well as others which may be due to no more than variant text types. Without fuller evidence, however, it is by no means easy to distinguish the one from the other; cf. W. E. Lemke, *HTR* 58 (1965), pp. 349–63. In addition, an unparalleled editorial assessment of Saul's reign is appended in vv. 13–14. The reader's knowledge of the events of 1 Samuel is apparently presupposed. In all these features, the chapter is thus quite typical of the nature of the Chronicler's narrative for passages which are based on a biblical source. In such cases, the reader is referred for questions of history, geography and the like to the commentaries on the earlier books, while we shall limit ourselves here to the Chronicler's own purpose in adopting and adapting such passages.

It has generally been thought that this chapter served only as 'a prelude to David's reign' (Elmslie), or at best as a dark foil to the brilliance of David's successes which follow (von Rad, *GCW*, p. 79; H. J. Boecker, *Die Beurteilung der Anfänge des Königtums* [1969], pp. 61–3). Less plausibly, some have argued that the whole chapter is a later insertion, whereas others have suggested that material may have been lost from its opening (Rudolph).

More recent studies, however (cf. especially K. Koch, *ThLZ* 90 [1965], cols. 659–70; Mosis, pp. 17–43; P. R. Ackroyd, *JSOT* 2 [1977], pp. 3–9), have succeeded in showing that the chapter serves a purpose in its own right. While some of the details of Mosis' arguments in particular are heavily overplayed, yet his general pos-

ition is well established that the chapter acts as what may be called
a paradigm of the exilic situation. The elements to be mentioned in
the following comments build up the picture of a situation which
keeps recurring in the subsequent history, and with which to some
extent (cf. Willi, pp. 9–12) the Israel of the Chronicler's own day,
deprived of its kingship and national independence, could identify
itself. This 'exilic' situation can then be balanced by the theme of
'restoration' in the following chapters, where David will be presented in part as fulfilling a saviour role.

1–5. These verses are adopted with only very minor changes from
the Chronicler's *Vorlage*. Since he assumes knowledge of the background of the incident, he can start straight in at that part of the
account which suits his purpose of portraying an 'exilic' situation,
namely, the rout of Israel by the enemy and the death of the king.

6. Two changes to 1 Sam. 31:6 by the Chronicler combine to
emphasise his view that Saul's dynasty came to a complete end in
this battle. First, by adding the word (they) **died** to the end of the
verse, and omitting the words 'on the same day', he has arranged
the verse in a chiastic manner with the word **died** at its opening and
close. It thus receives an added emphasis, picked up again in vv.
13–14. Secondly, the Chronicler has substituted the words **and all
his house** for 'and his armour-bearer, and all his men'. The dynastic
overtones of **house** (cf. 1 Chr. 17) are unmistakeable. We should
not suppose that the Chronicler was unaware of, or was trying to
deny, the ill-fated reign of Ishbosheth, Saul's son, over the northern
tribes (2 Sam. 2–4), for the story would have been far too well
known to his readers. Rather, he encourages them to see history
from the point of view of the purposes of God. In this theological
light, Saul's dynasty was judged, and was therefore to all intents
and purposes at an end. Its death-throes were in irrelevance, as was
the fact that part of the family survived. There is thus no reason to
deny 8:29–40; 9:35–40 to the Chronicler.

7. the army had fled: MT: 'they had fled'; by their punctuation,
the Massoretes clearly understood the verb to have an impersonal
subject (cf. GK §144*f*, *contra* Mosis, who suggests that **Saul and his
sons** are the subject). *RSV* is thus a reasonable paraphrase, since
the subject can be readily understood from the previous use of the
verb in v. 1. The result is that v. 7*a* becomes in effect a summary
of vv. 1–6. Though already present in the Chronicler's *Vorlage*, the
second half of the verse well serves his 'exilic' theme.

9–10. Whereas 1 Sam. 31 deals mainly with the Philistines' treatment of Saul's body, the Chronicler is more interested in the fate
of **his head.** Ackroyd (*JSOT* 2 [1977], p. 5) wisely notes that it is
not impossible that 'more than one version of the death of Saul and

the fate of his corpse had been preserved, so that the differences between Samuel and Chronicles must not be overpressed'. Rudolph even argues that v. 10*b* may have originally stood also in 1 Sam. 31. Rather we should inquire why the Chronicler was interested in this particular version. Two elements may have attracted him. First, the reference to **the temple of Dagon** reminds the reader of the situation in 1 Sam. 5:1-4. There, the presence of the ark caused Dagon to fall headlong with his head and his arms broken off; here, the head of Israel's king is hung up before him (Mosis, pp. 24-6). Secondly, Ackroyd points out (p. 6) that there is an equally striking contrast with the account in 1 Sam. 17 of David's victory over Goliath, the removal of his head to Jerusalem (v. 54) and the flight of the Philistines. Both elements thus serve the Chronicler's purpose of portraying an exilic situation by underlining the complete defeat of Israel, and hence apparently of her God.

11-12. Although on some later occasions the place of a king's burial implies an assessment of his reign (cf. 2 Chr. 21:19f.; 24:25; 26:23, etc.), there is no indication here that this applies also to the burial of Saul **under the oak in Jabesh** (*contra* Mosis), since burial in Jerusalem would, of course, have been impossible at this time. Rather the Chronicler omits the detail that Saul's body was burnt before burial; if this is not simply a matter of text, it may have been felt that this implied an unfair judgment on him personally in the light of Lev. 20:14; 21:9.

13-14. These two verses are undoubtedly the Chronicler's own composition. They are of significance because their assessment of Saul's reign is expressed in terms that occur frequently throughout the book, thereby underlining the paradigmatic nature of this chapter. (See further on 2 Chr. 7:14.) **So Saul died:** the causative theme of the same verb is used at 14*b*: **slew him.** For the emphasis of this *inclusio*, see v. 6. **for his unfaithfulness; he was unfaithful to the Lord:** this root (*m'l*) occurs frequently in Chronicles, but always in passages that are his own composition, or at least have no biblical parallel. Where the context makes its precise significance clear, it describes in particular religious unfaithfulness, usually in terms of an offence against the Jerusalem temple and the purity of its service (cf. 2 Chr. 26:16, 18; 28:19, 22; 29:5f., 19; 30:7; 33:19; 36:14; *IBC*, p. 53; J. Milgrom, *Cult and Conscience* [1976], pp. 16-35). In addition, Mosis (pp. 29-33) detects that there is frequently an allusion to the worship of foreign gods. Of particular significance for the present context is the observation that such unfaithfulness is regularly punished by military defeat and exile, including the final exile of both northern and southern kingdoms (1 Chr. 5:25; 9:1; 2 Chr. 36:14; for defeat alone, cf. 2 Chr. 12:2 and a number

of the references listed above). In the light of what has already been
noted of the nature of this chapter, a similar implication may underlie its use here.

he did not keep the command of the Lord: it has been usual for
commentators to specify the reference of these words by pointing
to 1 Sam. 13 or 15 (T further adds 22), chapters in which the
vocabulary used here certainly recurs, and both of which are regarded as in a measure responsible for the transfer of kingship from
Saul to David. Here again, however, Mosis points out that it is far
more appropriate to regard this as a general evaluation of Saul's
reign as a whole, for which any of the particular passages might be
safely regarded as an example without exhausting the phrase's total
significance. To further its understanding, he points to its use in
Dt. and Ps. 119, in both of which to **keep** (observe) **the command**
(word) **of the Lord** issues in life, rest, and possession of the land.
With this may then be contrasted not only the present passage, but
also, for instance, 2 Chr. 12:1 and 4; 13:11 and 13ff.; 14:4–5; 33:8;
34:2; 36:16, all passages in which either expressly or by implication
observance is rewarded in similar terms, and failure to observe by
foreign invasion and consequent exile.

and also consulted a medium, seeking guidance: cf. 1 Sam. 28:8–
25. The particular reference of this phrase is clear. Syntactically, it
is only loosely integrated into the verse. This suggests that it is not
one of the central elements of the section, but rather an example of
the more general principle of v. 14a (not the leading statement of
which the remainder of 13–14 is 'exegesis'; Willi, pp. 169–70). It
need not thus necessarily be regarded as a later gloss (Ackroyd,
JSOT 2 [1977], p. 8).

14. and did not seek guidance from the Lord: to 'seek the Lord'
is another favourite expression of the Chronicler, for it occurs nearly
forty times in his narrative. Although the immediate context might
seem to imply that it involves no more than a specific act of seeking
guidance, yet elsewhere in Chr., as in later biblical thought generally, it had acquired the far more general significance of an inner
attitude of loyalty towards God (cf. 2 Chr. 12:14; 15:2–7, etc., and
C. Westermann, *Kerygma und Dogma* 6 [1960], pp. 2–30). This
developed meaning, coupled with the fact that 1 Sam. 28:6 emphasises that Saul had endeavoured to seek God's guidance on this
particular occasion, suggests that once again the Chronicler is here
characterising the whole of Saul's life.

and turned the kingdom over to David: the Chronicler's narrative
and comment in this chapter have provided a comprehensive presentation of the failure of Saul when judged by his particular standards, a failure which was similar to that of several later kings who

led Israel to defeat and eventually to exile. In the Chronicler's view, however, the kingdom was God's (Introduction, Section G), and this turning of it over to David is, as Ackroyd (*JSOT* 2 [1977], p. 9) has well shown, quite as momentous as that 'turning' in 2 Chr. 10:15 which led to the division of the monarchy (see also 12:23 and 13:3). This underlines the independence in the Chronicler's scheme of the Saul narrative, leaving Israel at its close in a position of total defeat and 'exile', a situation from which only the faithfulness of a David could lift them.

David
1 Chr. 11–29

THE ESTABLISHMENT OF DAVID AS KING

11:1–12:40

It is stated several times in these two chapters (11:1–3, 10; 12:23, 31, 38) that the purpose of the various elements of which they are comprised is to depict the establishment of David as king over all Israel. However, whereas in 2 Sam. David is shown to be responsible for gradually reuniting the tribes into 'all Israel', here in Chronicles it is all Israel that is made responsible for David ever attaining the throne in the first place. Moreover, the narrative independence of the defeat of Saul and the downfall of his house in the previous chapter, followed by the abrupt elevation of David to the throne, combine to present him as the one chosen to save Israel from complete collapse. His military successes should thus be regarded not as purely personal triumphs but rather as saving events of considerable moment in the history of Israel, while the glory of his reign is for Israel's sake (cf. 11:10), not the reverse, as scholars have generally tended to think.

The whole passage has been given a well-planned structure by the Chronicler. It will be argued in the commentary that 11:10; 12:23 and 38–40 are his own editorial composition. It is then apparent that 11:1–3 and 12:38–40 are to be set side by side as dealing with the full number of those at Hebron to make David king. 11:10 and 12:23, however, may also be compared; their general purport is the same, and both indicate that David's coronation was 'according to the word of the Lord'. Finally, within 12:1–22 (see below) this chiastic structure is continued. Thus from the centre of the pattern (12:8 and 16) which refers to the early period of David's rise, through the Ziklag period (12:1 and 18f.) and the military personnel at Hebron (11:10 and 12:23) and on to the full extent of Israel at

Hebron (11:1–3 and 12:38–40), the picture is artfully presented of the increasing recognition of, and support for, David by the people. See further on 11:10, and *OTS* 21 (1981), pp. 164–76.

The Anointing of David

11:1–3

The account of the anointing of David as king over Israel follows 2 Sam. 5:1–3 very closely. However, because this paragraph immediately follows the notice of the death of Saul, thus passing over the account of the downfall of the kingdom of Ishbosheth (2 Sam. 2–4; see the comments on 10:6), it is clearly implied that '(all) Israel' (vv. 1 and 3) refers to all sections of the population without distinction, not just the northern tribes. This foreshortening of the steps taken towards a particular goal is repeated in the next paragraph. Once again, the Chronicler is seen to regard history from the point of view of its outcome as determined by God, in the light of which the intervening material may be passed over as irrelevant.

1. gathered together: 2 Sam. 5:1: 'came'; see below on 13:2. **at Hebron:** not regarded here as David's capital over a separate kingdom of Judah; see further, 3:1–9 and 29:26–7. For similar reasons, 2 Sam. 5:4–5 is not included at the end of this paragraph.

3. according to the word of the Lord by Samuel: although it could be argued that this phrase has been lost from Sam. by homoioteleuton (**Israel . . . Samuel**), it is most probably the Chronicler's own addition, since it conforms so closely to his general viewpoint of the direction of history by the prophetic word. Although we might be tempted to refer the phrase to the oracle of v. 2*b*, this latter is in fact much closer to the oracle of Nathan (cf. 2 Sam. 7:7–8; 1 Chr. 17:6–7) than to any recorded word of Samuel. Once again, therefore, we must infer that the Chronicler assumes extensive knowledge of the earlier histories by his readers, and in this case of 1 Sam. 15:28; 16:1–13 in particular. The addition underlines the implication of 2*b* that, as already noted, David's rule was the result of God's election for the sake of Israel.

The Capture of Jerusalem

11:4–9

The positioning here of the story of David's capture of Jerusalem is not simply determined by the Chronicler's adherence to the order of his *Vorlage*, 2 Sam. 5:6–10 (*contra* Rudolph), since (a) elsewhere he shows himself to be quite free of such restrictions (e.g. II:IIff.; 14; 2 Chr. I:I4ff.) and (b) vv. 10 and 12:38, which are probably both his own editorial comment, clearly show his awareness that the present paragraph was detached from its strictly chronological context. (For a discussion of the actual course events, cf. C. E. Hauer, *CBQ* 32 [1970], pp. 571–8.) His purpose, rather, will have been to develop the picture already begun in vv. I–3 of a united Israel (cf. v. 4) centred by David on Jerusalem. At this stage in the narrative, Jerusalem's significance is presented as a purely political focus for the nation; its religious significance as the site of the future temple is not mentioned here at all, and is developed only later. There is thus no need to follow Mosis (pp. 43–50) in his suggestion that this whole account, like every other feature recorded in Chronicles concerning David's reign, was included exclusively as part of the preparations for the building of the temple, which was to house the ark. The evidence cannot support this thesis which attempts to interpret the Chronicler's presentation of the Davidic monarchy as having no significance independently of the temple and its cult (see further, 2 Chr. 6:5–6).

The narrative itself as presented in Chronicles is straightforward by comparison with Samuel. There, as the commentaries show, there is a wide divergence of opinion as to the precise course of events; consequently, we have no reliable yardstick at present by which to evaluate the possible historicity of the elements found only in Chronicles (cf. v. 6). Again, it is usually suggested that the references to 'the blind and the lame' and to the *ṣinnôr* ('watershaft'?) were omitted by the Chronicler because he no longer understood them; while this is possible, we cannot be sure that it represents anything more than presumption on our part, or that the text of Samuel lay before him in its present form. It seems best, therefore, to reserve judgment on these matters for the time being.

4. and all Israel: 2 Sam. 5:6: 'and his men'. David's establishment of a neutral capital was, historically speaking, an important step in his uniting the tribes of Israel, and as such was probably a private undertaking by him and his personal mercenaries; cf. Alt, *KS* 3, pp. 253–5. The Chronicler's alteration presents a theological interpretation of this action, once more viewing history from the point of view of its outcome. **that is Jebus:** this phrase, and the words **The inhabitants of Jebus** in the next verse, are added by the Chronicler. There is no evidence that the city was ever called by any name other than **Jerusalem; Jebus** may have been the name of a nearby village (so J. M. Miller, *ZDPV* 90 [1974], pp. 115–27), or it may have been coined from the name of its inhabitants, **Jebusites**. Either way, it is used here, as occasionally elsewhere in the Bible, as a conventional means of referring to the city before its Israelite occupation.

6. The substance of this verse occurs only here, following the omission of most of 2 Sam. 5:8. Some scholars (e.g. H. W. Hertzberg, *I & II Samuel* [1964], pp. 266, 268–70, and, with a usually overlooked suggestion, Yadin, *The Art of Warfare*, pp. 267–70) still find this material necessary to an understanding of the account in 2 Sam., while others (notably H. J. Stoebe, *ZDPV* 73 [1957], pp. 73–99, followed most recently by Welten, pp. 34f., 59ff.) argue rather that nothing more than the present text of 2 Sam. was available to the Chronicler. In favour of the first position, it may be observed that (a) allowing the possibility that the Chronicler had access to sources since lost to us, the situation envisaged is in itself by no means implausible (cf. Jos. 15:16; *ANET*, p. 241, column *b*, top); and (b) some such event may be necessary to explain how **Joab** came to be **chief and commander** (*rō'š* and *śar*), a position which he undoubtedly held soon after (2 Sam. 8:13f. with 1 Kg. 11:15 and 21; 2 Sam. 8:16; 11:1; 19:13 [14], etc.), but which we might not have expected him to hold after he had incurred David's displeasure (2 Sam. 3:29, 39; 1 Kg. 2:5f., 32) for the murder of Abner, the previous commander (1 Sam. 26:5; 2 Sam. 2:8; 3:38; Goettsberger). Older commentators who favoured the second position, by contrast, observed the possibility that the reference to **Joab the son of Zeruiah** (*ben-ṣᵉrûyāh*) might have arisen from a misreading of the difficult word *baṣṣinnôr* ('in/to the watershaft'?) of 2 Sam. 5:8, while more recently it has been suggested that reference to him was supplied here both because it was felt to be missing from the list of David's chiefs which immediately follows and in order to provide an explanation for Joab's position in 18:15 (Rudolph). Neither of these latter suggestions is compelling, however, for it would have been more natural for the Chronicler to supply a reference to Joab in the following list itself had he been bothered by its absence, while he apparently did not feel it necessary to prepare in this way for all the other officials mentioned in 18:15ff. (Mosis, p. 46). Thus there is no compelling objection to the Chronicler's account, and some points favour it, but the confused state of the text in 2 Sam. precludes certainty in the matter.

went up: a quite general word in battle contexts; it cannot be used to support the theory that Joab gained entry into the city by climbing the Jebusite water-shaft.

8. The text and consequent interpretation of this verse are by no means agreed; thus it should not be made the basis for theories concerning the Chronicler's historicity (Welten, pp. 59–63) or theology (Mosis, pp. 45–8).

built: better 'rebuilt'. **the Millo**: 'filling'. This is now probably to be identified with the very elaborate 'terrace structure built by the Jebusites to support the houses on the eastern slope' (K. M. Kenyon, *Digging up Jerusalem* [1974], p. 100). Archaeological evidence suggests that the retaining walls of this terracing needed frequently to be repaired.

in complete circuit: the difficulties connected with this phrase ($we^{\epsilon}ad$ -$hass\bar{a}b\bar{i}b$) include the fact that (a) it is the only occurrence in the Hebrew Bible of $s\bar{a}b\bar{i}b$ as a substantive with the article, so that its precise meaning is uncertain. *RSV* seems to imply that David started at **the Millo** and worked right round the fortified city, in which case **the rest of the city** might apply to the suburbs outside. If MT is to be retained, however, *NEB*'s more general rendering is preferable: 'starting at the Millo and including its neighbourhood'; (b) suspicion raised by this unique use of the word is increased by the fact that $s\bar{a}b\bar{i}b$ is used two words previously in its more normal sense, **round about**; (c) the parallel in 2 Sam. 5:9 has $w\bar{a}bay^{e}t\bar{a}h$, which can mean either 'inwards' or 'to the house (palace)'. Thus a number of commentators prefer to emend the phrase in Chronicles to $^{\epsilon}ad$-$habbayit$, 'as far as the palace', or, less probably, to the unattested $s^{e}b\bar{i}b\hat{i}m$, 'surrounding wall' (Galling, Myers). Though attractive, these renderings remain totally conjectural, however, for the versions give no help (cf. Allen, 1, pp. 129f.).

repaired: though this use of the pi'el of hyh is usually justified on the basis of Neh. 4:2 [3:34], Sanballat's sarcasm there suggests that he may have had one of its more normal meanings, namely 'revive', in mind. It is thus by no means certain that *RSV*'s translation here can be justified. 'Preserved' may be a more accurate rendering. Furthermore, it is not generally recognised that the whole clause is probably to be construed as circumstantial (subject first; verb in the imperfect) rather than as consecutive. In that case, the clause may explain why David needed to attend to only a part of the city, Joab's assault having led to the destruction of only the weakest element in the city's structure. Alternatively, since **the city** ($h\bar{a}^{\epsilon}\hat{i}r$) can be used to refer to the inhabitants of a city (e.g. 1 Sam. 4:13; 5:12; Ru. 1:19; this obviates the need to follow the six MSS which actually read $h\bar{a}^{\epsilon}\bar{a}m$, 'the people'), the clause may be loosely attached to the whole account as a qualification of Joab's action in v. 6: apart from the first Jebusite(s) whom Joab slew (v. 6), he 'preserved the remainder of the city's population alive'. This would accord well with David's usual policy of incorporating the Canaanites into his kingdom (cf. H. J. Stoebe, *ZDPV* 73 [1957], pp. 73–99, and Hertzberg, *I & II Samuel*, p. 270).

9. Though adopted from the Chronicler's *Vorlage*, this concluding

verse accords well with the purpose of his collection of material in
chs II and I2.

the Lord of hosts: this divine title is used only three times in
Chronicles (cf. 17:7 and 24), each time in dependence on his source.
His dislike of the title is shown by the fact that he suppresses the
other references to it in his source (cf. 1 Chr. 13:6 ‖ 2 Sam. 6:2; 1
Chr. 16:2 ‖ 2 Sam. 6:18; 1 Chr. 17:25 ‖ 2 Sam. 7:27) and never
introduces it in material peculiar to himself (Japhet, *Ideology*, pp.
27–9). This contrasts with the popularity of the title in the editorial
material of Haggai and Zech. 1–8, and indicates that the Chronicler
may not have been so close to those circles as W. A. M. Beuken,
Haggai-Sacharja 1–8 (1967), has suggested.

The Chiefs of David's Mighty Men

11:10–47

10. See the introduction to chs II–I2 for the position of this
verse. A minor theme within the larger framework outlined there
is suggested by Willi, p. 224, n. 30, following Hummelauer, p. 215:
this verse, which is the Chronicler's introduction to 11:11–47, refers
to **the chiefs of David's mighty men**, 12:1 to 'the mighty men',
and 12:23 introduces the rank and file. Willi sees in this a progression in the unity of Israel which reaches its climax in 13:1–5. It
is difficult to be certain how much of this was intended by the
Chronicler, both because the lists of 11:11–47 and 12:1–22 do not
fully follow their introductions as regards these particulars, and
because, as argued above, chs 11–12 should be regarded as a single,
closed literary unit, with a new section starting at 13:1.

Most of the rest of ch. 11, which lists **the chiefs of David's
mighty men**, is drawn from 2 Sam. 23:8–39. There, it forms part
of an appendix to the books of Samuel, and has already passed
through more than one phase of compilation. Here, however, the
Chronicler sets it in a quite new context, for it becomes part of a
larger and impressive series of lists of those **who gave him** (David)
strong support in his kingdom, . . ., to make him king. Interest is
thus deflected from the individuals and their acts of bravery as such
in favour of the point that all these contributed to the overriding
concern of establishing David as king. As at v. 4, however, it is
emphasised that David's personal followers did not act alone, but
together with all Israel (cf. 12:38), and it is this which will have
led the Chronicler to include ch. 12, with its indication of support
for David by all the tribes. **according to the word of the Lord:** cf.
v. 3 and 12:23. **concerning Israel:** as noted in the introduction to

these chapters, God's purpose in establishing David as king was the salvation of Israel. His success was for their blessing rather than his personal aggrandisement (see further, 14:2).

11–47. Apart from the last six and a half verses, this list of **David's mighty men** is based on 2 Sam. 23:8–39. The differences between the two passages are again to be explained on mechanical grounds: it is the list as such that served the Chronicler's purpose, so that there is no need to speculate about his *Tendenz* in any of the changes. Only the most major differences can be noted here; for treatment of the list in its own right, see, in addition to the commentaries on 2 Sam., K. Elliger, *KS*, pp. 29–75, and B. Mazar, *VT* 13 (1963), pp. 310–20.

11. Jashobeam: for 'Ishbaal'; cf. 8:33–4. **the three:** *Kt.* has 'the thirty' and *Qr.* 'the officers'; 2 Sam. 23:8 may have 'the third part (of the army)'. The versional evidence is similarly divided. The context favours reading *haššᵉlôšāh*, **the three**, as in v. 12. **three hundred:** 2 Sam. 23:8 has 'eight hundred', which is undoubtedly original, since Ishbaal's exploit surpassed that of Abishai (vv. 20–21). Rudolph suggests that v. 20 was used to correct the unintelligible 2 Sam. 23:8 in connection with **his spear**, and that this opened the way for the smaller number which immediately follows there to be accidentally substituted here.

13. It is evident that, by a copyist's error, 2 Sam. 23:9b–11a has been omitted from its position following **for battle**. In consequence, the name of the third member of 'the three', Shammah, the son of Agee the Hararite, has been lost, and his exploit (vv. 13b–14) attributed to Eleazar.

14. he . . . his: in MT, the first half of this verse is in the plural. This was a change necessitated by the copyist's error noted above, since the subject in the present text is Eleazar and David (v. 13). *RSV* follows the text of 2 Sam. 23 without, however, restoring Shammah as the subject.

20–25. There is considerable confusion in these verses between **the thirty** and **the three**. *RSV* follows P and most commentators in making **Abishai** and **Benaiah** outstanding leaders of **the thirty**, but not yet attaining to the status of **the three**. MT refers to **the thirty** in v. 25 only. Though membership of **the three** may have changed, so that a full list would have included more than three names, an explanation along these lines seems to be ruled out here by vv. 21b and 25. (20b and 24 are less certain, there being versional and *Kt.-Qr.* variations.) MT, therefore, must be referring these men to a separate triad, perhaps the unnamed heroes of vv. 15–19.

20. and won a name beside the three: so *Qr.* 2 Sam. 23:18, many MSS and versions. Alternatives include *Kt.*, 'but he did not have a name amongst the three', and P, 'and he was famous among the thirty' (*NEB*).

22. ariels: probably 'heroes', 'champions' (*NEB*); cf. Albright, *Archaeology*, p. 218, and Baumgartner, *Lexikon*, 1, p. 80a, with refs.

23. five cubits tall . . . like a weaver's beam: both details are absent from 2 Sam. The latter phrase at least may have been influenced by the description of Goliath in 1 Sam. 17:7, for there is some evidence that the Chronicler had that story in mind at this point; cf. Willi, pp. 151f.

26. The mighty men of the armies were: this title is not found in 2 Sam. 23:24, and a reference there to 'the thirty' is here omitted. In neither list in their present form are there exactly thirty names. The Chronicler, therefore, probably 'regarded this list as independent of those mentioned above' (CM, p. 191), and introduced it accordingly, rather as with the various sections of ch. 12.

27. 'Elika of Harod' has probably been lost from the middle of this verse by homoioteleuton (cf. 2 Sam. 23:25).

34. MT has 'the sons of (*benê*)' **Hashem**, but this is rightly omitted by *RSV* as a dittography of the last three letters of 'the Shaalbonite' which immediately precedes.

35–36. Ur, Hepher: 2 Sam. 23:34 has 'Ahasbai, the son of . . .'. Though this latter is itself corrupt, it nevertheless probably indicates (together with the pattern of the rest of the list, here broken) that the Chronicler has erroneously made two separate names out of what was originally the name of **Eliphal**'s father.

41b–47. These verses are not found in the parallel passage of 2 Sam. Two factors mark them off from the preceding list and so suggest that they cannot have been its direct continuation which was either lost from, or never included in, 2 Sam. 23. First, there are several stylistic variations (cf. K. Elliger, *KS*, pp. 72–118): names are here sometimes linked by **and**, the place of origin is not always given, pairs of names are included, and in v. 47 there are two names without any further details supplied. None of these features is found in the preceding list in its textually corrected form. Second, there is the phrase **and with him thirty** (42). If MT (*we'ālāw šelôšîm*), as translated by *RSV*, is sound, this would quite contradict the original purpose of the list, which was simply to name the individuals who made up David's 'thirty'; such wider affiliations are not mentioned elsewhere. Several commentators, however, follow P and emend to *'al-haššelôšîm* (so *NEB*: 'was over these thirty'). Even if this reading is correct, the verse could still not be regarded as an original direct continuation of vv. 26–41, since (a) it would make the list number many more than thirty, and so be self-contradictory, and (b) it would not accord with notices

earlier in the chapter about who commanded the thirty. As already
noted, the evidence on this is not as clear as could be wished, but
it certainly does not support the view that **Adina** was the commander. Thus, for these various reasons, vv. 41*b*–47 cannot be
regarded as the original continuation of the list now preserved in
vv. 26–41*a* = 2 Sam. 23:24–39.

On the other hand, the list is unlikely to be a post-exilic fabri-
cation. The places mentioned which can be identified are all in
Transjordan: Reuben (42), Ashtaroth and Aroer (44), Moab (46).
In addition, many commentators emend **the Mahavite** (46) to 'the
Mahanite' (= from Mahanaim) and **the Mezobaite** (47) to 'from
Zoba' (*NEB*), providing two further links with the same area. Since
this area is already well represented in the lists included in ch. 12,
there is no reason for the Chronicler to have invented the paragraph.
Further, however, the area was regarded with such suspicion in the
post-exilic community that credence cannot be given to Noth's
suggestion (*US*, p. 136, n. 8) that certain families wished, by this
fiction, to trace their ancestry back to the early followers of David.
This must, therefore, be an additional fragment concerning David's
heroes, perhaps available to the Chronicler along with the material
which underlies ch. 12. (K. Budde, in fact, long ago suggested that
the paragraph had been misplaced from its position in front of 12:8,
reference here to **the Reubenites** paralleling 'the Gadites' there; cf.
Die Bücher Samuel [1902], p. 318. However, this is rightly rejected
by Rudolph, p. 101.) He may have placed it here because of the
formal similarity with the preceding. As he was not intending to list
'the thirty' (see v. 26), he will not have regarded this expansion as
in any way intrusive.

Early Support for David

12:1–22

N.B. In the Hebrew Bible, 12:4 is divided into two verses, so that thereafter the
English verse numbers are one lower than the Hebrew.

This section is made up of four short paragraphs, each one of which
illustrates the accumulating support for David in the period before
his elevation to the throne. The opening sentence of each paragraph
makes this theme clear: 'These are the men who came to David'
(1); 'there went over to David' (8); 'came . . . to David' (16);
'deserted to David' (19), while the concluding v. 22 stresses it even
more strongly. It is thus closely related to the aim of chs 11–12 as
a whole (cf. 11:1, 3, 9, 10; 12:23, 33, 38).

An associated emphasis is that of 'help' for David, encapsulated
in the poetic fragment in v. 18:

Peace to your helpers!
For your God helps you.

God's 'help' for the king has long been noted as a distinctive feature of the Chronicler's writing; cf. I Chr. 5:20; 2 Chr. 14:11 (twice); 18:31; 25:8; 26:7; 32:8 (and I Chr. 15:26 with the Levites as object). All these occurrences are peculiar to the Chronicler, sometimes even within an otherwise parallel passage. Conversely, to seek help of others leads to disaster: 2 Chr. 28:16 and 23; cf. 19:2. (See also v. 19 of this chapter.) The corollary of this is that of several kings it is noted that the (military?) leaders of Israel also helped them: Solomon (I Chr. 22:17); Uzziah (2 Chr. 26:13); Hezekiah (2 Chr. 32:3). This is the aspect which is particularly marked in the present section (cf. vv. 17, 18, 21, 22), and it too is linked with the remainder of the chapter (vv. 33 and 38).

As far as the chronological setting of the material is concerned, it has already been noted that in these chapters the Chronicler ordered his material by theme rather than strict historical order (see on 11:4–9, 10ff.), and furthermore 11:13f. and 15ff. similarly relate to the earlier period (cf. Goettsberger, p. 107). It is thus of interest to observe that the section itself is not chronologically arranged, a likely historical order being, in fact, (a) vv. 16–18; (b) vv. 8–15; (c) vv. 1–7; (d) vv. 19–21 (RH, p. 243). Rather we should observe that, according to the geographical indications supplied, the material is arranged in a chiastic structure, a device already noted more than once as a feature of the Chronicler's authorship. Including all the major lists in chs 11–12, the following pattern emerges:

Hebron	11:10	a
Ziklag	12:1	b
The Stronghold	12:8	c
The Stronghold	12:16	c'
Ziklag	12:20	b'
Hebron	12:23	a'

This pattern, since it brings 11:10 and 12:23 together, exactly dovetails with the larger structure outlined in the introduction to these two chapters as a whole. Its purpose is not hard to discern. Bearing in mind that the Chronicler passes over the seven years or so during which David ruled over Judah alone, and noting that once again he assumes knowledge of I Samuel on the part of his readers, we can see that David's residence at Ziklag (I Sam. 27:6) preceded the Hebron coronation, and that his stay at 'the stronghold' (I Sam. 22:1–5, 23:14 or 23:29 [24:1]) came before that. The centre of the pattern, therefore, goes back to the earliest time at which David began to attract support, and moves out until it encompasses 'all Israel' in the coronation at Hebron.

The theme and structure of this passage, together with various aspects of its literary style, thus point strongly to its inclusion in the work by the Chronicler. Finally, as far as the origin of the material is concerned, it would appear that the verses which introduce each paragraph and which conclude the whole should be attributed in their present form to the Chronicler. It is widely agreed that the lists and anecdotes themselves rest on good tradition, and may doubtless be attributed generally to the Davidic period, as in the case of 11:11ff. Only in the case of v. 18, however, does there seem to be the possibility of defining the question of origins more closely; for a more detailed discussion of all these matters, cf. *OTS* 21 (1981), pp. 164–76.

1. at Ziklag: cf. I Sam. 27. **among the mighty men:** see on 11:10. **who helped him in war:** literally, 'helpers in war', i.e. 'allies'. Although many have sought to identify here and elsewhere in the chapter a second root *ʿzr*, so translating this phrase as 'warriors' (cf. P. D. Miller, *UF* 2 [1970], pp. 159–75), this is unnecessary, as shown by A. F. Rainey, in H. A. Hoffner (ed.), *Orient and Occident* (1973), pp. 139–42, and Welten, p. 90, n. 67. A similar expression is found at v. 38.

2. with either the right or the left hand: a skill which compensated for their small number; cf. Jg. 3:15ff. and 20:16, both in connection with **Benjaminites. Saul's kinsmen:** cf. v. 29. In accordance with the purpose of the chapter as a whole, the Chronicler draws attention to the allegiance of even Saul's tribe to David from the start.

3–7. Such place names as can be identified all fall within Benjaminite territory (Myers).

4. a mighty man among the thirty and a leader over the thirty: since membership and leadership of **the thirty** will have changed over the years (Elliger), there is no need to identify **Ishmaiah** with either Abishai (11:20) or Amasai (12:18).

5. Bealiah: in a Benjaminite context, this name indicates an early date: see on 5:4–6 and 8:30.

6. the Korahites: Korah may be intended as an (otherwise unknown) place name; the view which links them with the Korahites of southern Judah (cf. J. M. Miller, *CBQ* 32 [1970], p. 66) is highly speculative.

7. of Gedor: against the practice in the rest of this list, the place name is introduced by *min-* ('from'). Such a town is not known inBenjaminite territory. Delete as a dittograph of the following words, with which it is virtually identical (Ehrlich; *BHS*).

8–15. Here again, the emphasis throughout is on the quality of the Gadite **warriors**. From the very start, men of the highest calibre were attracted to David.

8. at the stronghold in the wilderness: see the introduction to this chapter above. **expert with shield and spear:** in contrast with the Benjaminites (v. 2), their particular skill lay in fighting at close quarters. **lions . . . gazelles:** the comparison of heroic qualities with animals is very widespread indeed, to such an extent that animal names could even be used as metaphorical designations or titles of leaders and warriors; cf. P. D. Miller, *UF* 2 (1970), pp. 177–86.

14. the lesser over a hundred and the greater over a thousand: the Hebrew expression here is rather cryptic. *RSV*'s translation has the support of V, but we would then have expected the preposition *'al* rather than *lᵉ* (Keil). The alternative, supported by T and followed by the Jewish commentators, most modern commentators (e.g. Keil, CM, RH, Rudolph, Myers) and translators (e.g. *RV*, *NEB*) is thus more probably correct: 'the least of them a match for a hundred, the greatest a match for a thousand' (*NEB*). For the thought, compare Lev. 26:8; Dt. 32:30; Isa. 30:17. This verse cannot then be compared with 2 Sam. 18:1–4 to support A. Zeron's suggestion (*ThZ* 30 [1974], pp. 257–61) that this chapter reflects capitulation to David by various groups at and after the time of Absalom's rebellion (2 Sam. 15–20); cf. *OTS* 21 (1981), pp. 171f.

15. in the first month: i.e. springtime, when the river would be swollen with melting snow (cf. Jos. 3:15). In the second half of the verse, **those in** is not found in MT, and **all . . . the valleys** are a curious object for **put to flight**. Moreover, no connection between the two halves of the verse as translated by *RSV* is apparent. It makes better sense altogether to follow Rudolph in reading the verb as a denominative of *bᵉrîaḥ*, 'bar': 'and making all the valleys impassable . . . ' (cf. Myers; Ackroyd).

16–18. The interest of this paragraph, unlike the previous two, is in the poetic fragment. Given under inspiration, it overcame David's very natural hesitation in receiving all who declared allegiance. This would fit its *prima facie* historical setting at least as well as 2 Sam. 19:13, as suggested by Zeron.

16. Benjamin and Judah: the Chronicler may well have regarded this as of particular significance; see further on v. 18 below.

17. my heart will be knit to you: S. Talmon, *VT* 3 (1953), p. 136, finds in *yaḥad*, used here as a noun, the concept of covenant or community; thus Myers translates: 'I am eager for an alliancewith you'. This fits a period prior to David's coronation better than a later date, when such talk would be quite inappropriate.

rebuke: better, 'judge'; cf. H. W. Wolff, *Joel and Amos* (1977), p. 246, on Am. 5:10.

18. came upon: literally, 'clothed itself with', a very forceful expression; cf. Jg. 6:34 and 2 Chr. 24:20. Apparently this would be recognised by the onlookers. Particular attention is thus drawn to the words uttered.

Amasai: perhaps Absalom's general Amasa (Zeron), but others too had this name, so that identity is by no means certain. **chief of the thirty:** cf. v. 4.

The brief poetic utterance is a strong affirmation of loyalty to **David**; its word play on **help** in the last two lines demonstrates its appropriateness to the context (cf. v. 17, etc.). Ackroyd, p. 55, has suggested a contrast with 2 Chr. 10:16, and the suggestion is worth exploring. It may be noted that (a) there are formal correspondences which point up the contrast : **David** and **son of Jesse** are used in parallel in each passage; 'each of you to your own tents' is the opposite of **peace to your helpers**, and 'look now to your own house David' implies a negation of **For your God helps you;** (b) 2 Chr. 10:16 comes at the division of the kingdom. It may be significant that there, as here, the tribes of Judah and Benjamin remain loyal to the Davidic house; (c) the same fragment has occurred earlier at 2 Sam. 20:1, within David's lifetime, and suggests that even then the kingdom was not always so united as is often suggested.

It is thus possible that both fragments, together with others of a like nature which have survived, were coined in David's time with conscious reference to one another to reflect the opinions of opposing factions. The Chronicler, who remains the only witness to the fragment in this verse, perhaps saw the wider significance of both: just as 2 Sam. 20:1 had already been reapplied dynastically, by the addition of the line 'Look now to your own house, David', at the time of the division of the monarchy (1 Kg. 12:16; 2 Chr. 10:16), so too the Chronicler developed the old pro-Davidic saying in the present context with vocabulary and theology of his own in order to counter the denial of God's choice of the Davidic house which the last addition implies. Knowing this old, poetic fragment, he will have drawn attention to its importance by placing it at the heart of the chiastic structure analysed above; he then presented it as a prophetic saying underlining the divine choice of David as king from the earliest days of his career; see further *OTS* 21 (1981), pp. 164-76. **made them officers of his troops:** *NEB* may be more accurate with its 'attached them to the columns of his raiding parties' (cf. RH). David's suspicions were not totally allayed at once.

19-21. Every indication of this final paragraph points to its setting immediately before the death of Saul, which, in the Chronicler's presentation (1 Chr. 10–11) is followed by David's coronation at Hebron (cf. v. 23). On the basis of the pattern of this chapter outlined above, whereby chiasmus is used as a device to emphasise the increasing support for David up till the time of his coronation, there is thus no break before vv. 23ff.

19. This introduction exactly fits 1 Sam. 29, knowledge of which is presupposed (*contra* Zeron).

he did not help them: MT, 'they did not help them', which could refer to David and his men. The emendation affects the pointing only, but since 1 Sam. 29:2f. and 10f. suggest that it was partly the presence of David's men which caused **the rulers of the Philistines** concern, it may not strictly be necessary. The *caveat* itself was of importance to the Chronicler, because, in his presentation, for Israelites to **help**, or be helped by, Gentiles would mean that they themselves were no longer helped by God (see above).

At peril to our heads: better, 'at the price of our heads'; cf. 1 Sam. 29:4. This reference renders less likely the suggestion that an oath is intended: 'By our heads!' (cf. V. Rogers, *JBL* 74 [1955], p. 272).

20. David must have accompanied the Philistines at least as far as Aphek (1 Sam. 29:1), which lies near the territory of **Manasseh**, and if he had gone any further with them towards Jezreel (1 Sam. 29:11), he may even have passed through Manasseh. Either way, desertion to him at this point of **these men of Manasseh** is very credible.

thousands: probably a tribal sub-division (cf. G. E. Mendenhall, *JBL* 77 [1958], pp. 52–66). The men's status is being emphasised, without any implication that large numbers accompanied them.

21. the band of raiders: Amalekites, who had attacked Ziklag during David's absence (1 Sam. 30).

22. As noted above, this verse is the generalising composition of the Chronicler. It is unjustified to assume on account of it that the foregoing paragraphs imply that David had a following of this size during his outlaw days (*contra* Zeron); rather it acts as a bridge to the following verse: from small beginnings, support for David rapidly increased until he was acknowledged by all Israel at his coronation.

like an army of God: an expression for the superlative: either 'an immense army' (*NEB*), or perhaps again it is particularly the quality of support for David which is being stressed, as throughout this section.

David's Coronation at Hebron

12:23–40

This third list of those who came to Hebron in support of David at the start of his reign concentrates on enumerating the rank and file (see further, on 11:10). It achieves its purpose by including all the tribes of Israel, and by drawing attention to the large numbers involved in each case. It is very difficult in this passage to distinguish in detail between the Chronicler's own handling of the material and the source which he may have used. This in turn makes any attempt to reconstruct the source's original shape and purpose highly speculative. We may with reasonable confidence ascribe vv. 23, 31*b* and 33*b* to the Chronicler in view of their phraseology and evident links with other verses in this whole section. Less clear, by contrast, are, for instance, vv. 26–28 and 29*b* (see the comments below) and the order of the tribes. This latter is not strictly geographical (*contra* M. Noth, *Das System der zwölf Stämme Israels* [1930], p. 20); cf. the position of Simeon, Levi and Asher. Rather, it may reflect a similar outlook to 1 Chr. 2–8, with adherents to the later southern kingdom this time coming first (Simeon is linked to Judah as at 4:24ff.), then the core of the northern kingdom, followed by the tribes of the far north and the transjordanian tribes added at the close. But whether this is the Chronicler's responsibility, and he himself included Levi in order to achieve this effect, cannot now be determined. On the other hand, it seems highly unlikely that the whole list is his own fabrication; the curious relations between the tribes as regards the numbers (however understood) tells against this (see v. 29 below), as do some of the other snippets of tradition which are here preserved without contributing anything to the Chronicler's purpose in using the list (Ackroyd). A military census apparently underlies the passage (cf. 1 Chr. 7), but it would be hazardous to conjecture further.

The large numbers have been considered a problem by some. In a context such as this there is some justification for treating the issue separately from that of the large numbers in Chronicles generally. In a military census list, any of three similar possibilities may be entertained: (a) the word here translated **thousand** may originally have indicated 'unit'; thus v. 24 would read, 'The men of Judah bearing shield and spear numbered six units with eight hundred armed troops', and so on throughout the list; cf. G. E. Mendenhall, *JBL* 77 (1958), pp. 52–66, followed by Myers, p. 98; (b) each tribal clan (*mišpāḥāh*) may have been intended theoretically to provide a contingent of a thousand men, the number in fact being usually far smaller; cf. de Vaux, *AI*, p. 216; **thousand** should then be

retained in translation, but understood very loosely; (c) *'eleẹ*, **thousand**, may originally have been vocalised *'allūẹ*, 'chief', so that
Judah (v. 24), for instance, would have provided **eight hundred
armed troops** under six leaders; cf. J. Wenham, *TynB* 18 (1967),
pp. 19–53.

23. the divisions of: *rā'šê*, usually 'the heads of', but, despite
RV, that would be clearly inappropriate in an introduction to the
list which follows. *RSV* (and cf. *NEB*: 'bands') thus adopts a
reasonable translation which is attested in more than a dozen other
passages. A third possibility, that it is a general word for 'person'
(cf. Jg. 5:30; 1 Sam. 28:2), seems more remote.
to turn the kingdom of Saul over to him: see on 10:14.
according to the word of the Lord: see 11:3 and 10.

24. six thousand eight hundred: see v. 29 below.

26. The inclusion of **the Levites** is usually regarded as secondary
because, with Ephraim and Manasseh being treated separately rather
than as 'Joseph', thirteen tribes are listed instead of the usual twelve.
There is nothing in the form of the verse itself, however, to suggest
this.

27–28. Only here are individuals named. This points to a separate
origin for these two verses. Their inclusion is probably due to the
pro-priestly reviser (see the Introduction, section D), who, because
he maintained a more rigid distinction between priests and Levites
than the earlier sources, may have felt that the priests were not
adequately covered by v. 26.

27. The prince Jehoiada: the reviser may have intended an identification with the man of the same name at 27:5; 2 Sam. 8:18.

28. Zadok: the head of the later Zadokite priesthood. C. J. Hauer,
JBL 82 (1963), pp. 89–94, argues that this verse rests on good
tradition because of the small numbers involved (**twenty-two**) by
comparison with the rest of the list, because Zadok is not made
leader of the Levites and because he is not provided with a pedigree.
Accepting the view that Zadok was a priest of Jebusite Jerusalem
before its capture by David, he argues from this verse that he
defected to David at the start of his reign. This remains highly
speculative, however, not only because of the assumptions it makes
about Zadok's origins (cf. A. Cody, *A History of Old Testament
Priesthood* [1969], pp. 92–3), but also because, as has been stressed
above, it is by no means certain that the material gathered here
originally had reference to the start of David's reign.

29. The second half might be better translated, 'because until this
time the majority of them kept . . .'. It was felt necessary to explain
the small number of **Benjaminites**, which, at **three thousand**, is the
lowest in the list. With this may be coupled the observation that

the numbers from Judah and Levi are the next two lowest. It is usually suggested that the Chronicler wished to emphasise the extent of support for David by the members of the later northern kingdom. However, the explanation given in the present verse, which has to allude to the kingdom of Ishbosheth, a proceeding which the Chronicler strenuously avoids everywhere else, shows rather that he was embarrassed by the numbers. This makes it highly likely that he did not invent them, but found them already in his source (Rudolph). Whether this in turn reflects the fact that David had, historically speaking, already been king over Judah for some years (Keil) cannot now be determined.

32. who had understanding of the times: if this refers to astrological wisdom, it would point away from the Chronicler as the author. He himself might then have added **to know what Israel ought to do**, in order to give it a more neutral, political interpretation.

33. to help David: a very probable textual restoration and interpretation, bringing the statement into line with the repeated emphasis on 'help' elsewhere in the chapter (see above). It is thus the Chronicler's own comment, though curiously he uses an aramaising form here and in v. 39 (ʿdr for ʿzr).

38–40. An appropriate conclusion to chs 11–12, parallel in a number of ways with the opening in 11:1–3. The paragraph is so typical of the summaries of other great occasions in the Chronicler's work that we need look no further for its author.

38. arrayed in battle order (ʿōḏᵉrê maʿᵃrākāh): cf. vv. 1 and 33. **all the rest of Israel:** cf. 11:10. In his editorial passages, the Chronicler finds it hard to stress enough the nation's unity at this time.

39. eating and drinking: although this phrase by no means always has covenantal overtones (cf. E. W. Nicholson, *VT* 24 [1974], pp. 77–97; *VT* 26 [1976], pp. 148–50), it is probable that here it does in view of the corresponding passage in 11:1–3, where a covenant is referred to. That it also expresses joy is clear from the following verse. **their brethren:** another characteristic word of the Chronicler for expressing the inherent solidarity of Israel; cf. 13:2; 2 Chr. 11:4; 28:8, 11, 15.

40. The combination of feasting and of **joy in Israel** on major occasions was clearly regarded as appropriate by the Chronicler. Together with his emphasis on faith (see section G of the Introduction), it indicates that his religion was by no means the joyless ritualism that has sometimes been thought; see especially 1 Chr. 29:22; 2 Chr. 7:8–10 and 30:21–26, but also 1 Chr. 15:25 with 16:3; 29:7, 17; 2 Chr. 20:27f.; 23:16–18 and 29:30.

THE TRANSFER OF THE ARK TO JERUSALEM

13:1-16:43

From the establishment of David as king over all Israel, the Chronicler moves directly to the other of his great concerns, care for the
Ark, which was eventually to be housed in the temple. This involves
a rearrangement of the order of his *Vorlage* (cf. 2 Sam. 5-6), showing
once again that his material is presented on the basis of theme and
theology rather than strict chronology; cf. Brunet, *RB* 60 (1953),
p. 500.

In the earlier history, the whole account is given in one continuous
chapter (2 Sam. 6), probably drawn from an original 'Ark Narrative'
(on which see most recently A. F. Campbell, *The Ark Narrative*
[1975]; but contrast P. D. Miller and J. J. M. Roberts, *The Hand
of the Lord* [1977]). The Chronicler, however, has divided this
account between chs 13 and 15-16, using the indication in 2 Sam.
6:11 of a three month gap in the narrative to go back over the
material previously omitted from 2 Sam. 5; by its new position,
however, as well as some light editorial touches, this itself now
contributes in a fresh way to the development of the Chronicler's
main concerns (see below).

The First Attempt to Move the Ark

13:1-14

The main part of the narrative is based on 2 Sam. 6:2-11. Verses
1-5, however, are found only here. Their style and concerns again
point to the Chronicler as their author. His aim in their composition
is to draw out the significance of the story he is about to present,
and so point the way to its interpretation.

1-5. The first of these interpretative concerns is to stress that the
transfer of the Ark was the work of **all Israel** (5). In 2 Sam., it was
a more restricted undertaking, but here, following on immediately
from the gathering at Hebron (chs 11-12) together with David's
concern expressed in v. 2 and its sequel in v. 5, there are no such
limitations. The focus of the nation's worship, later identified with
the temple, is thus understood as the inheritance of all the people,
not just one section within it. This feature of assembling all the
people for major occasions is a recurrent theme of the Chronicler
(e.g. 11:1-3, 4; 23:1; 28:1; 2 Chr. 1:2; 5:2; 30:1ff., etc.). A secondary reason, consonant with our interpretation of David's significance as a whole (see above on 11-12), may have been 'the

Chronicler's desire to minimise the suggestion of the arbitrary authority of the King as seen in the books of S. and K.' (CM).

The second indication of the significance which the Chronicler saw in this account is made clear in v. 3. Neglect of the ark **in the days of Saul**, it is implied, was part of the reason for the defeat of Israel and Saul's death at the hand of the Philistines (see further, on 10:13-14). As Israel's 'saviour', David must thus put this right *before* undertaking his campaign against the Philistines (14:8-16). This is a clear pointer to the fact that David's faithful attitude towards Israel's cultic institutions is part of the way whereby the paradigmatic 'exilic' situation of ch. 10 may be overcome. The Chronicler's readers are thus encouraged to adopt a similar attitude.

2. let us send abroad (*nipre̊sāh nišle̊ḥāh*): the translation is possible, though not certain. *prṣ* ('break through/out upon') has been made a keyword in these chapters by the Chronicler (see below, 13:11; 14:11; 15:13), so that emendation or deletion (so Rudolph) is unlikely. It is thus attractive, with slight repunctuation, to render '. . . and if the Lord our God opens a way, let us send to . . .' (*NEB*). In the Chronicler's view, however, on this first occasion the ark was not carried 'in the way that is ordained', and so God 'broke forth' upon them (v. 11 and 15:13); but this was more than offset by God's 'breaking forth' on their behalf against the Philistines (14:11), which demonstrated his approval of their intention in general, if not the detail of their procedure. This word-play thus develops the contrast with the situation under Saul (cf. Mosis, pp. 6of.).

who remain (*hanniš'ārîm*): Welch (*WC*, pp. 16-18), followed by Elmslie (1954), suggested that this was an anachronism for 'the men of the North who survived the divine judgment in the exile under Sargon', and so took this as part of his evidence for the pro-Northern stance of the Chronicler. However, the term is not restricted to the sense proposed by Welch, and it is explicitly qualified by **in all the land of Israel. land** here being plural (*'arṣôt*), it is better rendered as 'regions' (cf. 2 Chr. 11:23 and 34:33; *IBC*, p. 124; *NEB*: 'districts'); it is further defined in v. 5. These considerations also rule out Mosis' understanding (pp. 51ff.) of a reference to the post-exilic diaspora. The phrase need therefore refer to no more than those who had not already come to Hebron, and as such fits exactly with 12:38 just above. **the priests and Levites:** a characteristic introduction of the Chronicler; however, they do not play any significant role in this chapter; contrast ch. 15.

in the cities that have pasture lands: cf. 6:54-81, and Japhet, *JBL* 98 (1979), pp. 205-18. **that they may come together** (*we̊yikkāb-e̊ṣû*: the same word that the Chronicler substituted for his *Vorlage* at 11:1. This is both a further indication of his stereotyped portrayal of the preparations for great religious occasions and a literary marker of the start of a new section following chs. 11–12.

3. let us bring again: literally 'let us bring round' (*nāsēbbāh*). This is a most unusual use of the verb (contrast its use elsewhere in the ark narrative: 1 Sam. 5:8f.). Does the Chronicler thus intend a word-play on the theme of 'turning' already noted at 10:14? David responds in kind, as it were, to God's turning over to him of Saul's kingdom. **neglected:** literally, 'did not seek'; a further allusion to 10:14.

5. from the Shihor of Egypt to the entrance of Hamath: the Chronicler's normal understanding of the full extent of the land of Israel is from Beersheba to Dan (cf. 1 Chr. 21:2), while the wider area defined here seems rather to cover his understanding of the empire (cf. *IBC*, pp. 123f.). His concern at this point is thus to maximise the extent of support for David's action. Japhet, *JBL* 98 (1979), pp. 205–18, reinforces this comment with her observation that this definition of the borders represents 'the most extreme concept of the Israelite territory to be found in the Bible'. Jos. 13:1–7 probably provided the inspiration for the Chronicler's composition. **from Kiriath-jearim:** knowledge of the earlier history of the ark is presupposed (cf. 1 Sam. 7:1).

6–14. The Chronicler now follows 2 Sam. 6:2–11, the commentaries on which may be consulted for the narrative. Although there is a considerable number of small divergences, these are generally of no more than textual interest, so that theological significance should not be read into them; cf. Rudolph, p. 113; Lemke, *HTR* 58 (1965), pp. 350–1; Ulrich, pp. 193–221.

6. and all Israel: for 2 Sam. 6:2: 'all the people who were with him', defined in 2 Sam 6:1 as thirty thousand chosen men of Israel. This is the same kind of extension as at 11:4.

The second half of the verse is textually difficult in both passages, and in its present form may be the result of secondary revision; cf. I. L. Seeligmann, *VT* 11 (1961), pp. 204f.

8. all Israel: for 2 Sam. 6:5, 'all the house of Israel'; cf. 15:28 and 2 Chr. 11:1. The Chronicler avoids 'terminology which might be confused with that used elsewhere in the Bible for the later political division' (*IBC*, p. 109).

before God: the first of several examples in this chapter of a change from 'the Lord' in 2 Sam. 6. This is taken by some, especially RH and von Rad, *GCW*, pp. 3–8, as evidence of a 'transcendentalising' of the divine name; Yahweh is increasingly detached from contact with the human world. A more balanced assessment, however, is offered by Japhet, *Ideology*, pp. 33–9, who observes that (a) such a position takes no account of the fact that 'Yahweh' is used some 500 times in Chronicles; (b) in many contexts, 'Yahweh' and *ᵉlôhîm* ('God') are clearly synonymous; and that (c) the textual evidence, particularly from LXX (cf. Allen, 2, pp. 146–8), suggests that this phenomenon is to be explained more on the basis of the practice of later scribes than the Chronicler himself. It may further be added that, as Lemke has shown, we can never be sure that such a slight change was not already present in the text of Sam.–Kg. that the Chronicler was using.

11. On **had broken forth** and **Perez-Uzza**, see v. 2 above.

14. in his house: *NEB*, 'in its tent', follows those commentators who think that the Chronicler 'could not conceive of the ark placed in an ordinary dwelling and modified the text accordingly' (CM, p. 206). This is unnecessary, however; if the Chronicler had intended 'tent', he would have used *'ōhel*, as at 15:1. Moreover, he may have thought that **Obed-edom** was a Levite; cf. 15:18 and 21 (Ackroyd, p. 58).

David Under Blessing

14:1–17

Although this chapter is drawn from 2 Sam. 5:11–25 (the commentaries on which may be consulted for questions of history and the like), it is clear that the Chronicler has purposes of his own for including it from the fact that he has repositioned it after the first attempt to bring the ark to Jerusalem. Though overpressed in some of its details, the explanation of the passage by Mosis (pp. 55–79) is the most illuminating. He points principally to the following factors: (a) the death of Uzzah (13:9–11) is reinterpreted by means of the word play on *prṣ* ('break through') noted above at 13:2; (b) the various blessings which this chapter describes are, because of their new position, to be seen as the result of seeking the ark; (c) consequently, the chapter shows in a number of details a reversal of the 'exilic' situation described in the account of Saul's death (ch. 10 above). Attention will be drawn to these in the following comments. This underlines the saviour role of David in Chronicles, and points to his actions as paradigmatic of the conditions for restoration. We may observe further that emphasis is placed on this theme of blessing at the opening and close of the chapter (cf. vv. 2 and 17), indicating that this is the correct approach to its interpretation.

1–2. The embassy of **Hiram** is presented as a gift, if not tribute, drawing attention to David's exaltation and contrasting with 10:13f., as 17:8, 11–14 demonstrates. Clearly this is out of its chronological position, which must come later in David's reign (and so too with the following paragraph!), but once again the Chronicler is content to pass straight to the God-given results of faithful conduct.

1. to build a house for him: cf. 15:1 (peculiar to Chronicles). This begins to introduce the circumstances which lead to a climax in ch. 17.

2. and that: *RSV* mistakenly follows 2 Sam. 5:12, for the Chronicler has himself here introduced a slight but significant change (omission of w^e), so that we should render 'because'. The force of this is to give prominence to the exaltation of David's kingdom **for the sake of his people Israel**, a theme already noted in the introduction to chs 11–12 and at 11:10. This is further emphasised by the Chronicler's introduction of **highly**, using an idiom ($l^ema'l\bar{a}h$) that is confined in the *OT* to his style alone (Japhet, *VT* 18 [1968], pp. 357f.).

3–7. For the list of David's **sons and daughters**, see on 3:1–9 above, in addition to 2 Sam. 5:13–16. Commentators usually think that the Chronicler included this paragraph simply because it came next in the text he was following; but Mosis is quite right to observe that such an explanation contrasts with the Chronicler's usual practice of careful composition, in which without hesitation he will omit any material from his *Vorlage* which does not suit his purpose. Rather, we should see here a further contrast with ch. 10. Attention was drawn at v. 6 of that chapter to the Chronicler's heightening of the description of the downfall of Saul's 'house', a word with evident dynastic overtones. Here, however, one of the blessings of David's faithfulness is a large family, including **Solomon**, the one through whom David's 'house' is to be established (ch. 17).

8–12. David's first defeat of **the Philistines**, a clear reversal of ch. 10. Had the Chronicler not wished to bring this into close association with the theme of seeking the ark, he would probably have grouped this paragraph with his collection of David's military successes in chs 18–20.

8. went out against them: 2 Sam. 5:17, 'went down to the stronghold'; cf. v. 11 below.

9. made a raid: this is substituted both here and in v. 13 for 2 Sam. 5:18 and 22, 'spread out'. Since the pi'el of the same root ($p\check{s}t$) is used at 10:8 and 9 (= 'to strip'), a further reversal of the situation there may be intended.

10. inquired: the same word ($\check{s}'l$) is used at 10:13 of Saul when he 'consulted' a medium. There, it is contrasted with 'seeking guidance' ($dr\check{s}$), a word which is itself drawn into the present context by its use in 13:3 above. Although the Chronicler here follows his

Vorlage, it seems certain that he did so because it so exactly suited his theme of contrast with ch. 10.

11. And he went up: 2 Sam. 5:20, 'came'. Together with the slight change in v. 8 above, there is the suggestion that the Chronicler may have thought that **Baal-perazim** was a hill or mountain, on the basis of Isa. 28:21; see further on v. 16 below.

Baal-perazim . . . has broken through . . . bursting: cf. 13:2.

12. That the **gods** of the Philistines fell into David's hands may be seen as a reversal of 10:10, where Saul's armour and head are taken as trophies to 'the temple of their gods'.

David gave command, and they were burned: 2 Sam. 5:21, 'David and his men carried them away'. This celebrated difference is generally explained as due to the Chronicler's desire to have David act in conformity with the law, and, further, to show that he was influenced as much by Deuteronomy (cf. Dt. 7:5, 25; 12:3) as P (cf. von Rad, *GCW*, p. 58). Lemke, *HTR* 58 (1965), pp. 351f., however, has argued on the basis of some LXX witnesses to the text in Sam. that the Chronicler here merely had a different *Vorlage* from MT, and did not necessarily introduce any change himself. The following observations may help keep the discussion in perspective: (a) since the Chronicler does not attempt systematically to present David as an 'ideal' character (cf. Japhet, *Ideology*, pp. 393–401), it is not certain that he would in any case have felt it necessary to change 2 Sam. 5:21; (b) if it is true that the Chronicler's main aim in this chapter is to portray the blessings David received in direct contrast to the situation in ch. 10, then it may be noted that either form of text would have accomplished this purpose; (c) while these factors may seem to support Lemke's case, and while the evidence of the text of Samuel from Qumran certainly demonstrates the correctness of his position in general, it must be remembered that assimilation of the Greek text of Sam. to either Chr. or Par. always remains a possibility in any individual case. This is particularly so here because the reading on which Lemke bases his suggestion is not supported by LXX^B; in 2 Sam. 10:1ff. (so J. D. Shenkel, *Chronology and Recensional Development in the Greek Text of Kings* [1968], pp. 117–20, rather than 11:2ff.) LXX^B and LXX^L (principally b o c$_2$ e$_2$) are generally opposed, but in the earlier chapters we would normally (though admittedly not inevitably) expect them to run together if they are to serve as a witness to a Hebrew text of the 4QSam type (cf. F. M. Cross, *Qumran and the History of the Biblical Text* [1975], pp. 188–93); (d) whatever be the truth of the matter, Lemke's position still does not overcome the historical problem raised by the two versions, since harmonisation in such a case does not carry conviction. It must therefore be concluded that the account of David's action has been conformed to the laws of Deuteronomy, but whether by the Chronicler or an earlier writer cannot now be determined, nor is it significant for an understanding of the Chronicler's own purpose.

13–16. David's second defeat of the Philistines.

13. made a raid: cf. v. 9. **in the valley:** defined in 2 Sam. 5:22 as 'of Rephaim', but that is omitted here as contrary to the Chronicler's interpretation of this passage in the light of Isa. 28:21 (see v. 16). Perhaps for similar reasons he omits the word *la⁽ᵃ⁾lôt*, 'came up'.

14. inquired: see v. 10. Further attention is drawn to the significant use of this word by the Chronicler's addition of **again**.

16. from Gibeon (2 Sam. 5:25: 'from Geba'): this slight change confirms the influence of Isa. 28:21 already alluded to, for each account of David's defeat of the Philistines has been conformed to the implications of that verse, despite the fact that the reference to Gibeon there is probably based on Jos. 10. In Isaiah, Mount Perazim and Gibeon are cited as examples of God's marvellous interventions in battle on behalf of his people (even though now turned against them in judgment). The Chronicler's allusions thus invite interpretation of his accounts as typical of such interventions, and he is to give many more comparable examples in his later narrative. Inclusion of them thus admirably suits his purpose in this chapter as a whole.

17. The Chronicler has himself added this summary of the main theme of the chapter, just as he did at 10:13–14, thus underlining the contrast between the two passages. As with vv. 1–7, it passes straight to effects of David's faithfulness that stretch beyond the immediate historical setting.

The Successful Completion of the Transfer

15:1–16:43

After the setback at Perez-uzza, the ark is now brought safely to Jerusalem. The core of the narrative (15:25–16:3, 43) is based on 2 Sam. 6:12–20, but the whole atmosphere has been changed in the Chronicler's account. Three main elements may be mentioned here, minor matters being reserved for the comments on individual verses below.

First, David's motive has been transformed. According to 2 Sam. 6:12*a* (omitted by the Chronicler), David acts because he has heard of the blessings which the presence of the ark has brought to Obed-edom's household. Here, however, the theme of blessing by association with the ark has already been reinterpreted in ch. 14 in David's favour. In these chapters, moreover, there is no suggestion that David had ever given up his intention of bringing the ark to Jerusalem; rather, more time was needed to make the necessary preparations both in terms of a home for the ark (15:1) and, most importantly, the ordering and sanctifying of the Levites. It was failure in this regard that led to the previous *débâcle* (see further on 15:2 and 13). Thus much of the material peculiar to Chronicles deals with the particular attention paid to them.

A second and related point, equally prominent in the Chronicler's overall concerns, centres on the change in the nature of the Levites' work after the ark has come to rest (see further on 6:31–2). Although this was not finally to happen until the dedication of the temple in Solomon's reign (2 Chr. 5:2–7:10), yet, as with every other aspect of the building and worship of the temple, the Chronicler was anxious to show that Solomon fulfilled the plans and arrangements of David his father (cf. *VT* 26 [1976] pp. 356–9). These chapters are thus the most suitable point for him to introduce the theme of the bearers of the ark becoming the temple singers of a later day (16:4–42).

Thirdly, the role of David appears in a quite different light in the Chronicler's account. A number of elements to be noted below contribute to this change (e.g. 15:3, 16, 27, etc.), but it is highlighted by the reinterpretation of the Michal episode. In 2 Sam. 6:20–23 the incident leads to Michal's having no further children, thus establishing a narrative tension with 2 Sam. 7 that is not finally resolved until Solomon's coronation. That is all omitted here, however, so that the one reference which remains (15:29) contributes instead to the contrast already noted between the differing approaches of Saul and David to the ark.

The material peculiar to Chronicles in these chapters falls into three clear categories. The first is narrative, principally 15:1–3 and 11–15. It will be argued below that each element of this either explains an allusion found by the Chronicler in his *Vorlage* interpreted in the light of the Mosaic law or develops a theme which he has already introduced earlier. There is thus no need to look for a further source. Secondly, there is the psalm of 16:8–36. Though adapted and arranged to suit the Chronicler's purpose, this is drawn from material known to us in the Psalter. The third category, however, consisting of lists of cultic officials with details of their duties, has occasioned much debate, particularly with regard to its origins and position in the present context.

We may start by accepting as probable the post-exilic development in the guilds of singers as analysed by Gese, 'Geschichte der

Kultsänger' (building on the earlier work of von Rad in particular). Although he believes that there is a continuity with the pre-exilic cult, Gese isolates the following stages for the later period:

I.   At the return from the exile, the singers are simply called 'sons of Asaph', and are not yet reckoned as Levites (Ezr. 2:41; Neh. 7:44);

II. Neh. 11:3–19 and 1 Chr. 9:1–18, from Nehemiah's time. The singers are now reckoned as Levites, and are in two groups, the sons of Asaph and the sons of Jeduthun;

IIIA. 1 Chr. 16:4ff.; 2 Chr. 5:12, 29:13f., 35:15. The levitical singers are now in three groups, Asaph, Heman and Jeduthun;

IIIB. 1 Chr. 6:31ff. and 15:16ff. Jeduthun is replaced by Ethan, and Heman is now more prominent than Asaph.

Gese then links this cult-historical outline with the results of the literary analysis of these chapters by RH, which has been adopted by many more recent commentators. Restricting the discussion for clarity's sake to ch. 15, this sees vv. 4–10 and 16–24 as later additions to the Chronicler's own composition. Thus, Gese argues that the Chronicler himself stood at stage IIIA, while IIIB reflects later accretion.

This last point, however, is not convincing, for the analysis of 1 Chr. 6 above attempted to show that vv. 31ff. were included by the Chronicler himself, and were not added secondarily. Might not the same be true, then, of 15:16ff., which, as Gese has shown, reflects a similar stage in the development? There is, of course, no difficulty in supposing that if Chr. = IIIB, material from IIIA should have been included in his work, for, as Gese himself admits, sometimes even stage I can still be reflected in his work. The question thus rests on a literary analysis alone.

In this regard, 15:4–10 are usually considered secondary because they are parallel to, and an expansion of, v. 11, so that if they were original v. 11 would be superfluous; and 16–24, because they break the narrative connection between 15 and 25 and because it is inappropriate to start ordering the Levitical classes after the ark has been shouldered (v. 15). These arguments, however, are less than compelling: (a) vv. 4–10, as several of the older commentators observed (e.g. Benzinger, Kittel), reflect a stage in the history of the Levites earlier than the Chronicler himself. The unparalleled six-fold Levitical division points away from an origin for this material within the Chronicler's immediate circle, while the comparatively small numbers involved suggest an earlier date. The repetitive

v. 11, far from being a difficulty, is just what we would expect if the Chronicler had added some material into his own composition; for this literary device, see, for instance, 4:1, 5:1, the remarks of Welten, pp. 190f., and, for the same technique in Ezra-Nehemiah, cf. S. Talmon, *IDBS*, p. 322. (b) Verse 25 is not a direct continuation of v. 15. (If anything, v. 26 is; so correctly Benzinger.) However, v. 25 marks the start of the Chronicler's use of 1 Sam. 6. There, it introduces the account; here, it serves to summarise the position to date, before the narrative moves on again in v. 26. On the basis of our slight alteration to Gese's analysis, vv. 16–24 will reflect the cultic practice of the Chronicler's own day (stage IIIB). It is thus no surprise to find that after his free narrative composition of vv. 1–3, 11–15 he should insert this paragraph as part of its Davidic justification and authorisation (for an appreciation of this procedure, see on 6:31–2) before moving on to pick up his source in v. 25. (For a comparable account of ch. 16, which may be broadly correct despite some exaggeration, cf. T. C. Butler, *VT* 28 [1978], p. 146.)

Thus, although the following comments will suggest that there may be some small addition in these chapters to the Chronicler's own composition (cf. 15:4, 11, 14, etc.), yet it may be argued that they essentially represent the shape he gave them. Of the cultic lists he included, some represent the situation of his own day (principally 15:16–24) and the rest somewhat earlier stages in the post-exilic development (15:4–10; see above. 16:37–42 = Gese's IIIA). These will then reflect traditions well known to him which he worked into his account where appropriate.

15:1–24. Preparations for the movement of the ark.

1. houses: apparently additional to 14:1, but the emphasis is on what follows. This is based on 2 Sam. 6:17, spelling out the presupposition of that verse that David had **pitched a tent** for the ark. This will have been a new construction, since the Mosaic tabernacle is said to have been at Gibeon at this time (16:39). **a place** (*mākôm*) often carries the implications of 'holy place'. It too is derived from 2 Sam. 6:17, its use here allowing the Chronicler to omit it in his parallel account, 16:1.

2. 2 Sam. 6:13 indicates without prior notice that on this occasion the ark was carried, not placed on an ox-cart. The law of Dt. 10:8 (whose terminology, together with that of Dt. 18:5, is used here) will have indicated to the Chronicler that this must have referred to **the Levites.** David's careful observance of the Deuteronomic law (the priestly laws of Num. 1:50ff., etc. are not so relevant, as stressed by von Rad, *GCW*, pp. 99f.) forms an important link in the Chronicler's claim for Levitical participation in the temple service; see further, 16:4-7; 2 Chr. 5-6.

3. 2 Sam. 6:12ff. initially suggests that David acted alone, but vv. 15 and 18f. indicate the participation of 'all the house of Israel'. Fully in line with his emphasis at 13:1-5, therefore (he uses exactly the same phrase here as at 13:5), the Chronicler again draws out the implication of his *Vorlage*. **its place, which he had prepared for it:** cf. v. 1.

4-10. The Chronicler here works in a suitable list of Levites (see above), providing it with his own introduction (v. 4) to fit it to the context.

4. the sons of Aaron: they are not mentioned in the more detailed list which follows (vv. 5-10). Again, though 'the priests Zadok and Abiathar' are mentioned in v. 11, David goes on to address only 'the heads of the fathers' house of the Levites' in v. 12. Further, although 'the priests and the Levites sanctified themselves to bring up the ark' in v. 14, vv. 15 and 25ff. refer only to the activity of the Levites, the priests not receiving attention until 16:39f. It is thus probable that mention of the priests here and in vv. 11 and 14 is secondary, perhaps included by a subsequent reviser who took his cue from the references to sacrifice later on (cf. RH and Welch, *WC*, pp. 65f.).

5-7 reflects a situation which may be compared closely with 6:16-30, the only difference being that the order of **Kohath, Merari** and **Gershom** (see on 6:1 for the spelling) is varied, and that **Joel** does not appear there in the family of **Gershom**, though cf. 23:8 and 26:22.

8-9. By contrast, **Hebron** and **Uzziah** are listed nowhere else as heads of Levitical families, and are probably to be identified with descendants of Kohath (cf. 6:18 and Exod. 6:22). If so, it is noteworthy that **Elizaphan** here appears as senior, since elsewhere he is junior to the other two (though cf. 2 Chr. 29:13). The names **Shemaiah, Eliel** and **Amminadab** occur elsewhere in Levitical lists, though not specifically in the relationships mentioned here. All these factors strengthen the view that the list reflects a slightly different situation from that which obtained in the Chronicler's day, and, since his narrative of v. 11 presupposes it, that it is likely to be earlier than him, not later. There is then no objection to his having worked the list into his original composition.

11. On this 'repetitive resumption' (Talmon) following an author's insertion of material into his narrative by the Chronicler and others, see above. On the secondary nature of **the priests Zadok and Abiathar, and,** see on v. 4. The case argued there is strengthened by the occurrence of **Abiathar**. The Chronicler is unlikely to have regarded him as a head of his father's house (v. 12) at this stage, since he does not feature at all prominently in his work (note especially his absence from 16:39). The addition of these two names specifically may reflect the influence of 2 Sam. 15:24–9.

12. sanctify yourselves: according to Exod. 19, the only passage which gives content to this word, the washing of clothes and abstinence from sexual intercourse were involved (vv. 14–15). In v. 22 of that chapter, the priests are particularly warned to sanctify themselves 'lest the Lord break out upon them' (and cf. v. 24). The use there of *prṣ*, already noted in 13:2, 11 and 14:11 above as a linking theme in the present section and recurring in v. 13 below in the same connection, will have suggested to the Chronicler that this aspect of preparation had not been attended to on the first occasion, and that it was of particular importance to remedy the defect this time. He therefore stresses fulfilment of the injunction in v. 14.

the place: see on v. 1. The word is not represented in MT. The text may be correct as it stands (cf. GK §155n), though some MSS and vrs suggest the reading *mᵉḳôm ʾᵃšer*, to be translated as in *RSV*; however, *hāʾōhel ha*, 'the tent which', would be a more plausible conjecture, since its loss could be easily explained by parablepsis after *yiśrāʾēl ʾel*, **Israel, to.**

13. This verse makes explicit the Chronicler's explanation of the first *débâcle* which has already been presupposed and commented on in earlier verses of the chapter (see especially 2 and 12). The text seems to have suffered some corruption in the first clause, though the general meaning is not in doubt. **carry** has been supplied by *RSV* on the basis of v. 2; alternatively, read *ʾittānû* (because you were not) with us'; cf. V and *NEB*: 'present'.

broke forth: see on 13:2. **we did not care for it:** lit., 'seek'; the object could equally well be 'God'. See on 13:1–5 and contrast 10:14.

in the way that is ordained: a characteristic note of the Chronicler; cf. 6:32, 23:31, 24:19; 2 Chr. 4:7 and 20, 8:14, 30:16 and 35:13. The law of God is, of course, referred to, generally understood as given through Moses (see v. 15), though David (2 Chr. 8:14) and even Aaron (24:19) are also mentioned.

14. the priests: see on v. 4. **sanctified themselves:** see on v. 12.

15. upon their shoulders: cf. Num. 7:9. **with the poles:** presumably, those of Exod. 25:13–15 are meant, though a different word is used.

16–24. As shown above, this section does not interrupt the Chronicler's narrative, but brings to a conclusion his account of the preparations for the movement of the ark before he resumes the story as found in 2 Sam. 6. Since v. 16 is in his own style and vv. 17 and

19 reflect what we have taken to be the cultic establishment of his own day (Gese's stage IIIB), the paragraph may be regarded as his own composition, though v. 24 (and perhaps 23) was added later. For David's link with the music of the cult and the relationship of texts like this to that tradition, see on 6:31–2.

16. The expressions **the chiefs of the Levites** (cf. *IBC*, p. 27) and **on harps and lyres and cymbals** (compare 13:8, some of whose changes from 2 Sam. 6:5 bring it closer to the present verse, 15:28, 16:5; 2 Chr. 5:12 and 29:25) suggest the Chronicler's hand in this verse.

17. Cf. 6:31–48 (where **Kushaiah** appears as 'Kishi') and the introductory comments to this chapter.

18. Most of these names, which are repeated in the following verses, recur elsewhere in Levitical lists, though any question of identity is highly uncertain.

the gatekeepers is a later gloss, reflecting the outlook of the reviser to be noted in v. 24 below (see also 16:38). For the Chronicler himself, **Obed-edom** was a Levitical singer (cf. v. 21 and 16:5), but at a later stage, he and his family (cf. 26:1–11) seem to have been demoted to the rank of gatekeepers. The incorporation of the gloss into the text may have led to the mistaken dropping of 'Azaziah' from the end of this verse, where his presence is demanded by v. 21; cf. L. C. Allen, *JTS* ns 22 (1971), pp. 143–50, for other examples of this textual process.

19–21. The Levites just mentioned are now divided into three groups according to the instruments which they played. Several technical terms are introduced which have given rise to much discussion, but there is no certainty about their meaning; for instance, **to lead** (*lᵉnaṣṣēaḥ*, 21) does not seem appropriate to **lyres**. **according to Alamoth** (20) and **according to the Sheminith** (21) have most often been taken as referring to soprano and bass respectively, but again, that hardly suits Ps. 46, where **Alamoth** occurs in the title. *NEB* omits the phrases altogether. See further, A. A. Anderson's commentary on the Psalms in this series, pp. 48–50.

22. music (*maśśā'*): disagreement over the correct translation goes back as far as the ancient versions. Two other possibilities are (a) 'carrying', as certainly at 2 Chr. 35:3, so that **Chenaniah** would then be expert in the correct way to carry the ark; and (b) 'oracle', as at 2 Chr. 24:27. On this view, there is a link between the Levitical singers and the postulated cultic prophets of pre-exilic times. The context here and especially in v. 27 below, however, supports *RSV*; see further, M. Gertner, *VT* 10 (1960), pp. 252–4.

23. The reference to **gatekeepers** seems to have no connection with David's initial command (v. 16) and so may well be secondary.

Perhaps a correction of 24*b*, also secondary, accounts for its inclusion.

24. As in v. 4 above, the sudden introduction of **the priests** arouses suspicion. The continuation of the story mentions **trumpets** among the instruments played in the procession (v. 28), but they have not been referred to in the list of 19–21. In the Pentateuch it was the priests alone who blew them (Num. 10:8; 31:6; cf. Neh. 12:35, 41), so that the priestly reviser, whose hand has already been noted in this chapter, added the present note to guard against any possible misunderstanding. The reference to **Obed-edom and Jehiah** as **gatekeepers for the ark** contradicts their role as singers earlier in the paragraph, and also seems to clash with v. 23. This probably reflects an element of tension in the position of some of the minor cultic officials, with the result that the same or another reviser brought the position into line with the situation of his own day, later than the Chronicler; see further on v. 18.

15:25–16:3. The Chronicler now follows his *Vorlage* (2 Sam. 6:12*b*–19) to recount the actual movement of the ark. All the significant differences are to be explained in terms of his distinctive approach to the whole episode already noted.

25. and the elders of Israel, and the commanders of thousands: the emphasis on the participation of all Israel is maintained by this addition; see on v. 3.

26. the Levites: the Chronicler's interpretation of his less explicit *Vorlage*; see on v. 2. The differences at the end of the verse from 2 Sam. 6:13 have the effect of conforming the sacrifices offered more closely with later practice (cf. Num. 23:1, 29; Ezek. 45:23; Job 42:8). Textual evidence suggests that this change was not introduced by the Chronicler himself, however, but was already found in his *Vorlage*; cf. Lemke, *HTR* 58 (1965), pp. 352–3, and Willi, p. 126.

27. The atmosphere of this verse is very different from 2 Sam. 6:14. The Chronicler is certainly responsible here, as elsewhere, for the introduction of **the Levites** and **the singers**, but the rest could be due to textual confusion. Either way, its effect is to see David as fully clad in **a robe of fine linen,** further described as **a linen ephod.** In the Samuel text, this means no more than a loin cloth, which will explain Michal's rebuke (2 Sam. 6:20); but the Chronicler probably understood it against the conditions of his own day, when it was a much more substantial garment, worn by the high priest (cf. de Vaux, *AI*, pp. 349–50). This change of meaning may help explain the differences between the accounts. **the leader of the music:** see on v. 22.

28. 2 Sam. 6:15 mentions only **the sound of the horn;** the Chron-

icler has added a number of other instruments in line with 13:8 and
15:19–21.

29. The Chronicler retains the note about how **Michal the daughter of Saul . . . despised** David, but omits the explanation of 2
Sam. 6:20–23. A reinterpretation of the incident is thereby intended,
the representative of Saul's family disapproving of David's care for
the ark, a theme already stressed in chs 13 and 14; cf. Mosis, p. 26.

16:1–3 follows 2 Sam. 6:17–19 without significant change; the
successful conclusion of the undertaking, the unity of the people
and David's provision for them all coinciding with the Chronicler's
own understanding.

16:4–42. Before including the conclusion of the narrative from
his *Vorlage* (v. 43), the Chronicler describes David's more permanent cultic appointments now that the ark has come to rest in
Jerusalem. The division between Jerusalem and Gibeon, however,
will not be resolved until the dedication of the temple under Solomon. Taken together with the temporary arrangements of ch. 15
for the transfer of the ark, these factors demonstrate the Chronicler's
awareness that institutions did develop through history, and that it
is hazardous to take any one passage in isolation as expressing his
understanding of a given matter. Often several passages need to be
studied together in order to gain an accurate appreciation of his
thought. See further, on ch. 17 below.

4. Until the dedication of the temple, the sacrificial cult was
restricted to the altar at Gibeon (vv. 39–40). Here, therefore, the
role of **the Levites as ministers before the ark** is limited at this
time to musical aspects of the cult, namely **to invoke** through the
Psalms of lament, **to thank** as in the thanksgiving Psalms, and **to
praise the Lord**, as in many of the hymns of the Psalter. Elements
of all three are to be found in the Psalm anthology which follows.
In the temple, of course, these were linked with appropriate forms
of sacrifice, in which the Levites were thus guaranteed a role (cf. 2
Chr. 7:5–6; 29:25–30; 30:21–22; 31:2).

5. Only some of those listed in 15:16–22 are mentioned here, the
rest being appointed to Gibeon (v. 41). There is thus no way of
telling precisely which stage of development in the Levitical office
is here reflected. However, since the names and musical functions
of this verse exactly parallel parts of 15:18–21, it is most probable
that here too the Chronicler is drawing attention to the Davidic
pedigree of the guilds of his own day.

and second to him: since this word is singular (*ûmišnēhû*), it can
govern only **Zechariah**. The remaining names are then more loosely
attached; cf. *NEB*: 'then came . . . '. **Jeiel:** the final name of 15:18

may be intended, but 'Jaaziel' from earlier in that verse (= 'Aziel', 15:20) seems more probable. The difference is very slight.

6. The reference to **priests** is again out of context, and suggests the work of the priestly reviser already noted; see especially 15:24 with reference to **trumpets**. An additional argument in this case is the clash with v. 42, where the Chronicler assumes that it was Levites who blew the **trumpets**. Although that refers to Gibeon, we can hardly suppose that he would have regarded the situation there as different from that associated with **the ark. Benaiah** is mentioned in the list at 15:24, but curiously **Jahaziel** is not.

7 is not just a repetition of v. 4, but is specifically composed to introduce the following psalm anthology, **thanksgiving . . . to the Lord** echoing the first phrase of v. 8. A colon would thus be a more appropriate punctuation mark at the end; cf. *NEB*. **first** balances the 'continually' of v. 37: this is the start of a continuing Levitical function. There is, of course, no clash with ch. 15, since that describes a unique event, but this a regular office.

8–36. The Psalm is drawn with only very slight changes from three of the canonical Psalms, as follows: vv. 8–22 = Ps. 105:1–15; vv. 23–33 = Ps. 96:1–13; v. 34 = Ps. 106:1 and vv. 35–36 = Ps. 106:47–48. It is generally agreed that the Chronicler is here dependent on the Psalter, not *vice versa*, so that the reader must be referred to the commentaries on the book of Psalms for questions of general exegesis.

It would be a mistake, however, to dismiss the passage as no more than an example of liturgical worship which the Chronicler deemed appropriate to the historical setting. He has been able to select from a wide variety of material, and to order it according to his own preference, so that it would be surprising if it did not reflect some of his major concerns. Moreover, since these Psalms were doubtless used regularly by his contemporaries in their worship, it is probable that he would be inviting them to renew their faith in the God who, having answered the prayers and aspirations expressed in these verses so abundantly in the days of David and Solomon, could be relied upon to do so again despite all appearances in a later day. At a time such as the Chronicler's when great caution had to be exercised in the expression of political aspirations, Israel's 'theological leaders turned to the collection of cultic poetry and edited it in such a manner as to rekindle fires of hope for a despondent people' (Butler, *VT* 28 [1978], p. 150). The use of Ps. 132 and Isa. 55:3 at 2 Chr. 6:41–2 is comparable.

Thus, after the hymnic introduction (8–13) he retains in 14–22 only that part of Ps. 105 which deals with the patriarchs who, though **few in number and of little account** (19), **wandering from**

nation to nation (20), were yet protected by God (21–22) because of his covenant promise (14–18) that they would inherit **the land of Canaan** (18; cf. 2 Chr. 20:7). Since the fulfilment of these promises, related in the remainder of Ps. 105 in terms of the exodus and conquest, is omitted, it would seem that the Chronicler expected the politically insignificant community of his own day to identify itself with the patriarchs. They too were protected and they too could look to a brighter future. Such a re-application of the patriarchal narratives finds a close parallel in their earlier use during the exile; cf. Ezek. 33:24; Isa. 51:1–3.

The hymn celebrating the Lord's kingship, 23–33, implicitly conveys a similar message of encouragement and hope. Despite every appearance to the contrary as the Chronicler wrote, **the gods of the peoples are idols** (26) whereas by contrast **The Lord reigns!** (31) and **he comes to judge the earth** (33).

In view of this, the Chronicler skilfully introduces at the close (35) a petition for deliverance and salvation **from among the nations**. In the reality of worship, Israel's eschatological role in the world is upheld, but in the harsh actuality of life in a minor province of a vast empire it is recognised that such a role can only be introduced by God's intervention. The anthology thus chooses a practical way of stimulating the faith which the work as a whole aims also to evoke.

13. Abraham is the reading of Ps. 105:6, but the Chronicler has changed this to 'Israel', which should certainly be read here. It is fully in line with his emphasis elsewhere; see the introduction to 1:1–2:2, and on 1:34.

15. He is mindful: *RSV* again follows the Psalm text, whereas MT of Chr. here has a plural imperative, 'be mindful!'. Despite the opinion of most commentators, who would support *RSV*, MT may be preferred if our understanding of the Chronicler's use of this Psalm as a whole is correct. **his covenant:** the Chronicler does not elsewhere refer explicitly to a covenant with the patriarchs. However, since he is familiar with the content of that covenant (cf. 2 Chr. 1:9 and 20:7), uncharacteristic terminology is no great problem in a passage where he is otherwise following his *Vorlage* so closely.

19. When they were: so Ps. 105:12. MT here has 'when you were', which again would fit well the Chronicler's application of the Psalm.

27. in his place: Ps. 96:6 has 'in his sanctuary', which the Chronicler clearly had to change as it was inappropriate in the setting he has given the Psalm.

29. before him replaces 'into his courts' (Ps. 96:8) for the same reason.

30–31. In Ps. 96, v. 31*b* follows 30*a*. This more logical order may have been accidentally disturbed during the later transmission of the Chronicles text.

35–36. of our salvation and **and save us** are added by the Chronicler to his *Vorlage* (Ps. 106:47) in order to emphasise the prayer which is far more appropriate to his own day (see above) than David's. The opening rubric **say also** and the response of the people at the end similarly draw particular attention to this closing petition.

37–42. A final note on David's ordering of the Levites.

37. Following the initial appointment of **Asaph and his brethren** (cf. v. 7), this necessary resumption of the situation following the inclusion of the Psalm anthology makes clear that this role was henceforth to be performed **continually . . . as each day required**.

38. For **his**, MT has 'their'. A more plausible solution than *RSV*'s is to suppose that 'and Jehiah' (cf. 15:24) has been accidentally omitted following the first mention of **Obed-edom** because of its close orthographic similarity to the word for **and** 'their' **brethren** (*waʾăḥêhem*) which immediately follows.

The apparent dispute over **Obed-edom**'s status is here heightened. The core of the verse is to be attributed to the corrector whose work has already been noted in 15:18 and 24. In his view, **Obed-edom** and his family were gatekeepers. The words **while Obed-edom, the son of Jeduthun** should be read as a self-contained sentence: 'but Obed-edom was the son of Jeduthun'. Since **Jeduthun** was head of one of the guilds of singers (cf. v. 42), this sentence is to be seen as a rejoinder to the corrector which in time was worked into the verse as a whole. **sixty-eight:** 26:8, which reflects the same outlook as the corrector, has 'sixty-two'. **Hosah:** not previously mentioned, but cf. 26:10f.

39. he left, not being in the Hebrew, has to be understood from v. 37, which, of course, it immediately followed in the Chronicler's original text.

the tabernacle of the Lord in the high place that was at Gibeon: this tradition is found only in Chronicles; see further 21:29 and 2 Chr. 1:3–6. It is unnecessary to follow Welch (*WC*, pp. 30–41) in his suggestion that all these references are secondary to Chronicles, for the division of the Levites between ministry before the ark and somewhere else, on which the whole of this chapter is based, presupposes the inclusion of this and the following verse for its explanation.

The tradition of the presence of the tent sanctuary **at Gibeon** is usually dismissed as a fabrication of the Chronicler, 'designed to justify Solomon's inaugural visit to Gibeon (1 Kg. 3:4; 2 Chr. 1:3) and bring his conduct into line with the Priestly law in Lev. xvii.

8-9' (J. Blenkinsopp, *Gibeon and Israel* [1972], p. 102; cf. Noth, *US*, p. 137; R. Schmitt, *Zelt und Lade* [1972], pp. 194-6), and inspired too by a desire to demonstrate the continuity between the old ways of worship and the new now being inaugurated (cf. de Vaux, *AI*, p. 297).

It is certainly the case that these features would have made the tradition attractive to the Chronicler, and in the absence of any other firm evidence, the view that he was himself its author cannot be ignored. Nevertheless, the responsible commentator should also collect such evidence as would support his text. This is especially so in the present case, because it is clear from 1 Kg. 3:3*b* that the Kings' account is as polemical against the legitimacy of Solomon's worship at Gibeon as the Chronicler is positive towards it; the silence of the Kings' account in this particular is therefore of no great significance. Secondly, whereas the explanations advanced above might account for the reference in 2 Chr. 1, they do not cover the present passage in which the introduction of the sanctuary at Gibeon, with its consequent necessity for a division of labour among the Levites, leads to a slight tension (though one which can quite easily be borne) with 6:31ff. There may therefore be the suggestion that the Chronicler was here working under the compulsion of inherited tradition. Thirdly, 2 Sam. 7:6 (strengthened, if anything, in 17:5 below) implies continuing respect for a tent sanctuary, and there are other indications too, some admittedly problematic, for this same outlook in the period before the temple was built (cf. W. Beyerlin, *Origins and History of the Oldest Sinaitic Traditions* [ET 1965], pp. 119-20). Fourthly, it is possible that such a sanctuary may have been located at some stage in Gibeon. Jos. 9:27 is most naturally understood as referring to an altar at Gibeon (cf. R. de Vaux, *The Early History of Israel* [ET 1978], p. 623), while the Deuteronomic addition at the end of the verse links it with the central sanctuary rather than an illegitimate high place. Finally, M. Görg, *Das Zelt der Begegnung* (1967), pp. 121-37 (cf. H. W. Hertzberg, *ZAW* 47 [1929], pp. 161-96) has argued strongly in favour of the Chronicler's presentation resting on earlier tradition on the basis of the identity or close proximity of the sanctuaries at Gibeon and Nob (1 Sam. 21), and the argument that the tent of 1 Kg. 1:39; 2:28 (cf. 1:50) cannot have been the tent which David pitched for the ark, but one which may have been at Gibeon.

The question of whether the Chronicler was here basing himself on earlier tradition should thus, from a historical point of view and in default of fuller evidence, be left open; meanwhile, the positive points noted above which led him to include the material, whatever its origin, remain of chief significance in the understanding of his work.

40. See on 6:49.

41. the rest of those chosen and expressly named: i.e. all those listed in 15:17-22 who have not already been mentioned in 16:5 as serving before the ark in Jerusalem. **to give thanks:** cf. 16:4. **for his steadfast love endures for ever:** a frequent and apparently standard refrain in the worship of the second temple (cf. *IBC*, p. 47). The Chronicler uses it as an indication of the type of psalmody most characteristic of the worship as led by the Levitical guilds; cf. 2 Chr. 5:13 and 20:21 together with 1 Chr. 15:34 and Ps. 106:1, 107:1, 118:1, 136:1, etc.

42. See on v. 6 above. **The sons of Jeduthun were appointed to the gate:** this is completely unexpected in the context, and there is no suggestion elsewhere that singers acted as gatekeepers. Unless the text is at fault (CM), we must see here either the hand of the glossator observed in v. 38 above, or else one who presupposed his work.

43. The Chronicler rounds off the whole section and prepares for the next by returning to his *Vorlage*, 2 Sam. 6:19*b*-20*a*. On his omission of David's altercation with Michal, see on 15:29 above.

THE DYNASTIC ORACLE

17:1-27

The remainder of 1 Chronicles, a long and apparently variegated passage, has been compiled by the Chronicler with one overriding aim in view—the steps taken towards the building of the temple. These include identification of the builder (ch. 17), the necessary political conditions (18-20), site (21), materials and plans (22, 28-29), and the personnel (the primary layer in 23-27). Though for convenience this section has been broken down into smaller units in this commentary, this should not be allowed to detract from the overall unity of the theme throughout.

The Chronicler starts in this chapter, then, with Nathan's oracle and David's response. He follows 2 Sam. 7 quite closely throughout. Although it has been argued that the Chronicler's *Vorlage* was a 'proto-Samuel' source, and that therefore 2 Sam. 7 should be re-garded as secondary (cf. H. van den Bussche, *ETL* 24 [1948], pp. 354-94, followed only by H. Gese, *Vom Sinai zum Zion* [1974], pp. 124-5), this view cannot be accepted in view of the fact that (a) a number of the slight differences can be most easily explained in the light of the Chronicler's position as a whole, and (b) such a view runs counter to the dependence of Chr. on Sam. elsewhere. For these reasons, scholars have normally upheld the priority of 2 Sam. 7 (cf. M. Simon, *RHPhR* 32 [1952], pp. 41–58, and, most recently, E. von Nordheim, *VT* 27 [1977], pp. 449–53). All this does not, of course, rule out the possibility that in particular instances the text of 2 Sam. 7 may have suffered corruption which 1 Chr. 17 has not, or that, as already noted elsewhere, the Chronicler's *Vorlage* may in certain particulars have been at variance with MT of 2 Sam. 7.

2 Sam. 7 presents students of the *OT* with many questions which have been endlessly discussed, but they cannot be our concern here; for recent statements with full bibliography, cf. T. N. D. Mettinger, *King and Messiah* (1976), pp. 48–63, and T. Ishida, *The Royal Dynasties in Ancient Israel* (1977), pp. 81–117. Although it is quite apparent that the Chronicler has followed his *Vorlage* in representing the divine decree that David's son, Solomon, should build the temple, scholars have not been in agreement over whether he limits the perspective of the oracle to Solomon alone, or whether conversely he heightens its 'messianic' significance.

In this debate, it may be suggested that proponents of both views have usually been in error in limiting their attention to this chapter in isolation. In fact, it should be taken in close conjunction with such later texts as 22:6–10; 28:2–10; 2 Chr. 6:15–17 and 7:17–18. Study of all these together reveals the following development. In 1 Chr. 17 itself and elsewhere there is a marked tendency to concentrate the attention of the oracle exclusively on Solomon (see below). In later echoes of it during David's and Solomon's reigns there is also an emphasis on various conditional elements. In the earlier, Deuteronomic history these had been intended primarily to refer to the failings of the later kings as an explanation for the fall of the dynasty in the Babylonian exile. At the same time, however, the Chronicler retains throughout the 'eternal' reference of the oracle.

These factors are to be explained on the basis of the Chronicler's distinctive concern to present the reigns of David and Solomon as a single, unified event within the divine economy for the life of the nation (cf. *VT* 26 [1976], pp. 351–61; Braun, *JBL* 92 [1973], pp. 503–16, and *JBL* 95 [1976], pp. 581–90). Whereas the Deuteronomic historian does not have Solomon make any particular contribution to the establishment of the dynasty, the Chronicler elevates his role to one of equal significance with that of David, and attempts thereby to harmonise the tensions of his *Vorlage* concerning the conditional or unconditional nature of the promise. Thus the dynastic oracle, delivered originally to David, is concentrated upon the person of his son Solomon; at the same time, however, the conditions of obedience, whose fulfilment will lead to the establish-

ment of an eternal dynasty, are also focused upon him (28:7). Thus
Solomon's role becomes as much a foundation for the future of the
dynasty as that of David, for the two elements of God's promise to
David and the carrying out of God's conditions by Solomon are
both necessary.

Since in his later narrative the Chronicler, as is well known,
presents Solomon as one who kept the conditions of the temple
building and obedience in as positive a way as it is possible to
conceive, it is evident that at the completion of the period of
Davidic-Solomonic rule he intends his readers to regard the dynasty
as indeed eternally established, and various later references further
make this explicit (2 Chr. 13:5, 21:7; 23:3). Although the term
'messianic' is perhaps too strong, it must be concluded that the
Chronicler still cherished the hope that one day the Davidic dynasty
would be re-established over Israel. For a more detailed defence of
this approach, with discussion of other viewpoints, cf. 'The Dynastic Oracle', and its development in *TynB* 28 (1977), pp. 115-54.

1. The Chronicler omits the comment that 'the Lord had given
him rest from all his enemies round about' (2 Sam. 7:1*b*). The fact
that chs 18-20 immediately following recount further wars of David,
or that there may be a desire to eliminate the suggestion that some
time elapsed before David turned his attention to a suitable resting
place for the ark will be only contributory factors at best. The
Chronicler's principal emphasis is that David himself was disqualified from building the temple because he had 'shed much blood'
and 'waged great wars' (22:8; cf. 28:3). His role is in every respect
preparatory, including the establishment of the political stability
necessary for such an undertaking (cf. Dt. 12:10f.). This has clearly
yet to be fully accomplished; see further, v. 10 below, and the
comments on 22:6-16.

4. You shall not build . . . replaces 2 Sam. 7:5, 'would you build
. . .?'. The emphasis of the Chronicler's version is placed upon the
you (*lō' 'attāh tibneh*), implying 'not you, but another'. This fits
in with his whole outlook which does not oppose temple building
as such (cf. 2 Chr. 6:8), but finds David himself to be unsuitable,
and his consequent increased focusing of the oracle on Solomon.
This may also account for his adding the definite article ('the') to
house (obscured in *RSV*, though cf. *GK* §127 *q–t*).

5-6. In view of what has already been seen, it is clear that the
Chronicler will not have regarded these verses as an outright rejection of a temple as such, but rather as an indication that there is no
need to rush into building one. David can accept his preparatory
role with patience (Goettsberger).

5. From dwelling to dwelling: a conjectural restoration, probably correct, *contra NEB:* 'I lived in a tent and a tabernacle'. See further, on 16:39 above.

6. Judges is correct against 2 Sam. 7:7 'tribes' (cf. v. 10), despite the contrary arguments of Ph. de Robert, *VT* 21 (1971), pp. 116–18, and P. V. Reid, *CBQ* 37 (1975), pp. 17–20.

10. and I will subdue for 2 Sam. 7:11, 'and I will give you rest'; see on v. 1 for an explanation. The Chronicler looks forward to the next three chapters, which will create the necessary political conditions for temple building (*contra* Mosis, pp. 82–7, who argues unconvincingly that throughout vv. 8–10 the verbs should be rendered in the perfect tense). **I declare:** for the correct use of the present tense in such a context, cf. C. Brockelmann, *Hebräische Syntax* (1956), §41d (with 42c). **will build:** Mosis' attempt (pp. 85–6) to render this as a perfect on the basis of 1 Chr. 11:8 and Isa 6:4 founders on his failure to observe that the word order of the latter two passages shows that they are circumstantial clauses, whereas the present verse is not.

11. one of your own sons: literally, 'who will be from your sons', replacing 2 Sam. 7:12, 'who shall come forth from your body'. Commentators have been sharply divided over the significance of this change, many following the interpretation of *RSV*, but some (e.g. Keil; von Rad, *GCW*, pp. 123–4; Galling) arguing rather that it looks further ahead than Solomon (i.e. 'who will come forth from one of your sons'). In fact, however, examination of the contentious phrase (*hāyāh min*, 'to be from') shows that it is ambiguous in this particular regard (e.g. contrast Ec. 3:20 and Gen. 17:16 with 1 Kg. 12:31 or Dt. 23:18, etc.). The context must thus determine its exegesis, and this clearly suggests a reference to Solomon (cf. v. 12a). However, it is equally mistaken to argue that an attempt has been made actually to intensify the individual reference to Solomon. The fact that sometimes *hāyāh min* (used in this verse) and *yāṣā' min* (used in 2 Sam. 7:12) occur in parallel (cf. Jer. 30:21, and Gen. 17:6 with 16) shows that they are virtually synonymous. This is also true of **your sons** and '(those who) come forth from your body' (2 Sam. 7:12), as the parallel passages 2 Kg. 19:37 (*Qr.*), Isa. 37:38 and 2 Chr. 32:21 shows (cf. Japhet, *Ideology*, p. 417; we would further add as closely comparable the MT and IQIsaᵃ reading of Isa. 39:7). Thus it would appear that the Chronicler understood his *Vorlage* to refer to Solomon and that he reproduced it accordingly with only a slight change, probably for no more than stylistic reasons.

13. The Chronicler omits 2 Sam. 7:14b, 'When he commits iniquity, I will chasten him with the rod of men, with the stripes of the sons of men'. Again, this is due neither to any messianic reference in the oracle nor to the simple fact that the whole passage refers to Solomon, whom the Chronicler presents as blameless, as commentators have generally thought. Rather it is to be linked to his understanding of the place of the oracle within the 'united' reign of David and Solomon, outlined above. In such a setting, the sentence is quite irrelevant: in the Samuel text, it refers to the whole future line of Davidic kings, to many of whom the saying could have applied, but in the Chronicler's text it would have to refer to Solomon, for whom it could have no application whatever. Either he was going to obey, in which case the dynasty would be established, or he would fail, and his house with him. What was not foreseen was the possibility that he would fail personally, but the dynasty nevertheless endure.

14. confirm him . . . his throne: contrast 2 Sam. 7:16, 'your house and your kingdom shall be made sure . . . your throne'. This shift in focus from David to Solomon is crucial. Its effect is to throw the promise of an established dynasty forward on to him. As noted above, however, this has in turn to be linked with later repetitions and expansions of the oracle in order to gain a full appreciation of the Chronicler's intention. **my house . . . my kingdom:** 2 Sam. 7:16, 'your house . . . your kingdom'. As well as switching attention from David to Solomon, the Chronicler here introduces a further characteristic thought. God is the real king of Israel, and the kingdom is his. Consequently, the only legitimate kings are those whom he has **confirmed** and **established**. On the basis of this oracle, David can thus later say that 'he has chosen Solomon my son to sit upon the throne of the kingdom of the Lord over Israel' (28:5), while it is further recorded that 'Solomon sat on the throne of the Lord as king' (29:23). After Solomon's reign, when the dynasty is regarded as established, Abijah uses the same thought in his appeal to the northerners to call off their rebellion: 'you think to withstand the kingdom of the Lord in the hand of the sons of David' (2 Chr. 13:8), whereas conversely it was seen above at 10:14 that after Saul's unfaithfulness the Lord 'turned the kingdom over to David'. This idea also comes to expression in 29:11 and 2 Chr.9:8. For the Chronicler's first readers, living at a time when prospects of a change in their politically subservient status may well have seemed unlikely, the implications of this message would not have been lost: Israel's kingdom was secure and everlasting, because it was in God's hands, no matter what the present contrary appearance. Just as he had entrusted it to the saviour David after the disaster of Saul's death (see on 10:13–14), so he was well able to intervene again to re-establish his kingdom 'in the hand of the sons of David'. See the Introduction, section G.

16–27. David's prayer in response to the oracle is adopted by the Chronicler without significant or tendentious alteration. Its emphasis on God's unique power, revealed especially in the Exodus, being now applied to the establishment of the Davidic house, and David's acceptance of the promise, will have suited his theme well. He probably understood the heart of the prayer (v. 25) to apply to Solomon, but the frequent repetition of **for ever** and similar phrases points forward to the fuller application of the promise which he will develop through the rest of his account of David's and Solomon's rule.

17. The text of the second half of this verse is very uncertain, and no suggestion has particularly commended itself. *RSV*'s **future generations** has been influenced by the preceding **for a great while to come**, while *NEB*, 'and now thou lookest upon me as a man already embarked on a high career', finds a contrast rather with **a small thing** earlier in the verse (cf. *AV*, *RV*).

21–22. This clear reference to the Exodus **from Egypt** should be contrasted with a tendency to suppress such references later on, especially in Solomon's prayer at the dedication of the temple (2 Chr. 6). This development highlights the importance of the Davidic covenant for the Chronicler. Here, the earlier saving events are made the basis for David's prayer, but by the time of Solomon that basis has given way to the new Davidic covenant as the foundation of the relationship between God and Israel (cf. *IBC*, pp. 64–6).

27. may it please thee to bless: *RSV* has reproduced the text of 2 Sam. 7:29. MT here has 'thou hast been pleased to bless', and this is to be preferred, for its greater definiteness is also reflected in the closing **what thou, O Lord, hast blessed is blessed for ever** (contrast 2 Sam. 7:29*b*). The Chronicler reflects a slightly greater certainty about the establishment of David's **house** than his *Vorlage*.

DAVID'S WARS

18:1–20:8

These three chapters, 18–20, are all extracted, with only minor variations, from 2 Sam. 8–21. The fact that they relate so obviously to a single theme, and that this concentration has been achieved by rigorous selection, suggests that the Chronicler was not concerned merely to omit material which might appear unfavourable to David (see further his inclusion of ch. 21 following). Rather he was governed positively by two main and related purposes.

First, these chapters go a long way towards explaining why, in the Chronicler's view, David did not himself build the temple. 22:8

and 28:3 show that this was because he was a man of war who had shed much blood, a theme more than adequately demonstrated here. Thus between the initially surprising prohibition by Nathan (ch. 17) and its later detailed explanation, the reader's understanding and agreement are awakened.

Secondly, it has already been noted above that at 17:1 the Chronicler did not regard David's reign as that period of 'rest' which Dt. had stipulated as necessary for the establishment of the central sanctuary, and that at 17:10 a further reference to 'rest' was replaced with the promise that God would subdue all his enemies, so that, we infer, those necessary conditions of peace might be secured (cf. 22:9–10). This promise now comes to fulfilment, as 22:18–19 states explicitly; note especially the 'refrain' of 18:6 and 13, and cf. 19:13.

To these two main themes, a third one may be added which, though not so prominent, was also germane to the Chronicler's purpose. In 2 Chr. 5:1, he retains a reference from his *Vorlage* to Solomon bringing to the temple all 'the things which David his father had dedicated'. It is probable that, on the basis of 18:8 and 11, we should in particular see here a reference to the spoil taken in war, which David dedicated to the work on the temple. The Chronicler was, therefore, pleased to include these chapters as illustrating the economic prosperity which would have been needed for the temple building, and which David was able to bequeath to his son.

A Survey of David's Victories

18:1–13

This survey is drawn from 2 Sam. 8:1–14. The only major omission is his treatment of the Moabites (2 Sam. 8:2), perhaps as much on the basis of 1 Sam. 22:3–4 as of an attempt to 'whitewash' David (CM).

1. Gath and its villages replaces the obscure 'Metheg-ammah' of 2 Sam. 8:1. It is generally agreed that the Chronicler's version is textually secondary. However, if David indeed **defeated the Philistines and subdued them**, it is likely to be factually correct. 1 Kg. 2:39–40 does not contradict this; cf. H. E. Kassis, *JBL* 84 (1965), pp. 259–71, and G. E. Wright, *BA* 29 (1966), pp. 81–2, *contra* Aharoni, *Land*, p. 261, and A. F. Rainey, *EI* 12 (1975), p. 72*.

4. Chariots is not found in 2 Sam. 8:4, and the number of **horsemen** is here considerably larger. Since these differences correspond with LXX of Sam., they were probably already found in the Chronicler's *Vorlage*.

6. garrisons is clearly correctly restored by *RSV*.

7. shields: more probably 'quivers' (*NEB*); cf. R. Borger, *VT* 22 (1972), pp. 385-98.

8. Tibhath = 'Tebah', which should also be read at 2 Sam. 8:8. **Cun** was in the Chronicler's day a better known town than 'Berothai' (2 Sam. 8:8), which was in the same area; cf. Simons, *GTTOT*, §§766-7; Willi, p. 120.

The second half of the verse, indicating that the captured **bronze** was used for the temple furnishings, is very much in line with the Chronicler's purpose in these chapters (see above), and since its equivalent is not found in the parallel passage it may well be his own addition, despite its appearance in LXX of Sam. (cf. *VT* 26 [1976], pp. 357-8, and Mosis, p. 104, *contra* Rudolph, p.135, and W. E. Lemke, *HTR* 58 [1965], pp. 354-5).

10. Hadoram: 2 Sam. 8:10 has 'Joram', which may be his second name, adopted under the influence of Israelite domination here attested; cf. A. Malamat, *JNES* 22 (1963), pp. 6-7. B. Peckham, in F. M. Cross, W. E. Lemke and P. D. Miller (eds), *Magnalia Dei* (1976), p. 243, denies Hadoram's vassal status, but without reasons.

11. Edom: 2 Sam. 8:12, 'Aram'. The former anticipates vv. 12-13; the latter looks back to vv. 5-6, but this does not speak decisively in its favour, since neither **the Ammonites** nor **Amalek** have been previously mentioned either.

12. For **Abishai**, the heading to Ps. 60 implies Joab, another **son of Zeruiah** (cf. v. 15), but 2 Sam. 8:13 makes David the subject. There are no certain grounds for deciding whether we have here variant traditions, a misreading of his *Vorlage* by the Chronicler (cf. Willi, pp. 74-5), or a case of textual corruption in all recensions of an original 'when he had returned from Zobah' (RH; Rudolph).

The Organisation of David's Kingdom

18:14-17

These brief notes about the organisation of David's kingdom are taken over from 2 Sam. 8:15-18. Although not directly about David's wars, they are clearly related closely to this theme (note the references to military leaders in vv. 15 and 17), while the favourable notice in v. 14 was no doubt also agreeable to him. For details of some of the titles, see, in addition to the commentaries on Sam., Mettinger, *Solomonic State Officials*, and J. A. Soggin in *IJH*, pp. 356-9.

16. Ahimelech: *RSV* correctly restores with 2 Sam. 8:17, several versions and MSS; MT has 'Abimelech'. In fact, however, it is widely agreed that the Sam. text itself should be re-ordered to read 'Zadok and Abiathar son of Ahimelech, son of Ahitub'; cf. *NEB*.

17. chief could equally well go with **sons** in the sense of 'eldest'. 2 Sam. 8:18, however, has 'and David's sons were priests'. The difference is usually attributed to the Chronicler's unwillingness to accept that non-Levites could be priests ('his regular solicitude for exclusiveness in priestly prerogatives', A. Cody, *A History of Old Testament Priesthood* [1969], p. 103). This seems improbable, however, in view of his references elsewhere to the priestly functions of David and Solomon (cf. 15:27; 16:2–3, 43; 21:26; 2 Chr. 6:3, 13). There is, in addition, a curious feature in the list in Sam., namely that 'priests' have already been treated in the previous verse, so that the present reference is evidently out of order. We are then left with two possibilities: (a) MT of Sam. is the result of a very early confusion (cf. Mettinger, pp. 6f.), which understandably posed a difficulty for the Chronicler which he solved by comparing the list with the similar one in 1 Kg. 4:2–6, and from which he concluded that **David's sons** must have exercised the same function as 'Ahishar [who] was in charge of the palace'; so Willi, p. 127. Alternatively (b) a strong case has been made out on the basis of versional evidence, context and comparison with 1 Kg. 4:5, for the suggestion that the Old Palestinian text of 2 Sam.8:18 originally read *sknym*, 'administrators (of the royal estates)' rather than *khnym*, 'priests'. Since by his day *skn* was rare, if not obsolete, the Chronicler gave **officials in the service of the king** as a reasonable paraphrase; cf. G. J. Wenham, *ZAW* 87 (1975), pp. 79–82.

Campaigns against the Ammonites

19:1–20:3

In the Samuel account (2 Sam. 10:1–11:1; 12:26 and 30–31), the latter part of this narrative also involves the affair of Bathsheba. By abstracting only that which was relevant to his theme, the Chronicler has introduced a slight unevenness into his account over David's location in 20:1–3, but probably, as already noted elsewhere, he assumes knowledge of the fuller account (Willi, pp. 57f.).

6–7 are a rather freely rewritten version of 2 Sam. 10:6 with the intention, apparently, of making it more intelligible to later readers, e.g. **Mesopotamia** (*ªram nahªrayim*) for the lesser-known 'Syrians of Beth-rehob' (*ªram bêt-rᵉḥôḇ*), omission of 'the men of Tob', totalling the numbers involved, etc., and of magnifying the strength of the enemy alliance, e.g. the introduction of **a thousand talents of silver** and of **chariots and horsemen** (though cf. v. 18). **Aram-**

maacah: see on 2:23. Since **Medeba** is in Moab (south of Ammon), this is usually regarded as an error for 'the water of Rabbah' (cf. 2 Sam. 12:27). B. Mazar, *BA* 25 (1962), p. 102, however, sees behind this account a struggle between David and Hadadezer (cf. 18:3) for control of the 'King's Highway', though this reference alone is hardly sufficient to support such a hypothesis.

9. the kings who had come: 2 Sam. 10:8 repeats the list of allies, which the Chronicler again simplifies by generalisation.

15. Joab's brother: MT, 'his brother', an addition to 2 Sam. 10:14, and perhaps originating in an abbreviation which *RSV* has correctly resolved; for a similar situation, cf. the comments of G. R. Driver on 2 Sam. 3:27 in *Textus* I (1960), p. 121; and see further, L. C. Allen, *JTS* ns 22 (1971), p. 144.

18. seven thousand: 2 Sam. 10:18 has 'seven hundred'. This tenfold increase (see also at 18:4) may be due to a desire by the Chronicler (or a predecessor of his) to magnify David's victory or to a mechanical error at some stage in the course of textual transmission—before, during or after the time of the composition of Chronicles. In this particular case, attraction to the **forty thousand** just following could have contributed to the error. **foot soldiers**: here it is widely agreed that Chr. preserves the correct interpretation in preference to Sam's. 'horsemen'.

20:3. set them to labour and **axes**: both emendations (cf. mg. and 2 Sam. 12:31) are undoubtedly correct and are widely accepted.

Further Victories over the Philistines

20:4–8

To conclude his survey of David's wars, the Chronicler returns rather appropriately to further victories over **the Philistines**, drawn from 2 Sam. 21:18–22.

4. Gezer: 2 Sam. 21:18: 'Gob', not otherwise certainly known. If Eissfeldt's topographical conjecture is sound (cf. *KS* 2 [1963], pp. 457–8), the Chronicler will have again substituted a better-known town in the same vicinity for the benefit of his readers. **and the Philistines** (MT: 'they') **were subdued**: lacking in 2 Sam. The word used here (*knʿ*) is a favourite with the Chronicler, some of whose uses of it are quite idiosyncratic (cf. Japhet, *VT* 18 [1968], pp. 359f.). He uses it on three other occasions as a summarising statement in connection with war – at 17:10, where it was suggested that his introduction of the word probably looked forward to these three chapters, and at 2 Chr. 13:18 and 28:19, where his own hand is probably also to be seen (cf. *IBC*, p. 116). It is therefore likely that he himself added the word here, his purpose being to give a more general application to a specific and personal incident. This helped draw the paragraph more closely into line with the theme of the section as a whole.

5. Lahmi the brother of Goliath: 2 Sam. 21:19 has 'the Bethlehemite (slew) Goliath'. It is generally held that the Chronicler found a discrepancy between 2 Sam. 21:19 and 1 Sam. 17 where it is David who slays Goliath (the continuation **the shaft of whose spear was like a weaver's beam** makes it clear that the same Goliath is being spoken of: cf. 1 Sam. 17:7), and that he deliberately altered his *Vorlage* in order to effect a harmonisation. While this remains likely, it is worth noting that the Sam. text itself is almost certainly corrupt, '-oregim' being a dittograph of the word translated **weaver** at the end of the verse. Was the Chronicler's *Vorlage* itself corrupt, or at any rate unclear? If so, he may have felt the need to correct textually, as much as historically, and did so correctly to start with. But the discrepancy in his *Vorlage* led him to continue the process further, and that in an intelligible manner: at 10:9 he has already rendered *bêt̲* by the accusative particle *ʾet̲*, **Lahmi** remains, but now as a proper name rather than an element of 'Bethlehemite', and *ʾēt̲* to *ʾaḥî* (**brother of**) is a slight change, which sense would have dictated (cf. Bertheau, followed by Willi, pp. 138f.). If something of this sort took place, we should have to abandon certainty as to what the true reading might originally have been, and attribute the Chronicler's motive more to a desire to make the Sam. text intelligible to his readers than to a deliberate harmonisation by falsification.

THE DESIGNATION OF THE TEMPLE SITE

21:1–22:1

The Chronicler has based himself on 2 Sam. 24, but he has used the chapter creatively for his own purpose. Whereas 2 Sam. 24 was originally closely linked with 2 Sam. 21 (note the use of 'again' at 24:1, and the parallel themes which run through the two chapters: the Lord's anger, the need for expiation, catastrophe, holy place and ultimate blessing, underlined by the use of identical phraseology in 21:14 and 24:25; cf. H. W. Hertzberg, *I & II Samuel* [1964], pp. 410 and 415f.), yet even in its new position it still does not mention explicitly that the threshing floor of Araunah which David purchased later became the site for the temple. For the Chronicler, however, this is the whole point of the account, as his own addition of 21:28–22:1 (and cf. 2 Chr. 3:1) makes clear. For an historical evaluation, cf. K. Rupprecht, *Der Tempel von Jerusalem* (1977), pp. 13f. This new focus to the chapter thus draws it closely into line with the purpose of his account of the second half of David's reign as a whole, namely, various aspects of preparation for Solomon's later temple building.

The Chronicler does not follow his *Vorlage* quite so closely as in the preceding chapters. In addition on the one hand to a number of 'mechanical' considerations already noted that help account for this, such as abbreviation or a *Vorlage* whose text evidently diverged from MT of 2 Sam. 24 (see especially on v. 16), and in addition on the other hand to the fact that, as at 10:13–14; 14:17, etc., the Chronicler has supplied his own ending (21:26b–22:1) to make clear his interpretation of the whole account, it should be noted that the chapter is rich in verbal allusions to other *OT* passages. It is clear from v. 16 that this process of allowing other texts to colour the detail of narration had already begun prior to the Chronicler's own composition, but, since textual evidence to the contrary is lacking, we must suppose that he continued this process, whether for theological (cf. v. 1) or more generally typological (cf. vv. 20–26) reasons.

1. The figure of **Satan** comes in only three passages in the *OT*, and the absence of the definite article in the present verse suggests that it has become a proper name, rather than a title, 'the Accuser'. In Zech. 3:1–2 he appears as a member of the heavenly court in just the role his title would lead us to expect, namely, 'to accuse' (*lᵉśiṭnô*) Joshua the high priest, while in Job 1–2 he is found among 'the sons of God', again with the primary role of accusing Job before God. In this latter passage, however, he also has power and permission to afflict Job, but only within the strict limits established by God (1:12; 2:6).

Both passages have influenced the Chronicler here, though it was reflection on Job in particular which led him to introduce the figure of **Satan** where 2 Sam. 24:1 has 'the anger of the Lord'. In Job 2:3, the verb **incite** (*wayyāseṯ*) is postulated of Satan; finding his *Vorlage* theologically difficult at this point, the Chronicler took the passage in Job as providing an explanation for it, and wrote accordingly (cf. Willi, pp. 155–6). It may further be observed that in 1 Kg. 11 the Lord's anger (v. 9) led him to raise up human 'adversaries' against Solomon (vv. 14, 23, 25), in contrast with 1 Kg. 5:4. However, it is clear from the fact that the outcome of the whole is the divine choice of the temple site, for the demonstration of which he has included the story in his narrative, that he still looked on Satan as one who, as in Job, was strictly limited by God's overriding sovereignty, and that indeed he could be an instrument of the ultimate divine will. His use of the figure is thus not to be seen as intended to contradict, but rather to elucidate, the text in Sam. **stood up against:** influence from the other *OT* passage where Satan is mentioned, Zech. 3:1, is apparent here, for the Chronicler has appropriately introduced this phrase directly from there (Ps. 109:6*b* is closely comparable). This further emphasises that the Chronicler's understanding of **Satan** is to be compared with his appearance elsewhere in the *OT* rather than with the development of his independence almost to the point of dualism in a number of later texts.

Israel: the Chronicler omits 'and Judah', perhaps 'to ignore the separation implied in the term "Israel and Judah". David's kingdom was one kingdom' (CM, p. 250; see above on chs 11–12).

2. from Beersheba to Dan: this 'south to north' definition (for the more usual 'from Dan to Beersheba') occurs only in Chronicles (see 2 Chr. 30:5, and compare 1 Chr. 13:5 and 2 Chr. 19:4). It may be a reflection of his emphasis on the importance of the southern kingdom (compare his arrangement of the tribal genealogies).

3. The objections of **Joab** to the taking of the census are expressed more strongly than in 2 Sam. 24:3, particularly by the addition of the final question, **Why should he bring guilt upon Israel?** (and cf. v. 6 below). Curiously, however, the basis for the objection is nowhere spelt out. Since the purpose of a census was usually for conscription, taxation or the introduction of forced labour, it may be that Joab himself regarded David's action as an infringement either upon God's own government of his people or upon the freedom of the people of Israel, and that he thus stood for 'an expression of conservative piety' (Ackroyd). The Chronicler, however, can hardly have regarded a census as invariably wrong in view of Exod. 30:12; Num. 1:2; 26:2. Perhaps he deduced from v. 5, from the fact that 'Joab and the commanders of the army' (v. 2) were in charge of the operation, and from the context of 2 Sam. 24, which immediately follows lists of David's warriors and their deeds in 2 Sam. 23, that this particular census was for military purposes (see further on the exclusion of Levi in v. 6 below), and thus represented a turning away from that absolute reliance upon God which characterises his accounts of successful battles and which makes numerical advantage insignificant (see especially 2 Chr. 14:9–15). Such an attitude would not stand in any tension with the genealogies of 1 Chr. 1–9, for although ironically some of these were drawn from a military census list (see above, p. 46), yet he himself did not include them for this purpose, but rather for more theological reasons.

4. The Chronicler here very briefly summarises 2 Sam. 24:5–8 which gives details of how **Joab** and 'the commanders of the army' (see v. 2 above, but omitted thereafter) actually conducted the census and the time that it took.

5. 2 Sam. 24:9 attributes 800,000 to Israel and 500,000 to Judah, a total of 1,300,000. The Chronicler's figure can easily be explained on this basis. His total for **all Israel**, which in the context (cf. vv. 1 and 4) and on the basis of the Chronicler's use of the expression elsewhere during the period of the united monarchy must refer to the total population, not just the northern tribes (*contra* Wenham, *TynB* 18 [1967], pp. 33–4), is 1,100,000. Since he normally regards Ephraim and Manasseh as separate tribes, he will have reckoned on thirteen tribes in all (including Levi). The figures in Sam. thus suggested to him an average of 100,000 for each tribe. In the next verse he has added the note that Levi and Benjamin were not included in the census; he therefore deducted 200,000 for them from the figure in Sam. to leave him with his present total.

It is probable, as most commentators agree, that the final clause (from **and in Judah**) is a later addition. It introduces a contradictory note to the stress of the Chronicler throughout on the unity of Israel, and the numbers cannot be made to fit his clear and simple scheme outlined above. They were arrived at by a glossator on the basis of 2 Sam. 24:9, with the deduction of 30,000 for Benjamin (though the reason for the latter figure is not clear). **Judah** was thus understood as a tribe (in 2 Sam. 24 as the southern kingdom), whose numbers are far above the average; this may give a clue to the glossator's motives.

6. The Chronicler himself has added this verse, and has perhaps concealed his own sentiments behind those of **Joab**. **Levi** will have been excluded from the **numbering** on the basis of Num. 1:49; 2:33, which forbad their inclusion in a military census (though cf. Num. 3:15 for a religious census; Num. 26:57ff. does occur in the context of a military census, but v. 62 indicates awareness of the anomaly). The reason for **Benjamin**'s exclusion is less clear, but probably relates to the presence of the tabernacle at Gibeon (v. 29) within its territory.

7. This addition by the Chronicler is necessitated by his rewriting of v. 1. The whole verse is a summarising introduction to the following paragraph, so that **and he smote Israel** refers to the pestilence of v. 14, not to some other and additional catastrophe.

8–14. This account of David's choice of punishment and its execution follows 2 Sam. 24:10b–15 more closely. Indeed, in several matters of detail the Chronicler's text has been better preserved, that of Sam. being usually emended in such cases to conform with it.

12. **devastation:** *RSV* apparently tries to translate the somewhat

obscure MT (*nispeh*, perhaps 'a snatching away'), but many commentators follow the parallel text, which has the almost identical
word 'flight'. **the sword of your enemies . . . . the sword of the
Lord**: the Chronicler (or the text he was following: see immediately
below) makes much clearer than MT of 2 Sam. the contrast between
human and divine agents of punishment, and this leads more easily
into David's contrasting of 'the hand of the Lord' and 'the hand of
man' in the next verse. **and the angel of the Lord destroying
throughout all the territory of Israel**: this is not found in the
parallel passage, and is the first of several places where the Chronicler has a reference to **the angel of the Lord** in addition to MT of
2 Sam. 24. It has usually been argued that this reflects the more
developed angelology of the later period, but in fact this solution
seems now not to be so satisfactory. In the first place, **the angel**
does appear twice in MT of 2 Sam. 24, so that the difference
between the two texts is at most one of degree, not of substance.
(Note also the comparable theology in Exod. 12:23 and 2
Kg. 19:35.) Secondly, however, it is now apparent from a fragment
of 4QSamᵃ (see p. 2) that some, at any rate, of this difference in
emphasis was already found in the text of Sam. which the Chronicler
followed as his *Vorlage* (see v. 16 below). Regrettably, this text has
still not been published, and is in any case fragmentary, so that we
are never likely to know the full story; it is nevertheless noteworthy
that **the angel** appears rather unexpectedly in 2 Sam. 24:16, whereas
in the Chronicler's form of the text, this is prepared for by the
present reference.

15–27 is clearly marked out as a single paragraph, for only with
v. 27 is there a resolution of the tension established in vv. 15–16 of
the angel hovering with his drawn sword stretched towards Jerusalem. Enclosed within the framework are the accounts of David's
repentance (17) and purchase of the threshing floor (18–25), and
God's acceptance of the sacrifices offered there (26). The whole thus
becomes a fine expression of repentance (17) consequent upon God's
prior grace (15f.) in a way which yet at the same time safeguards
the real significance of man's response (26 with 27). Undergirding
the whole, however, remains the steady purpose of God in focusing
the action upon the site which is to be purchased for the temple
(15, 18f. and 26).

15. And God sent the angel: MT omits the article (cf. *NEB*),
which some find curious in view of the fact that he has already been
introduced in v. 12. 2 Sam. 24:16 has 'And when the angel stretched
forth his hand', which many prefer, both because it resolves the
apparent difficulty of God 'repenting' of a command only just given,
and because, textually speaking, it is easy to see how the text in

Chr. could have arisen from that in Sam. Despite this, however, whether the change was made by the Chronicler or stood already in his *Vorlage*, we must agree with CM, p. 251, that 'the text of Ch. should not be changed, for it is the original of the Chronicler' (cf. Michaeli, p. 110). If it be allowed at all that God **repented of the evil** (cf. Gen. 6:6; Exod. 32:14, etc.), then, theologically speaking, the time between this and the giving of the original command is not really a problem, and was probably not felt by the Chronicler. **Ornan:** in 2 Sam., usually 'Araunah'; the Chronicler's version is linguistically secondary, but seems to have become the customary form in later times (cf. LXX of 2 Sam. and Josephus *Ant.* vii. 69 and 329ff., and H. B. Rosén, *VT* 5 [1955], p. 318).

16. Although the Chronicler's text here is much fuller than the parallel in 2 Sam., a fragment from the end of 4QSam^a has preserved enough to show us that the Chronicler was almost certainly not himself responsible for the expansion (cf. F. M. Cross, *The Ancient Library of Qumrân* [1958], p. 141, and *HTR* 57 [1964], p. 294. This, of course, does not settle the issue of ultimate priority). The longer text seems to have been influenced by Num. 22:31 and Jos. 5:13–15, though the portrayal of the angel **standing between earth and heaven** (which simply means 'in the air') is paralleled in the OT only in the visions of Daniel (cf. Dan. 8:16; 10:4ff.; 12:6ff.). From the story of Balaam, in particular, comes the idea of the angel barring the way forward, and perhaps also (Num. 22:35) of the angel revealing God's will (though see further on v. 18 below). The Chronicler makes both of these elements significant in guiding David to the threshing floor (vv. 18 and 30). Similarly Jos. 5:13–15, which is verbally slightly closer than Num. 22 to the present passage, leads to the revelation to Joshua that 'the place where you stand is holy' (cf. Mosis, pp. 115f.). Whatever the textual history that has led to the account in Chronicles, we can thus see that in the story as we now have it, for whose final form, at least, the Chronicler is evidently responsible, there is good use made of stereotyped language concerning the appearance of angels (see already on v. 12 above) and men's reaction to them, all harnessed for that single purpose for which the Chronicler has included the chapter in his narrative. **David and the elders, clothed in sackcloth:** we are evidently to understand that until this point there were in Jerusalem rituals of repentance and intercession on behalf of all the people. This highlights the personal acceptance of responsibility by David introduced in the next verse.

17. David's confession is more strongly worded than in 2 Sam. 24:17, though without any really material difference. **and done very wickedly:** a very slight emendation (*w^ehārō'eh* for *w^ehārēa'*), yielding the translation 'I, the shepherd, who did wrong' (*NEB*), provides a better contrast with the continuation **but these sheep**, and has long been suspected on the basis of some MSS of LXX of 2 Sam. and Josephus. It is now confirmed by 4QSamᵃ (cf. F. M. Cross, *HTR* 57 [1964], p. 294).

18. the angel of the Lord commanded Gad: in 2 Sam. 24, **Gad** appears to receive God's command directly, whereas here it is mediated through the same **angel** who previously was the agent of God's judgment, a theological development already attested in Num. 22:35 (when compared with v. 38), as suggested at v. 16 above. However, it is possible that the interpreting angel of Zechariah's visions (Zech. 1:7–6:15) should also be compared to show that the influence in this instance may not be so much from a single text as from a general refinement of the period in the understanding of the mediation of God's word, a refinement which was continued to a much greater degree in later literature, notably the Targums.

20. This verse in its present form has very little connection with 2 Sam. 24:20. While certain phrases could have arisen by textual corruption, the process is now beyond recovery. Equally, some may have already stood in the Chronicler's *Vorlage* (**Now Ornan was threshing wheat** is attested in 4QSamᵃ, according to F. M. Cross, *HTR* 57 [1964], p. 294), but at present we do not know how much. Certain it is, however, that in the text as it now stands there are a number of features which suggest that a deliberate comparison with the story of Gideon in Jg. 6 has been introduced (cf. Willi, p. 157). The basic theme is the same: the encounter of **the angel** with one who **was threshing wheat** (cf. Jg. 6:11), and we may note the offering received by supernatural fire (v. 26; cf. Jg. 6:21). Willi also compares **hid themselves** with Jg. 6:11, although the words used are different, **he turned** with Jg. 6:18, and **and saw**, in the sense of 'perceive', with Jg. 6:22. While some of this evidence is overplayed, the basic analogy is attractive. If valid, we may note once again that the appearance of the angel to Gideon led to the establishment of a permanent holy place to the Lord (Jg. 6:24), and, more tentatively, that Gideon went on from there to contend for the Lord against Baal (Jg. 6:25–32); did the Chronicler see in his account a similar development from a Jebusite sanctuary (note the use – only in Chronicles – of *māḵôm*, which can have the meaning of 'holy site' (see on 15:1), at vv. 22 and 25) to one consecrated to the Lord?

and his four sons who were with him: as the text stands, these can only be Ornan's sons, and their part in the narrative is inconsequential. Since in 2 Sam. 24 no one at the threshing floor actually sees the angel, the most that can be said is that 'the Chronicler desired to add more witnesses to the presence of the angel at this spot, since the fact consecrated the temple site . . . . The introduction of the four sons of Ornan is thus accounted for' (CM, p. 254). Some (e.g. Galling, p. 62; Mosis, pp. 113-15) have tried to argue that these were David's sons; since, according to 14:4, Solomon was David's fourth son, the temple builder would thus have been present at the designation of the site, as he is in the following chapters when the building materials are being prepared. However, this view can only be supported if **the angel** (*hammal'āk*) is read as 'the king' (*hammelek*; cf. 2 Sam. 24:20); but this then makes nonsense of v. 21, as well as destroying part of the analogy with Jg. 6. It is indeed possible that **his four sons** (*'arba'at bānâw*) has at some stage arisen by corruption from 'his servants coming on' (*ªbādâw 'ōbᵉrîm*) of 2 Sam. 24:20 (or, indeed, *vice versa*; cf. Goettsberger, p. 158); but it cannot have been by the Chronicler himself in view of the demands of the wider context in his version; thus the phrase probably already stood in his *Vorlage*, and he included it as adding slightly to the parallel with Jg. 6, but without its contributing further to the development of the narrative.

21. As David came to Ornan: this addition is made necessary by the insertion of v. 20.

22-5. David's purchase of the threshing floor from Ornan has been patterned by the Chronicler on Abraham's purchase of the cave of Machpelah from Ephron in Gen. 23. To the underlying similarity of the leading representative of the people of God buying a site for sacred purposes from a member of the indigenous population is added a number of details to make the analogy clear. Most noteworthy is the Chronicler's addition twice of the phrase **at its full price** (22), **for the full price** (24; *bᵉkesep mālē'*), exactly as at Gen. 23:9, and occurring nowhere else in the *OT*. Further, against his *Vorlage* he uses the word **give** for 'buy' at v. 22 (twice) as at Gen. 23:4 and 9, has David initiate the conversation (22) as at Gen. 23:3f., and in v. 23 gives added emphasis to **Ornan**'s initial response (which may well have been part of the bargaining process) of wishing to **give** (twice) the site to David, just as Ephron did with Abraham (Gen. 23:11). In the light of this, we may wonder whether the Chronicler's extension of the area to be purchased from **the threshing floor** to the whole **site** (vv. 22 and 25), as well as drawing attention to the sanctity of the spot (see above, on v. 20), was also influenced by the dispute in Gen. 23 over whether Abraham should purchase the cave alone or also the field in which it was found.

23. and the wheat for a cereal offering: lacking from 2 Sam., and usually explained as an introduction from the regulations of Exod. 29:38ff.; Num. 15:1ff., etc., which stipulate that **burnt offerings** should be accompanied by **a cereal offering**. However, in that case we should have expected a reference to wine and oil as well, while the **cereal offering** should have been of 'fine flour', not **wheat**. In fact, it is this latter which gives us the clue to the addition. The verse emphasises Ornan's willingness to offer everything within sight on the threshing floor. It was seen above at v. 20 that, unlike 2 Sam., the Chronicler's text has a reference to Ornan threshing wheat; this too is therefore appropriately included here.

25. The price which **David paid** is much larger here than in 2 Sam. 24:24, both because of the amount (**six hundred shekels** as against fifty) and the metal (**gold** as against silver). Several factors may have contributed: David should have paid more for the temple **site** than Abraham did for the cave ('four hundred shekels of silver', Gen. 23:16); **gold** was more appropriate since so much of it was used in the temple's construction (CM, p. 253), and an explanation of the figure **six hundred** which goes back at least as far as Rashi is that David paid fifty shekels for each of the twelve tribes: perhaps the Chronicler was seeking to emphasise thereby that 'the Temple should be the place of worship for all' (CM). More prosaically, the Chronicler thought of David buying the whole **site**, rather than just the threshing floor itself, so that he may have felt that a larger sum would be more appropriate.

26. At the second half of this verse, the Chronicler begins his own conclusion to the narrative, stressing first the acceptance of the **burnt offering** by **fire from heaven**. This confirms the choice of the site, establishes continuity with the worship at the altar of the Mosaic tabernacle (cf. Lev. 9:24) and points forward to the successful completion and dedication of the temple, whose acceptance was similarly marked by the Chronicler; cf. 2 Chr. 7:1.

27. The threat, suspended at v. 15, is now finally lifted. **Sheath** (*nāḏān*) is a Persian loan-word, and thus an important reminder that however much in this chapter concerning **the angel** may go back to a text-form of 2 Sam. different from MT (see above on vv. 14 and 16), the Chronicler has still himself determined the final shape of the narrative, a fact which should help guard against unduly exaggerated statements that might suggest the contrary (Lemke, *HTR* 58 [1965], p. 357).

21:28-22:1. Although there is a syntactical problem in v. 28 which has been much discussed (see below), it does not, fortunately, affect our understanding of the main point of the paragraph as a whole. The Chronicler aims to establish the divinely-willed continuity of worship (already alluded to in v. 26) between the Mosaic sanctuary and the future Jerusalem temple. Thus, although vv. 29–30 are clearly circumstantial, and so might almost be put in parentheses, there is a conscious contrasting of **the tabernacle of the**

Lord and **the altar of burnt offering** in v. 29 with **the house of the
Lord God** and **the altar of burnt offering** in 22:1, the latter verse
being the obvious climax of the whole. The importance of religious
and institutional continuity for fostering worship and service is well
known. By referring back in this paragraph to some of the central
themes of the previous story (e.g. **the sword of the angel of the
Lord** in v. 30), the Chronicler shows that he intends it to be its
interpretation. He invites us in reading the narrative to trace in it
the clear pointers of the divine will which, in spite of circumstances,
led David specifically to **the threshing floor of Ornan** rather than to
the expected **high place in Gibeon**, and then, through answering
by fire, demonstrated the transfer to this altar of the focus of the
nation's worship, formerly centred on the tabernacle.

28. At that time: attention is focused on this one event. There is
no necessary suggestion, as some have thought, that David never
again went to the tabernacle to worship, and Solomon certainly did,
in the Chronicler's view (cf. 2 Chr. 1:3ff.). **he made his sacrifices
there**: it is very hard to decide whether to translate this verse as a
complete sentence, as *RSV* does, or whether it should all be a
protasis to 22:1, with vv. 29–30 coming in brackets: 'At that time,
when David saw . . . and when he sacrificed there (now the tabernacle. . .) (22:1) then David said. . .'. Syntactically either are possible, so that a decision will finally rest on whether the **sacrifices** in
this verse are to be identified with the offerings of v. 26, or whether
David is thought to have sacrificed separately after that.

29. the tabernacle. . . .at Gibeon: see on 16:39.

30. could not: better, 'had been unable to'; cf. *NEB*. This is a
reference back to v. 16, not some new development. Once these
verses are understood as the Chronicler's interpretation of the whole
story, the reasons for regarding vv. 29–30 as secondary are elimin-
ated, and the contrast between 29 and 22:1 established.

22:1. Here shall be (*zeh hû'*): emphatic, and rightly understood
by *RSV* as referring to the future (the temple) rather than the
immediate present. The echo of Gen. 28:17 (RH; Rudolph), weak
at best, is thereby reduced still further, and certainly cannot support
an alleged anti-Samaritan polemic.

THE DESIGNATION OF THE TEMPLE BUILDER

22:2–19

Chapters 22–29, dealing with the closing period of David's reign,
have no parallel in other canonical books, although 'here and there
an allusion shows the Chronicler engaged in writing a kind of ex-

pansive commentary on the earlier material' (Ackroyd). If those scholars are right who regard all or most of chs. 23–7 as later additions to the Chronicler's work, then the remainder will be seen to be concentrated mainly on the integration of the reigns of David and Solomon by way of a further development of the theme of preparation for temple building. In the final form of the work, therefore, these chapters continue straight on from the preceding ones, and are thus not to be regarded as forming a separate section from that introduced at ch. 17.

Whether or not the Chronicler received any of his narrative material from earlier tradition, it cannot be denied that the chapters as we now have them are his own composition. This applies both at the level of language and style (for a study of ch. 22 in this regard, cf. J. Margain, *Semitica* 24 [1974], pp. 35–43) and, as the commentary will seek to show, at the level of broader theological structure and motifs (cf. *VT* 26 [1976], pp. 351–61, and Braun, *JBL* 95 [1976], pp. 581–90, who regards chs 22, 28 and 29 as 'of unexcelled importance for understanding these books').

Material Provision for the Temple

22:2–5

Particular stress is laid on the great quantities involved: **in quantities beyond weighing** (3); **without number. . . . great quantities** (4); **in great quantity** (5).

2. the aliens: non-Israelite inhabitants of **the land of Israel** (see further, on 2 Chr. 2:17–18). Although 2 Sam. does not recount David's levying of a corvée, it is clear that he did from the inclusion of 'Adoram (who) was in charge of the forced labour' in the list of officials of the latter part of his reign; 2 Sam. 20:24. It has usually been argued, on the basis of 1 Kg. 5:13, etc., that at any rate by the time of Solomon this included native Israelites, despite the apparently contradictory denial of 1 Kg. 9:20–22. However, Mettinger, *Solomonic State Officials*, pp. 128–39, concludes rather that only the aliens were subject to a permanent corvée (*mas ʿōbēd*), while the Israelites themselves were levied only for temporary conscription. (For an alternative account, cf. A. F. Rainey, *IEJ* 20 [1970], pp. 191–202.) In that case, the present verse will describe the origins of the permanent institution. Its description immediately after David's census may not be coincidental; cf. 2 Chr. 2:17f. For the Chronicler, the main point is to underline the comprehensive nature of David's preparations for building the temple. **dressed stones:** probably of *nari* limestone, which was widely used in Israel

at this period for ashlar masonry, and which could be quarried quite
close to Jerusalem; cf. Y. Shiloh and A. Horowitz, *BASOR* 217
(1975), pp. 37–48.

3. As already noted (18:8 and 11), some of the **bronze** came as
booty from David's wars. It may further be inferred from 1
Sam. 13:19–22 that after David's defeat of the Philistines, **iron**
would have become more plentiful. **clamps:** it may be conjectured
that these were horizontal 'bands', heavily decorated bronze forms
of which have been discovered at Balâwât, near Nineveh; cf. R.
D. Barnett, *Assyrian Palace Reliefs* (1961), pp. 12ff. and plates 138–
9.

4. cedar, from Lebanon, was highly regarded as a building material throughout the ancient Near East. The reference to **the Si-
donians and Tyrians** is echoed at Ezr. 3:7 in the building of the
second temple.

5. This verse explains why David undertook such lavish preparations: unaided, Solomon would be unable to meet the demands
posed by the task of temple building (see further 29:1–2). This
emphasis of the Chronicler's, lacking in Sam.–Kg., is balanced by
his heightened emphasis on David's inability to complete the task
as well; cf. 17:4; 22:7f.; 28:2f.; 2 Chr. 6:7–9. Thus the comple-
mentary nature of their reigns is underlined. Both were necessary
if the temple was to be built. This theme, which spans this whole
section, thus forges the reigns of these two kings into a united
monarchy indeed. **David said:** sc. 'to himself'. **young and inex-
perienced:** cf. 29:1. Ackroyd finds here an echo of Solomon's self-
description in his prayer at Gibeon (1 Kg. 3:7) as 'a mere child,
unskilled in leadership' (*NEB*), omitted by the Chronicler in his
version of that scene in 2 Chr. 1:8–10 (see also v. 12 below). If so,
it is noteworthy that the Chronicler has transposed the setting of
the story with its gift of wisdom to Solomon in such a way that it
too is integrally linked to the temple building (see on 2 Chr. 1).
Young (*na'ar*) is not nearly so narrowly defined as in English (cf. J.
Macdonald, *JNES* 35 [1976], pp. 147–70) and so cannot help determine Solomon's age at his accession.

David's Charge to Solomon

22:6–16

This important paragraph is in some senses parallel with 1 Kg. 2:1–
9, but, apart from the fact that it stands earlier in the narrative, the
Chronicler has so reworked it with themes and idioms of his own
that it must be regarded as a fresh composition. A particularly

dominant influence seems to have been reflection on the transition of leadership from Moses to Joshua (Dt. 31–Jos. 1; see the articles cited in the introduction to this chapter).

7. The Chronicler has appropriately put back into David's mouth the sentiments attributed to him by Solomon in his prayer at the dedication of the temple (1 Kg. 8:17; 2 Chr. 6:7).

8. In the oracle of Nathan to David (2 Sam. 7; 1 Chr. 17), no explicit reason is given for the prohibition to build the temple. In 1 Kg. 5:3–5, however, it is explained that he could not build 'because of the warfare with which his enemies surrounded him, until the Lord put them under the soles of his feet'. This passage, omitted by the Chronicler is his parallel section in 2 Chr. 2, is here given a further, theological interpretation. David's **great wars** not only left him insufficient time for so great a task, but caused him to **shed much blood** (see also 28:3 and 17:1, 10). It is anachronistic to read into these sentiments modern ideals concerning pacifism and the service of God (Rudolph, p. 151), for the Chronicler is second to none in the *OT* in his portrayal of God's activity in warfare on behalf of Israel in close conjunction with religious ceremonial and in answer to prayer (see, for instance, his rephrasing of 17:10, his interest in David's wars in 18–20, and especially his accounts of various battles in 2 Chr. 13ff.). Nor does the generalising statement here allow us to suppose that some particular fault, such as the removal of Urijah the Hittite, is in mind. There is thus a probably deliberate contrast, if not reinterpretation, intended of the accusations of Shimei in 2 Sam. 16:7f., where the phrase 'man of blood' is used of David with evident overtones of ethical culpability. Rather, the words **before me upon the earth** point to this activity as constituting a ritual uncleanness which debarred David from the particular task of temple building, just as in the Levitical and priestly laws many conditions and functions which can in no way be deemed ethically culpable similarly lead to periods of ritual uncleanness and hence exclusion for a while from the cult (Goettsberger).

9. In contrast to David, 'the man of wars' (*'îš milḥāmôt*, 28:3, rendered too simply as 'warrior' by *RSV*), Solomon is described as **a man of** 'rest' (*'îš mᵉnûḥāh*). **peace** is a quite misleading rendering here, for it is not distinguished from the second half of the verse, where a different word is used, and it further obscures a very important line of thought here being developed. Equally, **I will give him peace** (*waha̓nîḥôtî*) should be translated 'I will give him rest'. In the earlier history, there is confusion over this theme. It was precisely when the Lord 'had given (David) rest from all his enemies round about' (2 Sam. 7:1, and cf. v. 11) that David first expressed

his wish to build the temple, whereas in 1 Kg. 5:3–5 (whose influence on the present passage has already been noted in the previous verse), Solomon says that David was constantly engaged in war, 'but now the Lord has given me rest on every side'. Thus, in accordance with the Deuteronomic injunction (Dt. 12:9–11) that when the Lord gives his people 'rest' in the land they shall gather to a central sanctuary, Solomon was now in a position to build the temple. The Chronicler, however, smoothes out the confusion and makes the theme serve the interests of his wider purposes: the references to 'rest' in 2 Sam. 7:1 and 11 are omitted or altered at 1 Chr. 17:1 and 10 (q.v.), and in this verse he transfers them instead into part of the dynastic promise, thus involving Solomon personally, along with David, in the establishment of the dynasty; see the introduction to ch. 17. Moreover, it may be suggested that the theme is part of a Moses-Joshua typology in which Moses was disqualified from accomplishing the goal of his ministry in leading the people into the promised land, whereas Joshua, appointed as his successor for precisely this task, was the one who gave 'rest' and 'peace' to Israel; cf. Jos. 1:13, 15; 21:44; 22:4; 23:1.

This whole theme is supported in the second half of the verse by an exploitation of the very name **Solomon** (*šᵉlōmōh*) itself, for there will be **peace** (*šālôm*) **in his days**. Again it may be intentional that this is linked with **quiet** (*šeḳeṭ*), a word which comes twice at important stages in the description of Joshua's achievements (Jos. 11:23; 14:15. *RSV*, however, renders 'rest' on both occasions).

10. The continuation links the charge closely with the dynastic oracle. As at 17:11–14 above, it is applied at this stage to Solomon only (note the emphatic **he shall build . . . He shall be**). Thus, although this verse may have contributed to messianic formulations, it should not itself be so interpreted (*contra* Th. Lescow, *ZAW* 79 [1967], pp. 205–7, and Newsome, *JBL* 94 [1975], pp. 208–10). However, it is noteworthy that with the words **I will establish his royal throne in Israel for ever** (cf. 17:12 and 14), Solomon's role in establishing the dynasty's future is again introduced. Although the promise here appears to be unconditional (contrast 28:7, 9, etc.), it is isolated in this regard in the Chronicler's handling of the dynastic oracle, and it is probably intended to be modified in a conditional direction by David's heavy stress in the following verses on the need for obedience and carefulness; see further, the introduction to ch. 17 above.

11. Now, my son: with this verse, the charge proper begins. Its three elements closely resemble those of the installation of Joshua in Dt. 31:23 and Jos. 1:6, 9, namely (a) encouragement; (b) description of task; (c) assurance of divine aid, though they occur here in vv. 11–13 in the order (c), (a), (b) (see, in addition to the articles cited above, N. Lohfink, *Scholastik* 37 [1962], pp. 32–44; D. J. McCarthy, *JBL* 90 [1971], pp. 31–41, and K. Baltzer, *The Covenant Formulary* [1971], pp. 72–8). The form, if that is not too strong a term, recurs at 28:10 and 20, and perhaps in vv. 14–16 below. The phraseology is also closely comparable with that of Dt.–Jos., as will be pointed out below. While it is true, as Braun has observed (*JBL* 95 [1976], pp. 587–8), that at this point Solomon is installed exclusively to build **the house of the Lord your God**, other elements which are included in the parallel with Moses–Joshua relate more to Solomon's rule over Israel generally (see v. 12 and 29:23, 25, and 2 Chr. 1:1). Thus the purpose of drawing the parallel will have been rather to characterise the reigns of David and Solomon as a whole, even though in the Chronicler's presentation these are dominated by the theme of temple building.

the Lord be with you: cf. Dt. 31:6, 8, 23; Jos. 1:5, 9. **so that you may succeed**: 'apart from incidental uses. . ., Jos. 1:8 provides the only example of the hiphil of *ṣālaḥ* in Deuteronomy or the deuteronomistic history'; Braun, p. 587; see on 2 Chr. 7:11 below. **as he has spoken concerning you**: see the preceding verse.

12. discretion and understanding: again, David's prayer rather anticipates that of Solomon in 1 Kg. 3:6–9; see v. 5 above. **when he gives you charge** (*wîṣawwᵉkā*): only in Dt. 31:14, 23 and Jos. 1:9 is this verb used elsewhere in 'installation' contexts with God as the subject. In view of the many other parallels with those passages, there would seem to be no need to emend the text here (*contra BHS*), despite the slightly strained syntax.

12–13. The encouragement to **keep the law** and **to observe the statutes and the ordinances which the Lord commanded Moses** because then **you will prosper** has clearly been influenced by Jos. 1:7–9.

13. Be strong and of good courage: cf. Dt. 31:7, 23 and Jos. 1:6, 7, and 9, etc. **Fear not; be not dismayed**: cf. Dt. 31:8 and Jos. 1:9.

14–16. In view of the already vast figures of passages like 29:4 and 7 and vv. 2–5 above, it is clear that the quantities specified here are consciously and intentionally exaggerated, so that attempts to supply modern equivalents are futile. The exaggeration draws attention both to the magnificence of the future temple (cf. v. 5) and to the comprehensive nature of David's preparation for it. For a sense of proportion, compare the 420 (LXX: 120) talents of gold, already regarded as remarkable, which Solomon's fleet brought back from Ophir, 1 Kg. 9:28.

with great pains (*bᵉ῾onyî*): in view of the exactly parallel structure at 29:2 (obscured in *RSV*) where 'so far as I was able' is equivalent to the present phrase, *RSV*'s rendering is the most probable. Others, however, are possible, and fit the immediate context equally well; e.g. 'in my poverty' (LXX, V, *AV* mg.), 'in my humility' or 'in spite of all my troubles' (*NEB*).

16. Arise and be doing! The Lord be with you! These clauses correspond to elements (b) and (c) of the form of 'installation' outlined in v. 11 above. If David's account of the preparations he has made in vv. 14–16a may be described as 'encouragement', then all three elements are found again in these verses.

David's Charge to the Leaders of Israel
22:17–19

Just as David's charge to Solomon in the preceding verses was a private affair, so here 'this little pericope is directed to the officials alone' (Myers). Since chs 28 and 29 clearly record a fully public gathering (cf. 28:1, 8, etc.), there is no need to regard this paragraph as a secondary doublet. It again follows the same pattern as that outlined at v. 11 above, with element (c) in v. 18, (a) in 19a, and (b) in 19b.

18. Cf. v. 9. Again *RSV*'s **peace** might be more accurately translated 'rest'.

19. to seek: cf. 10:13–14 and 13:1–3. **the holy vessels of God:** it is clear from 2 Chr. 5:5 that this refers to the vessels that were in the tent, whereas 28:13ff. speaks of new ones that were to be made in addition for the temple. There would thus seem to be neither contradiction nor doublet (*contra* Rudolph).

DAVID'S ORGANISATION OF THE LEVITES
23:1–27:34

Two major and related problems face the commentator of this section of Chronicles. First, many have observed that there is a close link between 23:2 and 28:1, so that from a narrative point of view 23:3–27:34 seems to be intrusive. They therefore conclude that the whole of the intervening section is secondary to the Chronicler's original composition. Second, whatever be the attitude adopted to this first point, various literary levels have been detected even within these chapters. On the details of this, however, no particular analysis may be said to enjoy a consensus.

Since a full discussion of these issues would go beyond the scope of the present commentary, it has proved necessary to devote a special study to them; cf. *SVT* 30 (1979), pp. 251–68. Only the results can be summarised here. The context for the various lists is provided by 23:3–6a. This makes clear (a) that David was personally responsible for the organisation of the Levites into divisions; (b) that only Levites were involved at this stage; and (c) that the Levites were subdivided into four classes, namely, those who had charge of the work in the house of the Lord, officers and judges, gatekeepers, and singers.

When the lists are examined in this light, and when account is also taken of various discrepancies within the lists themselves, the whole of chs 23–27 is found to fall neatly into two, internally self-consistent layers. The primary, and much shorter, strand, is made up of 23:6b–13a, 15–24; 25:1–6; 26:1–3, 9–11, 19; and 26:20–32. Each of these four short sections is governed by one of the categories of Levite listed in 23:3–6a. In each case David is responsible for their organisation, and they each present a list based on genealogical principles.

The rest of the material is to be attributed to the same pro-priestly reviser whose hand has been detected elsewhere, especially in chs 15–16. Various factors point to his work being about a generation after the primary layer. One of the several ideological factors which bind this secondary material together is the introduction for the first time of the division of the priests and Levites into twenty-four courses, a system which then endured with relatively little change throughout the remainder of the second temple period. It thus appears that in the late Persian period the Jerusalem priesthood underwent a major reform, perhaps because of the defection of some of its leaders to the nascent Samaritan community at Shechem (cf. *SVT* 30 [1979], pp. 267f.). The reviser thus wished by his work to underline, amongst other things, the legitimacy of the reformed priesthood which remained.

A number of factors, some of which will be noted in the comments below, point to the inclusion of the primary layer by the Chronicler himself. It is sufficient to mention in this introduction that some such material is to be expected on the basis of the general context. From ch. 17 onwards the Chronicler's overriding concern has been David's preparation for the building of the temple. Just as in chs 15–16 he was concerned to explain the new role of the Levites after the ark had been brought to Jerusalem, so now it is not at all surprising to find that he goes on to make some reference to the preparation by David for their ordering in the future temple, a point further supported by such passages as 2 Chr. 8:14; 23:18 and 35:4, where explicit reference is made to David's ordering of the Levites.

On the apparent jump between 23:2 and 28:1, see the comments at 28:1 below, where it will be argued that that verse originally functioned as a literary device in the Chronicler's narrative to mark the inclusion of material germane to the author's main purpose but which does not, however, exactly fit his narrative sequence.

23:1 is intended as a general heading to the rest of the Chronicler's account of David's reign (cf. 29:22ff.); there is no suggestion that Solomon was made **king** at precisely this point, before the ordering of the Levites, etc. Once again, the Chronicler moves straight to the divinely ordained outcome, passing over the intrigues which characterise the end of 2 Samuel and the beginning of 1 Kings. Indeed, since **old and full of days** is a description which implies considerable honour (cf. 29:28; Gen. 25:8; 35:29; Job 42:17), there may even be intended a slight corrective to the rather negative portrayal of the end of David's reign in the earlier history (Rudolph; see further 29:24). On the co-regency of David and Solomon, cf. E. Ball, *VT* 27 (1977), pp. 268–79.

2. See on 28:1 for the literary purpose of this verse. It is possible that **and the priests** was added by the reviser of the following chapters, but more probably the Chronicler himself introduced it as part of the stereotyped threefold division of the population current in his time (cf., for instance, 13:2; 2 Chr. 30:25; 35:8; Ezr. 2:70, etc.).

The Introduction to David's Organisation of the Levitical Divisions

23:3–6a

3. thirty years old and upward: as in Num. 4. Elsewhere in Numbers, the age is given as 25, while later in the present chapter (vv. 24 and 27), in 2 Chr. 31:17 and in Ezr. 3:8 it is only 20. It does not seem possible, on any normal dating of these passages, to argue for a steady lowering of the age to ease the shortage of Levites. **were numbered:** cf. Num. 3:14ff. and 4. This might seem to contradict 21:6, but, as indicated there, there is a great difference between the general census of ch. 21 and the numbering here for the purpose of arrangement into divisions. **thirty-eight thousand:** is generally regarded as an exaggeration, in view of the much smaller numbers of Levites elsewhere in Chronicles as well as in Ezra-Nehemiah.

The three elements of this verse referred to above suggest that Rudolph may be right in regarding this paragraph as based on material earlier in date than the Chronicler. Our remarks have made clear, however, that the differences between it and other parts of

Chronicles are not so great as to oblige us to deny that the Chronicler could have incorporated it himself, especially when it is remembered that he was not responsible for the clash with vv. 24 and 27 (see below).

4-5. The four groups of Levites are listed here in descending numerical order. In the following more detailed lists, by contrast, they are dealt with on the basis of their relationship with the centre of worship in the temple. It is possible that the position of the musicians after the **gatekeepers,** and their comparatively small number, point again to an origin for this fragment independent of the Chronicler.

David said: not in MT, but added to make sense of the text in view of the first person **I have made** in v. 5. **Shall have charge of the work in the house of the Lord:** although it is true that later on the Levites are portrayed as having charge of temple maintenance (e.g. 2 Chr. 24; 29:5ff.; 34:12f.), there is no reason to limit the meaning of this phrase to that alone. It was evidently understood to have a much wider significance by the reviser in vv. 25ff.

6a. There should be a full stop after **divisions.** The first half of the verse then concludes this introductory paragraph.

The Temple Levites

23:6*b*-32

The bulk of this paragraph comprises a genealogically constructed list of the heads of the fathers' houses of the Levites. Although there are several points of contact with similar lists elsewhere (e.g. 1 Chr. 6), it also includes names found only here, while some of the differences are sufficiently striking (e.g. vv. 7f.) to show that the Chronicler has incorporated an originally independent piece. On the surface, no branch of the family comes down even as far as David's time. It is thus probable that the expression **the sons of** is to be understood loosely. The names of the heads of houses will then be those current at the time of the list's composition, linked directly to the main, well-known descendants of Levi.

Many scholars have thought that there should be twenty-four houses, in order to fit the passage to the twenty-four priestly courses, even though the present text gives only twenty-two (or twenty-three, according to CM). However, if the literary analysis of these chapters which was summarised above is correct, the twenty-four courses will have developed later than the Chronicler, so that the various textual speculations in this direction will have been unnecessary. It is, of course, possible that the text has suffered in places during the course of transmission, but there is no evidence beyond simple conjecture for emending it. In the circumstances, therefore, it is wisest to accept it, from the textual point of view, at face value.

6b. corresponding to: the preposition used here does not demand any link with what precedes. It can be used to introduce an independent list, and is best rendered 'concerning' (Welch, *WC*, p. 84) or even omitted in translation.

7. Ladan: elsewhere, the first son of **Gershon** is always Libni (6:17; Exod. 6:17; Num. 3:18). It has been suggested that Ladan was a descendant of Libni whose family became more prominent in later times.

9. Shimei: a different man from his namesake in vv. 7 and 10. This is not really a problem, though some have thought that another name, since lost to us, originally stood here, and that the present text arose through scribal confusion.

13–14. The explanatory expansion included in these verses is out of place in a list of heads of fathers' houses. It exactly reflects, however, the viewpoint of the priestly reviser whose hand has been detected elsewhere, and so should probably be attributed to him.

22. It is not clear whether the list intends to include **Eleazar** as a fathers' house or not. CM argue strongly that, since the regulations of Num. 27:4 and 36:6 were observed, his line was legitimately continued through his **daughters**.

24. The Chronicler added this conclusion to the list. He used verbal similarities with vv. 3–4 to show that he intended the list to be understood as an amplification of the first group mentioned in v. 4.

from twenty years old and upward: it is important to realise that this phrase, which contradicts v. 3, stands in MT at the very end of the verse. Verse 25, however, which comes at the head of the passage from the later reviser, is linked in sense by its first word 'for', not to this phrase, but to the substance of the verse with its reference to **the service of the house of the Lord** (Rudolph); this doubtless accounts for *RSV*'s rearrangement of the verse. The phrase under discussion must therefore have been added at an even later time. For Levitical service to start at **twenty years old** is not envisaged in the Pentateuch, though cf. 2 Chr. 31:17; Ezr. 3:8. Probably, the age was changed from time to time under the pressure of circumstances. We may then surmise either that the glossator wished to invoke Davidic authority for the practice current in his own time, or that he simply aimed at explaining away the difference between 23:3 and 2 Chr. 31:17.

25–32. It is widely agreed that this passage cannot come from the same hand as the earlier part of the chapter, first, because in vv.

30–31 it ignores the distinctions of vv. 4–5 which are carefully observed in vv. 6–24, and, second, because it is clear from vv. 28, 29 and 32 that its main purpose is to draw a careful distinction between priests and Levites. Such a concentration is out of place in the context as governed by the earlier part of the chapter, but is fully in line with the concerns of the priestly reviser.

25. The Lord . . . has given peace to his people: this reflects a different outlook from that of the Chronicler himself; see above on 17:1 and 10 and 22:9.

26. The need for changes in the nature of Levitical service after the establishment of a permanent cult in Jerusalem is recognised by the Chronicler (e.g. 6:31; 15–16). He, however, in dependence primarily on Deuteronomy, develops the theme in terms of the resting of the ark and the consequent rights of the Levites to participate in the temple cult. Here, by contrast, the priestly reviser follows the alternative tradition which stresses the role of **the Levites** as carriers rather of **the tabernacle** and **the things for its service** (cf. Num. 3–4; von Rad, *GCW*, pp. 107–9). Similarly, the theme is not used in the following verses to advance the rights of the Levites, but rather the subordinate nature of their duties is emphasised.

27. This verse disrupts the evident continuity between vv. 26 and 28. It is a misplaced gloss on v. 24*b*, seeking to explain the discrepancy with v. 3. It is not very apt, however, because the whole section, introduced at 23:1, is properly to be regarded as **the last words of David.**

28–29. The Levitical duties of cleaning and helping to prepare the offerings revolve round the periphery only of the temple cult, and reflect slightly less responsibility than 9:28–32. The attitude of the author seems to be that **to assist the sons of Aaron** is a way of suppressing, rather than exalting, their status. The various types of **offering** are dealt with more fully in Lev. 1–7.

30–31. The introduction here of Levites with responsibility for music shows the different outlook of this paragraph from that of the first half of the chapter. It was important for the reviser to deal with them in this way, however, because their duties involved close contact with the priests.

The Sons of Aaron

24:1–19

It is not surprising that, after having drawn so careful a distinction between the priests and the Levites, the reviser should now go on

to give details of priestly courses obtaining at his time. Fragments
of evidence from later times suggest that, once established, this
order continued with remarkably little change for most of the rest
of the period of the second temple. Needless to say, such treatment
of the priests is quite out of place in the Chronicler's own composition, which in this section is governed by 23:3–6a. Its secondary
nature is confirmed by its direct attachment to the end of the
previous chapter. Moreover, the organisation of the priests by lot
(v. 5) contradicts the system of royal appointment of 23:6a.

1–2. The fundamental **divisions of the sons of Aaron** follow the
common biblical tradition; cf. 6:3 and Exod. 6:23; Num. 3:2–4,
etc. However, the embarrassing reason for the death of **Nadab and
Abihu . . . before their father** (Num. 3:4) is suppressed, suggesting
where the sympathies of the reviser lay. Only the families of **Eleazar
and Ithamar** remained for priestly service.

3. A leading representative of each of these families is said to have
assisted David in the organisation. Both are drawn from 18:16.
Zadok, well known as a leading priest during both David's and
Solomon's reigns, was firmly established in the tradition (if not in
fact; see on 12:28) as one **of the sons of Eleazar. Ahimelech** may
well have been from the same family (compare 18:16 with 1
Sam. 22:20), but since this is not explicit in 18:16 by itself, the
author is able, for his schematic purposes, to have him represent
the sons of Ithamar, an association not attested elsewhere.

4. The superiority of **the sons of Eleazar** suggested in the previous verse, and doubtless actual at the time of the writer, is here
spelt out.

5. **all alike**: cf. 24:31; 25:8; and 26:13, all passages from the pen
of the reviser. The mechanics of lot-casting for groups of unequal
numbers are explained in the next verse. The point being stressed
here is that the larger group was not given precedence over the
smaller. This was because both families alike included **officers of
the sanctuary and officers of God**. The precise significance of these
titles is not certain, however. It has been suggested that the two
phrases represented the favoured titles of the two groups, which
were opposed to one another in the post-exilic period until they
were here reconciled (Welch, *WC*, p. 87). **officers of God**, however,
might well be an example of the use of the divine name as a
superlative (cf. D. Winton Thomas, *VT* 3 [1953], pp. 209–24; *VT*
18 [1968], pp. 120–4), to be rendered 'outstanding leaders'. (No
evidence has been advanced to support the alternative translation
'governors of the house of God'; cf. N. Avigad, *IEJ* 7 [1957],
pp. 149f.) Similarly, **officers of the sanctuary**, which otherwise
occurs only at Isa. 43:28 (a verse with difficulties of its own; cf. K.

Elliger, *Deuterojesaja* [1978], pp. 362f. and 368f.), is not an acceptable translation, since *ḳōdeš* would have to have the definite article
(as, for instance, at 23:32; 29:3; 2 Chr. 5:11; 29:5; 30:19, etc.).
When it does not, it is used descriptively; hence, 'holy officers' (e.g.
16:29, 'holy array'; cf. R. N. Whybray, *Isaiah 40–66* [1975], p. 93).
The two phrases are thus general descriptions rather than specific
titles, and stand virtually in apposition to one another, **and** having
the sense of 'even'.

6. **the scribe Shemaiah** is not found elsewhere. The text at the
end of the verse is uncertain, so that the procedure adopted cannot
be reconstructed in detail with any confidence, except that it is clear
that the lots of each family were kept separate so that they could be
drawn in a regular order. **one chosen for Ithamar** represents a
slight emendation based on several vrs., and favoured by many
commentators, for MT 'chosen, chosen'. This latter, however, could
be construed as a distributive use of repetition, which would mean
more or less the same as the emended text ('and then always one
chosen for. . .'; cf. Keil). Either way, the alternating draw could
only continue for the first sixteen names. The remaining eight would
all come from **Eleazar**. Since a similar procedure may have been
followed in ch. 25, this has been defended by many. Rudolph,
however, finds it unsatisfactory in view of v. 4*b*, which he thinks
suggests a 2:1 ratio throughout the draw. He therefore emends and
restores conjecturally to read 'one father's house and one father's
house being chosen for Eleazar. . .'. It is not certain, however, that
v. 4 demands this element of precision.

7–18. The order established by lot is presented in a straightforward manner, and reflects the final stage in the post-exilic development of the priestly courses for which we have evidence. As
already indicated, a number of those named are found in other lists,
both biblical (principally Ezr.-Neh.) and later, though they cannot
all be mentioned here.

7. **The first lot fell to Jehoiarib:** since the family of the Maccabees
was of this line (cf. 1 Mac. 2:1), it has often been argued that this
list must date from the Maccabean period at the earliest. In fact,
however, quite apart from the unlikelihood of so late a date even
for the reviser of Chronicles, this point alone could not establish
such a date for the list as a whole; cf. Liver, *Chapters in the History
of the Priests and Levites*, pp. 35ff. At the very most, it might point
to later editorial activity. It is, of course, possible that the family of
Jehoiarib was in any case prominent before the time of the
Maccabees.

10. **Abijah:** cf. Lk. 1:5.

The Rest of the Sons of Levi

24:20–31

This list shows itself as the work of the reviser from its connection
with what precedes, but it also presupposes the initial list of Levites
in 23:6–23 by recapitulating parts of it in the same order and then
extending them by one generation. Clearly, the reviser was bringing
the situation up to date. Verse 31 suggests he reached a final total
of twenty-four courses for the Levites, as for the priests, but quite
how is not so clear to us, especially as the sons of Gershon (23:7–
11) are not taken into account here.

   20. Jehdeiah is added to the genealogy of 23:16 (**Shubael** =
'Shebuel'). The rest of the information given is simply in order to
locate him accurately within the earlier list. The same procedure is
followed throughout this passage.

   21. Isshiah is added to 23:17.

   22. Jahath is added to 23:18.

   23. The start of this verse requires emendation. *RSV* has made
it follow 23:19 exactly; RH, by contrast, conjecture that originally
a further name was added to 'the sons of' **Jeriah**.

   24–25 add **Shamir** and **Zechariah** to the family of 23:20.

   26–27. MT, represented by *RSV*, seems to be corrupt because of
its disjointed nature. **Beno** simply means 'his son'. With a minimum
of emendation, Myers follows Rudolph in suggesting: 'The sons of
Merari were Mahli and Mushi; of his sons, Jaaziah his son. The
sons of Merari, by his son Jaaziah, were Shoham. . . '. This would
be the most extensive addition to the list of ch. 23, adding a third
son to **Merari** with three further sons of his own. On **Shoham**, cf.
L. Kopf, *VT* 8 (1958), p. 206.

   28 and **30** repeat the substance of 23:22*a*, 23 and 24*a*, while **29**
adds **Jerahmeel** to 23:22*b*.

   31. Cf. vv. 3 and 5. This summarising verse integrally links the
paragraph as a whole to what precedes.

The Singers

25:1–31

Our analysis of this list of singers in *SVT* 30 (1979), pp. 255–7,
suggests that vv. 1–6 were the Chronicler's composition, the remainder being the work of the reviser who wrote under the impact
of the institution of the twenty-four courses. The Chronicler's placing of this list immediately after that of the Levites was doubtless
due to the close association of their respective functions in the cult

(e.g. 2 Chr. 29:25ff.; cf. CM, p. 275). For further discussion of the Levitical singers, see on 6:31-32 and the introduction to chs 15-16. In the latter, an outline of the development of these guilds in the post-exilic period was supplied (following Gese). The order of Asaph, Heman and Jeduthun in the present passage (v. 1) is the same as stage IIIA, but the numbers attributed to each family indicate the increasing prominence of Heman (see v. 5) and so bring it close to stage IIIB, which (against Gese) we took to reflect the period of the Chronicler himself. This supports our attribution of these verses to him, and equally renders very questionable any attempt to make them later, for by that time Jeduthun had been replaced by Ethan.

1. **the chiefs of the service . . . for the service:** based primarily on Num. 8:25, CM have presented a strong case for the rendering 'for the chiefs of the serving host' (*sc.* 'of Levites'). **who should prophesy:** in vv. 2, 3 and 5 following, and at 2 Chr. 20:14; 29:25; 34:30 and 35:15, the Levitical singers are represented as standing in direct continuity with the cultic prophets of pre-exilic Israel (cf. A. R. Johnson, *The Cultic Prophet in Ancient Israel* [1962²], especially pp. 69-74; *The Cultic Prophet and Israel's Psalmody* [1979], pp. 130f.; there is less evidence for the view of Petersen that the Chronicler wished to present the singers as inheritors of the tradition of classical prophecy). The evidence of the present passage clearly shows, however, that no activity beyond regulated instrumental (and vocal?) performance is involved. This representation may have been facilitated by the fact that already in the earlier period these prophets are known to have made use of music (1 Sam. 10:5; 2 Kg. 3:15), and by the suggestion of their association with the musical guilds of the first temple, part of whose work may have survived in some of the Psalms.

The list (*mispār*): despite the objections of most commentators, this is an acceptable translation; cf. its use by the Chronicler in exactly this sense against his *Vorlage* at 11:11. By contrast the word is used by the reviser in its more normal sense of 'number' at v. 7 below.

2. With the exception of an occasional individual, neither these nor the other names included in this chapter are recorded elsewhere as Levitical singers. **Asharelah:** a mistaken conflation of 'Asharel. These are. . . ' (Goettsberger). It is less certain whether the number 'four', expected on the basis of vv. 3 and 5, has also dropped out (so Rudolph).

3. **Shimei:** though absent from MT, this name is correctly restored by *RSV* on the basis of v. 17 to make up the **six** sons of **Jeduthun.**

4-5. Since at least 1870 (cf. H. Ewald, *Ausführliches Lehrbuch der hebräischen Sprache des alten Bundes* [1870⁸], p. 680), it has been recognised that the names in the second half of v. 4 are onomastically unusual, and that with but slight redivision of a few words and some repointing it is possible to read them as (not quite regular) lines of poetry. There has been a good deal of discussion as to the detail of this reconstruction (in addition to the commentaries, cf. E. Kautzsch, *ZAW* 6 [1866], p. 260; P. Haupt, *ZAW* 34 [1914], pp. 142-5; J. Böhmer, *BZ* 22 [1934], pp. 93-100; H. Torczyner, *JBL* 68 [1949], pp. 247-9; Petersen, pp. 64ff.); but the consensus of moderate opinion is represented, for instance, by Myers, who renders:

> Be gracious to me, Yahweh, be gracious to me;
> My God art thou;
> I have magnified, and I will exalt [my] helper (Rudolph: 'thy help');
> Sitting [in] adversity I said,
> Clear signs give plentifully.

Assuming this to be at any rate approximately correct, it must first be observed that the names involved, though curious, were certainly regarded as genuine by the reviser in vv. 23ff., and by the Chronicler himself here, since they are needed to make up the **fourteen sons** of v. 5. If, as seems probable, these lists reflect conditions in the writer's own day, we have no alternative to regarding these as names in current use at that time. (The argument that the names were fabricated simply to make up the numbers of a utopian presentation is unable to explain why the Chronicler did not invent more ordinary names, for the present list would not have carried conviction with his contemporaries.)

On the other hand, it is implausible to suggest that, either by design or coincidence, nine names should have come together to form a single poem. This problem is eased, if not solved, by the observation that, despite attempts to suggest that even as a fragment they make sense form-critically, the lines are rather disjointed and were not necessarily connected with each other. More plausible is the view of Myers that we have here a catalogue of five 'incipits', i.e. the first lines of five separate Psalms which served as their titles. None consists of more than two names. Thus it may be suggested that members of five separate families or sections of the guilds were called, perhaps playfully, after the openings of Psalms which they were regularly accustomed to sing.

the king's seer: though a comparable title is used of Gad in 21:9, in the present context the term has no more significance than 'to prophesy' in the sense determined at v. 1 above. It is noteworthy

that at 2 Chr. 29:30 the title of **seer** is attributed to Asaph and at
2 Chr. 35:15 to Jeduthun, so that there is no distinction in this
regard between the heads of the three families of Levitical singers.
This complete picture, presented in three different parts of Chronicles, provides a further small pointer to the inclusion of the primary
layer of these chapters in the work of the Chronicler himself.
according to the promise of God: we know nothing about this,
unless it was seen in the fact of a large family itself. **to exalt him:**
Heman's family in fact came to occupy the leading position among
the Levitical singers. **and three daughters:** not listed. If their number is to be included, we have a total of twenty-seven heads of
houses. More probably, however, the intention is simply to emphasise the blessing of Heman's family.

6. A conclusion to vv. 4 and 5, parallel to 2*b* and 3*b*. The words
Asaph, Jeduthun and Heman (were) should thus be deleted as an
incorrect gloss on **They . . . all** (Rudolph).

7. This verse marks the introduction to the reviser's addition, the
number **two hundred and eighty-eight** clearly linking this verse
with the list which follows. **number:** see on v. 1 above. **singing:** this
word too is used differently from the previous paragraph, where its
association with various instruments (v. 6) shows that it must have
rather the sense of 'music'.

8. Cf. 24:5 and especially 26:13.

9–31. Despite the claim that this list was determined by **lot**, it is
in fact closely related to the order of names in vv. 1–6, suggesting
a measure of artificiality in presentation. The list may be analysed
by the three families of vv. 1–6 thus (cf. RH):

Asaph	*Jeduthun*	*Heman*
1. Joseph	2. Gedaliah	–
3. Zaccur	4. Izri	–
5. Nethaniah	–	6. Bukkiah
7. Jesharelah	8. Jeshaiah	9. Mattaniah
–	10. Shimei	11. Azarel
–	12. Hashabiah	13. Shubael
–	14. Mattithiah	15. Jeremoth
	16. Hananiah	17. Joshbekashah
	18. Hanani	19. Mallothi
	20. Eliathah	21. Hothir
	22. Giddalti	23. Mahazioth
	24. Romamti-ezer	

It is difficult to believe that this regular patterning, which has the effect of keeping the curious names of v. 4*b* together at the end, can be totally separate from the situation in vv. 1–6. On the other hand, there are sufficient small differences to show that it is not directly dependent on the earlier verses either. This slight divergence within substantial overall agreement points away from the literary dependence of vv. 9–31 on 1–6 towards an actual, historical continuity, but at a slightly later time. Thus while the development of the twenty-four courses will have caused a fundamental reorganisation, yet otherwise the guilds and their family connections apparently remained unchanged.

9. After **to Joseph**, we should supply 'his sons and his brethren, twelve', as in the following verses, and in partial dependence on LXX.

The Gatekeepers

26:1–19

The divisions of the gatekeepers follow the singers, as is usual. The literary division of this chapter is particularly clear. Verses 4–8 are intrusive, both because they interrupt the treatment of the family of Meshelemiah in vv. 1–3 and 9, and because the house of Obededom, with which they deal, is not linked genealogically with the Levites, whereas the other two main families in the list are (see below). In addition, the numbers attributed to Obed-edom (sixty-two, v. 8) are out of all proportion with those attributed to Meshelemiah (eighteen, v. 9) and Hosah (thirteen, v. 11). Verses 12–18 must then also be attributed to the reviser, since the reference there to Obed-edom is quite secure in its context. This conclusion is independently supported by the fact that Meshelemiah is called Shelemiah in v. 14, which would be surprising if the whole passage were from a single hand, and secondly by the fact that the lot-casting for duties by the gatekeepers themselves in this secondary passage contradicts the overall context, as established by 23:3–6, in which the organisation of the Levites was undertaken by David personally.

In vv. 1–11, the gatekeepers are divided amongst three families, but only the two which featured in the Chronicler's own composition are firmly linked with the Levitical genealogies, that of Meshelemiah through Korah (v. 1) and that of Hosah through Merari (v. 10). The late-comer to the list, Obed-edom (v. 4), has not yet been provided with a fuller genealogical assocation. The literary development of this list thus sheds welcome light on the growth of the Levitical genealogies, and may be compared with the similar situation postulated above at 6:26–28 in the case of Samuel, and with the uncertainty surrounding the status of Obed-edom himself seen in chs 15–16.

1. Asaph: since **the Korahites** belonged to the Levitical family of Kohath (cf. 6:22 and 37f.), whereas the well-known Asaph belonged to the family of Gershom (cf. 6:39–43), we should here read 'Ebiasaph', exactly as at 9:19 (and cf. LXX^B).

4. Obed-edom: see on 15:18, 24, and 16:38.

5. for God blessed him: a clear reference to 13:14, indicating the identity of this Obed-edom with the Gittite with whom the ark was temporarily housed. The general allusion there to God's blessing is here explained, as so often (e.g. 25:5), in terms of a large family.

8. able men qualified for the service: this has already been stressed in the two preceding verses, and may thus betray the anxiety of this family to establish its position amongst the minor cultic officials. **sixty-two**: 16:38 has 'sixty-eight', which is orthographically very similar. There can be no certainty, however, whether both passages originally had the same number, or, if so, which is the correct figure.

9. continues from v. 3, after the intrusion of vv. 4–8.

10. Apart from this chapter, **Hosah** appears only at 16:38, where he is also mentioned as a gatekeeper in association with Obed-edom.

12. As in the preceding chapters, the reviser is concerned to supply fuller details of the gatekeepers' **duties**. The evident presupposition of the existence of **the house of the Lord** throughout this paragraph (vv. 12–18) excludes any setting within the lifetime of David, who accordingly is nowhere mentioned. **just as their brethren did** (*lᵉˤummat ᵃḥêhem*): precisely the same phrase occurs at 24:31, where it indicates the division of the Levites into twenty-four courses corresponding to those of the priests. A comparable intention is probable here, even though the total of twenty-four in vv. 17 and 18 below relates to the numbers on duty each day rather than in rotation.

13. Cf. 24:5, 31, and 25:8.

14. Since the three families of vv. 1–11 had to be distributed among the four gates of the temple, **Zechariah** was counted as a division in his own right alongside his father **Shelemiah** (Meshelemiah). His prominence amongst the gatekeepers had already been noted at 9:21. The description of him as a **shrewd counselor** is evidently intended to explain this, though its reference to the work of a gatekeeper is not clear.

15. It is frequently suggested that no guard would have been needed for **the south** gate in the first temple, because the south wall of the temple is thought to have backed on to the royal palace (cf.

Ezek. 43:8), and this verse is therefore said to prove the post-exilic reference of this paragraph. While we have already noted the probability of this latter conclusion on the basis of the overall context of this section, this particular argument is quite conjectural. We are told very little about the gates of the first temple, most of our information being derived from incidental references only. Some have conjectured that in fact there was a means of access between the temple and the palace (cf. T. W. Davies, *HDB* 4, p. 702), and, if so, some kind of guard might be expected. The narrative of 2 Kg. 11:9–16 is suggestive, but the occasion was unique, and not all the references there are fully understood. The significance of **the storehouse** (cf. v. 17) may have been that it included the treasury.

16. For Shuppim: this is usually deleted as a dittograph of the preceding word, and certainly no other name is expected here. However, the dittograph would not be exact; could it then be a later copyist's note meaning 'erasures' to indicate some kind of damage or other difficulty in the text he was copying? For this suggestion with reference to 7:12, cf. G. R. Driver, *Or Bib Lov* I (1957), pp. 156f. **the gate of Shallecheth:** not mentioned elsewhere. The significance of the name is disputed.

18. the parbar: usually understood as the singular of *parwārîm*, 2 Kg. 23:11 (*RSV*: 'precincts'), though the reference is not, of course, the same as here. There is no agreement about the word's derivation (Persian or Egyptian seems most probable). It would appear from the recently published 'Temple Scroll' that in the second temple, at least, it referred to an area of free-standing pillars to the west of the sanctuary, used in connection with various types of offering; cf. J. Maier, *Die Tempelrolle vom Toten Meer* (1978), pp. 42 and 92f. The topographical difficulties of these verses are suggestive of a writer who presupposes intimate, and hence contemporary, knowledge of the temple precincts.

19. This verse serves best as a conclusion to vv. 1–3 with 9–11, and so may have been included originally by the Chronicler himself.

The Officers and Judges

26:20–32

Despite its division by many commentators, this paragraph clearly constitutes a single unit because of the overarching genealogical framework supplied by the four Kohathites listed in v. 23 (cf. 23:12). It seems probable that it has been extracted from some other more extensive source, because (a) despite their introduction in v. 23, and unlike the other three families mentioned there, the

Uzzielites are not referred to in the sequel, and (b) some of the people mentioned here have already been listed in 23:6bff.; as it is unlikely that they served simultaneously in two of the four categories of 23:4f., this discrepancy points to the separate origin of the material. The Chronicler included the passage chiefly because of its reference to 'officers and judges' (v. 29; cf. 23:4); there is no reason to suppose that, if he was aware of it, he was particularly bothered by the slight inconsistency with earlier material which this involved. Nothing with certainty can be said about the earlier history of this passage. As will be seen in the comments following, the allusions of the differing verses seem to stretch throughout the period of the monarchy and into the post-exilic period. Its position at the end of the primary layer of chs 23–27 is determined by the fact that the duties involved are furthest removed from the centre of cultic activity.

20. An introduction to vv. 20–28. **Ahijah** should thus be read with LXX as 'ahêhem, 'their brethren' (cf. *NEB*: 'fellow-Levites'). In this way the Chronicler integrated the paragraph into its wider context. Two **treasuries** are distinguished. Those of **the house of God** are dealt with in vv. 21–22, those **of the dedicated gifts** in 25–28. Since vv. 12–18 are secondary to the Chronicler's composition, there is no particular link with 'the storehouses' of vv. 15 and 17.

21–22. These two verses should be taken together. The text is uncertain (though not impossible; cf. Keil), but the main point is clear: **Zetham and Joel**, of the family of Gershon (cf. 23:7–8), were responsible for the first of the treasuries mentioned in v. 20. This contained principally what was needed for the regular services, such as the temple vessels (9:28–29).

23–24. Shebuel, a Kohathite through the family of **the Amram-ites** (cf. 23:12–16), seems to have been in overall charge of both types of treasury. We might thus have expected him at the head of the list. As already noted, however, the arrangement of this material is strictly genealogical, and from that point of view his position is correct.

25–28. The treasuries of the dedicated gifts were in the charge of **Shelomoth and his brethren** from the same family. Since the titles of 26b are military, it is clear that most of **the dedicated gifts** were the spoils of war; this is further spelt out in v. 27. For **David**, cf. 18:7f. and 11. The gifts of those listed in v. 28 are not mentioned elsewhere. Some have argued that the Chronicler could not have been responsible for so favourable a reference to **Saul**, but if, as was argued above, he drew on antecedent and popular tradition for this paragraph, that objection loses its force. There is evidence for the tendency to associate temple treasures with great figures of the past

(Ackroyd), though we have no means for testing its reliability in detail.

29–32. Although we have argued that the Chronicler included vv. 20ff. primarily on account of the reference in v. 29, these verses continue to puzzle commentators. On the one hand, such secular duties for the Levites are not attested until a comparatively late period (cf. 2 Chr. 19:8–11; Neh. 11:16), whereas on the other hand it is hard to envisage such authority over the area of Transjordan (31*b*, 32) at any time between the united monarchy and the Maccabean period (cf. 1 Mac. 5:8, 45ff.). It is possible, therefore, that we here have a somewhat utopian presentation of trends that are certainly attested in the post-exilic period (cf. Ezr. 7:25, perhaps with reference to Dt. 1:15; 16:18; Neh. 11:16, and CM, Myers, and Ackroyd; mention too should be made of K. Koch, *JSS* 19 [1974], pp. 173–95, some of whose observations are relevant at this point). However, if it is true that the Chronicler was here drawing on earlier material, we may with greater probability follow the suggestion of B. Mazar, *SVT* 7 (1960), pp. 197–9 (and cf. Aharoni, *Land*, pp. 269ff.), who, particularly because of the reference to **Jazer** (v. 31), linked this paragraph with the lists of Levitical cities whose establishment he took to be an important element in the administrative reorganisation of Israel during the period of the united monarchy. In this connection, the Levites, and **the Hebronites** especially, are regarded as a group on whose loyalty the Davidic house could depend.

29. the Izharites: cf. v. 23. The **outside duties** are clearly to be distinguished from 'the service of the king' (30) and 'the affairs of the king' (32), both of which were in the hands of the Hebronites. The explanation **as officers and judges** points to a judicial role (the **officers** seem to have been subordinate executives of the **judges**, despite the order; cf. J. van der Ploeg, *OTS* 10 [1954], pp. 185–96).

30. the work of the Lord and . . . the service of the king: no more plausible suggestion has been made than that these refer to religious and secular taxes, and that the terms in v. 32*b* are synonymous.

31. the fortieth year of David's reign: in other words, his last year; cf. 1 Kg. 2:11; 1 Chr. 29:27. While this might, therefore, derive from the setting the Chronicler has given this whole passage, it is less easy to explain in this way the curious fragment of tradition with which the verse continues. **Jazer** was one of the Levitical cities (6:81), though its precise location is disputed (cf. Noth, *Aufsätze* 1, pp. 535–42).

David's Secular Arrangements

27:1–34

The whole of this chapter is to be regarded as secondary, since it is neither related to the Levites, nor deals with David's final arrangements, but describes rather his reign in general. It is thus quite unrelated to the context governed by 23:3–6*a*. In addition, the numbers in vv. 1–15 (twelve divisions of 24,000 each) reflect the orderly outlook of the other secondary material.

The chapter is made up of four separate sections (vv. 1–15, 16–24, 25–31, 32–34) which may, as the comments following will suggest, have quite separate origins. Unless v. 1 is taken as an introduction to the chapter as a whole, there is no certain way of telling whether the redactor himself compiled the chapter from separate elements available to him, or whether they had already been joined before they reached him. The nature of vv. 1–15 may just favour the first alternative.

1–15. The commanders of the monthly relays. The artificial nature of this section is clear from the fact that (a) the names of the commanders are drawn from the list of David's heroes in 11:11ff., even though historically they could not also have been commanders of large divisions (see further, on v. 7). It may be noted, however, that there are enough small differences to suggest that the dependence is not direct; and (b) a national, conscripted army, unlike a professional standing army, was called to arms only in time of war (cf. de Vaux, *AI*, p. 227). There is no evidence whatever for the very improbable suggestion of this paragraph that civilians were conscripted for a month's service each year (though contrast the characteristically spirited discussion of this chapter by Yadin, *The Art of Warfare*, pp. 279–84). Thus, while it seems that David did take measures to arrange conscription procedures on a more organised basis (cf. ch. 21), this paragraph should not be used as evidence in that connection (and still less as evidence for the situation in the time of Josiah; *contra* Junge, pp. 65ff.). Most scholars think that the Chronicler drew his inspiration for the passage from 1 Kg. 4:7ff., which describes the monthly relays for providing food for Solomon's household. It may be suggested, however, that, if this is the work of the reviser of the previous chapters, he was working rather under the influence of the recently introduced priestly courses and that he read these back into the whole of David's organisation of the affairs of the kingdom in what can only be called a utopian manner. To a far greater extent than the Chronicler himself, he wished to describe the Davidic era as one in which the whole life of the nation was arranged in perfect order around the

temple and its service, and thereby, perhaps, both to justify the
recent cultic reforms and to express the nature of a future hope
which in this way has some points of contact with the programme
of Ezek. 40–48.

1. Despite several attempts, this verse cannot be made into a
heading for the chapter as a whole. **the heads of fathers' houses**
are not mentioned in vv. 16–24, and **their officers** ($\check{s}\bar{o}\underline{t}^e\hat{r}\hat{e}hem$;
cf. 26:29) do not come in vv. 25–31, whereas in each paragraph
other titles are used (cf. vv. 16, 22 and 31). Moreover, on this view
vv. 32–34 would be left without an introduction here, and the titles
in this verse would differ unexpectedly from the order of paragraphs
within the chapter. Since all the titles, however, are well attested
elsewhere in military contexts, the verse can be taken without difficulty as a heading to vv. 2–15 on their own.

2–3. Jashobeam is called 'a Hachmonite' in 11:11, but here he
is **the son of Zabdiel** of the family of **Perez**. This is typical of the
differences between the two lists, and they will not be noted hereafter. While it is theoretically possible to harmonise the two, it is
more important to observe the literary independence of the present
passage, suggesting that some earlier tradition may well have been
used by the reviser in his utopian reconstruction. **thousand:** see the
discussion at 12:22.

4. *RSV* mg gives the full MT, preferring with most commentators
to follow LXX in the text it chooses to translate. Rudolph suggests
that the obscure words are a marginal gloss, drawing attention to
the difference between this verse and 11:12: 'and concerning his
division, (the name of) the chief officer is corrupt'.

5–6. the priest: this seems to be an attempt to link **Jehoiada** the
father of **Benaiah** (cf. 11:22–24) with the man of the same name
at 12:27. It comes here as no surprise since it was argued that 12.27–
28 are also from the priestly reviser who was responsible for the
present passage.

7. Asahel (11:26) was killed before David became king over the
whole of Israel (2 Sam. 2:18–23). Mention of him here thus establishes the artificial nature of this section. The inclusion of **his son
Zebadiah after him** shows awareness of this difficulty, but it does
not in fact remove the anachronism.

16–24. This list of tribal chiefs is integrally linked with the note
about the census in vv. 23–24, and must therefore be intended as
a list of those responsible for each tribe in that particular connection.
Since vv. 23–24 aim at casting David's role in the affair in a better
light than ch. 21, CM may well be right in suggesting that the
purpose is to show how David acted in accordance with God's
command to Moses when he took a census (Num. 1:1–19). The

order in which the tribes are listed here is unique, but it is in further support of this view that it is as close to Num. 1:5–15 as to any other biblical list. Levi, omitted from Num. 1 on account of Num. 1:47ff., is included here in v. 17 in its regular third position, and Naphtali (v. 19) is out of place on the basis of any system, but the rest follow as expected. Asher and Gad are not included in the list, perhaps, in view of the separate inclusion of Ephraim and the two halves of Manasseh, in order to keep to the number twelve. Also noteworthy is the observation that many of the names are found only in Chronicles. All these factors combine to suggest the artificial nature of the list.

Other considerations, however, point in the opposite direction. Some scholars see the inclusion of such tribes as Reuben and Simeon and both halves of Manasseh as a mark of authenticity, though in itself this argument is not strong. More significant is the reference in v. 24 to 'the chronicles of King David'. Since the author seems to feel it necessary to explain the absence from these chronicles of the numbers included in the census, despite the fact that this explanation itself leads him into tension, if not contradiction, with 21:5, it is hard to escape the conclusion that he was drawing on older material for this list, rather than simply fabricating. Indeed, perhaps his *Vorlage* included Asher and Gad, and he himself omitted them in order to reduce his list to twelve; v. 17b provides further evidence of editorial handling of antecedent material (see below). We conclude, therefore, that some earlier material of unknown origin has here been heavily reworked by the reviser. (H. Seebass, *ZAW* 90 [1978], pp. 214f., dates the material to the period of Omri/Ahab, though on somewhat speculative grounds.) His aim was to tone down the criticism of David implied in ch. 21, and thus to portray his reign in an even more idyllic light than the Chronicler himself. This conforms to his purpose established above with regard to vv. 1–15.

17. for Aaron, Zadok: as part of the original list, this reference could only have stood right at the beginning (cf. Num. 1:3), for there is no evidence that **Aaron** was ever reckoned as a tribe separate from **Levi**. It also stands out from the context on account of the fact that **Zadok**'s father is not mentioned. Thus, whether the reviser moved the phrase or in fact added it himself, there is evidence here that he reshaped earlier, inherited material, probably with the aim of drawing attention to the status of the Aaronic family.

18. Elihu, one of David's brothers: this could be a scribal error for 'Eliab' (cf. 2:13 and LXX), or it could be the otherwise unnamed eighth son of Jesse indicated by 1 Sam. 16:10f.; 17:12, or 'brother' could have the wider sense of 'relative'. In any case, since no

particular purpose is served by it in the present context, this form
of identification, rather than a reference to the father's name as
elsewhere in the list, is further evidence that the author was drawing
on older material in this passage.

23–24. This note exonerates David from blame in the matter of
the census at Joab's expense; it thus represents a quite different
tradition from ch. 21. **those below twenty years of age:** here too,
David acts in conformity with Num. 1:3. The second half of the
verse indicates that to have done otherwise would have been to
doubt God's promise to Abraham (Gen. 15:5; 22:17). **began to
number but did not finish:** contrast 21:5. The implication here is
that **Joab** intended to finish, whereas at 21:6 he purposely excluded
Levi and Benjamin because he disapproved of David's actions.
wrath: this word is not used in the account of ch. 21; but again cf.
Num. 1:53.

25–31. A list of the stewards of David's property. Most kings in
the ancient near east became landowners on a large scale, acquiring
property by a wide variety of means (cf. de Vaux, *AI*, pp. 124–6).
This list, perhaps drawn from the same source as that which formed
the basis of the previous paragraph, shows concern for several
aspects of the king's estate, such as storehouses both in Jerusalem
and the provinces, landed property used for various kinds of agri-
culture, and livestock. There is no reason to doubt the essential
historicity of the list: several of the names are attested as early, the
inclusion of an Ishmaelite and a Hagrite (vv. 29–30) would be most
unusual in a late composition, and the territorial scope of the list
favours a date in the period of the united monarchy (cf. Rudolph;
Mettinger, *Solomonic State Officials*, p. 87). In addition, Myers observes that 'there is no indication of taxation in the time of David',
which suggests that he would have had a considerable private
income.

Exactly twelve names are listed. This may be coincidental, but it
suggests the editorial handling of the reviser, conforming the list to
the pattern of the previous two. Once again, we may suppose that
he included this material in order to enhance the glory of David
who had been blessed with such wealth.

27. wine cellars: this term has now been illustrated by the discovery of a 'winery' in the excavations at Gibeon; cf. W. L. Reed
in D. Winton Thomas (ed.), *Archaeology and Old Testament Study*
(1967), pp. 234f. and 241.

32–34. In contrast with 18:15–17, which gives a list of David's
official statesmen, this passage refers rather to 'influential persons
in the immediate entourage of the king' (Mettinger, p. 9; contrast
W. McKane, *Prophets and Wise Men* [1965], pp. 17f.).

32. Jonathan, David's uncle: not otherwise known, but this is no good reason for seeking an alternative translation such as 'lover' (CM, referring to Saul's son, who, however, died before David's accession) or 'favourite nephew' (*NEB*, presumably by comparison with 20:7, but less appropriate as **a counsellor**). **Jehiel the son of Hachmoni:** also mentioned only here. **attended:** i.e. 'were tutors to' (*NEB*).

33. Ahithophel is known as David's **counsellor** from 2 Sam. 15:12. Since he defected to Absalom (2 Sam. 15:31, etc.) during the latter's rebellion and soon after committed suicide (2 Sam. 17:23), it is clear that this list cannot refer to the close of David's reign. **Hushai the Archite** remained loyal to David (2 Sam. 15:32ff., etc.), and is elsewhere called **the king's friend** (2 Sam. 15:37; 16:16), while the pun on the title in 2 Sam. 16:17 suggests that it was clearly recognised as such at that time; cf. Mettinger, pp. 63-9, with full references to earlier discussions and attestation to Egyptian parallels.

34. Jehoiada the son of Benaiah is not otherwise known, though cf. 18:17 for his family. He succeeded Ahithopel as 'counsellor' (see previous verse) after the latter's suicide. **Abiathar** is known as a long standing associate of David (1 Sam. 22:20-23). The inclusion of **Joab** as **commander of the king's army** seems out of place, especially as he did not enjoy an especially close personal relationship with David (see on 11:6 above). A later scribe, who mistakenly compared this passage with 18:15-17, where Joab heads the list, may have included him as a sort of 'cross-reference'.

THE FINAL ASSEMBLY OF DAVID'S REIGN, AND THE ACCESSION OF SOLOMON

28:1-29:30

The account of David's last acts leading to Solomon's accession is picked up from 23:2. With the exception of only a few short fragments, there are no biblical parallels for this material. Its style and literary and historical status are the same as ch. 22; cf. the introductory comments on chs 22-29.

David's Public Commissioning of Solomon

28:1-10

22:6-16 recounted David's private charge to Solomon. It was argued there that the major themes were worked out by reflection on the commissioning of Joshua as Moses' successor at the end of Dt. and the beginning of Jos. The same consideration applies here, the private charge now being repeated 'in the sight of all Israel' (compare v. 8 with Dt. 31:7), and subsequently by an imperative command to put it into practice (see the literature cited at 22:11). Consequently, it is not surprising to find that most of the major themes in this paragraph, which centre around the related topics of temple building and establishment of the dynasty, are also repeated from that earlier section.

David's speech is couched in terms of what von Rad has titled 'A Levitical Sermon'. Examples of this form occur at a number of points in the Chronicler's narrative, and there can be little doubt that in their present shape they express the author's own viewpoint. They are characterised in particular by the use of earlier scriptures, and these will be noted below. Also distinctive to Chronicles is the use in these speeches of the introductory plural imperative, 'hear me', followed by the name of the addressees, in this case 'my brethren and my people' (cf. Japhet, *VT* 18 [1968], pp. 358f.; Newsome, *JBL* 94 [1975], pp. 210ff.). This form of introduction may be related to the tendency of the Chronicler, frequently noticed elsewhere, to involve all the people in the significant events of the nation's life; cf. Willi, p. 161.

1. It has often been thought that this verse, which repeats the substance of 23:2, demonstrates that all the material in between has been added secondarily. In fact, however, from the point of view of vocabulary, the two verses have little in common; the word for **assembled**, for instance, is different in each case. If the material had been inserted quite so clumsily as is suggested, we should not have expected any overlap at all, whereas if a later scribe were trying to point out the interruption we should have expected him to repeat the sentence exactly. It may therefore be suggested that this verse provides another example of 'repetitive resumption' (see above, p. 122, and *SVT* 30 [1979], pp. 264–5). In that case, most of this verse would be the Chronicler's own method of indicating the narrative continuity of this passage with 23:1–2 after his inclusion of the (quite short) primary layer of chs 23–27.

assembled: see on 15:3. Several of the titles in the middle of this verse relate directly to the various lists of **officials** in the previous chapter (CM), whereas there is no reference to the Levites who dominate chs 23–26. This suggests that the Chronicler himself included here only a general statement as a resumption of 23:2, but that it was expanded by the reviser in order to integrate his later additions more closely into the narrative.

2. Only in Ps. 132:7 is **the ark** spoken of as God's **footstool**. That

this Psalm is in the writer's mind is confirmed by the observation that the theme of **rest** is not used here in the way that is common in these chapters (see especially on 22:9), but rather in terms of God finding **rest** among his people, precisely as in the Psalm (cf. vv. 5, 7, 14, and von Rad, 'Levitical Sermon', p. 276). The influence of this Psalm on the Chronicler will be further noted at 2 Chr. 6:41f. **I made preparations for building:** this is not referred to elsewhere, and would be hard to fit in between 17:2 and 3. The sense of this context suggests not so much the preparations now in hand to aid Solomon as an expression of David's original intention.

3. God said to me: this introduces another summary of the dynastic oracle, and thus helps us further to understand how the Chronicler interpreted it. This is the situation also in 22:7ff., and both passages have to be read in conjunction with ch. 17. The introduction to this latter chapter summarises the conclusions which emerge. **a warrior:** literally, 'a man of wars', to be contrasted with the 'man of peace' in 22:9. **and have shed blood:** see the comments on 22:8.

4–5. Again, the initial application of the dynastic oracle is focused on **Solomon** in order then (v. 7) to make the dynasty's permanent establishment conditional upon his obedience. This focus is achieved here by reference to God's election of Solomon (cf. v. 10 and 29:1), and its importance may be judged by the fact that Chronicles is unique in the Bible in making Solomon the object of God's choice (cf. G. E. Mendenhall, *IDB* 2, p. 78; Japhet, *Ideology*, pp. 448–51; Braun, *JBL* 95 [1976], pp. 588–90). This receives particular emphasis by David's presenting the election in terms reminiscent of lot-casting (Jos. 7:16–18; 1 Sam. 10:20–21; cf. Jg. 6:15), starting with the tribe (**Judah**) and moving through the extended family (**my father's house**) and the immediate household (David himself) to the one chosen, **Solomon**. The purpose of this election is described equally in terms of dynastic rule (vv. 5 and 7) and temple building (v. 6). **the Lord has given me many sons:** this makes the election of Solomon even more remarkable. The intention of this comment is doubtless to draw attention to the 'Succession Narrative' in the second half of 2 Sam. and the beginning of 1 Kg. The Chronicler has thus in these verses given his theological commentary on the intriguing narrative of those chapters. **the throne of the kingdom of the Lord:** see the comments on 17:14.

6–7. Cf. 17:12f. and 22:10 for the substance of these verses. **as he is today:** this indicates that what is meant by **keeping my commandments and ordinances** is not an unatttainably high standard. The establishment of **his kingdom for ever** is a real possibility.

8. The plural forms of the verbs **observe and seek out** show that this exhortation is still part of the address to the leaders of Israel. Although to some extent it interrupts the development of the theme about Solomon and his kingdom, it is not unreasonable that the people's responsibility should be underlined before moving on to address Solomon personally (vv. 9–10), especially in view of the fact that it would have been so relevant to the Chronicler's first readers; cf. Neh. 9:33–37. There is thus no need to regard it as secondary. Scripture again underlies the injunction, e.g. Dt. 4:21f.; but, as Japhet has well observed (*Ideology*, pp. 327–33), the emphasis of **possess this good land, and leave it for an inheritance** is no longer on the conquest, but is a challenge which is presented afresh to each new generation. The verse thus forms what in other examples of the Levitical sermon has been called 'the exhortation', namely, 'a call to faith with the promise of reward' (von Rad, p. 271). It may be added that this is fully in line with the Chronicler's doctrine of retribution, the basis of which is the belief that each generation is confronted with either God's judgment or his salvation in all its fullness.

9–10. The charge to Solomon is now finally given in the hearing of all the people. A general exhortation, again rich in scriptural allusions (v. 9) is followed by the specific command to build.

9. Know: i.e. 'recognise the authority of'; cf. H. B. Huffmon, *BASOR* 181 (1966), p. 37. **every plan and thought** (*RV* 'the imaginations of the thoughts'): cf. Gen. 6:5; 8:21. **If you seek him. . .:** a succinct summary of an important part of the Chronicler's theology, couched in language which, though cited from other passages (cf. Dt. 4:29; Jer. 29:13f.; Isa. 55:6), he made very much his own; cf. especially 2 Chr. 15:2, the comments on 1 Chr. 10:13–14, and Braun, *SVT* 30 (1979), pp. 53–6.

10. See the comments on 22:11. **has chosen you:** cf. vv. 4–5 above.

The Plans for the Temple

28:11–21

A further aspect of the preparations which David made for the temple building was the provision of detailed plans. These are here handed over to Solomon. Rudolph ascribes much of the paragraph to a secondary hand, partly because some elements presuppose chs 23–27, and partly because he does not think the Chronicler would have gone into such detail over minor matters. On our analysis of chs 23–27, however, Rudolph's first point carries no weight, for all that is necessary for understanding these verses was included in the primary layer, which we attributed to the Chronicler himself. As for the detail accorded to the temple vessels in vv. 14-18, we may point to the remarks of P. R. Ackroyd in *SVT* 23 (1972), pp. 166–81. He observes that they are several times given more attention than we might have expected, and he finds in this 'a continuity theme' between the cult of the first temple period and that of the second temple as practised by the Chronicler's own readers, and moreover that they have the function of 'depicting the order to which practice must conform, the order which is itself linked to what the deity himself ordains' (p. 170).

11. **the plan:** the same word is used for 'the pattern' of the tabernacle and its furnishings, shown to Moses at Mount Sinai in Exod. 25:9, 40. Ezekiel's vision of the restored temple (Ezek. 40ff.) is comparable. In the present passage, however, there is no suggestion that David drew up a plan as a copy of something he had seen, but rather that his descriptive plan was written under inspiration (v. 19). Since there is so much in common between the basic plan of the tabernacle and temple, it may well thus be being implied that the temple stood in continuous tradition with the tabernacle in such a way that David did not need to 'see' the pattern, but rather merely adapt it under inspiration to the new conditions. Further evidence for this theme of continuity is provided by the fact that the Chronicler probably thought of the tabernacle eventually being housed in the completed temple (cf. 2 Chr. 5:5). This verse refers to the main components of the temple. They are described in greater detail in 2 Chr. 3.

12. **in mind:** some have suggested that this should be rendered 'by the Spirit', i.e. under inspiration, but on balance the evidence seems to favour *RSV*; cf. R. N. Whybray, *The Heavenly Counsellor in Isaiah xl.13-14* (1971), pp. 11-12. Particular attention may be paid to **the treasuries** because of their inclusion above at 26:22–28.

13. This verse clearly goes beyond the confines of a building plan, but is not inappropriate, especially following chs 23-27. Although it was argued that **the divisions of the priests** were not included by the Chronicler in 24:1–19, a reference to them in a general statement such as the present passage is not surprising; see also on 23:2. **all the vessels:** see above for their significance in the present context, and further at 2 Chr. 4 and 36:18. The theme is picked up also in Ezr. 1:7–11; 7:19; 8:25 and 33. In addition, the influence of Exod. 25:9, 40 may again be felt, with its reference to the pattern of both tabernacle and vessels.

14. A general statement, developed in greater detail in the following verses. Most of the **golden vessels** are referred to also elsewhere (e.g. 2 Chr. 4:7f., 16, 19–22). The **silver vessels**, however, are

itemised only here, though their existence is attested by the general
reference of 2 Kg. 25:15 (and cf. the implication behind 2
Kg. 12:13, spelt out by 2 Chr. 24:14).

18. By its position at the end of the list, and by the repetition of
plan, particular attention is given to the arrangements for **the ark**.

19. According to MT (cf. *RSV* mg), David's direct address is
here resumed. The verse is difficult to construe. Since **the hand of
the Lord** 'upon' is a common expression for divine inspiration (e.g.
2 Kg. 3:15; Ezek. 1:3; 3:14), the most reasonable interpretation
seems to be that the plans were **made clear** to David and that he
wrote them down under conscious inspiration (and not that God
himself wrote them down, *contra NEB*). See further on v. 11 above.

20–21. A third charge of David to Solomon. For the form and
major theme, see on 22:11–13 and 28:10. The new element is the
expansion of the expression of encouragement by reference to those
who will assist Solomon, and this opens the way to the major
concern of ch. 29.

Contributions for the Temple Building

29:1–9

The parallel with the account of the building of the tabernacle is
continued both in substance and in vocabulary as David first appeals
for offerings and the people then respond generously
(cf. Exod. 25:1–7; 35:4–9, 20–29). A new element, however, is introduced, namely, the example of generosity which David himself
set (vv. 2–5). This, of course, recapitulates the theme of 22:2–5,
but, as with the charge to Solomon in chs 22 and 28, so in this case
the matter is first brought to public notice here. The paragraph thus
well suits the structure of these chapters as it builds up towards the
public installation of Solomon (v. 22). Only Mosis (pp. 105f.) has
denied vv. 1–19 to the Chronicler, but on the basis of the analysis
presented here of chs 22 and 28–9 most of his arguments lose their
force.

1. whom alone God has chosen: see above on 28:4–5. For the
remainder of the verse, see on 22:5. **the palace:** this word (*habbî-
rāh*) is used only here and in v. 19 for the temple, though it occurs
several times in Neh., Est., and Dan. with the meaning 'castle',
'palace'. Clearly, it did not enter the Hebrew language as a loan
word until the post-exilic period (cf. Polzin, p. 130). No really
adequate explanation for the choice of this word has been suggested
(its occurrence in v. 19 precluding emendation to *habbayit, contra*
RH); perhaps in a context where so much attention is paid to

Solomon as the new king, the Chronicler chose a word whose overtones would remind the reader that the kingdom ultimately belongs to God (cf. v. 11, together with 17:14 above).

2. See on 22:3f. and especially 22:14. Again, many of these
materials, though not in every case identified with complete certainty, recur in the list of the people's gifts for the tabernacle.

3–5. As well as David's provision from the spoils of war, he gives
generously from his own personal **treasure** (M. Greenberg, *JAOS*
71 [1951], p. 174). For the figures involved, see on 22:14–16. **gold
of Ophir:** attested on an eighth-century ostracon from Tel Qasile (cf.
B. Maisler, *IEJ* 1 [1951], pp. 209f.), and mentioned also at 1
Kg. 9:28 in connection with Solomon's reign, but not otherwise
attested as early as David's time. For such an anachronism, see
further on v. 7 below.

6–9. Inspired by this example, the whole assembly (compare v. 6
with 28:1) brought **their freewill offerings**, the quantities again
being enormous.

7. darics: a Persian coin, not minted before 515 BC during the
reign of Darius I; for full details, with bibliography, cf. *TynB* 28
(1977), pp. 123–6. Such an anachronism, as others already noted in
this chapter, is understandable enough, and may be compared with
the attempts of some modern Bible translations to give up-to-date
equivalents when rendering sums of money. The fact that the
amount (**ten thousand darics of gold**) is not at all beyond reason
tends only to highlight the exaggeration of the figures for the other
sums involved.

8. Jehiel the Gershonite: cf. 26:21f., where his family are also
linked with **the treasury of the house of the Lord**. Rudolph feels
obliged in consequence to regard this reference as a secondary intrusion, after chapters 23–27 had been added to the Chronicler's
work. In our analysis, however, the reference comes in the layer
which we attributed to the Chronicler himself, and this verse may
be held to lend further support to that position.

9. rejoiced. . .rejoiced greatly: see on 12:40, where this element
was noted as characteristic of major occasions in the Chronicler's
history. Here, it extends even to the experience felt on giving materially **to the Lord**, which is far removed from caricatures of the
Chronicler as coldly ritualistic and legalistic.

David's Prayer of Thanksgiving

29:10–19

The climax of David's reign, as portrayed by the Chronicler, has now been reached. All the preparations for building the temple have been completed, and Solomon, chosen by God as the one who shall bring the plans to fruition, is about to be proclaimed as king over all Israel. And at this point the Chronicler reveals his true heart: the proper response to such a situation is a prayer which breathes joyful faith and simple humility.

From various points of view the prayer is straightforward enough. It concentrates on praise and thanksgiving, though it introduces petition at the close (vv. 18–19). Its form is thus unremarkable. Again, as so often in such theological passages where the Chronicler is responsible for the final form of composition, there is considerable use made of earlier scriptures (see on 28:1–10 above): for instance, compare v. 15 with Ps. 39:12 and Job 8:9; 14:2. In a liturgical setting, however, it is just as probable that these phrases reflect current usage which would have drawn on Israel's rich heritage of religious phraseology as that they are consciously drawn from their present biblical contexts. The thought of the prayer, too, is transparent, and indeed this is one of its great strengths. Its main themes stand out clearly and, as is appropriate at this point in the composition, draw together ideas which have been developed more fully elsewhere, and whose relevance to the Chronicler's own readers has already been noticed. Whereas they might well have despaired of ever seeing a return to such days as David's, it is made clear to them that theologically speaking their situation has much in common with his, both because they worship the same God, in whose hands remain **power** and **the kingdom** (vv. 11–12) and because the nature of man as a **stranger** and **sojourner. . .on the earth** (v. 15) is not altered even by the wealth and security which had been granted to David.

By way of illustration, it may be pointed out that these themes have a particularly close affinity with those of the Psalm anthology which the Chronicler assembled at 16:8–36. Three points were singled out in the comments on that passage as governing the Chronicler's selection and with direct relevance to his readers: (a) the theme of the landless patriarchs, 'few in number', who received the promise of the land. This dominates David's prayer here as well. There are references to the patriarchs (the **fathers**) at its opening and close (vv. 10 and 18), but more significantly the central verses of the prayer (vv. 14–16) build upon the same ideology: even within their secure boundaries the people of Israel are still **sojourners, as**

all our fathers were (cf. especially 16:19. On **abiding**, cf. P. A. H. de Boer, *OTS* 10 [1954], pp. 239f., and M. Wallenstein, *VT* 4 [1954], p. 214). If now they enjoy a prosperity unknown before, then that is only because they have inherited the substance of the promise of land to the patriarchs and because they have enjoyed God's protection against their enemies (cf. 16:18 and 21); thus they were no empty words of David when he acknowledged, **all things come from thee, and of thy own have we given thee** (v. 14), and they set the preparations made for the temple into their true perspective; (b) the celebration of the Lord's kingship (16:23-33). This has been seen several times as an essential and prominent aspect of the Chronicler's ideology (cf. 17:14), and expression of it comes to a climax in vv. 11-12 (**thine is the kingdom, O Lord**). Again, the theme is strikingly apt to the present context, preventing any misunderstanding of the significance of Solomon's imminent accession; (c) the Psalm of 1 Chr. 16 ended with petition. So too does David's prayer, though its content is adapted to the changed circumstances. He asks first that the people may always continue to serve God **freely and joyously** (v. 17; see the remarks at 12:40 and 29:9), and that beyond this their hearts would ever be directed towards God personally (v. 18). Finally (v. 19), David prays for **Solomon**, both that he too would fulfil the conditions necessary for the permanent establishment of the dynasty (see the introduction to ch. 17), and especially that he would successfully complete the building of the temple (**palace**; cf. v. 1).

It may be observed, therefore, that these two passages have much in common, and appropriately provide a framework to the whole section of chs 17-29, which has been totally dominated by David's preparations for building the temple. Plöger, 'Reden und Gebete', has sought rather to draw a parallel with David's prayer in 17:16-27, but except in the most general terms this does not extend beyond the phrase **But who am I, and what is my people** (v. 14), which shows clear influence from 17:16.

Solomon's Accession to the Throne

29:20-25

The concluding celebrations continued until the next day, when Solomon finally ascended the throne.

21. Sacrifices: in contrast with the **burnt offerings**, these will have been the 'peace offering', in which the worshippers participated, so adding to the joy mentioned in the next verse.

22. ate and drank. . . .with great gladness: cf. 12:39-40. **the**

second time: this is lacking in LXX[B] and P. Most commentators thus delete it as a later gloss, explaining that it was added by some one who failed to appreciate that 23:1 was a heading to this whole section rather than describing a separate event. This may be so, but an alternative explanation is possible. Several elements in this paragraph suggest that the Chronicler was writing here with 1 Kg. 1 in mind, e.g. contrast the sacrifices of v. 21 with 1 Kg. 1:9; with **prince**, compare 1 Kg. 1:35; the reference to the allegiance of 'all the sons of King David' in v. 24 no doubt has an eye on the whole account of Adonijah's rebellion in that chapter, etc. At the same time, however, there can be no question of this being an attempt to describe the same event. The Chronicler seems rather to have regarded that (no doubt rightly) as a somewhat hurried and semi-private anointing, whereas the event he describes here (whether historical or not) is intended to be a formal and public ceremony. Similarly, the points of contact with 1 Kg. 1 are more in the way of contrast than equation. Thus he may have intended **the second time** to refer, not to 23:1 (which, despite A. Bartel, *Beth Mikra* 47 [1971], pp. 500–6, is not a reference to the anointing of 1 Kg. 1 either, but a literary heading; see the comments there), but to the events of 1 Kg. 1. It would be another example of his manner already noted several times when an allusion on his part indicates that he presupposes his readers' knowledge of the earlier account, but that his own purpose is more in the way of theological interpretation of those events: 'He has chronicled the history of the kingdom from a religious point of view and follows a straight line rather than detours that would detract from his objective' (Myers, p. 198). **and Zadok as priest:** according to 1 Chr. 16:39, Zadok was already prominent, though according to 1 Kg. 2:35 it was not until later that Solomon installed him as Abiathar's successor. Either way, therefore, this reference seems to be somewhat out of place in the present context; we should expect the Chronicler to have thought of his anointing as earlier. Unless the phrase has been corrupted from an original indication that it was **Zadok** who **anointed** Solomon (cf. 1 Kg. 1:39), it is difficult to escape the feeling that it has been added later to the Chronicler's text by someone who, under the influence of the pro-priestly trends of the post-exilic hierocracy, thought that a reference to the installation of the high priest alongside that of the king was desirable, if not necessary.

23. This corresponds to 1 Kg. 2:12, though it is completely rewritten by the Chronicler to suit his own concerns. **the throne of the Lord:** cf. 17:14; 28:5, etc. **and all Israel obeyed him:** a further parallel with the installation of Joshua; cf. Dt. 34:9; Jos. 1:16–20.

24. This amplifies the content of the previous verse, with particular reference to Solomon's supremacy after Adonijah's rebellion in 1 Kg. 1.

25. And the Lord gave Solomon great repute (literally: 'magnified Solomon') **in the sight of all Israel**: this is repeated at 2 Chr. 1:1, and is similarly mentioned twice in connection with Joshua's succession; Jos. 3:7 and 4:14. The final clause of the verse should be understood as a strong assertion that Solomon was not inferior to **any king before him in Israel**, notably, of course, David himself; for this whole theme, cf. Braun, *JBL* 92 (1973), pp. 503–16. The unity of their reigns is thus further underlined.

The Close of David's Reign

29:26–30

Against his *Vorlage* (1 Kg. 2:10–12) and regular practice elsewhere, the Chronicler here has the notice of David's death following that of Solomon's accession. This detail represents a further dovetailing of the two kings' reigns (cf. *VT* 26 [1976], p. 356). He has, moreover, expanded this paragraph to include material usually found in such summaries, but lacking at 1 Kg. 2:10–12.

26. all Israel: see on 11:1–3.

27. Although this verse is taken straight from 1 Kg. 2:11, its position after the Chronicler's own composition in v. 26 goes even further than the *Vorlage* in suggesting that David's rule **in Hebron** was over all **Israel** rather than just Judah; cf. G. Botterweck, *ThQ* 136 (1956), pp. 431 and 433.

28. in a good old age, full of days: see on 23:1 for the slight correction implied here over the picture of the end of David's reign in the Deuteronomic history. This is emphasised here too by the additional reference to **riches, and honour**.

29–30. There is no passage in 1 Kg. 2 corresponding to v. 29, although such references to sources are normal at the end of the kings' reigns in Kg. as much as Chr. The Chronicler has merely assimilated this passage to that convention. It is widely agreed that he does not intend us to understand a source other than our Sam.–Kg.; but for the general significance of this type of formula, see the Introduction, section F. It need only be observed here that **Samuel** had died well before the point at which the Chronicler's narrative starts, suggesting again that he intends his readers to use his work in some way in conjunction with, rather than in opposition to, the earlier historical books. **the kingdoms of the countries**: an expression peculiar to the Chronicler. It refers to other countries close to Israel. In the present context they will be primarily those countries which came into contact with, and largely under the domination of, the Davidic empire; cf. chs 18–20.

2 Chronicles

Solomon

2 Chr. 1–9

The Chronicler's account of the reign of Solomon is dominated to an even greater extent than that of 1 Kg. 1–11 by the building of the temple. It may thus be regarded as the direct continuation and fulfilment of David's preparatory work which was the primary theme of 1 Chr. 17–29. Completion of this task was, however, seen to be the major condition for the eternal establishment of the Davidic dynasty. Such a concentration is therefore not surprising, and it is highlighted by the omission of otherwise quite neutral material such as the account of the building of Solomon's own palace (1 Kg. 7:1–12), attention to which was probably held to detract from the major theme.

The second condition which was imposed on Solomon (1 Chr. 28:7) was of more general obedience to God's commandments, and this fact will account for the other major group of omissions from the earlier account, namely, passages where criticism of Solomon is implied, especially 1 Kg. 1–2 and 11:1–40; but see also on 1:2–6 below, etc. In this way too, therefore, the unity of the reigns of David and Solomon in inaugurating what we must take to be the Chronicler's ideal of theocracy receives further emphasis.

The major literary structure of these chapters is straightforward. Chapters 2–8 are concerned directly with the temple; see the parallel introductory and concluding formulae at 2:1 and 8:16. Within this major section, similar summarising statements mark the principal divisions (e.g. 3:1 and 5:1; cf. Braun, *JBL* 92 [1973], pp. 503–16). The opening and concluding chapters (2 Chr. 1 and 9), which enclose the central block, each have as their principal component a story about Solomon's wisdom and accounts of his wealth. It is this, of course, for which Solomon was widely remembered in popular tradition. It looks very much as though the structure of the Chronicler's account is designed to indicate that these features found their true expression in the building of the temple, and this, indeed, is confirmed by various other explicit allusions that are found only in Chronicles (e.g. 2:12).

It may thus be seen that virtually the whole account of Solomon's reign is based on that in Kings, but that, as is typical of the Chronicler's method in handling his sources, he has managed to impress the stamp of his own interpretation on the material. This he achieves by selection, rearrangement, and sometimes a rewriting of his *Vorlage* on the basis of his understanding of the narrative, an understanding which has been moulded by reflection on a much wider range of biblical sources.

THE GREATNESS OF SOLOMON

1:1–17

After the introductory v. 1, there follow three short paragraphs which each illustrate a well-known characteristic of Solomon's reign. It is clear both from what has been omitted from 1 Kg. (e.g. 3:1–3) and from the radically new positioning of vv. 14–17 (cf. 1 Kg. 10:26–29) that this represents an intentional combination by the Chronicler, whose purpose is to show that these characteristics were directed towards, and most genuinely expressed in, the temple building, which immediately follows.

1. This introduction to the reign of **Solomon** continues directly the notices of 1 Chr. 29:23–30. The division of Chronicles into two books was introduced later for convenience only. **established himself:** where this expression is used elsewhere in such a position (12:13; 13:21; 17:1; 21:4; cf. 1 Chr. 11:10), there is always in the context the suggestion of accession either at a time of difficulty or as the result of some considerable effort. As at 1 Chr. 29:24, therefore, there may be an allusion here to the disorders which marked the close of David's reign (1 Kg. 1–2). The rest of the verse, however, emphasises that Solomon was God's own choice. **the Lord his God was with him:** cf. 1 Chr. 22:11, 16; 28:20, etc. **and made him exceedingly great:** cf. 1 Chr. 29:25 with Jos. 3:7 and 4:14.

Solomon's Worship

1:2–6

Whereas 1 Kg. 3:4, on which this paragraph is based, serves in its context merely as an introduction to the dream which follows, the Chronicler has here developed the material into an account in its own right, in which the king leads the people in a major act of sacrificial worship. Moreover, he has made it the first recorded incident of Solomon's reign. It thus serves as a pointer to the theme which the Chronicler judged to be of greatest significance, and encourages us to read the following chapters in the light of it.

There is a parallel here to the opening of David's reign: 1 Chr. 11–12 was concerned with the establishment of David as king over all Israel, and this was immediately followed in 1 Chr. 13 by the account of his gathering 'all Israel' (v. 5) to 'seek' (see the comment on 1 Chr. 13:3) the ark; see further on v. 5 below, where the same key word is introduced. These factors, together with what has already been established in 1 Chronicles, are sufficient to explain all the elements with which the Chronicler has amplified his *Vorlage*, as the following comments will indicate.

2. all Israel: there is no hint of this in 1 Kg. 3:4, but this recurrent feature of the Chronicler's accounts of major occasions has been noted several times; see especially on 1 Chr. 13:1–5. The list of officials which amplifies this heading may be compared with 1 Chr. 28:1. The first assembly in Solomon's reign thus shows elements of continuity with the last of David's.

3. all the assembly: as at 1 Chr. 13:2 and **4. for the tent of meeting . . . was there:** we know already from 1 Chr. 16:39 and 21:29 that this was the Chronicler's view, and he thus supplies this half verse as a most natural explanatory note on his *Vorlage*. Since he will have read the Kings' text in the light of this opinion, he will not have felt any need to explain away what might otherwise have been regarded in his time as a reprehensible act (cf. Lev. 17:8–9).

4. This verse adds nothing to the account of 1 Chr. 13 and 15–16. It may, in a discussion of the location of the primary cultic objects at the start of the reign, have been included for the sake of completeness; but perhaps, in the light of what has already been noted in this paragraph, its intention is rather to underline the parallel drawn with the first concern of David's reign.

5. the bronze altar: strictly speaking, acacia wood overlaid with bronze; cf. Exod. 38:1–2. It is introduced here by the Chronicler both because of the reference to sacrifice in the next verse, and as a link back to the Davidic dispositions following the transfer of the ark to Jerusalem; cf. 1 Chr. 16:39f. and 21:29. **Bezalel the son of Uri, the son of Hur:** cf. Exod. 31:2 and 9 and 1 Chr. 2:20. **sought the Lord:** the object of **sought** is expressed pronominally, 'him' or 'it'. The latter would refer to the altar, and it is to be preferred (so LXX, V, *AV*, *RV*, *contra RSV*) because of the obvious parallel with 1 Chr. 13:3, where *RSV*'s 'we neglected it (the ark)' is a loose translation of 'we did not seek it', and 15:13, where the same phrase is used (*RSV*: 'we did not care for it').

6. Though completely rewritten, this verse conveys the substance of 1 Kg. 3:4 from which the remainder of the paragraph has been deduced. There, it was the setting for the following narrative; here, it has become the first 'event' of Solomon's reign and was, for the Chronicler, a generous provision for the nation's worship.

Solomon's Wisdom

1:7–13

Although this paragraph tells basically the same story as 1 Kg. 3:5–15, the Chronicler has abbreviated it quite sharply, and does not follow his *Vorlage* nearly so closely as he usually does elsewhere. Although we can understand some of the changes and omissions, as the comments below will show, much remains in doubt: did his *Vorlage* here differ more markedly than usual from MT of 1 Kg. 3? Was he working more from memory than text? Or were his concerns homiletic (Ackroyd)? Such uncertainties demand caution before we rush to explain a particular feature. For instance, it is possible that the omission of the reference of God appearing to Solomon 'in a dream' (1 Kg. 3:5) may reflect later suspicions about such modes of revelation (e.g. Jer. 23:25ff.); but we cannot be sure that other more mechanical factors were not responsible.

We are on firmer ground, however, in observing that the Chronicler no longer has this story followed by the illustrative example of the exercise of Solomon's wisdom in the story of the judgment between the two prostitutes (1 Kg. 3:16–28). In his view, rather, the primary purpose of the gift of wisdom, and hence the best example of its exercise, was to equip Solomon for the task of temple-building. The paragraph thus takes its appropriate place in this chapter whose aim is to introduce the account of the building which follows.

8. This is a drastic shortening of 1 Kg. 3:6–7, though there is no appreciable difference in sense.

9–10. It has already been noted that part of the reference in 1 Kg. 3:7 to Solomon's weakness has been transposed by the Chronicler to 1 Chr. 22:5 (and cf. v. 12) and 29:1. As for its continuation, 'I do not know how to go out or come in', that has here been transformed into part of the request for **wisdom and knowledge** to rule effectively. **let thy promise. . . .be fulfilled:** this is additional to 1 Kg. 3, and is a clear reference back to the dynastic oracle in 1 Chr. 17. The form of words is similar to that found at 6:17 below, where it is drawn from the parallel in 1 Kg. 8:26; its importance to the Chronicler is further shown by its introduction against the *Vorlage* at 1 Chr. 17:23 and 24 (cf. *JSS* 23 [1978], p. 42). It is typical of the Chronicler to emphasise in this way the connection between God's promise to David and Solomon's obedience, for which wisdom was necessary, in terms of both temple-building and more generally effective rule over the nation. **as many as the dust of the earth:** since the significance of the patriarch Jacob to the Chronicler has been noted before (cf. 1 Chr. 1), it is probably not accidental that he here introduces a description of Israel that was also used to Jacob during his dream at Bethel (Gen. 28:14); see further, *IBC*, p. 64.

10–12. knowledge (*maddāʿ*): this word occurs in late biblical Hebrew only. The word *nᵉkāsîm* (**wealth**, v. 11; **possessions**, v. 12) is also probably late. This suggests that some, at least, of the differences from Kings in this passage are due to rewriting by the Chronicler.

13. It is not at all surprising that the Chronicler omits the reference to Solomon sacrificing before the ark on his return **to Jerusalem** (1 Kg. 3:15), since this would have conflicted with the picture of legitimate worship which he has taken such pains to develop in the foregoing. **And he reigned over Israel:** cf. 1 Kg. 4:1.

Solomon's Wealth

1:14–17

Rather in the manner of the previous paragraph, this section takes a well-known feature of Solomon's reign and suggests, by the new position allotted to it, that its main purpose was to provide for the building of the temple. It is further appropriate in its present setting because it illustrates the fulfilment of God's promise recorded in v. 12 above.

The Chronicler has here drawn with hardly any change at all on 1 Kg. 10:26–29. (Since only the overall element of wealth was of significance to him, as outlined above, the reader must refer to the commentaries on Kings for all matters of detail.) **and gold** has been added in v. 15 – unless its presence in LXX of 1 Kg. 10:27 suggests that the Chronicler already found it in his *Vorlage*. The verses recur less exactly at 9:25ff. below, together with material from 1 Kg. 4:21 and 26. The smaller number of **chariots** in this passage (**fourteen hundred** as opposed to stalls for 'forty thousand' or 'four thousand' chariot horses) may have made it seem to him the more appropriate to choose for the beginning of Solomon's reign, though, as will be seen, the literary status of some of the material in ch. 9 is questionable.

THE BUILDING OF THE TEMPLE

2:1–8:16

Both the introductory and concluding verses of this section represent considerable reworking and expansion of his *Vorlage* by the Chronicler. It is therefore reasonable to suppose that he was drawing renewed attention – if such were needed – to the centrality of the events here recorded for his work as a whole. It should be noted that he has not only included within these limits the narrative of physical building, but also the dedication of the temple to God with prayer and sacrifice, and God's acceptance by theophany and revelation of those theological values for which Solomon intended the temple to stand.

Preparation of the Labour Force

2:1–18

N.B. In the Hebrew Bible, 2:1 is numbered as 1:18, so that in ch. 2 the Hebrew verse numbers are one less than the English. It may also be noted that in the parallel 1 Kg. 5, Hebrew 5:1 = English 4:21, so that in ch. 5 the Hebrew verse numbers are 14 greater than the English. In the following, the English system is used throughout.

The main element of this chapter is an account of Solomon's negotiations with Hiram (vv. 3–16), reworked in such a way as to include, among other things, the leading skilled workman, Hura-mabi (v. 13). In the present text, this is flanked (vv. 2 and 17–18) by notes about the general labour force. The Chronicler has not slavishly followed his *Vorlage* for the most part, but reordered it, brought in elements from other biblical passages and further adapted much of the remainder. The result is that while at hardly any point are we in doubt as to his source, in fact very little indeed could strictly speaking be called 'parallel'. As elsewhere, the comments will concentrate primarily on the emphases which are thereby revealed as the Chronicler's own particular concerns. These chiefly relate to Solomon's initiative at this point in setting about the task, to an increased concentration on the primacy for his reign of temple building, and on a development of the temple-tabernacle typology, already noted especially at 1 Chr. 28:11 (cf. Mosis, pp. 136–9).

1. Solomon purposed to build. . .: the first half of this verse is lifted verbally from 1 Kg. 5:5. There, it is included as part of Solomon's letter to Hiram; here, it functions as a literary introduction in order to subsume the whole of that correspondence under the heading of Solomon's intention to build. **and a royal palace for himself:** cf. 2:12; 7:11; 8:1; 9:3 and 11 for later occasional references. However, unlike 1 Kg. 7:1–12, the Chronicler includes no details about its building; perhaps he felt that to do so would detract attention from the more important temple theme. The fact that he includes a reference here is sufficient to show once again, however, that his purpose was not to deceive in any way, but that he expects of his readers good knowledge of the earlier account.

2. This verse is repeated from v. 18 below. It is usually thought to have been added here as a preparation for the reference in v. 7 to the 'skilled workers'. Since this latter, however, clearly refers back to 1 Chr. 22:15, the present verse has to be regarded as secondary.

3. By omitting 1 Kg. 5:1, the Chronicler presents **Solomon** as taking the initiative in the correspondence with **Huram**: the merest suggestion that Solomon needed prompting to undertake the task of temple building is thus avoided (cf. v. 10). **Huram**: this is the usual, though less probable, spelling of 'Hiram' in Chronicles. **As you dealt with David my father:** cf. 1 Chr. 14:1, where there is the suggestion of tribute. In this passage too, Solomon is presented as the dominant partner. **so deal with me:** absent from the Hebrew. It may be right to supply such a phrase here; alternatively, the following verses may be regarded as a parenthesis, with the main sentence being resumed at vv. 7-8.

4. The Chronicler omits from 1 Kg. 5:3-5 the reasons why David did not build the temple, having already developed the theme fully in 1 Chr. 17; 22:7-10; 28:2-3. Instead, in this and the following two verses, he elaborates on the function of the temple in a religion that stressed heavily the transcendence of God. The list of cultic practices presented here is evidently intended as a comprehensive summarising formula of what should be done in the temple, for they have been **ordained for ever for Israel**. Thus it is not surprising to find that at certain key points in the later narrative (e.g. 2 Chr. 13; 28; 29-31) they become a yardstick by which the fidelity of the kings may be assessed, and thus contribute substantially to the work's literary structure (cf. *IBC*, pp. 121-2). Needless to say, regulations concerning each item are to be found in the Pentateuch: for **the burning of incense of sweet spices before him**, cf. Exod. 25:6 and 30:7-8; for **the continual offering of the show-bread**, cf. Exod. 25:30; 40:23; Lev. 24:5-9; **burnt offerings** are referred to frequently, but it would seem that Num. 28-29 in particular lies behind the description in this passage, for it follows the order of daily offerings, those for the **sabbath**, the **new moon** and the **appointed feasts**.

5. This recalls 1 Chr. 22:5 and 29:1.

6. This anticipates 6:18, but adds **except as a place to burn incense before him**. The temple retains its value as a focus for worship. By juxtaposing in these two verses references to themes developed elsewhere, the Chronicler underlines the paradox that though there is no question of God dwelling in the temple, yet it must still be 'great' as a reflection of his greatness.

7. So now: a transition-marker between the introduction to, and substance of, a letter. Though attested earlier (e.g. 1 Kg. 5:6, which is parallel to the next verse here), such a style was still part of the literary conventions of the Chronicler's own day; cf. P. S. Alexander, *JSS* 23 (1978), pp. 155–70. **send me a man skilled to work:** this request is lacking in the parallel. The Chronicler has anticipated, and so given much greater prominence to, the reference in 1 Kg. 7:13f. (see also vv. 13–14 below). In Kings, he appears merely as a skilled metal-worker, whereas here the request is for someone who will be skilled in addition in handling **fabrics** and in **engraving**. While part of this extension may have been influenced by the nature of the materials collected by David (1 Chr. 29:2), the various **fabrics** have not been referred to before. Since vv. 13–14 below suggest a typological comparison with the construction of the tabernacle, influence from that direction may also be felt here: see especially Exod. 35:35. The word used here for **purple**, *'arg^ewān*, is an Aramaic form of the Hebrew *'argāmān*, and the word for **crimson**, *karmîl*, is probably a Persian loan-word. Both factors point towards the hand of the Chronicler or a close contemporary for the presentation here; there is no need to look for otherwise unknown sources parallel to Kings or standing between Kings and Chronicles at this point.

the skilled workers . . . whom David my father provided: cf. 1 Chr. 22:15–16. **Judah and Jerusalem**: a common designation for the post-exilic community.

8. An expansion of the request in 1 Kg. 5:6a and c. **algum timber:** this is a transliteration (though cf. 1 Chr. 5:6 above) for a tree that has not been certainly identified, but which is known also from an Ugaritic list of tribute and which probably occurs in Akkadian texts as *elammakku*, also a valuable wood, but similarly unidentified as yet; cf. 9:10 and 11 below (parallel to 1 Kg. 10:11 and 12), and, for full discussion, J. C. Greenfield and M. Mayrhofer, *SVT* 16 (1967), pp. 83–9.

9. Since the Chronicler has already recorded David's abundant provision of timber for the temple (1 Chr. 22:4, 14; 29:2), he probably felt obliged to add this explanation of Solomon's need for yet more. Not surprisingly, it echoes 1 Chr. 22:5 and v. 5 above.

10. In 1 Kg. 5:6, Solomon leaves Hiram to set the wages for his workers, and the amount is recorded only later (v. 11). Here, by contrast, in line with developments already noted above, Solomon takes the initiative in fixing in advance the amount to be paid, and this comprises a single instalment, not an annual payment. Furthermore, it is noteworthy that in Kings the amount is given as 'food for his (Hiram's) household', which suggests that it was one of the terms included in the treaty of friendship between them (cf.

1 Kg. 5:12, and F. C. Fensham, *SVT* 17 [1969], pp. 76–9), whereas here it is retained strictly in the realm of wages **for your servants**.

1 Kg. 5:11 has no reference to **barley** or **wine**, and the amount of **oil** is greater in this passage. The LXX of the Kings account is sufficient to suggest, however, that the Chronicler may have been following a different *Vorlage* at this point, or at least continuing a development already reflected therein, rather than just indulging in exaggeration. **crushed**: this represents an unconvincing attempt to make sense of a corrupt text. With the parallel in 1 Kg. 5:11 and several versions we should read 'food', 'provisions' (*makkolet* for *makkôt*) **for your servants** (cf. *NEB*).

11. It has been suggested that a smoother reading would be obtained if this and the following verse were transposed. While there is truth in this, it is entirely conjectural. It may be, rather, that the Chronicler here retains an echo of the tradition of two messages from Hiram to Solomon, the first of which (1 Kg. 5:1) underlies v. 11 (note the possible development of **the Lord loves his people** from 'Hiram always loved David'), and the second of which incorporates both Hiram's reflection on the situation (1 Kg. 5:7, parallel to our v. 12) and his actual message (1 Kg. 5:8ff.). **in a letter**: this is not stated in 1 Kg. The Chronicler may have deduced it from the form of the message which coincides with epistolary conventions of his own day (cf. above, v. 7). He introduces similar references at 21:12 and 30:1 below.

12. This amplifies Hiram's reflections in 1 Kg. 5:7. First, addition of the words **God of Israel, who made heaven and earth** implies acknowledgement by Hiram of Solomon's confessional statement in v. 5. It is noteworthy that this is the only occurrence in the whole of Chronicles of an explicit statement that God is creator (though 1 Chr. 16:26 gets close to it, again in a passage where a contrast is being drawn with 'the peoples'), and its form may have been influenced by the acknowledgement of Abraham by Melchizedek in Gen. 14:19. The expression of so fundamental a confession in the God of Israel by a gentile king clearly demonstrates, therefore, that Solomon is being presented here as the dominant partner in the relationship. Second, Solomon's wisdom is again linked explicitly with his desire to **build a temple for the Lord** (see above on 1:7–13). **a royal palace for himself**: cf. v. 1.

13–14. Now: see. v. 7. In the substance of his letter, Hiram deals in turn with each of the matters raised by Solomon. To the request for a **skilled man** (v. 7), he sends **Huramabi**. These verses are clearly based on 1 Kg. 7:13–14, here brought forward to the very start of the building operation, with Huramabi being **sent** by Hiram, not merely 'brought' by Solomon. The extension of the list of his

skills has already been noted as one probable outcome of the Chronicler's desire to compare him with Bezalel in Exod. 31 and 35. To
this may now be added the ascription of his mother to **the daughters
of Dan** rather than Naphtali: Bezalel was helped in his work by one
Oholiab who belonged to the tribe of Dan (Exod. 31:6; 35:34), so
that in a way both builders of the tabernacle are brought together
in type in Huramabi. Indeed, it has been suggested, thirdly (Mosis,
p. 137), that the same explanation underlies the change in name
from Hiram to **Huramabi**, the additional -*ab* element being a reflection of the final syllable of Oholiab. It has also been suggested
(Rudolph) that this new final element should not be taken as part
of the name, but as a title, 'my master (craftsman)'; cf. Gen. 45:8,
and *NEB*, 'master Huram'. These proposals need not be regarded
as exclusive; since 'Oholi' (*'oh°lî*) means 'my tent', it is not impossible that the Chronicler (mis)understood the name as 'master of my
tent', which would have been appropriate for one involved in the
construction of the tabernacle (though it will not have been what
the name really meant; cf. M. Noth, *ZDMG* 81 [1927], p. 14, and
Die israelitischen Personennamen [1928], pp. 158-9), and that he introduced part of it here as a conscious word-play in order to underline the comparison he was drawing between the construction of the
tabernacle and of the temple. **craftsmen:** the root *ḥāḵām* is used
in this sense in association with building only in Exodus for the
tabernacle and in Chronicles for the temple.

15. The response to v. 10 above. **my lord:** the impression which
has been developing throughout this chapter that Huram is a vassal
of Solomon, rather than an equal as in 1 Kg. 5:12, is here finally
made explicit.

16. This reply to vv. 8-9 above is based on 1 Kg. 5:8-9, but has
been rewritten quite freely. The addition of the detail **to Joppa**
occasions no surprise, as it was the nearest port to Jerusalem in the
Chronicler's day; cf. Ezr. 3:7 and Jon. 1:3.

17-18. Following the order of his *Vorlage*, the Chronicler includes
a note about part of Solomon's own labour force for the building.
This is appropriate after his treatment of those employed from Tyre.

1 Kg. has two passages that refer to Solomon's forced labour,
5:13-18 and 9:20-22. The latter is reproduced fairly closely by the
Chronicler in 8:7-9 below, and it includes the clear statement that
the Israelites themselves were not subject to a forced levy. 1
Kg. 5:13-18 has often been held to contradict this, the words 'out
of all Israel' being taken to imply that Israelites *were* included in
the levy (though for a possible explanation of this apparent contradiction, cf. Mettinger, *Solomonic State Officials*, pp. 134-9). Whatever be the truth of the situation in Kings, however, the Chronicler

must have read the earlier text in the light of the later, and so made it clear that here too there was no question of the Israelites being levied. This he did by speaking specifically of **all the aliens who were in the land of Israel**, probably referring thereby to the remaining indigenous Canaanite population of the land. He may have hit upon this particular formula by reflection on the laws of Lev. 25:39–55, for it is there made clear that while one Israelite is not to rule over another 'with harshness' (vv. 43, 46, 53), yet Israelites may buy slaves 'from among the strangers who sojourn with you and their families that are with you, who have been born in your land' (v. 45), the word 'sojourn' here coming from the same root as **aliens** in the text under discussion.

The Chronicler's whole approach here, as elsewhere, may now be seen to provide a fine example of the exegetical principle to which he would doubtless have subconsciously subscribed that 'Scripture must interpret Scripture': thus his 'text' (*Vorlage*) is understood in the light of another, more explicit treatment of the same theme, with wording drawn from a relevant legal passage. The resulting presentation, though regarded as improbable by most scholars, can yet not be ruled out as impossible; cf. Willi, pp. 143–4. Indeed, by passing over 1 Kg. 5:13*b*–14, he may indicate awareness that the thirty thousand men there referred to were part of a *temporary* conscription of Israelites (cf. Mettinger), whereas vv. 15–16, which he reproduces in the following verse, were in the separate category of gentile conscripts.

after: i.e. 'on the model of', 'similar to' (*NEB*); cf. W. J. Peter Boyd, *JTS* ns 12 (1961), p. 54. **the census of them which David his father had taken**: cf. 1 Chr. 22:2, where the Chronicler's use of 'the aliens' is no doubt based on the same considerations which are more clearly seen to have influenced him in the present passage. It would seem most natural to refer **the census** to 1 Chr. 21, but in fact in Chronicles as well as 2 Sam. 24 it is apparent that that census related to native Israelites. **a hundred and fifty three thousand six hundred**: the Chronicler has worked out this total for himself. It is simply the sum of the numbers in the following verse.

18. Cf. v. 2, and 1 Kg. 5:15–16. **three thousand six hundred**: 1 Kg. 5:16 has 'three thousand three hundred', but it may well be this latter figure that is confused. For a full discussion of the textual problems (unfortunately inconclusive on precisely this point), cf. D. W. Gooding, *Relics of Ancient Exegesis* (1976), pp. 50–63.

The Building and its Furnishings

3:1–5:1

This section is clearly marked by its opening and closing verses and by the recurrent use of the clause 'and he made' noted at v. 8 below. At first sight it is striking to observe that, after the extensive, almost laboured, build-up to this point, the Chronicler has substantially shortened the account of his *Vorlage* (1 Kg. 6:1–7:51). Since for the material which he retains he follows the same order, and often the same wording, as Kings, there is no need to postulate an alternative source. Rather, examination shows that he has retained quite sufficient to direct his readers' attention to the earlier and fuller account, while at the same time adding or altering a number of details, to be noted below, that will encourage them to interpret the text in particular in terms of comparison with the Tabernacle – a procedure of his which is quite familiar by now. (This is more likely in general terms than the suggestion that he assimilated parts of the description to his knowledge of the second temple, both because it fits a pattern of interpretation already found elsewhere in his work, and because it is improbable that he would have wished to bring his description of Solomon's temple, so central to his concern, down to the level of what was in many respects an inferior institution.)

Location and Chronology

3:1–2

1. This verse is entirely the Chronicler's own, though it is probable that in every particular he is only making explicit the intention of earlier sources or tradition. First, and most striking, is his identification of the temple site with **Mount Moriah**, referred to elsewhere in the *OT* only at Gen. 22:2 as the site where Abraham was commanded to offer up Isaac. (For some later developments of the *Akedah*—temple association, cf. B. Grossfeld, *JJS* 28 [1977], pp. 60–64.) We may note in passing that one of the inscriptions from a burial cave at Khirbet Beit Lei, originally thought to date from about 700 BC and to read, 'The (Mount of) Moriah thou hast favoured, the dwelling of Yah, Yahveh' (cf. J. Naveh, *IEJ* 13 [1963], p. 86), should now most probably be read and dated differently, so that there is no direct attestation of this association earlier than the Chronicler himself; cf. Gibson, *Inscriptions* 1, pp. 57f.; F. M. Cross in J. A. Sanders (ed.), *Near Eastern Archaeology in the Twentieth Century* (1970), p. 302; and, most fully, A. Lemaire, *RB* 83 (1976), pp. 560f.

The important verses in Gen. 22 for our present concern are 2 and 14, though they contain several difficulties of their own. It is widely agreed that in their present form they already seek to interpret the narrative as a pointer towards the future temple. Noteworthy here is the use in v. 14 of the phrase 'the mount of the Lord', which clearly refers to the temple hill in Ps. 24:3; Isa. 2:3 and 30:29. Support for this conclusion comes from the words 'as it is said to this day', which suggest association with a well-known location, and the word-play between 'it shall be provided' (linking back to v. 8 of the narrative) and 'he will be seen', which could well be understood in cultic terms. In addition, if the popular view is right which regards part of the purpose of Gen. 22 as being originally an aetiology for the abolition of human sacrifice, then a reference to Jerusalem, apparently the centre of the 'Molech cult' which practised this form of sacrifice, is to be expected. Now, while it is clear that v. 14 is important for determining one aspect of the narrator's purpose, it cannot be divorced from v. 2. These are the only two verses which suggest that the altar was built on a mountain; the phrase 'one of the mountains of which I shall tell you', by its resemblance to the expression of God's choice of the sanctuary in, for instance, Dt. 12, seems to be making a similar allusion to that in v. 14; and finally, the name 'Moriah' itself (*môriyyāh*) may well, by a popular form of etymology, have been understood as 'the vision of the Lord', or the like, and so again be a pointer to one element in v. 14.

The Chronicler, we may now observe, has in our present verse picked up and made explicit these major interpretative themes from Gen. 22. First, the identity of **Moriah** with the temple site is, of course, plainly stated. Second, use of the word **Mount** relates to that feature already noted which seems only to have entered Gen. 22 as an element of interpretation, and thirdly the description **where the Lord had appeared to David his father** is subtly introduced to link an important feature of Gen. 22:14 ('he will be seen') with the more immediate designation of the temple site analysed above at 1 Chr. 21 in the story of **the threshing floor of Ornan the Jebusite**. The forging of this link between Gen. 22 and 1 Chr. 21 is sufficient to account for the slight anomaly that in fact it was the angel of the Lord who **appeared to David** in 1 Chr. 21:16 (unless the Chronicler has God's answer with fire from heaven in vv. 26 and 28 in mind). Either way, *RSV*'s interpretation is to be preferred to that of Ehrlich, pp. 355-6, and others who render 'which had been provided by David his father'. Not only is this very lame in such a theologically suggestive context, but it involves the absurd implication of identifying the whole of **Mount Moriah** with **the threshing floor**.

It has been argued by many commentators that 'Moriah' did not stand in the earliest version of Gen. 22:2, and because of this some have gone further in suggesting that in fact it was introduced there only under the influence of this verse in Chronicles; cf. R. Kilian, *Isaaks Opferung* (1970), pp. 31–46. This final step must be judged improbable for chronological reasons. As already noted, the name 'Moriah' is part of the whole interpretation offered in Gen. 22:2 and 14, and it is difficult to imagine that this had not been already introduced by the Chronicler's time. What does emerge with clarity, however, is that the Chronicler has not invented some arbitrary identification, but has drawn here on a tradition which was sufficiently deeply rooted and well established as to have influenced the Genesis text itself. His own contribution, rather, is first to spell out what is alluded to in the earlier texts (it was noted at 1 Chr. 21 that this was precisely what he did too in the case of **the threshing floor**, which is not explicitly linked to the temple site in 2 Sam. 24), and, second, to link these three episodes together in such a way as to emphasise the continuity of worship at this site and so indirectly to link the temple of his own day with some of the major religious leaders of Israel's past.

2. The date for the start of building is abbreviated from 1 Kg. 6:1. The omission of the 480 years from the Exodus is to be explained by the Chronicler's comparative lack of interest in this event (though see also on 36:21 below) in view of the new conditions inaugurated by David and Solomon; see on 1 Chr. 17:21–2 and 2 Chr. 6. MT includes an anomalous 'on the second' (*baššēnî*), which must refer to the day of the month. However, it is ungrammatical, poorly attested in the vrs., and is to be omitted, as in *RSV*, as a dittograph. **in the second month:** so too in the account of the building of the second temple; cf. Ezr. 3:8.

3–7. The Chronicler draws a distinction between the main structure of the temple and the elements contained within it, including the most holy place (see on v. 8). These first few verses supply details of the temple's overall size and appearance only. For discussion about the architecture of Solomon's temple, etc., the reader is referred to the commentaries on Kings and to Th. A. Busink, *Der Tempel von Jerusalem*, I (1970).

3. An introductory note of the **measurements** of the **house**; cf. 1 Kg. 6:2. This will have included the main holy place and the most holy place, but not the vestibule. The text of this verse is not certain. *RSV* represents a widely adopted emendation; but *NEB* may be correct to attempt a closer rendering of MT, 'These are the foundations which Solomon laid for building the house of God'. In that case, what follows would be merely the ground-plan (CM), and this would account for the fact that the Chronicler omits from his *Vorlage* both here and later a note of the height of the sanctuary.

of the old standard: it is clear from this passage and from Ezek. 40:5; 43:13 that there were at least two different **cubits** in ancient Israel, of which one had gone out of use by the time of the Chronicler. For a well-informed attempt to calculate the precise length of a cubit, cf. R. B. Y. Scott, *JBL* 77 (1958), pp. 205–14. It is not certain when one form of the cubit dropped out of regular use. The references in Ezekiel might suggest a date not long before his time. On the basis of a change in the size of the sanctuary at Arad, Y. Aharoni has suggested, in D. N. Freedman and F. M. Cross (eds), *New Directions in Biblical Archaeology* (1969), p. 40, that it was in the tenth to ninth centuries BC; but this may need revision downwards.

4. The vestibule: the text of this verse is corrupt, and many solutions have been proposed which cannot all be discussed here. MT appears to supply measurements for the length and height, while 1 Kg. 6:3 gives the length and breadth, as might be expected. In addition, something seems to have gone wrong with the first part of the verse ('and the vestibule which was in front of the length in front of the breadth of the house [was] twenty cubits'), while the **height** of **a hundred and twenty cubits** contradicts the expected thirty cubits, which was the height of the rest of the temple, and is in any case far too high for the first temple. Moreover, we do not expect a reference to height on the basis of the Chronicler's practice elsewhere. *RSV* responds to these difficulties by simply adopting parts of 1 Kg. 6:3; but for this there is no textual evidence. The best solution is proposed by CM: 'and the vestibule which was in front of the house (*habbayit*, restored with LXX): the length according to the breadth of the house was twenty cubits and the breadth ten cubits'. This has the advantage of supplying the information expected on the basis of 1 Kg 6:3, but of remaining close to MT. The last phrase (*weḥārōḥab ʾammôt ʿeśer*) is graphically very similar to MT, which may therefore simply represent corruption of it (so CM). It is more attractive to suppose, however, that the present text originated as a marginal gloss by someone who missed a reference to the height of the temple, and that, because of its similarity to part of the original text, this was later thought in fact to be a corruption of it and so came to displace it. For some other examples of this textual process, cf. L. C. Allen, *JTS* ns 22 (1971), pp. 143–50, and *JTS* ns 24 (1973), pp. 69–73. This must have taken place before the translation of LXX, and so cannot, as earlier commentators thought, be a reflection of the dimensions of the Herodian temple (Josephus, *Ant.* 15:391). Nevertheless, this later building shows that

such a tower-like structure as the glossator envisaged would not
have been inconceivable in his day.

He overlaid it on the inside with pure gold: at this point, the
Chronicler breaks away from 1 Kg. 6, which deals in the following
verse with the windows of the temple, its side-chambers, and so on.
He concentrates on the three main sections of the temple. Thus this
phrase, together with vv. 5-7, is his own composition, based generally on allusions in his earlier source. For the present sentence,
cf. 1 Kg. 6:22 and 30.

5. the nave: literally, 'the great house', i.e. the holy place. In 1
Kg. 6:15, **cypress** is used only for the floor, with cedar for the
remainder. **palms and chains:** cf. 1 Kg. 6:18, 29, 32, 35 and 7:17
for this type of decoration.

6. settings of precious stones: quite absent from 1 Kg.; but cf.
1 Chr. 29:2, where a link with the materials for the tabernacle was
noted. **gold of Parvaim:** despite the arguments of H. E. del Medico,
VT 13 (1963), pp. 158–86, this is to be understood as a place-name.
It was so translated by LXX and T, and it is also a place-name in
1QapGn 2.23 (cf. J. A. Fitzmyer, *The Genesis Apocryphon of Qumran
Cave 1* [1971²], pp. 52f. and 94f.). There, however, it has become
a strange and remote country, more in the realms of mythical than
actual geography. As such, it has been conjectured that it was
identified with 'the Garden of the Righteous', situated 'at the ends
of the earth' (cf. *Enoch* 60:23; 106:8, and P. Grelot, *VT* 11 [1961],
pp. 30–8, and *VT* 14 [1964], pp. 155–63). The Rabbis, who may
have still been aware of the literal meaning (cf. Grelot, p. 160, n. 3),
used etymology to derive some further meaning from it, linking the
word either with the root *pārāh*, 'to bear fruit', and so suggesting
that it produced gold fruit (Num.R. 11:3; cf. *B.Yoma* 21b and 39b),
or with *par*, 'a young bull', suggesting that the gold was like the
blood of bulls (Exod.R. 35:1). The first of these suggestions seems
also to be reflected in the apocryphal text published as the 'Traité
des Vases' by J. T. Milik, *RB* 66 (1959), pp. 567–75. Of these later
developments, however, there is no hint in our present text. It may
be that the Chronicler had a literal source for the gold still in mind
(compare the 'gold of Ophir' in 1 Chr. 29:4; indeed, R. North,
Fourth World Congress of Jewish Studies, 1 (1967), pp. 197–202, has
revived the view of Vigouroux that Ophir and Parwaim are the
same), in which case the most plausible identification would be *el-
farwain*, mentioned by the Arabic historian Hamdāni in north-east
Arabia. The suggestion that it was known as the site of a gold mine
lacks substantiation, however. In view of the developments traced
by Grelot in one branch of later tradition, it is also possible that
even by the Chronicler's time this literal meaning had been over-

shadowed, or even forgotten, so that the place-name was used more in the sense of a superlative for 'finest gold'. This seems to be the intention of V (cf. v. 7) and P, which both render along these lines without specific reference to Parwaim as a place-name.

7. This verse is largely resumptive of the foregoing, with the addition of **cherubim** to the carved decorations, on account of 1 Kg. 6:29. This does not, however, seem to be sufficient reason to regard 6*b*–7 as secondary.

The Furnishing of the Temple

3:8–5:1

The word *wayya'aś* (**And he made**) recurs with such regularity from now on, replacing other words of similar meaning in the *Vorlage* on several occasions, that it must point to part of a conscious shaping of his narrative by the Chronicler. The subject throughout is Solomon, as in the climax at 5:1. (In 4:11–16 the subject is Huram, but 4:10–22 may well be secondary; see below.) This is closely comparable with the shape of the narrative that tells of the construction of the tabernacle in Exod. 36:8–39:32, where *wayya'aś* occurs nearly forty times. Willi (pp. 96–8) and Mosis (pp. 140f.), believing that 4:10–22 are secondary, have argued that *wayya'aś* occurs twelve times in the remaining material, and they see in this evidence of the Chronicler's view that the temple was to be a sanctuary for all Israel. In fact, however, they are obliged to concede that the real figure is thirteen, and since it is agreed that 5:1 represents the climax, it is hardly legitimate to explain away the thirteenth occurrence in 4:9 as summarising, the more so when it is realised that 4:9–10 add a new element to the description rather than recapitulating what has gone before. Nearly all the items treated in this passage are without question to be grouped as 'furnishing' for the temple. It would thus be attractive to regard the only two possible exceptions in the same light. See further on vv. 3:8 and 4:9 below.

3:8. the most holy place: since this was included within the holy place, described earlier, there is no difficulty in supposing that the Chronicler regarded it as part of the temple 'furnishing', broadly speaking. This will have been, in his view, the central feature which the whole edifice was built to contain. Most of the material for this verse is adapted from 1 Kg. 6:19–20, though as already noted elsewhere, so too here the Chronicler does not specify the height.

six hundred talents: this is added by the Chronicler. Since he used the same figure at 1 Chr. 21:25 in connection with David's purchase of the temple site, and since there it is clearly twelve times the

figure of his *Vorlage* (50, in 2 Sam. 24:24), there is every reason to
suppose that he intended a comparable symbolism in the present
instance.

9. This verse, which has no parallel in Kings, is the Chronicler's
own composition. **nails** are not referred to in any other description
of the temple. Since their function was the same as the 'hooks' used
in the tabernacle (e.g. Exod. 26:32, 37), there can be little doubt
that the latter influenced the Chronicler at this point. **one shekel to
fifty shekels of gold:** an emendation suggested by LXX. The difficulty with MT ('the weight of the nails was fifty shekels of gold')
is that the weight (about 1¼ lbs.) is too heavy for a single nail and
not enough for the total. However, if the figure **fifty** is again inspired
by 2 Sam. 24:24 (see the previous verse), such considerations may
be irrelevant. **the upper chambers:** cf. 1 Chr. 28:11, though as
already noted 1 Kg. 6:5–6 and 8–10 have previously been omitted.

10–13. The **cherubim**. The Chronicler has rewritten and somewhat abbreviated 1 Kg. 6:23–8 with no substantial change of meaning. **of wood:** the Hebrew here has a word of uncertain meaning
($ṣa^{a}ṣu^{°}îm$), the usual understanding of which is represented by *NEB*,
'two images of cherubim' (literally, 'two cherubim of image work',
RV), relating the word's root ($ṣw^{°}$) to its Arabic cognate which means
'to form', 'to fashion' (by metal-casting). *RSV*, noting from 1
Kg. 6:23 that the cherubim were made of olivewood, prefers to
follow a hint from LXX that the present text may be corrupt and so
emends to $mē^{°}ēṣîm$.

13. extended: cf. 1 Chr. 28:18 and G. R. Driver, *JTS* 32 (1931),
pp. 251ff. The second half of the verse is not found in the Chronicler's *Vorlage*, but is a very probable deduction.

14. Nowhere else does the *OT* refer to such a **veil** in the temple.
The suggestion that a sentence to this effect has dropped out of 1
Kg. 6:21b is improbable from a textual point of view and it would
contradict 1 Kg. 6:31–32 (and 7:50), which speak of doors at this
point. Rather, influence from the design and construction of the
tabernacle is again apparent, for this verse verbally cites Exod. 26:31
and 36:35. See also on 2:7 above.

After this verse, there is a lengthy omission from Kings (1
Kg. 6:29–7:14). The reasons for this are mostly apparent. Some of
the material has already been substantially worked into the Chronicler's previous narrative (e.g. 6:29–30. For 7:13–14, see on 2:7 and
13–14 above). For the doors (6:31–2) he has substituted the veil, as
just noticed, while most of the remainder (7:1–12) relates not to the
temple, but to the palace (see on 2:1 above).

15–17. The description of the **two pillars** is abbreviated from 1
Kg. 7:15–22. It may be noted that the context there makes clear

that it was Hiram who was responsible for making them, not Solomon, as might be inferred from the Chronicler. The position of
the pillars, ambiguous in the Kings account, is here made explicit:
In front of the house (15); **in front of the temple** (17) (i.e. on either
side of the entrance into the holy place, rather than outside the
vestibule). This ties in with what is known from other comparable
sanctuaries such as the one at Hazor (cf. Y. Yadin, *Hazor* [1972],
p. 89) and Arad (cf. Y. Aharoni, *BA* 31 [1968], p. 22). **thirty-five
cubits high:** contrast 1 Kg. 7:15, 'eighteen cubits'. It is generally
agreed that the Chronicler added to this figure the circumference of
the pillar (12 cubits) and the height of the capital (5 cubits), but
unless his *Vorlage* was unclear there is no apparent reason for this.
like a necklace: with most commentators, *RSV* conjecturally reads
$k^e r\bar{a}b\hat{\imath}\underline{d}$ for MT $badd^e\underline{b}\hat{\imath}r$, 'in the oracle' (*RV*; i.e. in the most
holy place). The change is slight, and very probably correct. Rather
than assume simple corruption, however, we may conjecture that
the original text was glossed with the word 'in the oracle' from 1
Kg. 6:21 (so Barnes), and that this was mistakenly understood later
as a correction of the similar looking word in the text (see on v. 4
above for this process).

4:1. The **altar of bronze** appears accidentally to have been lost
from the description of the building in 1 Kg., though later references
both in Kg. and Chr. show that it originally stood in both books;
cf. Willi, p. 97, and Mosis, pp. 146f. The way in which the
measurements are listed does not conform to the Chronicler's own
style, and so it is likely to reflect the influence of his *Vorlage*. Less
probably, Mosis postulates influence rather from Exod. 27:1; 38:1.
Even without this, however, continuity with the tabernacle is suggested by comparison with 1:6. The large size of the altar suggests
that we are here given the dimensions of its base, from which steps
went up to the altar itself; cf. Ezek. 43:13-17 and de Vaux, *AI*,
p. 412.

2-5. **the molten sea:** cf. 1 Kg. 7:23-6, which is followed closely
for the most part. There are two slight differences: **gourds** (v. 3) of
1 Kg. has been replaced in MT of Chr. by 'what looked like oxen'.
The textual and theological speculation which has surrounded this
verse has now been undercut by Willi, who suggests (p. 139) that
the Chronicler did not understand his *Vorlage* here and so purposely
substituted this imprecise phrase. There is then no need for the
emendation suggested by *RSV*. The second difference concerns the
capacity of the sea, **three thousand baths** (**over** should be deleted)
in v. 5, but 'two thousand' in 1 Kg. 7:26. C. C. Wylie, *BA* 12
(1949), pp. 86-90, has neatly shown that the figure in Kings is

based upon a calculation that assumes a hemispherical shape for the sea while that in Chronicles assumes a cylindrical shape.

6. For the **ten lavers**, cf. 1 Kg. 7:38. However, as the Chronicler has omitted a long section dealing with the portable stands for the lavers (1 Kg. 7:27–37), he combines his description with a note about the placement of the stands from 1 Kg. 7:39. The Chronicler has himself added notes about the purpose of both the lavers – **in which to wash** and **to rinse off what was used for the burnt offering** – and **the sea – for the priests to wash in**. Once again, he has clearly been influenced by the description of the tabernacle, whose laver is said to have been for this same purpose; cf. Exod. 30:17–21. By contrast with the original symbolism of the sea, this may represent an element of 'demythologisation'.

7. The description and positioning of the **ten golden lampstands** are drawn from 1 Kg. 7:49 (cf. C. L. Meyers, *The Tabernacle Menorah* [1976], pp. 35–6). The addition of **as prescribed** (*kemiš-pāṭām*) singles out this item of furniture from the others, and puts it into the category of those particular institutions which were seen at 2:4 to have special significance for the Chronicler and his narrative. They will thus recur also at important points later on; cf. 13:11; 29:7, and *IBC*, pp. 121–2. This aspect seems to be more important than a reference back to the lamp in the tabernacle, Exod. 25:31ff.; 37:17ff., especially since the tabernacle had one seven-branched candlestick, whereas here there are **ten**. (Contrast 13:11, however, where the description clearly follows that of the tabernacle rather than the present verse.)

8. The **ten tables** are not referred to elsewhere. The context and their placement strongly suggest that the Chronicler thought that the lampstands were put on them. For the **basins of gold**, cf. 1 Kg. 7:50. The number, **a hundred**, is the Chronicler's own addition.

9. Although 1 Kg. 6:36 and 7:12 refer to the temple courts, the Chronicler has composed this verse himself in conformity with the design of the temple planned by Ezekiel (cf. Ezek. 40–48) and the temple of his own day, in which the inner **court** was for the **priests** and the outer or **great court** was for the laity. Although these courts can hardly be called part of the temple furnishing, they are nevertheless included by the Chronicler in this section which, if vv. 10–22 are indeed a secondary addition, will now be immediately concluded at 5:1. It may at least be noted that the section began at 3:8 with the most holy place, which it was seen could be loosely regarded as 'furnishing', and that there is thus a certain balance between opening and close.

10–22. At least since the time of Benzinger, this passage has been regarded as a secondary addition to the Chronicler's work (see especially Rudolph; Willi, pp. 94–5). It follows 1 Kg. 7:39–50 very closely indeed, which contrasts strongly with the Chronicler's looser attachment to his *Vorlage* in the preceding section; 4:12f. does not agree with 3:16, which the Chronicler had himself adapted; the reference to **the inner doors** in v. 22 may contradict the Chronicler's own view (cf. 3:14) that the temple had a veil here; a good deal of this section repeats items already treated previously by the Chronicler such as **the lavers** (v. 14), the **sea** with its **twelve oxen** (v. 15) and **the lampstands** (v. 20), whereas other material is included here which seems previously to have been deliberately omitted, such as **the stands** (v. 14). The passage includes all the material between 1 Kg. 7:39a, where the Chronicler broke away from his *Vorlage* (at 4:6) and 1 Kg. 7:51, where he rejoins it (5:1). This accounts for the abrupt and awkward introduction of the positioning of **the sea** in v. 10, which is otherwise quite out of place in the present context. It is thus generally supposed that some later worker felt the need to insert what in his opinion was missing from the Chronicler's account. There is much to be said in favour of this view, though no reason has yet been advanced to explain why such a later addition was made just here and not in the many other places where the Chronicler has omitted material from his *Vorlage*. Since the passage runs so closely parallel with 1 Kg. 7:39–50, little comment is needed here. Most of the slight differences are to be explained on mechanical, textual grounds.

11. the pots: the text is here better preserved than in 1 Kg. 7:40.

12. and the two capitals: comparison with the parallel passage suggests that this is an explicative use of the conjunction: 'even'.

16. Huramabi: cf. 2:13.

19. the tables: this is a mistaken assimilation to the tables of v. 8, which served a different purpose. There was only one table **for the bread of the Presence**, as in the *Vorlage* and as the Chronicler well knows; cf. 13:11; 29:18.

20. as prescribed: cf. v. 7 above.

22. *RSV* has here emended very slightly in order to conform the second half of the verse to 1 Kg. 7:50. MT has **the doors** themselves, not just **the sockets**, made **of gold**. It may be right to emend, but perhaps the later reviser was himself as capable as the Chronicler of highlighting the glory of the temple.

5:1. Cf. 1 Kg. 7:51. The Chronicler is able to use his *Vorlage* exactly here to round off his account of the building and its furnishings; see above on 3:1–5:1, and on 3:8. **the things which David his father had dedicated:** cf. 1 Chr. 18:8, 10f.; 22:3f., 14, 16; 26:26; 29:2–9. It is remarkable that though this sentence is taken straight from the Chronicler's *Vorlage*, neither Samuel nor Kings has any preceding account to explain it in the way that Chronicles has.

The Dedication of the Temple

5:2–7:11

The Chronicler closely follows the Kings' narrative for the account of the dedication of the temple (cf. 1 Kg. 8:1–66). His own contribution is considerably less than in the previous sections, so that only the significant differences need be noted in the following comments. There can be little doubt that this ceremony, together with God's response which immediately follows it, marks one of the major climaxes in the Chronicler's presentation. It falls into three well-defined parts: the movement of the ark to the temple (5:2–6:11), Solomon's prayer of dedication (6:12–42), and the concluding ceremonies of dedication (7:1–11).

The Movement of the Ark to the Temple

5:2–6:11

The prominence which the Chronicler gave to the ark in his account of David's reign was frequently noted in the commentary on 1 Chronicles, especially in chs 13–16. Also he has already made its coming to rest in the temple the basis for his explanation of the changed nature of Levitical service (cf. 1 Chr. 6:31–2). His concern to retain this account of its actual transfer to the temple is thus quite understandable.

2. This type of description of Solomon's assembling of the people agrees exactly with the Chronicler's practice elsewhere (see on 1 Chr. 13:1–5).

3. the feast which is in the seventh month: i.e. the feast of Tabernacles. As at 3:2, the Chronicler omits the older name for the month, 'Ethanim', though without substituting the later equivalent, 'Tishri'.

4. the Levites: substituted by the Chronicler for 'the priests' of 1 Kg. 8:3. This greater precision, based on the Deuteronomic law in particular, coincides with what was noted of David's prescription at 1 Chr. 15:2. However, when the ark reaches the sanctuary itself, the Chronicler leaves the priests as carriers, since only they are allowed to enter it; cf. Num. 4:5ff. and Ezek. 44:10ff.

5. the tent of meeting: whatever may be the situation in Kings, the reference here must be to the tabernacle which was in Gibeon (cf. 1 Chr. 16:39). Thus the division in the priestly and Levitical service which has obtained since 1 Chr. 16, and which was accentuated by 1 Chr. 21:28–22:1, is now to be regarded as resolved. **the priests and the Levites:** so 1 Kg. 8:4. MT here does not have the conjunction: 'the priests, the Levites', which should be understood as referring to only one category of official, namely the Levitical priests, as at Dt. 17:9; Jos. 3:3, etc. Since the same phrase occurs at 23:18 and 30:27, emendation is not a satisfactory solution; cf. von Rad, *GCW*, pp. 87f. Taken at face value, the clause seems to imply that **the holy vessels**, and perhaps also **the tent**, were carried by priests, but this both contradicts the law of Num. 1:50, etc., and fails to explain why this unusual phrase is introduced at precisely this point. Moreover, if the **ark** is included, there would be a clash with v. 4, where 'the Levites' must certainly be attributed to the Chronicler, for the words **brought them up** do not refer to the entry into the sanctuary, since this follows only at v. 7. The only possible solution seems to be that the whole clause is a later addition (syntactically, it is quite independent), probably designed to harmonise the apparent contradiction between Kings and Chronicles in v. 4 by using a title known from earlier literature that combined both words 'priests' and 'Levites' into one. Its appearance in Kings will then also be the work of a later redactor, with which several commentators on Kings agree; in support of this, it may be noted that the clause is more closely integrated with its context in Kings (*wayyaʿᵃlû* for *heʿᵉlû*), and that it eases the difficulty by the addition of the conjunction – 'the priests *and* the Levites'.

9. the holy place: so 1 Kg. 8:8. MT here has 'the ark', which *RSV* is right to emend. For an explanation of how the present text may have arisen, cf. L. C. Allen, *JTS* ns 22 (1971), p. 150.

11–13. From **for all the priests** to **endures for ever** is additional to Kings. The ceremony accompanying the placing of the ark in **the holy place** is elaborated in ways that are typical of the Chronicler, and which find particularly close parallels with the earlier account in 1 Chr. 15–16. Thus, for **had sanctified themselves**, see 1 Chr. 15:14; for **the Levitical singers**, see the introduction to 1 Chr. 15–16, and 25:1–6; the trio **Asaph, Heman, and Jeduthun** also occur at 1 Chr. 6:31ff.; 16:37 with 41; 25:1–6; 2 Chr. 29:13f.; 35:15; **arrayed in fine linen:** only at 1 Chr. 15:27 is this otherwise said of the Levites and the singers; for **cymbals, harps and lyres**, cf. 1 Chr. 15:16 and 25:1; 1 Chr. 13:8, which describes the musical accompaniment to the first, unsuccessful attempt to transport the ark to Jerusalem, is also comparable; finally, the Psalm fragment is the same as that which concluded the Psalm anthology at 1

Chr. 16:34. The material that is additional to Kings would thus seem to be just what we would expect of the Chronicler in such a situation. As on other similar occasions, the pageantry, the stress on **unison**, and the joy in worship are unmistakeable; cf. 2 Chr. 29:25–30.

Nevertheless, many scholars have argued that these verses were added only later. Rudolph's arguments may be taken as representative: (a) the reference to **divisions** of the priests is dependent on 1 Chr. 24, but that passage is itself secondary. This argument is not convincing. There are other places that speak of the divisions of the clergy which do come from the Chronicler (1 Chr. 23:6; 26:1, 19; 28:13, 21; 2 Chr. 8:14, 31:2, 15–17; 35:4, 10). It was shown above (and see in more detail *SVT* 30 [1979], pp. 251–68) that what the reviser introduced in 1 Chr. 23–27 was the fact of specifically twenty four divisions, but that is not mentioned here. The suggestion that the number of **a hundred and twenty priests who were trumpeters** is made up of 5 x 24 is quite without reason or foundation. (b) Rudolph argues that 1 Chr. 15:27*a* is a late gloss; there would then be no parallel for the singers wearing **fine linen**, normally reserved for the priests. This argument too is unconvincing. In his commentary on 1 Chr. 15:27 (p. 119), Rudolph acknowledges that the Chronicler had the Levites wearing fine linen, but to support his suggestion that 'the singers' were added later, he merely refers us forward to the present passage. The argument is thus entirely circular. (c) Rudolph's third argument includes an element that has impressed other commentators too, but also goes beyond it. Since 7:1–3 seems to be the Chronicler's own description of a theophany at the dedication of the temple (*contra* Welch, pp. 37ff.), it is thought that the present account of a theophany must be secondary. Rudolph refines this view. He thinks that the Chronicler's account at this point originally stopped at v. 10. A later editor then observed the difference with 1 Kg. 8, and so added what the Chronicler had deliberately omitted, namely, vv. 11*a*, 13*b* and 14. Since 11*b*–13*a* is embedded in this later material, it cannot have come from the Chronicler himself. In reply to this argument, leaving aside the question of general probability concerning such a process, it may be questioned whether the Chronicler may not himself have intended a double account of the theophany. In the present passage, in line with its *Vorlage*, **a cloud**, symbolising the Lord's **glory**, filled the house (cf. Exod. 40:34f.). This was appropriate as marking the divine approval of the ark's final resting place. In 7:1–3, however, there is a new element, fire from heaven. The echo of 1 Chr. 21:26–22:1 suggests that this marks acceptance of the temple as the place of sacrifice, as well as of the terms of Solomon's prayer. The state-

ment in 7:1 about the glory of the Lord should be taken as circumstantial, not necessarily as a further filling (see the commentary).
Then again it may be noted that in the present passage it is the holy
place which is filled, visible only to the priests, whereas in 7:1–3
the fire falls on the altar outside, in the sight of 'all the children of
Israel'. Understood in this way, 5:13–14 and 7:1–3 need not be
regarded as doublets but as separate acts of divine approval dealing
with somewhat different issues.

6:1. It is probable that the text of Kings from which the Chronicler drew these words was already in its present apparently corrupt
state (corrected by *RSV* at 1 Kg. 8:12). God's preference for dwelling **in thick darkness** had long been known (cf. Exod. 20:21) and
for this reason his presence was often symbolised by a cloud. This
then links with the cloud which filled the sanctuary at the end of
the previous chapter, and at the same time no doubt explains why
the most holy place was constructed in the way it was. A continuity
is thus forged between God's past revelation and the present temple
as a place where his people may meet with him.

4. Solomon's address to the people, which begins here, is clearly
seen as a comment on what has just transpired, not as an introduction to the later prayer (as seems generally to be assumed by commentators). Its major theme concerns the new temple as a permanent
resting place for the ark, something not achieved at any time since
the Exodus. But this inevitably involves too a reference to David's
previous desire to build and the dynastic promise to which this gave
rise. Thus, although the address follows its *Vorlage* closely, it again
reflects very much the Chronicler's own outlook.

5. I brought my people out of the land of Egypt: for the Chronicler's usual omission of reference to the Exodus in this chapter, see
the introduction to vv. 12–42 below. There, the reasons concern a
development in the covenantal basis for the people's relationship
with God. Here, however, the reference is purely for chronological
purposes, and is thus not deleted by the Chronicler.

5b–6a. and I chose. . . .may be there: these two clauses are
absent from the MT of 1 Kg. 8:16, but were only lost from there
by homoioteleuton after the time of the Chronicler. They are thus
not to be regarded as his addition, indicative of his particular
interests.

11. 1 Kg. 8:21b reads **the covenant of the Lord which he made
with** 'our fathers, when he brought them out of the land of Egypt'.
Though this would doubtless have been known to his readers, the
Chronicler omits the historical reference. What matters for him is
that **the covenant** is of effect now with **the people** (literally, 'children') **of Israel**. See further the paragraph immediately following.

Solomon's Prayer of Dedication

6:12–42

Solomon's prayer of dedication follows 1 Kg. 8:22–53 remarkably closely. Its major emphasis, on the temple as a centre for the prayers of the people in times of affliction, was as relevant to the Chronicler's readers as to any previous generation, and is abundantly illustrated in many other parts of his narrative where prayer is seen as the fundamental avenue for approach to God, with sacrifice being regarded rather as a response to God's goodness.

The major difference between Kings and Chronicles in this section is a decrease in the references to the Exodus and a consequent strengthening of the importance of God's word to David for the life and well-being of the nation; cf. Brunet, 'Théologie'; North, *JBL* 82 (1963), pp. 369–81; Japhet, *Ideology*, pp. 322–7; *IBC*, pp. 64–6. This difference, together with the new ending to the prayer in vv. 41–42, reflects an important element in the thought of the Chronicler, already noted above in part, for instance at 1 Chr. 17. The dedication of the temple marks a turning point in certain aspects of his presentation. Thus his well-known emphasis on the new role of singers which David gave to the Levites after the ark came to rest in the temple was seen in the previous chapter (and compare also 1 Chr. 16:7, 37–42; 2 Chr. 7:6; 8:14f.; 35:3), but the citation of Ps. 132:8–10 in vv. 41–42 draws renewed attention to this. Secondly, a major theme in 1 Chr. 17; 22 and 28–29 was seen to be that the completion of the temple would mark one phase in the fulfilment of the promises to the Davidic house through Nathan. These promises are the second main topic treated in Ps. 132, and the Chronicler's appreciation of this fact is made clear by his handling of the citation (see the comments on 41–42 below). It is therefore in no way surprising that he should also lay some emphasis on this fact, and thus see in the conclusion of the prayer (together with vv. 16–17) a request that God will now go on to fulfil the promise to David in its entirety by establishing his dynasty for ever. Chapter 7 then gives the divine response.

In all this, detraction from the Exodus is inevitable. In 1 Chr. 17 it formed the basis of God's relationship with his people, within the context of which a development was marked by the dynastic promise. Appropriately, therefore, the Chronicler retained the references of his *Vorlage* to it (especially in vv. 21f.). Now, however, that basis has for the Chronicler to lose ground to the stress on the new, Davidic covenant, whose fulfilment is heralded by this ceremony of dedication.

13. This verse is lacking in 1 Kg. 8, and has given rise to much

debate. Generally, it has been regarded as an addition by the Chronicler, and 'may have arisen from the desire to remove Solomon from
the place before the altar as a place sacred for the priests' (CM).
Rudolph, however, gave several reasons in support of the position
of one or two earlier commentators that this verse originally stood
in Kings, and was only later lost from it: (a) the manner in which
the dimensions of the **platform** are given contrasts with the Chronicler's usual practice elsewhere (see also on 4:1 above); (b) that
Solomon **knelt upon his knees** is presupposed by 1 Kg. 8:54, but
without the presence of this verse it would have to be assumed,
rather, that he was standing (cf. 1 Kg. 8:22); (c) the loss of the
verse can be explained by homoioteleuton: **and spread forth his
hands** comes at the end of both vv. 12 and 13.

This suggestion has impressed some scholars (e.g. Lemke, *HTR*
58 [1965], pp. 357–8), but not all, by any means. M. Noth, for
instance, argues that 1 Kg. 8:54 is itself a later addition (*Könige*
[1968], p. 173), while Mosis (pp. 144–6) finds the repetition of the
phrase **and spread forth his hands** precisely to betray this verse as
a later addition. From the point of view of style, this latter argument
is clearly justified, but that does not mean that the Chronicler
himself must have been responsible for the insertion. Since we know
that his *Vorlage* was not always identical with MT of Samuel and
Kings, it seems best on balance to regard this verse as an addition
indeed to 1 Kg. 8, but made prior to the Chronicler in a textual
tradition of that chapter no longer preserved for us.

a bronze platform: there are several representations from the ancient Near East of kings standing or kneeling on a chest or box of
some kind in an attitude of prayer; cf. Albright, *Archaeology*,
pp. 152–4, and Myers. This was no doubt necessary in order for
them to be seen and heard. In addition, however, it seems clear
from several passages in the *OT* that the king did have his own
particular place in the temple for ceremonial occasions, though
whether that is to be related to this platform is less certain, especially
as the words **had set it in the court** suggest that it was set up
temporarily for this occasion rather than being a permanent item of
temple furniture; cf. G. von Rad, *The Problem of the Hexateuch*
(1966), pp. 222–31, and G. Widengren, *JSS* 2 (1957), pp. 5–12.
Moreover, not even the position of this platform is certain; cf. N.
Poulssen, *König und Tempel* (1967), pp. 159–62. It might be assumed from v. 12 that it was near the altar. However, it was noted
at 4:9 that the Chronicler distinguished between 'the court of the
priests' and 'the great court', and in the present verse **the court**
(*hāᵃzārāh*) is the same word as is used for the latter. In addition,
since Solomon prayed **in the presence of all the assembly of Israel,**

it is most probable that the Chronicler would have envisaged the scene as being in the court for the laity.

14–17. The opening paragraph of the prayer shows clearly that although a measure of fulfilment of God's promises has been realised with the dedication of the temple (v. 15), this does not detract from, but rather, in the Chronicler's understanding, affords increased weight to, the prayer that God will now go on to fulfil his promise to establish the Davidic dynasty. Unlike in Kings, the prayer is made by the Chronicler to conclude on this same note.

16. in my law: 1 Kg. 8:25, 'before me'. Though this may be seen as a characteristic change by the Chronicler, by whose time the way of life for God's people was more fully described in the Pentateuch than had previously been the case (cf. Willi, pp. 125f.), there are many comparable expressions in the earlier books which suggest that this difference should not be overpressed; see, for instance, 1 Kg. 2:3.

24–39. Several of the petitions expressed in these verses concerning the life of Israel as a whole, though taken direct from 1 Kg. 8, could nevertheless have seemed of particular relevance to the community of the Chronicler's day. Unfortunately we do not know enough in detail about the conditions then prevailing to be sure of this in every case. One example, however, seems well attested on both literary and archaeological grounds, namely that in the middle of the fourth century BC the Jews were involved in the abortive revolt against the Persians led by the Sidonian Tennes and which may have resulted in the deportation of some of their number to Hyrcania (cf. D. Barag, *BASOR* 183 [1966], pp. 6–12). Verses 24–25, 34–35 and 36–39 might have been read especially with this, as well as the fact of continuing exile for many of the Jews in Babylon and elsewhere, in mind. Again, we certainly know from the much earlier post-exilic period of great difficulties which the community faced in its attempts to restore the agricultural prosperity of the land (cf. Hag. 1), and it is possible that drought (vv. 26–27) with its attendant famine and other afflictions (vv. 28–31) would have recurred from time to time. Finally, it is noteworthy that the open attitude towards the foreigner is retained in vv. 32–33, and suggests that the Chronicler was sympathetic towards that group within Judaism which saw Israel as having a role to play in the world of witness to God's uniqueness and power, and that through them the Gentiles too would come to acknowledge him.

39. The Chronicler omits from the end of this verse virtually the whole of 1 Kg. 8:50–51. Verse 51 refers back to the Exodus as the birth of the nation; for the omission of this, see above. Verse 50, however, is quite 'neutral' in this respect. Curiously, there is an echo of it at 2 Chr. 30:9 in the letter which Hezekiah sent to the remnant of the northern kingdom; this may be a small part of a much larger typological patterning of Hezekiah on Solomon.

40. The Chronicler draws the substance of this verse from his *Vorlage* again before departing from it radically at the close of the prayer. In Kings, the note of exile sounded in the previous verses suggests deliverance after the pattern of the Exodus from Egypt. This is again omitted by the Chronicler, who looks to other past aspects of God's deliverance to provide his model of future salvation.

41–42. With the exception of the last line, this poetic fragment is based on Ps. 132:8–10. The Psalm deals with the two related themes of the transfer of the ark to Jerusalem and God's promise to David. The verses cited here come at the point of transition from the first theme to the second, but by their new context both are given a much more far-ranging application. First, the **resting place** for **the ark** has become the final one of the temple itself. This marks an important development over the theme of rest which played such a vital role in the preparations for temple building in David's reign; see above, especially on 1 Chr. 22:9 and 28:2. In order for the temple to be built in the first place, 'rest' in terms of peace from war were a necessary precondition; now conversely the temple has itself become a resting-place for God. The use of the Psalm at this point thus marks a decisive turning point in the religious history of the nation. The later history is to show that such a peak did not last, and that it was lost to later generations. But we may suggest that it provided a pattern of what can only be called an eschatological rest, in which this passing glory would be replaced with the permanent dwelling of God amongst his people; cf. Ezek. 48:35; Heb. 4; Rev. 21:3.

42. This verse differs at two important points from Ps. 132:10, which reads:

> For thy servant David's sake
> do not turn away the face of thy anointed one.

First, the order of the two lines has been inverted; this has the effect of emphasising the last line. Secondly, though, the wording of this line has itself been changed by what must be regarded as an allusion to Isa. 55:3*b* ('And I will make with you an everlasting covenant, my steadfast sure love for David'): **Remember thy stead-fast love for David thy servant.**

In the Psalm, it is not entirely clear whether 'for thy servant David's sake' means because of David's faithfulness to God or because of God's promise to him. Here, however, the Chronicler seems certainly to have rephrased the line in order to make it refer to God's promise to David. First, this is its meaning at Isa. 55:3 (despite some who have argued to the contrary; see my discussion, with full references, in *JSS* 23 [1978], pp. 31–49). Second, as was observed at vv. 14–17 above, such an understanding balances what was said at the beginning of the prayer, where again there was the request that God should now go on to confirm his word of promise to David about a dynasty. Third, as was noted in the introduction to 1 Chr. 17, in the Chronicler's presentation of the united monarchy, the emphasis falls on the promise to David and obedience to the conditions by Solomon. Thus an appeal to David's pious deeds at this point would be less appropriate to his overall presentation. (Against the view defended here, see, most recently, G. Gerleman, *VT* 28 [1978], pp. 160f., while K. D. Sakenfeld, *The Meaning of Hesed in the Hebrew Bible* [1978], pp. 156–8, considers the expression deliberately ambiguous.)

The significance of this verse may now be appreciated (see further *TynB* 28 [1977], pp. 143–6). On the one hand, his allusion to Isa. 55:3 must be seen as an attempt to reassert the royalist interpretation of the promises to David, unlike Isa. 55:3 itself, which appears rather to transfer the promise to the people as a whole. On the other hand, the position of this verse at the end of Solomon's prayer of dedication shows that, with the task completed, the way is now clear for God eternally to establish the Davidic dynasty in accordance with his promise. As with the Chronicler's work as a whole, this cannot be termed 'messianic' in its full sense, but it certainly suggests strongly that, contrary to those commentators in whose view the promise is exhausted with the completion of the temple, he does rather see an abiding validity for the Davidic line, and that the temple building has confirmed, not absorbed, this hope.

Concluding Ceremonies of Dedication

7:1–11

The Chronicler has based himself somewhat more freely than in the preceding paragraphs on 1 Kg. 8:54–9:1, drawing the account into line with what is already known of his general outlook. The dedication of the temple is thus concluded with a dramatic and emphatic affirmation of Solomon's final appeal in his prayer and by a generous and joyful response from the congregation to this divine initiative.

1. The Chronicler omits the account of Solomon blessing the people (1 Kg. 8:54b–61), not because he thought that blessing was an exclusively priestly prerogative (cf. 6:3 and 1 Chr. 16:2), nor

because in his presentation Solomon was not standing before the altar but on a raised platform (6:13), but because he was anxious to show (in a way that the Kings' account does not) God's positive response to the prayer of 6:41.

fire came down. . . .and the sacrifices: a reference back to the account of David's purchase of the future temple site is apparent (1 Chr. 21:26). This continues the process which has emerged several times during the temple building of the uniting of what had previously been related but physically separated aspects of the Israelite cult, namely, the ark brought by David to Jerusalem and now installed in the temple, the Mosaic tabernacle, including especially the bronze altar (cf. 1:5f.), which had been at Gibeon, but on the pattern of which we have noted the Chronicler models the design of several aspects of the temple and which has also been brought into the new temple (see on 5:5), and now finally a reminder that as at its purchase, so now at its completion, the new site for the altar (1 Chr. 21:26—22:1) has been both designated and approved by God. It is thus significant to note further that this and the following two verses, which are found only in Chronicles, are also modelled on an account related to the approval of the earlier tabernacle cult, Lev. 9:23–4. In all this an apologetic motif may be discerned. It is quite likely that different groups within Israel laid particular claim to one or another of these diverse strands of religious tradition, just as later the Samaritans, for instance, were to do especially with regard to the tabernacle. The Chronicler, however, regards them all as having been taken up within the temple, which thus becomes a unifying symbol within a divided community, since all may see their own particular concerns brought to fulfilment within it. This is re-expressed in a more polemical style at 13:10–12 below. Equally and conversely, since so many traditions fed into the temple, it is implied that the temple community should be similarly open to the possibility of receiving those who may represent different shades of opinion or background within the total spectrum of Israelite, and later Jewish, faith.

and the glory of the Lord filled the temple; the word order (**and** followed by subject first and then verb — *mālē'* — which could as well be a present participle as in the perfect tense) marks this out as a circumstantial clause (cf. GK §156). In that case, it describes the circumstances which obtain at the time of the main action (**fire came down. . . .and consumed**), not a new development. Thus this refers back to what is recorded at 5:13f., and might perhaps be translated 'and all the while the glory of the Lord was filling the temple'. This verse is therefore no duplicate of 5:13f.; both passages have their own part to play in the Chronicler's narrative.

2. A similar note was included above at 5:14 from the *Vorlage*. The Chronicler's own phraseology in the present verse, however, is slightly closer still to the account of the dedication of the tabernacle (Exod. 40:35), showing that he was fully conscious of the typological parallel (cf. Mosis, pp. 147–9).

3. This verse too shows that the present paragraph is no mere replacement for 5:13f., for here, in addition to **the fire** (see v. 1), **the glory of the Lord** not only fills the sanctuary, marking approval of the transfer of the ark and affecting the priests, who alone were allowed in, but it is now seen **upon the temple**, so that **all the children of Israel** may know that God has consecrated it as a place of sacrifice and prayer. Since there is no suggestion in Kings that the glory was thus seen outside the sanctuary by the laity, we may again postulate influence on the Chronicler by Lev. 9:23f., and to a lesser extent Exod. 40:34. The people's response is described in the Chronicler's conventional manner.

4–7. The Chronicler here rejoins 1 Kg. 8:62–64. Rudolph's arguments for regarding the whole as a secondary expansion are quite insubstantial and raise the suspicion that his real reason is a desire to deny v. 6 to the Chronicler, since it accords less well with his analysis of 1 Chr. 23–27.

6. The Chronicler has himself added this characteristic verse, drawing attention to the full composition of the congregation (**priests . . . Levites . . . all Israel**) and to the musical aspects of the ceremony. **which king David had made:** cf. 1 Chr. 23:5 and 25:1–6, both from the primary layer in 23–27, and more generally the comments on 1 Chr. 6:31–2.

8–10. Cf. 1 Kg. 8:65f. In Kings, 'the feast' lasts seven days, and Solomon sends the people home on the eighth. (The addition in MT at the end of 1 Kg. 8:65, 'and seven days, fourteen days', is rightly relegated by *RSV* to the status of a marginal gloss, no doubt inspired by the Chronicler's account itself.) Because of the dates involved (cf. 5:3) the Chronicler understood this to be the feast of Tabernacles, which according to the law practised in his day was to be followed by an **eighth day** of **solemn assembly** (cf. Lev. 23:34–36, 39–43; the law of Dt. 16:13–15, which probably underlies the Kings narrative, has no reference to this additional day). He seems also to have felt, however, that it would not have been appropriate to celebrate the dedication of the temple during Tabernacles, and he further expands v. 9 to make **the dedication** fall during the **seven days** before **the feast** of Tabernacles.

8. from the entrance of Hamath to the brook of Egypt: coming at the conclusion of the dedication, this accords well with the first move towards a permanent home for the ark by David in 1 Chr. 13:5.

9. the dedication of the altar: the Chronicler regarded the temple as a house of sacrifice (cf. 2:4–6; v. 12 below, and 1 Chr. 22:1) as well as of prayer, and so it is not surprising that he should have coined this phrase, which does not occur in Kings.

10. and to Solomon: the Chronicler's own addition, pointing once more to his presentation of the reigns of **David** and **Solomon** as a single episode in the religious history of Israel; see also on 1 Chr. 17, and Braun, *JBL* 92 (1973), p. 514.

11. In 1 Kg. 9:1 this verse is a subordinate clause to introduce what follows. The Chronicler, however, has altered its syntax into that of an independent sentence. Both points are correctly rendered by *RSV*. It is probable that the Chronicler thus intended this verse as a summary conclusion of the dedication, for we have often seen that he likes to round off his literary sections with just such generalising statements. It is not entirely felicitous for this purpose, because it relates to building rather than dedication, even though the summary of the whole temple project does not come until 8:16. **the king's house:** see on 2:1 above. **he successfully accomplished** (*hiṣlîaḥ*): this is added by the Chronicler in order to note the fulfilment of the conditions laid on Solomon by David which would lead to the establishment of the dynasty; cf. 1 Chr. 22:11 and 13 above.

God's Reply to Solomon's Prayer

7:12–22

In view of the importance for the Chronicler of Solomon's completion of the temple and his prayer at its dedication, we would expect this paragraph, which contains God's answer to that prayer, to be equally significant in the presentation of this theological position. Naturally, like 1 Kg. 9:2–9, on which it is based, it first indicates God's choice of the new sanctuary. Beyond that, however, the Chronicler introduced a number of characteristic changes to his *Vorlage*. These will be noted in the comments below; but it should be pointed out here that one overall effect is to conform the answer more specifically to the prayer: vv. 13–15 deal with Solomon's request for his people, vv. 17–18 deal with his request concerning the status of the king, which 2 Chr. 6 was seen to intensify over against 1 Kg. 8, and finally 19–22 are now made to refer by way of summary to both king and people, rather than just the king and his descendants.

12. The introduction to the prayer is abbreviated from 1 Kg. 9:2 by omitting a reference back to God's earlier appearance to Solomon at Gibeon, though the addition of **by night** may be intended as a reminder of that occasion; cf. 1:7. A few of God's words are then retained from 1 Kg. 9:3 before the Chronicler branches off to make explicit what was only implicit in the earlier account, namely that God had **chosen this place** for himself (see also on 6:6). **a house of sacrifice:** cf. v. 9 above.

13-15. These verses are not found in Kings. The fact that they conform so completely to the Chronicler's ideology, thereby fulfilling a comparable role to his own addition in 1 Chr. 10:13-14, and that they interrupt a continuous sentence in 1 Kg. 9:3 without there being any suggestion that they originally stood there too, makes it virtually certain that these verses are added by the Chronicler himself. They supply an answer to the substance of the prayer of ch. 6, namely, that God would hear the prayers offered in or directed towards the temple.

13. As an introduction, reference is made to several of the calamitous situations which Solomon had described in 6:22-39. They are to be understood as representative of all.

14. It is quite extraordinary that none of the commentators has seen the vital significance of this verse for the Chronicler's theology, and in particular his doctrine of immediate retribution. Four avenues of repentance are mentioned which will lead God to forgive and restore, and these each get taken up at various points in the remainder of the narrative and illustrated, often with one of the remarkable interventions of God which are such a well-known feature of the Chronicler's work. That this is deliberate is shown by the fact that wherever these terms occur in the earlier narrative they are all quite neutral theologically and do not mark similar miraculous turning-points. It would thus seem clear that, as with regard to the establishment of the dynasty, so in terms of God's relationship with his people, the dedication of the temple was thought to have initiated a new phase. It can hardly be doubted that the intention behind this is fully kerygmatic; that is to say, there is an appeal here to the Chronicler's own readers to respond in like manner, for much of what follows is then designed to illustrate that no circumstances are too formidable to prevent God's immediate, direct and, if necessary, miraculous move to fulfil his promise. This verse, then, points the way towards salvation from the paradigmatic 'exilic' situation seen in the Chronicler's comments on the death of Saul, 1 Chr. 10:13-14. The two passages together summarise his basic concerns as regards God and his people as a whole. **if my people:** a response to Solomon's repeated 'if thy people' in 6:24ff. **humble themselves:**

earlier, and theologically neutral, occurrences of this word are found
at 1 Chr. 17:10; 18:1; 20:4, but after this it becomes a key element
on several occasions; cf. its use four times in the account of Shishak's
invasion during the reign of Rehoboam, the first king after Solomon
(12:6–7, 12), and also at 30:11; 32:26; 33:12, 19, 23; 34:7; and
36:12. **and pray:** contrast 32:20, 24 and 33:13 with 1 Chr. 17:25
and 2 Chr. 7:1. **and seek (my face):** cf. 11:16; 15:4, 15; 20:4, and
contrast 1 Chr. 4:39; 14:8; 16:10f.; 21:3. To **turn** is used frequently,
but with theological significance of the sort referred to here only at
15:4; 30:6, 9; and 36:13. It is true that **pray** and **turn** occur a
number of times in Solomon's prayer, but since this verse is the
direct answer to that prayer, this fact would seem to strengthen, not
undermine, the position outlined above. **hear. . . .forgive. . . .heal
their land:** expressive of full restoration. According to J. C. de
Moor, the last phrase indicates 'that YHWH comes to the rescue of
harassed nations and restores the *šalôm* on earth'; *ZAW* 88 (1976),
p. 336.

15. A response to the prayer of 6:40, which introduced the Chronicler's own conclusion in 41–42.

16. I have chosen: this is again from the Chronicler himself; cf.
v. 12 above. Thereafter he follows 1 Kg. 9:3*b*–9 for the most part
until the end of the prayer.

17–18. Since we have seen that the Chronicler has consciously
turned these verses into a specific response to Solomon's prayer
about the status of the dynasty, it is probable that two slight differences from his *Vorlage* (both in v. 18) should be regarded, not as
trivial, as some commentators have suggested, but rather as both
intentional and significant. **as I covenanted** (*kārattî*): contrast 1
Kg. 9:5, 'as I promised' (*dibbartî*). Although the possibility of
textual confusion cannot be ruled out here, there is no evidence to
support such a conjecture. It is thus better to regard this as an
indication that the Chronicler has intensified the reference to God's
covenant with David. **a man to rule Israel:** contrast 'a man upon
the throne of Israel' in 1 Kg. 9:5. Here, the echo of Mic. 5:2 (MT,
5:1) is unmistakable. Although there is no indication that this is
intended in a technical messianic sense here (*contra* Myers), there
can be no doubt that it does heighten the emphasis upon the promise
of an eternal dynasty, once Solomon has fulfilled the necessary
conditions.

19–22. Since in v. 19 the Chronicler has omitted the reference in
1 Kg. 9:6 to the sons of Solomon but retained the second person
plural form of address, he must, on the basis of the foregoing
context, have understood this warning to refer to Solomon and the
people. Previously, the conditions for the blessing of king and

people have been dealt with separately. Now, however, where the dangers of disobedience are spelt out, they are brought together. It is therefore all the more striking that although the full horrors of loss of national sovereignty and of exile are listed, there is no hint that this will entail the dynastic promise losing its validity.

Apart from this shift of addressees, the substance of the paragraph parallels 1 Kg. 9:6–9. That the Chronicler took its content with the utmost seriousness, however, is shown by his development elsewhere of its major themes; see, for instance, the discussion of **forsake** at 12:1 below. Verse 21a may represent an attempt by the Chronicler to make sense of what was an already corrupt *Vorlage*; cf. I. L. Seeligmann, *VT* 11 (1961), pp. 205f.

Concluding Appendices to the Building of the Temple

8:1–16

This chapter might appear at first sight to have little to do with the building of the temple, but the Chronicler's treatment of v. 16 shows that he, at least, did so regard it. He probably thought that the various topics treated here were connected with the consequences of the building and its completion, and the links in at least two cases with material in ch. 2, which dealt with the preparations for building, will have lent some substance to his view.

Thus vv. 1–2, which mention Solomon's dealings with Huram, may be compared with 2:3–16, and perhaps are intended to mark the conclusion of that particular set of negotiations. 2:2 and 17f. recorded the conscription of a levy for the temple building; vv. 7–10 of the present chapter suggest what became of them once the temple was completed. The link of vv. 11 and 12–15 with the completion of the temple are more obvious. This leaves only vv. 3–6 unaccounted for. It is possible that the Chronicler was merely content to follow the order of his *Vorlage* here, perhaps particularly because of the reference to building in Jerusalem in v. 6, but we should be reluctant to adopt this position in view of his rather careful composition elsewhere, which selects only such material as will contribute to the overall presentation. More probably, therefore, this section should be taken closely with vv. 7–10 following as illustrative of the type of building which the forced levy now undertook.

1–2. This is a celebrated passage in which the Chronicler appears to turn his *Vorlage* on its head, for according to 1 Kg. 9:10–14 Solomon gave twenty cities to Hiram in exchange, apparently, for the building materials which he had received. These cities, however, failed to please Hiram. A further note, somewhat disjointed in its present context, adds that Hiram also sent Solomon 120 talents of gold (v. 14). In the present passage, however, all this is reduced to a statement of Solomon's rebuilding and settlement of **the cities which Huram had given to him.**

Earlier scholars who thought that both Kings and Chronicles drew independently on a common source had little difficulty in harmonising this apparent discrepancy, the commonest suggestion being that Hiram returned the cities to Solomon (so that Chronicles retains the sequel to the Kings account), either because he was not satisfied with them, or because all along the intention had been to pay in gold, so that the cities 'may have been collateral until the time when payment could be made in gold' (Myers). The assumption of an independent source common to both Kings and Chronicles has now been generally abandoned, however, so that without other evidence that the Chronicler here had access to separate information, it is not possible to have any confidence in such harmonisations; it would be generally agreed today that in a case such as this the Chronicler was working from some form of the text of Kings.

Consequently, most scholars argue that the Chronicler was embarrassed by the story in Kings; it is thought that he would not have approved of Solomon parting with any of the land of Israel or have found credible the suggestion that Solomon was so short of money as to have to 'sell' territory in this way. Consequently, he rewrote the text to suit it better to his purpose.

This viewpoint too, however, has difficulties to face. For instance, since we have noted numerous examples where the Chronicler assumes close knowledge of the earlier account, it may be doubted whether he can have ever expected a flat contradiction of it to be accepted. It is more likely that he would have simply omitted the paragraph altogether, as he does with others towards the close of Solomon's reign. Secondly, since the Chronicler had no difficulty in including a reference in full to an earlier aspect of Solomon's payment of Hiram (cf. 2:10), it is not so certain that the passage in 1 Kg. 9 would have embarrassed him. Finally, this view does not deal satisfactorily with the Chronicler's omission of 1 Kg. 9:14. For whatever reason Hiram may originally have sent Solomon 120 talents of gold, in the present text there is no hint that it was payment for the cities; it appears rather as either a gift, or tribute, such as the Chronicler later reports in a general way at 9:24. It is probable that had the Chronicler's *Vorlage* included 1 Kg. 9:14, he would have been anxious to include it at this point.

This observation may then be added to the other evidence and suggestions of Willi, pp. 75-8, who argues that the Chronicler's

Vorlage was corrupt or divergent to a greater or lesser extent throughout vv. 1–6, and that his text represents the best reconstruction he could make. We know that the Chronicler's text of Samuel and Kings differed sometimes from MT (see the Introduction, section A). Some hints from LXX of Kings here suggest, as Willi has well shown, how very easily the question of who gave to whom could have become muddled, resulting in the present rather generalised statement which, it is postulated, the Chronicler managed to salvage. The consequence of this would be that little historical weight should be afforded the Chronicler's version here. Within his own work, however, it summarises the completion of one aspect of the temple building.

3–6. For the position of this paragraph within the chapter, see above. From a literary point of view, it is clearly linked with 1 Kg. 9:17–19, for by the end the two paragraphs are running parallel with identical wording. Earlier, however, while there are certainly some verbal contacts, they are far more spasmodic, and sometimes do not even follow the same order: compare, for instance, the respective positons of **Lower Beth-Horon** and **Tadmor** ('Tamar'). Moreover, the heading to the paragraph ('And this is the account of the forced labour. . .' etc., 1 Kg. 9:15f.), which on our understanding would have served the Chronicler's purpose well, does not occur in his version at all, even though the towns listed in vv. 4–6 depend upon it in the Kings' narrative. These facts point strongly towards the conclusion that the damage to the text of the Chronicler's *Vorlage* noted at v. 2 above continued into the first part of this paragraph, but not as far as the end of it. We may then endorse Willi's conjecture (pp. 76–7) that, for instance, the reference to **Hamath** in vv. 3 and 4 (but absent from 1 Kg. 9:15–19) arose through a misunderstanding of the word for 'wall' (*ḥômat*) in the damaged remains of 1 Kg. 9:15, that some of the Chronicler's omissions, such as the reference to Hazor and Megiddo, and the whole of 1 Kg. 9:16, are also due to damage sustained by the *Vorlage*, and that other elements are to be attributed to the Chronicler himself as he struggled to compose a continuous text out of the material available to him. Willi's appeal to the evidence of LXX in support of his case is, however, generally illegitimate. LXX clearly knew the present text of 1 Kg. 9:15–25, but has reordered it quite drastically for purposes of its own; cf. D. W. Gooding, *VT* 15 (1965), pp. 325–35. Thus 1 Kg. 9:16 is not missing in LXX, but has been moved to 1 Kg. 5:14*b*.

Should these conjectures be correct, the question of the historicity of the Chronicler's account has to be viewed in a rather different light. Unlike the account in Kings, he has Solomon campaigning

on the idealised northern borders of Israel. It has been argued of
late that this is reasonable (see Myers' commentary, with references
there, and add O. Eissfeldt, *BibOr* 9 [1952], p. 186; A. Malamat,
JNES 22 [1963], pp. 6–8; Aharoni, *Land*, p. 275; contrast Welten,
pp. 35–6), and it is not impossible that he should have been partly
influenced in his understanding of his damaged *Vorlage* by knowledge from some independent source that referred to such a campaign. But if so, as far as the present text is concerned, we shall
have to conclude that it was a matter of reaching the right conclusions for the wrong reasons.

3. If **Hamath** came into the Chronicler's text in the way postulated
above, it is probable that **-zobah** is his own addition, based on the
political system prevailing in his day under the Persian empire; cf.
Noth, *Aufsätze* 2, pp. 152f. If he understood his text to say that
Solomon built Tadmor (v. 4), which lay within that province, then
it will have been an obvious conjecture on his part to say that
Solomon **took it.**

4. Tadmor in the wilderness: the context shows that Palmyra is
intended, just as the presumed *Vorlage*'s 'Tamar' (1 Kg. 9:18) must
refer to some southern location, probably ʿAin Huṣb, 32 kilometres
SW of the Dead Sea; cf. Y. Aharoni, *IEJ* 13 (1963), pp. 30–42.
and all the store cities which he built in Hamath: it is easy to see
how on the basis of his new context the Chronicler could have
assumed that this was the sense of 1 Kg. 9:19a, and so have used
it here as well as at v. 6.

5–6. Deduced or derived from 1 Kg. 9:17–19.

7–10. This account of Solomon's levy follows 1 Kg. 9:20–23 fairly
closely. For a discussion of the topic and its presentation in Kings
and Chronicles, see on 2:17–18 above and the literature cited there.

8. had not destroyed: a slight alleviation of a possible embar-
rassment in 1 Kg. 9:21, 'were unable to destroy'.

10. two hundred and fifty: Kings has 'five hundred and fifty'. It
has been observed by J. Wenham, *TynB* 18 (1967), p. 49, that this
difference of 300 is matched by a similar difference at 2:18 over
against 1 Kg. 5:16, although in that case it is Chronicles that has
the higher number. Thus the total of overseers is the same, but
appears to have been reckoned up differently. This ingenious explanation, found already, and in greater detail, in Keil, is, however,
impossible, for the Chronicler is at pains to observe that gentile
foremen are involved in the earlier case, but Israelite foremen here;
so, rightly, D. W. Gooding, *Relics of Ancient Exegesis* (1976),
pp. 53–5. In fact, scribal error is very likely here, though whether
by a confused dittograph in Kings (*ḥᵃmiššîm waḥᵃmēš*) or by
haplography in Chr. is impossible to decide.

11. The Chronicler has not included earlier references to **Pharaoh's daughter** (1 Kg. 3:1; 7:8; 9:16, though this last reference may have been damaged in his *Vorlage*; see above), though once again the present verse, based on 1 Kg. 9:24, can hardly be understood without knowledge of the earlier account. He has included the reference on this occasion, however, because Solomon's action was a direct outcome of the completion of the temple, a view underlined by the second half of the verse, which is his own interpretative addition. Similar considerations may have caused him or a predecessor also to state that **Solomon brought** her **up**, rather than that she 'went up' (1 Kg. 9:24): his initiative in all that relates to the establishment of the temple and its worship is emphasised once again.

The reason supplied by the Chronicler for the move of Pharaoh's daughter is clearly based on considerations for cultic purity, and in particular on the fact that **the ark of the Lord** has now been brought into the temple (cf. 1 Chr. 13:9–13). Since the Chronicler had earlier stressed the importance of the right personnel to carry the ark (1 Chr. 15:2), he extended the principle to more remote contact, and so understood that Solomon's action was motivated by concern for his **wife's** safety: as a gentile and as a woman she should not be allowed contact with the **holy**. Ambiguity, however, surrounds one detail of this explanation. The word translated as **the places** in *RSV* is in fact a third person masculine plural pronoun, 'they'. Several suggestions have been advanced as to whom or what this refers: usually it is understood as the whole building complex, including both temple and palace, but Willi, p. 173, has argued rather for a personal reference. In fact, however, it has been well observed by C. F. Whitley, *JTS* ns 5 (1954), pp. 57–8, that the phrase *kî-qodeš hēmmāh* (lit., 'for holiness [are] they. . .') has quite a variety of different references in texts that would have been familiar to the Chronicler, e.g. Exod. 29:33 (the priests' portion of an atoning sacrifice); Num. 18:17 (firstborn domestic animals); Ezek. 42:14 (the priests' vestments); 2 Chr. 23:6 (priests and ministering Levites). We may thus conclude that the intention here is deliberately general; **the ark** should be surrounded by holiness in all respects.

12–15. The Chronicler considerably expands part of 1 Kg. 9:25 in order to illustrate Solomon's cultic arrangements for the new temple.

12. **Then:** as v. 13 shows, this does not apply to the occasion of dedication, but introduces a general account of Solomon's direction of the sacrifices. **burnt offerings:** there seems to be no particular significance in the Chronicler's omission of the 'peace offerings' of his *Vorlage*. **upon the altar of the Lord which he had built before**

the vestibule: I Kg. 9:25 refers to Solomon 'burning incense before the Lord'. The text there is difficult, and may have been corrupted from an earlier form which did not involve Solomon officiating within the holy place (cf. D. W. Gooding, *Relics of Ancient Exegesis*, pp. 63–6). However, its present form probably implies that he did so officiate, and this would have been unacceptable to the Chronicler, as 26:16–21 makes clear. He therefore not only omits the reference to incense, but also spells out that the altar at which Solomon officiated was not the one within the holy place, which was, of course, reserved for the priests.

13. I Kings refers to Solomon offering 'three times a year' (presumably at the major festivals). Lest the readers should have misunderstood this to mean that these were the only occasions on which Solomon offered, the Chronicler spells out other occasions too, **according to the commandment of Moses**, in this case especially Num. 28f. (Presumably **the duty of each day** is considered to cover the daily offerings.) This verse thus signifies the fulfilment of a major part of Solomon's purpose in building the temple, as set out at 2:4 above, where these various sacred occasions are also listed.

14. According to the ordinance of David his father: those who regard I Chr. 23–27 as completely secondary find this, and the similar clause at the end of the verse, a difficulty. On the understanding of those chapters summarised above, however, everything in this and the following verse comes within what was there described as the 'primary layer', and hence from the Chronicler himself, except for the detail about **the divisions of the priests**. For this, the situation is comparable to that explained at I Chr. 28:13 and 2 Chr. 5:11–13 above (and cf. I Chr. 23:2). The general issue of the relationship of the duties of **the Levites** to those of **the priests** was introduced by the Chronicler at I Chr. 16, and so does not need to depend on the secondary I Chr. 23:24ff. **the gatekeepers in their divisions:** cf. I Chr. 26:1–3, 9–11.

15. and concerning the treasuries: cf. I Chr. 26:20–32.

16. This verse represents a considerable expansion of the final clause of I Kg. 9:25. The somewhat laboured phraseology and the reference back to the time of **the foundation of the house** make it clear that the Chronicler intends this as a major literary mark in his narrative, concluding the long section which began at 2:1. Moreover, his use of a comparable idiom at 29:35 for the completion of the restoration of the temple service under Hezekiah was probably based on this verse, and so suggests a rather deliberate mode of composition here.

MORE ON THE GREATNESS OF SOLOMON

8:17–9:31

The concluding section of the Chronicler's account of Solomon's reign nicely balances the opening one in 2 Chr. 1. He has followed the text of 1 Kings just so far as it illustrates the twin themes of wisdom and wealth. The suggestion must be that as Solomon had been willing to channel these resources into the building of the temple, so now he was rewarded with an ever greater abundance of these selfsame gifts, with consequent esteem in the sight of the gentile nations. This theme of national reward for the establishment of correct religious priorities was also emphasised by the Chronicler in the reign of David (see, for instance, on 1 Chr. 14), while its opposite was seen to explain his inclusion of the fall of Saul's monarchy (1 Chr. 10). It is thus clear that it constitutes one of the major lessons which he wishes to impress upon his readers.

8:17–18. Following 1 Kg. 9:26–28, the Chronicler includes this brief note of a joint trading venture by **Solomon** and **Huram**. As in the building of the temple (see on 2:3ff.), Solomon appears as the dominant partner, with Huram providing materials and expertise. Though there are several differences between the two accounts, no particular bias can be detected to help account for them.

18. Huram sent him . . . ships: contrast 1 Kg. 9:27, 'sent with the fleet his servants'. Assuming that the Tyrian ships did not circumnavigate the whole continent of Africa, this would involve either transporting the ships by land, or taking them through a canal connecting the Nile with the Red Sea. For the former possibility, cf. Welten, pp. 37f.; for the latter, cf. G. Posener, *Chronique d'Égypte* 25–26 (1938), pp. 259–73, and K. W. Butzer, *Lexikon der Ägyptologie* 3 (1978), cols. 312f. Either is quite plausible in the Persian period, but less likely in Solomon's day, so that this may be an instance of the Chronicler misreading his text under the influence of the practices of his own time. To rewrite the text in order to avoid the difficulty (Rudolph) is pure conjecture. **Ophir:** cf. 1 Chr. 29:4. **four hundred and fifty:** 1 Kg. 9:28 has 'four hundred and twenty'. Scribal error is probably the cause of this discrepancy, though it is not possible now to say which version is original.

9:1–12. The account of the visit of the Queen of Sheba to Solomon is related with only the slightest variation from 1 Kg. 10: 1–13, the commentaries on which may be consulted for most of its details. Apart from the story's universal fascination, attested by its constant reuse and amplification in a wide variety of later texts and works of art, it will have appealed to the Chronicler as a fine illustration of his central themes in this section.

Precisely because the text is generally close to its *Vorlage*, it is all the more difficult to be sure in most cases (though cf. v. 8) whether the slight differences are intended by the Chronicler or are simply to be put down to the mechanics of textual transmission. For instance, in v. 1, the Chronicler has (literally) 'and she came to Solomon and spoke *with* him' rather than Kings '*to* him': is this perhaps the softening of a text in which the Queen of Sheba might have appeared as the dominant partner? Again, in v. 3 the Chronicler omits the word 'all' from 1 Kg. 10:4, 'And when the Queen of Sheba had seen all the wisdom of Solomon'; did he suppose that the earlier text implied that Solomon's wisdom was rather limited? In line with this might then be his addition of 'the greatness of your wisdom' in v. 6. Without further evidence there seems to be no way of assessing whether these changes are significant or not (nor can attention be drawn to them all in this commentary), but the passage stands as a parade example of the dilemma which constantly confronts the commentator on Chronicles.

4. his burnt offerings: so 1 Kg. 10:5; MT here has 'his roofchamber'. Either *RSV* should be followed, or perhaps both passages should be slightly emended to *ᵃlôtô*. This could then refer to 'his stairway (by which he went up to. . .)', or, perhaps more appropriately to the context, 'his ascent'. 'The reference would then be to the great processionals' (J. A. Montgomery and H. S. Gehman, *The Books of Kings* [1951], p. 217).

7. your wives: both here and at 1 Kg. 10:8 MT has 'your men'. In the Kings passage the versions suggest the emendation represented here, but since the Chronicler later omits the account of Solomon's wives it seems likely that we should attribute MT here to his own hand and thus not alter it.

8. and set you on his throne as king for the Lord your God: compare 1 Kg. 10:9, 'and set you on the throne of Israel'. This change is very characteristic of the Chronicler, who several times insists on the fact that the kingdom and the throne are God's; see on 1 Chr. 17:14. In line with this emphasis goes the thought which the Chronicler has also added here that through his king God **would establish** Israel **for ever.**

10-11. This paragraph is already inserted into the narrative in the Chronicler's *Vorlage*; cf. 8:17-18. **the servants of Huram and the servants of Solomon:** contrast 1 Kg. 10:11, 'the fleet of Hiram'. The Chronicler has ensured that Solomon is not outshone by his ally. **algum wood:** see on 2:8, though for reservations based on the present verse, cf. F. V. Winnett, in H. T. Frank and W. L. Reed (eds), *Translating and Understanding the Old Testament* (1970), pp. 184f.

12. The text of this verse differs a little from I Kg. 10:13, and is not easy to construe. *NEB*'s rendering is as good as any: '. . . whatever she asked, besides his gifts in return for what she had brought him'.

13–28. This miscellaneous collection of material, some detailed and some generalizing, but all centring on the main themes of this section, is reproduced with slight adaptations from I Kg. 10:14–28. Solomon's esteem amongst 'all the kings of the earth', already noted several times, becomes even more prominent here. Mosis, who collects all the material relevant to this theme on pp. 155–61, may, however, go a little too far in suggesting a comparison with the prophetic hope for a pilgrimage of the nations to Jerusalem in the end time, so that Solomon's reign becomes a paradigm of the eschatological age for whose return the Chronicler's readers can only look to God.

18. **a footstool of gold:** the Chronicler has substituted this for I Kg. 10:19, 'at the back of the throne was a calf's head', probably because of the latter's unacceptable religious overtones.

21. **the ships of Tarshish:** it is very probable that this is another example (cf. 3:6) of a place-name that has come to be used to describe a quality, so that the phrase will refer to ships capable of distant sea voyages. There is no need to follow W. F. Albright's more elaborate explanation that it means a 'refinery ship'; *BASOR* 83 (1941), p. 22. The cargoes carried suggest voyages south (to Ophir?) from Ezion-geber rather than across the Mediterranean to the town of Tarshish (Jon. 1–3). In that case **went to Tarshish** will represent a misunderstanding by the Chronicler of I Kg. 10:22 which starts, 'For the king had a fleet of ships of Tarshish at sea'. **with the servants of Huram** replaces 'with the fleet of Hiram', just as at v. 10 above, and probably for the same reason. **peacocks:** the meaning of this word is disputed. Many commentators now favour the view that it refers to another type of monkey, though certainty is not attainable at present (cf. M. Noth, *Könige* [1968], p. 205).

25–28. The textual history of these verses is obscure. This may be appreciated as soon as it is realised from what a wide variety of passages the material is collected: v. 25*a* = I Kg. 4:26 (with **four thousand** for 'forty thousand'); 25*b* = I Kg. 10:26*b*; v. 26 = I Kg. 4:21, and vv. 27–28 are based on I Kg. 10:27–28, though the texts diverge at the end and the continuation in I Kg. 10:29 is not included. In addition, I Kg. 10:26–29 has already been included by the Chronicler at 1:14–17 above, though without so many of the variations as are found in the present passage. Finally, it must be observed that the evidence of LXX of I Kings suggests that the material of this passage was rearranged in some traditions for exegetical purposes, the desire perhaps being to avoid the difficulties which later generations felt over Solomon's accumulation of gold and horses; cf. D. W. Gooding, *VT* 15 (1965), pp. 325–35, and especially *VT* 19 (1969), pp. 448–63.

The evidence from 1:14–17 shows that the Chronicler knew 1 Kg. 10:26–9 in roughly its present form. Since he had already included that material earlier, it is possible that he did not wish to repeat it in full here, but instead assembled vv. 25–26 as a final summarising statement. Verse 26 is clearly appropriate for this, but had not been included earlier. Verses 27–28 would then represent a later scribal expansion (for what reason one can only speculate) under the influence of the parallel passage which the Chronicler has closely followed throughout most of this chapter.

29–31. The Chronicler passes over in complete silence all the material in 1 Kg. 11 which indicates disapproval of Solomon, and which in the Deuteronomic history accounts for the division in the monarchy which is to follow. For reasons that have by now become fully clear (see on 1 Chr. 17 and the introductory remarks to 2 Chr. 1–9 as a whole), the Chronicler wished to present Solomon as one who fulfilled the conditions of obedience to the will of God that were necessary for the permanent establishment of the dynasty. Moreover, he takes a different, and rather more sophisticated, view of the division of the monarchy, which seeks to do justice both to the legitimate grievances of the northerners and to the element of rebellion against God's chosen instrument of rule over Israel (see the chapters which follow). He therefore passes straight from the account of Solomon in all his greatness to the concluding summary of Solomon's reign.

Being based on 1 Kg. 11:41–43, the paragraph's structure conforms to that of the regular notices of the death of kings in the Deuteronomic history. This contrasts with what was seen to be the case at 1 Chr. 29:26–30, where the attempt to bind together the reigns of David and Solomon was noted. As frequently in Chronicles, **from first to last** replaces the *Vorlage*'s 'and all that he did', but without any appreciable difference of meaning.

The only significant change which the Chronicler has introduced is in the citation of his sources. For the general questions involved, see the Introduction, section F. In our comments on Solomon's reign, no place has been found for any written source other than 1 Kings itself, interpreted in places, of course, on the basis of other biblical or oral traditions. It is thus very probable that the Chronicler is here imitating the notion of citation as a literary device under the influence of the earlier text, but showing too, and this is of considerable value, that he regarded that text primarily as prophetic.

Thus **the history of Nathan the prophet** points to 1 Kg. 1, and hence to the opening of Solomon's reign, while **the prophecy of Ahijah the Shilonite** is based on 1 Kg. 11:29ff. from the close of the reign. Again, it should be noted in passing, this presupposes that the Chronicler's readers will refer even to those parts of the earlier work which the Chronicler has omitted for ideological reasons (see also 10:15). **Iddo the seer**, included also at 12:15 and 13:22, is not mentioned by name in Kings, but is generally thought to be identified by the Chronicler (as by Josephus, *Ant.* 8.231ff.) with the unnamed prophet of 1 Kg. 13:1–10, and who may be supposed also to have worked in Solomon's reign. In this way the Chronicler was able to cite three prophetic 'sources', as he had done earlier for David; cf. 1 Chr. 29:29.

THE DIVIDED MONARCHY

2 Chr. 10–28

It is a well-known feature of the Chronicler's work that after the division of the monarchy he concentrates his attention on the southern kingdom of Judah. His presentation of the reigns of David and Solomon has shown how many of the earlier divergent traditions of Israel were incorporated into the twin institutions of Davidic dynasty and Jerusalem temple, and it is through these that he sees the continuity of true religious tradition to run. This does not, of course, mean that he presents the south as an ideal pattern of obedience; far from it! But he is clear that there can be no enduring salvation that disregards these fundamental institutions.

The history of the northern kingdom on its own, therefore, does not concern him. However, he is careful to preserve all the accounts of contact between north and south, including some not mentioned in Kings. Clearly, therefore, the northerners are not just 'written off', but as will be seen from the development from 2 Chr. 10 to 13, and then again at 2 Chr. 28, they remain part of 'Israel', but a part that has 'forsaken' God, and that needs to repent and hence to be restored. This is not so much because of the initial division, for which they are nowhere condemned, and which is regarded as due to God's will, as because of their continued independence after their legitimate grievances could be regarded as settled. Moreover, there are some indications that the Chronicler distinguished between the northern kingdom as a political institution and the population of the north as such. Since his main condemnation is reserved for the former, there is the suggestion of a much more open attitude towards the people in themselves.

REHOBOAM

10:1-12:16

The Chronicler includes nearly all the material concerning Rehoboam from 1 Kg. 12 and 14 but also adds to it in order to provide a pattern of failure (the division; 10:1-11:4) followed by success through obedience (11:5-23), and of disaster brought about by pride followed by a measure of restoration consequent upon self-humbling (ch. 12). This pattern sets the tone for much that is to follow.

The Division of the Monarchy

10:1-11:4

This account closely follows 1 Kg. 12:1-24. However, because the Chronicler omitted the material from 1 Kg. which was critical of Solomon, Rehoboam becomes personally more responsible for the division in this account. The emphasis on this being God's will is also retained, so that a full understanding of the Chronicler's attitude to the division cannot be derived from this passage alone, but must also take ch. 13 into consideration; cf. Welch, *Post-exilic Judaism*, pp. 189-91, and *IBC*, pp. 110-14. Only a few points of significant divergence from 1 Kg. 12 require comment here.

1. all Israel: whereas it is likely that in 1 Kg. 12 this is intended to refer to the northerners only, in Chronicles it will refer to the full number of the tribes. Later on it will be used of both the northern (10:16; 11:13) and southern (11:3; 12:1) kingdoms.

2. There is no doubt that the Chronicler wished **Jeroboam** to carry much of the responsibility on the northern side not only for the initial division of the monarchy in this chapter, but also for its continuation later (cf. 13:5ff.). There has been much discussion, however, whether the Chronicler reordered his *Vorlage* to achieve the emphasis, or whether it was already largely present in Kings. Those who adopt the former position have to argue that the present MT of 1 Kg. is the result of secondary editing under the influence of Chronicles, while LXX, it is claimed, gives evidence of the text's original order. The evidence of 2 Chr. 13 shows that, however he derived it, the Chronicler certainly intended what his own text here states. For discussion of the situation in his *Vorlage* which, though relevant, cannot be treated here in full, cf. D. W. Gooding, *VT* 17 (1967), pp. 173-89, and *JBL* 91 (1972), pp. 529-33; R. W. Klein, *JBL* 89 (1970), pp. 217-18, and 92 (1973), pp. 582-4. It should also be mentioned that LXX has a second, quite different, version of Jeroboam's rise, on which see R. P. Gordon, *VT* 25 (1975), pp. 368-

93. **he was in Egypt**: knowledge of 1 Kg. 11:26-40, omitted by the Chronicler, is presupposed.

4. Here again the allusions are to passages in Kings not included in the Chronicler's portrayal of Solomon.

7. kind. . . .and please them: an evident softening of 1 Kg. 12:7, 'a servant . . . and serve them'.

8. the young men: see further on 13:7.

14. My father made: so 1 Kg. 12:14 and many MSS and vrs here. The best witnesses to MT, however, have 'I will make'. Since a similar change is not made in the second half of the verse, it is probable that this is the result of textual confusion; otherwise it would be tempting to see it as a further example of shifting responsibility for the division on the southern side away from Solomon and on to Rehoboam's folly.

15. a turn of affairs: see on 1 Chr. 10:14. **brought about by God**: the importance of the Chronicler's retention of this phrase should not be underestimated. At this point in his narrative, as 11:4 further emphasises, he does not regard the rebellion by the notherners as reprehensible. It is their subsequent actions that lead to this development in his attitude. **his word, which he spoke by Ahijah the Shilonite**: knowledge of 1 Kg. 11:29-39 is presupposed.

16. *RSV* follows 1 Kg. 12:16, as do most commentators. However, MT lacks **and when . . . saw**. This may not be an accidental omission, for 15b-16a could then be translated, 'for it was a turn of affairs brought about by God that the Lord might fulfil his word, which he spake by Ahijah the Shilonite to Jeroboam the son of Nebat and all Israel, because the king did not hearken to them. And the people answered the king. . .'. If this is correct, it emphasises again that the division was God's will for **all Israel**; cf. *IBC*, p. 108. For the poetic fragment in this verse, see on 1 Chr. 12:18, and *OTS* 21 (1981), pp. 164-76.

11:1-4. The Chronicler omits from 1 Kg. 12:20 the account of Jeroboam's being made king over the northern tribes, but continues here in close dependence upon 1 Kg. 12:21-24.

3. all Israel in Judah and Benjamin: cf. 1 Kg. 12:23, 'all the house of Judah and Benjamin, and . . . the rest of the people'. Elaborate theories have in the past been constructed on this change, to the effect that the Chronicler now believed 'the true Israel' to be confined to the southern kingdom only; see especially von Rad, *GCW*, pp. 18-37. In fact, however, there is much evidence to the contrary of which this theory fails to take account. The Chronicler's view in brief is that for the period of the divided monarchy both north and south may legitimately be called 'Israel', so that the phrase **in Judah and Benjamin** is geographical only, just as in the similar 'Israel who dwelt in the cities of Judah' in 10:17; cf. Japhet, *Ideology*, pp. 233f. Throughout this description of the division of the monarchy, the Chronicler has made several slight changes (this one is the most marked) in the titles used for the people, his purpose apparently being to show that all the usual designations for Israel could be postulated equally of both kingdoms. Thus here he wished to call the south **all Israel**, just as he had the north in 10:16 (also with a slight change from the *Vorlage*); cf. *IBC*, *passim*, but especially pp. 97-110.

4. your brethren: that this relationship was taken seriously by the Chronicler is suggested by his use of it in the important passage which he has introduced in 28:8-15. **this thing is from me:** see on 10:15 above.

The Establishment of Rehoboam's Rule

11:5-23

The first period of Rehoboam's reign is portrayed in a favourable light. Each of the three short paragraphs which make up this section uses a motif (building; defection of the faithful from the north to the south; large family) which the Chronicler regularly uses to demonstrate God's reward for faithfulness.

5-12. It has long been recognised that the Chronicler uses the motif of building as an indication of prosperity and so reserves it for those kings or periods which he wishes to show as enjoying the blessing of God because of their obedience to him; cf., most recently and fully, Welten, pp. 9-78. That does not necessarily mean, however, that he has not drawn on earlier material for his composition, even though in most cases there is no parallel in Kings. Each example has to be examined on its own merits in this regard, and for the present passage scholars are almost unanimous in their agreement that an older source does, in fact, underlie the composition. Besides the commentaries the main studies are Beyer, *ZDPV* 54 (1931), pp. 113-34; Junge, pp. 73-80; A. Alt, *KS* 2, pp. 306-15; Aharoni, *Land*, pp. 290-4; P. Welten, *Die Königs-Stempel* (1969), pp. 167-71; Welten, pp. 11-15.

This confidence follows Beyer's demonstration that the list covers the most strategic points in any attempt to defend Judah from the east, south or west. Valleys leading up into the Judean hill country and important road junctions all appear to be covered. Debate has chiefly centred, therefore, around the date to be attributed to the list. Junge, followed more tentatively by Alt, argued for the reign of Josiah; but most recent studies have favoured the time of Rehoboam, as suggested by the Chronicler. This is because some of the major southern fortresses of the later period of the monarchy, such as Arad, are not included (see the survey by Y. Aharoni, *IEJ* 17 [1967], pp. 1–17), and because there is no fortification along the northern border, a direction from which Judah often came under threat after Rehoboam's reign. More positively, the boundaries suggested by the list suit what is known of Rehoboam's reign, while archaeological evidence from several of the sites mentioned has been thought to suggest fortification at this time. The strength of this latter argument, however, is rather diminished in the present state of knowledge. Many of the sites have not been excavated, while of those which have, several were excavated as early as the turn of the century, with the result that their conclusions cannot be relied upon, and indeed in some cases have been challenged by more recent work (see below for references). At present, only Lachish seems certainly to have been fortified at about this time, but then it had already had a well-established history as a major defensive position, so that this is hardly surprising. In addition, we have no way of knowing at present just how extensive this building operation would have been and hence what it would be reasonable to ask of archaeology to provide in the way of evidence. It is thus best not to press this line of argument either way.

Assuming, then, that the list does date from Rehoboam's reign, it is less certain whether he began to build before Shishak's invasion (ch. 12) or as a result of it. In favour of this latter view it is observed that the southern line is pulled back further than might otherwise have been expected. However, as a defensive line in relation to the contours it seems to make reasonable strategic sense (cf. Baly, *Geography*, p. 182). There is no compelling reason, therefore, why work should not have begun early in Rehoboam's reign, though such an enterprise could hardly have been completed as early as the fifth year of his reign (12:2), and so doubtless continued afterwards as well.

Some scholars have argued that the lack of a line of fortifications along the northern borders suggests that Rehoboam wished to keep open the possibility of a reunion of the divided kingdom. Alternatively, however, it must be said that, taking seriously his apparent policy of fortifying a minimal, but more securely defensible, position, it is not certain that any town satisfying these demands north of the approaches to Jerusalem itself (Mount Scopus) would have been available to him. Moreover, he may not have felt so threatened from that quarter, and so did not make its defence a first priority.

The order in which the places are mentioned has not yet been satisfactorily explained. The list starts off in an orderly manner, the first four names defining the eastern border from north to south. Then, however, there follow four from the southern part of the western front, three from the south, another three from the west, and finally Hebron (south). Assuming the list to have been in an originally coherent order, the presence of Hebron after Aijalon suggests that this order started out as:

(a) the eastern flank from north to south: 1. Bethlehem
2. Etam
3. Tekoa
4. Beth-zur
(b) the southern flank from west to east: 5. Lachish
6. Adoraim
7. Ziph
8. Hebron
(c) the western flank, also from north to south: 9. Aijalon
10. Zorah
11. Azekah
12. Soco
13. Adullam
14. Gath
15. Mareshah.

The present order, however, is 1 2 3 4 12 13 14 15 7 6 5 11 10 9 8. From this it is clear that Hebron came mistakenly to be joined to the third group, and that the names are then grouped in four internally coherent sets. How this order came about cannot be established, but it looks as though the order in which groups should be taken became confused, probably as a result of their having been listed in adjacent columns; cf. the somewhat similar position in 1 Chr. 25.

5. This verse will be all, or mostly, the Chronicler's own introduction to the list. It provides a perfect parallel to 1 Kg. 12:25, the verse which stands in an equivalent place in the earlier history, but which the Chronicler leaves out at this point because it deals with the northern kingdom alone.

6. Not all the places listed have been excavated. References are given below to some which have, and where fortifications have been thought to reflect the activity recorded here.

7. Beth-zur: archaeological evidence here is ambiguous; cf. R. W. Funk, *BASOR* 150 (1958), p. 14, and O. R. Sellers, *et al.*, *The 1957 Excavation at Beth-zur* (1968), p. 8.

8. Gath: this can hardly have been Gath of the Philistines. Aharoni, *Land*, p. 292, followed with further discussion by A. F. Rainey, *EI* 12 (1975), p. 72*, suggests that this is a scribal error for Moresheth–Gath (by confusion with **Mareshah** following). This is

probably to be identified with Tell Judeideh; but excavations there
from the turn of the century are insufficient to establish whether it
was fortified by Rehoboam; cf. M. Broshi, *EAEHL* 3, pp. 694–6.
Mareshah: the situation here is comparable. M. Avi-Yonah, *ibid.*,
pp. 782ff., favours a date later than Rehoboam for the finds.

9. Lachish: cf. O. Tufnell, *ibid*, pp. 735–46, and D. Ussishkin,
ibid., pp. 750–3. The usual identification of this site with Tell-ed-
Duweir has recently been challenged (unconvincingly) by G. W.
Ahlström, *PEQ* 112 (1980), pp. 7–9. **Azekah:** E. Stern, *EAEHL*
1, pp. 141–3, questions the earlier attribution of fortifications here
to Rehoboam.

10b–12. Several matters of style show that this is the Chronicler's
own concluding summary. Especially noteworthy is the inclusion of
and in Benjamin which contrasts with v. 5 and the data of the list
itself, but is the Chronicler's characteristic way of referring to the
southern kingdom. **So he held Judah and Benjamin:** Ackroyd suggests with good reason that this sentence should be rendered 'Now
Judah and Benjamin were his', and made the introduction to the
following paragraph.

13–17. This is an important paragraph in the development of the
Chronicler's narrative. First, it continues the major theme of showing how faithfulness to God is rewarded with his blessing. Second,
it introduces for the first time the apostasy which Jeroboam initiated
in the north. Though based on 1 Kg. 12:26–33, it has been entirely
reworked by the Chronicler to introduce items to which he will later
refer in his condemnation of the north (cf. 13:8–11). Third, and
arising out of these first two points, those in the north who remained
faithful are said to have come south to worship at Jerusalem. This
motif recurs several times in the Chronicler's history, and may well
constitute part of his appeal to the faithful inhabitants of the north
of his own day.

13. all Israel: see on 11:3 above. When not geographically qualified, this still refers to the northern kingdom. **resorted to him:**
more literally, 'took their stand with him'. There is no necessary
implication that they took up permanent residence (cf. v. 16),
though that is not definitely excluded.

14. The first half of this verse may be a later addition. Willi,
p. 211, notes that (a) the repetition from v. 13 of **the Levites** is
unnecessary; (b) whereas 14*b* speaks of expulsion, 14*a* suggests a
voluntary move; and (c) 14*b* clearly continues v. 13, the **because**
relating, as the explanation shows, to the priests alone. It is this
addition, rather than the Chronicler himself, which suggests that
they settled in the south. **and his sons:** probably in the sense of
successors. **cast them out:** this is the Chronicler's inference from

the account in 1 Kg. 12:31-32 and 13:33 of Jeroboam's establishment of non-Levites as priests, referred to here in the next verse.

15. the satyrs: not mentioned in the Kings' account of Jeroboam's apostasy, which is thus intensified here. They have generally been thought of as demons in the form of he-goats, though alternative proposals are advanced by H. H. Hirschberg, *VT* 11 (1961), pp. 381f., and by N. H. Snaith, *VT* 25 (1975), pp. 115-18. Probably by the time of the Chronicler the form of such worship was of less significance than the fact that the north was in contravention of Lev. 17:7. **the calves which he had made:** whatever Jeroboam originally intended by these (see the commentaries on 1 Kg. 12:28), they had long since become the focus of the south's condemnation of what was regarded as northern idolatry.

16. set their hearts to seek the Lord: a typical expression for those whom the Chronicler wished to commend; cf. 7:14. **to sacrifice:** wherever they lived, the faithful must worship in **Jerusalem**, according to the Chronicler.

17. they strengthened: by their allegiance rather than necessarily by their residence. Moreover, the continuation of the verse shows that **they** refers not only to those mentioned in the previous verse, but to the population of the south generally as well, so that this verse becomes a summary of the characteristics of the first period of Rehoboam's reign as a whole. **for three years:** this is deduced without difficulty from 12:1-2, which was taken to imply that Rehoboam 'forsook the law' in his fourth year. **and Solomon:** though this verse has no parallel in 1 Kings, the Chronicler's composition here, which would have been unthinkable for the earlier historian, was doubtless influenced by the same considerations as at 7:10 above.

18-23. For the Chronicler a large family was a sign of blessing (cf. 13:21; 1 Chr. 14:3-7). This paragraph thus fits into the pattern of this section as a whole, casting doubt on the interpretation of those who find here an adumbration of Rehoboam's later faithlessness. The passage is without a biblical parallel, though a few of the names are familiar from elsewhere. The tensions with such other passages are sufficient to suggest that the Chronicler has here drawn on some inherited source, but are hardly enough to deny that he was himself responsible for including it.

18. Mahalath is presented as a second cousin to **Rehoboam**. Her father **Jerimoth** is not mentioned elsewhere as a **son of David** (e.g. at 1 Chr. 3:1-9), so that presumably his mother was a concubine (cf. 1 Chr. 3:9). Moreover her mother, **Abihail**, was the daughter of David's eldest brother **Eliab** (cf. 1 Chr. 2:13), so that her own parents were also second cousins within the family of **Jesse**.

19. Nothing more is known of these three **sons**.

20. Maacah the daughter of Absalom: in 13:2, she is called
'Micaiah the daughter of Uriel of Gibeah', in 1 Kg. 15:2 'Maacah
the daughter of Abishalom', while in 1 Kg. 15:10 she is the mother
of Asa and hence the wife of **Abijah**, not his mother as here. It is
usually explained that she was in fact the granddaughter of **Absalom**, her parents being Uriel (13:2) and Tamar (2 Sam. 14:27), and
that she remained as 'queen mother' in the court even after her own
son's death. (For other suggestions, cf. Myers, p. 79.) This harmonisation, of course, depends on the identity of **Absalom** with
David's son, but this is far from certain. With so little of the
necessary information available it is more prudent simply to observe
what is said without assuming that it must be irreconcilable or that
it is necessary to harmonise. Nothing is known of Maacah's children
apart from **Abijah** (ch. 13; on the name see 12:16).

23. The text of both the beginning and the end of this verse is
uncertain. *RSV* represents one widely-held interpretation and may
be preferred if the understanding of the paragraph as a whole advanced here is correct. Others, however, favour the approach of
JB, which emends **he did wisely** to the more neutral 'he built', and
which emends the last clause to 'But he consulted the many gods of
his wives', thus transferring Solomon's sin (omitted by the Chronicler) to Rehoboam, and so explaining the unfaithful conduct referred to in the next chapter. However, if this is what was meant by
'he forsook the law of the Lord', it is difficult to imagine that 'all
Israel' did exactly the same. 12:1 seems to be more general in its
application than this, as its vocabulary shows; see the comments
below.

Shishak's Invasion

12:1-12

A brief account of Shishak's invasion is found at 1 Kg. 14:25-28.
It follows the record of Judah's cultic unfaithfulness under Rehoboam (1 Kg. 14:22-24), though there is no explicit connection between the two paragraphs. The Chronicler has drawn on this
material, and may well have had access to another account of the
affair also (see especially on v. 3), but he has certainly moulded it
all afresh in order to serve his purpose of illustrating the effects first
of unfaithfulness and then of repentance. To do this he employs
vocabulary characteristic of his theology of immediate retribution,
namely, 'forsake' (*'zb*; three times, in vv. 1 and 5), 'be unfaithful'
(*m'l*; v. 2) and 'humble oneself' (niph'al of *kn'*; four times, in vv. 6,

7 and 12). As so often in Chronicles, the historical narrative is thus
made into an example, a paradigm, of a situation that is likely to
recur, and to which his readers will be expected to make the appropriate response.

1. **was established and was strong:** in themselves these statements are quite neutral. The stress later on self-humbling, however,
indicates that here Rehoboam took a reprehensible pride in his own
achievements. **he forsook the law of the Lord:** this is the last major
item of the Chronicler's theological vocabulary to be discussed (for
the others, see principally 1 Chr. 10:13–14 and 2 Chr. 7:14). In this
passage 'to forsake' does not appear to be given much specific
content, but its use elsewhere shows that very often it implies either
irregular worship or, indeed, the worship of foreign gods; for the
former, see principally 13:10, 11; 21:10 as explained by v. 11; 28:6
(cf. vv. 1–4); and 29:6, and for the latter 7:19, 22; 24:18; and 34:25.
It is thus probable that the same is intended in the present passage,
so that this description may be taken as a summary of 1 Kg. 14:22–
24 which lists just such practices for the reign of Rehoboam.
Although it is not stated by his *Vorlage*, the Chronicler may be seen
to have drawn his own conclusions about cause and effect within
the earlier account and to have written up his version accordingly.
Punishment for 'forsaking' God in this way is also expressed in two
ways. The one is specific, namely defeat at the hand of foreign
enemies; cf. 7:19–22; 21:10; 24:24; 28:6; 29:6 with 8f.; and 34:25
with reference forward to the fall of Jerusalem. The other way in
which 'forsaking' God is punished is by God 'forsaking' his people,
usually with similar results, as. v. 5 of this chapter shows. This
word-play occurs explicitly three times, at 12:5; 15:2; and 24:20,
and it is implied at 1 Chr. 28:9 and 20, though in rather different
circumstances. Finally, it may be observed that a passage such as
15:2 suggests that to 'forsake' God is the exact opposite of 'seeking'
him; the word is thus drawn closely into that circle of ideas concerning paradigmatic 'exilic' situations outlined at 1 Chr. 10:13–14.
all Israel: see on 11:3.

2. Most of this verse is drawn directly from 1 Kg. 14:25. For the
details of the campaign of **Shishak king of Egypt** (Shoshenq I, c.
945–925 BC) reference should be made not only to the commentaries
on Kings, but also to Shishak's own account of the campaign in his
topographical list from Karnak. On this it is necessary to mention
only K. A. Kitchen, *The Third Intermediate Period in Egypt* (1973),
pp. 293–300 and 432–47, where there is a full discussion both of
Shishak's list and the major studies of it, and of the correlation of
the list with the biblical account. Here it should be noted, however,
that Kitchen bases his reconstruction of some aspects of the cam-

paign on the Chronicler's account alone (on pp. 298, 442f. and 446), so that though the coherence of his reconstruction lends plausibility to the Chronicler's version it cannot, without arguing in a circle, be said finally to establish its historicity. But see further on the next verse. **because they had been unfaithful to the Lord:** in the Hebrew text this clause comes at the end of the verse, and it marks the point at which the Chronicler introduces material of his own. He rejoins Kings at v. 9. There can be no doubt that this clause at least is his own comment on the cause of the invasion, as his use of the word **unfaithful** shows. For its importance to him, see on 1 Chr. 10:13.

3. twelve hundred chariots and sixty thousand horsemen: these numbers are generally regarded as exaggerated, but for the **chariots** the figure compares reasonably with that of other chariot-forces of the period known from extra-biblical sources (cf. Kitchen, p. 295). If **sixty thousand** is a scribal error for 'six thusand' (see on 9:25 and 1 Chr. 19:18 for this type of error), the proportion of **horsemen** to **chariots** would likewise be more reasonable. **Sukkiim:** probably the equivalent of the Egyptian $Tk(tn)$. 'From the Egyptian data of the thirteenth-twelfth centuries $\overline{BC}$, it is clear that, in part at least, the Tjuk(ten) were Libyan forces from the oases of the western desert — perhaps auxiliaries' (Kitchen, p. 295). The inclusion of this item suggests strongly that an independent account of the campaign was available to the Chronicler. The mention of **Libyans** and 'Nubians' (**Ethiopians**) is equally to be expected in the light of what is known of Shishak's reign.

4. the fortified cities of Judah: presumably a reference to 11:6–10, and so perhaps the Chronicler's own comment in order to underline the lesson that trust in human devices alone is misplaced. Of the towns mentioned there only Aijalon is included in Shishak's list, though there is reference to some other Judean towns, such as Gibeon.

5. Shemaiah the prophet: cf. 11:2. His brief analysis of the situation conveys exactly the Chronicler's theology; see on v. 1 above.

6. the princes of Israel: this is equivalent to 'the princes of Judah' in the previous verse. The Chronicler uses **Israel** in titles like this with reference to the southern kingdom on several occasions in his history of the divided monarchy. The intention is not to take an exclusive stance towards the north but to draw attention to the unbroken continuation of tradition in the south with the Israel of the united monarchy (cf. *IBC*, pp. 106f.). **humbled themselves:** see above and on 7:14. The stress on this action in this passage suggests that the Chronicler intended this story as a paradigm of the situation envisaged by Solomon's prayer and the divine response to it. "**The Lord is righteous**": cf. Exod. 9:27 and Dan. 9:14. In both these verses the expression is part of a more extended confession of sin, whereby the penitent confesses himself in the wrong and accepts that God is 'in the right'. The intention is the same in the present verse.

7–8. To the people's confession God responds in the way he had promised. The words spoken through the prophet resemble in certain respects both Ezr. 9:8f. and Neh. 9:36, though **some** should perhaps be rendered 'in a short while'. It is hard to avoid the impression that the Chronicler is aligning this whole account as closely as he can with the situation of his own readers. **that they may know my service:** i.e. that as a result of this experience they may learn that the service of God is not onerous by comparison with the service of foreign powers. By implication, therefore, it is mere folly to forsake God and his law (v. 1).

9–11. The first half of v. 9 is repeated from v. 2 in order to indicate that the Chronicler is now rejoining 1 Kg. 14:25–28; cf. I. L. Seeligmann, *ThZ* 18 (1962), p. 315. The absence of **Jerusalem** from Shishak's list suggests that he did indeed allow himself to be 'bought off'; the major areas in which he campaigned were the north and the Negeb.

12. This conclusion is again from the Chronicler himself. It underlines (if underlining were needed) his understanding of the incident he has just recorded. **conditions were good in Judah:** better, 'there were still some good things in Judah', with reference to cultic faithfulness, as the comparable 19:3 makes clear. This explains the positive start to the final section of Rehoboam's reign which follows.

The Conclusion of Rehoboam's Reign

12:13–16

13–14. This concluding assessment of Rehoboam's reign is based on 1 Kg. 14:21–22. The Chronicler has therefore moved it from the opening account of the reign there to its conclusion here. Moreover, although its factual content remains the same, he has rewritten it in part with vocabulary so characteristic of his style that it is very difficult to agree with Rudolph that the verses are a later addition by someone who missed the notice from 1 Kg. 14 and so included it here for the sake of completeness; had that been the case, we would have expected a more exact parallel, as at 4:10–22 above. Rudolph's main argument is the apparent contradiction between Rehoboam's age in v. 13 and the description of him as 'young' at his accession in 13:7; but see the comments on that verse and Willi, p. 93, n. 74.

13. **established himself:** this is from the Chronicler (see on 1:1 above). He has linked it with the account of Rehoboam's age (after **and reigned**) with the word 'because', omitted by *RSV*, but cf. *RV*. It is thus a general comment on his reign, as befits this paragraph's summary character, rather than a particular allusion to recovery from the effects of Shishak's invasion. **In Jerusalem:** contrast 'in Judah' of 1 Kg. 14:21.

14. **And he did evil:** the Chronicler has altered this judgment on Judah in Kings to one on Rehoboam alone. The clash with v. 12 has bothered some commentators. If once more, however, it is remembered that this is a summary of the whole reign, not just the effects of Shishak's invasion, then there need be no difficulty in understanding that the Chronicler has retained this general characterisation from his *Vorlage*. He has amplified it, however, by himself adding the explanatory clause. It was observed at v. 1 above that to **seek** is the opposite of 'to forsake' in the Chronicler's writing. He thus probably intends us to view the account of that specific act of apostasy as illustrative of the general nature of Rehoboam's reign. Despite the blessings of the opening years of his reign (11:5–23), Rehoboam is judged unfavourably on the whole in Chronicles; see further on 13:5–7.

15. The Chronicler follows 1 Kg. 14:29f. in referring to his sources here, but as at 9:29 and 1 Chr. 29:29 above he regards these as the works of prophets. As elsewhere the important point about his citation is the way he names his sources rather than their specific content. **Iddo:** see on 9:29. As *RSV* mg. indicates, MT adds a word whose translation in this context is uncertain; *RV*, 'after the manner of genealogies'; *NEB* mg., 'to be enrolled by genealogy'. The same word is used at 1 Chr. 9:1, where it seemed to be linked with a genuine source relating to a military census. While the text may be corrupt here, it could preserve an indication of a further source referred to by the Chronicler in which either the extra-biblical military material (the basis of 11:5–12 and 12:3–8), or the account of Rehoboam's family (11:18–23), or both, were recorded.

16. Cf. 1 Kg. 14:31, but the Chronicler omits the phrase 'with his fathers' after **was buried**. This could be either an accident of textual transmission, or in order to avoid repeating the phrase from earlier in the verse, but it could also imply a measure of adverse assessment of Rehoboam's reign. As will be seen, these burial notices are used systematically by the Chronicler for indicating such judgments, so that it is reasonable to assume that the same is true here. **Abijah:** 'Abijam' in Kings. There he is severely criticised,

whereas the Chronicler's presentation of his reign is favourable. Is this difference reflected in the varying forms of his name? The final element of 'Abijam' may perhaps be identified with the Canaanite god Yam, while in Chronicles this has been replaced with the more acceptable Yahwistic ending.

ABIJAH

13:1–14:1*a*

The presentation of Abijah in 1 Kg. 15:1–8 differs considerably from that in Chronicles. There he is briefly dismissed as unfaithful, it being then explained that despite this the dynasty continued for David's sake. Here, however, he is presented in a most favourable light. It is, of course, true that the Chronicler uses this favourable judgment as a basis for part of his developing ideology (see on 4–12 below), but it is still questionable whether he would have arrived at it in the first place had he not had in addition to Kings some account of a victory by Abijah over the north, from which in his usual way he would then have deduced Abijah's faithfulness (so Noth, *US*, p. 142, and Rudolph). Verse 19 is thought by some to contain the sort of details which might have been thus independently preserved. Be that as it may, it cannot be denied that for the development of the Chronicler's narrative this chapter is of crucial importance. The explanation it supplies of the situation within the divided monarchy prevails as far as ch. 28, and the principles on which that explanation is based were undoubtedly of abiding significance in the Chronicler's opinion.

1–2a. The introduction to **Abijah**'s reign is drawn from 1 Kg. 15:1–2. It provides the only place where the Chronicler preserves a synchronism with the northern kingdom, but it is appropriate here in view of the sequel.

2. Micaiah: 'Maacah' in 1 Kg. 15:2; probably only a scribal variant. **the daughter of Uriel of Gibeah:** contrast 1 Kg. 5:2, 'the daughter of Abishalom'; see on 11:20.

2b–20. The notice in Kings goes on to tell of Abijah's unfaithfulness. The Chronicler omits all this, but abstracts from the concluding formula of his reign the information that **there was war between Abijah and Jeroboam** (1 Kg. 15:7; note that he will later omit this clause when repeating the substance of 1 Kg. 15:7 at v. 22 below), and proceeds to give a lengthy account of one incident, doubtless intended as exemplary, of this war. While certain aspects of this may be accepted as historical (see above), the account itself bears all the marks of the Chronicler's own ideology and style and must be attributed directly to him in its present form.

3. The numbers of troops involved cannot be taken literally in their present form. There are two possible explanations. The first may be called 'symbolic'; the **eight hundred thousand** of the north is the same as the number of 'valiant men' recorded in the census of 2 Sam. 24:9. The implication is thus that **Jeroboam** made a full scale effort against the south, who only had half his numbers (**four hundred thousand**); the magnitude of the south's eventual victory is thus enhanced. The alternative approach is more 'rationalistic', the word for **thousand** (*'elep*) being understood as either a 'unit' (Myers) or even as a 'fully-armed soldier' (*'allûp*; cf. Wenham, *TynB* 18 [1967], pp. 25ff.) so as to reduce the numbers to a more readily acceptable size.

4-12. Before battle is joined, Abijah addresses the northern troops, ostensibly in an attempt to dissuade them from fighting. In reality the speech has many points of contact with its context in Chronicles, so that it should be regarded primarily as a thinly-veiled comment by the author in explanation of the theological reasons for the ensuing course of events. For further detail and rejection of the view which sees anti-Samaritan polemic here, cf. *IBC*, pp. 111-14.

The speech has two main points of focus, namely, the legitimacy of the Davidic dynasty and the purity of the Jerusalem cult as opposed to that of the northerners. Each point reflects a shift in the situation which prevailed at the time of the division of the monarchy, and in this way the Chronicler is able to reconcile the tension between the clear statement that the division was brought about by God and the evident and continuing state of rebellion by the northerners later on. Thus whereas some explanation of Rehoboam's weakness is provided (v. 7) so that the period of the division is regarded as abnormal, yet with the accession of the true Davidide Abijah normality has been restored, since the Chronicler regards each generation as being directly responsible to God for its actions without reference back to previous circumstances. This implies that on the political level there is now no reason why the northerners should not call off their rebellion. Secondly, since the division an account of the northerner's apostasy has intervened (11:14f.). The main points involved are rehearsed again here and contrasted with the situation in Jerusalem (vv. 9-11). Such a situation is incompatible with faithfulness to Israelite tradition.

The northerners' rejection of Abijah's appeal is reprehensible, but should not be taken to imply their forfeiture of the status of Israelite. They have 'forsaken' God (v. 11), but then so did the south sometimes, and their apostasy is no worse than that of Ahaz (ch. 28). They remain 'sons of Israel', and the Lord is still 'the God of their fathers' (v. 12). What is demanded is repentance and return to the twin foci of Davidic dynasty and Jerusalem temple, a theme to be developed further in the reigns of Ahaz and Hezekiah later on.

4. Mount Zemaraim: not certainly identified. A town of the same name appears to be located near Bethel in Jos. 18:22, and a hill in that region would suit the demands of the present context; because of the similarity of names, *rās ez-zēmara* is usually suggested. This is possible for the **mount** of Chronicles, but seems improbable for the town of Jos. 18:22 because of its close proximity to *et-Taiyibeh* (Ophrah) and *rammūn* (Rimmon). Moreover, surface explorations have revealed no trace of early settlement; cf. K. Koch, *ZDPV* 78 (1962), pp. 19–29. Koch, therefore, cautiously suggests a location for the town in the Jordan valley, some way north-east of Jericho; for other suggestions, cf. Welten, pp. 117f. One possibility that does not seem previously to have been seriously considered is whether there has not been confusion at some point with *Khirbet el-mazāri'a* (metathesis of the first two consonants), the most imposing peak of the whole district and some two kilometres to the west of *rās ez-zēmara*.

O Jeroboam and all Israel: it is significant that as the speech develops **Jeroboam** is spoken of in the third person (vv. 6 and 8) and that the appeal of v. 12 is addressed to the people without reference to him. It looks as though Abijah is trying to win the support of the people not only by appealing to them over Jeroboam's head but also by putting the blame for what has happened on him alone, thereby making the way back for them very much easier.

5. gave the kingship: cf. 1 Chr. 17:14. The importance of introducing the concept here is that to reject the rule of the Davidic king is tantamount to rejecting the rule of God himself. **for ever to David and his sons:** see on 1 Chr. 17 and 2 Chr. 6:42, etc. for the background to this in the Chronicler's thought. That he regarded the dynasty as eternally established is, of course, most emphatically supported by this verse. **a covenant of salt:** cf. Lev. 2:13 and especially Num. 18:19. The precise social origins of this expression are unknown, but it clearly means an eternal covenant.

6. a servant of Solomon: cf. 1 Kg. 11:26.

7. certain worthless scoundrels: this is usually understood as a reference to the representatives of the north, but no such small group is referred to in the account of the division; cf. 'Jeroboam and all Israel' at 10:3, etc. Moreover, the antecedent of **about him** is strictly speaking 'his lord' (i.e. Rehoboam) in the previous verse, and the word translated here as **defied** (*wayyiṯ'amm°ṣû 'al*) nowhere else has this meaning, but rather 'prevailed over', hence 'persuaded'. Josephus, *Ant.* 8.277 is therefore right to see here a reference to Rehoboam's young men (10:8ff.) who **gathered about him and** 'persuaded' **Rehoboam** to reject the wise advice of the elders, and who in the narrative we have must carry the real blame for the division. Thus Abijah is not here criticising the northerners for their failure to submit to Rehoboam.

The abnormality of the division is further underlined by the fact that the Davidic king at that time was **young and irresolute**. Almost identical language was used of Solomon at 1 Chr. 22:5 and 29:1. There it was made one of the reasons for David's ample provision for him and his securing the loyal aid of his trusted officials. Rehoboam, however, turned away from the elders towards 'the young men who had grown up with him' (10:8) and **could not withstand** their foolish counsel. (It may thus be seen that the word **young** has little to do with Rehoboam's age, *contra* Rudolph at 12:13, but is introduced (a) by way of typological comparison with Solomon, and (b) because of the implication of 10:8 that he was the same age as 'the young men'.)

8. The word-play on **withstand** shows that such a rebellion against the Davidic king is regarded as something that would not have succeeded in normal circumstances, because ultimately it is an attempt to withstand God himself. (Rudolph helpfully draws attention to Ps. 2 in this connection.) The outcome of the battle underlines this conclusion. **the kingdom of the Lord in the hand of the sons of David:** see on v. 5 above.

Abijah now moves on to the second part of his speech, dealing with the religious deviations which have been introduced in the north since the time of the division. **the golden calves:** cf. 11:15.

9. driven out the priests . . . and the Levites: cf. 11:14*b*; contrast 14*a*. The present verse supports our understanding of what was to be attributed to the Chronicler in that passage and hence indirectly confirms the secondary nature of 14*a*. **with a young bull or seven rams:** contrast Exod. 29:1, which prescribes 'one young bull and two rams'. It is not clear whether this discrepancy also reveals a mild polemic or is merely based on a variant legal tradition. **no gods:** this expression is used at Hos. 8:6 for 'the calf of Samaria', and so may here be a further reference to the golden calves. However, in view of the close parallel between this section and 11:14f., it is more attractive to see here a reference to the satyrs.

10–11. The contrast with the situation in the south is now drawn. They **have not forsaken** God, whereas the northerners **have forsaken him:** see on 12:1. On the cultic practices and items specifically listed here, see above on 2:4 and 4:7, where it was noted that there

2 CHRONICLES 13:12–19

too they were singled out as being of peculiar significance to the Chronicler.

12. See the introduction to vv. 4–12 for the force of this appeal and its implications for a correct understanding of the northerners' status. **his priests with their battle trumpets:** cf. Num. 10:8f. and 31:6, and note v. 14 below. As in ch. 20 later, the ideology of the holy war is believed implicitly.

13–17. The account of the battle is told in stylised fashion; cf. von Rad, *Der heilige Krieg*, pp. 79f. Most of its elements can be paralleled from battle narratives earlier in the *OT*, while others (compare vv. 16 and 17 with 28:5–6 and v. 18 with 28:19) are carefully phrased by the Chronicler with a view to his subsequent narrative. Finally, a statement like 'God defeated Jeroboam' (v. 15) is inaccessible, without further explanation or qualification, to the historian. If we are right in thinking that the Chronicler did know from some independent source of the capture of the three towns in v. 19, we cannot, in view of the nature of the account, do other than leave open the historical question of the actual course of the battle.

In order to appreciate the stylised nature of this account, it is necessary to point only to the most obvious parallels (cf. Welten, pp. 119–22). For the strategy of **an ambush**, cf. Jos. 8:2; Jg. 20:29; for **the battle** being **before and behind them**, cf. 2 Sam. 10:9; for **the trumpets** and **the battle shout**, cf. Jos. 6:16; for the course of the battle from the point of view of the southerners, see especially 1 Chr. 5:20–22, and cf. more generally D. M. Gunn, *The Story of King David* (1978), pp. 51–4, etc.

18. For the reversal of this situation, cf. 28:19. **they relied upon the Lord:** this is the decisive factor for the Chronicler. The word is used to the same end at 14:11 and 16:7–8, but the concept is found in several of his other battle reports.

19. It has been plausibly argued that this verse contains authentic information which has become the basis for the Chronicler's whole reinterpretation of Abijah (see above). Welten, pp. 116–29, has only suggested, not established, the alternative view which sees here a reflection of the claims of the post-exilic community. Moreover, his argument (p. 127) that the Chronicler's reinterpretation is based not on an alternative source of information but on a desire to present the first four kings of the south in a positive light carries little weight if our interpretation of Rehoboam's reign is correct; see on 12:14.

Studies which build on the assumption that the information in this verse is correct include F. M. Cross and G. E. Wright, *JBL* 75 (1956), pp. 222f.; Z. Kallai-Kleinmann, *VT* 8 (1958), pp. 139f.; Y. Aharoni, *VT* 9 (1959), pp. 230f.; and K.D. Schunck, *Benjamin*

(1963), p. 154. The subsequent history is not as clear as could be wished (see 15:8; 16:6; 17:2), but it is certainly known that by the eighth century BC **Bethel** was back in northern hands (e.g. Am. 7:10ff.). **Jeshanah** is usually identified with *Burj el-Isāne*, and **Ephron** (on the forms of the name, cf. K.D. Schunck, *VT* 11 [1961], pp. 188–200), or 'Ophrah', with *et-Taiyibeh*, though at present not enough is known about the sites to admit arguments from archaeology into the discussion of this verse's historicity.

20. This conclusion of the results of the battle is also probably the Chronicler's own deduction. According to 1 Kg. 15:9 **Jeroboam** in fact outlived **Abijah**, but an account of the death of the defeated leader often features in such battle reports (cf. Gunn), so that it will have seemed appropriate to the Chronicler. Note that **the Lord smote him** uses the same verb as 'God defeated Jeroboam' in v. 15.

13:21–14:1a. The summary of Abijah's reign.

21. grew mighty: a characteristic mark of the Chronicler's style. Once again a large family is taken as an indication of God's blessing; cf. 11:18–23. The source of the Chronicler's information, if any, is unknown.

22. The narrative here rejoins 1 Kg. 15:7, though cf. v. *2b* above. 'The Book of the Chronicles of the Kings of Judah', however, is replaced by **the story** (midrash) **of the prophet Iddo**: cf. 9:29 and 12:15. There is no reason to suppose that 'midrash' here has any particular significance; it need be no more than a stylistic variant on the Chronicler's other source citation formulae; cf. 24:27. See further, the Introduction, section F, and Willi, p. 236.

ASA

14:1b–16:14

N.B. 2 Chr. 14:1 is numbered 13:23 in the Hebrew Bible, and 14:2 as 14:1. Consequently, for the remainder of 2 Chr. 14 the verse numbers in *RSV* are one higher than in the Hebrew.

The Chronicler's treatment of Asa's reign represents a considerable expansion over the account in 1 Kg. 15:9–24. Inevitably, therefore, the question of possible additional sources must be raised. Secondly, problems of chronology arise when 16:1, which links Asa and Baasha, king of Israel, in Asa's thirty-sixth year, is compared with 1 Kg. 16:6 and 8, where Baasha is said to have died as early as the twenty-sixth year of Asa. Thirdly, further comparison of the two accounts has suggested to many scholars that, regardless of the issue of sources, the Chronicler has imposed a pattern on the account as a whole in order that it may illustrate his characteristic themes of reward for faithfulness and judgment for rebellion.

In seeking to explain these matters, commentators have generally taken one of two alternative approaches. They either bend over backwards in order to salvage the Chronicler's reputation as a historian, or they go to the other extreme of attributing virtually the whole of the account to his theological creativity. It will be argued here that both positions have an element of truth in them, and that justice must be done to both by treading a middle way. We will thus give a brief summary of the two major positions before going on to suggest how they may be brought closer together.

Rudolph's analysis has been generally followed by those who take the second approach (e.g. Michaeli; North). He observes, surely with justice, that the Chronicler would have been puzzled by two aspects of his Kings *Vorlage*: (1) since illness was regarded as punishment, why did the otherwise apparently virtuous king suffer so (1 Kg. 15:23); and (2) since faithfulness leads to peace, how can there have been continual war between Asa and Baasha (1 Kg. 15:16)? Rudolph then works backwards through Asa's reign to show how each event is supplied with its necessary cause: Asa's illness (16:12) is the result of his mistreatment of a prophet and his supporters (16:10), the peaceful start to his reign is the reward for his early piety, and so on. On this view, the chronology throughout is quite arbitrary, reflecting only what the Chronicler considered to be the necessary gaps between one event and the next: e.g., two years for Asa's illness (16:12–13); a space of three years before that (16:1) to allow for the negotiations and subsequent activity (16:2–6) which incurred the prophet's displeasure; peace during the period before that (15:19); and so on.

The alternative view, in contrast, starts from the chronological notices in the narrative, and treats them with the utmost seriousness. A pioneer in this direction is E. R. Thiele, *The Mysterious Numbers of the Hebrew Kings* (1951, ²1965), whose views are conveniently summarised in the article on 'Chronology in the OT' by S. J. De Vries, *IDB* 1, pp. 580–99, and cf. *IDBS*, pp. 161–6. He observes that taken at purely face value 15:19 is not even consistent with the Chronicler's own account, for its statement that 'there was no war until the thirty-fifth year of the reign of Asa' (there is no justification for the addition of the word 'more' in *AV*, *RSV*, etc.) conflicts with the account of Zerah's invasion in 14:9–15. He also points to the difficulty of 16:1, noted above. However, if it may be assumed as a working hypothesis that these references to the thirty-fifth and thirty-sixth years relate not to Asa's reign but to the division of the monarchy, all else falls neatly into place, for they would then correspond to the fifteenth and sixteenth years of Asa. Thus 15:19 would suggest that Zerah's invasion should be dated to Asa's fif-

teenth year, and this fits precisely with the implications of 15:10–
11. Moreover, such success would explain why many of the northerners came down to the south, so that precisely in the next year
(16:1) Baasha built Ramah in order to prevent their exodus (cf. I
Kg. 15:17).

In addition to the inherent attractiveness of this reconstruction,
there are one or two details which indicate that the chronology it
presupposes does in fact have a more objective basis than the suggestions of Rudolph would allow. First, Rudolph's reconstruction does
not adequately explain the thirty-fifth year of 15:19. On his view,
war only started in the thirty-sixth year (16:1), but the wording of
15:19 is most naturally taken to mean that it started in the previous
year. Second, Rudolph himself agrees that there was some further
source available to the Chronicler; this he regards as particularly
clear in the case of 15: (1) 8–15, which is a doublet of 14:2–4. If
this is so, it suggests that it is an appropriate method to attempt a
historical reconstruction, even though due regard must also be had
to the Chronicler's own contribution, to be discussed below. Finally,
if the Chronicler was really composing without the restraint of any
source at this point, why did he allow the apparent contradiction
between 15:19 and 14:9–15 to stand unresolved?

On this basis, therefore, we may suggest an outline of the actual
course of events as represented by the Chronicler's sources (including I Kg. 15). That this ultimately remains a hypothetical exercise
is fully recognised, as is the fact that the further question as to the
extent of these sources' dependence on historical reality is not hereby
settled. However, the latter issue is not directly relevant to an
attempt to appreciate what the Chronicler himself was seeking to
convey, which must remain our chief concern here, whereas without
some attempt at such an outline of his sources' presentation it
becomes less easy to distinguish his own contribution. In the following table, all the verses of chs. 14–16 are included, though, as
will be seen later, some are undoubtedly the Chronicler's own
composition.

Years 1–15 Reform and covenant; 14:1–8, parallel with 15:1–18; on
          I Kg. 15:16, see on 15:19 below; on the actual date of
          Asa's reform, see the introduction to 15:8–19.
Year 15   Zerah's offensive; 14:9–15; cf. 15:19
Year 16   Baasha's offensive; Asa's treaty with Benhadad and its
          consequences; 16:1–10
Year ?   Asa's illness and death; 16:11–14.

Should this outline be even approximately correct, the nature of
the Chronicler's contribution stands out with greater clarity. Four

main points may be singled out here, the remainder being reserved for the verse-by-verse commentary. First, he has brought forward the invasion of Zerah to the middle of the period of peace. In this way, and as interpreted by the Chronicler (cf. 14:11), it can be used as an example of Asa's piety in that he relied on God, and it was followed by further reward, rather than coming anomalously (on the Chronicler's view) at the end of the period of peace. Mosis, pp. 69f., well observes that in this the Chronicler has used just the same method as at 1 Chr. 14, where again an account of cultic reform is interrupted by a war in which victory for David is to be seen as a reward for 'seeking' God (cf. 1 Chr. 13:3; 2 Chr. 14:4, 7; 15:2).

Secondly, the covenant celebration (15:9-15) will have originally been the climax of Asa's reform only, but by a small addition in 15:11 he has made it also into a victory celebration, thereby further integrating the account of Zerah's invasion into this section of his narrative.

Thirdly, in order to prolong the period of peace with which Asa was rewarded for his faithfulness, the Chronicler has dated the Baasha incident some twenty years later than his source by the addition of the words 'of the reign of Asa' to the dates in 15:19 and 16:1. Thiele and those who follow him seem to suggest that this is the result of misunderstanding by later scribes (pp. 180f.; some even postulate scribal error in transmission), but we need look no further than the Chronicler, whose schematisation was well served by relegating the events of ch. 16 by this simple device to the closing years of Asa's reign.

Finally, the 'message' of the two halves of Asa's reign is characteristically drawn out for his readers by the Chronicler by the insertion of the speeches of the two seers, Azariah (15:1-7) and Hanani (16:7-9). The first underlines God's reward for the kind of reforms initiated and faith exercised by Asa at the first, while the second condemns lack of reliance on God, exemplified both by his league with Benhadad and later by his reaction to disease. These two speeches underline for us the clear pattern which the Chronicler has imposed on his material. The pattern is a familiar one in his narrative (cf. Mosis, pp. 173-5), and one whose rationale he is anxious to impress upon his readers.

Asa's Reform (1) and Prosperity

14:1b–8

The Chronicler's account of the opening years of Asa's reign largely represents his own expansion of 1 Kg. 15:11–12. The description there, however, of 'the male cult prostitutes' and 'all the idols that his fathers had made' did not accord well with his presentation of the previous reigns; consequently he has made Asa's reform much more 'Deuteronomic', thus anticipating the reforms of Hezekiah and Josiah, and suggesting that the abuses rectified were not wholly pagan, but rather 'internal' Israelite practices.

1b. In his days the land had rest: politically, this may be regarded as the result of Abijah's victory in the previous chapter; but for the Chronicler it was seen as reward for Asa's religious faithfulness, as the similar phraseology in vv. 5b, 6, 7b; 15:15b and 19 makes clear; see also on 1 Chr. 22:9, and G. von Rad, 'There remains still a Rest for the People of God', in *The Problem of the Hexateuch and Other Essays* (1966), pp. 94–102. The phrase is reminiscent of the one used in Judges where it applies, following some deliverance, to the period before the next rebellion of Israel against God which inevitably brings foreign oppression as its judgment. However much God may be regarded as having taken up his 'resting place' in Israel with the housing of the ark in the temple (6:41–42), the people's own enjoyment of rest remains an incentive for faithfulness which can all too easily be lost. On the contrast with 1 Kg. 15:16 and 32, see on 15:19 below.

for ten years: this presumably sets the Chronicler's date for Zerah's invasion (see above). It is somewhat arbitrarily chosen, the constraints being simply a round number which is less than fifteen (15:10–11).

3. Asa acts very much in the spirit of Dt. 7:5; 12:3 and 16:21–22, the cult objects listed here being no doubt regarded primarily as illegitimate expressions of Israelite worship. For discussion of the precise nature of these objects the reader must be referred to the commentaries on Deuteronomy, since they are not relevant to the work of the Chronicler itself. **the high places:** this appears flatly to contradict 1 Kg. 15:14, which would itself have clashed with the idealised portrayal of Asa which the Chronicler is offering. He gives his own harmonisation in 15:17, where he slightly alters the wording of his *Vorlage* in this matter.

4. to seek the Lord: a familiar summary of what the Chronicler regarded as man's chief duty; see on 1 Chr. 10:14. The use of such characteristic terminology both here and in v. 7 and 15:2 and 12 suggests that the account as a whole is intended by the Chronicler to be 'paradigmatic'. **to keep the law and the commandment:** further characteristic Deuteronomic terminology.

5. the incense altars: the meaning of this word (*ḥammānîm*) has been much discussed. *RSV* represents the consensus of opinion until recently, but now V. Fritz, in B. Benzing, O. Böcher and G. Mayer (eds), *Wort und Wirklichkeit* (1976), 1, pp. 41–50, has re-opened the issue, arguing on the basis of the word's occurrence in a number of extra-biblical inscriptions (and with full discussion of earlier treatments) that it must mean some kind of cultic building smaller than a temple — perhaps 'shrine' would be the best English equivalent. If Fritz is right, the word here may qualify, rather than add to, **the high places,** and indicate a difference between those situated in the cities of Judah and those mentioned in v. 3. There does not appear to be any other explanation for the repetition. **the kingdom had rest:** cf. v. 1.

6–7. For a general comment on the theme of building in Chronicles, see on 11:5–12 above. Here too the theme serves to illustrate the positive appraisal of the first years of Asa's reign. This is made more than usually clear by the reasons supplied for the building, namely that there was **no war,** but rather **peace** from God (see also on v. 1), and because the people **have sought the Lord** (see on v. 4). Since under such conditions of reliance upon God (as the following paragraph will show) conventional defensive equipment is hardly necessary, a tension is established between the activities of these verses and the impression of Asa which the Chronicler wishes to convey. This can only be resolved on the supposition that, in his view, good kings prosper, and prosperity is seen in building operations.

In the light of this, the question of a possible source behind the Chronicler's description becomes a secondary issue, and the evidence rather tells against it: (a) these two verses are closely joined to the preceding paragraph which, it has been argued, are the Chronicler's own expansion of his *Vorlage*; (b) the style is like that of the Chronicler elsewhere (cf. Welten, pp. 15–19, who nevertheless tends to overstate his case); and (c) there is none of the kind of detail which is found in 11:5–12 that would allow us to postulate such a source. Of course, it is highly probable that Asa did do some building; cf. 1 Kg. 15:23; Jer. 41:9, and 'the unsettled conditions of the time' (Myers), exemplified both in the following paragraph and the continuing difficulties to the north (ch. 16). But this is not sufficient to postulate source material here, nor need it relate to this period of Asa's long reign. It has been seen, however, that the Chronicler has adapted chronology to express his thought in these chapters; there can therefore be no objection to the view that he has done the same again here.

7. the land is still ours: i.e. while we still have opportunity. Post-exilic readers may have been quick to apply such language to themselves. **we have sought the Lord our God; we have sought him:** this emphasis by repetition is somewhat overdone. By simply repointing the second verb (following the lead of some of the versions) from *dārašnû* to *dᵉrāšānû*, sense comparable with 15:2 can be obtained: '(Because) we have sought . . . . he has sought us'. This attractive emendation is followed by many commentators and *NEB*. This short speech by Asa so repeats what the Chronicler has already said of him in the previous verses that we cannot doubt that he has again brought his own views to expression here.

8. Details of Asa's army. This is the first of several such notes included in the Chronicler's narrative; cf. 17:14–19; 25:5 and 26:11–15. The verse cannot therefore be evaluated in total isolation, but must be considered along with the others.

In three of the four passages, the description comes as part of the positive evaluation of a 'good' king. It thus serves a similar purpose, in the Chronicler's narrative, to the notes about building (vv. 6–7 above, and see on 11:5–12). However, 25:5 is a noteworthy exception, for the description there is both an integral part of its surrounding narrative context and comes in a passage where the king, Amaziah, is clearly acting in a way of which the Chronicler disapproves. This exception should be enough at once to warn that these notes cannot be automatically put on the same level as those about building (*contra* Welten).

The first systematic study of these passages was undertaken by Junge, pp. 37–45. Amongst the conclusions which he drew, we may note the following: (a) they differ from passages which are probably to be attributed to the Chronicler himself by their concise, clear and matter-of-fact style; (b) in themselves (that is, once removed from the context with which the Chronicler has supplied them) they are free of any moralising or religious element. Their purely factual content thus also marks them out from the Chronicler's own compositions; (c) they are therefore not to be attributed to him, but may legitimately be isolated and studied in their own right; (d) such a study reveals that they supply details, not of a standing army, but of the conscript army. This is shown by the divisions according to tribes, the large numbers involved (though Junge also thinks these may be exaggerated), the terms used to describe these troops which differ from those of a professional army, and the type of weapons listed, from which horses and chariots are notably absent. Up to this point, Junge's arguments have been followed by many scholars, though few, if any, are prepared to follow his further argument that all these passages date originally to Josiah's reign; in addition to the commentaries, cf. Noth, *US* p. 141, and de Vaux, *AI*, pp. 225–8.

We may here add two further points in favour of this general conclusion. First, it was suggested above (p. 46, following Johnson and Liver) that for another part of his work the Chronicler had available as a source some kind of military census-list, organised on a tribal basis. This renders more probable the view that such material was preserved until the Chronicler's time. Second, these notes are not nearly so widespread as those on building, and, as already observed, one is not used as part of the positive evaluation of a king's reign. This suggests that there was a measure of constraint placed on the Chronicler in his use of such material. The simplest explanation for this would seem to be that he had regard for the source from which he drew the material.

A quite different understanding, however, has recently been advocated by Welten, pp. 79–114. He regards these notes as no more than the Chronicler's own fiction, the model on which they are based being the Hellenistic armies of his own day. A full discussion of Welten's arguments would be out of place here; a few observations on some of the points he makes must suffice to indicate why the view outlined above may still be regarded as preferable.

(a) Welten has not been able to make out the case that the style of these notes points to their composition by the Chronicler. Needless to say, they have several features in common, such as the words used in the description of the weaponry, but this is only to be expected where comparable and technical material is being treated. It is true that there are some words or phrases used which occur only, or predominantly, in late biblical Hebrew. There are, however, various possible explanations for this which do not involve the suggestion that the Chronicler was himself responsible for these notes in their entirety without any earlier source.

(b) Welten's objections to the historicity of these notes are not compelling. For instance, he finds it remarkable that chariots are not mentioned, since these were so important in the period to which the notes purport to belong. However, it has already been noted that this is only to be expected in the case of enrolment figures for a conscript army, rather than a standing army.

(c) Welten also finds difficulty in the view that men of the tribes of Judah and Benjamin should so neatly have been skilled in the use of particular weapons. This is a most unimaginative objection, which completely ignores what we might now call 'regimental tradition', together with the possibility that with the passage of time the names 'Judah' and 'Benjamin' would in such contexts have tended

to lose their strictly tribal affiliation and become rather the names
of the 'heavy' and 'light' regiments respectively.

(d) Attention has already been drawn to the significance of 25:5.
Welten observes the difficulties which it poses to his view, but then
completely ignores them in his subsequent discussion. We may
therefore conclude that it remains more satisfactory to regard these
notes as based on older material, although it is recognised that
without further information it is not possible to say more about
either their specific accuracy or their particular chronological
attribution.

three hundred thousand. . . .two hundred and eighty thousand:
see on 13:3 for two possible approaches to these figures. It is noteworthy that once more the total is not far off half the stated size of
the opposing army (v. 9).

Victory over Zerah

14:9–15

Amidst considerable uncertainty concerning the origins of the material in this paragraph, two related features have rightly impressed
themselves on all commentators. First, its style demonstrates that
its present form is to be attributed to the Chronicler himself (so,
most recently and thoroughly, Welten, pp. 133–5). Secondly, he
has clearly introduced the account to illustrate a further aspect of
Asa's faithfulness, namely, his complete 'reliance' (cf. v. 11) upon
God. As in the similar case of Abijah earlier (13:18), this attitude
resulted in a famous and remarkable victory. Indeed, several literary
parallels are to be observed between the two accounts, no doubt
deriving ultimately from the stylised reports of battles to which the
label 'Holy War' has often been attached. In the ensuing discussion,
sight must not be lost of these agreed matters, for it is they which
are of most importance in terms of understanding the Chronicler's
text itself.

It is inevitable, however, that scholars should have gone beyond
this to inquire after the historical nature (if any) of this encounter.
A few examples of the positions adopted will illustrate the diversity
of their conclusions. (a) Some take the account at more or less its
face value, drawing in additionally the remark of 16:8 which, by
linking the Ethiopians with the Libyans, suggests that *hakkûšî*,
'the Cushite', should indeed be understood as 'Ethiopian' (so *RSV*)
rather than anything else. While it would now be generally agreed
that Zerah cannot be identified with Osorkon I, both because the
names differ entirely and because Osorkon I was of Libyan, not

Ethiopian (Nubian), origin, K. A. Kitchen, *The Third Intermediate Period in Egypt* (1973), p. 309, for instance, can suggest as a reconstruction that 'by 897 BC, Osorkon I was already an old man, and so he may well have sent a general of Nubian extraction to lead a force into Palestine, to emulate his father's [Shoshenq; see on 12:1–2] exploit, bring home some fresh booty, and dismantle the military build-up of king Asa'. The lack of an Egyptian record of the affair would be understandable in view of the Judean victory.

(b) An alternative, but comparable, view, first suggested by W. F. Albright, *JPOS* 4 (1924), pp. 146–7, and adopted by a number of others, postulates that after his successful Palestinian campaign Shoshenq established a buffer state around Gerar, peopled by Nubian mercenaries. For one reason or another, these eventually invaded Judah. Against this view, however, S. Hidal, *SEA* 41–2 (1976–7), pp. 100–1, correctly observes both that there is no evidence whatever that such a garrison or buffer state was ever established by Shoshenq at Gerar, and that the account here does not state that Zerah came from Gerar, only that he was pursued thither.

(c) Hidal himself adopts what is probably the majority view. This severs all connection of the episode with the Egyptians, but recognises in the prominence of the place-names involved the marks of an originally historical tradition. Noteworthy too is the indication from v. 15 of Bedouin involvement. On this basis it is suggested that the episode was on a much smaller and more local scale than the Chronicler indicates. 'Cush might then be the name of an ethnic group, living in the vicinity of Judaea' (Hidal), with which some compare 'Cushan' in Hab. 3:7, and the whole incident might reflect a bedouin raid or a clash under the pressure of a group seeking better pasture at Judah's expense.

(d) Finally, Welten, pp. 129–40, is the most recent advocate of the view which regards the whole paragraph as no more than the Chronicler's fabrication. (He is followed without further discussion by Mosis, p. 174.) He points first to the fact, noted above, that the style of the Chronicler himself is prominent throughout the account, there being no stylistic evidence for part being extracted from some older source. Second, while admitting that the places named would fit well in the pre-exilic period, he observes that they were equally prominent later. Third, he argues against Noth, *US*, p. 142, that it is not at all surprising that such a victory should be attributed to the insignificant Asa; it is part of the Chronicler's purpose to present the first four kings of Judah in a favourable light.

Welten used this same argument against the battle report in ch. 13, and it is no more convincing here than there; see on 13:19 and the introduction to ch. 13. His first two arguments, moreover, again only offer an alternative suggestion without establishing its preferability. Evidence that the Chronicler did have another source besides 1 Kings for Asa's reign has been offered above, while the concrete details of this account (including v. 15, which sits somewhat uneasily with what is evidently the Chronicler's own interpretation of the incident, but which is not fully dealt with by Welten) are still pointers towards some alternative, possibly local, tradition.

In sum, therefore, and in the total lack of any extra-biblical evidence, the third view outlined above seems to be the most satisfying from a historical point of view. That the Chronicler has, however, rewritten his source extensively is the abiding value of Welten's study. Moreover, his inclusion of the Libyans at 16:8 shows that he presented it as a major international engagement, comparable to Shishak's invasion in ch. 12. By this substantial representation he clearly felt that the theological lessons outlined above, for the sake of which he included this account in the first place, could be more effectively pressed home.

9. a million men: see on 13:3. If the final possibility suggested there were adopted here, it would give a total of a thousand warriors. However, if the understanding of the nature of this encounter outlined above is correct, even this would be inappropriate, and suggests that such rationalising explanations of the Chronicler's numbers are not always to be preferred. 'A thousand thousands' need be no more than a way of expressing a huge number. Equally, the **three hundred chariots**, though modest in numbers for a major encounter, are also to be attributed to the Chronicler's (or an intermediate predecessor's) version of the tradition, since chariots as such would have been quite out of place amongst the Bedouin. **Mareshah:** cf. 11:8. As one of the sites of Rehoboam's defensive fortifications, its occurrence in this context makes good sense.

10. Zephathah: otherwise unknown. LXX suggests 'north of', which is orthographically extremely similar in Hebrew script ($ṣāp̄-ônāh$ for $ṣ^e p̄ātāh$). This reading is favoured by many, and may be right, though the possibility cannot be excluded that it is LXX which, being the easier text, is secondary.

11. between the mighty and the weak: it is not entirely clear whether this means 'either the mighty or the weak' or 'in an encounter between forces that are unequally matched', and hence by implication to help the weak. The remainder of Asa's prayer is couched in familiar terms which reflect the Chronicler's own viewpoint; cf. especially 13:14 and 18. Ackroyd also points to a possible link with Isa. 10:20. Such reliance upon God turns any army, however small, into an 'overwhelming minority', because **man** cannot

prevail against him. The reverse of this truth is to be the theme of ch. 16.

12. See 13:15 and 16, where the same phraseology is used, though even the Judeans' small role there is unmentioned here; cf. Exod. 14:14; Dt. 20:4; 1 Sam. 17:47, etc.

13. Gerar: Y. Aharoni's identification (*IEJ* 6 [1956], pp. 26–32) with Tell Abu Hureira is now generally accepted. **remained alive:** the word has in it the idea of recovery; cf. Myers: 'so many of the Ethiopians fell that they were unable to rally'. **before the Lord and his army:** the so-called 'holy war' theme is here continued, even though it is not clear whether **his army** (literally, 'his camp'; cf. Gen. 32:2; 1 Chr. 12:22) is a reference to the heavenly host or Asa's troops; the latter is favoured by Welten, p. 134.

14. the fear of the Lord was upon them: that the Lord would paralyse Israel's enemies with fear and panic is a familiar theme in accounts of the 'holy war'; cf. Exod. 23:28; Dt. 7:20, 23; Jos. 24:12 (all as translated in *NEB*); Jg. 7, etc.

15. the tents of those who had cattle (*'oh°lê miqneh*, literally 'tents of cattle'): *NEB*, 'the herdsmen', follows the now widely-accepted view that as well as meaning 'tent', *'ohel* can be extended to cover those who live in tents; cf. Arabic *'ahl*, 'people who inhabit the same tent or place'. The view that tents were sometimes used as stables for cattle (K. Koch, *TDOT* 1, p. 120) seems unlikely. This, together with the reference to **camels**, points to the association of the enemy 'Cushites' with nomadic herdsmen of some sort.

Azariah's Sermon

15:1-7

The victorious returning army is met by an otherwise unknown prophet, whose inspired address encourages Asa to press ahead with his reform. A number of commentators have felt, however, that the content of the address is unsuitable to the occasion, because its apparent references to the past do not fit anything that the Chronicler records of Asa's reign (though cf. in part 1 Kg. 15:16). Such an approach fails to appreciate the purpose of this section. As is often the case with these 'Levitical sermons', it constitutes the Chronicler's theological commentary on the events he is recording. Thus v. 2 draws out the lesson to be learnt from the victory over Zerah against all the odds, while v. 7, in context, is to be taken as a warning against 'resting on one's laurels', and hence explains why the parallel reform accounts have been treated separately by the Chronicler.

There has also been a certain amount of discussion over whether the central section of the sermon refers to the past or future. On the basis of a form-critical examination of this *genre* (cf. von Rad, 'The Levitical Sermon'), the references must be to the past, for it is on the basis of this that the hortatory element is introduced. However, the interpretation of some of these elements as future goes back at least as far as LXX, being no doubt influenced by the use in the sermon of prophetic texts, and by indications (e.g. vv. 1 and 8) that this passage was a prophecy. It is therefore possible that MT itself has been influenced by this very early interpretation (so Rudolph; see on v. 4 below), and if so it would help account for the difficulties which later interpreters have felt.

1. The Spirit of God came upon: such language is regularly used by the Chronicler to indicate prophetic inspiration, e.g. 20:14. On his conception of prophecy, cf. Willi, pp. 216–29, and Seeligmann, *SVT* 29 (1978), pp. 270–9. **Azariah the son of Oded:** not otherwise known. We have already seen (and will see again), however, that it is the Chronicler's practice to attribute this type of address to historically attested prophets. It is likely, therefore, that he derived the name from his extra-biblical source or sources for Asa's reign, evidence for which has been briefly noted above.

2. This verse states the basic theological postulate which the previous chapter has served to illustrate; cf. 14:4 and 7. It will also recur at the end of the covenant ceremony in v. 15 below. *RSV*'s translation with a timeless present tense is therefore appropriate. The phraseology is very familiar to the reader of Chronicles; cf. especially 1 Chr. 28:9 (with the reference to Dt. 4:29; Jer. 29:13f.; Isa. 55:6) and 2 Chr. 12:1.

3. As there is no finite verb in this verse, it has been thought by some to refer to the future, a view which the allusion to Hos. 3:4 might appear to strengthen. However, attention to the context in Hosea will at once make clear that the Chronicler's method is here very free, constituting little more than a use of familiar phraseology. The verse is most naturally understood as referring to the troubled period of the judges (e.g. Jg. 2:11–13; 17:5–6, etc.). **teaching priest** and **law**, derivatives of the same root, are to be taken closely together. J. Weingreen, *JSS* 6 (1961), p. 171, paraphrases the first word as 'priest giving authoritative direction', and explains that this 'refers to the lost priestly function of issuing authoritative directions on matters of ritual and religious law. Appropriately, then, this priestly function which is absent is referred to by the noun *tôrāh*' (**law**), which Weingreen translates 'authoritative direction'.

4. Cf. Jg. 2:18, which sets the pattern for the stories of deliverance throughout Judges; e.g. 3:9, etc. Rudolph observes that this verse appears to interrupt the connection between 3 and 5f., both of which deal with the times of distress and which the salvific element in this verse should logically follow. He also notes that the connection between **distress** at the beginning of this verse and the end of v. 6 would be restored if this verse were transposed to follow v. 6. He explains the present order as due to interpretative activity which referred vv. 3f. to the past but 5f. to the future (see also on 5b). An alternative approach, however, which preserves the present order, would be to observe that, just as this verse shows that restoration was possible even after the horrors of v. 3, so (v. 7) it will be possible again for the Chronicler's contemporaries, even though conditions in the present may be as bad as, or worse than, those which obtained under the judges. **sought . . . found:** cf. v. 2.

5. For historical references, cf. Jg. 5:6 and 6:2ff., etc., together with Zech. 8:10. However, if the suggestion advanced above in v. 4 is correct, the Chronicler will have expected his readers to see parallels here with their own day too. This will explain also the broadening of the perspective to include **all the inhabitants of the lands.** Rudolph thinks this is a later addition under the influence of Zech. 14:13a, inserted only after this passage had come to be interpreted as referring to the future. Alternatively, however, the Chronicler may have chosen carefully to paint an exaggerated picture of the past in terms which his readers would have recognised as parallel to their own, out of which also, no doubt, the prophet constructed his impression of the future. In favour of this latter view it is noteworthy that the verbal parallel with Zech. 14:13 is less close than at times when the Chronicler appears consciously to cite a prophetic text.

6. Again, this verse can be easily referred to the judges period from a historical point of view, but the conceptual parallels with such passages of prophecy as Isa. 9:18–21; Ezek. 38:21; Hag. 2:22; Zech. 8:10b and 14:13f. will not have been lost on the readers, and will have encouraged them to see a reflection of the **distress** of their own day.

7. In good homiletical style, the conclusion of the sermon presses home the lessons of the foregoing on the listeners. To object that Asa has already shown himself a faithful reformer in the previous chapter and that this passage is somehow misplaced fails to appreciate both its function in the immediate narrative context and in the Chronicler's purpose as a whole. As to the former, there is nothing here specifically to suggest that a completely fresh start is being urged, but rather encouragement to continue, following the interruption caused by Zerah's invasion; as to the latter, the fact that the Chronicler cites Jer. 31:16 and Zeph. 3:16 indicates that he

intended this exhortation to be heeded also by his own community, for by now they doubtless recognised these prophecies as authoritative. His whole narrative in this section thus becomes exemplary to his readers.

Asa's Reform (2) and Covenant

15:8–19

It has already been noted that from a literary point of view part of this account of Asa's reform represents a parallel account with that at the start of ch. 14. Indeed, the source which lies behind it has certain features which appear historically more probable than the alternative account, which is based on Kings. The latter suggests that Asa's reform began at the start of his reign; however, Asa was probably very young when he succeeded to the throne, and it is implied (cf. v. 16) that it was owing to his mother that the religious state of Judah deteriorated. This is most likely to have been during the period of her greatest influence, namely, when Asa was a minor. A reform starting later on in his reign, perhaps leading to a renewal ceremony in his fifteenth year (v. 10), is thus plausible (see further on v. 8 below). For reasons already outlined, however, it suited the Chronicler to develop the portrayal already presented in Kings of the reform starting much earlier, and to use this alternative version of it as a description of its continuation and successful conclusion.

8. of Azariah the son of: these words are a conjectural restoration by *RSV*. However, the process that has to be postulated in order to explain how the present form of the text arose if this conjecture is correct is rather complicated and unconvincing. It is better to regard 'Oded the prophet', which is the reading of MT, as a misplaced explanatory gloss on v. 1. **abominable idols:** these may be comparable to 'the idols' of the parallel account in 1 Kg. 15:12. **the cities which he had taken in the hill country of Ephraim:** this poses an obvious difficulty, since no such capture has been mentioned. The usual suggestions made by the commentators are unsatisfactory. For instance, the sentence cannot simply be referred to 13:19, since it explicitly states that Asa took the cities. (Rudolph's suggestions for rewriting the verse in order to overcome this difficulty are without any textual warrant whatever.) Equally, however, reference cannot be made forward to 16:6, since, apart from the chronological problems which this would raise, Geba and Mizpah are not sufficiently far north to be located **in the hill country of Ephraim.** Since, moreover, we can hardly suppose that the Chronicler would himself have invented this passage which is at variance with his general presentation of Asa's reign, we are obliged to seek an explanation in terms of his source, whose historical value has already been noted. It is clear from 16:1 (1 Kg. 15:17) that Abijah's conquests (13:19) were not held for long. It seems reasonable to suppose that they were lost during Asa's minority (Myers). Now 1 Kg. 15:16 and 32 state that 'there was war between Asa and Baasha king of Israel all their days', so that the present verse could well refer to one phase in that protracted (though doubtless intermittent) struggle. We thus conclude that this sentence adds weight to our contention that the Chronicler was here drawing on an independent source which at this point he did not fully harmonise with his wider presentation. This may have been an oversight on his part, or it may have suited him to retain this reference for other reasons; cf. v. 17. **the altar:** its position shows this to have been the altar for the burnt offerings (8:12); it will presumably have needed to be **repaired** from time to time; there is no necessary implication here of prior desecration.

9. And he gathered: this inclusive concern of the Davidic kings at important religious ceremonies has been repeatedly noted from 1 Chr. 13:1–5 onwards. This is again stressed in the present instance by the inclusion of some from the north; cf. 11:13–17. It would seem to be the Chronicler's view that firm, legitimate and godly leadership in Jerusalem will always attract back the religious allegiance of some, at least, from **Israel**. The presence of **Simeon** poses a problem that has not been satisfactorily resolved. Though located to the south of Judah (1 Chr. 4:24ff.), this tribe nevertheless seems occasionally to be included with the north; cf. *IBC*, p. 104.

10. the third month: the assembly will thus have come close to, if not coincided with, the Feast of Weeks (cf. Exod. 23:16; 34:22; Lev. 23:15–21; Num. 28:26; Dt. 16:9–10). It is possible that the writer intends us to make this connection because of the close verbal similarity between 'Weeks' (*šābūʿôt*) and the root for 'to swear', 'to take on oath' (*šābaʿ*), which is prominent in vv. 14f. Some have gone even further, however, in seeking to draw on the Jewish tradition of celebrating the giving of the law at Sinai at this festival (based on Exod. 19:1). This is mistaken, however, both because that tradition is very much later in date, and so was probably not established as early as the Chronicler's day (cf. de Vaux, *AI*, pp. 493–5; J. C. Rylaarsdam, *IDB* 4, pp. 827f.), and because this interpretation may rest on a false understanding of the nature of the covenant in v. 12. **the fifteenth year of the reign of Asa:** see the introduction to the reign of Asa for the acceptance of this date, which, besides, there seems no reason to doubt once it is agreed that a source of some kind underlies this account.

11. from the spoil which they had brought: stylistically, this phrase stands rather apart from its context (it either includes a relative clause without *ªšer* or should be rendered as an independent sentence: 'they brought [some] of the spoil'). If our analysis of Asa's reign has been correct, it must be an addition by the Chronicler himself to bring together the victory over Zerah and this cultic celebration. It was argued above that the fifteenth year was indeed the year of Zerah's invasion, but the victory can hardly have been won as early as the third month since as a general rule campaigning only began at this time of the year. As noted at 14:1 above, the Chronicler leaves his own dating of the campaign deliberately vague.

12. they entered into a covenant: it is not entirely clear who are to be regarded as the partners in this covenant, the king and the people or God and the people. Some linguistic justification can be found for both interpretations, though it slightly favours the former (cf. Japhet, *Ideology*, pp. 99f.), while the continuation, **to seek the Lord. . . .,** would sound strange if God were himself a party to the covenant. Thus to see in this celebration a renewal of the Sinai covenant (so, for instance, Kraus, *Worship*, p. 194) is probably mistaken. We should think rather of the people entering a binding agreement amongst themselves to continue whole-heartedly the life of faithfulness demonstrated by the king. For the importance of **to seek the Lord**, see on 14:4. Many commentators find in this covenant ceremony a backprojection of comparable ceremonies in the days of Josiah (2 Kg. 23) and Nehemiah (Neh. 10). This may well be true. It should be remembered, however, that evidence has been adduced that an independent source underlies the Chronicler's account here, and that it has marks of historical sobriety. Thus, (a) that source may itself have been influenced by the literary parallels, (b) the Chronicler may have further embellished it, or (c) some of the similarities may be due to the conservative nature of religious ritual which means that similar elements are to be expected in similar circumstances.

13. Though this penalty clause seems harsh to us, it is closely comparable to Dt. 13:6–10 and 17:2–7.

14. They took oath to the Lord: this will in fact describe the covenant ceremony. For the remainder, cf. 1 Chr. 15:28.

15. This verse is full of features characteristic of the Chronicler himself. For joy as a keynote of the ceremonies he describes, see on 1 Chr. 12:40. **had sought him . . . he was found by them:** see on 15:2, etc. Once again the Chronicler demonstrates that his narrative is to be understood as exemplary. **the Lord gave them rest round about:** see on 14:1. Their faithfulness had, in his view, to be further rewarded, even though on our understanding of the history of Asa's reign the war with Baasha (16:1) in fact followed almost immediately. The phrase may also act as a literary marker, indicating the resumption of dependence (whether close or remote) on 1 Kg. 15 as a source, broken off with similar words at 14:7.

16–18. This passage is taken for the most part from 1 Kg. 15:13–15, the commentaries on which should be consulted for most aspects of the content. This description of the continuing reform might more logically have been included earlier on. However, the Chronicler seems to have followed his sources in blocks as far as possible (he will continue to follow 1 Kg. 15 at the start of the next chapter), and, as the comment at the end of the previous verse suggests, to have left markers which indicate his procedure. Beyond such considerations, it must be concluded that Asa's actions here described, painful to him personally as they may have been, are intended to show how he himself fulfilled the stipulations of the covenant so recently agreed.

17. out of Israel: this is the Chronicler's own addition to his *Vorlage*. Without it, there would have been an irreconcilable contradiction with 14:3 and 5. As already noted, he has retained a hint from his source that at one stage Asa exercised authority over part of the northern kingdom (cf. v. 8), and it is to the north that **Israel** here undoubtedly refers. He is thus able to use this as a way of harmonising his own account with that of his *Vorlage*.

19. *RSV* is wrong to insert the word **more**. Coming just here this verse ought to parallel 1 Kg. 15:16, which, however, it seems flatly to contradict. Three points must be borne in mind. First, full justice must be done to the fact that the Chronicler's theology demanded of him that he present Asa's faithfulness being rewarded with an era of peace. Nonetheless, Baasha's move against him in the following verse seems to come before Asa's defection, so that that argument should not be pressed into being the whole explanation. Second, the Chronicler has clearly included in 14:9–15, and less certainly at 15:8, references to encounters which he himself dates to the earlier part of Asa's reign. This is a pointer to the fact, substantiated in the introduction to Asa's reign above, that his source was also in part responsible for his composition here. Finally, apart from the hint in 15:8, no real evidence will have been available to the Chronicler of open conflict between north and south before the events of the next chapter. He may, therefore, have interpreted his *Vorlage* as indicating that there was certainly what we should now call a 'cold war' between Asa and Baasha, which he will not have needed to deny, but that there was no war in the full sense that he intended until much later. **the thirty-fifth year:** see above, p. 256, for this date.

War with Baasha

16:1–6

The Chronicler continues in close dependence on his *Vorlage*, I Kg. 15:17–22. It is of significance to him because its account of Asa's league with the Syrian Benhadad shows a falling away from that complete reliance upon God which Asa manifested earlier in his reign (e.g. 14:11) and which the Chronicler wished to impress upon his readers. This interpretation is drawn out more fully by Hanani's address in the following paragraph. Of the minor differences between Chr. and Kg. in this passage, several are due to stylistic variation, or to the desire to express place-names in terms of their later equivalents, while for others the textual condition of the Chronicler's *Vorlage* may again not have coincided exactly with our MT (Willi gives examples of each of these ponts; cf. his index). Only one or two points of more significant difference can be mentioned here.

1. **the thirty-sixth year of the reign of Asa:** according to the chronology in Kings, Baasha died long before this. For our explanation, both in terms of history and of the Chronicler's intention at this point, see above, pp. 256f. W. F. Albright, *BASOR* 87 (1942), pp. 23–9, and 100 (1945), pp. 16–22, however, took this date as literally correct and made it the corner-stone for his chronology of the divided monarchy which involved the 'correction' of many of the dates in Kings. His confidence in this regard was based on his interpretation of the stele of Benhadad which, he argued, demonstrated that this Benhadad must be the same as Ahab's arch-enemy, and that this can only be done if the incident related here was as late as the Chronicler suggests. This, however, seems precarious evidence on which to base so extensive a revision of Israelite chronology, not least because the reading of the stele in question is itself not certain; cf. F. M. Cross, *BASOR* 205 (1972), pp. 36–42, and Gibson, *Inscriptions* 2, pp. 1–4. Further objections of a quite different sort are advanced by E. R. Thiele, *VT* 4 (1954), pp. 185–91.

2. **silver and gold:** the Chronicler here abbreviates his *Vorlage* in order (a) not to draw renewed attention to Shishak's plundering of the temple and (b) not to give the impression that Asa completely stripped the temple of all that remained.

6. See also on 15:8.

Hanani's Sermon

16:7–10

Just as the Chronicler inserted Azariah's sermon in 15:2–7 to interpret to his readers the positive period of Asa's reign, so here he
draws out the lessons to be learned from his falling away. They
coincide very closely with the teaching of Isa. 1–39, to which he
makes appropriate allusions.

7. **Hanani the seer**: from 1 Kg. 16:1 and 7 the Chronicler will
have known of 'the prophet Jehu the son of Hanani', and he refers
to him at 19:2 and 20:34 during Jehoshaphat's reign. What is more
natural than that Jehu's father should have prophesied during the
reign of Jehoshaphat's father?

Hanani's condemnation of Asa reminds the reader forcibly of
Isaiah's condemnation of Ahaz (Isa. 7) in a similar situation. Both
kings were faced by a threat from the north; both appealed for help
to a superior third power; both are condemned for their failure to
rely on the Lord (cf. Isa. 7:9*b*, 'If you will not believe, surely you
shall not be established'); and for both worse disasters yet to come
are predicted as a result of their lack of faith (v. 9*b*; Isa. 7:17ff.).
The Chronicler's keyword here is to **rely**; Asa has failed to do now
what previously he had done (cf. 14:11). Isaiah does not use this
keyword in ch. 7, but his use in comparable contexts at 10:20 and
31:1 shows that his thought is similar.

the army of the king of Syria: at first sight this seems curious, and
it is not surprising that a number of commentators (and the *NEB*)
have followed the Lucianic MSS of LXX in reading 'Israel' for Aram.
Textually, however, the case for this is weak; it is far more probable
that 'Israel' represents a secondary easing of the difficulty. What the
prophet means rather is that if Asa had remained faithful, 'he would
not only have conquered Baasha, but also the Syrians who were in
league with him' (CM; cf. v. 3). As it was, the continued power of
Syria was to involve not only the north, but also Judah, in costly
wars (cf. ch. 18) which could have been avoided.

8. The contrast between the two periods of Asa's reign, already
noted above, is here drawn out explicitly, again with characteristic
terminology. **the Libyans**: cf. 12:3. They are not mentioned in
ch. 14. Their inclusion shows that, probably against his source, the
Chronicler regarded Zerah and his army as Egyptian.

9. **the eyes of the Lord run to and fro throughout the whole
earth**: a citation, in the regular manner of these Levitical sermons,
of Zech. 4:10. This produces a frequently overlooked pointer to the
date of the Chronicler, for sufficient time must have elapsed for
Zechariah to be regarded in the same light as the pre-exilic prophets.

As with the hint at 1 Chr. 29:7, this suggests that the very early date recently advocated by several scholars is improbable (see further, pp. 15f.). The explanation of the citation shows that it is interpreted as implying the universality of God's protection towards **those whose heart is blameless towards him**, whether the threat is from the south (ch. 14) or the north (ch. 16). **You have done foolishly in this:** a clear echo of 1 Sam. 13:13. This, together with the only other occurrence in Chronicles (1 Chr. 21:8, drawn from 2 Sam. 24:10), shows that the folly cannot be limited to either the religious or the secular, political realm alone. Faith should influence political action, so that to neglect the one is to court disaster in the other. In this case, it will lead to **wars**. Since Asa's reign is nearly at an end with no conflicts recorded in its closing years, this appears to constitute a rare occurrence in Chronicles of the actions of one king having consequences in the reign of another (cf. 18; 22:5).

10. Hanani's rejection by Asa is based on the comparable experience of Jeremiah (Jer. 20:2-3), who was also put **in the stocks** (*RSV*'s addition of **in prison** is unnecessary). Asa's attitude here, including the torture of some who, presumably, supported Hanani, is quite uncharacteristic; there is no hint of such a turnabout in 1 Kg. 15. Asa's otherwise unexplained illness in the following paragraph may well, therefore, have led the Chronicler to postulate that such must have been the case.

The Conclusion of Asa's Reign

16:11-14

Although based on 1 Kg. 15:23-4, with which it is in general agreement, this paragraph has been substantially rewritten by the Chronicler, but whether on the basis of an alternative source or not there is not sufficient evidence available to determine.

11. The Chronicler follows his *Vorlage* in including at this point a reference to his sources. This is the first occasion on which he refers to **the Book of the Kings of Judah and Israel**, but from now on that title, or its near equivalents, becomes quite common. We have seen that the Chronicler probably did have an independent source for some of the material which he has included in Asa's reign, but whether it all formed part of a larger single history, as this source citation might imply, is uncertain; on the general issue, cf. the Introduction, section F. It is of importance to notice here that the Chronicler has added the words **and Israel** to the title as given in his *Vorlage*, and this too will be his regular practice; in fact, not once does he refer to 'the book of the kings of Judah' (and

equivalents) on its own, but always makes such an addition or substitution. This suggests that in these references to sources it was the names by which he called them, rather than their specific content, that was of significance to him. It was part of his way of showing that, despite her name, Judah was still a part of that inclusive Israel which he maintained before his readers as an ideal; cf. *IBC*, pp. 106f. and 128.

12. The diagnosis of Asa's disease **in his feet** has been much discussed. Traditional Jewish interpretation favours gout, some moderns favour dropsy (e.g. Myers), while the majority argue for a form of senile gangrene, e.g. A. de Vries and A. Weinberger, *New York State Journal of Medicine*, February, 1975, pp. 452–5: 'peripheral obstructive vascular disease with ensuing gangrene'. However, many of the elements in the text on which such diagnoses are based are very uncertain: (a) the sources of the detail in the Chronicler's description are unknown. For instance, the date of the onset of the disease, **the thirty-ninth year of his reign**, may be accurate, but equally may simply be part of the artificial chronological structure with which we have seen the Chronicler supplied Asa's reign. If so, it becomes pointless discussing whether gangrene can last up to two years or not; (b) the interpretation of some of the detail is also uncertain. For instance, much has been made by those who favour the diagnosis as gangrene of the description in v. 14 of the sweet-smelling spices; it is thought that they were to drown the stench of gangrene. However, it is possible that the description there is quite unrelated to the disease, and that it is simply part of the Chronicler's description of Asa's honourable burial; (c) the possibility should certainly not be ruled out that **feet** is a euphemism for the genital organs, as elsewhere in the *OT*; cf. P. Humbert, *RHPhR* 44 (1964), p. 5; (d) we are not even told that Asa died as a direct result of his disease; (e) finally, some linguistic arguments that have been invoked to help settle the issue are extremely weak; cf. G. R. Driver, in M. Black and G. Fohrer (eds), *In Memoriam Paul Kahle* (BZAW 103, 1968), pp. 100f., and in A. Caquot and M. Philonenko (eds), *Hommages à André Dupont-Sommer* (1971), pp. 283f. For instance, to argue on the basis of the root of the word that **became severe** really means that the disease spread upward from his feet (*'ad-lema'lāh*) is completely to disregard the consistent and characteristic usage of the Chronicler (cf. Japhet, *VT* 18 [1968], p. 357). Moreover, not too much should be made of the suggested (though uncertain) distinction between *ḥlh* and *ḥl'*, since it is even possible, as Rudolph has argued, that in *wayyeḥeʾleʾ*, **was diseased**, from *ḥl'*, the final *aleph* should be deleted as a dittograph, and the word be repointed as *wayyaḥal*, from *ḥlh*. We may thus conclude

that, even if the Chronicler had a specific disease in mind, he has
not left us with sufficient clear evidence to determine what it was.

This discussion must not deflect us from appreciating what the
Chronicler *has* made clear, namely, that Asa's disease should have
acted as a warning of God's displeasure at the events recorded earlier
in the chapter. Its remedy, therefore, should have been to put right
what had gone wrong, to return to the attitude which characterised
the longer first part of his reign when, as we have seen, he did **seek
the Lord**; cf. 14:4, 7; 15:2 and 12. This particular cause of his
disease, moreover, explains his folly when he **sought help from
physicians**; such action was inappropriate in the circumstances, and
by it the Chronicler demonstrates that Asa's falling away, seen
initially in his relying not on God but on a league with the Syrians
(vv. 2f., 7f.), marked also the closing years of his reign. This close
link between the Chronicler's condemnation of Asa and the very
particular circumstances of the context renders unnecessary the
prolonged discussion about whether **physicians** are here condemned
because they indulged in magical practices or necromancy, or
whether resort to doctors should be accompanied by, rather than
substituted for, prayer. **sought help from**: the syntax here is unusual, and some have thought that the use of the preposition *b* implies
a contrast with the use of the accusative for **the Lord**. It is not easy,
however, to see quite what point the contrast is intended to make.
It may be noted that *dāraš bᵉ* does occur in a few other passages
with no appreciable difference in meaning; cf. 2 Kg. 1:2ff.; 1
Chr. 10:14.

14. The burial notice is much more elaborate than the stereotyped
formula of 1 Kg. 15:24, and implies that the overall assessment of
Asa's reign is positive, despite the falling away in his closing years
(see also 17:3). No more than this need necessarily be read into the
reference to the **various kinds of spices**, while such is clearly the
intention of the **very great fire in his honour**, as the contrast with
21:19 shows, for it demonstrates that this was a regular practice
rather than a special occurrence in the case of Asa only.

JEHOSHAPHAT

17:1–21:1

The Chronicler's extensive treatment of Jehoshaphat stands in contrast with the presentation in Kings. There, apart from the regular
notices introducing and concluding his reign (1 Kg. 15:24; 22:41–
50), he appears only in connection with actions undertaken jointly
with the king of Israel, and it is the latter who on each occasion

appears as the dominant partner (1 Kg. 22:1–38; 2 Kg. 3:4–27. 1 Kg. 22:48f. provides only a partial exception). Here, however, much new material is introduced which makes of Jehoshaphat one of the major kings in the Chronicler's narrative, and when he refers to him later on, it is in terms of unqualified approval; cf. 2 Chr. 21:12 and especially 22:9.

The first point to notice is that it is unlikely to have been the account in Kings alone which led the Chronicler to this evaluation. This is evident, first, from the fact that in the case of both narratives which he takes over from his *Vorlage* (18:3–34; 20:35–37) he makes it clear by the addition of prophetic words of condemnation (19:1–3; 20:37) that Jehoshaphat was at fault in undertaking these joint ventures. Second, even where Kings speaks approvingly of Jehoshaphat, that approval is qualified; this qualification is retained by the Chronicler (20:33), unlike his own unqualified evaluation at 22:9. There can thus be no question but that the Chronicler interpreted the presentation of his Kings *Vorlage* as expressing a negative opinion of Jehoshaphat, and indeed, contrary to what might appear to have been his own understanding, he has gone out of his way to underline this point of view. From this it must be concluded that the Chronicler had access to other material whose apparently sympathetic stance towards Jehoshaphat has influenced his final overall presentation. Discussion of the extent to which it is possible still to identify this other material must be reserved for the later section-by-section commentary.

Next, it is of interest to observe how the Chronicler has integrated this disparate material, for this will reveal the lessons he sought to convey. There is a marked contrast with the situation under Asa. There it was seen how the Chronicler adapted the chronological framework which he inherited in order to illustrate the two sides of 'reliance'. In the case of Jehoshaphat, however, there is an equally noticeable lack of a rigid chronological framework. Most of the references to time are general in the extreme: 'After some years', 18:2; none at all at 19:4; 'After this', 20:1, and 'after this' again at 20:35. Only 'the third year of his reign' in 17:7 appears at all specific, but even this, it will be argued, is but a concealed reference to the first year of his effective rule. Thus, instead of chronological progression we find rather the juxtapositioning of varying episodes in order to illustrate, to an even greater degree than in the somewhat comparable case of Rehoboam, the blessings of faithfulness in 'seeking the Lord' and the dangers of association with the wicked (19:2; 20:35), exemplified in this case by Israel.

This alternation of light and shade which runs throughout Jehoshaphat's reign is thus certainly in one sense paradigmatic; but within this pattern there is also the muted introduction of a further note, namely, that alongside the usually rigid outworkings of the doctrine of retribution the Chronicler envisages the possibility that judgment can be mollified, if not altogether averted, by subsequent actions (see also 12:1–12). This, of course, necessitates a certain thematic linking between the various episodes. Mosis (pp. 175–8) denies that there are any such links, but more careful examination reveals that the Chronicler has after all left just sufficient indication for us to be confident that he intended us to read one episode in the light of the next. Thus, chs 17 and 18 are joined by the repetition in 18:1*a* of the statement from 17:5*b* of the theme of the opening chapter that 'Jehoshaphat had great riches and honour'. His culpability in an alliance by marriage with Ahab (18:1*b*) and in being impressed by Ahab's show of wealth into going with him into battle (18:2), both peculiar to Chronicles, is thus increased and underlined. Consequently 'wrath (*qeṣep*) has gone out against you from the Lord' (19:2). Precisely to help avert this Jehoshaphat next undertakes his judicial reform (cf. the use of the same word at 19:10).

The story in 20:1–30, which comes next, might seem to have no connection with this developing theme, unless it be that Jehoshaphat's fear (v. 3) and consequent turning to God are a reflection of how seriously he took the threat of 19:2 (Ellison). In fact, however, there is much more to it than that. Older commentators used to compare this account with 2 Kg. 3:4–27. More recent work has rightly shown that after all there is no direct literary or historical connection between them; the Chronicler's source is to be sought elsewhere. Because of this 2 Kg. 3 seems to have been ignored altogether in modern discussions; that too, however, is mistaken. Naturally the Chronicler will have known of it. Moreover, like all the other material which he adopted from Kings for his account of Jehoshaphat it too tells of joint action with Israel and might easily therefore have been worked in. Why, then, does he appear to replace it with this quite separate account, which indeed has certain resemblances with 2 Kg. 3 (namely, an attack from east of the Jordan), but which also has some fundamental differences? We would suggest that a clue lies in the concluding verse of that account (3:27): 'And there came great wrath (*qeṣep*) upon Israel; and they withdrew from him and returned to their own land'. The Chronicler, however, as already noted, wishes to show how such wrath can be averted. He has therefore substituted another story in which this time Jehoshaphat acts without an alliance with Israel and in perfect dependence upon God, and on this occasion the result is exactly the opposite: an outstanding triumph.

Finally, the concluding paragraph may also be integrated into this theme. In the words of Eliezer's prophecy (20:37), which are, as in other such cases, to be attributed to the Chronicler himself, he predicts the destruction of Jehoshaphat's fleet because they again represent a joint venture with Israel. The word he uses for this, however, is *pāraṣ*, which was seen to be an evident connecting link between the narratives of 1 Chr. 13–15 (see on 13:2 and the subsequent references listed there). At the heart of those narratives stands 13:10, 'And the anger of the Lord was kindled against Uzzah; and he smote him . . . ', with its interpretation in the next verse that 'God had broken forth (*pāraṣ*) upon Uzzah'. It is thus probable that by the use of this word in 2 Chr. 20:37 Jehoshaphat was now indeed experiencing the effects of God's wrath, even though his faithfulness in between showed how reduced this was by comparison with the heavy defeat of 2 Kg. 3.

The Character of Jehoshaphat's Reign

17:1–19

In this introductory chapter the Chronicler portrays Jehoshaphat's reign in a wholly favourable light. To achieve this he uses some types of material already familiar in such contexts (e.g. notes about building and the army), but also adduces a new element in the teaching mission of vv. 7–9.

The nature and process of composition in this chapter emerge from the following observations. There is a certain amount of repetition and overlap of the major themes handled, and closer examination reveals that this is because some of the major statements of the very generalised introductory vv. 1–6 are amplified in the following paragraphs; compare vv. 2 and 13*b*–19; 5 and 10–13*a*; 3, 6 and 7–9. Arguments will be adduced in the commentary below to show that much of the material in the latter part of the chapter is based on earlier sources. It may thus be concluded that this material was one of the factors which prompted the Chronicler's positive judgment of Jehoshaphat, and that on its basis, together with one or two other snippets from his *Vorlage* (v. 1*a*) and earlier narrative (v. 2*b*), he himself composed vv. 1–6 to set the tone for the remainder. (Against Rudolph's arguments that vv. 1*b*–2 must come from a source, cf. *IBC*, pp. 104f.)

A further influence on the construction of the chapter may have been a desire to achieve an impact similar to that in the case of Solomon, for there are some points of correspondence which appear to be by design. Verbal parallels are noted at vv. 1 and 3, for instance, but more importantly the themes which marked the start of Solomon's reign also find an echo here: for attention to Israel's worship, cf. v. 6; to balance the gift of wisdom, the teaching mission of vv. 7–9 might be adduced; for the theme of wealth, cf. vv. 5 and 11; finally, the Chronicler's tendency to make Solomon into a dominant partner in his relationship with Hiram of Tyre, together with such later general passages as 8:3–6 and 9:14, 22ff., is not unlike vv. 10–11 here.

1. The Chronicler continues on from the previous chapter with his *Vorlage* (1 Kg. 15:24) for the first clause of this verse only. **and strengthened himself against Israel:** the use of this verb elsewhere (cf. 1:1) suggests that 'and established himself over Israel' (referring to the southern kingdom) is another possible translation. In its favour we should note that Jehoshaphat's reign was not at all marked by hostility towards the north, and that **Israel** is used of the southern kingdom elsewhere in connection with Jehosphat's reign (cf. 21:2). Moreover, v. 2 cannot be taken, strictly speaking, as an amplification of this verse, since it refers to more than fortification along the northern boundary alone. Equally, however, the troubles from that direction during Asa's reign (ch. 16) would suggest that the more traditional rendering, as in *RSV*, might still be correct, despite the Chronicler's practice elsewhere. The issue cannot be satisfactorily resolved at present.

2. forces: see vv. 13–19 below. **all the fortified cities of Judah:** cf. 11:5–12. There too such a statement was seen as a mark of prosperity brought about by God's favour. **the cities of Ephraim which Asa his father had taken:** see on 15:8.

3–4. The Lord was with Jehoshaphat: there may be here another echo of 1:1. What it meant in concrete terms is spelt out in v. 5. **his father:** MT here includes 'David'. However, since David is portrayed in a consistently favourable light by the Chronicler, the expression **the earlier ways** would then be meaningless. *RSV* is thus probably correct to drop the name, so that the reference intended is, appropriately, to Asa. **did not seek . . . but sought:** contrast 1 Chr. 10:13f., and compare the frequent references to this, the Chronicler's favourite word, in assessing the faithfulness of the kings. **the Baals . . . the ways of Israel:** since Jehoshaphat's reign was largely parallel with that of Ahab in the north, the Chronicler may well have had in mind the various stories in the closing chapters of 1 Kings where the influence of Jezebel led to widespread Baal-worship in Israel for a time. Knowledge of the whole of the earlier history is thus again presupposed by the Chronicler.

5. established the kingdom: cf. 1:1, though a different verb is used. The continuation of the verse may similarly be compared with 1:12b and 1 Chr. 29:23–25, though the theme of **great riches and**

honour for a faithful king is common enough; cf. Japhet, *VT* 18 (1968), p. 366.

6. Apart from its being the mark of any king who was, in the Chronicler's opinion, **courageous in the ways of the Lord**, the removal of **the high places and the Asherim** was probably thought to be necessary after Asa's falling away towards the end of his reign. **furthermore** might thus be better translated 'again'; cf. 14:3. On the contradiction with the statement of his *Vorlage*, see on 20:33.

7–9. As a more particular example of Jehoshaphat's zeal for the Lord, the Chronicler includes this brief paragraph concerning the teaching mission which he established throughout his kingdom. He doubtless regarded it as being based on what we now call the Pentateuch, and as being primarily religious in character.

It is thus not surprising that many scholars have seen here a doublet of 19:4ff., and in view of the nature of this chapter as a whole, there is no particular objection to that suggestion. The question concerning a possible source or tradition underlying the account is more difficult to decide, and is to some extent linked with a judgment about 19:4–11. Most of the evidence which has been adduced in its favour merely shows its possibility without establishing its probability. For instance, it is likely that there was a law code in Judah as in most ancient near eastern monarchies; cf. S. Yeivin, *VT* 3 (1953), pp. 149–66. It is true that the king was probably thought of as responsible for instruction in the law; cf. G. Widengren, *JSS* 2 (1957), pp. 16f. None of this, however, adds up to historical proof. A better approach is to observe the prominence of the laity and the listing of Levites before priests as a pointer to the likelihood of pre-Chronistic material here, but the details of the account are too vague to permit more specific conclusions. If our analysis above of the Chronicler's method in the composition of this chapter is correct, it would provide a further independent indication of the presence of an earlier source behind this paragraph.

7. In the third year of his reign: in view of 16:12–13, the Chronicler may have thought that for the first two years of his reign Jehoshaphat was merely a co-regent with the ailing Asa. If so, this date will mark the beginning of his own effective rule. Thus reforming zeal characterised his reign from its start. Five **princes** (i.e. lay officials) head the mission, followed by ten religious leaders (eight Levites and two priests). In view of the vast increase in our knowledge of personal names in Israel on the basis of seals and the like, the analyses of older handbooks which pointed towards the late date of such lists as this one now stand in need of revision; cf. M. Heltzer and M. Ohana, *The Extra-Biblical Tradition of Hebrew Personal Names* (Hebrew; 1978). From at least the eighth century BC onwards (cf. Hos. 4:6) it was the priests' duty **to teach** the *Torah* **in the cities of Judah**. However, since any authentic tradition underlying this paragraph (rather than what the Chronicler has made of it) is more likely to have dealt with a royal law code (Myers), no conclusions about the early date of the material can legitimately be drawn on this basis.

8. The teaching role of **the Levites** is well attested for the post-exilic period; cf. especially Neh. 8:7–8. However, this verse is not therefore to be regarded as an addition by the Chronicler to his older source (Rudolph) since, as Willi (p. 198) observes, he regularly puts **the priests** before **the Levites. and Tobadonijah:** this name is generally deleted as an accidental recopying of the previous two names.

9. the book of the law of the Lord: see above.

10–13a. Further indications of God's blessing on a faithful king follow. All the elements are familiar from other comparable sections of the Chronicler's work. It may be noted in particular that vv. 10–11, which deal with external relationships, balance the description of v. 5 of Jehoshaphat's relationship with his own people.

10. the fear of the Lord: cf. 14:14; 20:29 and 1 Chr. 14:17, etc. **they made no war:** peace was also noted as a characteristic blessing at the start of Asa's reign; see on 14:1.

11. See above for the comparison with 9:14, 22ff., etc. The reference to **the Philistines** naturally also reminds the reader of 1 Chr. 14, whose paradigmatic quality as an indication of the rewards that follow upon 'seeking the Lord' was discussed in the commentary; see also Mosis, pp. 70–72. **the Arabs:** 21:16 suggests that these were neighbours of the Cushites ('Ethiopians') of 14:9ff. Although the Chronicler has undoubtedly written up this material to add to his favourable presentation of Jehoshaphat as a whole in this chapter, it is probable that sound tradition underlies it: the area from which tribute is brought is localised, assuming our understanding of **Arabs** to be correct, and is restricted to the area where Asa, Jehoshaphat's father, had campaigned victoriously towards the end of his reign (see above, p. 257, for a possible chronological outline of Asa's reign). Moreover, the rather guarded opening, **some of the Philistines**, creates a favourable historical impression (Rudolph), as does the modest nature of the tribute brought (though the actual numbers of **rams** and **he-goats** appears stylised). We may thus conclude that the Chronicler here based himself on an earlier, extra-biblical tradition.

12–13a. This inflow of wealth enabled Jehoshaphat to continue the policy of Rehoboam (11:5–12) and Asa (14:6); see also v. 2. A neat transition is thus effected to the material of the next paragraph which the Chronicler wished to introduce.

13b–19. Details of Jehoshaphat's army. This paragraph may be seen as an expansion of v. 2, for which also it formed the historical basis. It is the second of the four statistical notices about the Judean army. The reasons for regarding them as being based on one of the sources available to the Chronicler were set out at 14:8 above, so that only a few additional points need be mentioned here.

Confusion seems to have arisen at some stage (perhaps by the Chronicler himself) between the standing and the conscript armies. Elements that refer to the standing army include particularly the statement of v. 19 that **these were in the service of the king**, the personal names of individual **commanders**, and the fact of their being stationed **in Jerusalem** (13b). Details of the conscript army, however, lie behind **the muster of them by fathers' houses** (14a), the divisions based on tribal affiliation (**Of Judah . . . of Benjamin**) and the huge (and doubtless exaggerated; see on 14:8) numbers. While this confusion makes hazardous any attempt at historical reconstruction, it has at least the advantage of strengthening the case for the view that inherited material underlies the paragraph.

16. a volunteer for the service of the Lord: this description is unlikely to derive from the Chronicler because it is not explained in any way and because it is quite unparalleled in other comparable cases. It has rather the appearance of an unedited fragment of the type common in the list of David's heroes (1 Chr. 11:11ff.), and is thus a further possible pointer to the use of a source.

Jehoshaphat and Ahab

18:1–19:3

The bulk of this long story is taken over directly from 1 Kg. 22, but the Chronicler has supplied his own introduction and conclusion. It emerges from these (see below) that he is strong in his condemnation of Jehoshaphat for entering into alliance with Ahab. This at once renders highly improbable the view of most commentators that he included the account merely for the sake of the appearance of a true prophet, Micaiah the son of Imlah, for were that the case the condemnation of a king whom he generally regards so favourably would be unnecessary and confusing to the reader. Rather, as outlined above, it is precisely for the sake of the condemnation (which is, to be sure, only heightened by Jehoshaphat's failure to heed the prophetic warning) that the story is included, for it then offers the Chronicler the opportunity of presenting a paradigmatic example of how the faithful should respond when 'wrath has gone out against' them (cf. 19:2), especially in the case of ch. 20, which from so many points of view provides a complete contrast with this chapter. Once again, we should not fail to see in all this a message to the Chronicler's own readers; the problems of mixed marriages with 'those who hate the Lord' (19:2) had dragged on long after Ezra and Nehemiah (cf. *IBC*, p. 138), and it is not impossible that they too were living in the aftermath of a military disaster (cf. the Introduction, section E). If so, unlike the rigorous exclusivists, he will have wished to encourage his people along the road of repentance and restoration by showing them first how low even a Jehoshaphat could sink and then how marvellously the consequences of that failure could be reversed.

18:1. The first half of this verse repeats 17:5*b*. Since there thus seems to be intended a contrast between the blessings of ch. 17 and Jehoshaphat's action here, the meaning might be more clearly brought out by translating as a concessive clause: 'Now although Jehoshaphat . . .', with Rudolph and Myers. In the ancient world **a marriage alliance** between the families of rulers was often for the sake of the dowry or other political gain, but the Chronicler implies that this would not have been necessary in the present case. The historical consideration that the alliance may have brought, or at least sealed, a much-needed peace between the two kingdoms will naturally not have entered into the Chronicler's reckoning. The marriage in question was between Jehoshaphat's son, Jehoram, and Athaliah, a daughter of Ahab (cf. 21:6; 22:2), no doubt arranged some time before this incident.

2. After some years: the Chronicler purposely makes vague the more specific reference of 1 Kg. 22:2; see above, p. 278. A second failing of Jehoshaphat now emerges, for it is implied that he was impressed by Ahab's display in feasting him and his retinue on **an abundance of sheep and oxen** in spite of the wealth with which God had already blessed him. Indeed, Ackroyd aptly observes that when the Chronicler records that Ahab **induced him to go up**, he uses a word which in Dt. 13:6 means to entice into apostasy. His condemnation of Jehoshaphat's action is thus very strong indeed.

3. At this point the Chronicler picks up his source at 1 Kg. 22:4, and follows it very closely through to the end of this chapter. The variations are mostly of the textual or stylistic variety familiar from other such parallel passages. The commentaries on Kings should be consulted for an analysis of the account.

27. And he said, "Hear, all you peoples!": for arguments against *NEB*'s omission of this sentence, together with a discussion of its significance, cf. E. Ball, *JTS* ns 28 (1977), pp. 90–4.

31. and the Lord helped him. God drew them away from him:
these words are added by the Chronicler himself. The theme of
God's help, especially in a military context, as a response to prayer
is a favourite with him; cf. *OTS* 21 (1981), pp. 166f. Moreover, the
verb translated **drew . . . away** is the same as that which he used
with such negative overtones in v. 2 (where it is translated 'induced'). Even in the middle of a battle which he should never have
been fighting, Jehoshaphat could find the kind of deliverance which
the Chronicler always delights to relate.

34. The Chronicler abbreviates the end of his account quite drastically, since the details of Ahab's death, recounted in some detail at
1 Kg. 22:35–38, were irrelevant for his purposes and furthermore
involved the fulfilment of a prophecy which he himself had not
recorded.

19:1–3. The Chronicler adds his own conclusion to the narrative,
in which a prophet once again expresses the Chronicler's own theological comment on the situation.

1. The Chronicler has phrased this verse as a fulfilment of Micaiah's prophecy in 18:16. The verbal agreement is much closer in
the Hebrew than appears from *RSV*; 'in peace' and **in safety** translate the same Hebrew word, as do 'home' and **house**. A contrast
with Ahab's fate is also clearly intended.

2. Jehu the son of Hanani the seer: see on 16:7. His condemnation of Jehoshaphat is much as we would expect, adding little to
what is already known of his view of the north; see on 13:4–12. On
help, cf. 18:31 above, and for **love** and **hate** as political rather than
purely emotional terms, cf. J. A. Thompson, *VT* 29 (1979),
pp. 200–5. Needless to say, there is no suggestion here that Israel's
position might not change in the future. **wrath has gone out against
you from the Lord:** for this statement as introducing a connecting
theme for the following three narratives, see above p. 279.

3. This verse does not of itself mollify the judgment of v. 2,
though Jehoshaphat's subsequent behaviour will show how that too
might be achieved. It is simply to show that failure need not necessarily cause one to change his overall assessment of a king's reign:
see the remarks at 16:14 for the similar situation at the end of Asa's
reign. **you destroyed the Asherahs:** cf. 17:6. **and have set your
heart to seek God:** cf. 17:3, though the whole of ch. 17 exemplifies
the kind of actions and their consequences which were involved for
the Chronicler in this his favourite term for faithful religious
practice.

Jehoshaphat's Judicial Reform

19:4–11

The position and purpose of this paragraph within the context of the Chronicler's account of Jehoshaphat's reign has already been discussed (pp. 277ff.). On the question of the origins of the material there has been the greatest possible variety of opinion, stretching from those who have followed Wellhausen, *Prolegomena*, p. 191, in believing that the judicial institutions here described derive in fact from the Chronicler's own day, being attributed to Jehoshaphat simply because of his name ('The Lord is Judge') to those who have followed Albright, 'The Judicial Reform', in his argument that 'the narrative in II Chron. 19 is a substantially correct account of the judicial reform of Jehoshaphat, though it does not tell the whole story'.

Any attempt to resolve this dilemma should pay far more attention than has usually been the case to the literary variety of material here: (a) v. 4 is both very generalised and in tension with the account which follows. In it, Jehoshaphat moves around his kingdom, and personally encourages a return to following the Lord; in vv. 5–11, however, he appoints judges and other officials to act on behalf of himself and the Lord. Moreover, it may be questioned whether the functions assigned to them are really the same as what the Chronicler would have termed 'bringing them back to the Lord'; (b) in vv. 5–11 there is a substantial block of parenetic material couched in Deuteronomic language (cf. vv. 6–7, 9–10 and 11*b*); (c) the remainder (vv. 5, 8 and 11*a*) provides a brief, but intelligible, framework. On the one hand, judges are appointed to serve in the fortified cities; on the other, Levites, priests and heads of families are appointed to serve in Jerusalem with a double function, first, to act as a court of appeal in civil cases, with Zebadiah presiding and, second, to deal with disputes relating more particularly to the cult, with Amariah, 'the chief priest', appropriately presiding. It thus does not seem necessary to find such contradictions within these spheres of jurisdiction as to oblige us to postulate different sources, as Michaeli does.

It may be suggested on the basis of this analysis that the introductory v. 4 is probably from the Chronicler himself, and that he intended vv. 5–11 to serve as an illustration of his generalised comment. The outlook of the verse is very much his own, and we may note two particular stylistic devices in addition: the country is described from south to north ('from Beersheba to the hill country of Ephraim') which compares with his practice elsewhere, but contrasts with the normal biblical pattern (see on 1 Chr. 21:2); similarly the

title 'the God of their fathers' has been noted as one that is particularly characteristic of him (cf. Japhet, *Ideology*, pp. 19–23). Finally,
it should be remembered that we have several times found the
Chronicler to provide just such generalising introductions elsewhere.
This was seen to be the case in particular in ch. 17, the introduction
to Jehoshaphat's reign itself. In such passages we have either been
able to see from his biblical *Vorlage* (e.g. in 1 Chr. 13; 15, etc.), or
to deduce on other grounds, that the material so introduced is not
his own free composition but is based on his inherited sources. The
same is thus likely to be the case here.

This conclusion receives support, secondly, from the tension
already noted between vv. 4 and 5–11. It is easier to imagine that
this arose because the Chronicler wanted to use a source to make a
point which was not the source's original intention than to imagine
that the Chronicler was incapable of himself composing a more
harmonious passage.

Thirdly, as in 17:7–9, the listing of Levites before priests in v. 8
is contrary to the Chronicler's own practice, and thus provides a
further small pointer to the independent origin of this material.

Fourthly, it was observed earlier that the Chronicler did not
derive his favourable impression of Jehoshaphat from the books of
Kings. Some positive material has already been isolated in ch. 17,
but his thinking becomes much easier to understand if part, at least,
of the present chapter can be added to them.

So far we have argued on the basis of an analysis internal to
Chronicles only towards the conclusion that vv. 5–11 include material earlier than the Chronicler himself, but that those verses
themselves need not be a unity. We must now introduce the comparison often observed (e.g. by Junge, pp. 81–92) with some of the
laws contained in Dt. 16:18–17:13. This is particularly striking in
the case of the parenetic material, so that it is hard to escape the
suspicion that this may be directly dependent on Deuteronomy. For
the brief framework of vv. 5, 8 and 11*a*, however, the reverse is the
case: here, only 'the fortified cities of Judah' are mentioned, in
contrast with the more extensive 'all your towns' of Dt. 16:18. R.
Knierim, *ZAW* 73 (1961), pp. 146–71, has reasonably suggested
that in the transition from the older, tribal system of justice to the
more centralised, royal administration, the step would have first
been taken in those garrison cities where the king's authority was
uppermost before passing on to other towns in general. Again, the
officials are more developed in Deuteronomy, with the addition of
'the judge' in Dt. 17:9 to the central court of appeal, whereas
Chronicles has the apparently more primitive 'governor of the house
of Judah' (v. 11; cf. Rudolph). Similarly the 'heads of families' of

v. 8, who seem to be related to the earlier, locally based institutions of justice, have dropped out in Deuteronomy. It would thus appear that the essential elements of the judicial reform as described in Chronicles are earlier than the present form of Deuteronomy, but that the parenetic expansion is later, perhaps from the Chronicler himself.

Finally, attention should be drawn to histories of Israelite law which seem to demand some such reform as described here (cf. Knierim, *op. cit.*; A. Phillips, *Ancient Israel's Criminal Law* [1970], pp. 18ff.; G. C. Macholz, *ZAW* 84 [1972], pp. 314–40; K. W. Whitelam, *The Just King* [1979], pp. 185–206; and see the comments on Dt. 16:18–17:13 in A. D. H. Mayes, *Deuteronomy* [1979]). Clearly, the tradition of tribally-based systems of justice must have given way at some stage to the more central and royally appointed institutions outlined here, and various texts in the eighth-century prophets, such as Isa. 1:21–26; 3:2; Mic. 3:1–2, 9–11, suggest that this was before their time. To attribute such a reform to Jehoshaphat is thus eminently reasonable, though of course it cannot ultimately be proved beyond doubt; for a contrary opinion, cf. A. Rofé, *Beth Mikra* 65 (1976), pp. 199–210.

4. Jehoshaphat dwelt at Jerusalem: in the context this can mean only that he did not go to the northern kingdom again. **he went out again:** a reference back to 17:7–9, even though there he acted indirectly through his emissaries. **the hill country of Ephraim:** cf. 17:2. **and brought them back to the Lord:** the Chronicler envisages a time of religious revival, as under several of the kings (e.g. Asa in 15:8–15), thus involving factors rather different from those of the following verses. It would seem that, after the judgment expressed in vv. 1–3, Jehoshaphat acts in accordance with God's promise of 7:14, already noted several times as a key verse in such situations; 'turn' and **brought . . . back** are from the same root. Thus his actions bespeak a measure of repentance.

5. Cf Dt. 16:18 and the comments above.

6. The start of the first parenetic section. Its sentiments are based largely on Dt. 1:17. In Israel it was believed that all judgments should be ultimately under God's direction. This is not, however, at all the same thing as saying that they were unable to distinguish between sacral and secular cases. There is thus no tension between this verse and vv. 8 and 11.

7. This is similar to Dt. 16:19, but combined with Dt. 10:17 where these qualities are said to be in God himself. Since he will be with the judges in their work (v. 6), it is right that they should undertake this task with due reverence and circumspection.

8. The composition of the court set up **in Jerusalem** is reasonably

clear, for, as fitted its wider functions, it was representative of both
religious and lay leadership. The **heads of families of Israel** will
have stood in continuity with the older judicial system of elders (cf.
IBC, p. 107), so that **Israel** in this case reflects the continued usage
in Judah of a title from before the division of the monarchy. By the
time of the Chronicler, however, it could also be used simply in the
sense of 'laity' (e.g. Ezr. 10:25, etc.), and he himself may have
understood it here in this way.

Because of a textual difficulty at the end of the verse, there is less
certainty about the details of the court's jurisdiction. Two points
are clear and generally agreed: first, the court in Jerusalem served
as a court of appeal for disputed and capital cases referred to them
from the provincial courts of v. 5. This is plainly stated in v. 10.
Second, a distinction was drawn between sacral and secular cases,
and v. 11 refers to the appointment of different presidents for the
different types of case. But how should the prescriptions of v. 8 be
fitted into this pattern? *RSV* appears to suggest that **to give judgment for the Lord** is the same as 'all matters of the Lord' in v. 11,
and that **to decide disputed cases** is the same as 'all the king's
matters' in v. 11 and that it refers to the appeals procedure of v. 10.
There are two objections to this view, however. First, the word
translated **disputed cases** is in fact singular (*rîb*), and, second, this
reconstruction leaves no place for a lower court for the citizens of
Jerusalem. To these difficulties a third point must be added: *RSV*'s
rendering of the last clause of the verse, **They had their seat at
Jerusalem**, presupposes an alteration to the vocalisation of MT; the
latter itself is better represented by *RV*, 'And they returned to
Jerusalem'. This, however, contradicts the evident implication of
the start of the verse, and, moreover, since the verb is plural, it
cannot be meant, as some have supposed, to describe Jehoshaphat's
return after his tour described earlier in v. 4. There is thus much
to be said in favour of a very slight emendation here, which enjoys
the support of LXX and V, and which has been adopted by many
commentators and by *NEB*, namely, to read *ûlᵉrîbê yōšᵉbê
yᵉrûšālaim*, 'and (to decide) the disputed cases of the inhabitants
of Jerusalem'. If this is correct, then **judgment for the Lord** is
better referred to disputed cases from elsewhere (v. 10), while v. 11
marks a development to show that sacral and secular cases were
dealt with differently.

Though the emendation favoured here is very slight, and may
therefore have arisen simply through an accident in transmission,
an alternative explanation may be suggested. It was noted earlier
that there is a measure of tension between the account of vv. 5, 8
and 11*a* and the use to which the Chronicler has put it in his

introductory v. 4. It is stated there that he 'brought them back to
the Lord'. The verb used there is the same one as that found in
MT of v. 8. We may therefore postulate that a scribe, expecting this
account to describe how v. 4 was fulfilled, was influenced slightly
to misread v. 8 as *wayyāšîḇû yᵉrûšālaim*, 'and they brought
back Jerusalem'. This represents the consonantal text of MT; for a
suggestion as to how its vocalisation developed, cf. J. Heller, *VT* 24
(1974), pp. 371–3. If this is correct, it will support our general
thesis because it both highlights the tension felt between v. 4 and
the remainder, and because it shows how the levelling process,
begun already by the Chronicler, continued even after his time.

9–10. The second parenetic section (see above) draws in particular
on Dt. 17:8ff. for its legal presupposition, but the words of installation echo a wider variety of texts which the Chronicler has already
used in other contexts, such as 1 Chr. 28:9–10. For **wrath may not
come upon you**, see above, p. 279.

11. See the introduction to vv. 4–11 and the comments on v. 8
above. **Amariah:** cf. 1 Chr. 6:11. **the chief priest:** for the possible
judicial significance of this title, cf. J. R. Bartlett, *VT* 19 (1969),
p. 6. **officers:** see on 1 Chr. 26:29. The final exhortation is again
from the Chronicler; cf. 1 Chr. 22:6; 28:10, etc.

Jehoshaphat's Victory

20:1–30

It was seen above (p. 279) that this lengthy narrative marks in one
sense the climax of the theme which the Chronicler traces throughout his account of the reign of Jehoshaphat, and that in order to
achieve this he has deliberately used this story in preference to that
of 2 Kg. 3. It is thus not surprising to find that its style and
presentation throughout bear the unmistakable marks of being his
personal composition. The comments below will be able to note
only the most prominent examples of this. The major emphasis of
self-humbling, repentance and complete dependence on God in the
face of a grave threat to the nation (pictured here as a religious
community rather than a sovereign state) is one which the Chronicler
never tired of pressing home to his readers. Moreover he has used
throughout liturgical forms and practices familiar in their own day
and described 'the battle' along such conventional and stereotyped
literary lines as a 'holy war' that again the spiritual message of the
narrative stands out in deliberate prominence over against its apparent historical content.

Whereas without question we must respect this predominant concern of the text, the modern reader will nevertheless inevitably ask what historical kernel, if any, underlies the description. Once again, critical scholarship can offer no consensus of opinion. (For a fuller survey of opinions, cf. Petersen, pp. 70–1.)

Welten, pp. 140–53, is the most recent of those who find no historical material here of any worth, though it should be noted that not all his fundamental assumptions are justified: for instance, it ought to be quite obvious by now that Jehoshaphat is not judged completely positively by the Chronicler throughout his reign. Again, Welten builds a good deal on an understanding of the Meunites which is by no means certain (see v. 1), and he dismisses without discussion the literary evidence in favour of an earlier layer of material in this chapter (see below). Finally, it should always be remembered that while full allowance must be made for the Chronicler's contribution to a chapter such as this one, and while it is clear that he has shaped it to suit his wider purposes, that fact does not of itself constitute proof that the whole underlying situation is total fabrication.

Second, an intermediate position was adopted in an influential article by Noth, *ZDPV* 67 (1944–5), pp. 45–71. Basing himself on a study of the place-names involved in the text (e.g. vv. 2, 16, 24 and 26), Noth argued that an intelligible route was here being traced from the Dead Sea to the area round Tekoa. Indeed, more recent studies have served only to confirm this opinion; see the comments below on the relevant verses and the survey of Z. Ilan, *Beth Mikra* 53 (1973), pp. 205–11. Noth maintained that detailed local knowledge thus lay behind the account, and that this could best be accounted for on the basis of an oral, local tradition of a Nabataean invasion early in the third century BC.

Finally, Rudolph (followed by Myers) has sought further to refine Noth's position in order to find a good historical tradition lying behind the passage. He rejects Noth's association of the Meunites with the Nabataeans, sees no reason why a local tradition should not already have been taken up by the Chronicler's source, and argues that there is a hint that the Chronicler was dependent on earlier written material in his addition of the explanation 'that is, Engedi' to the more precise place name Hazazon-tamar of his source (v. 2).

In my opinion, while full justice must be done to the Chronicler's positive contribution to this chapter, as stressed earlier, and observed with renewed emphasis by Welten, Rudolph's position on the probability of a source here has not been overthrown by subsequent studies. Moreover, in view of what we have noted on a number of previous occasions in similar situations, it seems more in keeping with the Chronicler's method as a whole than the assumption of wholesale invention on his part. Finally, a further small pointer to the presence of more than one layer in the literary or tradition-history of the account may be detected in the aetiology of v. 26. The relative unimportance of the verse to the narrative as a whole shows that there can be no question of the story having grown out of the name 'Valley of Beracah' (blessing). Rather, the use in this case of the phrase 'to this day' provides an excellent example of what B. S. Childs, *JBL* 82 (1963), pp. 279–92, has called 'a formula of personal testimony added to, and confirming, a received tradition'. In other words, it takes its place alongside the many other examples of the use of this phrase which indicate that a later writer is commenting on earlier, received material. That this is so may be additionally seen from the rather loose attachment of v. 26*b* ('for there they blessed . . .') to 26*a*; cf. B. O. Long, *The Problem of Etiological Narrative in the Old Testament* (1968), pp. 10f. Once again, therefore, we seem to have at least two separate layers within the development of the narrative, pointing to some kind of a source underlying the Chronicler's account. (See also on vv. 10–11 below.) In this case, however, his own reworking of it seems to have been so extensive, for the reasons already seen, that it is no longer possible to determine the source's extent and hence to judge its likely original date or point of reference. It would not be surprising, however (and the localisation of the incident would tend to suggest this), if once again the Chronicler had taken up an originally fairly insignificant incident and magnified it for didactic reasons.

1. **the Meunites:** considerable uncertainty surrounds the identification of this third group in the coalition. MT has 'the Ammonites', which cannot be right after they have been mentioned earlier in the verse. Nevertheless, it must not be forgotten that any alternative proposal is ultimately conjectural. Initially, one would suppose that the word is only a confused dittography of the previous word, **and with them** (compare the close similarity of the consonants in *w'mhm* and *mh'mwnym*). However, vv. 10 and 22f. indicate that there was a third group involved, so that a reference to them here is probable. There, however, they are consistently called '(the inhabitants of) Mount Seir', and no one has been able to explain why they are apparently referred to by a quite different name here. A final point in establishing the scope of the problem is to observe that they are set apart slightly from the other partners in the coalition, **the Moabites and Ammonites**. This is clear both from the addition of the words **and with them**, and by the fact that it was against the inhabitants of Mount Seir that the others turned in v. 23.

The normal solution to the problem is that favoured also by *RSV*.

The textual change to read **the Meunites** is slight, and since there is a town called Ma'an some twelve miles south-east of Petra with which their name might be connected, it has been assumed that they came from that region, and hence could be loosely associated with Mount Seir. This solution faces certain difficulties, however, principally that it does not tie up at all well with the only other certain reference to Meunites in Chronicles (see 26:7, and the comments there; also cf. 1 Chr. 4:41), which clearly places them to the west of the Dead Sea. In addition, the suggestion is unable to offer an explanation for the fact that, as noted, they are set apart from the other members of the coalition.

If **the Meunites** still remains the most attractive reading, and if the evidence of 26:7 is to be taken seriously, an alternative identification should be explored, namely, one which sees in them a people living to the west of the Arabah. Their link with Mount Seir is no objection to this proposal, for there have always been those who have argued that Seir was located somewhere in the southern Negeb, and in recent years strong arguments have been advanced in its support; cf. J. R. Bartlett, *JTS* ns 20 (1969), pp. 1–20, and G. I. Davies, *PEQ* 111 (1979), pp. 97–100. In connection with the present verse, Bartlett (p. 6) notes in addition a number of references to 'Maon' in the Negeb (Jos. 15:55; 1 Sam. 23:24; 25:2ff.; 1 Chr. 2:45). Perhaps, therefore, the striking nature of this coalition was precisely its diverse make-up, and the difference in origins of its members would explain the different treatment of the Meunites in this verse and the inherent tensions which led to the strife of v. 23. The nature of the present text does not allow for more than guesswork on the likely historical background to such a coalition, but an advance up the western coast of the Dead Sea as far as Engedi (v. 2) would fit well with a gathering to the south of the Dead Sea of troops from such areas.

2. Edom: MT has 'Aram' (Syria). If we are right in rejecting above a link between the Meunites and **Edom**, MT should perhaps be preferred; in view of the widespread power of Aram-Damascus, it is by no means unreasonable in itself (cf. Aharoni, *Land*, p. 293). **Hazazon-tamar**: although the precise location has long been disputed, Noth (pp. 50–3) has made out a strong case for an identification with *el-ḥaṣāṣa*, on the route between Engedi and Bethlehem. This links well with the topographical information of v. 16. No doubt this route was followed because the more normal approaches into the heartland of Judah were still defended by Rehoboam's system of fortifications (11:5ff.) and in order to achieve an element of surprise. **that is, Engedi**: roughly on the centre of the west bank of the Dead Sea. The identification, probably from the Chronicler

himself, is only approximate, but undoubtedly marks the point at
which the invaders turned inland, 'by the ascent of Ziz' (v. 16).

3. It is with Jehoshaphat's reaction to the news that the Chronicler's interest is really aroused. The king's fear indicates his awareness of the threat of 19:2 to which only a religious response is
appropriate. **to seek the Lord** has been frequently noted as the
Chronicler's general expression for this, and the following verses
will spell out what specifically was involved. For the particular
idiom in the present instance, cf. U. Cassuto, *Biblical and Oriental
Studies 2* (1975), pp. 22–3. **proclaimed a fast:** a symbol of earnest
repentance; cf. Jl 2:12ff.; Jon. 3:7ff. Jehoshaphat clearly acts within
the spirit of the paradigmatic 7:14.

4. A widely representative assembling of the people is typical of
solemn religious occasions in the Chronicler's narrative; see on 1
Chr. 13:1–5.

5. This gathering **in the house of the Lord** immediately recalls
Solomon's role at the dedication of the temple. His prayer at that
time envisaged just such situations as the crisis described here. At
the same time, however, it will have given the Chronicler's readers
a specific point in the story with which they could begin to identify
in terms of the practices of their own day. This will have been
increased by the reference to **the new court**, seen at 4:9 ('the great
court') to have been a reflection of the second rather than the first
temple.

6–12. Jeshoshaphat's prayer takes the form of a national lament,
familiar from a number of the Psalms (cf. Petersen, pp. 72–3). Just
as it is generally assumed that such laments were answered by an
oracle of salvation in the temple liturgy, so we find it to be the case
here also (vv. 15ff.). After its general introduction, which grounds
the appeal in the incomparable nature of God's power, the lament
stresses God's past mercies, appropriately citing as examples those
that relate to security in the land. It then moves on to a protestation
of the worshippers' innocence of anything worthy of the impending
judgment and a reminder of God's promises to save. Finally, the
prayer returns to a declaration of the people's complete dependence
on God; cf. the comparable, though briefer, prayer of Asa, 14:11.

6. God of our fathers: this especially favourite title in the Chronicler's composition is particularly apt at the start of a national prayer
of lamentation. **art thou not. . . ?:** the use of rhetorical questions
in these opening verses reflects the influence of the 'disputation' (cf.
A. Schoors, *I am God your Saviour* [1973], pp. 188–9, 245–95). Its
purpose is to move from a general and widely agreed proposition to
a more controversial but highly apposite affirmation (v. 7). **God in
heaven:** the purpose of this phrase, together with the rest of the

verse, is to stress God's complete omnipotence. Some of the expressions are already familiar (e.g. 1 Chr. 29:11–12), but there is a movement here in the direction of the apocalyptic writers: God's rule **in heaven** is contrasted with the apparent independence of **all the kingdoms of the nations**, who in turn oppress the faithful people of God. But this appearance is deceptive, and God may be confidently expected soon to intervene to rectify the present injustice. The continuation of the present story thus becomes paradigmatic of the final deliverance for those who are prepared for it by repentance and faith; for the phraseology, cf., for example, Dan. 2:17–23; 4:17, 34–35, etc., and for the underlying thought, cf. Dan. 7, etc. Though we have no evidence of prolonged, sustained oppression of the Jews by the Persians, there certainly were periods of considerable stress which, together with a continuing sense of frustration at the lack of national freedom, would doubtless have nurtured the development of such a theology.

7. This is the climax of the first part of the prayer: the initial conquest and settlement of the land in accordance with the earlier promises to Abraham are taken as timeless guarantees of God's blessing upon his people, and typical of deliverance in any time of threat. **Abraham thy friend:** cf. Isa. 41:8, where the expression is used as part of God's word of assurance to those in exile.

8–9. Jehoshaphat now moves on to plead not only the fundamental saving events of Israel's history, but also the importance of temple-centred worship for the preservation of the life of Israel. Verse 9 in effect summarises the substance of Solomon's prayer at the dedication of the temple (ch. 6) which God had promised to answer (7:12ff.). The emphasis on prayer as the ultimate expression of repentance and dependance upon God is as noteworthy here as it was there. **judgment:** in view of the context, where Jehoshaphat seems to have regarded the invasion as an expression of God's judgment against him (see above), the marginal reading 'the sword of judgment' seems appropriate. Some, however, finding this to link less well with the situations envisaged in Solomon's prayer, prefer to emend slightly by rearranging the consonants of *špwṭ*, **judgment**, to *wšṭp*, 'and flood'.

10–11. All this is now related to the specific case in hand, a situation only aggravated by the fact that **Israel** had been obliged not to invade **the men of Ammon and Moab and Mount Seir** on their journey under Moses **from the land of Egypt**. The events described here are combined from a variety of earlier texts (Num. 20:14ff.; Dt. 2:1–19; Jg. 11:16f.; cf. von Rad, *GCW*, pp. 77f.) and are of significance as showing that, despite his usual silence about the Exodus, wilderness and conquest traditions, he was neither unaware of them nor wished to deny their relevance to the later community where appropriate. For a different appreciation, which regrettably makes no mention of the present passage, cf. Japhet, *JBL* 98 (1979), pp. 205–18. **Mount Seir:** cf. v. 1. In this verse, where the Chronicler himself may be presumed as the author, the later view is adopted which places Seir in Edom, contrary to the apparently earlier view of vv. 1 with 22f. In this difference there may be a further slight indication of the use of an antecedent source by the Chronicler.

12. The lament's final appeal well expresses both confidence in God's power to save and man's own inability. In such a situation, faith rather than activism is the only practical attitude. This has been noted several times as expressive of the Chronicler's position, though the expectation of deliverance, so fully vindicated in the sequel, demonstrates that this should not be confused, as some commentators have done, with an appeal for the Chronicler's readers to acquiesce in their subservient status to the Persian rulers. Deliverance is eagerly awaited, but it must be entirely of God's own doing, unaided by human contrivance.

13. Cf. v. 4 and Jl 2:16.

14–17. The divine response to the lament comes in the form of an oracle of salvation. This is of considerable interest as it is one of the very few certain examples of this form in a specifically liturgical context, even though on other grounds it has been frequently invoked by scholars to explain the sudden change of mood in a number of the Psalms of lament in the Psalter. Other examples are found in Isa. 40–55 in particular. An extensive literature discussing this form has developed; recent treatments, which also refer back to earlier works, include A. Schoors, *I am God your Saviour* (1973), pp. 32–175; T. M. Raitt, *A Theology of Exile* (1977), pp. 128–73, and M. Weinfeld, *VT* 27 (1977), pp. 183f.

It should be noted with Petersen, pp. 75f. (though cf. P. E. Dion, *CBQ* 32 [1970], pp. 565–70), however, that in its present context this oracle also serves the function of providing one of the elements which go together to pattern this account along the lines of a 'holy war'; cf. G. von Rad, *Der heilige Krieg im alten Israel* (1951), and more briefly de Vaux, *AI*, pp. 258–65. Others will be noted later. It need not be supposed that the holy war was an institution as such (as some imply); it represents rather a literary device for expressing the conviction of God's involvement in the wars of Israel. There is thus, as in the present case, an inevitable association, if not identification, of the oracle of salvation and the assurance to 'fear not' before a battle; cf. von Rad, pp. 9–10. This being so, there is no need to regard this oracle as a 'levitical sermon' *sensu stricto* (*contra* von Rad, 'The Levitical Sermon', pp. 272f.). The other biblical citations (cf. vv. 15 and 17) are similarly taken from descriptions of the holy war rather than the prophetical writings.

14. the Spirit of the Lord came upon: see on 15:1. Appropriate to a liturgical setting, this prophetic inspiration falls on **a Levite**, who, being one of **the sons of Asaph**, will in particular have been one of the singers; see on 1 Chr. 25:1. The unusually long genealogy of **Jahaziel** is probably intended to trace his pedigree as far back as the time of David and his definitive reorganisation of the Levitical offices.

15. The three main components of the oracle of salvation are all present in this verse: the definition of the addressees, the 'fear not' formula, and the substantiation; cf. the comparable Isa. 41:8–13. The comprehensive definition of those addressed is noteworthy as a recurring feature of the Chronicler's conception of prophecy, and may well arise from reflection on the work of the classical prophets; cf. Seeligmann, *SVT* 29 (1978), p. 274. **Fear not:** while this formula is to be expected, its direct link with v. 3, and hence with the theme of the Chronicler's presentation of Jehoshaphat's reign as a whole, should not thereby be overlooked. **for the battle is not yours but God's:** cf. 1 Sam. 17:47. This expresses the fundamental conviction of the 'holy war', and as a tenet of faith it has no doubt influenced the presentation of the 'battle' later on; cf. v. 17 below and von Rad, *Der heilige Krieg*, p. 9.

16. The element of substantiation is now backed up with specific details, drawn, we must assume, from the Chronicler's source. That he has worked these into one of his speeches is an indication of the extent of his rewriting. **the ascent of Ziz:** Noth (p. 55) was not able to identify this, and argued that, as in the case of some of the other names in this passage, it was virtually a nickname, known only to local inhabitants. Though the name remains unattested, it is now probably to be equated with an ascent from a point on the western shore of the Dead Sea near Engedi (cf. v. 2) up into the Judean desert. There is evidence for its use from the period of the Judean monarchy onwards; cf. M. Harel, *IEJ* 17 (1967), pp. 18–25. It has been conjectured that some of the forts found along the route were built after this invasion in order to prevent the possibility of its ever being repeated; cf. Aharoni, *Land* p. 293. **the end of the valley, east of the wilderness of Jeruel:** otherwise unknown. The nature of the description again suggests local knowledge. A situation on the route up from the south-east towards Tekoa is presumably implied.

17. This recapitulates the substance of the oracle, this time with a citation from Exod. 14:13; see on v. 15 above.

18–19. As the change from lament to praise in a number of the Psalms shows, it was usual for the oracle of salvation to be followed by worship. In this case, it is appropriately led by **the Levites. and the Korahites:** since they are part of the larger family of **the Kohathites** (cf. 1 Chr. 6:22, 37f.), it seems probable that **and** should here be translated 'even'. The present context, together with the appearance of **the Korahites** in a number of the Psalm headings (e.g. Ps. 42–49), suggests that they are regarded as Levitical singers. Elsewhere in Chronicles, however, they occur as gatekeepers (cf. 1 Chr. 9:19; 26:1). The difficulty which Gese, 'Zur Geschichte der Kultsänger', pp. 230–4 (and cf. Petersen, pp. 75f.) has in integrating this into his outline of the development of the Levitical singers in the post-exilic period (see on 1 Chr. 15–16 above) suggests that this element may not have come originally from the Chronicler himself; cf. J. M. Miller, *CBQ* 32 (1970), pp. 58–68, who for similar reasons regards this verse as probably 'a remnant of the old tradition'.

20. And they rose early in the morning: 'often the moment of divine victory' (Ackroyd). There is the suggestion of confidence, based on the prophetic word. **the wilderness of Tekoa:** cf. v. 16. **as they went out, Jehoshaphat stood and said:** the king here fulfils the role of the priest of Dt. 20:1–4, who is to give the army an assurance of divine aid in the 'holy war'. He does so, however, in a brief example of the Levitical sermon, which we have seen elsewhere often to contain the Chronicler's own theological commentary on the narrative (cf. 15:1–7) and which is regularly based on earlier written prophecy. Both features are evident again here. Isa. 7:9 underlies part of Jehoshaphat's words, and indeed 'the quotation is undeniably appropriate, for the situation in which the Chronicler depicts Jehoshaphat is very similar to that in which Ahaz is shown in the book of Isaiah. In both instances there is an explicit test of faith' (von Rad, 'The Levitical Sermon', p. 274). However, the Chronicler himself adds **believe his prophets, and you will succeed.** By his day, knowledge of God is increasingly through the written, perhaps even canonical, word. Prophecy is now primarily a matter for reinterpretation and application, and the message which he seems to want to convey on that basis from this whole story is one of waiting in faith for a new intervention by God; see on v. 6 above.

21. when he had taken counsel: cf. 1 Chr. 13:1. The two poetic lines are a frequent refrain in the Psalms which the Chronicler intends as illustrative of the praise offered; cf. 1 Chr. 16:34; 2 Chr. 5:13.

22. The account of the battle is highly stylised, and is not to be

understood apart from the tradition of the 'holy war'; to invoke
brilliant military use of the terrain as an explanation for the victory
(Yadin, *The Art of Warfare*, pp. 310f.) is completely to deny the
emphasis of vv. 15–17 at the level of the Chronicler's own presentation, even if it may be an interesting speculation about the underlying narrative now lost to us. However, it can be seen that the
Chronicler has pressed matters still further, in that the great 'shout'
which is such a feature of the earlier narratives (e.g. Jos. 6:5; Jg.
7:20; I Sam. 17:20 and 52; 2 Chr. 13:15) is now replaced by musical
worship (**when they began to sing and praise**; cf. von Rad, *Der
heilige Krieg*, pp. 80f.). Again, whereas the use of **an ambush** is
found elsewhere in connection with the 'holy war' (e.g. Jos. 8:2,
and cf. 2 Chr. 13:13), only here is it **set** by **the Lord**. The word in
question is strictly a personal plural participle ('liers in wait'), by
which supernatural agencies seem to be implied. This element,
therefore, as its outcome demonstrates, is comparable with the 'panic' which God is often said to have induced amongst Israel's oppo-
nents in the earlier accounts (e.g. Exod. 23:27; Jos. 10:10, etc., and
cf. von Rad, *Der heilige Krieg*, p. 12). **and Mount Seir**: see on v. 1.
so that they were routed: a summary of the following verses.

    23. For the self-destruction of Israel's enemies, cf. Jg.7:22; I
Sam. 14:20, and in prophetical texts Ezek. 38:21; Hag. 2:22; Zech.
14:13. The complete lack of any participation by Jehoshaphat's
army certainly marks an ideological advance over such passages as
13:14ff. and 14:12ff.

    24–25. the watchtower of the wilderness: cf. v. 16. Local know-
ledge is again presupposed. **they were dead bodies . . . none had
escaped**: in earlier accounts of a 'holy war', it was Israel's responsibility to 'dedicate' the opposing forces and all their goods to the
Lord by the ban; cf. de Vaux, *AI*, p. 260. In this case, however,
we again see how God's role has been magnified still further in that
nothing remained to be done in this respect except **to take the spoil**.
No exact parallel for this exists, though there are points of comparison in 2 Kg. 7:3–16 and 19:35. The huge quantities of spoil further
emphasise the magnitude of the victory. **cattle**: this represents a
slight emendation which has the support of LXX and may well be
right. It is a slightly curious item in the context, however; the syntax
of MT would seem to be not impossible for the Chronicler, and
gives good sense; literally: 'and they found amongst them abundantly, even goods,. . .'. **clothing**: an emendation for MT's 'corp-
ses', and almost certainly right.

    26–28. the valley of Beracah: the name is still retained in both
Khirbet Berekut and the Wadi Berekut, both situated near Tekoa.
For the aetiological element in v. 26, see above, p. 293. The fitting

climax to such an account is undoubtedly praise, both near the site
of deliverance, and then, after a festal procession **to Jerusalem** with
Jehoshaphat at their head, in the temple itself, since it was here
that God's deliverance had initially been invoked (v. 5). The rejoic-
ing is reminiscent of the occasion when David brought the ark to
Jerusalem; cf. 1 Chr. 15:28.

29. Cf. 17:10. Ch. 17 was seen to be introductory to Jehoshaphat's
reign as a whole, whereas the incident in this chapter has been seen
to derive from a failure in faith on Jehoshaphat's part. It thus
furnishes an exception to the general rule of 17:10. When that
failure was put right, however, the more normal conditions were
restored. **when they heard:** cf. Jos. 2:9–11; 9:1–3, etc.

30. God gave him rest: this has been noted several times as a
mark of blessing: see on 14:1*b*.

The Conclusion of Jehoshaphat's Reign

20:31–21:1

The Chronicler follows 1 Kg. 22:41–50 for the concluding notices
about Jehoshaphat's reign. This is sufficient to account for the
curious order; otherwise we would have expected vv. 35–37 to come
earlier.

31. As usual (cf. Willi, p. 98), the Chronicler omits the synchronism of his *Vorlage* between the reigns of the kings of Israel and
Judah.

32. He walked in the way of Asa his father: contrast the Chronicler's own assessment in 17:3, where a distinction is made, according to his presentation of Asa's reign, between his earlier faithfulness
and later falling away. **and did not turn aside from it:** the Chronicler
must have allowed this generalisation to stand on the grounds that
it coincides with his final judgment on Jehoshaphat's reign (cf.
p. 278), even though his own presentation of the reign has introduced some temporary elements which contradict it. Moreover, he
has retained the qualification of the next verse.

33. The high places: contrast 17:6. There is no evidence to
support a harmonisation along the line that the earlier passage speaks
of idolatrous high places whereas this verse speaks of high places
dedicated to the Lord (Goettsberger). Nor on the other hand, however, is it necessary to go as far as Rudolph, who, on the basis of
this apparent contradiction, suggests that vv. 31–33 are a secondary
addition by some one who wished to bring the Chronicler's text into
closer conformity with that of Kings. Willi, pp. 61–2, well observes
that this is not the only case of such a tension and that Rudolph's

view does not account for the amelioration of the tension in the second half of this verse or for the other differences between the two texts which fit the pattern of the Chronicler's own composition (see on v. 31 above).

It must be presumed, therefore, that the Chronicler both wished to retain his *Vorlage* intact as far as he could, and yet that he was aware of a tension, not only with 17:6, but also with the attitude of the people as presented earlier in this chapter. His solution is to be sought in his substitution of **the people had not yet set their hearts upon the God of their fathers** for 1 Kg. 22:43*b*, 'the people still sacrificed and burned incense on the high places'. We have often seen how the Chronicler makes important play of human fickleness (e.g. the reigns of Rehoboam and Asa). His phraseology here suggests that he invoked the same device to explain the apparent contradiction: 17:6 stands in line with his generally positive appraisal of Jehoshaphat's character and reign, but that need not mean that either he (ch. 18 and vv. 35–37 below) or **the people** had so permanently **set their hearts** that there was not always the danger that they would fall away. Needless to say, the Chronicler will have wished his readers to draw from this the moral of the need for constant faithfulness and vigilance.

34. This largely replaces a notice to similar effect in 1 Kg. 22:45. **the chronicles of Jehu the son of Hanani:** for this prophet, see on 16:7 and 19:2. Once again, the Chronicler likes to be able to indicate that his historical source is to be regarded as a prophetic work (see the Introduction, section F). **which are recorded in:** this makes clear his view, already noted above, that his 'prophetic' sources were not independent works, but parts of a larger book. **the Book of the Kings of Israel: Israel** is here substituted for 'Judah'; see on 16:11.

35–37. Jehoshaphat's disastrous maritime venture. 1 Kg. 22:48–49 tells how Jehoshaphat built a fleet, which, however, was wrecked at Ezion-geber before ever it sailed. Then Ahaziah offered the assistance of his servants, which Jehoshaphat refused. Here, however, the two kings are allied from the start of the venture, and the shipwreck concludes the narrative.

Older commentators, such as Keil, found no difficulty in harmonising on the assumption that each account retained only part of an original full account, but the view that the parallel passages of Kings and Chronicles are both independently drawn from an anterior source is no longer tenable. More recent commentators have tended to argue that the Chronicler simply rewrote his *Vorlage* in order to explain why such a disaster befell an otherwise good king, while Rudolph suggested that the Chronicler took this paragraph from a different source, the Kings' account being historically secondary because it tries to cover over Jehoshaphat's dependence on the northern kingdom.

Willi, p. 219, however, has advanced a much more convincing suggestion which obviates the need for further speculation, because it provides a coherent explanation of how the Chronicler's version developed directly from that in Kings. The Chronicler would have regarded as bizarre the offer of Ahaziah, 'Let my servants go with your servants in the ships' and Jehoshaphat's refusal (1 Kg. 22:49) at a time after the ships were already wrecked. Consequently, he was obliged to interpret the verb 'āmar, 'said' (1 Kg. 22:49a) as pluperfect ('had said'; this in itself is, of course, quite reasonable), and the 'then' ('āz) at the beginning of the verse as meaning 'at that time'. Ahaziah's offer could then refer not only to the journey, but also to the building, which will also at once have made clear to the Chronicler why the venture failed, namely, because of his culpable alliance. This explanation the Chronicler then, in his usual fashion, put into the mouth of a prophet. This fits well with our view (above, p. 280) that the explanation derives from the Chronicler himself.

36. ships to go to Tarshish: this represents the same misunderstanding of the *Vorlage*'s expression 'ships of Tarshish' as at 9:21, confirming that it is indeed the Chronicler who has rewritten this passage on the basis of Kings.

37. Eliezer the son of Dodavahu: otherwise completely unknown. **will destroy:** cf. GK §106n. For the significance of this word (*pāraṣ*) in the present context, see above, p. 280.

JEHORAM

21:2–20

The Chronicler's account of Jehoram's reign, comparatively brief though it is, represents a considerable expansion over the meagre treatment of 2 Kg. 8:16–24. As will be seen, there is no good reason to doubt that much of the additional material here comes from earlier, and probably fully authentic, sources. Nevertheless, the whole has been ordered by the Chronicler in such a way as to illustrate once more one of his fundamental principles, namely that faithlessness will inevitably lead both to personal tragedy and to domination by foreign enemies; cf. the comments on 1 Chr. 10.

Jehoram is the first king of the Davidic line of whom the Chronicler's judgment is totally negative. His strengthening of the wording of v. 7 is thus of particular significance. It should be noted, moreover, that in some respects the account of Jehoram's reign should be taken closely with that of Ahaziah's which immediately follows it; see on 22:1–9 and Mosis, pp. 178–9.

Jehoram's Establishment of his Rule

21:2–4

This passage is peculiar to Chronicles. It owes its present position, prior to the usual introductory remarks to a king's reign (cf. v. 5), partly to the fact that the Chronicler preferred to follow his source consecutively if possible once he had started with it (cf. Willi, pp. 63–4), and so chose not to allow this paragraph to interrupt it. In addition, however, it should be noted that it introduces a theme which is to dominate the next two chapters, namely, a very serious threat to the continuation of the Davidic line. Four times (here, at v. 17, at 22:8–9, and at 22:10–11) violence is perpetrated against the royal family in such a way that the line is all but cut off. The Chronicler draws attention to this theme by placing this paragraph prominently at the start of Jehoram's reign.

The removal by a new king of any possible rival claimants to the throne is by no means improbable (cf. Jg. 9:5; 2 Kg. 10:11; 11:1). The matter-of-fact nature of the account, its circumstantial details (e.g. v. 3) and the lack of any obvious marks of the Chronicler's style have allowed the majority of commentators to agree that this passage has probably been taken from one of his sources. He will have included it in particular because of the unfavourable impression which it creates of the character of Jehoram's rule, especially in the light of his later comment that these brothers 'were better than yourself' (v. 13), an allusion, no doubt, to Jehoram's religious policy (v. 11).

2. Azariah: it is unlikely that two **brothers** would have the same name. Either one occurrence should be deleted, or the second emended to 'Uzziah'. **Judah:** MT has 'Israel', which should certainly be preferred as the harder reading. While such a title is not incompatible with the Chronicler's usage elsewhere, there is no obvious motive for its occurrence just here. It may reflect the influence of his source; cf. *IBC*, pp. 102–10.

3. together with fortified cities in Judah: cf. 11:23 and 19:5. **because he was the first-born:** the need felt to add this otherwise rather obvious explanation may indicate that even from early times Jehoram's reign was regarded unfavourably.

4. and was established: cf. 1:1. **and also some of the princes of Israel:** see on 12:6.

The Character of Jehoram's Reign

21:5–11

With the exception of v. 11, this paragraph is drawn from 2 Kg. 8:17–22, the commentaries on which should be consulted for details about the history of the period. The Chronicler has adopted it because its presentation of the revolt of Edom and Libnah (vv. 8–10) following the description of Jehoram's apostasy (v. 6) precisely coincides with his understanding of divine retribution. The few touches from the Chronicler's own hand may be recognised without difficulty.

6. daughter: Athaliah was probably a daughter of Omri and so a sister of **Ahab**, but it is not therefore necessary to emend the text (*contra* Rudolph); cf. H. J. Katzenstein, *IEJ* 5 (1955), pp. 194–7.

7. The Chronicler has introduced two significant changes into this verse. 'Judah' of 2 Kg. 8:19 has become **the house of David**, and 'for the sake of David his servant' has become **because of the covenant which he had made with David**. The effect of both changes is to strengthen the allusion to the unconditional promise to the Davidic dynasty. During a reign which has no redeeming features, in the Chronicler's view, the promise shines out all the more brightly; see further on 1 Chr. 17; 2 Chr. 6:42; 13:5, and *TynB* 28 (1977), p. 148. The second half of the verse, adopted unaltered from the *Vorlage*, fully supports this view, even if it is uncertain what is meant by **a lamp**. Various suggestions are discussed by H.-J. Kraus, *Psalmen II* (1961²), pp. 887f.; J. Coppens, *Le Messianisme royal* (1968), p. 51; P. D. Hanson, *HTR* 61 (1968), pp. 297–320. Nor can we be sure that the Chronicler would have understood the expression in the same way as Kings. The general sense of the phrase, however, is clear. **and to his sons:** the word **and** has been added by the Chronicler, perhaps 'to bring the idea more prominently forward' (Keil): in a time when the promise appears most under threat, there is a tendency always to look forward to future generations for its fulfilment.

9. and smote the Edomites: the Chronicler here follows his *Vorlage*, itself unclear. The context shows that there can be no question of general defeat of the Edomites by Jehoram. Either we should emend to 'and the Edomites smote him' (Rudolph; cf. *NEB*), or understand that Jehoram just managed to break out of the position where he had been **surrounded**, and so to escape with his life.

10. The last part of the verse (from **from his rule, . . .**) is added by the Chronicler, as its characteristic style demonstrates; see on 12:1 and 15:2. It provides just the explanation for the loss of terri-

tory which we would expect of him. Further details of what he will
have thought was involved are supplied by him in the next verse.

11. The Chronicler adopts from the Deuteronomic history the
attitude of the kings to the **high places** as a criterion for assessing
their faithfulness to God. Despite fluctuation, the tendency of the
previous kings, Asa and Jehoshaphat, is regarded as having been
towards their abolition (see v. 12 with 14:2–5; 15:8; 17:6), but to
underline his condemnation of Jehoram (cf. v. 6) the Chronicler
adds this note about how he reversed the favourable trend with the
result that he led the people **astray**, an action which in the case of
the northern kingdom was to lead to final exile; cf. 1 Chr. 5:25. **hill
country:** some commentators follow a number of MSS, LXX and V
in reading 'cities', but MT makes acceptable sense.

The Letter from Elijah

21:12–15

Whereas comparison with the Chronicler's account of other kings
might lead us to expect that he would interject his own comment in
the form of a 'Levitical sermon', we find instead that he uses the
device of a 'letter' sent by Elijah to Jehoram. Such a device will
have been attractive to him because in the books of Kings Elijah
stands as the champion of Yahwism against the inroads of Baal-
worship into the northern kingdom during the reigns of Ahab and
Ahaziah. Since Jehoram was allied by marriage to the house of Ahab
and 'walked in the way of the kings of Israel, as the house of Ahab
had done' (v. 6), it was considered fitting that the rebuke should
come to him too from Elijah.

It is generally agreed now that this letter is the Chronicler's own
composition. On the one hand we have repeatedly seen that it is his
practice elsewhere to comment in similar fashion on the events he
is recording while on the other hand it has been argued that had
there existed such a letter from Elijah the Deuteronomic historian
would undoubtedly have included it. The second argument is not
strong. Not only is it based on silence, but had such a letter been
sent to Jehoram we would not have expected it to be included with
the Kings' Elijah cycle, since the latter's literary history must have
started in the north and might well have been sufficiently determined early on for no convenient place for the inclusion of this
letter to have been found. Despite this, however, the balance of
probability must still be said to lie against the letter's authenticity.

That the Chronicler should have thought of Elijah sending a
written message is not in itself surprising, despite the lack in Kings

of any indication of a written ministry by the prophet. He will not, of course, have been aware of the possible precedent for such activity suggested by at least one text from Mari; cf. H. B. Huffmon, *BA* 31 (1968), pp. 101–24 (107f.). Rather it should be noted that already by his time most prophecy will have been known only in a written form that was approachirg canonical status (Ackroyd helpfully points to Zech. 1:5f.), while the view that the prophets wrote down their own oracles would have been gaining credence.

The contents of the letter itself, viewed from the angle of the Chronicler, present no serious problems of interpretation. Jehoram is condemned for his faithlessness by comparison with his predecessors and for his treatment of his family. As a result both he personally and his kingdom will suffer.

12. a letter came to him from Elijah: it is not clear whether the Chronicler thought that Elijah was still alive. The chronology of the period is uncertain. 2 Kg. 3:11 and the position of 2 Kg. 2 would suggest that he was already dead, but 2 Kg. 1:17 might be taken to mean that he was alive for part, at least, of Jehoram's reign. Some earlier commentators made much of the wording of this phrase, contrasting it with the more normally expected 'Elijah sent a letter. . .', to suggest either that the letter came direct from Elijah in heaven or that he wrote it 'prophetically' before his death. While the former suggestion would be without any kind of *OT* analogy, it is not impossible to believe that the Chronicler could have thought in terms of the latter. The evidence is insufficient to decide. **the God of David your father:** the title is accommodated to Jehoram's situation, but is close to one of the Chronicler's favourite and characteristic expressions for God; cf. Japhet, *Ideology*, pp. 19ff. **Jehoshaphat. . .Asa:** cf. v. 11 above.

13. you have killed your brothers: see on vv. 2–4 above, the theme of which is here carried a step further: Jehoram's murder of his brothers will be rewarded by the violent death of his sons.

14–15. The various judgments predicted here are worked out exactly and in detail in the following paragraph, and, indeed, assuming that material for the latter lay already in the Chronicler's source, they may well have been written up out of it.

The End of Jehoram's Reign

21:16–20

In two paragraphs the Chronicler deals with the judgment against the people (vv. 16–17) and against Jehoram personally (vv. 18–20).

16–17. No other account of this raid by the **Philistines** and **Arabs**

is preserved. It reflects very much the same nature and geographical background as that considered to have been the account underlying 14:9–15 above, and may therefore have been derived from the same source; see also 17:11. A further pointer towards the use of a source here by the Chronicler may be seen in the name **Jehoahaz** (v. 17), which contradicts his normal usage. Once again, though not on quite the same scale, the Chronicler will have magnified a local border raid, such as must frequently have occurred, into an event of national significance.

16. stirred up. . .the anger: as at 1 Chr. 5:26. Outside the Chronicler's own writing, the expression may have a positive application; cf. Ezr. 1:1 (= the secondary 2 Chr. 36:22); Hag. 1:14; but contrast Jer. 51:11. **the Ethiopians**: as at 14:9–15, these are better regarded as 'Cushites', a bedouin tribe to the south of Judah.

17. the king's house: this need not (and in the present context cannot) refer to the palace in Jerusalem. The practice of stationing members of the royal household in the fortified cities has already been noted (v. 3, etc.), and that appears to be presupposed here. It is clear, moreover, from 22:1 that **his sons and his wives** were not given as part of a price to buy off the invaders, but were captured during the course of the invasion, and eventually killed. **his youngest son**, together, as ch. 22 makes clear, with his mother, was not involved; no doubt they remained with the king in Jerusalem. **Jehoahaz**: this is the same name as 'Ahaziah', but it is the latter form which the Chronicler himself uses (ch. 22). This variation in usage may indicate dependence on an earlier source.

18–19. Again in accordance with the prophecy of v. 15, Jehoram is personally judged, and dies in agony. His disease is not recorded in Kings, and we have no real way of assessing how the Chronicler came by his account. Rudolph argues that it cannot be his own invention because of the detail of the description, and to this may be added the possibility, supported by the analogy of vv. 16–17, that the Chronicler wrote up the prophecy on the basis of the account found in his source rather than inventing both *de novo*; but neither argument amounts to a fully convincing case, so that the issue must remain open.

As in the case of Asa (see on 16:12), no firm modern diagnosis of the disease is ultimately possible from a text of this nature from antiquity. 'Chronic diarrhoea' (CM) is usually postulated, though more recently G. R. Driver, in A. Caquot and M. Philonenko (eds), *Hommages à André Dupont-Sommer* (1971), p. 284, has resorted to a mild conjecture in order to suggest ulcers leading to chronic rectal prolapse, a view which underlies the translation of *NEB* both here and in v. 15.

19. The text of the first part of this verse is uncertain, and commentators have suggested a number of conjectural emendations without any carrying full conviction. *RSV* reflects one widely held view, though the word translated **years** is more naturally understood of 'days'. Should it be taken so here, **the end** will refer to his life, and the description in this verse will represent an advance over v. 18, and refer to the final stages of the illness.

19b–20. Cf. 2 Kg. 8:23f. Jehoram's unpopularity is expressed both by the lack of honours accorded him on his death and, more contemporaneously for the Chronicler's readers, by the exceptional fact that on this occasion the Chronicler omits a reference to his sources for fuller information even though such a reference is present in his *Vorlage*. (The exceptional nature of this omission cannot merely be overcome by suggesting, with Rudolph, that he was here following an alternative account, for it still remains to be explained why he chose to do this rather than to follow his usual procedure.) For such a reference he substitutes the observation that **he departed with no man's regret.**

Jehoram's unpopularity even in his own life-time is expressed in the information (found only here) that **his people made no fire in his honour** (contrast 16:14) and that his tomb lay apart from **the tombs of the kings.** It is impossible to say whether these represent more than the Chronicler's own additions, but it may be noted that an indication was found in v.3 to suggest that this would indeed have been the general attitude to Jehoram as early as the contemporary recorders of his reign.

AHAZIAH

22:1–9

In two ways the Chronicler's presentation of Ahaziah's reign should be seen as a close continuation of Jehoram's. The influence of Athaliah remains dominant, with all that that meant in terms of religious policy and close cooperation with the north. The Chronicler makes some small additions in vv. 3 and 4 in order to emphasise this. Secondly, the theme of threat to the Davidic dynasty is also carried forward (see on 22:2–4). Ahaziah, the sole surviving son of Jehoram, meets a premature and violent death, thus perhaps completing the underlying sense of the prophecy of 21:13–14, while Athaliah will shortly thereafter destroy all the remainder of the royal family with the exception of Joash (vv. 10–11). Thus the conclusion of the account is the Chronicler's own comment that 'the house of Ahaziah had no one able to rule the kingdom' (v. 9), while v. 7

points to this situation as 'ordained by God'. Mosis, p. 179, is thus right to draw out the parallel with the paradigmatic account of Saul's reign in 1 Chr. 10. There is an obvious similarity with v. 6 of that chapter, while the theme of religious faithlessness resulting in 'exilic' conditions (1 Chr. 10:13-14) dominates the whole account. See also on v. 7 below for a further possible point of contact. In the light of all this, the providential preservation of the royal line may be seen as confirmation of the promise referred to in 21:7, and may have been intended to encourage the readers' own hopes in this direction, despite the 'exilic'-type conditions which they had long endured in this regard.

1. **the inhabitants of Jerusalem:** nowhere else are they said to act in this manner (e.g. contrast 26:1; 33:25 and 36:1). If this verse is drawn from an authentic source (see below), there will be an indication here of confusion concerning the matter of succession. **the band of men that came with the Arabs to the camp. . .:** cf. 21:16-17. The scale of the invasion suggested in the present verse is noticeably more modest. It may be assumed that both passages are taken from the source suggested at 21:16-17, and that this verse confirms the conjecture advanced there that the Chronicler magnified the original account somewhat.

2-6. For this general characterisation of Ahaziah's reign, the Chronicler follows 2 Kg. 8:26-29 quite closely. While the major differences, noted below, fit well with the Chronicler's own viewpoint and should therefore probably be attributed to him, the possibility should not be forgotten that in such passages his *Vorlage* may have already differed slightly from MT of Kings (see the Introduction, section A).

2. **forty-two:** this is impossible, as it would make Ahaziah older than his father (cf. 21:5 and 20). 2 Kg. 8:26 has 'twenty-two', for which there is some versional support here, and the major LXX mss 'twenty'. Myers supposes that 'the MT of Chronicles may represent the conflation of two traditions and exhibits a striking example of the effort to preserve two divergent traditions'. Alternatively, it may be a simple case of scribal error, for which various explanations are possible, depending on what system of recording numerals is presupposed (cf. Keil and Rudolph). **granddaughter:** this represents an interpretation by *RSV* of the MT, which simply has 'daughter'. It is more probable that MT should be preferred in its literal sense; see on 21:6.

3. **He also:** this is added by the Chronicler, and it indicates the link in his mind between the reigns of Ahaziah and Jehoram. **for his mother. . .:** the second half of the verse is also added to

2 Kg. 8:27. It clearly shows his attitude to the quality of Ahaziah's rule.

4–5. for after the death. . .their counsel: this passage is again added by the Chronicler, with similar effects. Such contacts with the north would, in his view, inevitably lead to disaster, as the sequel shows.

7–9. The narrative of this paragraph seems to be based on 2 Kg. 9:1–28 with 10:12–14. Though it can be understood in its present form, the Chronicler probably expected his readers to be familiar with the longer account, and so did not feel the need to explain who Jehu was, and so on. He simply included the briefest amount of material commensurate with his aim of tracing the fortunes of Ahaziah and his family. In addition, as is quite often his practice, he has added a sentence at the beginning and end of the paragraph to supply the narrative with an interpretative framework. It shows that the events are to be regarded as the judgment of God on the king's faithlessness, and that it brought the Davidic dynasty to the brink of extinction, from which, we may infer, it was rescued only by God's saving intervention in accordance with his promise.

Even allowing for the Chronicler's drastic abbreviation of the material, there are to be observed, however, a number of differences between this paragraph and the fuller account in Kings. (a) The princes of Judah are here murdered before Ahaziah, but after him in 2 Kg. 10:12–14. (b) In 2 Kg. 9:27 Ahaziah is wounded near Ibleam as he flees, but manages to escape to Megiddo, where he dies. Here, he is captured while hiding in Samaria, brought to Jehu at some unnamed place and put to death. (c) It is implied here that he was buried at the place of his death, whereas in 2 Kg. 9:28 it is stated that he was brought by his servants to Jerusalem and there buried 'with his fathers in the city of David'.

These differences are of such a kind that any attempt at harmonization must at once appear forced and unconvincing. It has usually been supposed, however, that since the differences do not materially serve the Chronicler's purpose, he was in fact basing himself on an alternative account at this point. This conclusion is questionable, however. As far as point (a) is concerned, there is no difficulty in supposing that the Chronicler could have brought this incident forward in order to be able to conclude the narrative with the death of Ahaziah. Moreover its importance for his overall theme has been noted (see on 21:2–4, etc.), whereas earlier commentators did not observe it, and his inclusion of 21:17 and 22:1 is sufficient to explain the change from 'kinsmen (literally, brothers) of Ahaziah' (2 Kg. 10:13) to 'the sons of Ahaziah's brothers' here. Concerning point (c), we have again already seen several times that the place and circumstances of a king's burial can be one means whereby the Chronicler expressed a theological judgment on the quality of the reign; e.g. 16:14; 21:19f., etc. The difference in this respect between the two passages under discussion could be fully accounted for in this way too. Finally, although point (b) appears to betray the least marks of the Chronicler's theological bias, his emphasis on Ahaziah's culpability in visiting the northern king may have caused him to want to picture Ahaziah as hiding specifically in Samaria, and the remainder of the account would then follow naturally enough.

It is thus not necessary to postulate an alternative, but irreconcilable, source. We may suggest rather that the Chronicler presupposed knowledge of the earlier story by his readers (see above), and therefore could expect them to read his version not as an alternative historical account but as a theological commentary on the original story which drew out his perception of the outworkings of God's retributive justice.

7. downfall (*te̱bûsa*t̲): this *hapax legomenon* literally means 'down-treading', and is slightly surprising in the present context. It is thus extremely attractive (though conjectural) to adopt a slight emendation to *ne̱sibbat̲* (Rudolph) or *te̱subbat̲* (Ackroyd), meaning 'a turn of affairs'; see the highly-charged theological use of this root by the Chronicler at 1 Chr. 10:14 and 2 Chr. 10:15.

8. brothers: this can be understood to mean 'relatives' more generally. It is therefore unnecessary to discuss whether Ahaziah could have had nephews of sufficient age at this time.

9. for they said: there is no warrant for the remainder of this verse in the Kings' account. It represents the Chronicler's own reflections. Ahaziah was not sufficiently honourable for the usual notice about a burial in Jerusalem to be recorded. On the other hand, as **the grandson of Jehoshaphat**, it would not be fitting that his corpse should simply be left exposed. **who sought the Lord with all his heart**: this, the Chronicler's own final evaluation of Jehoshaphat, needs to be read in the light of his presentation of chs. 17-20 as a whole; see above, pp. 277ff. No doubt he will have been inclined towards such a favourable appreciation by reflecting on the contrast with the reigns of Jehoram and Ahaziah just recorded.

JOASH

22:10-24:27

For most of his account of the reign of Joash, the Chronicler is dependent on 2 Kg. 11-12 alone. Only for parts of ch. 24 can there be any serious suggestion of an alternative source. Nevertheless, the Chronicler has firmly stamped his own interpretation on the material so that it becomes illustrative of some of his central concerns. The reign is clearly divided into three main periods. The scene is set for the first by the reduction of the Davidic house to its lowest ebb during Athaliah's interregnum (22:10–12), a situation whose parallel with the close of Saul's reign has already been noted (see the introduction to 22:1–9). It is thus not surprising to find that a number of the differences between the Chronicler's account of the coronation of Joash (ch. 23) and that of Kings are due to his desire to point out comparisons with the elevation of David to the throne of Israel in 1 Chr. 11ff. The most obvious example of this is the emphasis on the willing and joyful participation of all the people, while at the same time the Chronicler adds another of his significant references to the promise of God to David (23:3). The first episode, therefore, illustrates again the transition from a position of apostasy rewarded by death and defeat to one in which God, wellnigh miraculously (Rudolph, p. 273), brings salvation centred upon the Davidic dynasty.

Second, there follows a period during which Joash's rule is regarded most favourably by the Chronicler. It too has close correspondences with his presentation of David's rule, for it is dominated by concern for the purity of the nation's worship. Just as David inherited a situation in which under Saul the ark had been neglected (1 Chr. 13:3), so the Chronicler adds the comment in 24:7 that Athaliah's family had abused the temple and its 'dedicated things' (cf. Mosis, p. 181).

The Chronicler introduces a third period into the reign of Joash in a way which does not have immediately obvious warrant in 2 Kings. Following the death of the high priest Jehoiada, Joash reverses his policy of faithfulness and, rather as in the case of Asa (chs. 14–16), his reign closes with the rejection of prophetic warning leading to military defeat for the nation and, in this case, a violent death for the king. Whether or not additional sources lie behind parts of this material, there can be no doubt that the Chronicler himself put the account together as an illustration of the outworkings of divine retribution which might serve as a solemn warning to his readers.

One further introductory point deserves mention, though its interpretation is disputed, namely, the role of the high priest Jehoiada. It is at his initiative that Joash is brought to the throne and under his influence that the nation is restored to something of its former status of faithfulness, while specifically after his death decline rapidly sets in. A number of commentators have observed that in the

Chronicler's own day the high priesthood exercised considerable power and influence, and that it was tending to combine the roles of political and religious leadership. The question then arises whether, as has generally been thought, the Chronicler's very favourable portrayal of Jehoiada was aimed at furthering this development, seeing in his leading role a possible substitute in the post-exilic period for the kingship of earlier times.

In my opinion, and taking the Chronicler's position as a whole into account, just the reverse is the case. The work of Jehoiada, the Chronicler's ideal high priest (cf. 24:15–16), is not at any point that of substitute for the king, but rather of preserver of the dynastic household, of king-maker and of faithful adviser to the crown. We have already noted that by the end of ch. 22 there are certain parallels to be drawn with the Chronicler's own situation, not least as regards the fortunes of the royal household. Precisely in the glowing description of Jehoiada's role at this time we may see a mild polemic against the tendency of the post-exilic high priest to usurp all authority in Jerusalem and an encouragement rather for them to maintain a vision for, and where possible to work towards the realisation of, what the Chronicler always regarded as the ideal for the theocracy of a balance between royal and religious leadership.

The Elevation of Joash to the Throne
22:10–23:21

22:10–12. The interregnum under Athaliah; cf. 2 Kg. 11:1–3. The absence of the usual opening and closing formulae shows that this is not regarded as a proper reign.

10. destroyed: while the sense of this passage is not in doubt, it remains uncertain whether this word, *watt⁽e⁾dabbēr*, is an example of the postulated root *dbr*, cognate with Akkadian *dabāru*, 'overthrow', or whether, in the case of so late a text as Chronicles, it is not easier to suppose a simple corruption of the similar *watt⁽e⁾'abbēd* of the *Vorlage*. **of the house of Judah:** lacking in Kings. If it is added by the Chronicler himself, Willi (p. 131) may be right in seeing a hint that while Athaliah may have struck a blow at the 'earthly manifestation' of the kingdom, she could not, of course, eliminate the true kingdom, which the Chronicler regards as being God's alone, entrusted to the Davidic family as his representatives; cf. 1 Chr. 17:14.

11. the daughter of the king: cf. N. Avigad, *IEJ* 28 (1978), pp. 146–51. **and wife of Jehoiada the priest:** it has often been thought that this addition is intended to justify **Jehoshabeath's**

presence in the temple, but since in any case women were not admitted such a supposition is unnecessary. The addition may, of course, be 'a mere surmise on the part of the Chronicler due to the fact that the infant prince enjoyed the protection of Jehoiada' (CM), but the possibility cannot be ruled out that in fact the text of Kings is defective at this point. The repetitious nature of the verse is generally agreed to testify to some confusion in its transmission; perhaps the same is true of Kings.

23:1–21. For the account of Joash's coronation and the killing of Athaliah the Chronicler has no other source than 2 Kg. 11:4–20. Two main points govern the many alterations he has introduced. (a) His concern has already been noted (p. 313) to make the elevation of Joash to the throne an act of all the people, not just the result of a palace intrigue. (b) In verse 6a he adds to the speech of Jehoiada a prohibition which no doubt reflects his own convictions and which is certainly a principle that was intended to be the practice of his own day: 'Let no one enter the house of the Lord except the priests and ministering Levites; they may enter, for they are holy'. In order to conform his account to this, the Chronicler has had consistently to alter references to 'the Carites' and 'the guards' (foreign mercenaries) of 2 Kg. 11 to expressions for the priestly and Levitical temple guard; in addition to the commentaries, cf. Welch, *Post-Exilic Judaism*, pp. 207–9. Other differences will be noted in the comments below.

23:1. entered into a compact with: cf. D. J. McCarthy, *SVT* 23 (1972), pp. 77–80. **the commanders of hundreds:** contrast 2 Kg. 11:4: 'the captains of the Carites and of the guards'. This illustrates point (b) above, for the names of these **commanders** (as well as the sequel) show that they are to be understood as Levites. As Rudolph notes, with the exception of the otherwise unattested **Elishaphat**, all the names are found elsewhere in priestly or Levitical lists.

2. This is entirely the Chronicler's addition; see point (a) above. It is strongly reminiscent of his well-known theological bias in the early chapters of his account of David's reign. His use of the title **heads of fathers' houses of Israel** is thus particularly appropriate; cf. *IBC*, p. 107. **to Jerusalem:** rather than just to 'the house of the Lord', which befitted the smaller scale plot of 2 Kg. 11:4.

3. all the assembly: cf. 1 Chr. 13:4; Kings implies that only 'the captains' **made a covenant** (=a). **with the king:** the Chronicler evidently regarded Joash as the legitimate, because Davidic, king even during the period of Athaliah's interregnum. **Let him reign, as the Lord spoke concerning the sons of David:** for this important addition by the Chronicler, see above, p. 134, and *TynB* 28 (1977), pp. 148f. Priest and people are united in their resolve to establish a king of the true line of promise on the throne.

4–5. Neither the arrangements envisaged here nor in 2 Kg. 11:5–7 are entirely clear, due to our ignorance about the detail of the routines that are presupposed and to the fact that there is possible textual corruption in both passages; contrast, for instance, *RSV* and *NEB*. The main points, however, are not in doubt. Jehoiada wished to have as many men present and strategically placed as possible without arousing suspicion. To this, the Chronicler is careful, in conformity with his two guiding principles already noted, to add that the guards were made up of **priests and Levites**, and that **all the people shall be in the courts of the house of the Lord**. The fact that this last addition somewhat conflicts with the secrecy implied by his *Vorlage* will not have concerned him. Such gatherings on the Sabbath may have been a commonplace in his day. **gatekeepers**: literally, 'porters of the thresholds', as at 1 Chr. 9:19 and 22.

6. See point (b) above. **all the people**: the Kings *Vorlage* does not envisage an address to any other but the guards (=a). Thus the expression 'keep the watch of the house of the Lord' (11:7; *RV*) there is to be understood in a fully secular sense, while here it has become **keep the charge of the Lord** in terms of religious duty.

7. The Levites: again added by the Chronicler. **the house**: 2 Kg. 11:8: 'the ranks'. Since this latter word is retained in v. 14, Willi's suggestion (p. 116) that the Chronicler changed it because he no longer understood it is improbable. Rather his concern here is again for the sanctity of the temple.

8. The Levites and all Judah: 2 Kg. 11:9: 'The captains over hundreds' (*RV*) = (b) and (a). **did not dismiss the divisions**: this addition by the Chronicler represents a combination of factors: now that the leading participants are regarded as priests and Levites, the Chronicler will have been picturing their involvement against the background of their service by 'divisions' as practised in his own day (cf. 1 Chr. 23–26, etc.). He has therefore rewritten his source in these terms to indicate that those going off duty did not leave the temple area.

9. small shields: see on 1 Chr. 18:7. It has generally been assumed that this verse originated with the Chronicler and was later added to 2 Kg. 11:10, because the guard of 2 Kg. 11 would be expected already to be armed. However, if the weapons are ceremonial here, as seems likely, the supposition becomes unnecessary, and no contradiction need be found with v. 7.

10. and he set all the people: 2 Kg. 11:11: 'and the guards stood' = (a).

11. The ritual here described has been much discussed, but the scope of the present commentary precludes our entering into this debate; for the Chronicler's secondary addition of **Jehoiada and his sons**, cf. A. Schoors, *OTS* 20 (1977), pp. 93f.

12. the people running (*hāʿām hārāṣîm*): 2 Kg. 11:13 has these two words in reverse order, *hārāṣîn* in the context of that chapter (cf. v. 4) meaning 'guards' and it or 'the people' being probably a secondary gloss; contrast W. Rudolph, *Festschrift Alfred Bertholet zum 80. Geburtstag* (1950), pp. 477f., with the majority of commentators on Kings. The Chronicler, however, knew the text in its present form and was led by the principles which governed his reading of the text as a whole to understand it quite differently.

13. his pillar: we should perhaps follow LXX (and cf. 34:31) and repoint as *ʿomedô*, 'his place'. Either way, the addition of the pronominal suffix shows that it is intended as the equivalent of the *Vorlage*'s 'standing by the pillar, according to the custom', though possibly from a time when 'the custom' itself was no longer known. **at the entrance:** this is the Chronicler's own addition. It probably refers to the entrance from the court of laity to the inner court, according to the plan of the second temple, known to the Chronicler; see the discussion at 6:13. He will not have expected the king normally to enter the areas reserved for the priests. **and the singers with their musical instruments leading in the celebration:** the Chronicler is responsible for this highly characteristic addition.

16. The Chronicler has somewhat simplified his *Vorlage* so as to make of it no more than a solemn act of rededication to God by the whole nation; see the discussion of the similar case of Asa at 15:12, and cf. Japhet, *Ideology*, pp. 98f.; D. J. McCarthy, *SVT* 23 (1972), pp. 77–80; M. Noth, *The Laws in the Pentateuch* (1966), pp. 115f.

17. Though following his *Vorlage* quite closely at this point, the Chronicler will have been in thorough sympathy with the view that rededication to God should immediately express itself in removal of the trappings of foreign cults, especially those introduced under the period of influence from the north, as in the present case.

18. The first part of this verse comes from 2 Kg. 11:18, but the Chronicler then expands considerably (from **under the direction of. . .to the end of v. 19**) in order to illustrate that the cult was restored according to the pattern which he regards as correct. **whom David had organised. . .according to the order of David:** cf. 1 Chr. 15–16 and especially the primary layer of 1 Chr. 23–27. It may be noted again that this passage from the Chronicler clearly presupposes some such ordering as is there described and so tells against the common attribution of the whole of that passage to a later addition. As regularly in the Chronicler's own view, the general arrangements for **the house of the Lord** and for the **singing** are traced back to David, but the prescriptions for the **burnt offerings** go back to what **is written in the law of Moses**; cf. 1 Chr. 6:48–49; 16:39–40, etc. The general tenor of this verse is thus not in doubt. Nevertheless it is slightly awkwardly expressed, so that several commentators prefer to follow the longer and clearer reading of LXX: **under the direction of the** 'priests and the Levites and he appointed the courses of the priests and the Levites' **whom David**. . .

19. the gatekeepers: a reference to the third of the four Levitical divisions in the primary layer of 1 Chr. 23–27. **so that no one should enter who was in any way unclean:** this continues the concern already expressed in v. 6 above.

20–21. The Chronicler now rejoins 2 Kg. 11:19–20, though with the same kind of alterations as those noted earlier in the chapter. Thus **the nobles, the governors of the people** are substituted for 'the Carites, the guards', and **the upper gate** replaces 'the gate of the guards', though according to 27:3 it would not have been built by this time.

Joash under Blessing

24:1–16

The first period of Joash's reign proper is dominated by the beneficial influence of Jehoiada the high priest, and deals on the whole with the restoration of the temple (vv. 4–14). While certainty on such matters is unattainable, there is no point at which the differences from 2 Kg. 12:1–16, many and varied though they be, are of such a kind as to demand the postulation of an alternative source. Furthermore, attempts at harmonisation are far too speculative to be critically satisfying, and, indeed, in the recent case of B. Z. Luria, *Beth Mikra* 52 (1972), pp. 11–20, involve utilising as historically reliable material such as vv. 20–22 which should almost certainly be attributed to the Chronicler himself. Rather, since the differences from 2 Kg. 12 can all be explained on the basis of what we know from elsewhere to be the Chronicler's own interests and methods, and since there are some slight points of verbal contact with 2 Kg. 12, it remains the simplest hypothesis to suppose that the Chronicler has in this passage radically rewritten his *Vorlage*. (For the only point of substance in favour of Rudolph's contrary position, see on vv. 5–6 below.) This very fact should serve as a warning that for other passages which reflect his style and for which we have no copy of his *Vorlage* there may nevertheless be some alternative source which he has similarly drastically rewritten.

1. This verse is parallel with 2 Kg. 12:1, with the regular omission of the synchronism with the northern kingdom; see on 20:31, etc.

2. **all the days of Jehoiada the priest**: contrast 2 Kg. 12:2: 'all his days, because Jehoiada the priest instructed him'. The latter certainly means that the Deuteronomic historian judged the whole of Joash's reign favourably, though he goes on immediately to qualify this with a note about the non-removal of the high places. The Chronicler, by contrast, has omitted this qualification and instead, noting the difficulties which confronted Joash at the end of his reign and his violent death, has divided the reign into two periods, to the first of which the present verse then serves as an introduction.

3. There is no equivalent for this verse in Kings. While it is possible that the information derives from an alternative source, it should not be forgotten that the Chronicler has elsewhere used this device as an indication of God's blessing (see on 1 Chr. 14:3–7; 2 Chr. 11:18–23; 13:21), and that, moreover, the dynasty had all but been extinguished under Athaliah, so that this verse represents its restoration. The role of **Jehoiada** in finding **two wives** for Joash is thus appropriate as an illustration of the Chronicler's reinterpretation of v. 2.

4–14. The restoration of the temple. This account certainly differs radically from 2 Kg. 12:4–16. However, once it is realised that vv. 5b–6 are a secondary addition (see below) it can be more readily appreciated that the Chronicler has not rewritten, but simply passed over, 2 Kg. 12:4–8, a passage which represents quite a sharp criticism of the priesthood. Thereafter the differences can be attributed to three of the major emphases of his work as a whole: (a) He has involved the Levites in the restoration. This fits well with his emphasis on part of their role as temple ministers (cf. 1 Chr. 23:4, etc.). (b) His concern to draw out the parallels between the Jerusalem temple and the tabernacle has been repeatedly noted, especially during the account of its building under Solomon. This is sufficient to explain the reference to 'the tax' which Moses collected in vv. 9–10 and to the joyful way in which the people contributed. (c) It is generally agreed that the arrangements made in 2 Kg. 12:4–16 were intended to, and did, establish a continuing system for the maintenance of the temple (cf. 2 Kg. 22:4ff.). The Chronicler, however, as is well known, was more concerned to examine and explain the response to God of each individual generation. Consequently, he has chosen to present this as a single act of restoration (v. 4), which was necessitated by a particular situation (v. 7; cf. Kittel). Moreover, we can thus understand how it was possible for there to be money left over to devote to other purposes (v. 14)

which explicitly contrasts with the presentation of 2 Kg. 12:13-14.
Other minor points of difference will be explained below.

4. This represents the Chronicler's own heading to the account,
and it at once explains his different understanding of it; see point
(c) above.

5-6. Welch (*WC*, pp. 78-80) argued that these verses were a later
addition, a position merely rejected, not refuted, by Rudolph. However, Welch's arguments were, perhaps, stronger than Rudolph
realised, and more can be added to them, though against Welch it
will be maintained that v. 5a also belongs to the Chronicler. It must
first be observed that there has evidently been some kind of intrusion
before v. 7 since that verse explains why Joash wanted to repair the
temple and is quite unsuitable as a sequel to v. 6. Second, as the
narrative stands, verse 8 represents a new idea by the king, a means
for collecting the tax to replace the failed plan of vv. 5-6. This,
however, then leads to an unsatisfactory form of narration, for we
are left without any indication of the final outcome of the arrangements made in v. 5. Third, the expression used in v. 6 for **the tent
of testimony** (*'ōhel hāʿēḏûṯ*) occurs only here in Chronicles; contrast 1 Chr. 16:39; 21:29, etc. Fourth, **the chief** (*hārōʾš*, v. 6) is
found only here in this absolute form; contrast the Chronicler's own
regular use of 'the chief priest', e.g. in v. 11. Fifth, whereas in 5a
the priests and the Levites are summoned, in 5b-6 it is only **the
Levites** who are reprimanded; the role of the priests is thus left
unexplained. Sixth, it would be surprising to find such a criticism
of the Levites in the Chronicler's work. Rudolph used this point to
argue that the material here must therefore come from another
source. However, since there is no other substantial evidence to
support this case, and since there is no hint of this unfavourable
attitude elsewhere in the story, it seems rather to point to the
secondary status of this section. Finally, the expression **from year
to year** conflicts with what we have seen to be the clear understanding of this incident by the Chronicler as a single act of repair.

It may therefore be concluded that vv. 5b (from **from year. . .**)
and 6 have been added later to the Chronicler's original account.
(In saying this it is, of course, recognised that such precision is
highly speculative; what is really meant is that the substance of 5a
accords well with the Chronicler's narrative, and the substance of
5b-6 does not. Certainty about the exact form of the Chronicler's
own text is now unattainable.) Their criticism of the Levites alone,
together with indications from the vocabulary used, suggest that
they may come from the pro-priestly reviser whose hand has been
seen particularly in 1 Chronicles, and that they were intended both
to draw the whole account closer to that in 2 Kg. 12 (note the

attempt to turn it into the start of a continuing arrangement as well as the verbal parallel between 6*a* and 2 Kg. 12:7*a*) and at the same time to soften the criticism of the priesthood expressed in the earlier version.

Meanwhile, for the Chonicler himself, the arrangements made in v. 5*a* are the same as those executed in vv. 8ff. The order to **go out to the cities of Judah** is picked up in the proclamation made in v. 9. **and gather:** this is used quite generally. The detail of how it was to be done follows in vv. 8ff. **all Israel:** the use in v. 9 demonstrates that this title is here used once again as a symbol of continuity with the generations of earlier times; cf. 12:6. **the tax levied by Moses:** see on v. 9, whose language has influenced the reviser at this point.

7. In the Chronicler's original text, this could represent a continuation of Joash's words from v. 5*a*, in which case the verbs should be rendered in the perfect, not pluperfect, tense. Either way, they continue to be part of the Chronicler's own introduction to the narrative, before he picks up the outline of his *Vorlage* in the next verse. Although the events described have not been previously referred to, the Chronicler may well have supposed that the temple had been thus violated. **the sons of Athaliah:** MT is awkward here. We should perhaps rather read 'Athaliah . . . and her sons', with a number of the versions. The significance of **sons** is disputed; it could be taken literally and so refer to the time before Athaliah murdered them all (22:10). Others think it means rather 'her adherents' (*NEB*), while alternative pointing (*bōneyhā* for *bāneyhā*) would give 'her builders', suggesting that the temple materials, as well as its **dedicated things,** had been used for building the temples of **the Baals.**

8. The Chronicler now loosely follows the account of 2 Kg. 12:9ff. **outside the gate:** contrast 2 Kg. 12:9: 'beside the altar'. Once again, the Chronicler conforms the narrative to the practice of his own day when the laity were not permitted inside the court; see on 23:13, etc.

9. proclamation was made: by the priests and the Levites in conformity with the king's instructions in 5*a*; see above. **the tax that Moses the servant of God laid upon Israel in the wilderness:** not in 2 Kings. The reference is to the half-shekel tax of Exod. 30:11–16 and 38:25f., which was used for the construction of the tabernacle. The Chronicler drew this parallel against his *Vorlage* to further his tabernacle-temple typology noted as point (b) in the introduction to vv. 4–14 above.

10. rejoiced: cf. 1 Chr. 29:9, etc. This is a characteristic mark of the Chronicler's description of the performance of cultic service, as well as perhaps reflecting a more recent well-known event of a similar nature; cf. Neh. 12:44. **until they had finished:** better, 'until it was full' (*NEB*).

11. the Levites (see point (a) above) **brought** the full **chest** to **the king's officers,** more closely defined, in near conformity with 2 Kg. 12:10, as **the king's secretary and the officer of the chief priest.** This latter official may simply be an invention of the Chronicler's so as to provide a parallel for **the king's secretary. when they saw that there was much money in it:** again, a close literary echo of 2 Kg. 12:10.

12. This verse is the equivalent of 2 Kg. 12:11-12. It is largely rewritten, though there are some points of verbal contact. **those who had charge of the work of the house of the Lord:** see on 1 Chr. 23:4.

14. As explained in point (c) of the introduction to this paragraph, the difference between this verse and 2 Kg. 12:13-14 is to be accounted for on the basis of the two works' different understandings of the nature of the task being described. There may also be a further point of comparison with the Mosaic tax, part of which had been used for furnishing the tabernacle (Exod. 35:10ff.; cf. point (b) above). For the last sentence of this verse, see on v. 2. The reference to regular **burnt offerings** is intended as a symbol of full cultic faithfulness throughout the period of Jehoiada's lifetime.

15-16. Details of Jehoiada's death and burial are supplied by the Chronicler. There is no clear evidence to suggest an alternative source for this material, as in his presentation each item is to be regarded as symbolic rather than necessarily literal. **old and full of days:** see on 1 Chr. 23:1 for this indication of honour. **a hundred and thirty years old:** long life is a well-known mark of blessing. At his death Jehoiada was older than such great figures as Sarah (Gen. 23:1); Joseph (Gen. 50:26), Aaron (Num 33:39), Moses (Dt. 34:7) and Joshua (Jos. 24:29). **they buried him in the city of David among the kings:** we have already seen several times that the Chronicler uses the place of burial as a means of expressing his assessment of the quality of a person's life; e.g. 21:20; 22:9, and contrast v. 25 below. Clearly no greater honour in this respect was possible than that recorded here of Jehoiada. The explanation provided by the Chronicler makes it quite plain that this is his intention: there is no suggestion that he is hereby favouring the tendency in the post-exilic period to merge the roles of king and high priest.

Joash under Judgment

24:17-27

The Chronicler will have known from 2 Kg. 12:17-21 and perhaps from some other sources that, despite the reform which marked the start of Joash's reign, he had eventually to submit to the Syrians and was himself assassinated. No religious explanation is offered by Kings for these disasters, but the Chronicler provides for them a framework which is familiar from other parts of his work, and he links the whole with the loss of the good counsel of Jehoiada. The framework opens with a falling into sin described in very general terms and with some characteristic vocabulary of the Chronicler himself.

Contrary to what is often thought, punishment does not follow automatically, but rather prophets are sent in order first to urge repentance leading to forgiveness; compare the similar cases of Rehoboam (12:1-12) and Jehoshaphat (17-20) amongst others. As with Asa (16:7ff.), it was the rejection of these prophetic warnings which led to judgment, a pattern which is repeated in Chronicles until the final punishment of the exile itself (cf. 36:15f.). Moreover, S. Zalevsky, *Beth Mikra* 65 (1976), pp. 278-88, has helpfully pointed out that the Chronicler is careful to establish a close connection between sin and punishment. As will be noted below, there are several examples of an exact correspondence in this regard. The section as a whole, therefore, serves as a warning to the Chronicler's readers, but holds open as always the possibility of avoiding disaster if they will only be awakened by such an example to the necessity for their own repentance.

Although it is by no means certain that the Chronicler had access to other sources for his composition here, it seems easiest to assume that he did have some tradition about Zechariah (see on v. 20), together with an alternative account of the Syrian invasion and its after-effects (see on vv. 23-26). Even here, however, there are many marks of his own hand, and he has certainly reshaped the narrative in order to use it as a means of conveying the theological lessons just noted.

17. after the death of Jehoiada: contrast vv. 2 and 14. **the princes of Judah:** cf. 12:5 and 6. As the change there suggests, so here too the Chronicler may have used this title in specific preference to 'princes of Israel' as an indication of his disapproval. **the king hearkened to them:** the scene is reminiscent of the account of the division of the monarchy under Rehoboam, 10:1-6.

18. they forsook the house of the Lord: this verb is familiar as one of the Chronicler's favourites; see on 12:1, and note vv. 20 and

24 below. Its punishment is that God will 'forsake them' (cf. 15:2), so that military defeat becomes an inevitability; it is only those who 'rely on' him whom he 'helps'. The same word is also used in v. 25, translated in *RSV* by 'leaving him (severely wounded)'. Although the use there may be quite neutral, it is tempting to think that the Chronicler intended this as a further pointer to the equivalence of sin and punishment. **the house of the Lord:** though an unusual object for 'forsake', it is fully intelligible in the context of this chapter and is in line with the Chronicler's ideology (see on 12:1). **and served the Asherim and the idols:** see on v. 23 for the punishment. **wrath:** cf. 19:2; 29:8 and 32:25f.

19. The language of this verse is somewhat stereotyped, recurring both in Chronicles (e.g. 36:15f.) and elsewhere (e.g. 2 Kg. 17:13ff.; Jer. 7:25f.; 25:4; Neh. 9:26, 29f.); on this function of the prophets in Chronicles, cf. Japhet, *Ideology*, pp. 154–66, and Seeligmann, *SVT* 29 (1978), pp. 275f.

20. the Spirit of God took possession of (literally, 'clothed itself with'): cf. 1 Chr. 12:18, and more generally 2 Chr. 15:1. **Zechariah:** not mentioned elsewhere in *OT*. As noted at 15:1, it is usually the Chronicler's practice to attribute 'sermons' to prophetical figures already known from tradition. It may be that on this occasion he was content just to postulate a **son of Jehoiada the priest** to serve as a foil to Joash and to underline the contrast between the two parts of the reign, but on the whole it seems more likely that he inherited the name, and perhaps some information about his death. His brief sermon, however, as in other such cases, must be attributed to the Chronicler himself. **the commandments of the Lord:** contrast the evil 'command of the king' which is obeyed in the next verse. **prosper:** cf. 1 Chr. 22:11 and 13; 2 Chr. 7:11; 13:12; 20:20; 26:5; 31:21 and 32:30. **Because you have forsaken. . .:** cf. 15:2 and v. 18 above.

21. they conspired against him: note v. 25 below, where the equivalence is explicitly spelt out. A procedure similar to the case of Naboth may be envisaged; cf. 1 Kg. 21:8–14. **in the court of the house of the Lord:** contrast the care to prevent such an occurrence in the case of Athaliah taken earlier by Zechariah's father; 23:14. It is probable that Mt. 23:35; Lk. 11:51 refer to this same incident, indicating that Chronicles stood last in the canon at that time.

22. kindness: K. D. Sakenfeld, *The Meaning of Hesed in the Hebrew Bible* (1978), pp. 158f., finds here the pre-exilic, secular meaning of 'deliverance' for *ḥesed*, though in itself that is scarcely sufficient evidence to postulate dependence on an earlier source. **killed:** appropriately, the same word is used in v. 25 below ('slew him'). **"May the Lord see and avenge!":** Zechariah's last words echo the cry of Exod. 5:21, except that there 'judge' replaces **avenge** here, though with little difference of meaning. This may have continued in the Chronicler's mind to the end of v. 24, where he carefully records that 'they executed judgment on Joash'. It is difficult not to point out the contrast with Lk. 23:34 and Ac. 7:60.

23-24. This account of an Aramaean invasion differs markedly from 2 Kg. 12:7-18. There Hazael, king of Syria, is bought off by Joash before he attacks Jerusalem. Here, however, (a) Hazael is not referred to by name, but is merely **the king of Damascus**; (b) it is clearly implied that whereas **the army of the Syrians came up against Joash** their king was not with them, but stayed behind in Syria; and (c) a battle is recorded here which cannot be reconciled with the account in 2 Kg. 12. Thus the only substantial point of contact is the reference to **spoil**. Because of these differences, not all of which serve any positive purpose in the Chronicler's presentation, it is probable that the account derives from an alternative source. As will be shown, however, it has been so worked over by the Chronicler in order to contribute to the purpose of the passage as a whole that it is impossible now to be sure what shape the original account had and what its connection was, if any, with that of 2 Kg. 12:17-18.

and destroyed all the princes of the people from among the people: this expression of careful selection is intended to show that it was those who had sinned (vv. 17-18) who now were punished. Moreover, whereas the word **destroyed** might appear curious in this context, it in fact exactly fits on the basis of the Chronicler's usage elsewhere. At 12:7 and 25:15-16 the same word occurs as the punishment, either potential or actual, for adopting the worship of foreign gods, and it is this of which the princes were guilty in v. 18. **with few men:** several times the Chronicler has stressed that a small Judean army could defeat an enemy which was numerically superior if they would rely on God (cf. 13:3 with 13-18; 14:9-13 and 20:2 with 20-23). Now, however, the tables are turned **because they had forsaken the Lord** (see on v. 18). Thus the whole of v. 24 must be attributed to the Chronicler in its present expression. **Thus they executed judgment on Joash:** see on v. 22 above. On the basis of Deuteronomic phraseology, Zalevsky further suggests that there is here intended a deliberate punishment for 'transgressing the commandments' in v. 20, but this is over-subtle.

25. The death of Joash is more closely connected with the foregoing than in 2 Kg. 12:20. Despite a number of differences between the two accounts, most can be attributed to the Chronicler's scheme described above, so that there is no need to postulate an alternative source. **leaving him:** see on v. 18 above. **severely wounded:** this may have been the Chronicler's own conjecture, based on the fact that in his account of the Aramaean invasion Joash was involved in a battle. **his servants conspired against him:** as in 2 Kg. 12:20, which may also have encouraged the Chronicler to frame Joash's sin in the way he has done at v. 20 above. **because of the blood of the son of Jehoiada the priest:** this is clearly the Chronicler's own interpretation, both drawing out the exact nature of divine retribution noted throughout this section and reminding the reader, by way of this somewhat contrived manner of bringing in a reference to **Jehoiada**, of the two phases of Joash's reign. **and slew him:** see on v. 22 for an explanation of the Chronicler's change of verb here (*hārag* for *hikkāh*). **on his bed:** this need be no more than a conjecture by the Chronicler for the difficult phrase of 2 Kg. 12:20, 'in the house of Millo, on the way that goes down to Silla' (Willi, p. 122). **but they did not bury him in the tombs of the kings:** according to 2 Kg. 12:21, he was nevertheless buried 'with his fathers'. Though it would be possible to conjecture a harmonisation, that would miss the point of the Chronicler's modification, which once again is intended to express his evaluation of Joash's reign; see on v. 16 above.

26. The names of the conspirators differ slightly from 2 Kg. 12:21, but in ways that can be explained in terms of textual corruption. Only here, however, is one linked with Ammon and the other with Moab. At what point this entered the tradition is unclear. Ackroyd appears to attribute it to the Chronicler himself, suggesting that 'when king (or people) turn to alien gods, their judgment will be at the hands of alien instruments of divine wrath', a suggestion which accords well with the Chronicler's method in this passage.

27. Commentary: this same word ('midrash') is translated as 'story' by *RSV* in its only other occurrence, 13:22, where it was connected with a prophet. We have noted the possibility that the Chronicler had access to an alternative source at vv. 20 and 23, but that otherwise he has followed the account in Kings, often with radical, though intelligible, rewriting. This at once raises the suspicion that in fact he did not have much else to go on. This is reinforced by his statement that the commentary included **many oracles against him.** Judging by his practice elsewhere, we might have expected the Chronicler to include more of these, had they really been available to him. It is thus doubtful whether, as many commentators have done, we should seize on this particular title as a significant clue to unravelling the complex question of the nature of the Chronicler's sources. As at 13:22, it need be no more than another variation on his source citation formulae; see the Introduction, section F.

AMAZIAH

25:1–28

For the opening and concluding parts of Amaziah's reign, the Chronicler has based himself closely on the parallel in 2 Kg. 14:1–22. The central section of the Chronicler's account (vv. 5–16), however, includes much otherwise unknown material, and is paralleled only by the brief account of Amaziah's defeat of the Edomites in 2 Kg 14:7. Evidence which suggests that part of this material at least came from an earlier source will be presented at two or three points in the comments below.

Despite this measure of dependence on inherited material, however, the Chronicler has clearly managed once again to use it all to illustrate themes which are by now familiar. Indeed, these themes are picked out by what are probably his own explanatory insertions (e.g. vv. 14–16 and 20), which show that part of his concern has been to provide a theological explanation for the events recorded in his *Vorlage*. The first period of Amaziah's reign is mainly judged favourably, and thus is marked by victory over the Edomites. This is not to say that he never fell into error; clearly, his hiring of Israelite mercenaries was, to the Chronicler, reprehensible, as a prophet warns, but the underlying character of this period of Amaziah's reign is demonstrated by the fact of his heeding the prophetic warning and taking action in the light of it.

The second half of his reign, however, contrasts explicitly with the first. After turning to the worship of the Edomite idols, Amaziah this time rejects the warning from a prophet, becomes proud (contrast 7:14) rather than 'reliant', and so suffers military defeat and personal tragedy (see the notes on v. 27). The pattern is clearly reminiscent of the second half of Joash's reign just recorded (see on 24:17–27), as of several others before him. Attention may again be drawn in particular to the role of the prophet; retribution for sin is not inevitable, and it usually only follows the rejection of an appeal for repentance. When that appeal is heeded, however, the Chronicler is anxious to stress God's restoring forgiveness. Both possibilities are well illustrated in this chapter.

1–4. The initial characterisation of Amaziah's reign is based on 2 Kg. 14:2–6 with some slight, but familiar, variations (see, for instance, on 20:31). **yet not with a blameless heart:** this alteration by the Chronicler of 2 Kg. 14:3 is necessitated both by his reinterpretation of the second half of the reign and by the qualification which he has introduced into the first.

5–13. Amaziah's successful campaign against Edom; cf. 2 Kg. 14:7, which the Chronicler has expanded with the help of additional material, the precise extent of which, however, it is not always easy to determine.

5. The substance of this notice concerning the conscript army is undoubtedly drawn from an older source; for a full discussion, see on 14:8. **and Benjamin:** Welten, p. 92, argues that this is a later gloss, since it does not fit well with the first part of the verse. More likely, however, it is a redactional insertion by the Chronicler himself, as sometimes elsewhere (cf. Welten, p. 81), and thus in itself an additional pointer to the fact that the Chronicler is here handling inherited material. **three hundred thousand:** it is not clear how this large number is to be interpreted. See on 13:3 for some possibilities. Unlike there and 14:8, however, it is not possible in the present case to relate this figure to the size of the opposing army. CM observe that the army of Amaziah is much smaller than Asa's or Jehoshaphat's, and that this may help explain his action in the next verse.

6. This introduces the account of Amaziah's fateful attempt to hire mercenaries **from Israel** (vv. 6–10, 13), of which there is no hint in Kings. Two arguments suggest that the basis of the story derives from a separate source: (a) the action of the mercenaries in v. 13 contrasts with the implications of the promise in v. 9. Since the latter probably expresses the Chronicler's own viewpoint, this would suggest that in v. 13 he was writing under the constraint of a source; (b) this is reinforced by the observation that in the Chronicler's own view Amaziah had done nothing to deserve the treatment meted out in v. 13. It is thus difficult to see what motive could have guided him were the whole account pure fabrication. It is more probable that he felt obliged to include an account which was in itself somewhat embarrassing to him, but that he has been able to turn this to his advantage in making it the vehicle for an example of response to prophetic warning without being able fully to integrate all the details of the story into his pattern. If this conjecture is correct, vv. 6 and 13 will include most, if not all, of the account in the Chronicler's source, though the historical reason for the Israelite's rampage on their way home is left without explanation. If we might guess that it was without adequate cause, but was simply prompted by a desire for personal gain, it might help explain Amaziah's otherwise foolish challenge to Jehoahaz of Israel which followed. Since the material relates to the history of the Judean army, it could well have come from the same source as v. 5.

7. a man of God: a general title for a prophet. The fact that he is unnamed suggests, by comparison with the Chronicler's practice in this matter elsewhere, that he may be composing freely. He gives two reasons why Amaziah should **not let the army of Israel go with**

him. First, **the Lord is not with Israel.** The basis for this has been explained at 13:4–12 above, so that no further detail is supplied here. It is to be noted that this statement does not necessarily imply the irrevocable rejection of Israel, as comparison with 15:2 makes clear. It will last for so long as Israel continues to reject God. Meanwhile, to ally with them is to court disaster, as the history of Jehoshaphat has shown (chs 17–20). **all these Ephraimites:** this explanatory note may simply be intended to make clear that in this verse **Israel** refers to the northern kingdom. However, since that is in any case not in doubt, it more probably alludes to the fact that the mercenaries were hired specifically from the border region with Judah.

8. This verse provides the second reason why Amaziah should not use his mercenaries. Unfortunately MT appears to be corrupt, though the general sense is not in serious doubt. (*RSV* conveys this sense, though not by the most probable emendation.) The Chronicler has already provided examples to show that **God has power to help or to cast down,** irrespective of numbers (e.g. 13:13ff.; 14:9ff., etc.). What he requires is that the armies of Judah should 'rely' on him. Since the hiring of the mercenaries betrays Amaziah's lack of faith, however, **God will cast you down before the enemy** in spite of his apparent superiority.

9. Amaziah's reply, though somewhat feeble in itself, is sufficient to indicate his acceptance of what the prophet has said, and on this basis he is assured that the Lord will not allow him to lose by the exercise of faith. This assurance, which continues the free composition of the Chronicler (see on v. 7) and which reflects his viewpoint as seen repeatedly elsewhere, nevertheless clashes with the outcome in v. 13; see on v. 6 for the consequences of this observation.

10. Amaziah discharged the army: as a historical conjecture, J. R. Bartlett, *JTS* ns 20 (1969), p. 14, noting the good relationships between Israel and Edom, has suggested that 'possibly the Israelite soldiers were not thought to be reliable against the Edomites'. The reaction of the discharged mercenaries (**very angry . . . in fierce anger**) is to be explained by the fact that they would normally have expected to share in the spoils of the campaign. Thus the Chronicler has neatly managed to provide a rational motive for their action in v. 13, even though it still does not square with his ideology.

11. The campaign against Edom is told in dependence upon 2 Kg. 14:7, the first half of which corresponds with the essence of the present verse.

12. 2 Kg. 14:7*b* reads 'and took Sela by storm, and called it Joktheel, which is its name to this day'. Since 'Sela' can be both a proper name and a word meaning **rock,** and since it has been suggested that 'Joktheel' may mean 'God destroys', it seems likely that the Chronicler has preserved a variant tradition which is alluded to, but not explained, in his *Vorlage*. The identity of the site referred to is uncertain, despite many attempts to link it with Petra; cf. C.-M. Bennett, *PEQ* 98 (1966), pp. 123-6.

13. See on vv. 6 and 10 above for the origins of this material and its explanation. **Samaria** is out of place here, since it is well within the northern kingdom. It must be an error for a Judean town. Rudolph suggests Migron (cf. 1 Sam. 14:2; Isa. 10:28), which is orthographically similar.

14-16. None of this paragraph is found in 2 Kg. 14. It can all be explained on the basis of the theological constraints which the Chronicler will have felt, so that there is no need to look further for the origins of the material. The points of contact with 1 Kg. 13 and Am. 7 which P. R. Ackroyd observes, in G. W. Coats and B. O. Long (eds), *Canon and Authority* (1977), pp. 80-1, are quite general and so do not demand that 'the Chronicler was making use of a form of the same tradition which we have in the other two passages'; it may simply be that, perhaps even unconsciously, these earlier narratives have themselves exerted some influence on his shaping of the narrative.

14. According to J. R. Bartlett, *JSOT* 4 (1977), p. 7, this is the only passage in *OT* where the gods of **the Edomites** are condemned (see also M. Rose, *ibid.*, p. 30). Moreover, such worship of the gods of a defeated nation by a Judean king is also unique, and historically improbable. When we add to this the fact that this narrative is used in v. 20, which is the Chronicler's own insertion into the Kings *Vorlage*, to explain Amaziah's defeat by Joash of Israel, it becomes hard to escape the conclusion that he has composed this verse too for that very purpose. Very little is known of **the gods of the men of Seir** (Edom), but cf. the article of M. Rose mentioned above and J. R. Bartlett, *JSOT* 5 (1978), pp. 29-38.

15. Once again, retribution is not the immediate sequel of **the Lord** being **angry**, but first **Amaziah** is warned of the folly of his actions by **a prophet**, again unnamed (see on v. 7). Though his speech is cut short, the Chronicler has him say enough to reveal the absurdity of the situation (contrast 28:23).

16. The king's rejection of the prophetic warning seals his fate, as the prophet's rejoinder makes clear. The irony of a king who rejects God's **counsel**, and then takes human counsel (v. 17) to his own undoing is underlined by a word-play that is quite typical of the Chronicler (cf. 13:7-8). Thus from the same root ($y's$) come **counsellor, has determined, counsel** and 'took counsel' (v. 17). **to**

destroy you: for the rather technical use of this verb in Chronicles, see on 24:23. **and have not listened:** as also at v. 20.

17-28. The remainder of the account of Amaziah's reign is drawn from 2 Kg. 14:8–14, 17–20. For details, see the commentaries on Kings. By his handling of the previous narrative, the Chronicler has already set up the situation in such a way that he can follow his *Vorlage* quite closely in order to convey his message. Here and there, however, as will be pointed out below, he adds an occasional touch to remove all doubt as to his intentions. The Chronicler's whole presentation of Amaziah's reign is thus bound together in a way that is not true of 2 Kg. 14.

17. Then Amaziah king of Judah took counsel: this is the Chronicler's own introduction, in which he uses a forceful play on words to connect the following narrative with what precedes; see on v. 16.

19. I have smitten: a conjectural emendation. MT has 'you have smitten', following 2 Kg. 14:10. **your heart has lifted you up in boastfulness:** while found also in the *Vorlage*, reflection on this condemnation may well have influenced the Chronicler in his overall shaping of his account of Amaziah's reign, since pride, which implies a lack of dependence upon God, was in his view a particularly heinous sin; cf. 26:16, etc.

20. Apart from the first phrase, this is the Chronicler's own explanatory comment, expressed with some of his most characteristic vocabulary. See also the comments on v. 14. Theologically, the verse is closely comparable with 10:15 and 22:7.

24. and Obed-edom with them: *NEB* translates more accurately, 'in the care of Obed-edom'. This phrase is not found in 2 Kg. 14:14. According to the Chronicler himself, Obed-edom was a Levitical singer (see on 1 Chr. 15:18). Only later did he and his family become gatekeepers with particular responsibility for the storehouse (1 Chr. 26:15). This phrase is thus probably a later marginal comment.

26. and Israel: added by the Chronicler; see on 16:11.

27. From the time when he turned away from the Lord: this is added by the Chronicler in order to link Amaziah's violent death with his worship of the Edomite gods (vv. 14 and 20). The artificial nature of the explanation is shown by the fact that the **conspiracy** (see also 24:26) would have had to last at least fifteen years (cf. v. 25).

28. David: a well-attested emendation for MT 'Judah', and probably correct, although MT is possible, since Jerusalem is referred to as 'the city of Judah' in extra-biblical sources (CM and Myers).

UZZIAH

26:1–23

Although Uzziah reigned for fifty-two years, the Deuteronomic historian has chosen to record only the briefest outline of his reign, 2 Kg. 14:21–22; 15:1–7. The only two points of any historical substance to emerge from this outline are that 'he built Elath and restored it to Judah' (14:22), and that 'the Lord smote the king, so that he was a leper to the day of his death' (15:5).

It is not difficult to see either the questions which this would have raised in the Chronicler's mind or how he would have chosen to answer them. On the one hand, the length of Uzziah's reign, together with the restoration of Elath, would have indicated to him that Uzziah enjoyed God's blessing; on the other hand, the statement that 'the Lord smote the king' would have suggested that he was being punished for some otherwise unrecorded sin. The solution to this difficulty lay to hand in 2 Kg. 15:3 (cf. 2 Chr. 26:4): 'And he did what was right in the eyes of the Lord, according to all that his father Amaziah had done'. Whereas in Kings this is intended in a fully positive sense, the Chronicler has already presented his account of Amaziah according to a two-part structure (see on ch. 25 above). It is not surprising, therefore, to find that he has done the same in the case of Uzziah, thereby managing to explain the evidence of both blessing and of judgment included in his *Vorlage*.

The effects of this restructuring may be easily seen in the chapter, and indeed, as regularly noted elsewhere, the Chronicler has highlighted them by the addition of some phrases which are so clearly editorial, and which so reflect his vocabulary and theology, that they must be attributed to him personally. Thus after the opening notices about the reign (vv. 1–4), he has added a note in v. 5 which points to a parallel with the reign of Joash (ch. 24) in that the first and good period of each king was under the guidance of a faithful spiritual mentor, and which then invites the reader to expect that a change will come later by adding that 'as long as he sought the Lord, God made him prosper'. (On the characteristic vocabulary of this passage and the others mentioned in this paragraph, see the detailed comments below.) The positive period of the reign (vv. 6–15) is then divided into two parts by the catchword 'for he became very strong' (v. 8) and 'till he was strong' (v. 15); the passages deal with foreign and home affairs respectively. In both cases God 'helped' him (vv. 7 and 16), and, as in the case of David in particular, 'his fame spread' far and wide (vv. 8 and 15; cf. 1 Chr. 14:17. 2 Chr. 9 and 17 are similar). Pride in achievement, however, led to Uzziah's downfall, exactly as in the case of Rehoboam (12:1), though the accounts of Joash and Amaziah are comparable. Moreover, his sin is twice described by the verb *m'l* (see on 1 Chr. 10:13), and judgment falls only after a warning by the high priest has been rejected (cf. 24:20–22; 25:14–16, etc.). It is thus apparent that by his almost stereotyped presentation the Chronicler has not only provided an explanatory interpretation of his *Vorlage*, but has also brought forcefully home to his readers that such patterns or paradigms of behaviour and of divine recompense recur with almost monotonous regularity. The lessons to be drawn from this are obvious.

As already indicated, the main part of this chapter (vv. 5–20) is found only in Chronicles. In addition, we have seen that the Chronicler's own hand is evident throughout. Nevertheless, there is an extraordinarily wide consensus of opinion that some, at least, of the notices relating to the first period of the regin, vv. 6–15, are drawn from earlier and authentic sources. Naturally, each item will need to be discussed below on its own merits. Two general points, though, will need to be borne in mind throughout. First, it is a virtual certainty that for so long a reign as Uzziah's there must have been more recorded than was included in Kings. Since we have repeatedly found evidence elsewhere that the Chronicler did have access to some extra-biblical material of pre-exilic origin, it is not unreasonable to suppose in principle that the same may have been the case here. Secondly, the reign of Uzziah, much of which was paralleled by that of Jeroboam II of Israel, was probably a time of comparative prosperity and even territorial expansion for the two kingdoms (cf. H. Tadmor, *Scripta Hierosolymitana* 8 [1961], pp. 232–71; H. Donner, in *IJH*, p. 395). External conditions for such a brief expansion were right, and the biblical testimony is impressive; cf. the record of the eighth-century prophets as well as 2 Kg. 14:22, 25–27, etc. There is thus much to be said in general terms in favour of the Chronicler's portrayal of the character of Uzziah's reign.

1–4. These introductory verses reproduce 2 Kg. 14:21–22 and 15:2–3 without substantial change.

1. Uzziah: so consistently in 2 Chr. (though contrast 1 Chr. 3:12), whereas in 2 Kg. he is more usually (though not always) called 'Azariah'. Some have argued that this reflects the difference between his regnal or throne name and his personal name (so A. M. Honeyman, *JBL* 67 [1948], pp. 20–22). However, since both names are used interchangeably even for the period of his rule, and since the two verbal roots *'zr* and *'zz* which underlie the names converged in the course of time so that each could stand for the other (G. Brin, *Leshonenu* 24 [1959–60], pp. 8–14), it now appears probable to most scholars that the two forms are simply variants of the same name. The Chronicler may have preferred **Uzziah** in order to avoid confusion with Azariah the high priest in vv. 17–20, though the name Azariah itself may have also influenced him in that ʿzr, 'help', is a leading theme of the chapter as a whole.

4. according to all that his father Amaziah had done: see the introduction above. Since for the Chronicler this already involves a qualification of the first half of the verse in temporal terms, he has omitted 2 Kg. 15:4 (as with 2 Kg. 14:4 at 25:2), since this would imply a qualification of the whole of Uzziah's reign.

5. This is the Chronicler's own introduction to the first half of the reign; see above. **to seek God . . . he sought the Lord:** see on 1 Chr. 10:14. **in the days of Zechariah:** cf. 24:2. Zechariah, a common name, is not otherwise known. In view of the Chronicler's practice elsewhere (see on 15:1), it is probable that he found a reference to a Zechariah in association with Uzziah in one of his sources. Thus neither the Zechariah of 24:20 nor of Isa. 8:2 can be the direct origin of this tradition, though one or the other may in a confused manner have entered the tradition prior to the Chronicler. **God made him prosper:** this is one of the Chronicler's favourite expressions for indicating God's blessing; see the passages listed at 24:20.

6–8. This first additional paragraph from the Chronicler, intended to illustrate how Uzziah prospered, gives some account of his foreign affairs. There is no reason to doubt its substantial accuracy. (Even Welten, pp. 153–63, concedes that v. 6a was drawn from a reliable source.) Unlike many of the Chronicler's battle reports, this passage is concise and specific, with none of the lengthy expansions which we have come to recognise as characteristic of his own composition. Moreover, the place-names involved, all relating to the south and south-western borders of the kingdom, make excellent geo-political sense; cf. Rinaldi, *SVT* 9 (1963), pp. 225–35, and J. Gray, in *TI*, p. 76. Expansion to the north was out of the question, in view of the strength of Jeroboam's rule in Israel at the time, but the south offered opportunities not only for internal economic advance (see on v. 10), but also for trade. This is the probable explanation for Uzziah's restoration of the strategic port of Elath (v. 2), and an attempt to control the trade routes provides an intelligible motive for Uzziah's further activities described here. Finally, a number of fortresses and other building installations found in the Negeb and elsewhere have been taken in a general way as evidence of this expansion under Uzziah; for bibliography, see on v. 10.

6. Jabneh: only here in *OT*, though Jabneel (Jos. 15:11) refers to the same place. It is not otherwise found in literary sources before

the Maccabean period, a fact which argues against pure invention
here by the Chronicler. **and he built cities in the territory of
Ashdod and elsewhere among the Philistines:** this translates only
four words in the Hebrew, and they include a grammatical anomaly
(the unapocopated form *wayyibneh*) and a syntactical problem (**the
territory of** has to be supplied; **Ashdod** and **the Philistines** are
syntactically parallel but do not make a satisfactory pair. There is
no word here for **elsewhere**). In the consonantal text, **and he built**
and **Jabneh** are the same. Two of the remaining three words (**Ashdod** and **the Philistines**) also occur in the first half of the verse. It
is thus probable that the whole of this second half has arisen secondarily as a confused dittograph. It is true that there is some
evidence for building in this area at the time (Myers), but that
would be likely enough without reference to this verse.

7. God helped him: doubtless the Chronicler's own interpretation, further marking this paragraph as an indication of God's
blessing; cf. *OTS* 21 (1981), pp. 166f. Consequently, the underlying
source will have referred to campaigns against two other groups,
both, we suggest, most probably to be located in the Negeb. The
first is described as **the Arabs that dwelt in Gur** (baal should
probably be emended to $w^{e\,c}al$, meaning **and against**, which is otherwise unexpressed; cf. Ehrlich, p. 373). By **Arabs** will be meant
Bedouin tribes. **Gur** is most probably to be identified with the *Gari*
of the Tel el-Amarna letters, an area situated to the east of Beersheba; cf. Alt, *KS* III, pp. 396–409, and Rinaldi, pp. 229f. **the
Meunites:** cf. 20:1. The evidence of this verse points strongly to
their location in the south as well, and it has now been claimed that
there is a reference to them that would fit this; cf. H. Tadmor, 'The
Me'unites in the Book of Chronicles in the light of an Assyrian
Document', *J. Liver Memorial Volume* (1971), pp. 222–30; and cf.
BA 29 (1966), p. 89, citing in restored form a text published by D.
J. Wiseman, *Iraq* 13 (1951), pp. 21–6. If this identification is cor-
rect, it would place the Meunites somewhere in the region of Kadesh
Barnea, another strategic trading centre.

8. the Ammonites: this is contrary to the Chronicler's normal
usage (cf. Welten, p. 160) and unsuitable in the context. LXX suggests that we should again read 'Meunites'. If Tadmor's identification is correct, this will then fit admirably with the Chronicler's own
additional comment that **his fame spread even to the border of
Egypt;** see above, p. 332, and 1 Chr. 14:17, where a similar expression serves likewise as a summary statement for God's blessing on
David. **for he became very strong:** here too the language is typical
of the Chronicler (see the list in CM, pp. 28–36, numbers 38, 39,
87 and 127).

9–15. The second paragraph dealing with the period of Uzziah's prosperity concentrates on internal affairs, principally building (vv. 9–10) and the army (vv. 11–15).

9. That **Uzziah** should have undertaken defensive rebuilding **in Jerusalem** is a virtual certainty following the destruction sustained at the hands of Joash of Israel during the previous reign (25:23). Moreover, in view of the character of the rest of the material in vv. 6–15 it seems quite likely that the information of this verse could similarly have been drawn from some authentic source. Welten, pp. 63–6, however, has cast doubt on this widely-held opinion, principally because in its present form the verse seems more suitable to the period of the Chronicler's own composition. Thus the word **towers** is clearly being used in a quite different sense from v. 10, and its sense here is predominantly attested in the post-exilic period; cf. especially Neh. 3. **The Corner Gate** (at the north-west angle of the city wall) could have been deduced from 25:23, and was still known in later times (Zech. 14:10). **The Valley Gate** is attested only in post-exilic sources, though Neh. 2:13 shows that it was certainly in existence under the monarchy. Though its location has been disputed, a position at the southern end of the city seems most reasonable on the basis of Neh. 3:13 (cf. Alt, *KS* III, pp. 326–47). This, however, is not the stretch of wall which we expect Uzziah to have been repairing. The position is rather similar with **the Angle** (cf. Neh. 3:19f. and 24f.), though it can no longer be precisely identified. It is thus not possible to establish the Chronicler's dependence on a source, although nothing which has been said here is sufficient to disprove that hypothesis either.

10. By contrast, widespread archaeological finds are impressive in their testimony to the authenticity of the notice in this verse. A full survey is impossible here, but mention may be made of appropriate finds at such sites as Qumran (cf. de Vaux, *Archaeology and the Dead Sea Scrolls* [1973], p. 94; P. Benoit *et al.*, *Discoveries in the Judaean Desert II: Les Grottes de Murabba'at* [1960], p. 95), in the Negeb around Beersheba at Hurvat 'Uzzah and Khirbet al-Gharra (cf. Y. Aharoni, *IEJ* 8 [1958], p. 37; N. Glueck, *Rivers in the Desert* [1959], pp. 168–80), in the Nahal Seelim area (cf. Y. Aharoni *IEJ* 11 [1961], pp. 15f.), at Kadesh Barnea (M. Dothan, *IEJ* 15 [1965], pp. 134–51), Arad (Y. Aharoni and R. Amiran, *IEJ* 14 [1964], pp. 131–47), and so on. (It should be noted that the evidence from some of these sites is ambiguous, a date in Jehoshaphat's reign, for instance, being preferred by some scholars.) For more general surveys, see, in addition to the commentaries, Y. Aharoni, *Land*, p. 314; A. Feuillet, *VT* 11 (1961), pp. 270–91; Rinaldi, *SVT* 9

(1963), pp. 226-8; Welten, pp. 24-7; W. Zimmerli, *ZDPV* 75 (1959), pp. 148-51.

towers: watchtowers, for the defence of the **herds**; cf. 1 Chr. 27:25. **the wilderness:** of Judah and the Negeb. Archaeological surveys have shown that by careful management these areas were opened up for agricultural development at certain periods. **the Shephelah:** the foothills towards the coastal plain, west of Jerusalem. This ties in well with his defeat of the Philistines (v. 6). It is likely that the following three regional indicators should also be translated as proper names. The reference to **the plain** (note the slightly odd singular here) could thus be transliterated (Mishor), and perhaps be identified with the plain of Sharon, though others look, less probably, for a transjordanian setting. **the hills:** clearly the hill-country of Judah. **the fertile lands:** again this is better taken as a place name, the Carmel, not to be confused, of course, with the well-known mountain of the same name. Rather, a district near Maon, some way south of Hebron, is intended; cf. 1 Sam. 25 and A. Jepsen, *ZDPV* 75 (1959), pp. 74-5. **farmers and vinedressers:** cf. S. Yeivin, *Leshonenu* 24 (1960), pp. 40-6, and H. Gese, *VT* 12 (1962), pp. 422f.

11-15. Details of the army and its equipment complete the review of Uzziah's prosperity. For a general discussion, suggesting the authenticity of such a notice, see on 14:8.

12-13. Once again, it is difficult to be sure how to interpret these figures, though many commentators point to the reasonableness of the suggested 120 soldiers per unit. Could the figure of v. 12 represent the actual figure, and the Chronicler have assumed that they were commanders, from which he computed the figure in v. 13? Certainly **to help the king against the enemy** is suggestive of his own composition; cf. v. 7.

14. Uzziah prepared for all the army: this is a pointer to the increasing sophistication of warfare. Previously, the conscript army would have provided its own more simple armour. For an introductory study of the various terms, cf. Yadin, *The Art of Warfare*.

15. engines: *RSV* clearly favours the interpretation that these were some form of catapult. Since the word is coined from the root *ḥšb*, 'to think', 'inventions' would be a more neutral rendering. If the information is authentic, as the overall context would suggest, catapults are unlikely, since there is no reliable evidence for their existence as early as this; cf. Welten, pp. 111-114. Rather we should see here a reference to defensive constructions **on the towers and the corners** that enabled the soldiers **to shoot arrows and great stones** from a position of safety. The Assyrian reliefs of the siege of Lachish, which come from a period only shortly after Uzziah, portray just this kind of construction, which has hardly any other known parallels; cf. Y. Sukenik (Yadin), *BJPES* 13 (1946–7), pp. 19–24. While this is the explanation preferred in this commentary, the possibility has been mentioned that the reference is to catapults. If that is so, it will be an anachronism from the Chronicler's own day. The matter is of some importance, because Welten has used this argument to date Chronicles in the Hellenistic period. This was not unreasonable, in view of the literary evidence (Diodorus Siculus 14.42.1) that catapults were invented in Syracuse about 400 BC. Their development into defensive weapons, as here, would then probably not have been known in Judah until the third century BC. Recent evidence, however, has now shown that the Persians may well have used some kind of device (whether exactly a catapult or not cannot be determined) for hurling **great stones** at a date considerably earlier than Diodorus Siculus implies; cf. the discovery of some 422 shaped, heavy stone balls dating from 498 BC at Old Paphos; E. Erdmann, *Nordosttor und persische Belagerungsrampe in Alt-Paphos* (1977), pp. 80–2. Thus, even allowing for the possibility that the present phrase is anachronistic, it need no longer demand a date as late as Welten has supposed. **And his fame spread far:** see on v. 8. **for he was marvellously helped:** cf. v. 7. **till he was strong:** v. 8. This last sentence is thus clearly the Chronicler's own summary of the leading themes of the positive period of Uzziah's reign.

16–21. The account of Uzziah's pride and downfall is similarly found only in Chronicles. 2 Kg. 15:5 records that 'the Lord smote the king, so that he was a leper to the day of his death', but gives no explanation. Moreover, attempts to demonstrate dependence on an earlier source have been unable to produce convincing arguments. Thus Rudolph finds the account highly dramatic, something of which he regards the Chronicler as being incapable, while J. Morgenstern, *HUCA* 12–13 (1937–8), pp. 1–20, has to draw both on the retelling of the story by Josephus and on his own highly speculative reconstruction of the cultic calendar of ancient Israel in order to reconstruct a possible underlying account.

It is perhaps more illuminating to observe how many features are suggestive of the Chronicler himself. At the level of vocabulary, words like **when he was strong, destruction, was false** (v. 16) and **you have done wrong** (v. 18) are characteristic of his style. Second, the theme of judgment falling only after explicit rejection of a warning from God (vv. 18–19) is familiar by now. Third, the outlook of the passage, with its rigid demarcation between royal and priestly functions, its ascription of authority to the high priest, and so on, is at least suggestive of the post-exilic period, and seems out of place in an earlier historical setting. Finally, Zeron, *ThZ* 33 (1977), pp. 65–8, has successfully shown that many of the details of the narrative are either echoes of, or the result of probable reflection on, other biblical texts (for some examples, see below). This style of composition, too, we have noted as characteristic of the Chronicler (e.g. 1 Chr. 21). While certainty is, of course, unattainable, we must nevertheless conclude that it is unnecessary to postulate dependence on a source. It may be that the source or sources which underlie the earlier part of the chapter made reference to Uzziah officiating in the temple (so Zeron), and that, in the light of 2 Kg. 15:5 and the practices of his own day, the Chronicler deduced the remainder; but such a suggestion cannot be more than hypothetical. On the setting of this paragraph within the chapter as a whole, see above, p. 332.

16. But when he was strong: with this word the Chronicler links the two halves of Uzziah's reign together. Exactly as with Rehoboam (cf. 12:1), this blessing leads to pride, which this time is not alleviated by self-humbling, but rather results in **his destruction** (see on 24:23, though the usage here is more general). **he was false:** see on 1 Chr. 10:13. **and entered the temple of the Lord:** though this would probably have been acceptable in pre-exilic times, it certainly was not in the Chronicler's own day. We have already noted examples of his care to avoid any such implication; cf. 4:9; 6:12; 23:6, etc. But Uzziah's real offence lay in his intention **to burn incense on the altar of incense.** This may reflect what also seems to be intended as the climax of the condemnation of Jeroboam, who 'went up to the altar to burn incense', for it both comes at the very end of the description (1 Kg. 12:33) and is emphasised by repetition in the next verse (13:1). Moreover, as in the present case, so just at that moment Jeroboam was confronted by a man of God. See also on vv. 18–19. For the use of **incense** in Israelite ritual, cf. Haran, *Temples and Temple Service*, pp. 230–45.

17. Azariah the priest: not mentioned elsewhere, though two other high priests of the same name are listed in 1 Chr. 6:1–15. Was the Chronicler attracted to this name because of its link (*'zr* = to help) with one of his leading themes in this chapter? See also on v. 1 and 31:10. **men of valour:** better, 'courageous men', with *NEB*.

18. The priests here express the view of the priestly legislation in Exod. 30:7ff. and Num. 18:1ff. It is disputed to what extent such legislation was already operative in pre-exilic times; see also 13:10f. **Go out of the sanctuary:** this is intended as a warning to Uzziah. The clear statement of the law here functions with the same im-

mediate authority as the word of the inspired prophets elsewhere
(e.g. 24:20ff.; 25:14–16).

19. The probable influence of 1 Kg. 13 on this paragraph has
already been noted. It is thus of interest to note the comparable
dramatic nature of the onset of judgment in the two accounts; cf.
1 Kg. 13:4. **leprosy:** the evidence of other passages suggests that
this is not to be identified with the modern disease of the same
name; cf. E. V. Hulse, *PEQ* 107 (1975), pp. 87–105, and S. G.
Browne, *Leprosy in the Bible* (³1979).

20. The wording of the first half of this verse is clearly based on
the description of the onset of Miriam's leprosy in Num. 12:10.
because the Lord had smitten him: the Chronicler here rejoins 2
Kg. 15:5, which he follows, with some characteristic differences, to
the end of the chapter.

21. in a separate house: the exact significance of this designation,
though much discussed, remains uncertain; see the commentaries
on Kings and, most recently, W. Rudolph, *ZAW* 89 (1977), p. 418.
for he was excluded from the house of the Lord: added by the
Chronicler, in conformity with Lev. 13:46. See also L. Delekat, *VT*
14 (1964), p. 12.

22. The citation of other sources is adapted towards the Chronicler's usual formula. The reference to **Isaiah the prophet the son
of Amoz** is thus probably to be understood in the same way as in
the similar cases at 1 Chr. 29:29; 2 Chr. 9:29; 12:15, etc. In addition
to the appearance of Isaiah in Kings in association with Hezekiah,
influence was probably felt from Isa. 1:1 and 6:1. Zeron (see above)
makes much of this in his suggestion that part of the story of
Uzziah's leprosy has arisen from reflection on the call of Isaiah in
Isa. 6, but the correspondences seem rather remote.

23. The burial notice is changed somewhat from 2 Kg. 15:7,
probably with the intention of stressing (against the implication of
the phrase **with his fathers**) that Uzziah was buried separately. On
this occasion there is some evidence which might lead us to suppose
that the Chronicler's version is correct. S. Yeivin, *JNES* 7 (1948),
pp. 30–45, has pointed to the bearing of the 'Uzziah inscription' on
this passage. The inscription, which dates from the second temple
period, implies that Uzziah's remains were removed from their
original resting place; cf. J. A. Fitzmyer and D. J. Harrington, *A
Manual of Palestinian Aramaic Texts* (1978), pp. 168f. and 223f.
Their isolated treatment in this regard would be curious indeed if
he had been buried 'with his fathers', as Kings states without further
qualification. It would be more probable that a solitary tomb of
Uzziah was uncovered during later building operations. (Yeivin's
arguments in favour of the authenticity of all the Chronicler's burial

notices are, however, less convincing.) W. F. Albright, *BASOR* 44 (1931), pp. 8–10, however, has reasonably observed that the identification might in the first place have depended upon the Chronicler's statement that he was buried separately, and so have no independent value. The Chronicler would then have been influenced in his composition by the treatment as unclean of lepers in his own day.

JOTHAM

27:1–9

To the brief account of Jotham's reign in 2 Kg. 15:32–38 the Chronicler has added some further details about his building activities (vv. 3*b*–4) and his campaign against the Ammonites (vv. 5–6), but omitted the note that 'in those days the Lord began to send Rezin the king of Syria and Pekah the son of Remaliah against Judah' (2 Kg. 15:37). Details of this latter campaign are held over to the account of the next king, Ahaz, where they contribute to the Chronicler's consistently negative portrayal of that monarch.

The effect of these changes is to produce a fully positive account of Jotham's reign, thus indicating a break in the pattern which has persisted through the last few chapters of presenting an alternation between good and evil within each individual reign. This new pattern will last only as far as the end of Hezekiah's reign (chs 29–32). This fact suggests that the Chronicler may have wished to draw particular attention to the characteristics of these three reigns. The discussion later will suggest that this is so primarily in terms of the break that he has emphasised between Ahaz and Hezekiah. In the case of Jotham, therefore, to whom the Chronicler does not otherwise seem to attach great significance, it is probable that his presentation is designed to prepare the reader for what is to come, succeeding by its unqualified approval in deepening the darkness of the account of Ahaz which immediately follows.

1–2. Cf. 2 Kg. 15:33–35*a*. **Only he did not invade** (better, 'come to') **the temple of the Lord**: this is the Chronicler's own addition necessitated by his reinterpretation of the reign of **Uzziah**. It is true that Hebrew *raḳ*, **only**, normally suggests a qualification of what precedes it, so that this clause might appear to limit the approval of Jotham: for some reason he neglected the sanctuary altogether (Myers, following Cazelles). The overall context tells against such an interpretation, however. Either, therefore, the word is intended to qualify only the second of the two preceding clauses, the Chronicler fearing that otherwise it might be taken to mean that Jotham too fell into disobedience, or *rak* should here be given asseverative force, 'surely' (cf. BDB, p. 956B, e). **But the people still followed corrupt practices:** a summary of 2 Kg. 15:35*a*. Were Cazelles and Myers correct in their understanding of the previous sentence, **But** could be better translated 'and'.

3–4. The first half of v. 3 is drawn from 2 Kg. 15:35*b*, but the remainder is found only here. We have repeatedly noted that the theme of **building** is used by the Chronicler to enhance the positive portrayal of a king's reign (see on 11:5–12), and this will be its function here too. Many commentators assume that the additional material is drawn from some otherwise unknown source. However, the manner in which it runs on from the notice in Kings and the rather generalised description arouse suspicion. Moreover, Welten (pp. 27–9 and 66–8) has made out a strong case on the basis of style for attributing some of this material to the Chronicler himself. Thus, while it may well be that in fact Jotham did undertake some such activities, it may be suggested that the Chronicler has composed the description here himself in a conscious attempt to develop the parallel, to which v. 2 has already drawn attention, with the positive period of his father's reign, and to show that he continued his father's policy, for Uzziah too undertook building in Jerusalem (cf. 26:9 and 15; **the wall of Ophel** may, in the Chronicler's terminology, refer in particular to the northern part of the city, though more normally it is identified with the spur running south from the temple mount) and **in the hill country of Judah** (cf. 26:10).

5. No other account of Jotham's war with **the king of the Ammonites** is preserved. Though Judah and Ammon did not share a common border at this time, such an encounter would not be impossible in view of the rapid decline in the influence of the northern kingdom; cf. H. Tadmor, *Scripta Hierosolymitana* 8 (1961), p. 248. Moreover, Rudolph refers to 1 Chr. 5:17 and to the build-up to the Syro-Ephraimite war in support of the historicity of this account. Alternatively, there may have again been confusion between **the Ammonites** and the Meunites (cf. 20:1), in which case this verse would describe another example of Jotham continuing his father's policy (cf. 26:7). The amount of tribute paid is generally thought to be exaggerated, though on the basis of its style Kropat, pp. 47 and 53, has argued that it too derives from an earlier source (see also Polzin, pp. 61–4, but contast Welten, pp. 163–6). In fact, with no hard evidence on which to come to a decision, the question of the historicity of this verse cannot be decided with any certainty whatever. All we can do is to observe how it introduces another element (successful war and tribute) which the Chronicler regularly uses to portray a king under God's blessing.

6. This is clearly the Chronicler's own comment, underlining the cause of Jotham's success. **became mighty:** a typical mark of the Chronicler's hand; see on 1:1, though it is not used here, of course, in connection with Jotham's accession.

7. Cf. 2 Kg. 15:36. **and all his wars, and his ways:** substituted for 'and all that he did'. Perhaps a reference is intended to the note of the first Syro-Ephraimite invasion (2 Kg. 15:37) which the Chronicler has omitted. **Israel and:** this addition conforms to the Chronicler's regular practice; see on 16:11.

8. This seems to be an unnecessary repetition of v. 1. Rudolph suggests that it may originally have been intended as a corrective gloss on 28:1.

AHAZ

28:1–27

From a number of points of view the reigns of Ahaz and Hezekiah are of particular importance to the Chronicler, for in them he presents his solution to the problem which was posed for him by the division of the monarchy following the death of Solomon. Up to that point (2 Chr. 10), he stresses time and again and in a variety of ways the unity of Israel, the people of God, and we have noted various ways in which he insists on that ideological unity even in the face of the historical division. That he was able to do so was in no small measure the consequence of his conviction that ultimately he would be able to present a resolution of the paradox and that it did not endure permanently. Thus, after a long series of reigns whose primary purpose was to impress upon his readers the attitudes and standards which they should either adopt or eschew, the attention now switches rather to concentrate on an important development, as he sees it, in the nation's history. Naturally, however, this will in no way exclude the possibility of other themes being included at the same time.

The first step is taken in this chapter by the reworking of the reign of Ahaz (cf. 2 Kg. 16), by which the Chronicler manages to effect a complete reversal in the relationship between north and south to that outlined in the programmatic ch. 13; cf. *IBC*, pp. 114–18. Thus, while the details will be treated more fully below, it may be noted here that the apostasy of Ahaz has been heightened over against 2 Kg. 16 in ways which show that the religious faithfulness of the southern kingdom as expounded by Abijah has been completely overthrown. Secondly, the northerners are here presented by contrast in a most favourable light (vv. 8–15), and most significantly this includes an apparently genuine statement and act of repentance not just for the sin of the moment, but of their whole situation. This was seen at 13:4–12 to be one of the vital steps necessary for the reunification of the people, and many of the Chronicler's stories since have underlined its efficacy. Thirdly, it is suggested by the language of v. 12, and made clear by 30:6, that in the Chronicler's view it was at just this time that the northern regime fell to the Assyrians. Thus by the end of the reign of Ahaz, at any rate, there is only one king reigning in Israel. This too eliminates one of the major stumbling blocks to reunification noted in 13:4–12. Fourthly, it will be seen especially in vv. 5–6 that the military fortunes of the two kingdoms are here explicitly reversed by comparison with 2 Chr. 13, suggestive of God's favour towards the north and judgment of the south. Finally, the fortunes of both kingdoms are virtually the same by the end of this chapter (see also 29:5ff. and 30:6ff., which are also descriptive of the situation at Hezekiah's accession), with much of the population in captivity and exile, but with the possibility of restoration resting on the faithfulness of those who remain in the land. Much of the language of the paradigmatic treatment of Saul (1 Chr. 10) is echoed here, as if to emphasise the 'exilic' atmosphere which prevails throughout. The scene is thus set for the vigorous moves towards restoration which Hezekiah is portrayed as undertaking.

From this analysis it should be evident that the Chronicler's own hand is clearly to be seen in this chapter, and indeed it is replete with his most characteristic vocabulary. However, that need not rule out the possibility that, just as he can be seen to have adapted his biblical *Vorlage* to suit his purpose, so other older sources may underlie other parts of his presentation. Indications which strongly support such a conjecture will be noted in what follows; see also McKay.

1–4. The substance of this introductory evaluation is taken straight from 2 Kg. 16:2–4, but the description of the apostasy of Ahaz has been heightened by the addition of 2b and 3a.

2. but walked in the ways of the kings of Israel: if our general analysis of this chapter is correct, the Chronicler will have taken this otherwise stereotyped formula with utmost seriousness. **He even made molten images for the Baals:** unlike 2 Kg. 16, the Chronicler makes explicit both here and later in the chapter (vv. 23 and 25) that Ahaz practised the worship of foreign gods. This exactly reverses Abijah's accusation that after the division the northerners looked to the golden calves as gods and had priests to 'what are no gods' (13:8–9). Isa 2:8 and 20 indicate that the Chronicler's description is accurate.

3. and he burned incense in the valley of the son of Hinnom: possibly deduced by the Chronicler from the following clause, on which see now D. Plataroti, *VT* 28 (1978), pp. 293–8.

5–7. The Chronicler's account of the Syro-Ephraimite war differs in certain respects from any other known to us (cf. 2 Kg. 15:37; 16:5; Isa. 7; Hos. 5:8–6:6). In the present paragraph he maintains a distinction between the two partners to the northern coalition, while in vv. 16–21 he relates the appeal of Ahaz to Tiglath-Pileser to an apparently quite separate invasion of Edomites and Philistines, a point which may well reflect the historical situation (see below). Since these matters are not demanded by the Chronicler's message nor suggested by any other passage (beyond a possible hint in 2 Kg. 16:6), it may be confidently concluded that he had access to a separate and valuable alternative source. The names in v. 7 may also be regarded as deriving from it. However, as with the rest of the material in this chapter, the Chronicler has used it freely to convey his particular interpretation of the reign of Ahaz, as the comments following will demonstrate.

5. and took captive: this is only the first of a number of such notices in this chapter (and cf. 29:8–9). Their purpose is both to create the impression of an 'exilic' situation, and to parallel in certain respects the fortunes of both northern and southern kingdoms. **given into the hand of the king of Israel, who defeated him with great slaughter:** this exactly reverses, as the use of the same vocabulary shows, the situation in 2 Chr. 13:15–17, where Judah's faithfulness was vindicated in their defeat of Israel.

6. Though such a defeat of Judah is not directly attested in any other known account, it is very likely in view of the fact that the northern coalition got as far as besieging Jerusalem (2 Kg. 16:5). Moreover, 'if Ahaz and his people were terrified at the approach of the Syro-Ephraimite armies (Isa. 7.2, 4), then it is highly probable that many of Judah's villages had fallen and that fighting men had been slain', McKay, p. 78. At the same time, the large numbers involved present the usual difficulties (see on 13:3 and 14:9), while **in one day** may also be added for effect. **because they had forsaken the Lord, the God of their fathers:** both vocabulary and ideology mark this as the Chronicler's own interpretation (cf., for instance, 21:10; 24:24). In particular it may be noted that it expresses precisely the condemnation of the south which Abijah levelled against the north in 13:11–12.

7. The otherwise unattested details of this verse are strongly suggestive of an antecedent source. Thus, while it is true that the office of the one **next in authority** (= 'second') **to the king** occurs otherwise only at Est. 10:3, it need not for that reason alone be regarded as exclusively post-exilic. **the king's son:** cf. A. F. Rainey, *UF* 7 (1975), pp. 427–32, who defends a literal understanding of this phrase.

8–15. The importance of this paragraph for the development of the Chronicler's narrative has already been discussed (p. 344). Moreover, the device of introducing a prophet to give expression to the dominant theological interest of the surrounding narrative is characteristic of the Chronicler. It is thus probable that at the very least he has substantially rewritten whatever source may underlie this account.

Commentators have often argued that the favourable impression of the north conveyed here is so at odds with the Chronicler's usual stance that he must have been using an older source. Clearly, however, the interpretation of the Chronicler's narrative presented in this commentary robs that argument of any weight. Nevertheless, we have seen above (vv. 5–7) that the Chronicler probably did have access to an alternative account of the Syro-Ephraimite war, and there is a strong indication from the first clause of v. 15 (hidden by *RSV*; see below) that the basis of the present narrative may have been drawn from it. The names of v. 12, together with the unexpected reference to Jericho in v. 15, further support this conclusion. However, the whole has now been so worked over by the Chronicler that it is idle to speculate on the precise form of the earlier account.

8. took captive: cf. v. 5. **kinsfolk:** literally, 'brothers'. The relationship between north and south is so termed three times in this passage (see also vv. 11 and 15), and this may represent a deliberate emphasis by the Chronicler to remind his readers both of the accession of David, when the unity of the nation was a dominant feature (cf. 1 Chr. 12:39), and of the time of the division of the monarchy (11:4) when it was first disrupted. This emphasis thus serves as a further pointer to the fact that the Chronicler is here moving towards a solution of that dilemma.

9. Oded: not otherwise known, but see on 15:1. His brief sermon again reads like an exact reversal of the situation in ch. 13. Although he does not 'quote' the canonical prophets in the same way as other such Levitical sermons, his outlook may be closely compared with them. Thus the view that the Lord might use military defeat as a punishment for Judah's sin because he **was angry with** them, but that his instrument might then overstep the mark (**in a rage which has reached up to heaven**) recalls Isa. 10:5–19, and cf. Zech. 1:15. **the Lord, the God of your fathers:** it is worth noting the recurrence of this title (cf. 13:12). Even in rebellion the northern kingdom has been consistently viewed as a part of the people of God.

10–11. as your slaves: though not explicitly stated, this seems to allude to such a passage as Lev. 25:46 which, while allowing short-term slavery of one Israelite to another, prohibits the ruling 'with harshness' 'over your brethren'. **Have you not sins of your own against the Lord your God?**: together with the observation that **the fierce wrath of the Lord is upon you,** this question amounts to an invitation to repentance, unheard of heretofore in the north. It finds a ready response in the echo of the leaders in v. 13. It should be noted that at this time the south too stands under God's **wrath** (cf. v. 25 and 29:8, 10). **send back**: repentance should be expressed in actions, even though under normal circumstances such a demand would be regarded as preposterous.

12. It is possible that the authority assumed by these **chiefs of the men of Ephraim** is intended as an indication that the northern monarchy had already fallen.

13. Cf. vv. 10–11. **in addition to our present sins and guilt. For our guilt is already great:** this constitutes a clear acknowledgement by the men of the north not just that they are at fault in this particular event, but that they stand in a general state of sin, to be identified, for the Chronicler, with the points outlined in 13:4–12.

14. 'The result is as remarkable as the appeal' (Ackroyd). As portrayed by the Chronicler the unhesitating response in releasing **the captives** is tantamount to an acknowledgement of the confession of v. 13.

15. the men who have been mentioned by name: *RSV* refers to the men of v. 12. It has been reasonably queried, however, whether they alone would have been sufficient for such a task. When the phrase occurs elsewhere (31:19; 1 Chr. 12:31; 16:41), it has rather the meaning of being designated for a particular task; thus *NEB* is preferable: 'men nominated for this duty'. This indicates that the Chronicler had access to a full list which he has chosen not to include. It is not clear why the captives were brought specifically to **Jericho,** except that it is presented as a border town on the northern side ('Jericho. . .beside their kinsfolk' is a more literal rendering). Such otherwise unexpected and unmotivated detail may again point to dependence on an older source.

16–21. The historical substance of this paragraph comprises an appeal by Ahaz to Tiglath-pileser III of Assyria because of invasions by the Philistines and the Edomites in addition to (this is the force of **again** in v. 17) the Syro-Ephraimite invasion of vv. 5ff. This situation is not described in any other biblical text, though 2 Kg. 16:6 points in the same direction. However, increased knowledge of Assyrian movements from texts discovered at Nimrud has convinced most scholars that this represents an accurate portrayal of the situation; cf. J. Gray, *ET* 63 (1952), pp. 263–5; H. W. F.

Saggs, *Iraq* 17 (1955), pp. 133, 152; H. Tadmor, *BA* 29 (1966), p. 88.

This conclusion must not blind us to the fact, however, that the Chronicler has turned this material to his own purpose. We may confidently see his own hand in the verses which explain that (a) Judah's low state under Ahaz was in the first place due to his unfaithfulness (v. 19), (b) his appeal to Assyria instead of relying upon God was demonstrably wrong, because it involved plundering the temple (v. 21), and (c) such a policy secured relief from one direction only to open the door to an even worse disaster in the other (v. 20). This latter point in particular is in line with, and may have been derived by the Chronicler directly from, the interpretation of the same event in Isa. 7.

16. for help: we have often noted that the Chronicler delights to record of faithful kings that God 'helps' them (cf. 1 Chr. 5:20; 2 Chr. 14:11; 18:31; 25:8; 26:7, 15; 32:8), so that the use of the word here draws attention to Ahaz's lack of faith. There is a bitter play on the word in the closing sentence of the paragraph, at the end of v. 21, and in v. 23.

17. Such an attack by **the Edomites** is fully compatible with what is known of their growing strength and their increasing interest in the Negeb at this time; cf. J. R. Bartlett, *PEQ* 104 (1972), p. 33, who adds (with reference to Am. 1:6; Ezek. 16:57; 25:12-17; Ob. 19) that 'indeed, the Edomites and the Philistines were natural allies against Judah', an observation well supported by this and the following verse. **carried away captives:** see on v. 5.

18. the Philistines no doubt exploited the first sign of weakness by Judah to recover their losses suffered under Uzziah, 26:6. The cities mentioned all lie 'to the west of Jerusalem, on the border of the hill country' (Myers). One might speculate that the Chronicler would have seen here a reflection of his paradigmatic account of Saul's reign, 1 Chr. 10.

19. the Lord brought Judah low: this exactly reverses 13:18, though *RSV* has obscured the use of identical vocabulary. **king of Israel:** it is curious at first sight that this title should be used of so faithless a king, but it should be noted that it is common from here to the end of the chapter (cf. vv. 23, 26, 27). With the northern king removed by now (in the Chronicler's view), and with those who remained in the north having begun, at least, on the road to repentance (vv. 8-15), there was apparently nothing left to prevent the Chronicler from moving towards a presentation of the people as once again united. This he develops in his characterisation of Hezekiah (chs 29-32). **and had been faithless:** see on 1 Chr. 10:13.

20. Tilgath-pilneser: see on 1 Chr. 5:6. **and afflicted him instead**

of strengthening him: the Chronicler's point is theological (see above). It is nevertheless true both that in the long run Ahaz's policy did not gain him material advantage, since the Philistine states were incorporated into the Assyrian empire rather than being returned to Judah, and that Ahaz had to pay heavily in terms of tribute in order to maintain his own independence.

21. but it did not help him: see on v. 16.

22-25. far from heeding the warning implicit in the disasters of the previous verses, Ahaz slides further into apostasy and idolatry. This section is related to 2 Kg. 16:10-18, but it has been completely reworked by the Chronicler.

22. yet more faithless: cf. v. 19.

23. he sacrificed to the gods of Damascus: see on v. 2. According to 2 Kg. 16:10-11, Ahaz had a copy of an altar which he saw in Damascus built for the temple in Jerusalem, but the sacrifices made upon it would still appear to have been offered to the God of Israel (vv. 13 and 15). The Chronicler, however, perhaps with the aid (though hardly the explicit statement) of an alternative source (cf. McKay, p. 6), interprets this as an act of wholesale apostasy. **which had defeated him:** cf. v. 5. However, since the Syrians had by now themselves been defeated by Assyria, it must be concluded that the Chronicler is aiming at underlining the utter folly of Ahaz's policy rather than recording a probable historical development. **helped. . .help:** cf. vv. 16 and 21. The word-play draws out the irony of Ahaz turning in all directions—to the Assyrians and to **the gods of the kings of Syria**—except to the Lord, from whom alone, in the Chronicler's narrative, true **help** can come. **they were the ruin of him, and of all Israel:** this anticipates the exile, averted at this stage only by the timely reformation of Hezekiah. Here again it is noteworthy that the Chronicler's phraseology aids his development of a levelling process between north and south.

24. The Chronicler interprets the plundering of the temple in order to raise tribute for Assyria (2 Kg. 16:17-18) as a religious desecration, designed effectively to prevent further worship in the temple.

25. Cf. vv. 2 and 3. **provoking to anger the Lord, the God of his fathers:** a further adumbration of the exile (cf. 36:16) as well as another point of contact with the conditions in the north (vv. 9, 11 and 13).

26-27. For the conclusion of Ahaz's reign, the Chronicler rejoins 2 Kg. 16:19-20, though with several differences familiar from other such sections. **and Israel:** see on 16:11.

27. Contrary to the statement of 2 Kg. 16:20, the Chronicler has Ahaz **buried** apart from the royal tombs, presumably because of his apostasy. A comparable situation has been noted at 21:20; 24:25 and 26:23 above. **kings of Israel:** i.e. Judah; see on v. 19.

HEZEKIAH TO THE BABYLONIAN EXILE

2 Chr. 29–36

Although the Chronicler's interest throughout the period of the divided monarchy has been primarily centred on the southern kingdom, and although he does not include the account of the fall of Samaria to the Assyrians (2 Kg. 17), it has nevertheless been briefly noted in connection with the reign of Ahaz that he was fully aware of this fact, and that he has allowed it to influence the general shape of his narrative. With the reign of Hezekiah he presents the final step in this development, and thereafter traces through the history of the kingdom to the point of exile. Despite the work thus ending on an apparently negative note, he has left sufficient indication at its close to point the way forward to the restoration in the Persian period. The typological patterns which have been noted throughout from the reign of Saul onwards are here continued, the themes of restoration and exile thus being ones in the light of which he will have expected his readers to assess their own situation.

HEZEKIAH

29:1–32:33

The Chronicler's great interest in Hezekiah may be seen at once from two superficial observations. First, he has devoted more space to the account of his reign than of any king other than David and Solomon themselves. Second, he has completely reordered the emphasis of his *Vorlage* (2 Kg. 18–20) in order to bring its balance into line with that of David and Solomon. Thus, while Kings devotes only a single verse to his religious reform and the bulk of its material to an account of his political and military affairs, in Chronicles the reform occupies three chapters, and deals with the cleansing and rededication of the temple (ch. 29), the celebration of the passover by representatives of all Israel (ch. 30) and subsequent arrangements for the continuing temple worship (ch. 31). The remainder of the narrative is then heavily condensed and reapplied to serve as an illustration of the fortunes of one who has thus shown himself religiously faithful.

Not only in these general points, but also in many matters of detail, it may be said more specifically that the Chronicler has gone

out of his way to present Hezekiah as a second Solomon; cf. the
notes below, and the summary in *IBC*, pp. 119–25. That this should
be said of the first king following the fall of the northern monarchy
is no accident. As already noted, and as Hezekiah's own words
reaffirm (29:5–11; 30:6–9), the situation in the two countries at the
end of the reign of Ahaz was closely comparable, while the major
barriers which had hitherto divided them were now crumbling.
Thus in Hezekiah's recapitulation of Solomon's achievements it is
as though the Chronicler is taking us back prior to the point of
division where the one Israel is united around a single temple under
the authority of the Davidic king.

The Cleansing and Rededication of the Temple

2 Chr. 29:1–36

It was seen at 2 Chr. 1 that in his introduction to Solomon's reign
the Chronicler took up three of its well-known characteristics and
showed how from the first they were directed primarily towards the
task of temple building. The effect of the present chapter is similar,
in that he has Hezekiah plunge straight into the work of restoring
the temple at the very start of his reign (v. 3). Similarly, at the end
of the chapter (v. 35*b*) there is a conscious echo of the Chronicler's
own conclusion of his account of Solomon's building (see on 8:16),
suggesting that he regards the work of restoration as in large measure
parallel with that of the initial building.

Apart from the first two verses, the material of this chapter is
found only in Chronicles. Unfortunately, while in some cases (such
as vv. 5–11) it is highly probable that the Chronicler is himself
directly responsible for the composition, there seems on the whole
to be no tangible evidence that would enable us to decide whether
or not he also had access to an alternative account of this particular
phase of the reform (though for other aspects of his reform in
general, see the introduction to ch. 30 and on 31:1 in particular).
While some scholars have argued in general terms that he may have
done (cf. Moriarty, *CBQ* 27 [1965], pp. 399–406; McKay, pp.
15ff.), it is perhaps wiser in the present context to leave the issue
open and to concentrate attention on the Chronicler's own intention
alone.

A final introductory issue concerns the unity of the chapter. Since
the time of A. Büchler, at least (*ZAW* 19 [1899], pp. 109–14), a
number of scholars have suggested differing forms of secondary
expansion of an original chronistic narrative, usually with the result
of seeing references to the priests and their work as later; especially

noteworthy are the contributions of Welch, *WC*, pp. 103–8, and, most recently, Petersen, pp. 77–85. On the other hand, Rudolph has argued forcibly in favour of the unity of the chapter throughout. Both sides have strong arguments in their support, so that a decision on this issue may not be lightly taken and any judgment cannot be more than tentative. Some of the points will be noted at vv. 5, 11, 16 and 20ff. below. Although the expansion envisaged by Welch, for instance, would be fully compatible with that of the pro-priestly reviser whose hand has been detected elsewhere (e.g. 1 Chr. 15–16; 23–27), nevertheless it will be suggested that there are one or two indications which, despite tensions in the account, point rather to a single composition of this particular chapter as a whole by the Chronicler himself.

29:1–2. The Chronicler draws this introduction to his account from 2 Kg. 18:2–3 before departing completely from the earlier biblical source for the next three chapters. **according to all that David his father had done:** this is adopted by the Chronicler from his source as a stereotyped expression of commendation. It has no reference to the detailed ('Solomonic') characteristics of Hezekiah's reign.

3–11. Hezekiah's charge to the Levites is carefully composed by the Chronicler in such a way as to draw out the significance of the events he relates for the broader development of his narrative. Frequent points of contact will be noted with earlier passages where similar concerns are highlighted.

3. In the first year of his reign, in the first month: in v. 17 this is further specified as 'the first day of the first month'. It is probable, in the light of ch. 30, that the Chronicler meant by this the first month of Hezekiah's first regnal year, rather than necessarily the first month after the death of his father. Either way, however, his aim is to show that concern for the temple, here summarised by the opening and repairing of **the doors of the house of the Lord** (contrast 28:24), characterised Hezekiah's reign from the start and completely overshadowed all other considerations. The actual chronology of Hezekiah's accession has been much debated, and the relationship between his reform and the fall of Samaria is of considerable importance to the historian. The Chronicler, however, shows no interest in such an approach, and it would be unwise to use his account as evidence in such discussions. As in the later case of 32:1 ('After these things'; cf. vv. 9 and 24), he introduces chronological notices as part of his way of characterising a reign in a way that gives them typological significance.

4. the square on the east: we should perhaps compare Neh. 8:1

and 3. A location outside the still unclean temple itself is clearly indicated by the context.

5. Levites: the absence of a reference to 'the priests' has led some to suspect that they have been added only secondarily in v. 4, rather as in the comparable case of 1 Chr. 15:4ff. On this occasion, however, it would seem from v. 11 that they must also be included, even if they are not addressed directly. Rudolph suggests that it was the Chronicler's particular feeling for the Levites that led him to highlight them here in this way.

sanctify yourselves: cf. 1 Chr. 15:12. **sanctify the house of the Lord:** a general and introductory command. The reader is expected to fill out its meaning both from his knowledge of the situation following the reign of Ahaz and from the description of the remainder of this chapter. **the filth:** a strong word relating to ritual impurity and occurring primarily in priestly literature. While the effects of Ahaz's desecration come chiefly to mind (cf. 28:23f.), the following explanation is more generalised, and is suggestive of a long-term failure. Once again, therefore, the emphasis falls on the opening of a fresh chapter in the Chronicler's history, where the types of restoration and exile outweigh more time-bound considerations.

6. have been unfaithful: cf. 1 Chr. 10:13. **they have forsaken him:** cf. 12:1 and contrast 13:10. The vocabulary of this verse is thus strongly suggestive of that 'exilic' pattern on which we have seen the Chronicler often models his description of judgment brought about by neglect of God and his temple.

7. The details are clearly the result of Ahaz's action in 28:24. The effect, however, is precisely to reverse the situation initiated by Solomon (cf. 2:4 and 4:7) and reaffirmed by Abijah (13:11). Restoration, therefore, will involve a return to Solomonic conditions.

8–9. the wrath of the Lord: Judah and Jerusalem are thus in the same situation as the north (cf. 28:9, 11, 13), as 28:25 has already suggested. Moreover, comparison of the remainder of these verses with Jer. 29:18 in particular (though see also Dt. 28:25, 41; Jer. 15:4; 19:8; 25:9, 18; 34:17; Ezek. 23:46 and cf. 6:36–38 above) shows clearly that this situation is being consciously described in language used elsewhere of the Babylonian exile. Thus while in one sense Hezekiah's words can again be referred back to the reign of Ahaz (see on 28:5), yet in another they are carefully phrased in order to encourage a wider application.

10. it is in my heart: cf. 1 Chr. 22:7; 28:2; 2 Chr. 6:7. Language used elsewhere of the preparations for the initial building is here taken up again at its rededication. **to make a covenant with the Lord:** the expression used here reflects 'a late and irregular usage'; M. Weinfeld, *TDOT* 2, p. 259. Comparison with the similar idiom at Ezr. 10:3-5 suggests that **with** is not the best translation; rather, Hezekiah is expressing his intention of taking a solemn oath before God to put right what is wrong; cf. Japhet, *Ideology*, pp. 101-3. Thus this passage is similar to 15:12 in expressing a one-sided commitment on the part of the king and perhaps the people; it is not to be understood as a renewal of the covenant between God and Israel.

11. the Lord has chosen you: cf. I Chr. 15:2, where the reference is exclusively to the Levites. The conclusion of the present verse, however (**and burn incense to him**), shows that priests must also be included, for it would be unthinkable for the Chronicler, following his emphatic assertions in 26:16-21, to contemplate anyone else undertaking this duty. Unless, therefore, this verse has been expanded by a later redactor—a gratuitous assumption for which there is no tangible evidence, and which the reference to incense in v. 7 renders improbable—the priests must, despite v. 5, have been in view alongside the Levites throughout Hezekiah's address. **to stand . . . to minister:** cf. Dt. 10:8, where the commentators agree that specifically priestly duties are in view. **to be his ministers:** this phrase, by contrast, will refer primarily to the Levites, thus balancing the priestly reference of the following phrase.

12-19. The cleansing of the temple. The Levites are again prominent, the priests apparently doing only the minimum required of them. The specific favour of the Chronicler for the former group is thus maintained (see on v. 5), and will be clearly stated later (v. 34).

12-14. Fourteen **Levites** are listed as responding prominently to Hezekiah's command. They fall into two groups. The first eight are made up of two from each of the great Levitical families, **the Kohathites, of Merari, the Gershonites**, and **of Elizaphan**. The closest parallel for this ordering comes in I Chr. 15:5ff. (though see also I Chr. 6), where it was argued against many commentators that, as is accepted without question here, the material could well have been included by the Chronicler. The second group is made up of two each from the three families of Levitical singers, **Asaph, Heman**, and **Jeduthun**. This too is a familiar form of listing in Chronicles; see the introduction to I Chr. 15-16 (Gese's group IIIA), and 25:1 (primary layer, and hence to be attributed to the Chronicler), etc. It is thus clear that this somewhat stylised presentation is intended to show that all the main branches of the Levitical family responded with equal enthusiasm. The names themselves are mostly familiar from other Levitical lists, though attempts at specific identification are inevitably hazardous. A few also feature in the later narratives of Hezekiah's reign (cf. 31:13 and 15).

15. as the king had commanded: several features of Hezekiah's charge (vv. 5–11) suggest that the Chronicler has consciously moulded it in the form of a 'Levitical sermon' (see on 1 Chr. 28:1–10); note, for instance, the characteristic introduction (v. 5), the use of citations from canonical texts (v. 8), and the parenetic style at the close (v. 11). Elsewhere, such sermons may be found in the mouths of prophets or other inspired speakers. Here, the same effect is achieved by the addition of the descriptive **by the words of the Lord**. It is thus unnecessary to try to identify passages in the law to which this might refer.

16. the inner part of the house of the Lord: this will refer to the most holy place, where the ark was kept (cf. 3:8ff.; Lev. 10:18). It has already been noted at 5:4 (and cf. von Rad, *GCW*, p. 92) that the Chronicler follows Pentateuchal prescription in permitting only **the priests** to enter it. Thus, although they are certainly somewhat overshadowed in this chapter by **the Levites** (who are introduced as doing as much of the work of cleansing as they are allowed), there is no need to regard the present verse as a later addition. It is just what we should expect of the Chronicler. **the brook Kidron:** cf. 15:16; 30:14; 2 Kg. 23:4, 6 and 12. As a burial site it would have been regarded as unclean and so was used on several occasions for the destruction of items of foreign worship.

17. the first day of the first month: see on v. 3. The first week seems to have been taken up with the courts and only in the second week did they reach the sanctuary itself (**the house of the Lord**), for part of which the priests were responsible. The positioning of v. 16 might thus appear a little premature. However, the problem is not serious in view of the fact that this verse aims to summarise only the chronology of the operation, not its detailed nature. **on the sixteenth day of the first month:** i.e. two days after the normal start of Passover. Together with other points, this is picked up again in 30:3, where there is the implication that the operation might have been concluded sooner had more priests been actively involved (and cf. 29:34).

18–19. The importance of the temple vessels, or **utensils**, as a symbol of religious continuity through the disruptions of exile and restoration has been stressed by P. R. Ackroyd, *SVT* 23 (1972), pp. 166–81. Their prominence here, therefore, following their desecration by **King Ahaz** (cf. 28:24), suggests a restoration of Solomonic conditions (cf. 2 Chr. 4). **when he was faithless:** cf. 28:19, 22.

20–36. The ceremony of rededication. This section is made up of three paragraphs, the first two of which are simultaneous. They deal, broadly speaking, with the sacrifices offered by the leaders of the people as a sin offering and a burnt offering for the nation (vv.

20–24), the accompanying musical worship (vv. 25–30), and finally the sacrificial offerings brought by the whole assembly (vv. 31–36). The first part of the ceremony is treated in two separate paragraphs in order to give particular prominence to the role of the Levitical singers. This, however, has led to a certain duplication in the narrative (vv. 21 and 27), which, together with various other minor points to be noted in the detailed comments below, has been taken by many as a sign that the original text has undergone later expansion, though there is little agreement as to what is primary and what secondary; in addition to the monographs noted in the introduction to this chapter and several of the commentaries, cf. J. Hänel, *ZAW* 55 (1937), pp. 46ff.; von Rad, *GCW*, p. 104; Willi, p. 200. Such a conclusion, however, is not necessary; the comments below, which generally follow Rudolph's line of interpretation, will endeavour to show that the passage can be understood as a unity.

21. It is evident from the sequel that the **bulls, rams,** and **lambs** were for the burnt offering and only the **he-goats** were **for a sin offering.** Consequently, some favour restoring 'for the whole-offering' (*lᵉ ʿōlāh*; cf. *NEB*) after **lambs.** The general situation finds its closest parallel in Ezekiel, where the **sin offering** is prescribed for such comparable settings as the cleansing and consecration of the altar (Ezek. 43:18–27), the cleansing of the sanctuary (45:18–20), the return of a priest to his duties after defilement and purification (44:27), and the preparation of the prince and people for the celebration of the passover (45:21–3). Here, the offering is specified for **the kingdom,** which must mean rather 'the royal house', **the sanctuary,** including especially the cultic personnel, and **for Judah,** the nation as a whole, though cf. v. 24 below. All three groups were equally involved in the apostasy under Ahaz in the previous chapter. **the priests the sons of Aaron:** as those responsible for the actual offering of the sacrifices on the altar (e.g. Lev. 1:7–9), they alone are mentioned in this introductory verse. The following verses, however, which go into greater procedural detail, draw a careful distinction between the functions of the priests and the laity in other aspects of the ceremony. It is similarly appropriate that they should be given their full title here, but referred to more simply as 'the priests' hereafter. None of this furnishes any evidence for a literary division of the text.

22. they killed the bulls: since **the priests** are specifically mentioned as the subject of the next clause, which deals with the manipulation of **the blood,** and as those who actually killed the sin offering in v. 24, it is clear that this verb must be understood as having an impersonal plural subject. In the Levitical laws of sacrifice (e.g. Lev. 1:5) the one bringing the offering himself kills the animal, while the blood is handled by the priest. Precisely the same procedure is described here, so that the king and officials of v. 20 must be understood as the subject. With this pattern clearly established in the case of **the bulls**, the same will obviously apply to **the rams** and **the lambs** following, so that the change of subject does not need to be spelt out in each case. Note that *RSV*'s use of the passive **was thrown**, though reflecting the change of subject correctly enough, is itself without warrant in the Hebrew, which simply says 'and they threw' in each case. For the blood rite itself, cf. Exod. 29:16; Lev. 1:5, 11, etc.

23. Although the practice of **laying hands** upon the sacrificial victim was current also for the burnt offering (cf. Lev. 1:4), it receives particular emphasis in the case of the **sin offering** (cf. Lev. 4) as an indication of the identification of the offerer (**the king and the assembly**) with the victim (**the he-goats**). There may also be intended an allusion to Lev. 16:21, the day of atonement ritual, though there are also some important points of difference; cf. R. Péter, *VT* 27 (1977), pp. 48–55.

24. and the priests killed them: contrast v. 22. It is not entirely clear why the Chronicler has made this distinction, which is not demanded by the Levitical laws of sacrifice. Our problem here is compounded by the fact that the regulations for the sin offering are in any case not as clear as we could wish; cf. B. A. Levine, *In the Presence of the Lord* (1974), and J. Milgrom, *VT* 26 (1976), pp. 333–7. Perhaps the solemnity of this unique occasion led the Chronicler to base certain of its elements on the annual day of atonement, where the (high) priest killed the goat of the sin offering (Lev. 16:15). **all Israel:** this contrasts with 'Judah' in v. 21, and is a further small point of apparent tension in the narrative which some have exploited in favour of a literary division. Rudolph harmonises by suggesting that 'Israel' here simply means Judah. However, while this equation is sometimes made in Chronicles, such a usage here would contradict the Chronicler's unvarying practice throughout the whole section from Hezekiah to the exile, in which he uses it to stress the completeness of the people following the fall of the northern monarchy (cf. *IBC*, pp. 126–30). Rather, we may note that the continuation of this verse suggests a different solution. The word order is emphatic, literally 'because for all Israel commanded the king (that) the burnt offering and the sin offering (should be made)'. This word order stresses that the offering was to cover an unexpectedly wider group of people than was originally envisaged in v. 21, implying a correction by **the king** of what the priests and officials apparently thought there. The phrase thus refers to the full extent of the population, without regard for the former political division.

By this device the Chronicler brings forcibly to the reader's attention Hezekiah's personal concern for the inhabitants of the old northern kingdom, a concern which is further developed in the following chapters.

25-30. This paragraph describes the role of the Levitical musicians in leading the worship of the assembly. Its simultaneity with the preceding paragraph is stressed (v. 27), and this accounts for any duplication in the narrative. The Chronicler's particular interest in the Levites, evident throughout this chapter, is sufficient to explain why he brought their role into prominence in this way. It is often attractively suggested that procedures from the Chronicler's own day underlie the description. At the same time the close parallel with the original dedication of the temple under Solomon (cf. 7:6, etc.) should not be overlooked.

25. cymbals, harps, and lyres: cf. 1 Chr. 15:16. **according to the commandment of David:** cf. 8:14 with 1 Chr. 15-16 and 25:1-6. **and of Gad the king's seer and of Nathan the prophet:** only here are they related to David's arrangements for the music of the cult, though for their importance in connection with David's reign generally, cf. 1 Chr. 29:29. The continuation of the verse makes clear that we need not look for some otherwise unattested tradition. The Chronicler was anxious to stress that these arrangements followed a word of **commandment . . . from the Lord**, and for his readers this would be accepted as most authoritative if it was understood as having been mediated **through his prophets**.

26. the instruments of David: cf. 1 Chr. 23:5, again part of the primary layer of 1 Chr. 23-27. **the priests with the trumpets:** in 1 Chr. 15:24 a similar reference was seen perhaps to be secondary as a caution against misunderstanding of the more casual introduction of trumpets in the list of instruments in v. 28 following. That does not mean, however, that the Chronicler was unaware of the law which made clear that they should be blown only by priests (cf. 5:12), so that there is no reason in the present context why he should not be responsible for this reference.

27. the burnt offering: the same as in v. 22. **began . . . began:** this is the emphasis of the paragraph. Priests, Levites and laity are all caught up together in the act of worship, each with their necessary part to play. Perhaps in this idealised description the Chronicler is again urging a conciliatory attitude in his own troubled times.

28. The whole assembly worshipped: Rudolph, believing this to imply an act of prostration, links it to the previous verse in order to allow for a separate prostration at the end of the ceremony in v. 29. Syntactically, however, the phrase is exactly parallel with the two which follow, from which in consequence it can hardly be detached. But in fact Rudolph's difficulty is only apparent. When the Chronicler intends a specific act of prostration he explicitly says so; cf. 'bowed themselves', v. 29, and 'bowed down', v. 30. By his day, **worshipped** need not of necessity have included this act, but had come to have the more general sense of attitude which we associate with it. Thus this verse again points to the participation of all classes in the service, namely, the laity (**the whole assembly**), the Levites (**the singers**) and the priests (**the trumpeters**), and to the fact that **this continued until the burnt offering was finished**.

30. This verse is a summarising conclusion, and so need not represent a further ceremony. **Asaph the seer**: see on 1 Chr. 25:5.

31–36. Following the formal acts of sin-offering and rededication of the sanctuary by the nation's leaders, the people are invited to bring their own tributes of worship and gratitude. In this way the regular round of temple services is reintroduced (v. 35b).

31. You have now consecrated yourselves to the Lord: the idiom used here normally refers to priestly investiture, but such an interpretation would be extremely difficult in view of the clear application to the whole **assembly** in what follows. Consequently several commentators have sought to avoid this difficulty by emendation. This is not necessary, however, since the use of the same idiom at 1 Chr. 29:5 shows that it can be taken in this wider sense when the context so demands. A further pointer to the relevance of 1 Chr. 29 may be found in the expression **a willing heart**, for the root *ndb* occurs seven times in that chapter (in vv. 5, 6, 9, 14 and 17), but only very rarely elsewhere in Chronicles. The word for **sacrifices** (*zᵉbāḥîm*) is an abbreviation for 'sacrifices of peace offerings' (cf. v. 35), of which **thank offerings** were one category (cf. Lev. 7:11ff.); it is thus probable that the conjunction **and** should be regarded as epexegetical, 'sacrifices which are (were) thank offerings'. Clearly they are appropriate in the circumstances to head the list of offerings that were brought.

32. Reference is next made to **burnt offerings**. Being offered in their entirety on the altar to God (Lev. 1), they were expressive of total self-giving worship in which the offerer himself enjoys no share. This may account for the smaller numbers by contrast with the following verse, and for the fact that they were brought by 'all who were of a willing heart' (v. 31).

33. consecrated offerings: these are generally thought to refer to the sacrifices of v. 31. The worshippers participated in these offerings, only certain parts being burnt on the altar or reserved for the priests.

34. and could not flay: this is curious in view of the fact that according to Lev. 1 it was the task of the offerer, not **the priest**.

However, there is evidence that 'the practice wavered after the return from the Exile' (R. de Vaux, *Studies in Old Testament Sacrifice* [1964], p. 29), and the polemical manner in which this verse continues suggests that it may be reflecting precisely such a controversy in which the Chronicler takes the part of **the Levites**. The reason why the priests were **too few** is that not enough had yet **sanctified themselves**, i.e., responded to the initial injunction of Hezekiah (v. 5). Thus, rather as with the underlying tone of vv. 12–16, the Chronicler follows up his factual statement that **the Levites helped them** with an additional comment which stands apart from the narrative sequence and which points to their more prompt response in this same particular.

35. This verse lists two further duties of the priests, in addition to the flaying of such a **great number of burnt offerings**, which also helps explain why they could not do their work unaided. **the fat of the peace offerings** was that part of the sacrifices of vv. 31 and 33 which had to be burnt on the altar (cf. Lev. 3), while **the libations** of wine were also prescribed to accompany **the burnt offerings** (cf. Exod. 29:40; Num. 15:1–15). **Thus the service of the house of the Lord was restored:** this summary clearly reflects the terminology of 8:16, which was also seen to be phrased by the Chronicler himself and which brought to a conclusion his account of the building and dedication of the temple by Solomon. The parallel drawn between the two kings is thus further underlined.

36. had done: more literally, 'prepared', 'established'. The same root is used as for the significant word 'restored' in the previous verse. **suddenly:** apparently less than three weeks (see vv. 17 and 20), and dating from the first day of Hezekiah's first regnal year at that (v. 3). This dramatic reversal in the situation prevailing under Ahaz was the cause of reverent joy for **Hezekiah and all the people**, and was doubtless intended by the Chronicler as a source of inspiration for his readers.

The Celebration of the Passover by all Israel

30:1–31:1

Following the restoration of the temple and its services in ch. 29, the emphasis now falls heavily upon Hezekiah's strenuous efforts to reunite in worship the hitherto separated peoples of the north and south. The interest of commentators has sometimes been so taken up with the question of the historicity of the Passover celebration itself that attention has tended to be diverted from this chief concern of the Chronicler. Yet it can be seen to be dominant throughout the

first half of the chapter (vv. 1–13), prominent in the concluding
section (note especially 30:25 and 31:1) and certainly to be present
also in the central section which describes the celebration itself,
since the Chronicler here shows particular interest in Hezekiah's
prayer on behalf of those from the north who strictly speaking were
not in the necessary state of ritual purity (vv. 17–20). This primary
theme of the chapter represents, of course, another major step in
the Chronicler's portrayal of Hezekiah as a second Solomon (cf. v.
26) and, as he presents it, it marks something of a return to the
conditions which had been disrupted by the division of the
monarchy.

While it is undoubtedly the case that the bulk of this chapter
reflects the Chronicler's own interests and style, yet his portrayal of
Hezekiah as showing particular interest in the north is certainly true
to history, even though he cannot have deduced it from the account
in 2 Kings; cf. Myers; E. W. Todd, *SJT* 9 (1956), pp. 289–91; E.
W. Nicholson, *Deuteronomy and Tradition* (1967), pp. 98–9; McKay,
p. 17; B. Oded, in *IJH*, pp. 443f. First, the political conditions for
such an interest were right early in Hezekiah's reign, for the northern kingdom had fallen but Assyria was for a short time preoccupied
with other parts of its extensive empire (cf. H. W. F. Saggs, in D.
J. Wiseman [ed.], *Peoples of Old Testament Times* [1973], p. 162);
thus an expansion northwards by Hezekiah was almost an inevitability, given his desire to reform with its probable political implications (31:1). Second, it is highly significant that Hezekiah named
his son Manasseh, one of the leading tribes of the north and one
which, when linked with Ephraim (cf. 31:1), can virtually stand for
the northern region itself. Finally, the possibility may be noted of
links by marriage between the royal house and the inhabitants of
the old northern kingdom, though this is more speculative; cf. W.
F. Albright, *The Biblical Period* (1950), p. 45.

Turning now to the issue of Hezekiah's celebration of the Passover, we confront a problem which is much less easy to resolve and
over which there is great disagreement amongst scholars. This is the
result of uncertainty about the history of Passover and its association
with the feast of Unleavened Bread on the one hand, and on the
other of the relationship between the account of the celebration here
and that of the Passover in Josiah's time (2 Kg. 23:21–23, expanded
considerably in 2 Chr. 35:1–19). Some of the issues involved, relevant though they be, go far beyond the scope of the present commentary. It is therefore here acknowledged that many of the points
only touched on in the following comments deserve much fuller
discussion. Equally it is possible to list as examples only a few of
the many works which have been devoted to these questions.

(1) First, we must note that there are a few scholars who argue that the Chronicler had access to a reliable tradition. It would be agreed that many of the details reflect later developments, but nevertheless, it is maintained, it need not be doubted that Hezekiah did celebrate the Passover in Jerusalem. S. Talmon, for instance, *VT* 8 (1958), pp. 48–74, argues that 'we are confronted here with a genuine historical source, accurate even in details', on the grounds that the celebration of the Passover in the second month was necessary in order to accommodate those who came from the north because ever since the time of Jeroboam their calendar had lagged one month behind that in the south; cf. 1 Kg. 12:32–33. This accounts for the derision with which Hezekiah's invitation was initially greeted (v. 10) and the reason for its deferment by one month (v. 2); see also M. Gaster, *ET* 24 (1913), pp. 198–201.

Moriarty, *CBQ* 27 (1965), pp. 399–406, disagrees with Talmon, pointing out with justice that the invitation to the north was issued for a celebration in the second month from the outset (vv. 2–4). Nevertheless, he too accepts the basic historicity of the account precisely because of its irregularities, namely the celebration in the second month and the lack of preparation even then on the part of many who participated (vv. 17–20). This, he suggests, rules out the possibility that the Chronicler has merely constructed the account out of his own imagination in an attempt to magnify Hezekiah at the expense of Josiah. 'The greater probability seems to be that the Chronicler was faced with an unusual and an unorthodox historical event.'

Finally, we may note amongst those who take a positive approach to the account in this chapter the view of A. Phillips, *Ancient Israel's Criminal Law* (1970), pp. 167–79. Phillips contends that 'the nature of Hezekiah's reform has in fact been summarised in Exod. 34:10ff., which has been created as the climax to the pre-priestly Sinai material by the JE redactor writing in Judah in the light of that reform'. Thus he sees Hezekiah's celebration of the Passover to lie behind Exod. 34:18ff., though he admits that the present account also betrays some misunderstandings of his source by the Chronicler.

(2) Secondly, we may turn to note the view of the majority of scholars who, in complete contrast with the foregoing, find no historical basis in the Chronicler's account whatever. Apart from considerations of general probability, which will vary according to one's attitude to such questions as the nature and extent of other sources that may have been available to the Chronicler, three main arguments are advanced in connection with this narrative in particular.

First, there seems to be a contradiction between v. 26, which

asserts that 'there had been nothing like this in Jerusalem' since the
time of Solomon, and 35:18 (based loosely on 2 Kg. 23:22), which
claims with regard to Josiah's Passover that there had not been the
like since the days of Samuel. This is regarded as decisive by, for
instance, J. B. Segal, *The Hebrew Passover* (1963), pp. 18–19. He
also dismisses Rudolph's attempt at harmonisation along the line
that 30:26 alludes only to the joy of the occasion as having 'little to
commend it' (though see further on 35:18 below).

Second, Rudolph's own objection to the historicity of the account
arises rather from his opinion that the prescription ordering that the
Passover should be celebrated together at the central sanctuary in
Jerusalem is found only in Dt. 16:5f., and that this would have
been unknown as early as Hezekiah's reign.

Finally, others such as E. Kutsch, *ZThK* 55 (1958), pp. 1–35,
argue for the same conclusion on the basis of the history of the
related festivals of Passover and Unleavened Bread. It is generally
thought that these two festivals were of separate origin and that for
most of the monarchical period they were also celebrated separately.
It was only in Josiah's time that the two were combined, this being
the inevitable outcome of the Deuteronomic legislation: once Passover, observed at the same time of the year, came also to be
regarded as a pilgrimage festival, it was natural that the two should
come to be celebrated together. The Chronicler's portrayal of this
taking place already in Hezekiah's time is thus anachronistic.

If, for such reasons, the Chronicler's account is regarded as un-
historical, what factors influenced him in his composition? The most
widely adopted view is stated succinctly by CM: 'Since Hezekiah
was held to have been a reformer equally with Josiah, it was felt he
too must have celebrated in a similar manner the Passover'. In
addition, Segal (pp. 19 and 228–30) observes a number of details in
the narrative which closely reflect the practice of later times, so that
his own experience of Passover will also have contributed to his
description. Finally, Hezekiah's handling of the issue of participation by the northerners is also taken by some to reflect the con-
troversies of his own day with the Samaritan community; cf.
Rudolph, and Kraus, *Worship in Israel*, pp. 49–55.

(3) Before moving to a fresh evaluation of this major difference
of opinion between scholars, notice must be taken of a third, intermediate position, which has been advocated in particular by H.
Haag, in H. Gese and H. P. Rüger (eds), *Wort und Geschichte*
(1973), pp. 87–94, though in some important respects he was anticipated by Welch, *WC*, pp. 108ff. Haag attempts a somewhat
intricate literary analysis of the chapter from which, he claims, four
stages in its composition emerge. A brief, pre-chronistic core told

of a celebration of Unleavened Bread. This was taken up and developed by the Chronicler himself. Third, this account was later worked over by a reviser, and only at this stage were the references to Passover introduced under the influence of ch. 35. Finally, a number of harmonising glosses brought the text into its present form.

In my opinion, Haag's literary analysis is not successful. The whole chapter betrays too many features of the Chronicler's own style to allow for such a major later revision. Moreover the account displays a literary unity which precludes so elaborate a division. Thus, for instance, Haag opens his analysis by finding a conflict between vv. 1 and 2 which overlooks the correct assessment of Rudolph that v. 1 is a summary introduction to the whole of the following paragraph. Nevertheless, at the historical level Haag has suggested a line of approach which deserves further investigation. Can the hypothesis be substantiated that the Chronicler was working on the basis of an earlier tradition which told of a celebration of the feast of Unleavened Bread alone by Hezekiah?

Several points may be made in support of such a hypothesis. Inevitably they fall short of proof, but they have the merit of drawing the Chronicler's presumed method of composition here into line with what we have seen elsewhere to be the case. First, this suggestion enables us to do justice to Moriarty's arguments for a historical nucleus noted above, since those arguments (and, come to that, those of Talmon and possibly of Phillips too) do not specifically relate to Passover. They would apply equally well to an unusual and irregular celebration of Unleavened Bread. It would certainly be odd if the Chronicler introduced such irregularities into an invented and idealising portrayal if there were not some constraint upon him from tradition to do so. Secondly, the arguments of those who deny any historicity to the account lose their force on this hypothesis. There would be no contradiction with 35:18, since that explicitly refers to the Passover. That Hezekiah did move in the direction of centralisation will be argued at 31:1 below, and the force of that point may be given full weight without having to introduce the specific issue of when a centralised Passover was first introduced. Similarly, the question of the combination of Passover and Unleavened Bread is also irrelevant to this new phase of the discussion.

Third, and most important, however, comparison between the Chronicler's description here and in ch. 35 reveals a significant difference of emphasis. At 35:1–19, under the influence of the brief notice of his *Vorlage*, the Chronicler sets out to provide an elaborate account of a Passover celebration. In this, there is only one passing

reference to the feast of Unleavened Bread (v. 17). No doubt this
was introduced because the two were inseparably joined in his own
day. It should be noted, however, that it seems to be added almost
as an afterthought, and it plays no significant part in the description
whatsoever. The heading to the present chapter (v. 1), with its
reference to Passover, seems to suggest that the Chronicler is likely
to proceed in the same manner here. However, when we come to
the account of the celebration itself, we find that the feast of Unleavened Bread is far more prominent, and indeed in certain important respects it overshadows the Passover itself. Particularly
striking is the fact that in both the heading (v. 13) and the conclusion
(vv. 21–22) of the account it stands alone, without any allusion to
the Passover whatsoever. The contrast with the Chronicler's approach in ch. 35 gives rise to the strong suspicion that this is an
inherited element to which, understandably enough in the conditions of his own day, he has himself added the description of a
Passover.

As one of the three long-standing pilgrim feasts of Israel, Unleavened Bread would be a natural occasion for Hezekiah to use as
part both of his reform and his attempt to reunite the people. We
may thus conclude that the Chronicler had access to the account of
such an event. The shape of that account cannot now, however, be
recovered, for he has rewritten it almost completely under the influence of the equivalent festival of his own day, as demonstrated
by Segal. Consequently, in commenting on this chapter we must
inevitably respect the now unified composition with which the
Chronicler has presented us.

1–12. The preparations for the celebration of the Passover are
primarily concerned with the gathering to Jerusalem of representatives of the whole of Israel.

30:1. As rightly noted by Rudolph, this verse stands as a heading.
The following verses will fill out the details. **all Israel:** though the
reference here must, as the sequel shows, be to the northern territory, it is clear from the context that it is part of an inclusive
description of the land and its people. As if to avoid any possible
misunderstanding on this very point, the Chronicler clarifies his
intention with the parallel addition of **and wrote letters also to
Ephraim and Manasseh.** The oral proclamation of the heralds was
supported with written authorisation, as well-known royal procedure in the Persian period; cf. E. J. Bickerman, *JBL* 65 (1946),
pp. 247–75. **that they should come to the house of the Lord at
Jerusalem:** on the possibility that Hezekiah's reform may have
influenced the Deuteronomic movement, see 31:1.

2. had taken counsel: though obscured by *RSV*, precisely the same idiom is used as at 1 Chr. 13:1, where David showed a similar concern to gather all Israel together for the 'cultic reform' which marked the start of his reign. **in the second month:** this irregularity may be one of the elements which the Chronicler derived from his earlier source (see above). However this might be explained at the historical level, he provides two reasons in the next verse which derive directly from his own particular interpretation of Hezekiah's reign.

3. The first reason was that **the priests had not sanctified themselves in sufficient number:** this is a somewhat artificial explanation, for it can hardly be supposed that all would have been ready in any case by the fourteenth day of the first month, the normal date for Passover. This, then, seems to be the continuation of the theme of criticism of the priesthood already noted several times in ch. 29, and probably reflecting a dispute in the Chronicler's own day. Secondly, **nor had the people assembled in Jerusalem:** this will have been the more important reason for the Chronicler, as already noted in the introduction to this chapter above. In his view it was for this very purpose that the celebration was being held in the first place.

4. Legal justification for agreeing to a postponement of the Passover will no doubt have been found in Num. 9:9–12, which allows an individual who is unclean or absent abroad to celebrate in the second month. Exceptionally, this was here applied to the whole community.

5. all Israel, from Beersheba to Dan: it is noteworthy that under Hezekiah the land is regarded as having returned to its full Solomonic extent. See also on 1 Chr. 21:2, and *IBC*, pp. 123f. and 128. **in great numbers as prescribed:** as a reference to the written law, this would seem to imply knowledge of Dt. 16:1–8, although Haran, *Temples and Temple Service*, pp. 341–8, has argued that Passover had long been regarded as a pilgrim-feast, and that this is reflected in the early legal codes as well.

6–9. The text of **the letters from the king and his princes** plays the same role here as the so-called 'Levitical sermon' does elsewhere. It reflects the Chronicler's own application of his narrative, reinforced by citation or allusion to Scripture. Several general themes of considerable significance emerge. First, the letters are addressed to the whole population, **all Israel and Judah**, not just the north alone, and the reaction to it of both north and south is subsequently recorded (vv. 10–12). This fact reinforces our earlier interpretation of the reign of Ahaz (ch. 28), where a process of 'levelling down' of both Israel and Judah was noted. Thus in the Chronicler's presentation there is nothing here that cannot apply to Judah as much as

Israel, for she too was given over to **desolation** (v. 7), came under God's **fierce anger** (v. 8), was partly led captive (v. 9; see on 28:5), and, on the basis of 28:20f., could even be called **the remnant of you who have escaped from the hand of the kings of Assyria** (v. 6). These letters, therefore, provide further helpful evidence of the reuniting under Hezekiah of the formerly divided people.

Secondly, the repeated appeal not to be **like your fathers** (vv. 7 and 8) is to be understood against the background of the Chronicler's doctrine of individual retribution. There is evidence from the literature of the post-exilic period that despair often beset the community of Jerusalem because they felt that they were heirs to a situation which left them in every way in such a low state that full restoration was no longer possible and therefore no longer worth striving for. The emphasis of the Chronicler in the present passage, however, points in quite the opposite direction. Each generation stands or falls on its own merits before God, whose ability to intervene dramatically has been frequently noted. Thus he appeals to his readers to turn from a deadening obsession with the failures of the past and to grasp the possibilities of the present and future by yielding to the Lord (v. 8) with the full assurance that he is **gracious and merciful** (v. 9).

Thirdly, we find expressed in this passage a new theme which is rather distinctive in *OT*, namely, that the continuity of tradition runs through the community in the land rather than through those in exile. Moreover, the Chronicler here picks up and develops the theme of Solomon's prayer at the dedication of the temple to the effect that if those who remain will **return to the Lord**, those in captivity **will find compassion with their captors** (v. 9). This too may be seen as a powerful appeal to, and motivation for, the Chronicler's own readers.

Finally, the importance of the canonical prophets in shaping both the Chronicler's thought and his terminology must not be overlooked. This applies particularly to the four-fold use of the root *šûb*, to **return**, to **turn again**. In vv. 6, 8 and 9 it is employed equally to express repentance by the people, the turning again towards them by God, the removal from them of God's anger, and the return home of those in exile. Such word-play on this root is associated in particular with Jeremiah, although it is also found in Zech. 1:3 and Mal. 3:7; for a full study, cf. W. L. Holladay, *The Root šûbh in the Old Testament* (1958). Also from Zech. 1:2–6 comes the appeal **Do not be like your fathers**, and perhaps the reference to God's **fierce anger**, so that clearly those verses were particularly in the Chronicler's mind; see further W. A. M. Beuken, *Haggai-Sacharja 1–8* (1967), pp. 84–115, though he unnecessarily rules out the possibility of direct literary dependence (p. 92). This is of further interest, because already there in Zechariah the words of the pre-exilic prophets, and presumably of Jeremiah in particular, have begun to take on canonical status through their vindication in the exile. The Chronicler is thus seen to be continuing a process of development already attested by the prophetic literature itself. More than that, however, we must note that he has also begun to detach the word from its immediate historical context. Both Jeremiah and Zechariah have the Babylonian exile in mind as their point of reference, whereas we have seen that the Chronicler has made the exile into a recurring, 'typical' situation within the continuing life of the community. In this way he is able to reapply the originally historically-bound prophetic word and to actualise it even for those who remained in the land. The final step towards this universalising of the originally quite specific promise may be noted in the inclusion of the theme of return in the programmatic divine statement in 7:14, whose influence on many parts of the Chronicler's narrative has been repeatedly noted. In fact it is most striking that all four of the verbs describing repentance in that verse are featured with some prominence in the Chronicler's account of Hezekiah's reign; cf. vv. 11, 18, 19, 32:20 and 24 below.

6. the remnant of you who have escaped: of all *OT* writers, only the Chronicler applies this expression either to those left in the north or to the whole population remaining in the land after the fall of Samaria; see further on 34:9 and 21.

7. who were faithless: see on 1 Chr. 10:13. It is particularly appropriate in a description of the generation of Ahaz; cf. 28:19 and 22.

8. yield yourselves to the Lord: for the suggestion that 'the current legal usage at the formation of covenants provided the background for the phrase' used here, cf. Z. W. Falk, *JSS* 4 (1959), p. 269.

9. There is a clear echo here of 1 Kg. 8:50. There, it occurs in Solomon's prayer at the dedication of the temple, but precisely this verse was omitted by the Chronicler in his parallel account at 6:39 above. This transference to Hezekiah of the same promise and assurance that Solomon had given earlier is fully intelligible in view of his patterning of the one upon the other.

10–12. The response of both north and south to Hezekiah's invitation is now recorded.

11. as far as Zebulun: there is such variety and inconsistency in the Chronicler's naming of the tribes of the north in this chapter that the references should probably be taken as representative or exemplary only. Thus, contrast this statement with v. 5 above, and for the response contrast vv. 12 and 18 below. In fact, if we include the references to Simeon and Naphtali in 34:6, it is only the two and a half transjordanian tribes that remain unmentioned in a reform context in this last major section of the Chronicler's work, an omission which may perhaps reflect the conditions of his own time. **they laughed them to scorn, and mocked them:** see also 36:16.

11. a few: an unnecessary addition by *RSV*. That the Chronicler did *not* take such a pessimistic view is demonstrated by v. 18. **humbled themselves:** see on 7:14 and on vv. 6–9 above. No doubt with an eye on the difficulties of his own day, the Chronicler will go on to show how concessions were made by Hezekiah towards those who came from the north to Jerusalem in this condition.

12. also: the use of this word further supports our contention that the response mentioned in the previous verse should be judged most positively.

13–22. The celebration of the feast of Unleavened Bread and the Passover itself. Once again the primary emphasis is on the numbers who joined together for the celebration.

13. For the suggestion that the Chronicler's inherited material mentioned **the feast of unleavened bread** alone, without reference to Passover, as would have fitted Hezekiah's time, see the introduction to this chapter. **in the second month:** see on vv. 2–4.

14. The Chronicler can hardly be expected to have envisaged such a major festival without at the very least the removal of **the altars that were in Jerusalem** which Ahaz had set up (28:24). **and all the altars for burning incense:** perhaps an explanation of the foregoing phrase in the light of 28:4 and 25. **the Kidron valley:** see on 29:16.

15. And they killed: the context indicates that this refers to the laity. However, the sequel shows that not all were able to do this because they were not in a state of ritual purity. Thus the next few verses concentrate on the particular arrangements that were made for this group. To describe these arrangements, the second half of this verse in fact has to start somewhat further back in time. Since the killing of **the passover lamb** had to be done on a single and particular evening, and since the next verse tells us that **the priests and the Levites** were ready at their places for this occasion, it is clear that their actions described here had already been accomplished earlier, presumably under the impact of seeing so many lay people gathering enthusiastically. The verbs should therefore be translated in the pluperfect tense: 'had been' **put to shame** . . . 'had' **sanctified themselves . . . and** 'had' **brought** . . . Contrast also 29:34. **burnt offerings:** not the Passover lambs, but contributions as part of the priests' self-preparation (cf. 29:31–36).

16. according to the law of Moses: this is a purely general reference to the priestly sections of the Pentateuchal law which assume the prominence of the cultic officials on all such occasions. Again it should be noted that the manipulation of **the blood** by **the priests** relates only to the offerings of those specified in the following verses, as the action of **the Levites** here and in v. 17 shows.

17. Finally, the Chronicler reaches the explanation for the fore-going special arrangements. His narrative through this section is thus somewhat involved, but not for that reason open to alternative explanation. **many in the assembly:** primarily those from the north. The Chronicler may be writing here with pointed intent in showing that it was precisely this group whom the officials of the Jerusalem cult went out of their way to assist.

18–20. These verses are important in revealing that the intent of the heart and the effectiveness of prayer override purely ritual con-siderations in the opinion of the Chronicler. **Ephraim, Manasseh, Issachar, and Zebulun:** see on v. 11. Even though these people **had not cleansed themselves** (cf. Num. 9:6), they were still not ex-cluded from eating the Passover because of Hezekiah's prevailing (v. 20) prayer for forgiveness. **Hezekiah had prayed:** this introduces (together with 32:20 and 24) the third element of repentance listed in 7:14 (see on vv. 6–9 and 11 for the first two), and it is immediately followed by a near equivalent of the fourth with the expression **sets his heart to seek God.** The divine response there was threefold: 'I will hear from heaven, and will forgive their sin and heal their land'. Each of these elements too is picked up here. Two are explicit in v. 20: **the Lord heard Hezekiah, and healed the people.** The other is not verbally exact, but is certainly reflected in the request for **pardon.** The Chronicler's readers are thus forcibly reminded that the stipulations of 7:14 are not necessarily to be interpreted cultically, and indeed the prayer of Solomon to which they form part of the answer further makes this clear.

21–22. The summarising conclusion again concentrates exclu-sively on **the feast of unleavened bread.** However, some of the accompanying celebrations reflect later practices, according to Segal, *op.cit.*, p. 19, notably the ceremonial **singing** (though this could equally well be a typical addition of the Chronicler in line with his descriptions of major celebrations elsewhere) and the sacrifice of **peace offerings** during the **seven days** of the festival. See also on v. 27. The reference to **all the Levites who showed good skill in the service of the Lord** is to be attributed to that same strand of polemic which has been noted repeatedly in this and the previous chapter.

30:23–31:1. The celebration is continued for a second week and the people's enthusiasm finds further expression in the removal of high places throughout the land.

23. the whole assembly: further defined in v. 25. The emphasis on the united action of all the people is again prominent in this paragraph. **another seven days:** a conscious reflection of the extended festival which marked the original dedication of the temple under Solomon (7:8–9). **with gladness:** see on 1 Chr. 12:40.

24. The extension of the festival was made possible both because of the enormous contributions of **bulls** and **sheep for offerings** by **Hezekiah** and **the princes** (note that the same group was responsible for initiating the united celebration, vv. 2, 6 and 12) and because **the priests sanctified themselves in great numbers,** thus finally overcoming the hitherto most persistent hindrance to the reform movement.

25. The joy already noted in v. 23 is said to have been shared by **the whole assembly,** here given an extensive definition. **the sojourners:** in pre-exilic times these were 'resident aliens' who had both settled in Israel and adopted her religion. Unlike more casual visitors, they were permitted a share in the Passover (cf. Exod. 12:48f.). By the Chronicler's time, however, it is probable that the word had already begun to cover those known later as proselytes.

26. Since the time of Solomon: while the immediate emphasis is on the **great joy in Jerusalem,** the position of this verse in the summary of the festival as a whole suggests that the Chronicler also intended it to characterise his entire description, and we have noted many points at which Hezekiah appears indeed as a 'second Solomon'. Not the least significant point in this connection is that the joy is attributed, by way of the inclusion of the previous verse, to the reuniting of the people. This is certainly the most obvious link between Hezekiah and Solomon and it is one which could not be said of any of the intervening kings.

27. the priests and the Levites: MT does not include the copula: 'the priests, the Levites', often rendered 'the Levitical priests'. The sudden introduction of this Deuteronomic phraseology, which runs counter to the Chronicler's more normal designation (see on 5:5), has puzzled many commentators. It is, however, noteworthy that his description of the removal of the high places which immediately follows is also expressed in Deuteronomic terms and yet seems to rest on some form of inherited material in addition to 2 Kg. 18:4, and that the arrangements for the priestly and Levitical 'portions' in the next paragraph are based on the Deuteronomic law of the tithe. We may thus conclude either that the Chronicler was influenced by all this in his phraseology, if he was himself composing freely here, or that we have here a small indication that he was drawing in part on a fuller account of Hezekiah's reform than that preserved in 2 Kg. 18 which itself employed Deuteronomic language. Such a speculation is by no means improbable, for the notice of 2 Kg. 18:4 could well have invited expansion in fuller texts than our MT within the Deuteronomic school. Alternatively, if we are correct in supposing that Deuteronomy is itself not a totally new composition from Josiah's time, but has incorporated much earlier material (see, for instance, on 19:4–11), we must clearly allow both for the possible influence of Hezekiah's reform on the composition of Deuteronomy itself without automatically assuming that any point of contact with Deuteronomy is inevitably the result of its own later influence on the historical record, and for the possible influence of some early form of Deuteronomy on Hezekiah's reform in the first place; cf. McKay, pp. 17f., though contrast the novel opinion of Haran, *Temples and Temple Service*, pp. 132–48, that Hezekiah's reform was based on the ideology of P. **and blessed the people:** cf. Num. 6:22–27. According to Segal, p. 19, this is another element in the Chronicler's description which was 'the accepted practice in later times', though here, of course, it can hardly be called part of the Passover celebration itself. **their voice was heard:** no specific outcome is recorded. However, the final part of the verse reminds the reader very much of the repeated requests in Solomon's prayer of dedication (e.g. 2 Chr. 6:21, etc.), so that the general well-being of the nation will be primarily in view.

31:1. Before the people return home, they destroy **the high places** with their related cult objects not only in **the cities of Judah**, but also in **Ephraim and Manasseh**, a title here standing for the region of the old northern kingdom. For the Chronicler, therefore, this serves admirably as a conclusion to his foregoing account.

A few words of the account have a parallel in 2 Kg. 18:4, although the reference in that verse to the destruction of Nehushtan, 'the bronze serpent that Moses had made', is omitted out of pietistic considerations. However, despite this parallel the Chronicler's account is more detailed, both expanding on the fact that they **broke down the high places and the altars throughout all Judah and Benjamin** and adding the reference to the extension of the activity into the north.

It is generally agreed now that Hezekiah did undertake some form of cult centralisation. The biblical witness to this is not confined to a single verse, but can appeal also to a reference to it in the report of the Rabshakeh's speech in 2 Kg. 18:22 and to the evident implication of Jer. 26:19, which refers to Hezekiah's reformation under the impact of Micah's preaching. It should be noted, however, that the archaeological evidence which has been adduced in support of this literary evidence is itself uncertain; cf. Y. Yadin, *BASOR* 222 (1976), pp. 5–18. As for the extension of centralisation to the north as well, we have already noted the probability that Hezekiah was particularly concerned in this direction. More specifically, however, it has been argued independently by both E. W. Nicholson, *VT* 13 (1963), pp. 380–9, and M. Weinfeld, *JNES* 23 (1964), pp. 202–12, that part of the reason for centralisation in the first place was precisely the desire to undo the work of Jeroboam I and to reunite the people around Jerusalem as the religious centre for the nation as a whole. This, of course, need not conflict in any way with the possibility noted in the previous verse that Hezekiah's thinking in this direction was influenced by an early form of Deuteronomism.

Arrangements for the Continuing Temple Worship

31:2–21

In the idealised portrayal of the previous two chapters the Chronicler has compressed what is likely to have been a lengthy period of reform into little more than two months, starting from the very outset of Hezekiah's reign. In this way the undoing of Ahaz's apostasy has been turned into more or less a single act, reminiscent of the original building and dedication of the temple under Solomon. Following this auspicious beginning, therefore, he will have felt the need to go on to describe the provision and arrangements for the continuation of the regular services in the temple; cf. 8:12–15.

2. The first need was to restore **the divisions of the priests and of the Levites.** This marks a return to the order introduced by Solomon (see on 8:14), who was himself acting under David's instructions. As is usual in the Chronicler's composition, the handling of **the burnt offerings and peace offerings** will have been the responsibility of the priests, while the Levites acted primarily as gatekeepers and singers—**to give thanks and praise. the camp of the Lord:** cf. 1 Chr. 9:18, where the explanation provided in the following verse makes clear that this is used as a figurative expression for the temple, based on the account of the Tabernacle in the wilderness narratives (Num. 2).

3. Next comes the need of provision for the **burnt offerings** both for the daily and more occasional festival services. Again, just like Solomon before him (8:12f.), Hezekiah himself makes this contribution **from his own possessions.** A further link with Solomon is to be observed by comparison of this verse with 2:4; see the comments there, which point to the importance of the present verse in the literary structure of Chronicles. **as it is written in the law of**

the Lord: this refers to the offerings themselves, not to a require-
ment that the king should provide for them. Specific references are
also given at 2:4 above.

4-19. Thirdly, Hezekiah arranges for the proper collection and
storage of the tithes and other contributions of the people on which
the priests and Levites were dependent for their livelihood if they
were to be able to devote themselves full-time to their duties. There
is good evidence that this was a recurring problem in the post-exilic
period (cf. Neh. 10:35-9; 12:47; 13:10-13; Mal. 3:8-10), so that
the Chronicler may well have hoped to challenge his readers in this
regard by his description of the people's enthusiastic response.

4. The command is initially directed only to **the people who lived
in Jerusalem**. The contrast with what follows emphasises the people's willingness to contribute. The **portion due** will have included
tithes, first fruits, and parts of some of the sacrifices. Here, however,
no further detail is given since the emphasis of the paragraph is on
the unexpected sequel to which this verse provides only a foil. **that
they might give themselves to the law of the Lord:** this is usually
explained as referring to their temple duties. There may also, however, be an allusion to the increasing importance of study of the law
for its own sake in the post-exilic period; cf. Pss. 1 and 119; Mal.
2:6-7, etc.

5. was spread abroad: this is the only place in *OT* where this
verb (*prṣ*) is used of a command or speech. Since it usually has
overtones of violence, the meaning is probably that, contrary to
Hezekiah's intention, his command to the residents of Jerusalem
became unexpectedly widely known. **the people of Israel** here will
then refer to the whole of the population (including the remaining
inhabitants of the old northern kingdom), not just those mentioned
in the previous verse. The manner in which this wider circle responded suggests a dependence upon the Deuteronomic law; cf. Dt.
12:5-12; 14:22-27, and *IBC*, pp. 129f. **grain, wine, oil:** in Dt.
12:17 it is expressly forbidden to eat the tithe of these three com-
modities 'within thy gates'. They had to be brought by all in kind
to the sanctuary. **first fruits . . . tithe:** according to the probably
later law of Num. 18:12f. and 21 the former were for the priests
and the latter for the Levites, though Dt. 18:4 already points in that
direction. **honey:** cf. Lev. 2:11f. **all the produce of the field:** Dt.
14:22.

6. This verse introduces a further act, to be distinguished from
that of the previous verse, namely, the bringing of **the tithe of
cattle and sheep**, i.e. livestock as opposed to produce. To bring
livestock in kind to the sanctuary was not a practicable proposition
for the whole population, and the Deuteronomic law makes pro-

vision for this. The present verse, therefore, must be dealing only with those for whom 'the way' was not 'too long' (cf. Dt. 14:24 with 12:15f.), not the whole population as previously. This will explain the carefully defined subject at the start of the verse with its restriction **who lived in the cities of Judah**. Since in this part of his narrative the Chronicler generally uses the expression **the people of Israel** to refer to the whole of the population without regard for the former division, **and Judah** should probably be omitted. For the Chronicler here to be contradicting his usual practice by referring to those who came south to Judah from the north during the period of the divided monarchy (cf. 15:9), as most commentators assume, would lead to a hopeless clash with the use of the same phrase in the previous verse. **the dedicated things**: MT has 'the tithe of the dedicated things', but since they were dedicated in their entirety, this cannot be right. *RSV* therefore deletes 'the tithe' with earlier commentators. *NEB* follows approximately the alternative suggestion of Rudolph who adds *kol-t^ebû'at śādeh* so as to read 'and the tithe of all the produce of the field as dedicated things'.

7. the third month is the time of the grain harvest, and **the seventh month** marks the end of the vine and fruit harvesting; cf. Exod. 23:16.

8–10. Because of the people's willing response, more than enough is collected; there may be a further reference here to 1 Chr. 29 as well as to 2 Chr. 24:8–14.

8. Hezekiah and the princes: see on 30:24. **they blessed the Lord and his people Israel**: as v. 10 explains, the people's initial response in giving was more than matched by God's blessing in the harvest; both are therefore legitimately praised.

10. Azariah the chief priest, who was of the house of Zadok: if the genealogy of 1 Chr. 6:1–15 is taken at its face value, it would be difficult to link this Azariah with the one mentioned in vv. 13–14 on chronological grounds. However, it was noted that that list was not complete, so that the Chronicler may have intended the identification nevertheless. He cannot, however, have believed that this was also the Azariah of 26:17. Since there is now a considerable weight of evidence to suggest that papponymy (the practice of naming a child after his grandfather) was common in the Chronicler's own day, especially amongst priestly and other leading families (cf. *JTS* ns 28 [1977], pp. 61–4), it may be that he assumed this practice to have been current also in earlier times and that this will then explain how he arrived at the names either here or at 26:17 or both.

11–19. Hezekiah makes careful provision for the storage and distribution of all these contributions. Rooms are prepared in the temple (vv. 11–12), and two Levites with ten assistants are put in charge of the storage (vv. 12–13). Distribution, however, is in the hands of another Levite with 6 assistants who lived in the priestly cities (vv. 14–15). Considerable care is exercised to define precisely who is entitled to a share of these offerings (vv. 16–19), though unfortunately the significance of some of the details is far from clear.

11. to prepare: there is nothing to indicate whether this involved new building or the adaptation of existing facilities.

12–13. Little of interest for our present purposes can be gathered from these names, most of which are known from elsewhere, often in Levitical lists. **Azariah**, the high priest of v. 10, is here called **the chief officer of the house of God:** cf. 1 Chr. 9:11.

14. keeper of the east gate: 1 Chr. 9:18 indicates the prominence of such an official. **freewill offerings . . . the contribution . . . the most holy offerings:** these refer specifically to the priestly contributions.

15. In addition to being in charge of the priestly portions in the temple, Kore was also responsible for the distribution of the general priestly and Levitical portions to those resident **in the cities of the priests**. For this work he had the assistance of six other Levites. **their brethren:** it is not clear whether this refers to priests and Levites together, or to the Levites alone. The introductory nature of the verse would suggest the former, with more specific details following in vv. 17–19, while the addition of **by divisions** might point rather to the latter possibility. However, it may be misleading to press the force of **by divisions** in such an introductory verse, while the continuation in v. 16, as translated by *RSV*, would in any case make clear that the writer was aware of the problem and took steps to avoid such a misunderstanding.

16. those enrolled by genealogy: i.e. the priests, as the next verse shows. However, the translation of the whole of this first phrase is quite uncertain; cf. *NEB*, 'irrespective of their registration'. Regardless of the precise translation, the purpose of the phrase is to stress the inclusive nature of the distribution. The verse as a whole is thus somewhat parenthetical. **from three years old and upwards:** that is, from the time at which they were weaned. Verse 18 makes clear that children of priests were included in the distribution; it is thus not necessary to emend to 'thirty'. **all who entered the house of the Lord:** it would seem that when a priestly family went to Jerusalem from one of the priestly cities to fulfil their term of service, their family went with them and drew support from the distribution in the temple.

17. Since **the priests** were organised by families, their enrolment was **according to their fathers' houses**. (This may have changed shortly after the Chronicler's time with the introduction of the

twenty-four priestly courses.) The Levites, however, were divided
on the basis of their duties (see the primary layer of 1 Chr. 23–27),
so that they were appropriately enrolled **according to their offices,
by their divisions. from twenty years old and upwards:** cf. 1 Chr.
23:3, 24 and 27. It is evident that the figure changed under the
pressure of developing circumstances.

18. The translation and meaning of this verse are again quite
uncertain. *RSV* relates it specifically to **the priests,** for which there
is no justification in MT, and indeed **the whole multitude** (better,
'company') might suggest that the reference is to both priests and
Levites without distinction. In that case the purpose of the verse
will be to stress that families were included with their fathers in the
registration. **their little children:** this may refer to those under three
years of age; cf. v. 16. **their wives, their sons, and their daughters:**
Rudolph argues that this must be a later addition since v. 16 refers
only to males over three years old. However, this suggestion fails to
distinguish between the fact that v. 16 relates only to those on
temple duty in Jerusalem whereas the present verse relates to the
more permanent residence in the cities of the priests. In the latter
case we should expect to find consideration made for families.

19. Since v. 15 has already dealt with distribution to those who
lived in the cities of the priests, it would appear that the Chronicler
drew a distinction between them and those **who were in the fields
of common land belonging to their cities;** he thus makes clear that
the latter group were not forgotten either, but received **their portions** from some who lived in the cities themselves and who were
designated by name for this task. **and to everyone among the
Levites who was enrolled:** it is difficult to see how this can be
fitted into the verse, which is specifically dealing with a particular
group amongst **the sons of Aaron, the priests** only. It is probably
either an addition by the Chronicler to his inherited material or else
a later misplaced corrective gloss on part of the preceding paragraph,
which may well have been as opaque to readers in antiquity as it is
to us.

20–21. A summarising assessment of Hezekiah's reform. The first
part of v. 20 refers back to vv. 4–19 in particular, but thereafter
there is a clear echo of 29:2 as well as of 2 Kg. 18:3–7. This suggests
first that this summary is to be understood as a literary marker,
indicating that the Chronicler is now rejoining the account of his
Vorlage, which he has so expanded by the account of the reform
and Passover. Second, however, there are also some striking points
of contact with 7:11, which was seen to have been deliberately
shaped by the Chronicler into a conclusion of the dedication of the
temple under Solomon. The situation here is thus comparable to

that at 29:35 with its echo of 8:16 and suggests again that he has
been careful to present Hezekiah as a second Solomon. **and faithful:**
cf. 32:1. **and prospered:** in addition to 7:11, cf. 32:30.

The Rewards for Hezekiah's Faithfulness

32:1–33

It has already been noted that the Chronicler reversed the emphasis
of the account of Hezekiah's reign in Kings by giving such prominence to the reform. The other events of the reign, which are
dominant in Kings, are presented more briefly in the present chapter
as illustrative of the blessings which faithfulness brings. This is
made particularly clear by the word-play between the summary
passage at the end of the reform (31:20–21) and the opening (v. 1)
and close (v. 30) of the substance of the present chapter. The
Chronicler has thus conformed his presentation to the pattern
already seen elsewhere, notably in the case of David, Solomon and
Asa.

1–23. Deliverance from Sennacherib. It might at first seem
strange to use deliverance from an invasion as an example of blessing. However, the situation is exactly analogous to the invasion of
Zerah in 14:9–15 (where there is a similar emphasis on trust in the
Lord alone leading to a remarkable victory), while military success
has been repeatedly emphasised by the Chronicler as a reward for
obedience. Furthermore, the account of the invasion itself has been
considerably modified by the Chronicler so that the kingdom does
not appear to suffer nearly as much as in the earlier accounts (2 Kg.
18–19; Isa. 36–37). For instance, there is no mention here of a siege
of Jerusalem, of Hezekiah paying tribute, or even of Sennacherib's
capture of many of the towns of Judah (v. 1).

These general observations raise the more particular issue of the
nature of the Chronicler's composition at this point. B. S. Childs
has devoted an illuminating study to this question in *Isaiah and the
Assyrian Crisis* (1967), pp. 104–11. He notes as of first importance
that the Chronicler is dependent on written biblical sources. (Contrast the less satisfactory view of H. Haag, *RB* 58 [1951], pp. 348–
59, who believes that Chronicles is here based on an earlier form of
the narrative from which the duplicate accounts in Kings have
subsequently developed.) These would have been known to the
Chronicler's readers (indeed, some parts of this chapter would be
virtually unintelligible without the assumption of such knowledge),
but would also have presented them, as they have more recent
scholars, with considerable difficulties of both interpretation and

contemporary application. The Chronicler's account aims by its retelling to offer guidelines for the overcoming of such difficulties. It may therefore be appropriately labelled as 'midrash'.

Aware of the many different ways in which the word midrash is used, Childs offers a careful definition which, it may readily be agreed, certainly does justice to the Chronicler's method in this paragraph: 'By midrash we mean a specific form of literature which is the product of an exegetical activity by a circle of scholars in interpreting a sacred text . . . This process functions in terms of a dialectic movement which proceeds from the interpreter to the text, and *vice versa*, from the text to the interpreter. On the one hand, the form of the midrash is structured by a serious wrestling with the problems arising from the text itself. On the other hand, categories of interpretation which are independent of the text in origin are brought to bear upon it' (p. 107).

To appreciate the first point, it needs to be remembered that the Chronicler, together with many modern scholars, took the two accounts in 2 Kg. 18:17–19:9*a*, 36–37 and in 2 Kg. 19:9*b*–35 to be parallel and that he summarised them into one. In the process, however, he also offered various harmonisations which make clear that he had reflected seriously on the problems which the double account poses. Childs is able to provide convincing examples of this, and they will be noted in the comments below.

The second point, the bringing to bear on the text of independent categories of interpretation, reveals the presuppositions which were uppermost in the Chronicler's mind as he wrote. Dominant here, of course, will be the concerns already outlined above to present Hezekiah as a man both of faith and faithfulness, whose trust God rewarded with security and protection. This will account for such features as the omission of his surrender to the Assyrians (2 Kg. 18:14–16), the Chronicler's presentation of the nature of the threat posed by the Assyrians, and the consequent prominence given to what might be called the 'spiritual' response of Hezekiah and the miraculous nature of the deliverance. Characteristically, these points are highlighted for the reader by the inclusion of a short address by Hezekiah (vv. 7–8) which is similar to the 'Levitical sermons' noted elsewhere. Thus the Chronicler's presentation may indeed be seen to have been determined by the two-fold influence of his written source and his more familiar patterning of events which caused him to select and arrange his material in the way that he did.

The formidable historical questions raised by the various accounts of Sennacherib's invasion go beyond the scope of the present commentary, since the Chronicler was already working at one remove from first hand accounts; only in vv. 2–6 can there be any serious question of an alternative source. For an introduction to the historical discussion, cf. B. Oded in *IJH*, pp. 446–51, with further bibliography on p. 441, to which add A. K. Jenkins, *VT* 26 (1976), pp. 284–98; N. Na'aman, *VT* 29 (1979), pp. 61–86; and R. E. Clements, *Isaiah and the Deliverance of Jerusalem* (1980).

32:1. After these things: contrast 2 Kg. 18:13, 'in the fourteenth year of King Hezekiah'. The Chronicler shows by this change that his concern is not for history as such, but for the patterns which he detects in events from which abiding truths may be learned. His aim here is to draw the story of deliverance into a direct relationship with the account of the reform, regardless of specific chronological considerations; see also on 29:3. **and these acts of faithfulness:** this emphasises the same point by its allusion to the summary verse 31:20 just before. **thinking to win them for himself:** for reasons already noted, this replaces 'and took them' at 2 Kg. 18:13.

2–6. Hezekiah's preparations for Sennacherib's invasion. At first sight this paragraph seems to stand in contrast to the insistence on complete trust in God's power to deliver expressed both in Hezekiah's address immediately following (vv. 7–8) and in the miraculous manner of the deliverance later on. The same tension was found in the similar case of Asa (14:7ff.). It was suggested there that this could only be resolved on the basis of the Chronicler's conviction that part of the blessing which faithful kings enjoyed was their success in building operations. The same explanation will apply here, together with the additional, and almost universally accepted, probability that he had access to a reliable source which supplied some of the details included in this paragraph. The measures undertaken covered the city's water supply, improvement of its fortifications, and organisation of the conscript army. The same points are mentioned in Isa. 22:8–11. It is difficult to see how the Chronicler could have constructed the present passage directly out of that one, because there are several quite striking differences between them; it therefore serves as a useful, though general, confirmation of the accuracy of the Chronicler's source here.

3. to stop the water: an intelligible defensive measure, as explained in the following verse. Nothing is said here about the construction of 'Hezekiah's tunnel', which links the Gihon spring with the Pool of Siloam (cf. v. 30); from a historical point of view, therefore, it had probably been built earlier. It is in any case unlikely that so large an undertaking could have been completed in time after the immediate Assyrian threat had become known. **the springs that were outside the city:** the precise development of Jerusalem's water system at this time is a matter of continuing uncertainty, and many varying proposals have been advanced in recent years. It appears, however, that before the construction of 'Hezekiah's tunnel' there was an earlier system which took some of the water from the Gihon spring round to the south of the city. The remains show that this was partly an open channel and partly tunnelled. In places, outlets were cut to allow some of the water to flow down into the Kidron valley for irrigation purposes, and it has been suggested that this system may be referred to in Isa. 8:6 as 'the waters of Shiloah that flow gently'. Some of these openings were found deliberately to have been blocked in the period of the late monarchy; cf. J. Simons, *Jerusalem in the Old Testament* (1952), p. 177. Y. Shiloh, *BA* 42 (1979), p. 168; contrast G. Brunet, *Essai sur l'Isaïe de l'histoire* (1975), pp. 198–203. Since these 'springs' all originated from one source which could now be diverted through the tunnel, Hezekiah's plan here was a practical one, unlike any attempt to block a natural spring, such as En-Rogel to the south of the city, which could never be permanently successful. It was also necessary in order to deny the Assyrians knowledge of the location of Jerusalem's water supply. (For the question of the unobtrusive disposal of the overflow from Siloam itself, cf. N. Shaheen, *PEQ* 109 [1977], pp. 197–202, and J. Wilkinson, *Levant* 10 [1978], pp. 116 ff.)

4. the brook that flowed through the land: 'the little stream at the bottom of Kedron made up of all the rivulets which descended from the slope' (J. Simons, p. 177). This natural explanation does full justice to the demands of the context. The attempt by Ackroyd, *JSOT* 2 (1977), pp. 11f., to link this with the 'cosmic' stream of waters that are said to flow from Jerusalem in Ps. 46:4 and Ezek. 47, and to associate **much water** with a mythological context, is less plausible. There is, however, value in his observation that Hezekiah is here seen to have taken measures that forestalled Sennecherib's boast of drinking 'foreign waters' in his taunt song at 2 Kg. 19:24. **the kings of Assyria:** for this seemingly curious, though in fact by no means unparalleled, use of the plural, cf. Willi, p. 164.

5. Confirmation that Hezekiah devoted much attention to the city walls in his defensive measures comes from Isa. 22:8–11. Moreover, recent archaeological evidence points in the same direction. K. M. Kenyon, *Digging up Jerusalem* (1974), pp. 150f., attributes some of her finds on the eastern slope to this activity, and the history of the wall along that slope would suggest that this is the most probable site for **all the wall that was broken down** and for **the Millo in the city of David** (see on 1 Chr. 11:8). **and outside it he built another wall:** this cannot be identified with certainty. Some conjecture an outer defensive wall. An attractive alternative, however, is to link this statement with the accumulating evidence for a considerable growth in Jerusalem's population at this time (cf. M. Broshi, *IEJ*

24 [1974], pp. 21–6), and with the discovery of a section of a massive new wall in the modern Jewish Quarter of the Old City of Jerusalem. This wall is dated by N. Avigad, *IEJ* 20 (1970), pp. 129–40, to the reign of Hezekiah. What area it originally enclosed is quite uncertain; the main options are surveyed by N. Shaheen, *PEQ* 109 (1977), p. 108. It certainly suggests, however, a considerable expansion in the defended area of the city, and this would fit well with the implications of this verse.

5b–6a. The equipment and organisation of the conscript army; cf. Isa. 22:8b. Although little of detail is recounted here, the notice may come from the same type of source material as that discussed at 14:8.

6b–8. Hezekiah's address to the military leaders. This short 'Levitical sermon' provides a most striking example of how with the passage of time reflection on the message of Scripture influenced the interpretation of the historical tradition. In Isa. 22 and elsewhere, Hezekiah's defensive measures were condemned because 'you did not look to him who did it, or have regard for him who planned it long ago'. By the time of the Chronicler, however, Hezekiah had become a model of the faithful king; the earlier accounts themselves indicate development in this direction. In this sermon, therefore, he in fact puts into Hezekiah's mouth words from Isaiah himself, as well as from other passages, to make clear that Hezekiah's trust was indeed in God, and not in the precautionary measures just recorded. This trust is fully vindicated in vv. 20ff. below. Hezekiah, like Asa, Jehoshaphat and others before him, thus paradoxically becomes an example of the man of faith for whom the Chronicler will have believed Isaiah was seeking, and whom certainly he wished to hold as a pattern before his readers.

the square at the gate of the city: cf. 29:4. 'The assembly of the military leaders provides a neat counterpart to that of the religious leaders' (Ackroyd).

7. Be strong and of good courage. Do not be afraid or dismayed: a clear echo of the charge to Joshua (Dt. 31:6, 8; Jos. 1:9), whose influence on that of David to Solomon has already been noted; cf. 1 Chr. 22:13, etc. Just as Joshua was himself able to pick up these words and encourage his people with them, suggesting an application of them against 'all your enemies against whom you fight' (Jos. 10:25), so now Hezekiah, the second Solomon, can also apply them in the context of this specific confrontation; see also 20:15 and 17. **there is one greater with us than with him:** cf. 2 Kg. 6:16. Ackroyd further suggests an allusion to the Immanuel (= 'God with us') passage of Isa. 7:14.

8. an arm of flesh: cf. Jer. 17:5. The continuation with the contrasting **but with us is the Lord** is, however, more particularly reminiscent of Isa. 31:1 and 3. **to help us and to fight our battles:** see on 20:15–17.

9–23. Using the principles of composition outlined above, the Chronicler constructed this account out of the parallel versions in 1 Kg. 18:17–19:37. While the resulting combination forms a new account with a unity in its own right, the following comments will seek to isolate the sources from which the material is drawn, together with an indication of the force of the Chronicler's own additions or adaptations.

9. Cf. 2 Kg. 18:17. **who was besieging Lachish with all his forces:** the *Vorlage* merely states that the envoys were sent 'from Lachish'. The Chronicler has deduced the fuller version from his understanding of the various references to Lachish in 2 Kg. 18:13–14, 17 and 19:8 (cf. Childs, pp. 107f.). It should further be noted that the Chronicler omits any reference to the 'great army' which accompanied Sennacherib's **servants to Jerusalem** in 2 Kg. 18:17. Since this army is not referred to again until, apparently, 19:35, where many are killed, it might be deduced that the siege of Jerusalem was started by them immediately. The Chronicler, however, has also to reckon with the word of Isaiah in 19:32 that the Assyrians would not besiege Jerusalem. He therefore leaves the Assyrian army at Lachish, and so implies that they were also cut off there (v. 21) without ever mounting a siege of Jerusalem. His omission in the present verse thus resolves a certain discrepancy in his *Vorlage*.

10. Abbreviated from 2 Kg. 18:19–20. **to Hezekiah . . . and to all the people:** this harmonises the implications of 2 Kg. 18:18, 26, and 19:9. **On what are you relying?** This is the crux of the matter for the Chronicler, who has already indicated the answer in vv. 7–8. He therefore omits from 2 Kg. 18:21 even the suggestion that Hezekiah might have been relying on Egypt.

stand siege in: in view of the comments at the previous verse, this might better be rendered 'stay in the fortress of'; cf. Myers.

11. This verse is based on 2 Kg. 18:32, though with possible reflection on 18:27.

12. Cf. 2 Kg. 18:22. **one altar:** a slight strengthening which accords with the more marked conformity of the Chronicler's account of Hezekiah's reform to the demands of Deuteronomy. 'By a slight change in syntax the argument of the Rabshakeh concerning the removal of Yahweh's altars is redirected. In Kings the suggestion is made that Yahweh has been insulted and therefore will not help Israel. In Chronicles the reform is used by the enemy to show that Hezekiah cannot be trusted. Naturally for the reader the effect is just the opposite since he has been taught to value the reform as Hezekiah's greatest act of faithfulness' (Childs, p. 110).

13–15. These verses take elements from both 2 Kg. 19:11f. and 18:29, 33 and 35. **I and my fathers** is another typical harmonisation of the two accounts. It is especially noteworthy that the Chronicler has selected those passages from the earlier accounts which most emphasise the theological issues at stake. The question has shifted from whether Hezekiah to whether **your God should be able to deliver you from my hand**. This emphasis is fully in line with the speech in vv. 7–8 and with the eventual outcome.

16. This is the Chronicler's own summary addition. From the literary point of view it demonstrates his conscious dependence on a written *Vorlage* and his frank admission that he has abbreviated it. Theologically, it underlies his interpretation of the challenge posed by the Assyrians as being essentially concerned with the reliability of God. **against the Lord God and against his servant Hezekiah** is an echo of Ps. 2:2, the whole thought of which is very close to the Chronicler's in this chapter.

17. And he wrote letters: this is the form in which the Assyrian challenge was delivered in the second of the parallel accounts in Kings (cf. 2 Kg. 19:14). Its relation to the oral delivery of the first account is not explained. Here again, the Chronicler suggests an interpretation by sandwiching this reference parenthetically between the speech of vv. 10–15 and the shouting of the Assyrian envoys to the people of Judah on the walls (v. 18). **to cast contempt on the Lord:** this root occurs four times in the earlier accounts (2 Kg. 19:4, 16, 22, 23), but Childs (pp. 88–90) has shown that its intention in the present verse is again more theologically heightened, putting at stake, as it does, the honour of God by indicating that he is no more than another of **the gods of the nations of the lands**.

18. And they shouted: cf. 2 Kg. 18:28. There, the purpose was to direct their arguments to the whole population; here, however, it has simply become a gesture of defiance **to frighten and terrify them**. It may thus be regarded as the reverse of the typical 'Holy War' descriptions; cf. 13:13–17; 14:14; 20:22.

19. In typical fashion the Chronicler rounds off this section of the account with a summary in his own words which highlights the primary theme of what has gone before, namely, the equation of **the God of Jerusalem** with **the gods of the peoples of the earth, which are the work of men's hands** (cf. v. 17).

20–23. The juxtaposition of Hezekiah's address (vv. 7–8) with the Assyrian taunts has elevated the confrontation from a simple issue of military superiority into a direct challenge to God's sovereignty and power. Thus in this concluding paragraph, Hezekiah acts in the only appropriate manner—prayer—and the outcome is decided entirely by divine intervention as a vindication of faith.

20. Hezekiah the king and Isaiah the prophet: another conflation of the earlier parallel accounts; cf. 2 Kg. 19:2-4 and 14f. **prayed . . . and cried to heaven:** they act in accordance with the programmatic 7:14. This may help account for the absence of a reference to their going to the temple to pray, which is prominent in Kings, for 7:14 is addressed to some situations where that would be impossible (cf. 6:36ff.). Thus inasmuch as the Chronicler wishes his narrative to be exemplary, he has removed such a particularity which might have proved a hindrance to its application by his readers.

21. A summary based on 2 Kg. 19:35-37. **the Lord sent an angel:** contrast Kings, 'the angel of the Lord went forth'. The Chronicler heightens the direct intervention of God. **in the camp of the King of Assyria:** located by the Chronicler at Lachish; cf. v. 9. He thus avoids the evident implication of his *Vorlage* that Jerusalem was under siege. **with shame of face:** this element is added by the Chronicler, and is of a piece with his heightening of the confrontation between the Assyrian and God himself, for it is likely that he intends us to understand it in the light of many passages in the Psalms which speak of God's enemies being 'put to shame' (e.g. Ps. 31:17; 83:16f.; 97:7).

22-23. The Chronicler adds here his own conclusion, which introduces some familiar themes to describe the blessings which Hezekiah now enjoyed. **So the Lord saved:** he first emphasises the vindication of Hezekiah's faith in the face of the Assyrian taunts. **and from the hand of all his enemies:** the last two words are added by *RSV* on the basis of a few MSS. The effect is to turn the foregoing narrative into an exemplary account which, it is implied, can be repeated for all who share Hezekiah's faith. **and he gave them rest on every side:** this represents a slight, and very probable, emendation of MT's 'and he guided them on every side'; cf. LXX and V. This was seen to be a blessing enjoyed as reward for faithfulness by Asa (14:1, 5-7; 15:15) and Jehoshaphat (20:30), but most especially by Solomon; see on 1 Chr. 22:9.

23. The same can be said of the theme of foreign tribute and exaltation **in the sight of all nations,** referred to in connection with David (1 Chr. 14:17), Jehoshaphat (2 Chr. 17:10f.; 20:29) and Uzziah (26:8), but again perhaps especially reminiscent of Solomon (2 Chr. 9, especially vv. 23f.).

24-32. In those days suggests that the following paragraphs should be read in close connection with the preceding narrative. For a study of this material see, in addition to the commentaries, Ackroyd, *JSOT* 2 (1977), pp. 10-14.

24. This brief reference to Hezekiah's illness could hardly be understood without knowledge of the fuller account in 2 Kg. 20:1-11. **and he prayed to the Lord:** though referred to in Kings, this highlighting of Hezekiah's response to danger is reminiscent of v. 20 and so also of 7:14. The latter verse receives further illustration in v. 26. **a sign:** a reference to the shadow going back ten steps in 2 Kg. 20:8-11. In v. 31 the Chronicler uses this to link together the two separate accounts in Kings of Hezekiah's illness and the visit of the Babylonian envoys (2 Kg. 20:12ff.). The Chronicler's drastic abbreviation of his *Vorlage* would thus seem to have been carefully composed, and not to be a simple mechanical procedure, as suggested by S. Talmon, in F. M. Cross and S. Talmon (eds), *Qumran and the History of the Biblical Text* (1975), p. 329.

25-26. This section too demonstrates the integration which the Chronicler has forged between the two incidents, for the element of judgment which it involves is clearly dependent on Isaiah's threat following the reception given to the Babylonian envoys; yet here that reception is itself explained as due to pride brought on by his recovery from illness. This too could not have been appreciated if the Chronicler had not been able to count on his readers' knowledge of the fuller account. **wrath came upon him:** the same word (*qeṣep*) is used, without any influence from the *Vorlage*, as the one seen to act as an important thematic link in the reign of Jehoshaphat (see the introduction to chs 17-20). It serves the same purpose here in miniature, as its resumption in v. 26 (**the wrath of the Lord did not come upon them in the days of Hezekiah**) shows. As in the case of Jehoshaphat, such judgment can be averted by repentance. **Hezekiah humbled himself:** deduced from 2 Kg. 20:19*a*. Not surprisingly, the Chronicler uses one of his key verbs from 7:14 (and cf. 12:1-12 and 30:11) to describe this repentance; contrast the fate of Uzziah, of whom it is also said with an identical phrase that **his heart was proud** (*gābah libbô*; 26:16), but who refused to repent. **and Judah and Jerusalem:** by this repeated addition, the Chronicler may perhaps be encouraging his readers to apply the lessons of this section to themselves. **in the days of Hezekiah:** in 2 Kg. 20:19, from which this is deduced, the reference forward is clearly to the Babylonian exile. The Chronicler, however, probably intends his readers in addition to read the 'exile' of Manasseh (33:11) in the light of this passage.

27-29. The theme of **very great riches and honour** is familiar as illustrative of the blessings enjoyed by 'good' kings especially Solomon; see, for instance, the references listed at v. 23 above. There is no biblical parallel for this passage. The Chronicler probably elaborated it into a separate unit from the description of Hezekiah

showing off his riches to the Babylonian envoys in 2 Kg. 20:13. In
general terms it nevertheless accords well with the hints of archaeological evidence which suggest that Hezekiah enjoyed a measure of
prosperity during his reign; cf. Myers, and J. Gray in *TI*, p. 77.

27. shields: slightly out of context here. A very small, though
conjectural, emendation to a word for 'precious objects' would fit
better.

29. cities: this word, again unsuitable in the context, is very
similar to that translated 'sheepfolds' at the end of the previous
verse. This suggests that it may have arisen as the result of scribal
confusion.

30. The successful construction of the well-known 'Hezekiah's
tunnel' (see also on vv. 3-4) will also have been seen by the Chronicler as a mark of divine favour. Though 2 Kg. 20:20 refers to this,
the greater detail of this verse, together with considerations of the
Hebrew style at this point, strongly suggest that he drew this notice
from an alternative source; cf. Welten, pp. 30 and 39. **outlet:** exactly
the same word (*môṣāʾ*) is used in the Siloam Tunnel inscription
(line 5; cf. Gibson, *Inscriptions* 1, pp. 21-3), which is a contemporary
record of the undertaking. **And Hezekiah prospered in all his
works:** this should be taken closely with the following verse (so
NEB), indicating that he came successfully through God's time of
testing. There is a further link back to the summary in 31:21 (see
also on v. 1 of this chapter), so that this chapter as a whole may
legitimately be interpreted as illustrative of the reward granted him
for his faithfulness in the reform.

31. A somewhat radical reinterpretation of the visit of the Babylonian envoys in 2 Kg. 20:12-19. First, the Chronicler draws on the
well-known Babylonian interest in astrology to explain the purpose
of the visit in the first place: **to inquire about the sign that had
been done in the land;** see also on v. 24. The suggestion of political
intrigue found in the Kings account is thus entirely suppressed, and
together with it Hezekiah's display of wealth, which has been developed as a separate unit in vv. 27-29. Secondly, the element of
judgment is also omitted, because that too has already been
abstracted by the Chronicler and used in vv. 25-26 in closer association with Hezekiah's recovery from illness. Thirdly, he explains
the whole episode as a time of divine testing, **to try him and know
all that was in his heart.** This is considered necessary after his
deviation and repentance in vv. 25-26, the question being whether
that repentance was genuine and lasting. **God left him to himself:**
this is the normal *OT* understanding of divine testing. Finally, the
Chronicler seems to have deduced from Hezekiah's confession to
Isaiah in 2 Kg. 20:19 ('The word of the Lord which you have

spoken is good') that he came through this testing successfully (this despite the continuation in the *Vorlage* which interprets Hezekiah's confession rather differently). Thus the verse serves to round off Hezekiah's reign on a fully positive note.

32–33. The regular form of conclusion to the reign as a whole. **his good deeds** (*ḥªsādāyw*): cf. 35:26 and Neh. 13:14. It would be possible grammatically to translate 'the deeds of loyalty shown towards him', but the context favours *RSV*'s rendering. The parallel passage (2 Kg. 20:20) has 'and all his might', which, as again in the later case of Josiah, the Chronicler interprets as deeds of piety, seen especially in his account of the reform. There is thus no need to attribute a different meaning to *ḥesed* here; cf. *JSS* 23 (1978), pp. 36f. **the vision of Isaiah the prophet:** see on 9:29. Again, there is a considerable amount of material about Isaiah in 2 Kings. The use of the word **vision**, however, may imply influence too from the book of the prophet; cf. Isa. 1:1. Nevertheless, the immediate continuation, **in the Book of the Kings of Judah and Israel** (see on 16:11) shows that the Chronicler is not referring directly to the book of Isaiah.

33. The Chronicler has expanded the Kings burial notice as a means of passing his final approving judgment on the reign of Hezekiah; cf. the similar device at 16:14; 21:19f., etc. **in the ascent:** this literalistic rendering makes no sense. In view of the Chronicler's frequent use of this root to express the superlative (and its use later with the meaning 'excellence'), it may be better rendered 'in a privileged place amongst'; cf. Rudolph, following Ehrlich.

MANASSEH

33:1–20

The evaluation of Manasseh's reign in 2 Kg. 21:1–18 is, without any exception, negative; indeed, it is stated several times that the eventual fall of Jerusalem to the Babylonians and the exile of the population was due to his grim catalogue of sins. With this, the Chronicler's portrayal presents us with a striking contrast, for whereas he opens his account by following his *Vorlage* quite closely (vv. 1–10) in describing Manasseh's apostasy, he then adds to it the otherwise unattested record of Manasseh's being led away as a captive of the Assyrians to Babylon, of his repentance there and subsequent restoration to his throne, and of a partial reform of the cult which he then carried through.

Needless to say, this raises a number of historical questions to which a wide variety of solutions has been suggested. Some discussion of this is included in the comments below. It is important, however, that this should not detract from an appreciation of the Chronicler's own purposes in this chapter, and these may therefore be appropriately outlined here.

First, in terms of the experience of an individual, Manasseh furnishes the most explicit and dramatic example of the efficacy of repentance in the whole of the Chronicler's work. A number of such stories have already been noted (e.g. 12:1–12; 19–20; 32:25–26, etc.); but this one goes further both in that Manasseh initially refused God's warning (v. 10), which hitherto has led straight to disaster (e.g. 16:7ff.; 24:19ff.), and in that he is actually taken into 'exile' before he repents. Even in such dire circumstances, it is implied, restoration remains a possibility. That the account is intended to be exemplary is made certain by the use of the highly charged vocabulary of the Chronicler's theology in vv. 12–13, and by the fact that the restoration is illustrated first and foremost by his characteristic theme of building (v. 14) regarded as blessing (see on 11:5–12).

Secondly, however, it has recently been argued (Ackroyd; Mosis, pp. 192–4) that this account should not be regarded simply as arising out of a rigid doctrine of 'individual retribution'. Rather it should be viewed within the typological pattern of exile and restoration, already observed elsewhere; cf. 1 Chr. 10:13–14. The experience of Manasseh is thus to be read as a paradigm of the people's experience, a reflection of their own Babylonian exile, which will aid them in the interpretation of their current situation and encourage them on the way forward towards a regaining of the blessings they have lost.

It may be readily agreed that there are a number of points which show that this is indeed part of his intention. On the negative side, it should be recalled that many commentators have explained the Chronicler's purpose here as being to reconcile Manasseh's apostasy with the fact that he ruled longer than any other king in Jerusalem (fifty-five years; v. 1). Now while it is true that, like other biblical writers, the Chronicler regarded long life as a sign of God's favour, Mosis is justified in pointing out that nothing is made of this element in the account of Manasseh's restoration, so that it is unlikely to have been amongst the Chronicler's dominant concerns in this chapter.

On the positive side there are several points to be made: (a) the two preceding reigns, those of Ahaz (ch. 28) and Hezekiah (chs 29–32), have been seen to have this prefigurement of exile and restoration as a major interpretative theme. We can thus well understand that the Chronicler should now have wanted to reinforce this by illustrating the pattern within the reign of a single monarch; (b) it was observed at 32:25-26 above that the Chronicler left the way open for a reference in his *Vorlage* to the Babylonian exile to be picked up more immediately in the reign of Manasseh; (c) whatever is made of possible historical sources for the account of Manasseh's captivity, the reference to Babylon in v. 11, superficially curious as a seat of Assyrian power, must have been consciously included as a pointer to the national exile later on; (d) the reference to God's warning of Manasseh and his people and their rejection of his word in v. 10 look very like a prefiguration of the Chronicler's explanation of the exile in 36:15f., while the continuation in each case (v. 11 and 36:17) is also comparable.

It seems less certain, however, that the rigid 'either/or' which Mosis sets up for the understanding of this chapter is really necessary. The two themes outlined above are not in any way contradictory, and indeed it has been frequently noted that the Chronicler is anxious to link the individual experiences of the kings with those of his people. Provided we accept that his overriding concern here is hortatory, rather than simply explanatory of a certain theological difficulty in his *Vorlage*, there is no good reason to limit him to a single inflexible message; depending on circumstances, he may well have allowed his readers more than one specific application of his coherent underlying theology.

33:1-9. For this first half of the reign, the Chronicler follows 2 Kg. 21:1-9 quite closely. In addition to the commentaries on Kings, see McKay, pp. 20-7 for an analysis of the origin and nature of the pagan cults here described.

1. The Chronicler omits a reference to Manasseh's mother, and this sets a pattern for all the remaining kings, contrary to the Chronicler's regular practice up to this point. Not previously understood, this omission has now been convincingly explained by McKay, pp. 23-5. In the case of the mothers of Manasseh, Amon and Josiah, he establishes their Arabian origins and shows how their religion will have influenced Judah at this time (see further on v. 20). Thus, just as the Chronicler omitted the name of Maacah, the mother of Asa, at 14:1 because of her introduction of foreign cults (cf. 15:16), so now, in similar circumstances, he adopts the same procedure.

3. Baals, Asherahs: the use of the plural here against the *Vorlage*'s singular may be intended to accentuate Manasseh's apostasy; see also v. 6. A reference to 'Ahab king of Israel' is omitted, perhaps because the Chronicler has not given an account of his reign earlier, or perhaps because the slight changes earlier in the verse have in any case obscured the parallel between Ahab's and Manasseh's apostasy: cf. McKay, p. 91.

6. his sons: this plural too is from the Chronicler; cf. v. 3. At 28:3 he has made precisely the same alteration, and also added, as here, a reference to **the valley of the son of Hinnom**.

7. the idol: cf. 2 Kg. 21:7, 'Asherah'. According to McKay, pp. 22f., the word used here, *semel*, is of Phoenician origin. 'Indeed, it is possible that the Chronicler referred to Manasseh's idol as a *semel* precisely because it represented some imported Phoenician goddess.' If so, the change probably already stood in the text of Kings that the Chronicler was following, since it is unlikely that he himself would have still known the precise significance of the word.

10. On the importance of this verse, see the introduction to the chapter. The first half stands as a summary of 2 Kg. 21:10–15, while the second half is based on 2 Kg. 21:9*a*, previously omitted by the Chronicler.

11–13. Manasseh's captivity, repentance, and restoration. The importance of this paragraph for an understanding of the Chronicler's presentation of Manasseh's reign has been outlined above. The question of a possible historical account underlying it cannot be so simply answered.

First, it must be clearly stated that no single aspect of this account receives any direct confirmation from other sources; indeed, in certain important respects they contradict it. For instance, not only the account of Manasseh's reign in 2 Kings, but also its subsequent interpretation as a primary cause of the exile, present, at the very least, a totally different picture from that of the present chapter. At the same time, the only direct references to Manasseh known so far from Assyrian sources show him to have been a loyal vassal (cf. *ANET*, pp. 291 and 294), whereas the account here has generally been taken to imply that he was involved in some form of rebellion against Assyria. These facts, taken together with evidence from the passage of the Chronicler's own style and theological interest, have long persuaded a considerable number of scholars that the whole account is no more than fabrication on his part; cf., for instance, R. North, 'Does Archeology Prove Chronicles Sources?', pp. 383–6.

On the other hand, it is equally clear that the Deuteronomic historian as much as the Chronicler had a message of his own to convey which will have influenced his selection of material, while the Assyrian records known to us are by no means sufficiently comprehensive for the argument from silence to carry much weight. Consequently there is a similarly strong body of opinion which feels that, however much it may have been worked over by the Chronicler, some historical event must underlie his narrative. Discussion then centres on determining by way of circumstantial evidence the most likely setting for a capture of Manasseh.

By far the most popular view is to suggest that Manasseh may
have been involved in the widespread unrest throughout the Assyrian empire generated by the rebellion of Shamash-shum-ukin, the
brother of Asshurbanipal, in 652–648 BC; cf. E. L. Ehrlich, *ThZ* 21
(1965), pp. 281–6; McKay, pp. 25f. It is known that at the time of
this rebellion disaffection spread rapidly in Syria-Palestine; Egypt
had already withheld tribute a few years previously and was never
reconquered, and Arab tribes overran much of the territory to the
east of the Jordan. In 648 BC Babylon fell to Asshurbanipal who
then turned to deal with the situation in the west, particularly the
Arab incursions. Evidence for his activity in Palestine is indirect,
but may be supported by the resettlement referred to in Ezr. 4:10.
Such a background, particularly with the reference to Babylon
(v. 11), provides an attractive setting for the captivity of Manasseh.
McKay has made out a good case for Manasseh's friendship with
both the Arabs and the Phoenicians, which could well have drawn
him into the rebellion, or at least been sufficient for suspicion to
have fallen on him; moreover, McKay's arguments thus provide
material to answer M. Cogan's objection to this reconstruction (*Imperialism and Religion* [1974], p. 69), namely, that Asshurbanipal's
campaign in the west was concerned only with maintaining control
over the major Arabian trade routes. At the same time there are
several parallels known for the apparently lenient treatment afforded
Manasseh thereafter; cf. B. Oded in *IJH*, pp. 455f. While involvement with one of the several other rebellions attested during the
reigns of Esarhaddon and Asshurbanipal has been suggested by
different scholars, none has the inherent attractiveness of this the
majority view.

The only other approach to the problem which deserves serious
consideration centres on an attested gathering of Assyrian vassals in
672 BC in order to safeguard the succession from Esarhaddon to
Asshurbanipal. The vassals, who with the highest degree of probability will have included Manasseh, were made to swear an oath of
allegiance to the Assyrian throne, as attested by the vassal treaties
of Esarhaddon; cf. D. J. Wiseman, *Iraq* 20 (1958), pp. 1–99; R.
Frankena, *OTS* 14 (1965), pp. 122–54. It is possible that the Chronicler would have known of this, since a copy of the treaty would
have been deposited in Jerusalem, and that from this he constructed
his own, more elaborate account.

A decision as to where the balance of probability lies in this
discussion must inevitably be influenced finally by the general stance
adopted towards the Chronicler's procedures of composition as a
whole. In the present commentary, several examples have been
suggested of the Chronicler taking up a relatively local or trivial

incident and magnifying it by way of his own ideological presuppositions into an account of major and significant proportions. It would thus not be surprising if he had followed the same method here. Certainly the fact that no reference is made to Manasseh's long reign being a reward for his repentance tells against those who argue that the Chronicler invented the whole story in order to defend an alleged doctrine of rigidly individualistic retribution. But along the historical front we cannot advance beyond such a tentative suggestion that there are two or three occasions when either as a loyal vassal or a discomfited rebel Manasseh may have found himself taken to the Assyrian court. This consciously makes a distinction between his removal to 'Babylon' and his repentance as presented by the Chronicler, for of course none of the evidence advanced above enables us to make any historical pronouncement whatever about the latter; on its apparent outworking in Manasseh's subsequent reform, see further below.

11. **with hooks:** while this may be understood quite literally (cf. *ANEP*, p. 152), the Chronicler probably intends his readers to see rather more in it as well. On the one hand, the treatment of Manasseh here is reminiscent of that thought later to have been afforded to Jehoiachin; cf. Ezek. 19:9, and compare **brought him to Babylon** with 36:10. This, then, accords well with the interpretation of Manasseh's capture as a type of the Babylonian exile. At the same time, there may also be a reference intended to the threat uttered against the king of Assyria in Hezekiah's time; cf. 2 Kg. 19:28. It has already been noted that the Chronicler has linked the reigns of Hezekiah and Manasseh by way of judgment; in the present case the Chronicler would be aiming simply at showing how, on the 'table-turning' principle, a faithless king of Judah could expect similar treatment.

12. **when he was in distress:** contrast the reaction of Ahaz in 28:22. **he entreated the favour of:** though not identical, this is a close equivalent of 'seek my face' in 7:14. **and humbled himself greatly:** taken with the evidence of the next verse, there can be no doubt that Manasseh's repentance has been deliberately composed by the Chronicler on the basis of 7:14. Frankena, p. 152, has tried to defend the Chronicler's account even at this point: 'if we are right in supposing that Yahweh had been a witness to the making of the vassal-treaty of Manasseh, the rebellion of Manasseh must have been against the will of Yahweh, whereas his repentance must have been in accordance with the will of Yahweh.' Yet it can hardly be supposed that the Chronicler would have regarded the affair in this light, and the opinion of the majority of commentators that he

has composed this particular aspect of the account under the influence of his wider theology remains the most likely.

13. He prayed to him: again we find the same language as in the programmatic 7:14. This reference, together with v. 19, became the source for later reflection in the apocryphal 'Prayer of Manasseh'. **heard his supplication:** God is portrayed as acting in accordance with his promise to Solomon. **and brought him again to Jerusalem:** though initially surprising, this would in fact be historically quite intelligible (see above). The Chronicler, however, again saw it as an expression of divine faithfulness which should have encouraged his readers to share in Manasseh's confession that **the Lord was God.**

14-17. Manasseh's reform. The influence of 7:14 on the preceding paragraph is quite evident. The last clause of that verse refers to the promise that God will 'heal their land'. The present section serves as an eloquent example of and commentary on this.

14. Although some have suggested that historically this verse would have described Manasseh's preparations for joining one of the anti-Assyrian rebellions (as with Hezekiah at 32:5), the Chronicler is explicit in placing it afterwards. Theologically, this makes it illustrative once more of the blessings enjoyed by faithful kings (see on 11:5-12); historically, it might refer either to an Assyrian desire to encourage Judah to act as a strong buffer-state with Egypt (Rudolph), or to the general needs of the city whose population was continuing to expand rapidly at this time (cf. M. Broshi, *IEJ* 24 [1974], pp. 21-6), or a combination of both. This verse is not without topographical as well as textual problems, however, from which Welten, pp. 72-8, draws the conclusion that it reflects no more than the Chronicler's own composition, based on his knowledge of the post-exilic Jerusalem.

15-17. Clearly a repentant king should undo the worst effects of his previous apostasy. However, not only does no other biblical passage support this description, but it seems to run deliberately counter to such passages as 2 Kg. 23:4ff. and Jer. 15:4, to say nothing of v. 22 of this very chapter immediately below, which clearly indicate that the idols installed earlier by Manasseh were not removed until Josiah's reign. To attempt to harmonise this discrepancy by suggesting that Amon reinstalled the idols once 'thrown out' (cf. v. 15) is to read more into the text of v. 22 than it can legitimately be made to bear. The very most that could be said from the historical point of view would be that, if McKay is right in stressing Phoenician and Arabian influence on Manasseh in his initial apostasy, and if it is further correct to link his captivity in Babylon with a rebellion in which he acted in alliance with those same groups of people, then possibly the Assyrians might have

insisted on his dismantling of some of the more blatant symbols of
their religion as a condition for his restoration to the throne. This
suggestion, however, speculative as it is, is very far from the positive
reformation of the cult with which the Chronicler here credits
Manasseh.

17. By this qualification, the Chronicler concedes that Manasseh's
reformation was not as far-reaching as his previous enthusiastic
description might have led us to suppose. Even this, however, is
insufficient to explain away the discrepancies noted above, for it is
clear from 34:3f. and 2 Kg. 23:4ff. that Josiah's reform was aimed
at idolatrous worship.

18–20. This summary and conclusion of Manasseh's reign represents an expansion by the Chronicler of 2 Kg. 21:17f.

18–19. The Chronicler's *Vorlage* refers only to 'all that he did,
and the sin that he committed'. This has been expanded in these
two verses to highlight once again the leading themes of the Chronicler's distinctive presentation. Note the use of his favourite theological vocabulary: **his prayer, his faithlessness** (see on 1 Chr.
10:13), **humbled himself,** etc. **the words of the seers who spoke
to him:** a reference to v. 10, which is itself merely a summary of 2
Kg. 21:10–15. **the Chronicles of the Kings of Israel:** see on 16:11.
Israel is here tellingly substituted for 'Judah' in his *Vorlage*. **the
Seers:** 'his seers' is a more convincing emendation of MT's impossible 'my seers'. Comparison of these two verses suggests
strongly that **the Chronicles of the Seers** are to be identified with
the Chronicles of the Kings, since the latter are said to include **the
words of the seers.** Once again, therefore, the interest of the citation
rests in its title rather than its content.

20. in his house: contrast 2 Kg. 21:18, 'in the garden of his
house, in the garden of Uzza'. According to McKay, pp. 24f.,
'Uzza' is to be equated with the Arabian astral god *Al-ʿUzzā*, and
'the garden of Uzza' will have been a plot of land in Jerusalem
dedicated to this god under the influence of Manasseh's wife (see
on v. 1). In conformity with his practice of using the place of a
king's burial as a means of passing a final theological judgment on
his reign, the Chronicler will have been anxious to avoid this reminder of Manasseh's apostasy, conflicting, as it would, with his
otherwise positive appraisal following Manasseh's repentance.

AMON

33:21-25

The brief account of Amon's reign is extracted from 2 Kg. 21:19–26. The only changes which it introduces are those caused by the Chronicler's special handling of the second half of Manasseh's reign. It thus serves as a necessary prelude of renewed apostasy before the reform of Josiah which follows. For the somewhat artificial nature of this device, see on vv. 15–17.

21. For the omission of a reference to Amon's mother, see on v. 1 above.

23. This verse is added by the Chronicler himself, in clear dependence on his own account at v. 12.

24–25. In addition to the commentaries on Kings, cf. M. Cogan, *Imperialism and Religion* (1974), pp. 70f., and the literature cited there. The final notice of Amon's reign (2 Kg. 21:25–26) may have simply been lost in the course of transmission by homoioteleuton (Benzinger).

JOSIAH

34:1–35:27

The Chronicler follows the Deuteronomic historian in his positive evaluation of the reign of Josiah, and indeed enhances it in certain respects. The characteristic features of his presentation are the earlier dating of Josiah's reform, the more elaborate description of his Passover celebration, and the more detailed account of his death in the battle of Megiddo. Despite this, however, Josiah is not so significant a monarch overall for the Chronicler as he is for the earlier historian. Much that he records is now to be understood as recapitulation of Hezekiah's work, who stands out as the real innovator in Chronicles. In addition (see on 34:3–7), one aspect of Josiah's reform is transferred back to the reign of Manasseh. Finally, the Chronicler's explanation of Josiah's death (35:20–24) also implies a stronger measure of censure. Josiah thus does not mark a particular turning point in the Chronicler's narrative, but rather he takes his position as one, albeit an important one, amongst others in a longer succession.

Introduction and Cultic Reform

34:1–13

The Chronicler takes his introductory notice of Josiah's reign with only slight changes from 2 Kg. 22:1–2; on the omission of the reference to Josiah's mother, cf. 33:1. However, unlike Kings, which at this point jumps straight over to the eighteenth year of Josiah's reign, the Chronicler clearly felt the need to illustrate the positive evaluation of v. 2 by showing evidence of Josiah's piety from a much earlier time (v. 3). He thus introduces the account of Josiah's cultic reform at an earlier point in his reign than in Kings. Moreover, it follows inevitably that this aspect of the reform is severed from its apparent connection with the finding of the book of the law.

There has been much discussion in consequence of the historical value of the Chronicler's revised chronology. It has frequently been argued in general terms that the discovery of the book of the law in 621 BC itself presupposes that some such reform must already have been under way (cf. H. H. Rowley [ed.], *Studies in Old Testament Prophecy* [1950], pp. 164f.); more specifically, an attractive claim has been made for the influence of Zephaniah and the early ministry of Jeremiah on Josiah before 621 BC (cf. D. W. B. Robinson, *Josiah's Reform and the Book of the Law* [1951]), while as an extreme example it has been suggested that each step of the Chronicler's outline corresponds exactly with the declining influence of Assyria in the Levant; cf. F. M. Cross and D. N. Freedman, *JNES* 12 (1953), pp. 56–8, followed in principle by J. Bright, *A History of Israel* (1972²), pp. 316f., and Myers, amongst others.

The following points need to be borne in mind in any attempt to evaluate this discussion. (a) There is no evidence from the literary side to suggest that the Chronicler is following an alternative source in this passage. The comments below will show that the material can mostly be satisfactorily explained as being based on Kings, while stylistic considerations suggest that for the first half of v. 3 we must reckon with his own composition. Only the two dates of v. 3 cannot be explained in this way. However, if they were drawn from an alternative source, it would be surprising that no other trace of it survived. Moreover, we have seen elsewhere (e.g. 17:7; 29:3, etc.) that he sometimes uses the date of a king's reforming activity as a means of indicating his approval. These dates too, therefore, must be attributed to the Chronicler's own reckoning; contrast J. R. Lundbom, *CBQ* 38 (1976), pp. 293–302. It is possible to suggest the factors which may have influenced him in this (see below). (b) Attempts to relate in detail the steps in Josiah's reform

as outlined by the Chronicler and the decline of Assyrian influence
rest on two uncertainties. One is Assyrian chronology. The other is
the assumption that Josiah's reform was almost entirely politically
motivated. This, however, has been forcefully challenged by
McKay, who has shown in addition that the Chronicler's account
cannot be used to distinguish between two phases in the reform,
one based on the removal of foreign cults and the other more directly
on the book of the law. (c) It is certainly possible that Josiah's
reform was started before the discovery of the book of the law, and
even that the lessening of Assyrian influence may have been a
contributory factor. Recent studies of 2 Kg. 22–23 have tended to
detach the reform from its historical dependence on the finding of
the book (see A. D. H. Mayes, *Deuteronomy* [1979], pp. 85–103).
This reminds us that the Deuteronomic historian also had his own
point of view to convey, a fact reinforced by the amount of activity
which he has packed into Josiah's eighteenth year. Nevertheless,
even if this is so, that does not prove that the Chronicler has
preserved an independent record of it. Thus it is illegitimate to use
his account in such a way as to suggest that it gives us an alternative
and more authentic record of Josiah's reign than does Kings.

3. in the eighth year of his reign: Josiah will then have been
sixteen. The addition **while he was yet a boy** is intended to explain
why Josiah did not take public action at this time: no doubt he was
still ruling under the constraint of a regent. Yet from an early age
his personal piety began to manifest itself. No particular significance
appears to attach to the age of sixteen, unless it was considered to
be the age of responsibility in the Chronicler's community; nor does
the Hebrew allow us to follow the otherwise attractive suggestion of
some rabbinic commentators, who understand this to mean 'in his
eighth year, when he began to reign'. **to seek the God of David his
father:** this familiar idiom betrays the Chronicler's own hand in this
verse. **in the twelfth year:** i.e. twenty years old, probably to be
understood as the age of majority. Josiah thus acts at the earliest
practical date. According to 2 Kg. 23:4–20, there were three main
aspects to the reform: the cleansing of the temple, the destruction
of the high places in Jerusalem and Judah, and the desecration of
the sanctuaries in the territory of the old northern kingdom. The
Chronicler has already transferred the first of these back to the reign
of Manasseh (33:15f.), and this does not appear to have been reversed by Amon (33:22). Consequently, he says very little about a
purification of the temple in his account of Josiah's reform, though
its repair is given greater prominence in vv. 8–13. Here and in the
following two verses, therefore, he summarises the second aspect of
the reform, namely, purging **Judah and Jerusalem of the high**

places with their attendant cult objects; cf. 2 Kg. 23:8, 13, etc. **the graven . . . images:** as honoured by Amon, 33:22.

4–5. These verses continue the summary of the Kings' account, using generalised expressions whose origin in the earlier text is nevertheless clear; for instance, compare 4*b* with 2 Kg. 23:6 and 5*a* with 2 Kg. 23:14, 16 and 20. **the incense altars:** see on 14:5.

6–7. The third aspect of the reform, namely, its extension into the old northern kingdom (cf. 2 Kg. 23:15–20), is similarly summarised here. The listing of a few representative tribal names, **Manasseh, Ephraim and Simeon, and as far as Naphtali,** is typical of the Chronicler in such contexts; cf. 15:9; 30:10f. and 18, and G. S. Ogden, *ABR* 26 (1978), pp. 26–33. On his inclusion of **Simeon** with the northern tribes, cf. 15:9. **in their ruins:** this is one conjectural emendation of the corrupt MT; another is 'in their squares'. Most convincing, however, is the proposal of I. L. Seeligmann, *VT* 11 (1961), p. 202, n. 1, who finds here an instance of the common interchange of the laryngals *ḥ* (of the *Kt. bḥr*) and ʿ. He thus reads *biʿēr bātêhem*, 'he destroyed their sanctuaries'; both words are found in 2 Kg. 23:19 and 24, which the Chronicler is here summarising; or indeed he may have misread them both from 2 Kg. 23:19 alone (mistaking *beʿārê* for *biʿēr*). **Then he returned to Jerusalem:** this also concludes the fuller account of 2 Kg. 23:4–20, confirming that the Chronicler has based his summary on that passage and not on some otherwise unknown source.

8–13. In 2 Kg. 22:3–7, on which these verses are based, Josiah commands one of his officials to go to the temple to make arrangements for the start of repair-work. When he goes, he is informed of the discovery of the book of the law. There is thus no suggestion that repairs were already in hand or that the book was discovered as a result of their undertaking. The whole section is of secondary importance in itself: it merely sets the scene for an announcement of the discovery.

The Chronicler's treatment here, therefore, marks a two-fold shift of emphasis (cf. Mosis, pp. 196f.). First, the manner in which he has dated the incident, **in the eighteenth year of his reign** (contrast 2 Kg. 22:3), explicitly turns this into one episode in the series begun earlier in v. 3. The repairs to the temple thus become part of Josiah's reform, rather as in the case of Hezekiah (ch. 29). Second, the Chronicler has turned the king's command into a narrative of what actually happened. Far from being a setting for the discovery of the book, the repairs to the temple have now become an episode in their own right.

8. when he had purged the land and the house: this is the Chronicler's own addition, providing further evidence that he regarded the repairs as an integral part of the reform. Only here does he refer to a purging of the temple (cf. 2 Kg. 23:4ff.), since he has transferred that operation back to Manasseh's reign (33:15f.). **Maaseiah the governor of the City, and Joah the son of Joahaz, the recorder:** these two officials are not included in the parallel account in Kings. There is nothing here, however, to suggest invention by the Chronicler. The names themselves are common, and the titles are well attested from the pre-exilic period; for the former, in addition to various biblical passages, see now its appearance on a seal published by N. Avigad, *IEJ* 26 (1976), pp. 178–82; for the latter, cf. Mettinger, *Solomonic State Officials*, pp. 51–62. It is thus probable that these names stood in the Chronicler's *Vorlage*, which was only subsequently corrupted. **to repair:** this is added by the Chronicler, making clear his different understanding of the episode. The narrative from this point on is constructed out of the king's command in the *Vorlage*.

9. **and delivered:** this contradicts v. 10, which states that the money was delivered directly to the workmen rather than to **Hilkiah the high priest**. Attention to the wording of v. 17 has suggested to Rudolph that here too we should read 'and emptied out' (*wayyattiḳû* for *wayyittᵉnû*). This has the further advantage of making this account closer to Josiah's command in 2 Kg. 22:4. **the Levites:** a typical addition by the Chronicler; cf. 24:4–14. **from Manasseh and Ephraim and from all the remnant of Israel and from all Judah and Benjamin and from the inhabitants of Jerusalem:** this is the Chronicler's own expression of his *Vorlage*'s 'from the people'. Clearly he is aiming at as comprehensive a definition of the people of both north and south as possible. As in Hezekiah's time, all have a share in the community which focussed on the temple (contrast 24:6). It is noteworthy that only the Chronicler uses the word **remnant** for the inhabitants of the northern kingdom after the fall of Samaria (see also v. 21). It is possible that this is intended to serve as a further pointer to his belief that from the time of Hezekiah on the prophetic hopes for the reunification of Israel had already been realised in principle; cf. *IBC*, pp. 125f.

11. **which the kings of Judah had let go to ruin:** the Chronicler has himself added this explanation. The reference can only be to Manasseh and Amon.

12. **faithfully:** in 2 Kg. 22:7 this is referred to the workmen's handling of the money, but here to **the work** itself. From this point to the end of the paragraph, the Chronicler adds his own conclusion, in which he stresses that **the Levites** had oversight of the work. There is no indication of this in the *Vorlage*, but it coincides precisely with the Chronicler's own view; cf. chs 24 and 29, and v. 9

above. It no doubt reflects the practice of his own day. The names listed are all common in such contexts. On the basis of 29:12 a reference to the Gershonites might also have been expected.

12–13. The use of **music** to accompany the work of building in ancient times is well attested (cf. Rudolph). **scribes, and officials, and gatekeepers:** it is natural to suppose that such functions would be necessary in a major building operation. Several other passages have indicated that some Levites were alloted to such tasks, e.g. 1 Chr. 26.

The Discovery of the Book of the Law

34:14–33

For most of this account, the Chronicler follows 2 Kg. 22:8–23:3 quite closely. As so often, however, he has himself supplied the opening and closing verses, and these provide clues to the reasons for his inclusion of the narrative in the first place.

In Kings, it is clear that the discovery of the book is made the basis for the account of the reform which follows. As already noted, the Chronicler has reversed this. Verse 14 re-emphasises that only because of the undertaking of repairs to the temple (an integral part of the reform for the Chronicler) was the book found in the first place. It is thus to be regarded as a reward for faithfulness as well as a springboard for further acts of obedience (von Rad, *GCW*, p. 14). Its discovery clearly takes the place of other forms of reward for faithfulness included by the Chronicler in his account of other pious kings; building enterprises, success in war, wealth and so on: all these have been noted on numerous occasions. Only for Josiah, the last major king of his history, does reward take the form of 'the book of the law of the Lord given through Moses' (v. 14). This may be intended both to reflect and encourage the high value placed on the Torah in the Chronicler's community.

Second, as a result of Josiah's positive response to the book's demands, the Chronicler adds a note at the end of the passage that he redoubled his efforts to make Israel serve the Lord and that 'all his days they did not turn away from following the Lord the God of their fathers' (v. 33). This is probably intended to draw attention to the favourable promises made to Josiah by Huldah the prophetess (vv. 26–28). Though based on the Kings account, it will be noted below that the Chronicler took a particular interest in this passage. Although he must have realised that part of the promise was not fulfilled, it certainly was the case that Josiah did not live to 'see all the evil which I will bring upon this place and its inhabitants' (v.

28). The Chronicler then emphasised by his addition in v. 33 that this blessing was again a reward for Josiah's obedience to the demands of the book, and that it staved off the by now inevitable disaster for a certain period of time at least (cf. Mosis, p. 198). We may thus conclude that, quite in contrast with his *Vorlage*, the Chronicler has included this lengthy passage in order to illustrate two aspects of his familiar theme of righteousness rewarded.

14. This verse picks up the narrative again from v. 9. **the book of the law:** it is probable that the Chronicler understood this as a reference to the whole of the Pentateuch, and not just to (part of) Deuteronomy, as Kings implies; for this reason, he omits the statement from the next verse that Shaphan read it (cf. 2 Kg. 22:8), and also modifies the phraseology of v. 18.

16. The differences at the start of this verse from 2 Kg. 22:9 depend on alternative ways of vocalising the consonantal text; the Chronicler's version is inferior.

18. read it: so 2 Kg. 22:10. MT here has 'read therein' (*RV*): see on v. 14 above.

21. for those who are left in Israel and in Judah: contrast 2 Kg. 22:13, 'for the people, and for all Judah'. The Chronicler's introduction of a reference to the remnant of the northern kingdom again here is of significance; see on v. 9 above.

24. all the curses: this is more specific than the *Vorlage*'s 'all the words'. The Chronicler will have had passages such as Lev. 26 and Dt. 27–29 particularly in mind.

27. and you have humbled yourself: this favourite verb of the Chronicler (see on 7:14) stands once already in 2 Kg. 22:19. The Chronicler has drawn particular attention to it, however, by repeating it. This suggests that he wishes Josiah's actions to be regarded as an example by his readers, and that the reward promised is held out also to them as not beyond their grasp; see further the introduction to this paragraph above.

30. the Levites: 2 Kg. 23:2 has 'the prophets'; cf. von Rad, *GCW*, p. 114; Petersen, p. 85. While this change may be a quite insignificant assimilation to the usual sociological division of the post-exilic community (priests, Levites, laity; cf. Willi, p. 196), it has normally been thought to reflect his more conscious intention of placing the Levites of his own day within the tradition of the prophets of earlier times; see on 1 Chr. 25:1 and the references cited there. It should be noted, however, that there is no reference to the Levitical singers here. The preaching tradition of the Levites as reflected in Chronicles may have influenced him at this point.

32. While this verse represents an expansion by the Chronicler of 2 Kg. 23:3*b*, its meaning is essentially the same. **to it:** these words are supplied by *RSV*. It is preferable to suppose that **and in Benjamin** represents a corruption of 'in the covenant' (*babbᵉrît*) of the *Vorlage*; cf. *NEB*.

33. The Chronicler has himself added this conclusion to the account. It represents in effect an allusion to the reforms of 2 Kg. 23:4–20, and the tension which results with vv. 3–7 above is a further pointer to the fact that the Chronicler had no other source than Kings for this whole chapter. However, for the reasons already noted in the introduction to this section above it was important for him to include this summary, despite the difficulties. The further stress on the reform's coverage of all **the territory that belonged to the people of Israel** is again noteworthy.

Josiah's Passover

35:1–19

The Chronicler's account of Josiah's Passover provides a great deal more detail than the brief notice in 2 Kg. 23:21–23. For several reasons, however, it is improbable that he has here drawn on any independent written source. First, the opening (v. 1) and close (vv. 18f.) of the account are clearly dependent on Kings, indicating that the Chronicler has himself expanded this notice rather than replaced it with an alternative account. Secondly, it has been argued in the previous chapter that he had no additional source for his variant presentation of Josiah's reform. Since the Passover and reform were closely related, it would be surprising if an alternative account of one part had survived, but not of the other. Third, in contrast with what was found to be the case for Hezekiah's Passover (ch. 30), the narrative presents itself as a unity without the internal tensions which would invite either a source-critical or a traditio-historical analysis. (This latter point, it may be observed in passing, also tells against the attempts of earlier scholars to isolate various secondary additions to this narrative; see, for instance, Rudolph's convincing arguments against Welch, pp. 139–48.)

It must thus be concluded that the paragraph represents the Chronicler's own composition. It is probable that it combines a reflection of the practices of his own day with a limited amount of material which expresses his hopes for developments in the future. Two related features may here be singled out as being of particular interest. One is the prominence of the Levites and the very favourable portrayal of their role in the proceedings. This closely matches what has been noted elsewhere (e.g. chs 29–30), and derives from the Chronicler's concern to establish their position within the

post-exilic cult. The other point is the application to the Passover
of language more appropriate to regular sacrifices. Aspects of this
too may derive from current practice (cf. J. B. Segal, *The Hebrew
Passover* [1963], pp. 226–8), consequent upon the centralisation of
Passover, but it would seem probable that part may also be dependent on the same desire to advance the cause of the Levites. It is
then noteworthy that neither point appears to have become normative in later practice.

In accordance with Kings, the underlying legal prescriptions are
those of Dt. 16; cf. von Rad, *GCW*, pp. 52f. This was inevitable in
view of the centralised nature of the celebration. It is clear, however,
that there has also been an attempt to harmonise this position where
possible with that of Exod. 12. This is typical of the Chronicler's
relationship to the law as a whole (von Rad), and doubtless reflects
one stage in the long process through which post-exilic Judaism
passed in its attempts to reduce the various traditions of the Pentateuch to a united and all-embracing code of practice. There is thus
no need to see in this fact evidence for a core of earlier, pre-Chronistic material (*contra* L. Rost, in S. Herrmann and O. Söhngen
[eds], *Theologie in Geschichte und Kunst* [1968], pp. 169–75).

35:1. Loosely based on 2 Kg. 23:21. **in Jerusalem:** this was the
new and significant point for the Deuteronomic historian; for the
Chronicler, however, it merely follows Hezekiah's precedent. For
rather similar reasons, he also omits the words 'as it is written in
this book of the covenant'. It has been seen in the previous chapter
that the Chronicler was anxious to tone down the emphasis in Kings
on the reform being solely based on the discovery of the book;
similarly, he here wishes to avoid the impression that such a celebration would have been impossible earlier. Rather, the account is
introduced as an illustration of the principle of 34:33 immediately
preceding. The prominence of the initiative taken throughout by
Josiah himself is thus also explained. **on the fourteenth day of the
first month:** this is one of the points which betray the influence of
Exod. 12. There may also be an allusion to Hezekiah's celebration
(ch. 30; cf. Welch, pp. 139f.); in that pioneering enterprise, it was
not possible to adhere to the prescribed date. Now that a precedent
had been established, however, all could be undertaken quite
normally.

2–9. The preparations for the Passover. Josiah arranges the duties
of the priests and Levites, with considerable emphasis on the latter,
and takes the lead in providing animals for the sacrifices.

2. and encouraged them: this rather implies that **the priests**
needed such encouragement in contrast with the eager willingness
of the Levites to serve (cf. vv. 12–15); cf. 29:12–19, 34; 30:3.

3. **the Levites who taught all Israel:** cf. 17:7-9. This contrasts
with the earlier practice in Israel where such important work was
more normally the task of priests (e.g. Hos. 4:6; Jer. 5:31; 18:18).
and who were holy to the Lord: this may represent a further
ascription to the Levites of a status more normally thought of in
association with the priesthood (Rudolph). **Put the holy ark in the
house:** this command is difficult to understand, since (a) we have
no evidence that the ark had been removed from the temple; if the
Chronicler thought that Manasseh or Amon had removed it, we
might have expected him to say so. Moreover it would more probably have been returned at the time of the repairs to the temple
rather than during the preparations for the Passover. (b) In the
Chronicler's view, only the priests were permitted to enter the most
holy place, so that this command should have been addressed to
them rather than the Levites; cf. his careful observation of this at
5:7. (c) The emphasis of the king's command falls on the later words
Now serve the Lord . . . and his people, but as the verse stands
in *RSV* this is not linked with the words under consideration. (d)
It is not clear why **the house** is so emphatically qualified with the
words **which Solomon the son of David, king of Israel, built**.

These difficulties can all be overcome if the first part of the speech
is made subordinate to the second, and this can be done in various
ways. Keil, for instance, argued that **Put** should be translated
'Leave'. Others conjecture various slight emendations to give such
renderings as 'since the holy ark has been put in the house, . . .
you no longer have anything to carry about on your shoulders; now,
therefore, serve . . . '; cf. Welch, pp. 69f.; Rudolph, etc. On this
view, the reference will be back to the initial dedication of the
temple (hence the emphasis on **Solomon**), since which time the
Levites have had greater freedom for other duties. This then links
with the Chronicler's view expressed elsewhere (e.g. at 1 Chr. 16:4)
that some of the Levites became singers when the ark came to rest.
Here, he seems to be broadening the idea to include other aspects
of cultic service, and this is amplified in the sequel. (For the view
that in fact the ark had already been destroyed by this time, cf.
Haran, *Temples and Temple Service*, pp. 276-88.)

4. **by your divisions, following the directions of David king of
Israel:** cf. the primary layer of 1 Chr. 23-27. This verse provides
further evidence that that layer should be attributed to the Chronicler himself. **and the directions of Solomon his son:** cf. 8:14.

5. Each extended family grouping of **the lay people** was to be
served by a part of a Levitical family.

6. The service of the Levites consisted of killing **the passover
lamb** and assisting more generally in preparation **for your brethren**

(the laity; cf. v. 5). In the account of Hezekiah's Passover, the Levites acted in this way only because 'there were many in the assembly who had not sanctified themselves' (30:17), whereas here this practice seems to be regarded as the norm. Since it was certainly not the custom in later times, it is possible that the Chronicler is here only expressing his personal aspirations. **to do according to the word of the Lord by Moses**: since the Pentateuch certainly does not legislate for the slaughter of the Passover lamb by the Levites, this phrase must be intended to qualify only the immediately preceding clause, and to refer forwards to v. 13.

7–9. As in the case of Hezekiah's Passover, so here the king and **his princes** (and other officials) made liberal provision for the sacrifices, the former for the laity (**all that were present**) and the latter for **the priests** and **the Levites**. According to Dt. 16:2 (contrast Exod. 12), the Passover sacrifice could come 'from the flock or the herd', and this seems to be sufficient to account for the gift of **bulls**. It is also possible, though not clearly stated, that some may also have been intended for the more general sacrifices which were offered during the week of Unleavened Bread (v. 17). Either way, the numbers involved are exaggerated for effect. The names mentioned in vv. 8–9 are reasonable in a Levitical setting, but most cannot be otherwise identified. **Hilkiah** was the high priest; cf. 34:9.

10–15. The celebration itself is now described.

10. had been prepared for: see on 8:16 and 29:35. The same verb is used at v. 16 below to introduce the conclusion of the account. This is therefore strongly suggestive of the Chronicler's own composition.

11. The Levites both **killed the passover lamb** (cf. v. 6) and **flayed the victims** (cf. 29:34), while **the priests** manipulated **the blood** (cf. 29:22; 30:16). All these actions were largely dictated by the centralised nature of this celebration. Clearly the family involvement and blood rite of Exod. 12 would have been inappropriate in the temple setting. These factors will have then encouraged the blurring of the distinctions between the Passover and the other more regular sacrifices.

12. the burnt offerings: Rudolph argues convincingly that in the context this must refer to the parts of the sacrifice which were burnt on the altar (v. 14), not to a completely different set of offerings. Here too, therefore, there is a marked assimilation of the Passover to the 'sacrifice of peace offering' of Lev. 3 in particular. The treatment of the blood and several parts is similar. This will then justify what would otherwise be an inaccurate comment: **as it is written in the book of Moses**. As part of the Passover sacrifice (see on vv. 7–9), **the bulls** were appropriately treated in the same way.

13. And they roasted (literally, 'boiled') **the passover lamb with fire:** this incongruous and unparalleled expression arises from the desire to combine the regulations of Dt. 16:7 and Exod. 12:8f. In contrast, the bulls (v. 12), to which **the holy offerings** presumably refers, were **boiled.** This was certainly an ancient practice (e.g. 1 Sam. 2:13f.; 1 Kg. 19:21), but in the Pentateuch is expressly mentioned only in connection with rather particular ceremonies (e.g. Exod. 29:31; Lev. 6:28; 8:31). **carried them quickly:** the eager and willing service of the Levites is again emphasised. The following verses develop this still further.

14. And afterward: this implies selflessness. **the burnt offerings and the fat parts:** as interpreted above, these will both refer to the same thing—a perfectly acceptable grammatical construction.

15. For **the singers,** see the introduction to 1 Chr. 15–16; 1 Chr. 25, and 2 Chr. 29:12–14. The preparation of the Passover for the priests, singers and gatekeepers by the Levites in fact surpasses the king's command in vv. 3–6.

16–19. A concluding summary, which towards its close draws once again on 2 Kg. 23:21–23.

16. was prepared: see on v. 10. **according to the command of King Josiah:** this emphasis is explained at v. 18 below.

17. the people of Israel who were present: the next verse makes clear that, as in the case of Hezekiah, people came from north and south without distinction. **and the feast of unleavened bread:** the Chronicler adds this almost as an afterthought, reflecting the established practice of his own time. Contrast the feast's prominence in 2 Chr. 30.

18. No passover like it: for the Deuteronomic historian, this referred to the centralised celebration in Jerusalem. The Chronicler, however, has already anticipated this with his account of Hezekiah's Passover. Rudolph is therefore right to point to the only really new element in the account—the prominent role of the Levites—as being in the Chronicler's mind at this point. Moreover, it was specifically to this element that 'the command of King Josiah' (v. 16) related; cf. vv. 3–6. His reference to **the days of Samuel** and to the fact that **none of the kings of Israel had kept such a passover** will then suggest that he is claiming a role for the Levites which was theirs by right as early as the period of the initial settlement of the people in the land. **Samuel the prophet** is regarded as the last of the judges, and so replaces the more general reference to them in 2 Kg. 23:22. **the kings of Israel:** the Chronicler omits 'and Judah' from his *Vorlage*; the unity of the people of God is again his concern. This is underlined by his own addition of the closing part of the verse, the purpose of whose detail is to make the same point in a different way.

19. Cf. 2 Kg. 23:23 and 34:8 above.

Josiah's Death

35:20–27

Following Josiah's reform and Passover, his premature death clearly came as a considerable shock to his contemporaries, and there is evidence that they were not able immediately or with a single move to accept and explain this reversal to their hopes. The account in Kings is brief and obscure as to detail. It follows the final summary of the reign (2 Kg. 23:28) and thus has the appearance of a somewhat embarrassed appendix. Chronicles supplies much fuller details, an important element of which is taken up with explaining that Josiah refused a (rather odd form of) prophetic warning and that this was the direct cause of his death. In this way an explanation is supplied which bears the marks of having reflected seriously on the problems of the clash between the actual course of events and the prophecy of Huldah recorded earlier (34:23–28; see further, below).

The question of the historical reliability of the Chronicler's version of events has naturally loomed large in scholarly discussion. A solution will always depend in part upon the interpretation of the Kings' account, for there continues to be a minority opinion which thinks that it does not intend to record a battle at Megiddo in the first place; cf. most recently G. Pfeifer, *MIO* 15 (1969) pp. 297–307. More generally, however, it has been accepted since the publication of the Babylonian Chronicle that the Chronicler was dependent upon a reliable account which in fact even corrects one misleading point of detail in Kings. Finally, attention should be drawn to the recent very detailed studies of this whole incident by Malamat. These have succeeded in illuminating its background and development in a number of fresh ways; cf. most fully *JANES* 5 (1973), pp. 267–78. The account in Chronicles dovetails nicely with this reconstruction. While this does not amount to a demonstration of its reliability, it provides an additional pointer in that direction.

Commentators have not usually considered how this account reached the Chronicler. There are, however, one or two factors which suggest that it may have assumed substantially its present shape within the development of his *Vorlage*, and not been either his own free composition or worked in from some fully independent source.

(a) Uniquely in this passage the Chronicler does not follow precisely the order of his *Vorlage* as regards his source citation formula (contrast verses 26–27 and 2 Kg. 23:28, and cf. section F of the Introduction). There is no apparent reason for this quite exceptional circumstance. It is thus reasonable to suppose that the form of Kings which he was following, and which we know was not always identical with our MT, already reflected this change of order. If so, it is probable that the Chronicler's *Vorlage* represented an intermediate stage between Kings and Chronicles.

(b) The message of Neco to Josiah (v. 21), though it may well reflect historical circumstances, is not in its detail what we should expect either historically or of the Chronicler. On the one hand it is hard to suppose that Neco would have explained his movements theologically, while on the other hand we have seen on numerous occasions that, given a free hand, the Chronicler will introduce these kinds of warning as Levitical sermons on the lips of inspired prophets or Levites. Rudolph is thus right to find here evidence that the Chronicler was composing under the restraint of prior tradition, but over-optimistic if he supposes that such a conclusion necessarily implies historicity. Rather, it looks again as though the Chronicler's *Vorlage* represents a step in his direction from the account in Kings, but developed as regards this particular detail within an Israelite context, presumably for apologetic purposes.

(c) It is noteworthy that the incident is recounted without the use of the Chronicler's particularly characteristic vocabulary, but that it does reflect knowledge of the Deuteronomic history. The important words in v. 22 ('He did not listen to the words of Neco from the mouth of God') are clearly intended as a contrast with the emphasis on 'listening' or 'hearing' in the prophecy of Huldah, 34:26–27 (= 2 Kg. 22:18–19). The death of Josiah is patterned closely on the account of the death of Ahab in 1 Kg. 22:30, 34–37 (cf. 2 Chr. 18:29, 33–34). Finally, the death of Josiah back in Jerusalem (v. 24) as opposed to the statement of 2 Kg. 23:29 that 'Pharaoh Neco slew him at Megiddo' may be intended as a step towards ameliorating the problem of the non-fulfilment of Huldah's prophecy that Josiah would 'be gathered to your grave in peace' (2 Kg. 22:20; cf. 2 Chr. 34:28). It would thus appear that the passage has been composed by some one who was aware of the difficulties of the narrative in Kings and who reflected on them within the wider context of the Deuteronomic history as a whole, and probably also with fuller knowledge of the actual course of events, but that there is really no evidence to identify him directly with the Chronicler. Thus a revised and expanded form of Kings, which the Chronicler has worked over only lightly, seems to be the best way of accounting for the literary development of this passage.

(d) A final small pointer in this same direction may be found in the aetiological element of v. 25*b*. Though not impossible from the Chronicler's own day, the references to the continued singing of laments for Josiah would fit an earlier date more easily.

20. when Josiah had prepared the temple: it is likely that this connection derives from the Chronicler himself; cf. vv. 10 and 16 above. **to fight at Carchemish:** it has often been thought that the Chronicler derived this name from Jer. 46:2, where it relates to a battle several years after Josiah's death. Malamat, *JANES* 5 (1973), p. 274, has shown, however, that already in 610 BC (half a year before the battle at Megiddo) Ashur-uballit, the Assyrian king, had established his new capital at Carchemish, whither the Babylonians and their allies had driven him. Egyptian involvement in helping the Assyrians is attested for this period, and it is also known that by the following summer (609 BC) 'a great Egyptian army' had again joined the Assyrians in their counter-offensive; cf. A. K. Grayson, *Assyrian and Babylonian Chronicles* (1975), p. 96. There can thus be no doubt that **Neco king of Egypt** was on his way with reinforcements in order further to strengthen his Assyrian ally (not to fight *against* the king of Assyria, as 2 Kg. 23:29 has it). In view of the Egyptian set-back only a few months previously, and with account taken of the wider political situation (cf. A. Malamat, *JNES* 9 [1950], pp. 219f.), it becomes clear that Josiah's move **against him** at Megiddo was 'a bold decision based on far-reaching political and military considerations', aimed at cutting off this Egyptian aid.

21. he sent envoys to him: it is by no means impossible that historically speaking Neco should have sent word to Josiah before he passed through Israel explaining his purpose, and seeking safe passage in view of his undoubted need to **make haste.** Y. Yadin, *IEJ* 26 (1976), pp. 9–14, has similarly suggested an interpretation of one of the Arad inscriptions which would indicate that Ashur-uballit too had written to Josiah requesting permission for Neco to pass through his territory without interference. Josiah would thus have been in a position to prepare for a completely surprise attack on Neco as he passed; if Megiddo was indeed an Egyptian base at this time, as argued carefully by Malamat, there would have been no difficulty in deducing the route which Neco proposed to follow.

As recorded here, however, the message goes further than just this, and it must be assumed that it has been written up within an Israelite context in order to make of it a word of **God** to Josiah, the rejection of which then serves to explain his death. The latter part of the message assumes that Josiah is already opposing Neco, thereby betraying its secondary nature (*contra* B. Couroyer, *RB* 55 [1948], pp. 388–96, *et al.*). The absence of any of the Chronicler's

characteristic vocabulary at this point is particularly striking.
against the house with which I am at war: it seems certain that
Neco would be specific in explaining his intentions to Josiah. Of
the many suggestions that have been advanced to explain this enig-
matic phrase, two make particularly good sense in the context,
though it is difficult to choose between them. One has been proposed
by B. Alfrink, *Biblica* 15 (1934), pp. 173–84, and is followed in
particular by Malamat. Observing that the phrase can be translated
literally as 'the house of my war', he suggests that it means 'my
fortified base' or 'my garrison city'. It could then refer to the
Egyptian base at Carchemish or Riblah (Alfrink) or perhaps even
Megiddo itself (Malamat). The other proposal is to emend conjecturally by adding 'Babylon' or 'the king of Babylon' so as to render:
'Not with you, but with the house of (the king of) Babylon am I at
war today' (Rudolph).

22. disguised himself: the first indication of the influence of 1
Kg. 22:30. There seems little point, therefore, in proposing emendations or alternative meanings for this word which separate it from
the earlier passage. **He did not listen:** see above.

23–24. The influence of 1 Kg. 22 is here continued. **brought him
to Jerusalem. And he died:** on the contrast with 2 Kg. 23:29f., see
above. **the tombs of his fathers:** Kings has 'his own tomb', which
probably comes to the same thing.

25. Jeremiah also uttered a lament: though there is no good
reason to doubt this, in view of Jeremiah's high regard for Josiah
(cf. Jer. 22:15–16, though contrast 22:10), the lament appears not
to have been preserved; cf. C. Wolff, *Jeremia im Frühjudentum und
Urchristentum* (1976), pp. 2–4. **behold they are written in the Laments:** this is often referred to the book of Lamentations. Since
that book does not deal with the death of Josiah, however, this
clause is then dismissed as a later gloss. Since the title here is not
the same as that regularly used for Lamentations, the possibility
should be remembered that this too may refer to some other book,
since lost.

26–27. This concluding notice corresponds to 2 Kg. 23:28; on its
different position, see above. **his good deeds:** see on 32:32. **the law
of the Lord:** in line with the Chronicler's understanding of the
Book of the Law discovered during Josiah's reign (see on 34:14),
this will refer to the Mosaic law generally, not just Deuteronomy.
Israel and: added by the Chronicler in his regular manner, even
after the fall of the northern kingdom; see on 16:11.

FINAL JUDGMENT AND EXILE

36:1–21

This section covers briefly the reigns of the last four kings of Judah, an explanation for the exile to Babylon, and a hint at the eventual restoration. It is nevertheless probable that the Chronicler regarded it as a single unit in his composition. First, he has heavily abbreviated (and once even contradicted; cf. v. 6) his *Vorlage* in order to emphasise throughout the common fate of each of these kings, as of the people, namely, that they were each led away into exile. Secondly, he has carefully omitted from Kings the notice of the death of each king (*Mosis*, pp. 205–8); contrast 2 Kg. 23:34; 24:6; 25:30. This too has the effect of toning down the rigid separation between each of their reigns. Thirdly, he has carefully included by way of additional information only such points as concern the fate of the temple. He has traced from its muted beginnings (v. 3) a crescendo in terms of the temple's deprivation (vv. 7, 10, and 18), and this reaches its climax in its eventual destruction (v. 19). Thus there is a sense in which the Chronicler has drawn a deliberate parallel between the fate of the temple and that of the Davidic dynasty.

The effect of this procedure by the Chronicler is to turn the chapter exclusively into an account of, and justification for, the exile, understood both in the usual terms of deportation, but also, as so often previously in his history, as an interruption in the regular worship and service of God, centred on the temple in Jerusalem. While he does not leave his readers without a clear indication of the way forward to restoration (vv. 20–21), the main result of his composition here is thus to close his history on the same note as the start of the narrative portion of his work, namely the 'exilic' conditions noted in his account of the death of Saul in 1 Chr. 10.

There is no need to look for extra-biblical sources to account for most of the material in this chapter. For the political history of the period, see the commentaries on Kings, the standard histories of Israel, and in particular an extensive series of studies by A. Malamat; cf. *JNES* 9 (1950), pp. 218–27; *IEJ* 18 (1968), pp. 137–56; *SVT* 28 (1974), pp. 123–45.

Jehoahaz

36:1–4

This paragraph is abbreviated slightly from 2 Kg. 23:30–34. Most of the omissions are intelligible enough (e.g. see above and on 33:1),

though it is not clear why he should have omitted the negative
judgment on Jehoahaz from 2 Kg. 23:32.

3. The notice about **tribute** is the only information which the
Chronicler retains other than details concerning the king himself.
He probably thought that it would have been paid, in part at least,
out of the temple treasury. This, therefore, marks the start of one
of the major themes of the chapter (see above). It is probably
significant that, against his *Vorlage*, he shows no interest in the fate
of either the kings or of the temple spoils once they are removed
from **the land**. The close association of people and land, noted
already in 1 Chr. 1–9, continues here, paradoxically, in spite of the
'exilic' atmosphere; see further, on v. 21.

Jehoiakim

36:5–8

The framework for this paragraph is supplied by 2 Kg. 23:36–24:7,
abbreviated in the usual manner. The narrative portion (vv. 6–7),
however, is selected from elsewhere by the Chronicler in order to
continue his twin themes of despoiling of the temple and exile of
the king.

6. and bound him in fetters to take him to Babylon: at this
point, the Chronicler departs from 2 Kg. 24:1. It is probable that
we should draw a careful distinction between the historicity of the
Chronicler's conjectured source and the use to which he himself has
put it.

Our improved knowledge of the events of this period since the
publication of the Babylonian Chronicle reveals that there is no
objection to be raised against Judah's subjugation to Babylon following the Battle of Carchemish and during the reign of Jehoiakim,
but that the date, unmentioned here, remains uncertain; see the
commentaries on Dan. 1:1, etc. Though *OT* would be the only
record of such an event, it is by no means impossible that Jehoiakim
was 'personally required to go to Babylon to take part in the victory
celebrations as a conquered and vassal king . . . as had Manasseh
in the days of Esarhaddon' (33:11); D. J. Wiseman, *Notes on Some
Problems in the Book of Daniel* (1965), p. 18. The removal of some
of the temple vessels (v. 7), also unmentioned in Kings, would be
intelligible as tribute in such a setting. Alternatively, some commentators suggest that Jehoiakim was not actually taken to Babylon
at this time, but only bound and threatened so as to bring him into
submission. This is certainly a possible interpretation of the Hebrew
expression used here.

Either way, it is clear that the most plausible setting for this incident is during Jehoiakim's reign, and that he continued in power for some time after, eventually dying in Jerusalem shortly before its first major siege; cf. 2 Kg. 24:1-10. The Chronicler, however, in line with his interpretation of this chapter as a whole, has made of the incident an exile of Jehoiakim to Babylon from which, it is implied, he did not return. He has thus dated it to the very end of the reign and appropriately omitted the reference to Jehoiakim's death.

7. For the possible historical setting of these events, see on v. 6. **part of the vessels of the house of the Lord:** this is more direct than v. 3, but not yet as strong as vv. 10 or 18. The Chronicler's interest in the vessels has already been noted several times as a theme of continuity; see on 1 Chr. 28:11-19.

8. the abominations: a strengthening of the *Vorlage*'s wording. **and what was found against him:** an addition by the Chronicler, signifying either 'and what happened to him' (Myers) or 'and everything of which he was held guilty' (*NEB*). The Chronicler may have had in mind the unfavourable portrayal of Jehoiakim in the book of Jeremiah (e.g. Jer. 22:18f.; 30). **Israel and:** cf. 35:27.

Jehoiachin

36:9-10

The Chronicler has here abbreviated his *Vorlage*, 2 Kg. 24:8-17, even more drastically than for the previous two reigns. Apart from the essential details about the accession and succession, he again retains only the statement of his twin themes in v. 10: the exile of Jehoiachin to Babylon and the further spoiling of the temple.

9. eight years old: contrast 2 Kg. 24:8, 'eighteen'. The present text has arisen by a simple scribal error. **and ten days:** lacking in 2 Kg. 24:8. It has probably arisen by mistake from a marginal correction of the error earlier in the verse.

10. In the spring of the year: supplied by the Chronicler to indicate that a military campaign was involved (cf. 1 Chr. 20:1), even though he has not included the details of it from Kings so as not to deflect attention from his primary theme. **his brother:** strictly speaking, his uncle; cf. 2 Kg. 24:17; Jer. 37:1. This may be an example of the use of **brother** in the sense of relative, but more probably there has been some confusion from 1 Chr. 3:15-16, where two different Zedekiahs are mentioned.

Zedekiah

36:11–21

The Chronicler draws the opening notices of Zedekiah's reign (vv. 11–12*a*) from 2 Kg. 24:18–19 before going his own way entirely to describe and explain the final downfall of the nation and its chief institutions. Four points should be noted concerning this concluding paragraph of the Chronicler's work.

First, the pattern already noted for the first three reigns in this chapter is continued here. Although there is fuller explanatory material than previously, the narrative is largely restricted again to the essential aspects of exile and desecration of the temple and its vessels. This latter theme, which has been increasing throughout the chapter, naturally reaches its climax in vv. 18–19. Equally, no interest is shown in the personal fate of Zedekiah, while again the only abiding factor of significance is the land itself (v. 21) rather than the community in exile as such.

Second, unlike the previous three reigns, greater interest is shown here in the population at large. Their condemnation closely parallels that of the king himself, however. In this way the 'democratic' aspect of the Chronicler's work which has been observed from time to time, especially in connection with the addresses of the prophets in the form of Levitical sermons, is here maintained. This is particularly appropriate in the present paragraph, where the exile is largely explained as due to the persistent rejection of just such prophetic warnings.

This leads directly to the third point of importance concerning this passage: the exile is explained with the use of some of the Chronicler's most characteristic theological vocabulary; cf. vv. 12–16. This marks a point of significant contrast with the Deuteronomic history. There is no suggestion here that Manasseh's sin in particular was the cause of the exile, as at 2 Kg. 21:10–16; 22:16f.; 24:3f., 20. Rather, by the use of familiar vocabulary, the Chronicler has assimilated the exile to that pattern of sin and judgment which has recurred so often throughout his work. Moreover, in this same connection it should be noted that it is not the sin itself which leads directly to the exile. Rather, again as usually elsewhere, it was the failure to heed the prophetic warning which finally brought down judgment upon them. Thus ultimately the exile was due to a failure of faith in the reliability of God's word rather than to a catalogue of particular and specific 'sins'.

Fourthly, this form of explanation for the exile, together with the material of vv. 20–21, provides a pointer for the Chronicler's readers to the pattern for future restoration. Since the exile has now become

one in a recurring series of judgments, there is no good reason why
it should not similarly be followed by the kind of reversal which he
has also regularly illustrated. Again, it may be assumed that the way
towards such an objective will be by giving greater heed to the
teaching of the prophets as mediated in their own day through the
Levitical preachers. Thus the work of the Chronicler himself may
in a sense be regarded as an extended form of this same preaching.
Finally, although the interpretation of v. 21 is not easy, part of its
purpose would seem to be the attempt to demonstrate that another
possible hindrance to full restoration had been removed (see the
Introduction, section G). Thus the Chronicler can end his work
with a reference to 'the establishment of the kingdom of Persia' (v.
20). This would have directed his readers towards the next major
phase in their history, with which they would have been familiar.
Since it was also probably the kingdom under which they were still
living, albeit very much later on, the Chronicler would appear to be
encouraging them towards a realisation of the restoration which he
still believed to be available to them.

12. He did not humble himself: for this key word, cf. 7:14.
before Jeremiah the prophet: a specific example in the case of
Zedekiah of the fault of the people at large; cf. vv. 15f. The Chronicler will here have been dependent on the many passages in the
book of Jeremiah which treat the prophet's dealings with Zedekiah;
cf. especially Jer. 37:2. It is noteworthy that some of Jeremiah's
characteristic phraseology has influenced the Chronicler in his development of this passage. Jeremiah frequently urged the surrender
of Jerusalem to the Babylonians; the next verse demonstrates how
Zedekiah rejected this advice.

13. He also rebelled against King Nebuchadnezzar: cf. 2 Kg.
24:20*b*. This is interpreted by the Chronicler not simply as political
folly, but as disobedience to God. **who had made him swear by
God:** it is made particularly clear in Ezek. 17:11–21 that Zedekiah
was in a covenant relationship with Nebuchadnezzar. His rebellion
thus involved contradicting his oath sworn in God's name. **he stiff-
ened his neck:** thus Jeremiah frequently condemns his contemporaries; cf. Jer. 7:26; 17:23; 19:15, etc. **against turning to the Lord:**
another key word from 7:14, also characteristic of Jeremiah's
preaching.

14. The Chronicler now goes on to show that the people were no
better than their king. **the leading priests:** in the context we do not
expect this one group to be singled out to the apparent exclusion of
others. The Greek versions suggest that a word has been accidentally
omitted. By restoring it, we can read, 'All the chiefs of Judah and
the priests' (*NEB*). **were exceedingly unfaithful:** see on 1 Chr.

10:13 for this familiar condemnation. **they polluted the house of the Lord**: it is clear from Ezek. 8 that the effect of Josiah's reforms did not last long.

15–16. With language which again echoes Jeremiah (e.g. Jer. 26:5; 29:19, etc.), the Chronicler summarises the root cause of the exile. Despite God's **compassion**, which led him to send **persistently to them by his messengers**, the people refused to listen. **his words** and **his prophets** are again presented as virtually parallel; cf. 20:20. **till there was no remedy**: this is another echo of 7:14, where the same word is translated 'heal (their land)'.

17–20a. The Chronicler summarises the final judgment as a comprehensive destruction and exile. In line with the teaching of the prophets, he asserts emphatically that it was God who **brought up against them the king of the Chaldeans**; there is no suggestion of divine weakness or failure. Many of the people were killed (v. 17), while all who **had escaped from the sword** were taken into exile in Babylon (v. 20). As is his usual practice, the Chronicler paints with broad strokes; he shows no interest in the fact, amply attested by his *Vorlage* and so undoubtedly known to him, that part of the population continued to live in the land. The theological importance to him of the desolation of the land shortly becomes apparent (v. 21). The other major point of focus for the Chronicler in these verses is the complete spoiling (v. 18) and then the destruction (v. 19) of **the house of God**; see above, p. 412.

20b–21. The Chronicler concludes his work on a note of hope, which looks forward to the restoration. This is made clear by the specific reference **until the establishment of the kingdom of Persia. to fulfil the word of the Lord by the mouth of Jeremiah**: it is not certain whether this refers back to v. 20 or forward to v. 21. Either would be appropriate. The former would underline that the exiles would **become servants to** the Babylonians for only a limited period (e.g. Jer. 25:11; 27:7). The latter would look forward to the end of v. 21, and echo specifically Jer. 25:11 and 29:10. Either way, it is striking to observe how a prophetic word has been linked with, and so interpreted by, a clear allusion to a legal passage, Lev. 26:34f. This is part of a long catalogue of punishments for disobedience, and explains that the purpose of an exile would be to allow **the land** to enjoy **its sabbaths** 'which it had not in your sabbaths when you dwelt upon it'. The way the Chronicler has linked the passages together demonstrates that this judgment has fully passed and no longer stands as a threat to his readers.

to fulfil seventy years: this phrase has been almost endlessly discussed; the following list mentions only some of the more significant contributions: C. F. Whitley, *VT* 4 (1954), pp. 60–72, and 7 (1957), pp. 416–18; A. Orr, *VT* 6 (1956), pp. 304–6; P. R. Ackroyd, *JNES* 17 (1958), pp. 23–7; R. Borger, *JNES* 18 (1959), p. 74; P. Grelot, *Biblica* 50 (1969), pp. 169–86; O. Plöger, *Aus der Spätzeit des Alten Testaments* (1971), pp. 67–73; M. Weinfeld, *Deuteronomy and the Deuteronomic School* (1972), pp. 143–6; K. Koch, *VT* 28 (1978), pp. 433–41. By way of summary, it may be suggested that the words have both a forward and a backward look. As spoken originally by Jeremiah with reference to the exile, they may well have been intended as a general period of punishment, based either on an individual's life–span or on three generations; there are extra-biblical as well as *OT* parallels for this usage. In time, however, it came to be appreciated that, although the exile itself lasted only some fifty years, yet in two ways the prophecy had a rather more accurate fulfilment; reckoning from the Babylonian victory at Carchemish (605 BC), the time of servitude to them was in fact quite close to seventy years. Even more striking, however, is the period of exactly seventy years between the destruction of the first temple and the dedication of the second (586–516 BC), and it may be that the Chronicler would by his time have had this particularly in mind rather than the original Jeremianic intention.

The phrase has also clearly been given a reference backwards, however, by its association with **the land** enjoying **its sabbath**. This suggests that the Chronicler has a period of 490 years in mind. Although the dedication of the first temple might be considered, it is not sufficiently close to the figure in question. In fact, the Chronicler has incorporated that into a separate 'chronological' scheme based on the genealogies; cf. 1 Chr. 6:1ff. and Koch. Equally, the suggestion that by omitting from the reckoning such good kings as David, Solomon and Hezekiah one might reach back to the time of the conquest is also too vague and uncertain. In fact, on the basis of the lengths of reign which the Chronicler himself supplies, it would seem clear that he intends the reference to cover the period of the monarchy, which is more or less co-extensive with his narrative history: to the beginning of David's reign gives a total of 474 years. If some allowance is made for the uncertain length of Saul's reign (cf. 1 Sam. 13:1), it will be seen that the figures could coincide almost exactly. Thus the Chronicler seems to suggest that the whole legacy of neglect which the land had suffered has been fully 'paid off' by the period of exile.

APPENDIX

36:22-23

The Chronicler's own work finished at v. 21 (cf. *IBC*, pp. 7–10).
These final two verses have been added subsequently from Ezr. 1:1–
3 (the commentaries on which should be consulted for details). The
reason for this is probably liturgical. It may have been felt inappropriate to end reading on what was considered to be a pessimistic
note. These two verses were thus borrowed from Ezra in order to
point up the hopeful elements in the Chronicler's concluding words.
At the same time, they have the effect of directing the reader to the
books where the continuation of the people's history may be found.

INDEX OF AUTHORS

GENERAL INDEX